CREATING Keepsakes SCRAPBOOK MAGAZINE

Y0-IWC-281
R0230295

more than 300 never-before-published layouts

Scrapbooking with Lisa Bearnson

Tips, techniques and examples of how to use products to their fullest potential!

PRIMEDIA Inc.
P.O. Box 469007, Escondido, CA 92046-9007 Toll-free number: 888/247-5282 International: 760/745-2809

Creating Keepsakes

Founding Editor	Lisa Bearnson
Co-founder	Don Lambson
Editor-in-Chief	Tracy White
Special Projects Editor	Catherine Weber Scott
Copy Editors	Kim Sandoval, Kerri Bradford
Contributors	Kristy Banks, Kerri Bradford, Marci Leishman, Loni Stevens, Angela Ash, Jennifer Burke, Heather Uppencamp, Skye Johansen, Cori Dahmen, Cherish Larsen
Art Director	Brian Tippetts
Designer	Celeste Rockwood-Jones
Production Designers	Just Scan Me!
Production Manager	Gary Whitehead
Publisher	Mark Seastrand
Business Sales Manager	Tara Green
Business Sales Assistants	Jacque Jensen, Melanie Cain
Vice President, Group Publisher	David O'Neil
Circulation Marketing Directors	Dena Spar, Janice Martin
Promotions Director	Dana Smith

PRIMEDIA
Consumer Magazine & Internet Group

PRIMEDIA, Inc.

Chairman	Dean Nelson
President & *CEO*	Kelly Conlin
Vice-Chairman	Beverly C. Chell

PRIMEDIA Consumer Media and Magazine Group

President & CEO	David G. Ferm
Chief Operating Officer	Daniel E. Aks
EVP, Consumer Marketing/Circulation	Steve Aster
SVP, Chief Financial Officer	David P. Kirchhoff
SVP, Mfg., Production & Distribution	Kevin Mullan
SVP, Finance	Kevin Neary
SVP, Chief Information Officer	Debra C. Robinson
VP, Consumer Marketing	Bobbi Gutman
VP, Manufacturing	Gregory Catsaros
VP, Business Development	Jasja de Smedt
VP, Direct Response & Classified Advertising	Carolyn N. Everson
VP, Single Copy Sales	Thomas L. Fogarty
VP, Manufacturing Budgets & Operations	Lilia Golia
VP, Database/e-Commerce	Suti Prakash

NOTICE OF LIABILITY

The information in this book is distributed on an "as is" basis, without warranty. While every precaution has been taken in the preparation of this book, neither the author nor PRIMEDIA Inc. shall have any liability to any person or entity with respect to any liability, loss or damage caused or alleged to be caused directly or indirectly by the instructions contained in this book.

TRADEMARKS

Trademarked names are used throughout this book. Rather than put a trademark symbol in every occurrence of a trademarked name, we state we are using the names only in an editorial fashion and to the benefit of the trademark owner with no intention of infringement of the trademark.

Copyright © 2003 Primedia Inc. All rights reserved. No part of this book may be reproduced or transmitted in any form or by any means, without the prior written permission of the publisher, excepting brief quotations in connection with reviews written specifically for inclusion in magazines or newspapers, or single copies for strictly personal use.

Printed and bound in Hong Kong, China.
ISBN 1-929180-51-9

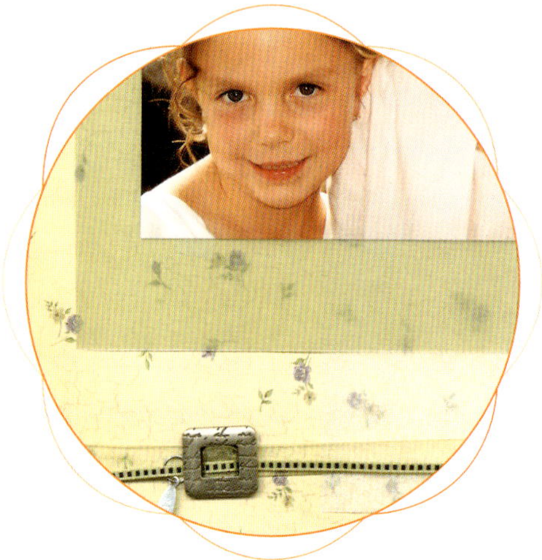

15

contents

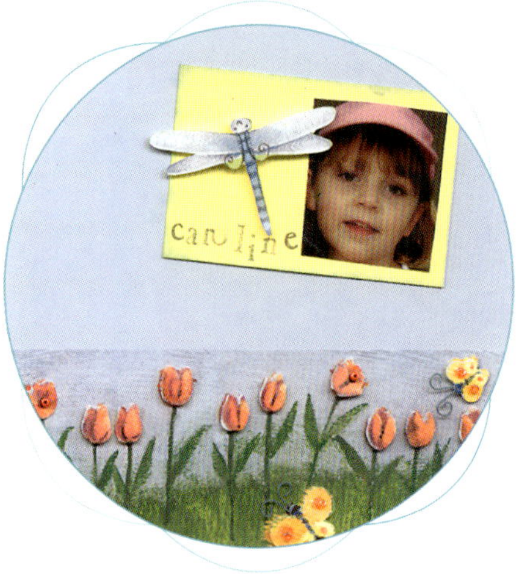

51

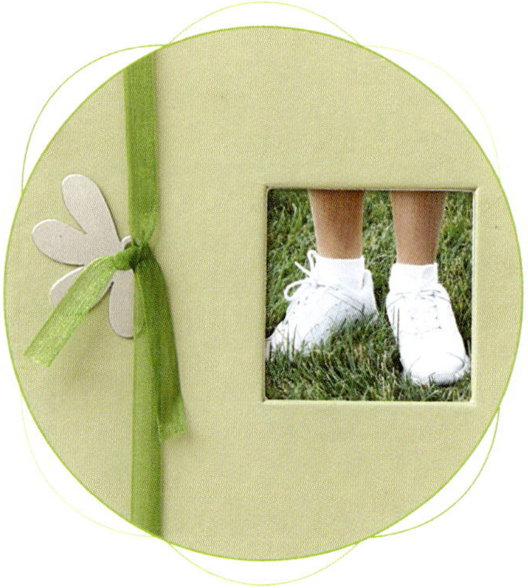

150

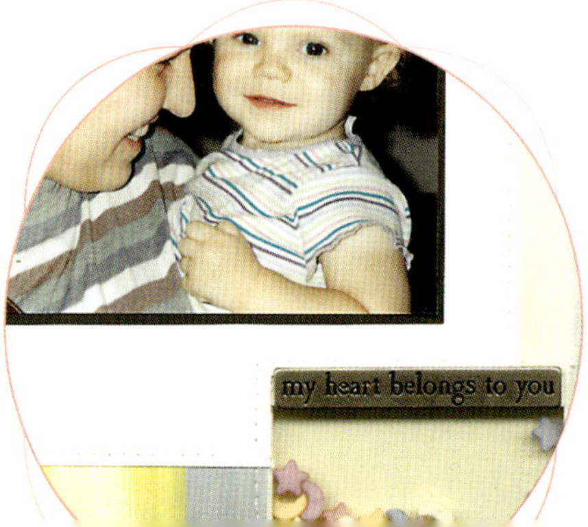
my heart belongs to you

169

editor's note

it's finally here!

DURING THE PAST SEVEN YEARS as the founding editor of *Creating Keepsakes* magazine, I've been asked a lot of questions. However, 10 to one, the number-one question I'm asked is, "When are you going to publish a book with all those great layouts you show on television?" Subscribers and viewers go on to tell me they tape all my shows and later freeze-frame page ideas when they receive their supplies, then go crazy trying to scrapbook while looking at a fuzzy TV screen.

We listened and your request is granted—this book is a result of all the feedback. On the following pages, you'll find the best of the best scrapbook pages that I've shown on television over the past few years.

You'll love the format of the book—it's divided into "product" chapters, then sections in each chapter separated by technique or idea. We also created a unique spine so the book will lie flat when opened.

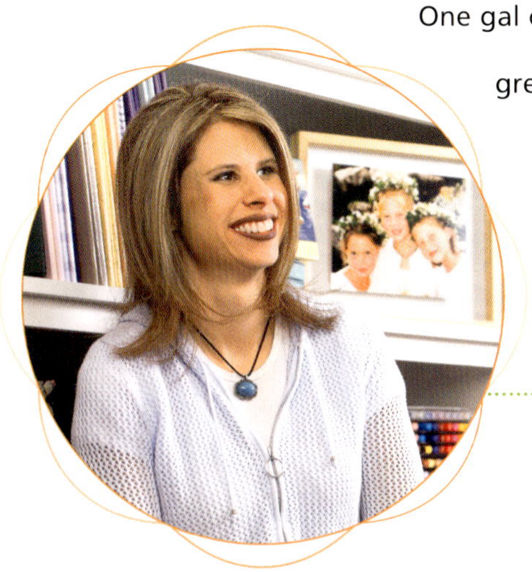

One gal on our staff looked through the book and said, "This is the greatest book ever; it gets back to the basics of scrapbooking." Best of all, this book has something for everyone—there's a wonderful representation of styles and designs.

"Creativity is what makes life worth living."
—MARION WOODMAN

Most of the layouts can be created in a short amount of time and use items you already have in your scrapbook stash. The "I Love It" sidebars point out elements on each page that I want you to try.

Thanks to my wonderful staff for making my television show and this book such a success: Kristy Banks for being my personal assistant and close confidante, and for always laughing with me for the past four years. Kerri Bradford for stepping up to the plate when Kristy had her baby and being so dependable and such a great friend. Both these gals are amazing, versatile scrapbookers. Every page they create is a masterpiece.

Thanks to the other page designers who are so awesome at what they do: Marci Leishman, Loni Stevens, Angela Ash, Jennifer Burke, Heather Uppencamp, Skye Johansen, Cori Dahmen and Cherish Larsen. You all are the best! Also, hats off to Catherine Scott, the editor of the book, and Celeste Rockwood-Jones for the design. Both did a stellar job working under such tight deadlines.

The next time I'm on television, I'll wave "hi" and think of you scrapbooking in your own little corner of the world. Happy memories and enjoy!

Lisa Bearnson

····> LISA BEARNSON

lisa says:

"*Paper is the foundation of every scrapbook page.* The paper you choose will set the *tone* of the layout: is it playful, thoughtful, masculine, formal or subtle? Paper provides the *perfect* background for your cherished photographs. Learning to use paper creatively and *effectively* is the first step to becoming a *master* scrapbooker!"

PAPER

ch. 1

playing with paper

PAPER *n. a felted sheet of usually vegetable fibers laid down on a fine screen from a water suspension*

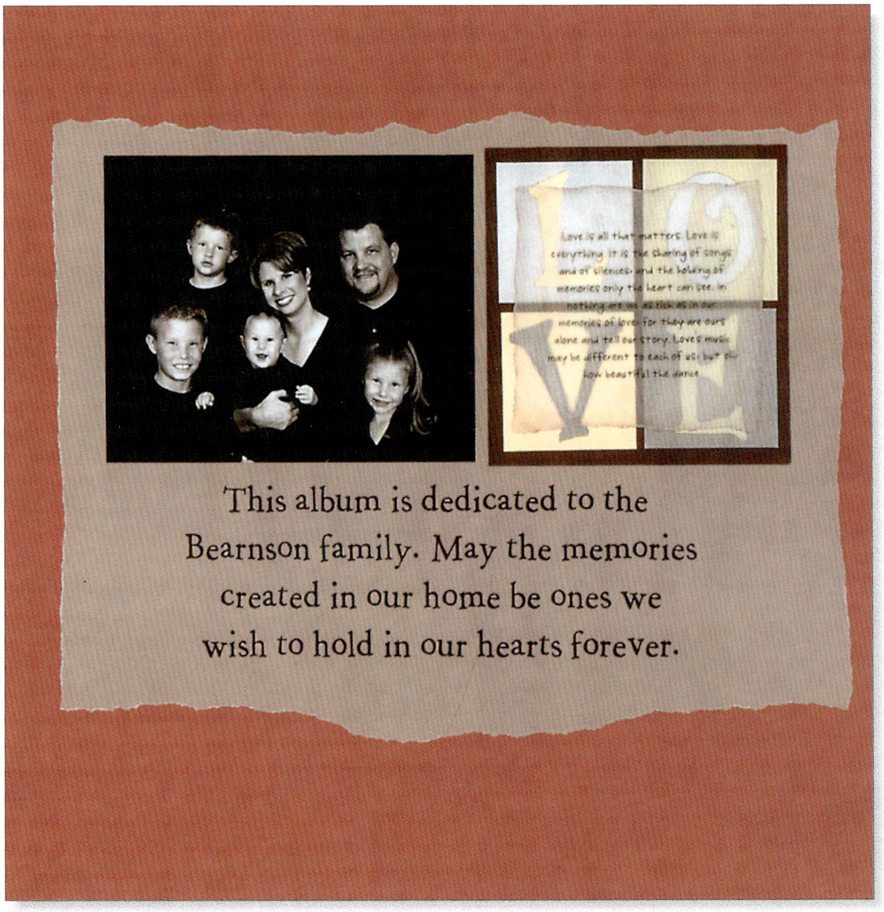
This album is dedicated to the
Bearnson family. May the memories
created in our home be ones we
wish to hold in our hearts forever.

Love

Supplies
Vellum: Provo Craft
Letter die cuts: Sizzix
Computer fonts: CK Jot, "The Art of Creative Lettering" CD; CK Constitution, "Fresh Fonts" CD, *Creating Keepsakes*
Chalks: Craf-T Products

♥ **I Love It!:** *Create an artistic background to layer your journaling over—with vellum, the background will show through while maintaining the visibility of the smaller journaling.*

tip **1**

coordinate
papers in different patterns and colors.

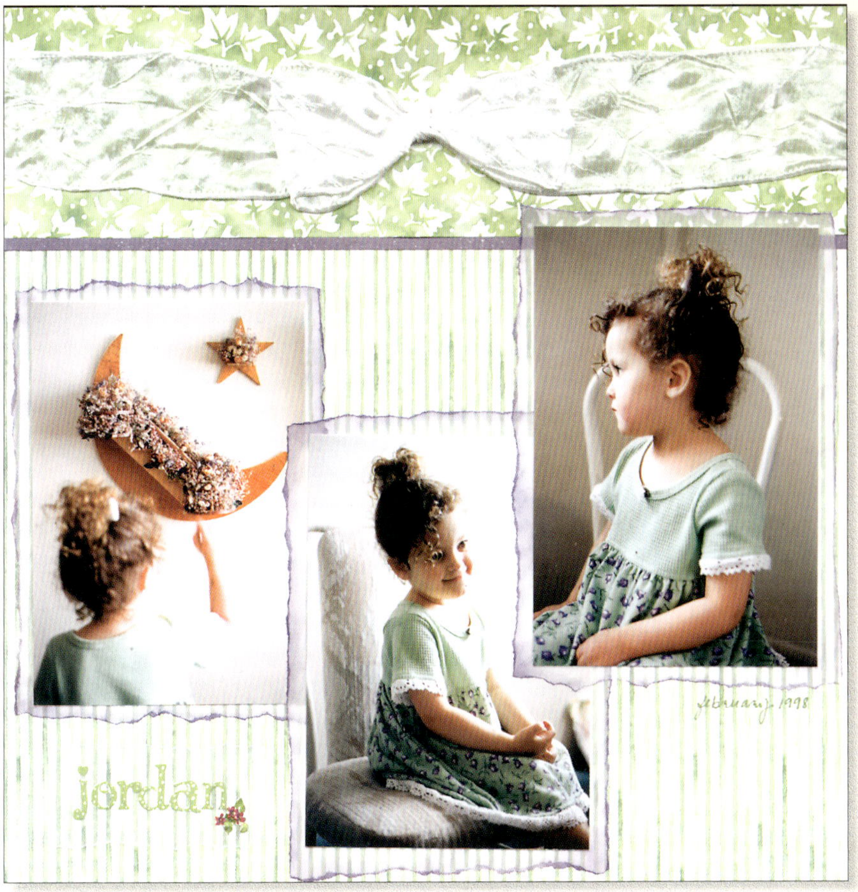
jordan

Jordan

Supplies
Patterned papers and letter stickers: Susan Branch, Colorbök
Vellum: Autumn Leaves
Chalks: Craf-T Products
Pen: Zig Writer, EK Success
Other: Ribbon

♥ **I Love It!:** *An easy design rule to remember is to choose a dominant color for your layout (in this case, green), then choose an accent color (in this case, purple). Try to use the accent color sparingly (but not so sparingly it looks "out of place" or draws attention because it's different).*

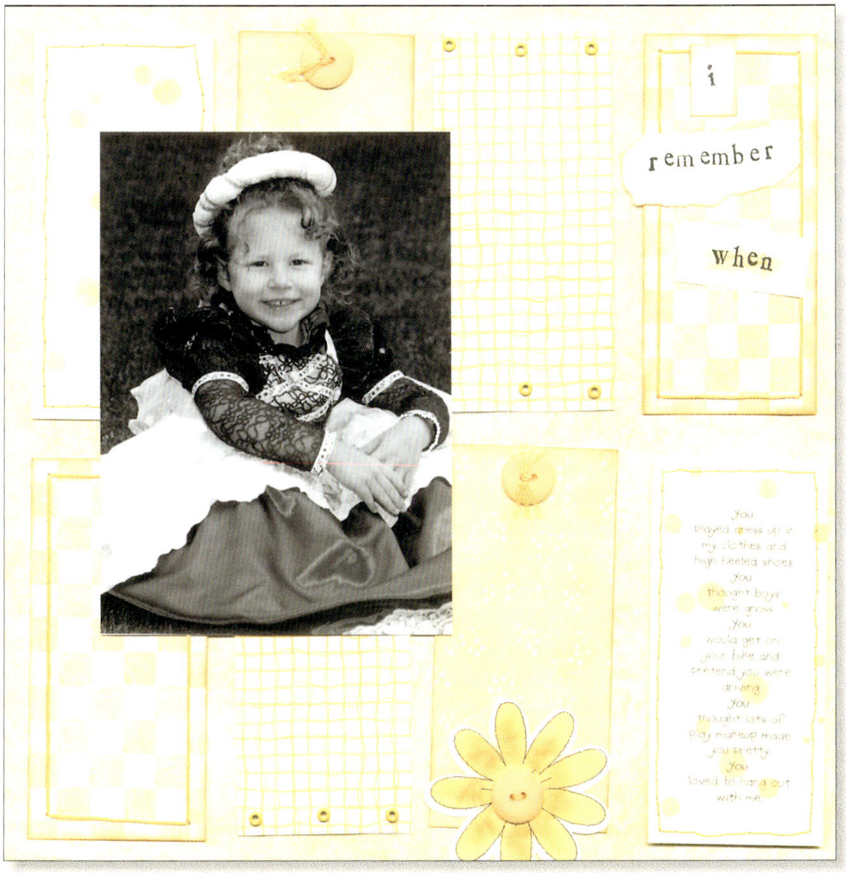
i
remember
when

I Remember When

Supplies
Patterned papers: Provo Craft
Vellum: Autumn Leaves
Computer fonts: CK Toggle, "The Best of Creative Lettering" CD Vol. 3, *Creating Keepsakes*
Buttons, eyelets and embroidery floss: Making Memories
Flower accent: My Mind's Eye
Letter stamps: PSX Design
Stamping ink: ColorBox, Clearsnap
Chalks: Craf-T Products

♥ **I Love It!:** *Many paper manufacturers have created different patterns of paper with the same dye lot. Notice how these five different patterns are effectively used on this layout—thanks to the same shades of yellow in all the papers.*

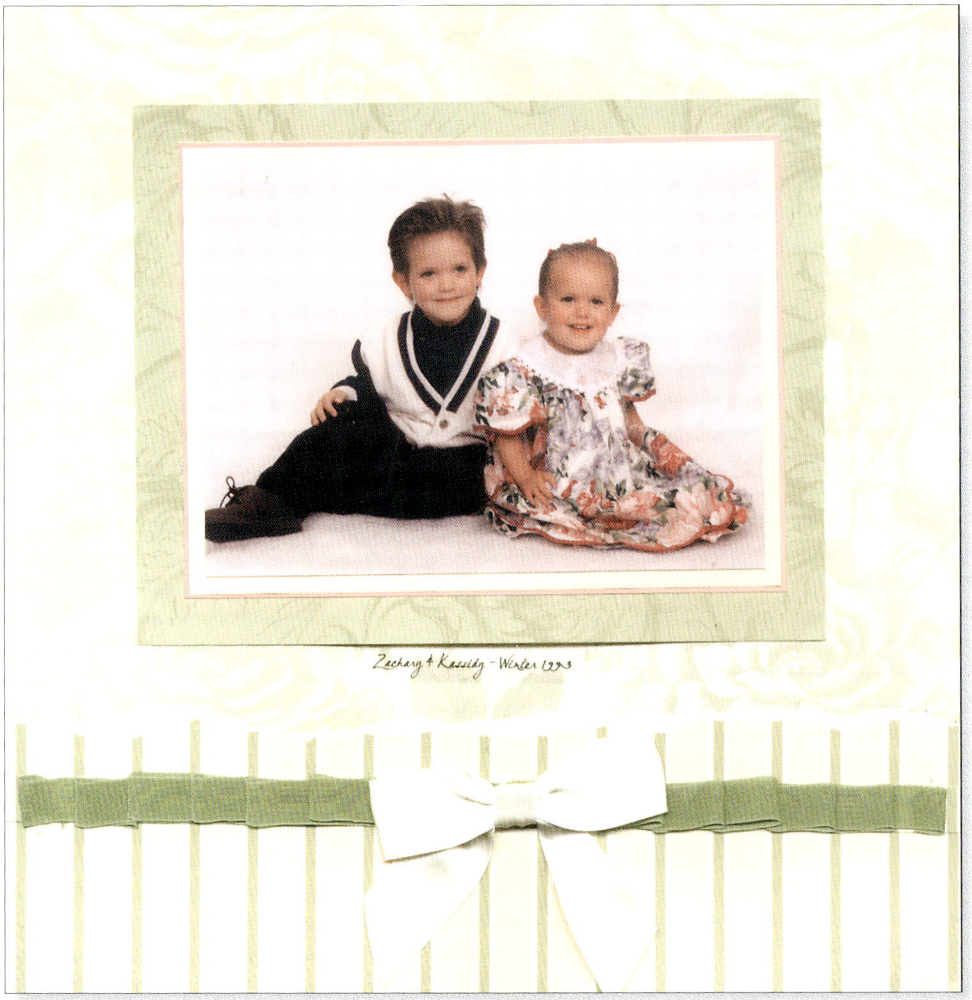

Zachary & Kassidy

Supplies
Patterned papers, ribbon and bow: Anna Griffin
Computer font: CK Bella, "The Best of Creative Lettering" CD Vol. 4, *Creating Keepsakes*

♥ **I Love It!:** *This simple ribbon border was pleated to correspond with each stripe in the patterned paper. This feminine page was simple to create!*

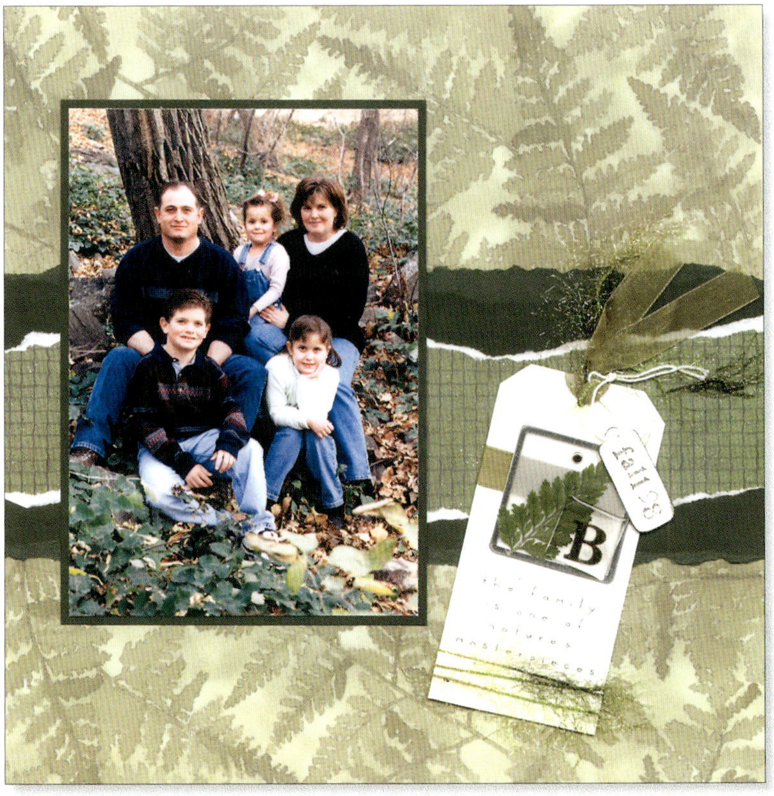

The Family

Supplies
Patterned papers: Provo Craft
Metal-rimmed tag and pebble accent: Making Memories
Fibers: Adornaments, EK Success
Pressed fern: Nature's Pressed
Rubber stamps: PSX Design (small letters and numbers), The Missing Link Stamp Co. (capital "B")
Stamping ink: Brilliance, Tsukineko
Computer font: 2Peas Think Small, downloaded from *www.twopeasinabucket.com*
Other: Ribbon, brad and tag

♥ **I Love It!:** *Tags are all the rage in scrapbooking! This beautiful tag, comprised of two small tags layered onto a larger tag, is a fun, innovative twist on an often-seen accent.*

tip 2

tear paper to create a textured, uneven edge.

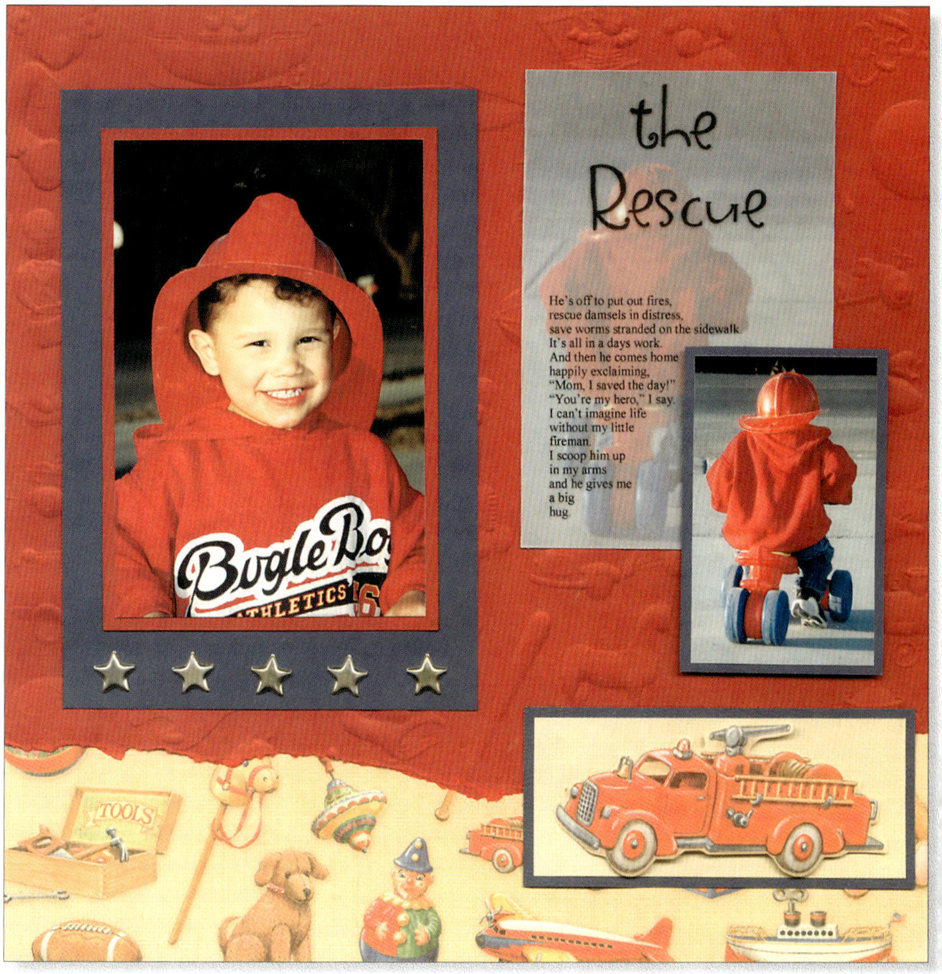

the Rescue
He's off to put out fires,
rescue damsels in distress,
save worms stranded on the sidewalk.
It's all in a days work.
And then he comes home
happily exclaiming,
"Mom, I saved the day!"
"You're my hero," I say.
I can't imagine life
without my little
fireman.
I scoop him up
in my arms
and he gives me
a big
hug.
TOOLS

The Rescue

Supplies
Patterned and embossed papers: K & Company
Vellum: Autumn Leaves
Letter stickers: David Walker, Colorbök
Computer font: Garamond, Microsoft Word
Other: Star-shaped brads and 3-D foam adhesive

♥ **I Love It!:** *Cut a shape or picture from the patterned paper you're using on your layout, adhere it with 3-D foam adhesive to raise it slightly, and mat it with coordinating patterned paper or cardstock. This is a quick and easy way to create a perfectly matching accent!*

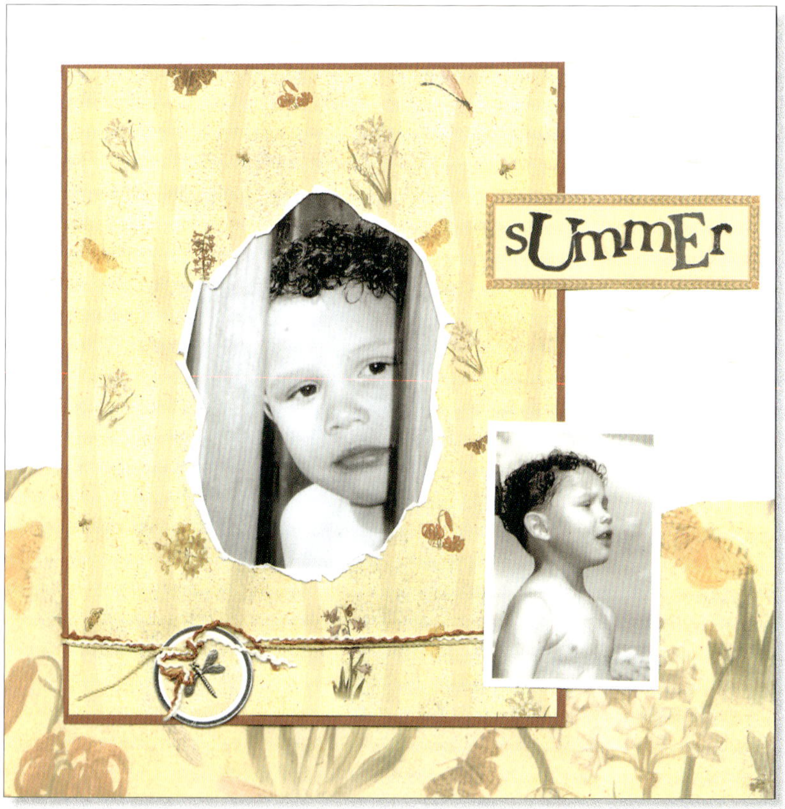

sUmmEr

Summer

Supplies
Patterned paper, and embossed vellum and cardstock: K & Company
Charm: Buttons Galore
Fibers: On The Surface
Metal-rimmed tag and letter charms: Making Memories

♥ **I Love It!:** *Create this easy, rip-and-reveal frame with paper tearing. First, cut a piece of patterned paper larger than your photograph to act as a photo mat. Starting in the middle, make a small cut with your scissors, then tear away the paper slowly until the subject of your photograph is visible. Gently fold the torn edges back to create a nicely curled "frame" for your photo. Wetting the paper before tearing and folding it will help the edges curl.*

♥ **I Love It!:** *Not all photographs have to look "picture-perfect." For rustic or aged-looking photographs, try scanning your photos and printing them onto cardstock or printing them using a low-quality setting on your printer. Make sure your page also follows the more rustic feeling of the photos as well.*

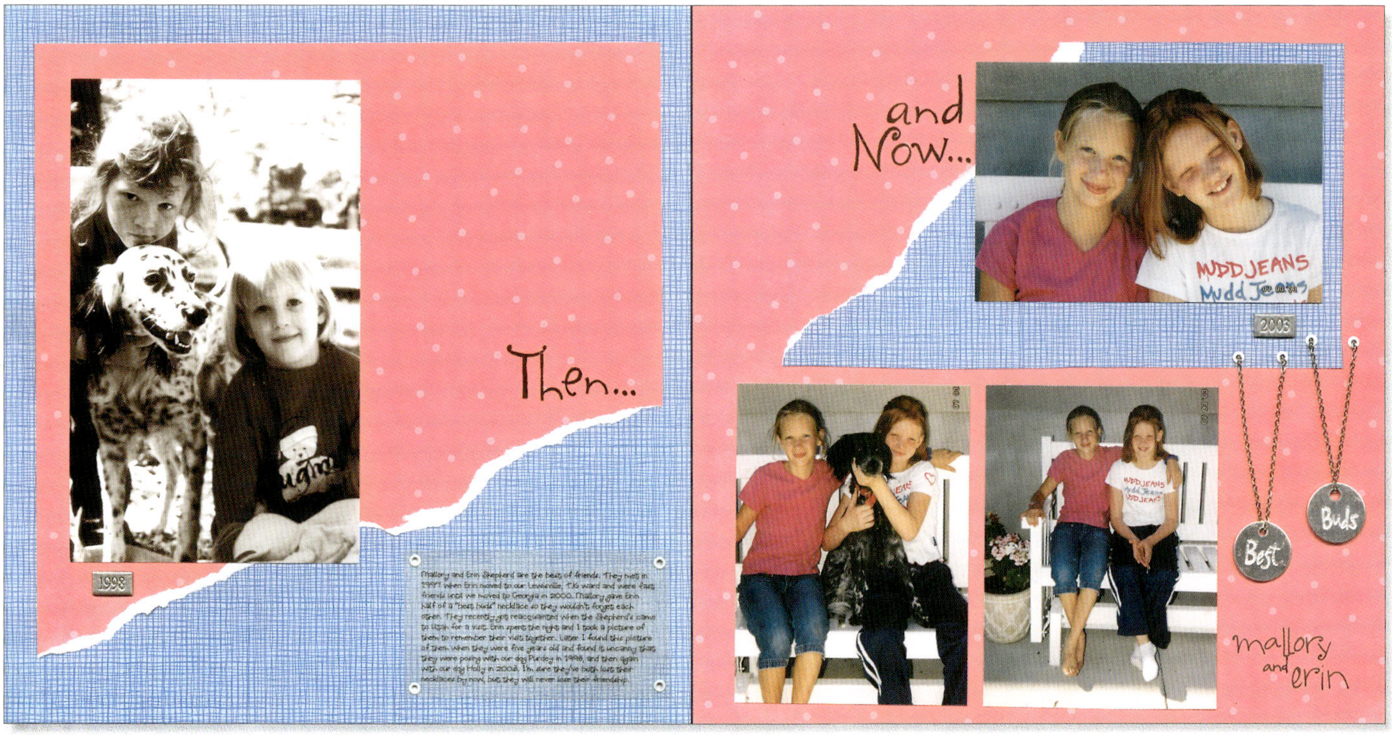
Then...
1998
Mallory and Erin Shepherd are the best of friends. They met in 1997 when Erin moved to our Lewisville, TX ward and were fast friends until we moved to Georgia in 2000. Mallory gave Erin half of a "best buds" necklace so they wouldn't forget each other. They recently got reacquainted when the Shepherd's came to Utah for a visit. Erin spent the night and I took a picture of them to remember their visit together. Later I found this picture of them when they were five years old and found it uncanny that they were posing with our dog Purdey in 1998, and then again with our dog Holly in 2003. I'm sure they've both lost their necklaces by now, but they will never lose their friendship.
and Now...
2003
Best
Buds
mallory and erin

Then ... and Now

Supplies

Patterned papers, eyelets and metal year accents: Making Memories
Letter stickers: David Walker, Colorbök
Round medallions and chains: Magic Scraps
Computer font: CK Daydream, Becky Higgins' "Creative Clips & Fonts" CD, *Creating Keepsakes*
Pen: Pigma Micron, Sakura
Other: Transparency paper

♥ **I Love It!:** *Create a whimsical yet unified two-page layout by using the same patterned papers on both pages but reversing the background and accent papers. Here, the first page uses a blue plaid paper as the background and a pink dot paper as an accent paper. The second page uses the pink dot paper as the background and the blue plaid paper as the accent paper. What a playful way to add some variety to your layouts!*

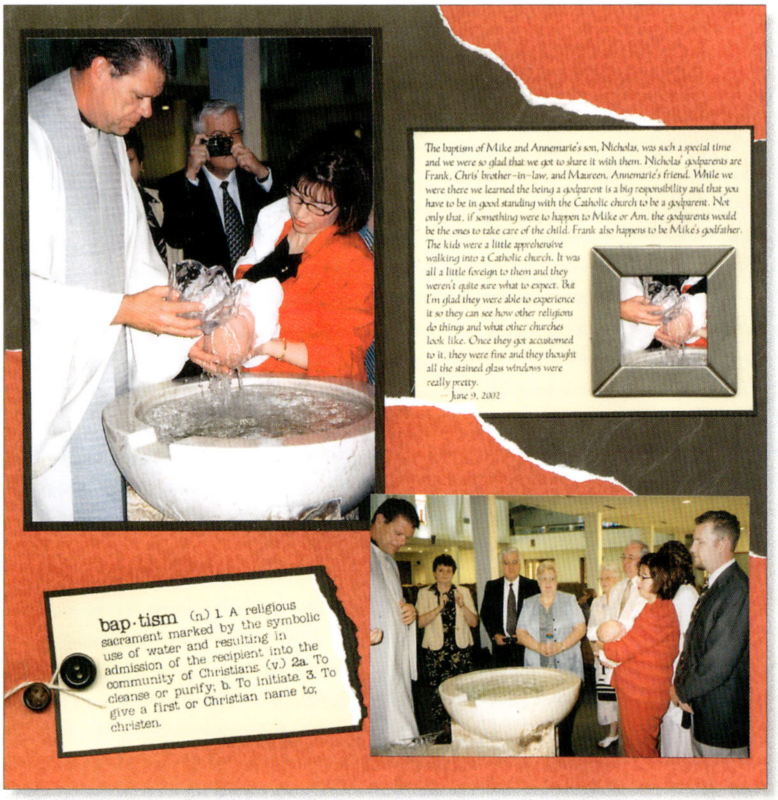
The baptism of Mike and Annemarie's son, Nicholas, was such a special time and we were so glad that we got to share it with them. Nicholas' godparents are Frank, Chris' brother-in-law, and Maureen, Annemarie's friend. While we were there we learned the being a godparent is a big responsibility and that you have to be in good standing with the Catholic church to be a godparent. Not only that, if something were to happen to Mike or Am, the godparents would be the ones to take care of the child. Frank also happens to be Mike's godfather. The kids were a little apprehensive walking into a Catholic church. It was all a little foreign to them and they weren't quite sure what to expect. But I'm glad they were able to experience it so they can see how other religions do things and what other churches look like. Once they got accustomed to it, they were fine and they thought all the stained glass windows were really pretty.
— June 9, 2002
bap·tism (n.) 1. A religious sacrament marked by the symbolic use of water and resulting in admission of the recipient into the community of Christians. (v.) 2a. To cleanse or purify; b. To initiate. 3. To give a first or Christian name to; christen.

Baptism

Supplies

Patterned papers and metal frame: Making Memories
Computer fonts: Problem Secretary (baptism definition tag), downloaded from the Internet; PC Callihan (journaling), "Fontmania" CD, Provo Craft
Other: Buttons and jute

♥ **I Love It!:** *Tear a strip from the top piece of patterned paper to reveal the patterned paper beneath. Although this layout shows the technique on a diagonal, the torn lines can be horizontal or vertical as well.*

♥ **I Love It!:** *A repeated portion of a photograph (as seen on this layout in the frame) makes an interesting accent or element on a page.*

tip 3

layer papers to create a new look.

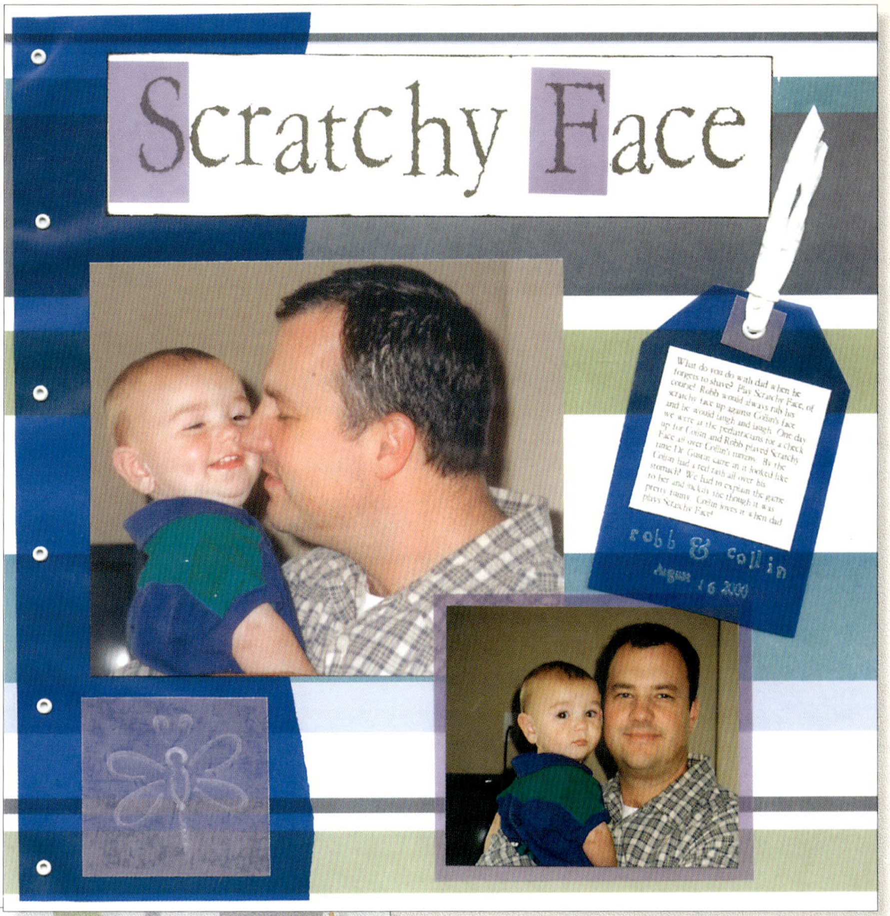
Scratchy Face
robb & collin
August 16 2000

Scratchy Face

Supplies

Patterned paper: American Crafts
Vellum: Autumn Leaves
Dragonfly template: Lasting Impressions for Paper
Computer font: CK Extra, "Fresh Fonts" CD, *Creating Keepsakes*
Rubber stamps: Hero Arts
Stamping ink: ColorBox, Clearsnap
Embossing powder: Stampa Rosa
Large eyelet: Impress Rubber Stamps
Small eyelets: Making Memories
Other: White raffia

♥ **I Love It!:** *Dry embossing on vellum creates a unique, frosted look. Experiment with different colors and weights of vellum to make the most of this fun technique.*

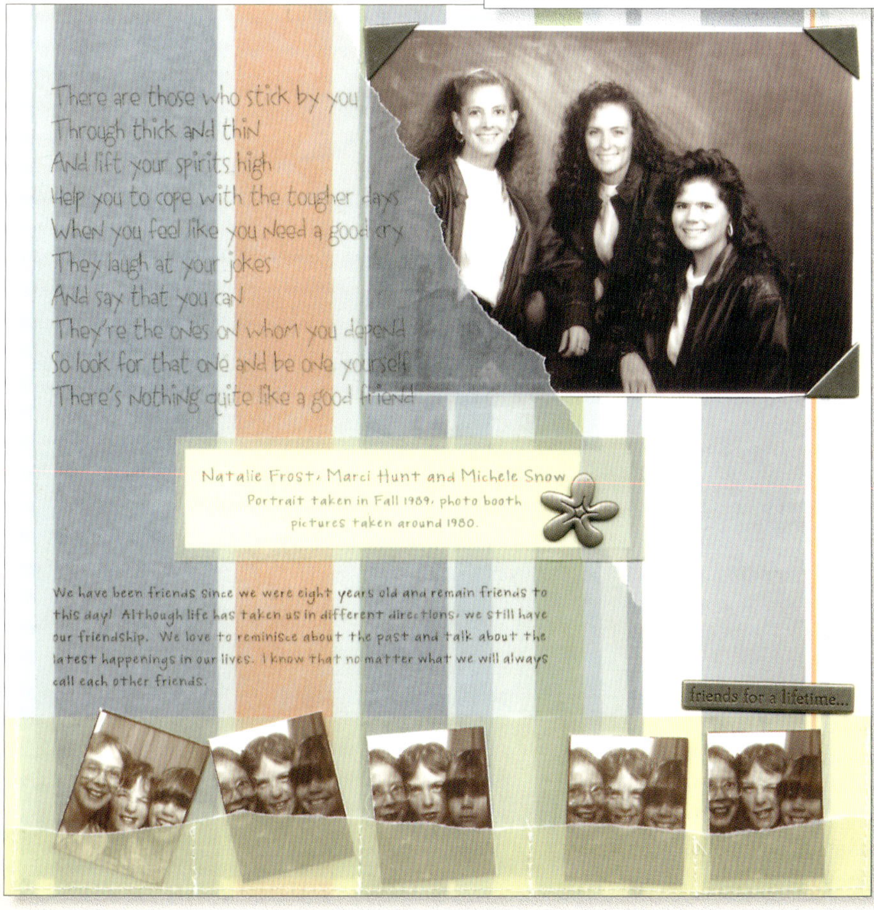
There are those who stick by you
Through thick and thin
And lift your spirits high
Help you to cope with the tougher days
When you feel like you need a good cry
They laugh at your jokes
And say that you can
They're the ones on whom you depend
So look for that one and be one yourself
There's nothing quite like a good friend
Natalie Frost, Marci Hunt and Michele Snow
Portrait taken in Fall 1989, photo booth pictures taken around 1980.
We have been friends since we were eight years old and remain friends to this day! Although life has taken us in different directions, we still have our friendship. We love to reminisce about the past and talk about the latest happenings in our lives. I know that no matter what we will always call each other friends.
friends for a lifetime...

Friends for a Lifetime

Supplies

Patterned paper: American Crafts
Vellum: Autumn Leaves
Metal accents: Making Memories
Computer fonts: CK Eclectic, Becky Higgins' "Creative Clips & Fonts" CD; CK Jot, "The Best of Creative Lettering" CD Vol. 4, *Creating Keepsakes*
Poem: Tiny Tales, My Mind's Eye

♥ **I Love It!:** *Are you handy with a sewing machine? This adorable photo border was created by sewing pockets in two strips of vellum and slipping small photographs into each pocket.*

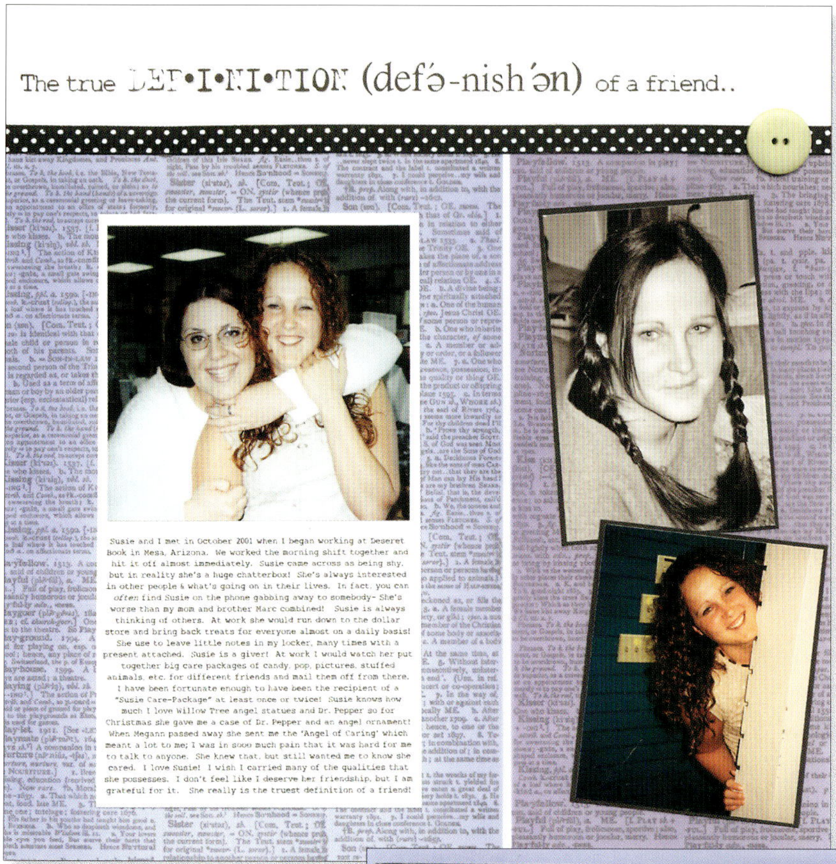
The true DEF•I•NI•TION (def'ə-nish'ən) of a friend..
Susie and I met in October 2001 when I began working at Deseret Book in Mesa, Arizona. We worked the morning shift together and hit it off almost immediately. Susie came across as being shy, but in reality she's a huge chatterbox! She's always interested in other people & what's going on in their lives. In fact, you can often find Susie on the phone gabbing away to somebody- She's worse than my mom and brother Marc combined! Susie is always thinking of others. At work she would run down to the dollar store and bring back treats for everyone almost on a daily basis! She use to leave little notes in my locker, many times with a present attached. Susie is a giver! At work I would watch her put together big care packages of candy, pop, pictures, stuffed animals, etc. for different friends and mail them off from there. I have been fortunate enough to have been the recipient of a "Susie Care-Package" at least once or twice! Susie knows how much I love Willow Tree angel statues and Dr. Pepper so for Christmas she gave me a case of Dr. Pepper and an angel ornament! When Megann passed away she sent me the 'Angel of Caring' which meant a lot to me; I was in sooo much pain that it was hard for me to talk to anyone. She knew that, but still wanted me to know she cared. I love Susie! I wish I carried many of the qualities that she possesses. I don't feel like I deserve her friendship, but I am grateful for it. She really is the truest definition of a friend!

Definition of a Friend

Supplies
Patterned paper: 7 Gypsies
Colored vellum: Autumn Leaves
Computer fonts: Last Words and Linenstroke, downloaded from the Internet
Button: Making Memories
Other: Ribbon

♥ **I Love It!:** *Simply layering two different shades of purple vellum over printed dictionary paper creates a striking look.*

♥ **I Love It!:** *Definitions are a fun trend in scrapbooking. You can create your own definition, including the funky-looking pronunciation guide for the word, using the symbols menu in Microsoft Word.*

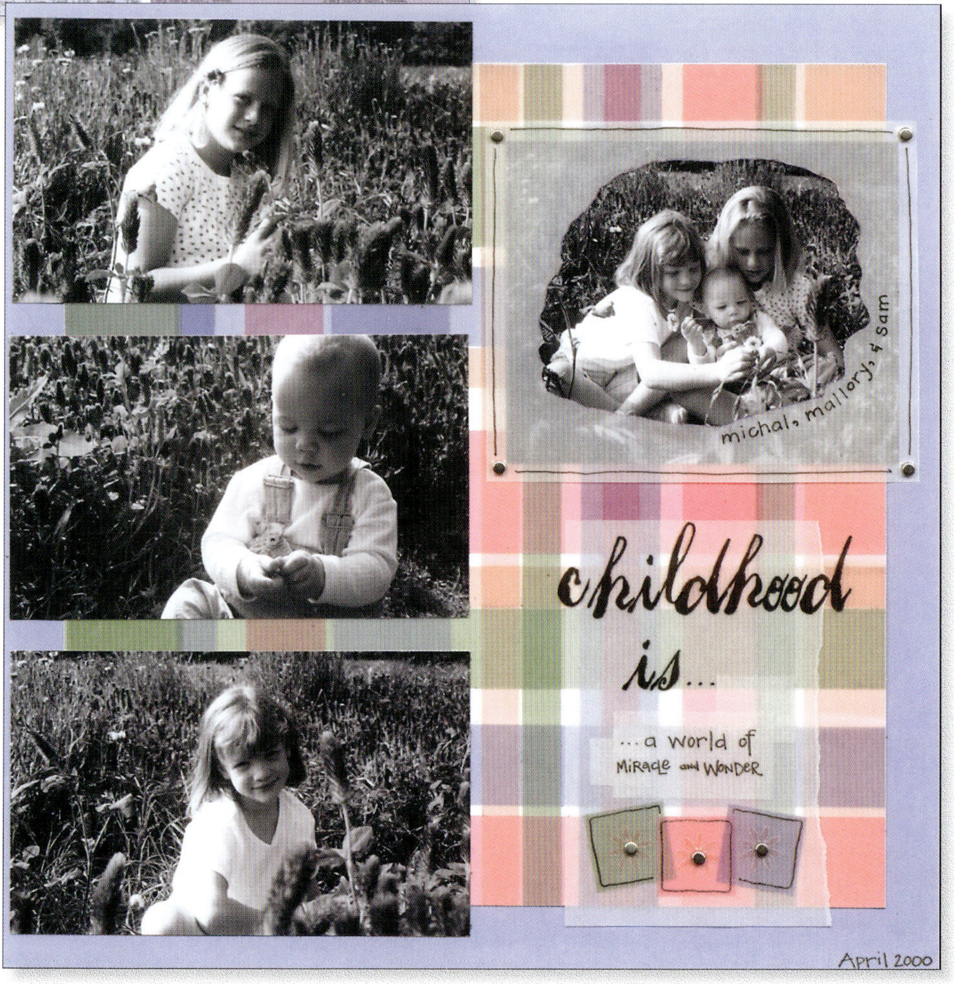
michal, mallory, & Sam
childhood is...
...a world of
MiRacle and WonDER
April 2000

Childhood Is ...

Supplies
Vellum: Autumn Leaves
Letter stickers: Flavia, Colorbök
Daisy punch: Family Treasures
Pen: Zig Writer, EK Success
Other: Brads

♥ **I Love It!:** *Weaving different-sized strips of vellum in different colors creates a true plaid, since overlapping colors blend into each other. Try different color combinations for different page themes, and mount the entire woven plaid on white to ensure the colors stay true.*

tip 4
color-block backgrounds for your layouts using a variety of papers.

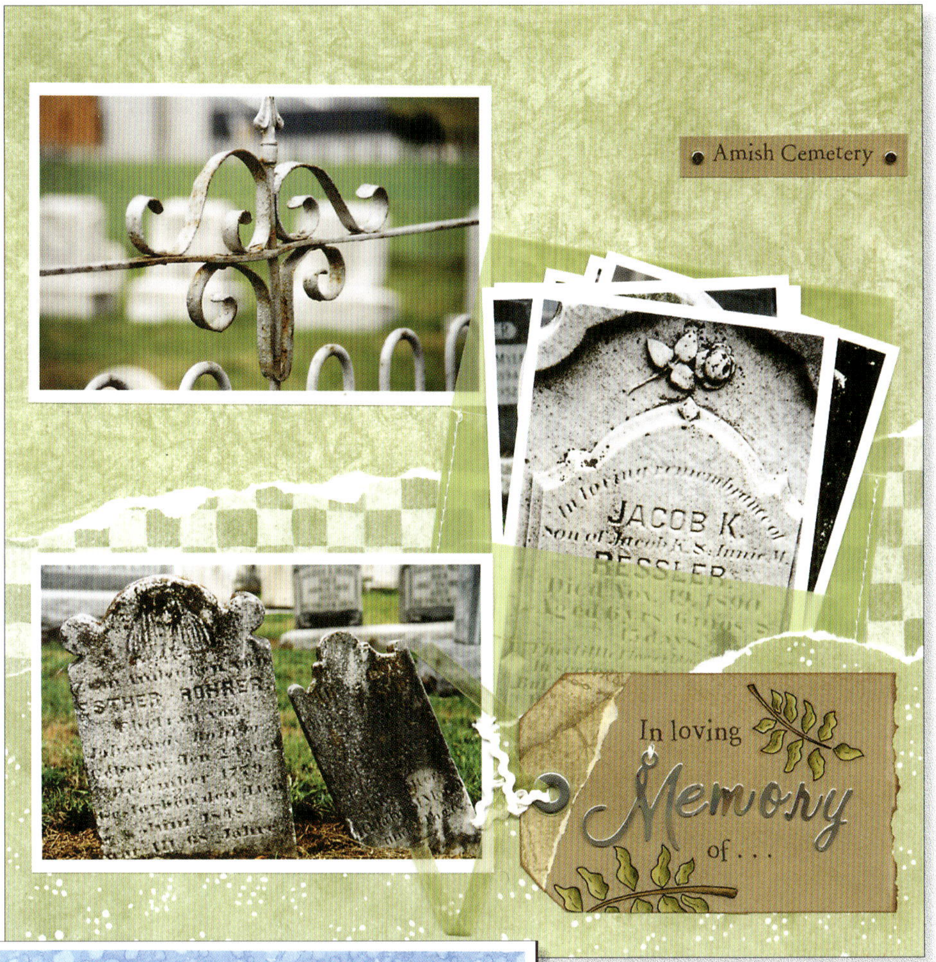
Amish Cemetery
In loving
Memory
of . . .

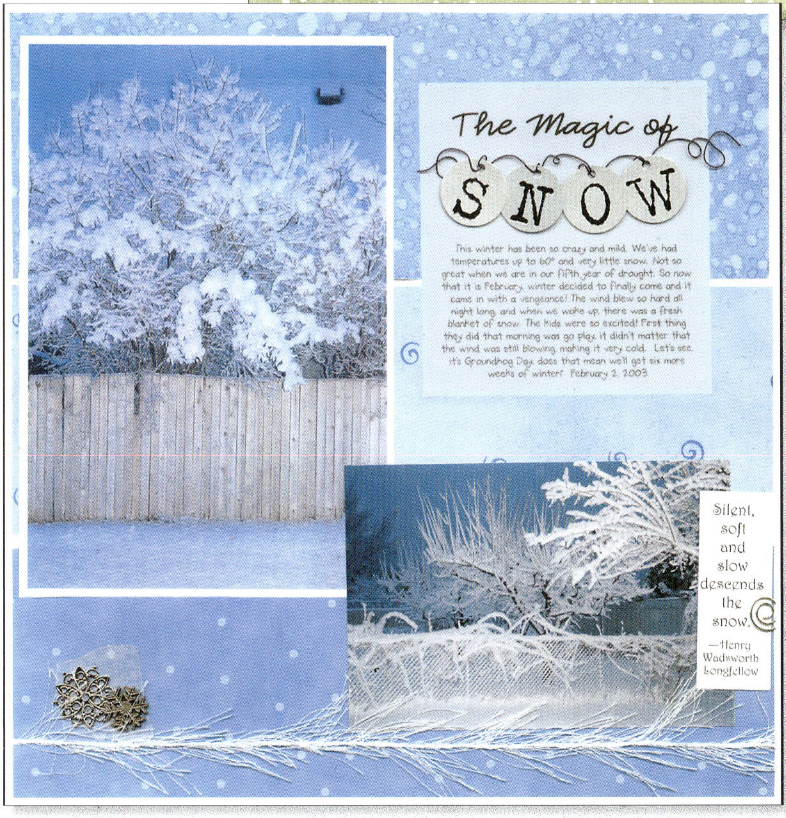
The Magic of
SNOW
This winter has been so crazy and mild. We've had temperatures up to 60° and very little snow. Not so great when we are in our fifth year of drought. So now that it is February, winter decided to finally come and it came in with a vengeance! The wind blew so hard all night long, and when we woke up, there was a fresh blanket of snow. The kids were so excited! First thing they did that morning was go play. It didn't matter that the wind was still blowing, making it very cold. Let's see, it's Groundhog Day, does that mean we'll get six more weeks of winter? February 2, 2003
Silent, soft and slow descends the snow.
—Henry Wadsworth Longfellow

In Loving Memory

Supplies
Patterned papers and stickers: Provo Craft
Metal letters and brads: Making Memories
Computer font: CK Newsprint, "Fresh Fonts" CD, *Creating Keepsakes*
Other: Vellum envelope, fibers and washer

♥ **I Love It!:** *Use decorative envelopes to hold extra photos, accents or journaling. For an extra-nice touch, accent the envelope further by sewing it to your background.*

The Magic of Snow

Supplies
Patterned papers, metal accents and craft wire: Making Memories
Snowflake charm: American Tag Co.
Fiber: Adornaments, EK Success
Quote: Tiny Tales, My Mind's Eye
Computer fonts: CK Toggle, "The Best of Creative Lettering" CD Vol. 4; CK Script, "The Best of Creative Lettering" CD Vol. 1, *Creating Keepsakes*

♥ **I Love It!:** *Print a favorite quote, trim it to size and clip it to the side or top of your layout with a decorative paper clip.*

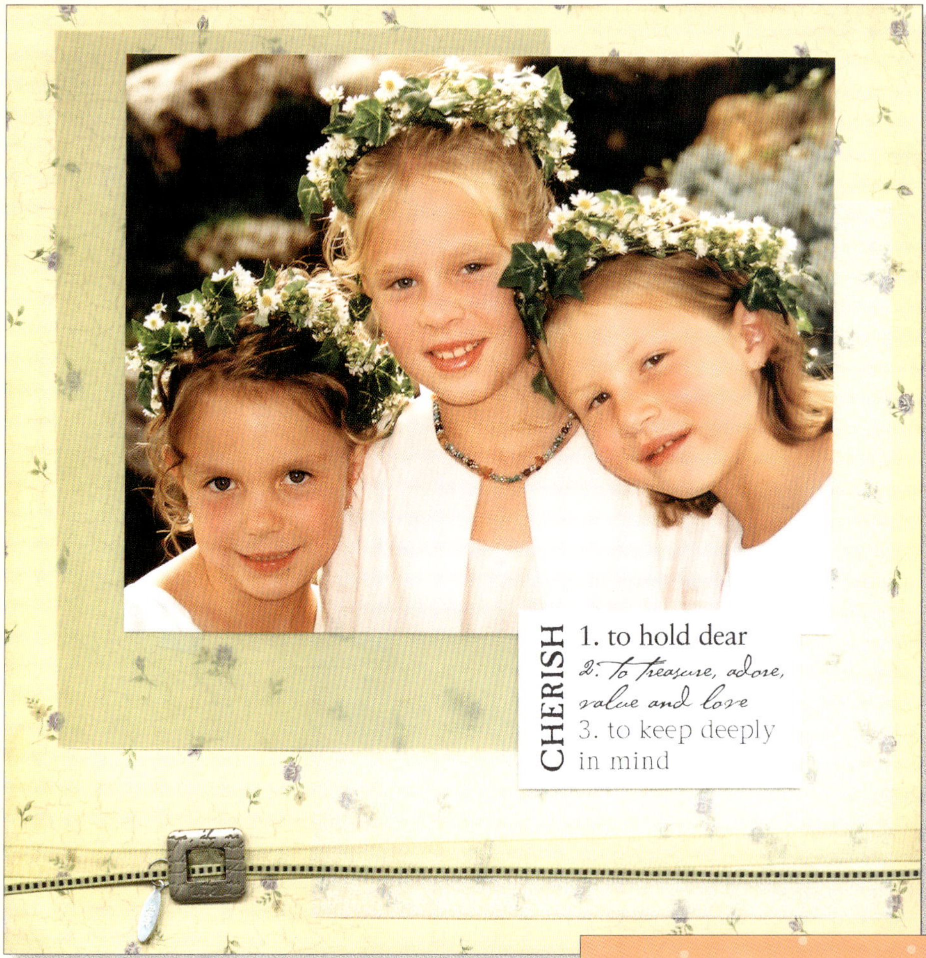
CHERISH
1. to hold dear
2. to treasure, adore, value and love
3. to keep deeply in mind

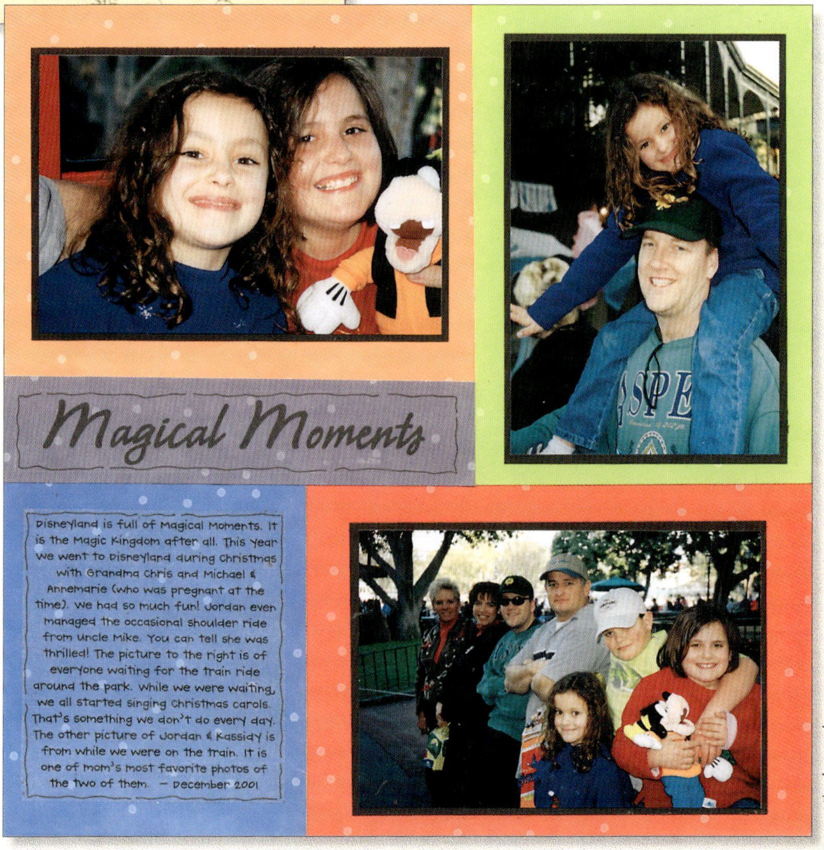
Magical Moments
Disneyland is full of Magical Moments. It is the Magic Kingdom after all. This year we went to Disneyland during Christmas with Grandma Chris and Michael & Annemarie (who was pregnant at the time). We had so much fun! Jordan even managed the occasional shoulder ride from Uncle Mike. You can tell she was thrilled! The picture to the right is of everyone waiting for the train ride around the park. While we were waiting, we all started singing Christmas carols. That's something we don't do every day. The other picture of Jordan & Kassidy is from while we were on the train. It is one of mom's most favorite photos of the two of them. – December 2001

Cherish

Supplies
Patterned paper, vellum, ribbon buckle, charm and preprinted definition accent: Making Memories
Ribbon: Making Memories

♥ **I Love It!:** *Every once in a while, fill a layout with an enlargement of your favorite photograph. Include any sentiments or a personal letter to the subject of the photograph in an envelope on the back of the layout.*

Magical Moments

Supplies
Patterned papers: Making Memories
Computer font: CAC Leslie (title), downloaded from the Internet; CK Handprint, "The Best of Creative Lettering" CD Vol. 4, *Creating Keepsakes*
Pen: Zig Writer, EK Success

♥ **I Love It!:** *Scrapbookers generally reach for white cardstock when matting their photographs, but this fun layout shows that black cardstock can provide an effective, pleasing photo mat as well. When your photographs are vivid or dark, hold them up to a piece of white and a piece of black cardstock to see which is more effective.*

tip 5
create geometric accents for a simple layout.

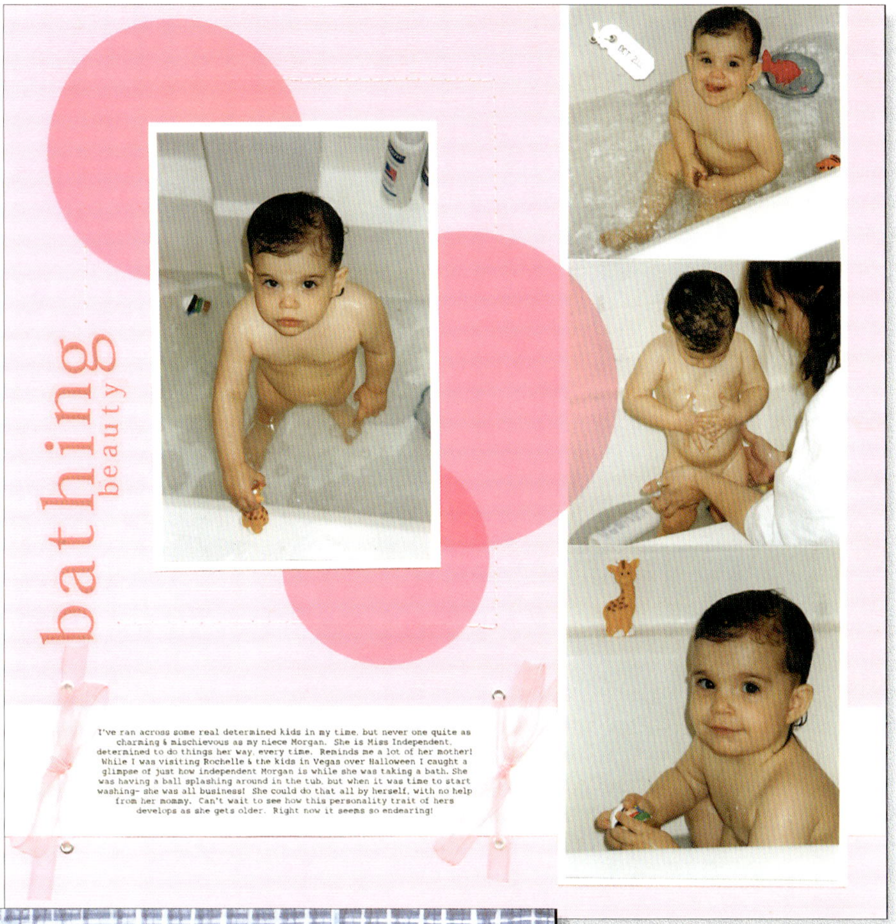

bathing beauty
I've ran across some real determined kids in my time, but never one quite as charming & mischievous as my niece Morgan. She is Miss Independent, determined to do things her way, every time. Reminds me a lot of her mother! While I was visiting Rochelle & the kids in Vegas over Halloween I caught a glimpse of just how independent Morgan is while she was taking a bath. She was having a ball splashing around in the tub, but when it was time to start washing- she was all business! She could do that all by herself, with no help from her mommy. Can't wait to see how this personality trait of hers develops as she gets older. Right now it seems so endearing!

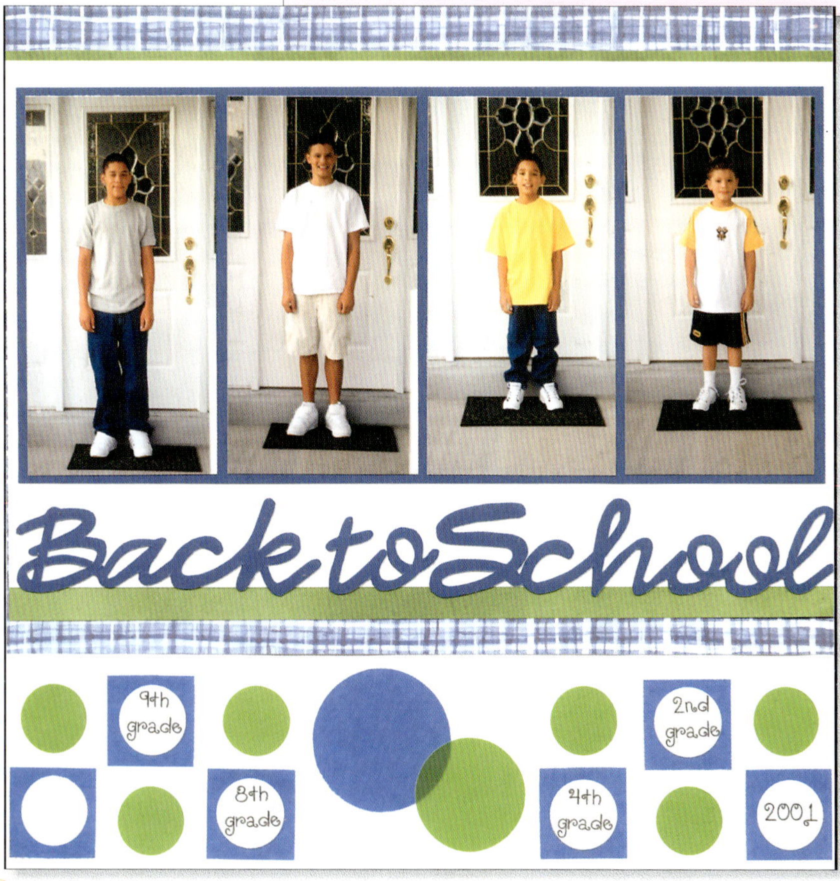

Back to School
9th grade
2nd grade
8th grade
4th grade
2001

Bathing Beauty

Supplies
Vellum: Autumn Leaves
Letter stickers: SEI
Eyelets: Making Memories
Computer font: Linenstroke, downloaded from the Internet
Other: Date stamp, tag and ribbon

♥ **I Love It!:** *Every once in a while, add some variety by running your title along the side of your layout instead of across the top or bottom.*

♥ **I Love It!:** *Create a "visual photo mat" by sewing an even border around your photograph. The stitches are just enough to draw the eye but not as obvious as a paper photo mat.*

Back to School

Supplies
Patterned paper: Karen Foster Design
Vellum: Autumn Leaves
Circle punch: Family Treasures
Computer fonts: CK Script, "The Best of Creative Lettering" CD Vol. 1; CK Diva, "The Best of Creative Lettering" CD Vol. 4, *Creating Keepsakes*

♥ **I Love It!:** *These are great photographs of the first day of school. They line up perfectly on the layout because they were all taken in exactly the same spot. When you have photos that line up well, you can save time by matting all of them on the same photo mat instead of cutting separate mats for each photograph.*

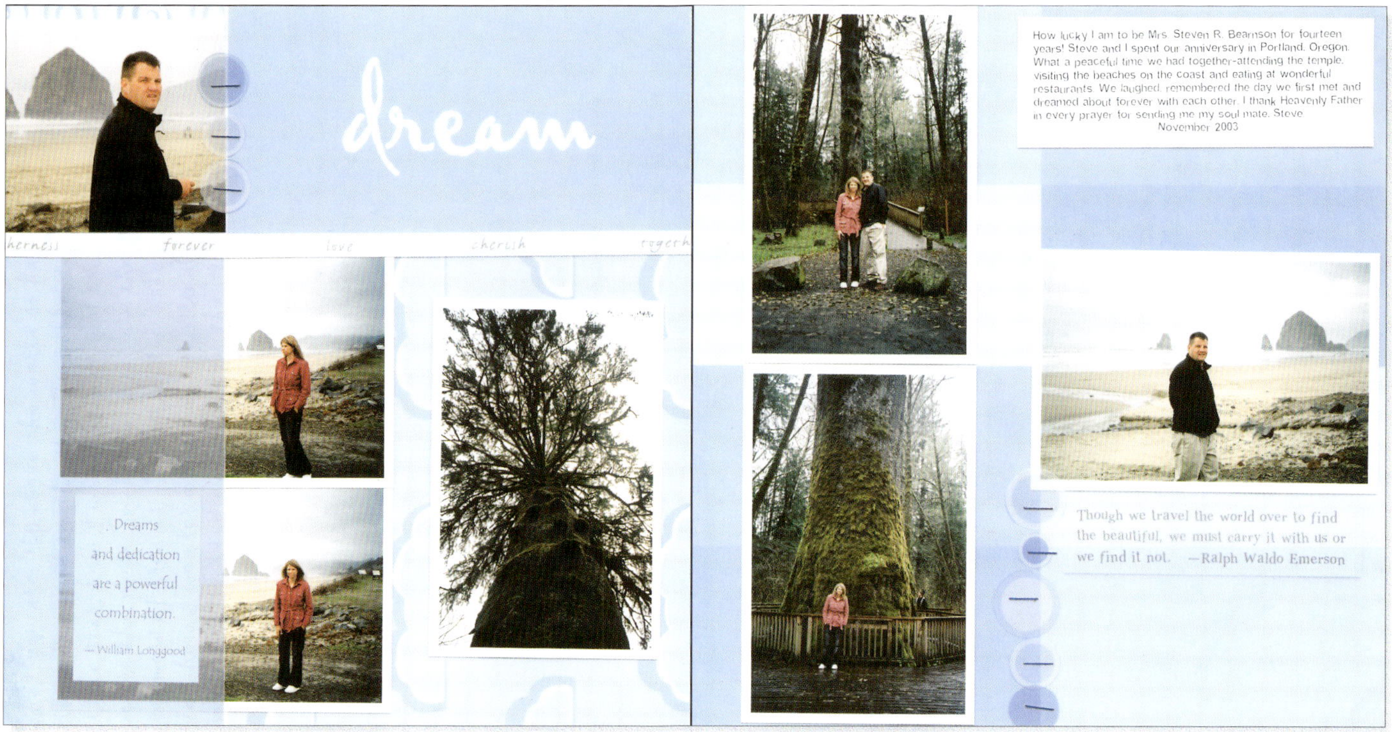

dream
forever
love
cherish
Dreams and dedication are a powerful combination.
— William Longgood
How lucky I am to be Mrs. Steven R. Bearnson for fourteen years! Steve and I spent our anniversary in Portland, Oregon. What a peaceful time we had together-attending the temple, visiting the beaches on the coast and eating at wonderful restaurants. We laughed, remembered the day we first met and dreamed about forever with each other. I thank Heavenly Father in every prayer for sending me my soul mate. Steve
November 2003
Though we travel the world over to find the beautiful, we must carry it with us or we find it not. —Ralph Waldo Emerson

Dream

Supplies
Vellum: American Crafts
Preprinted quote accent: Tiny Tales, My Mind's Eye
Colored staples and printed ribbon: Making Memories
Computer font: CK Elusive, "Fresh Fonts" CD, *Creating Keepsakes*

♥ **I Love It!:** *Cut a slit in the vellum and slide the ends of photographs under the vellum for an artistic look.*

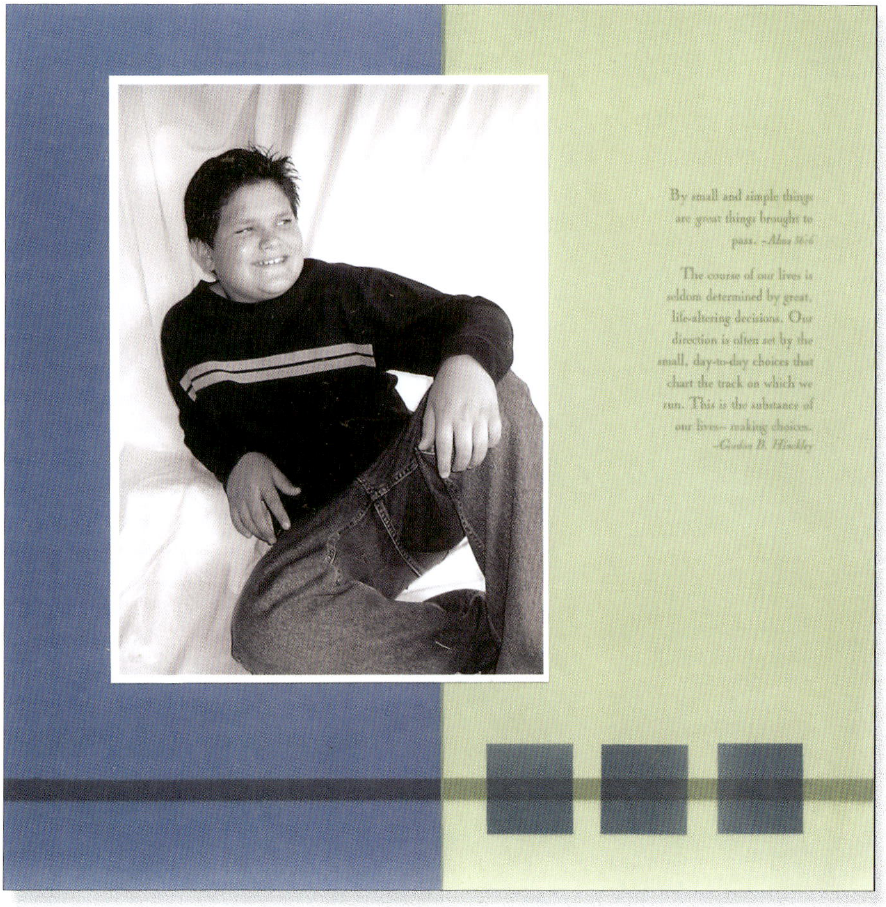

By small and simple things are great things brought to pass.
The course of our lives is seldom determined by great, life-altering decisions. Our direction is often set by the small, day-to-day choices that chart the track on which we run. This is the substance of our lives– making choices.
–Gordon B. Hinckley

Small and Simple Things

Supplies
Vellum: Autumn Leaves
Computer font: Bernhard Modern BT, Microsoft Word

♥ **I Love It!:** *Printing the journaling on white cardstock and placing it on the vellum background would have stolen attention from the focus of the page—the photograph. Instead, the journaling was printed on white cardstock and slipped under the vellum. The words are clear but not dominant on the page.*

tip 6

hold photos, journaling or memorabilia in a pocket.

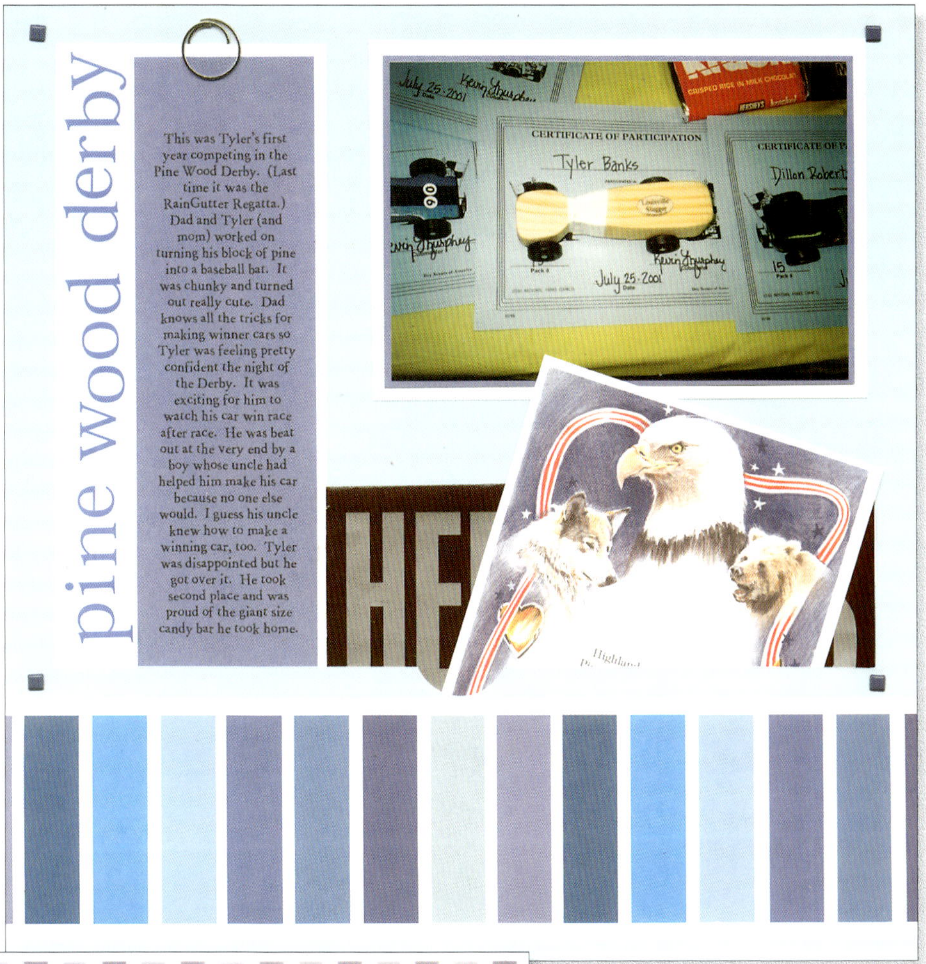

pine wood derby
This was Tyler's first year competing in the Pine Wood Derby. (Last time it was the RainGutter Regatta.) Dad and Tyler (and mom) worked on turning his block of pine into a baseball bat. It was chunky and turned out really cute. Dad knows all the tricks for making winner cars so Tyler was feeling pretty confident the night of the Derby. It was exciting for him to watch his car win race after race. He was beat out at the very end by a boy whose uncle had helped him make his car because no one else would. I guess his uncle knew how to make a winning car, too. Tyler was disappointed but he got over it. He took second place and was proud of the giant size candy bar he took home.
CERTIFICATE OF PARTICIPATION
Tyler Banks

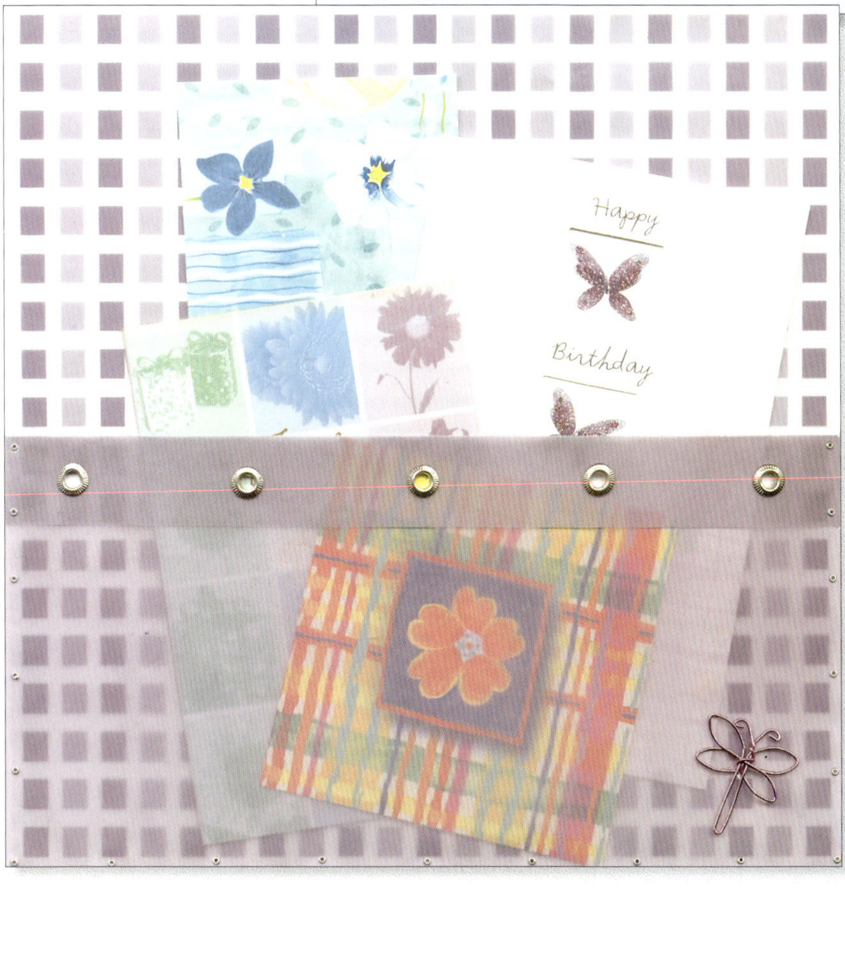

Happy
Birthday

Pinewood Derby

Supplies

Patterned paper and letter stickers: SEI
Circle punch: Family Treasures
Brads: Provo Craft
Computer font: CK Newsprint, "Fresh Fonts" CD, *Creating Keepsakes*
Other: Spiral paper clip

♥ **I Love It!:** *Using pocket pages as a solution to your memorabilia storage problems means you can save more memorabilia. I love that this layout includes not only the certificate that was won that night, but also the wrapper from the candy bar prize!*

Happy Birthday

Supplies

Vellum: American Crafts
Small eyelets: Making Memories
Large eyelets: Creative Imaginations
Wire dragonfly accent: Westrim Crafts

♥ **I Love It!:** *When using vellum to make a pocket page, fold the top edge over to layer the vellum, creating a slightly darker border along the pocket edge. This simple technique will dress up the pocket and give it a finished look.*

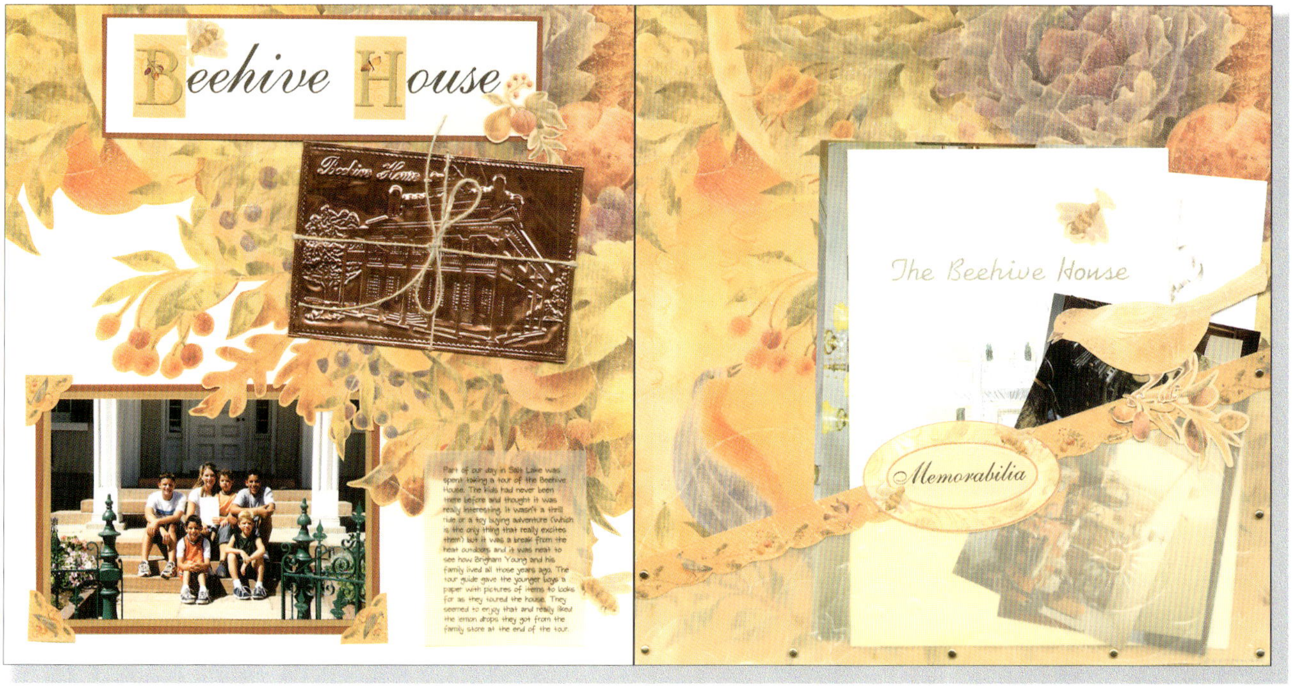
Beehive House
The Beehive House
Memorabilia
Part of our day in Salt Lake was spent taking a tour of the Beehive House. The kids had never been there before and thought it was really interesting. It wasn't a thrill ride or a toy buying adventure (which is the only thing that really excites them) but it was a break from the heat outdoors and it was neat to see how Brigham Young and his family lived all those years ago. The tour guide gave the younger boys a paper with pictures of items to looks for as they toured the house. They seemed to enjoy that and really liked the lemon drops they got from the family store at the end of the tour.

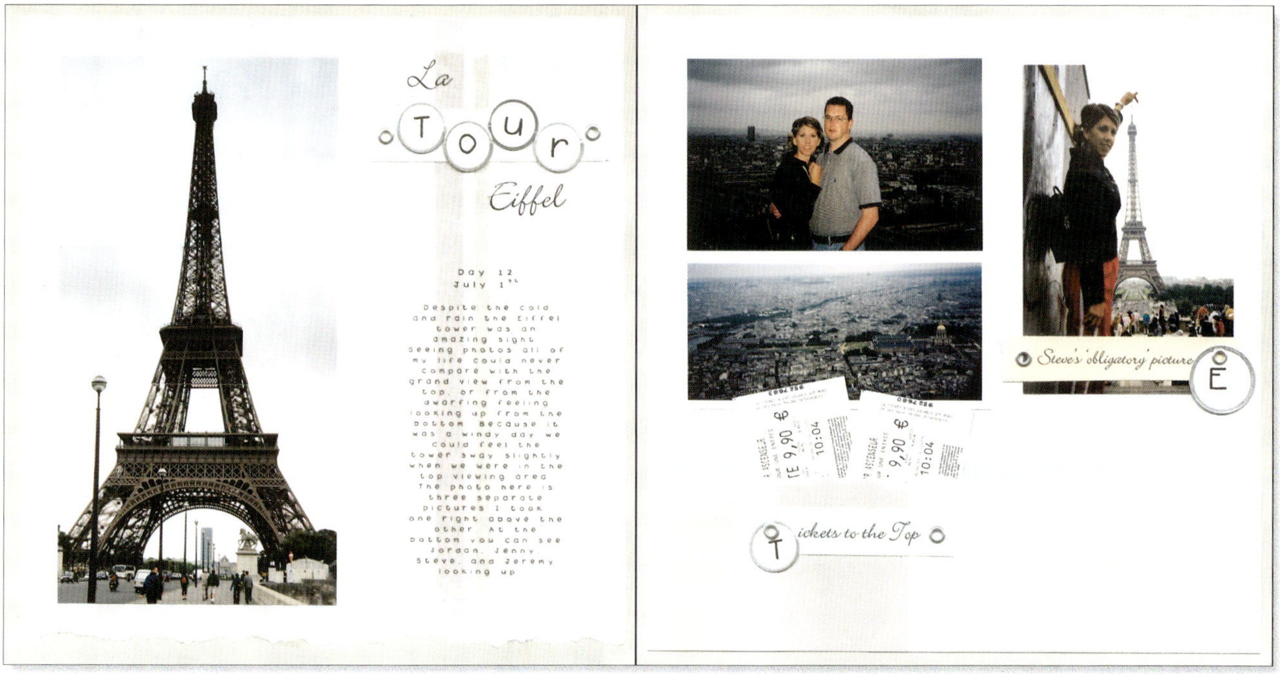
La Tour Eiffel
Day 12
July 1st
Despite the cold and rain the Eiffel tower was an amazing sight seeing photos all of my life could never compare with the grand view from the top, or from the dwarfing feeling looking up from the bottom Because it was a windy day we could feel the tower sway slightly when we were in the top viewing area The photo here is three separate pictures I took one right above the other. At the bottom you can see Jordan, Jenny, Steve, and Jeremy looking up
Steve's 'obligatory' picture
Tickets to the Top

Beehive House

Supplies
Patterned paper, embossed vellum and stickers: K & Company
Vellum: Autumn Leaves
Computer font: CK Journaling, "The Best of Creative Lettering" CD Vol. 2, *Creating Keepsakes*
Other: Copper postcard and twine

♥ **I Love It!:** *Creating pockets out of paper is a great way to include memorabilia or several photographs on a layout. If your pocket is too thick to use traditional adhesive, try attaching it to your page using brads or eyelets.*

♥ **I Love It!:** *Cutting a portion of the patterned paper, silhouetting around the printed pattern as you cut, and mounting it on a matching color of solid cardstock emphasizes the beauty of the pattern while still keeping the focus on the photographs.*

La Tour Eiffel

Supplies
Patterned paper: SEI
Vellum: Autumn Leaves
Tags: Making Memories
Eyelets: Memory Lane Paper Company
Computer fonts: 2Peas Spread Sunshine, downloaded from *www.twopeasinabucket.com*; Bickley Script LET, Macromedia

♥ **I Love It!:** *Some things are too large to fit in the viewfinder of your camera—unless you stand so far away you can barely see what the object is! For subjects like these, take a series of photographs to capture the entire object, then piece the photos together on your layout. What a cool way to get a close-up of important but large things!*

tip 7

mute distracting page elements.

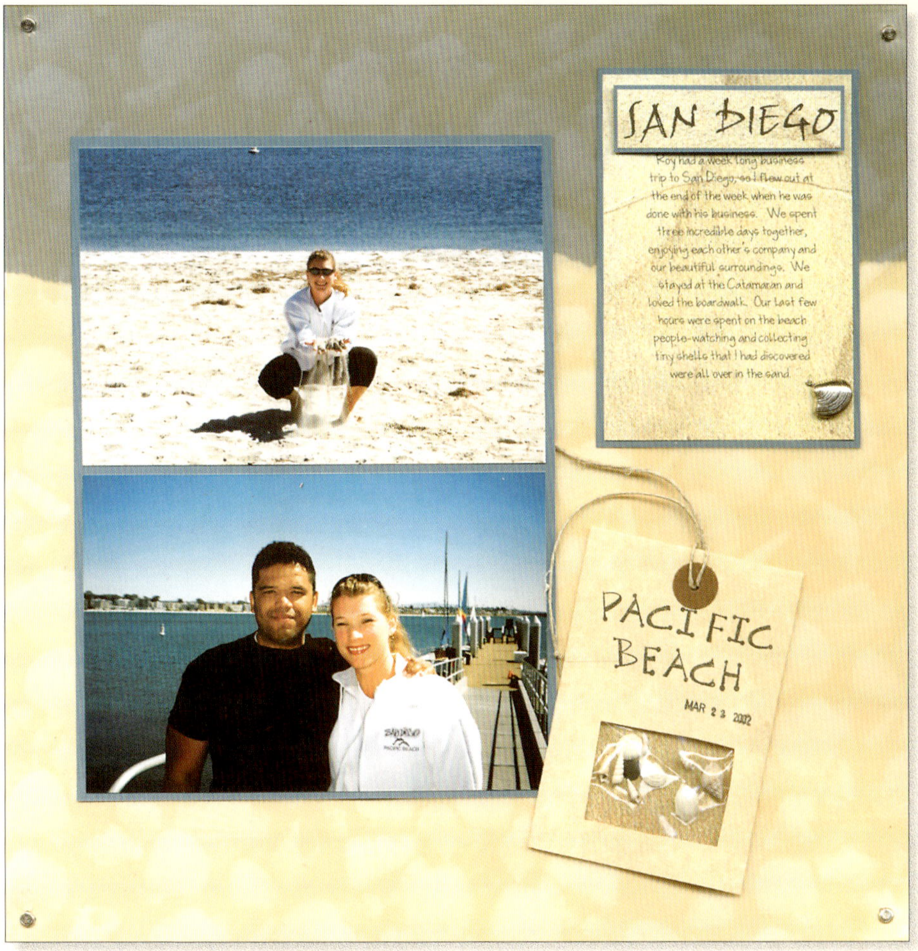
SAN DIEGO
Roy had a week long business trip to San Diego, so I flew out at the end of the week when he was done with his business. We spent three incredible days together, enjoying each other's company and our beautiful surroundings. We stayed at the Catamaran and loved the boardwalk. Our last few hours were spent on the beach people-watching and collecting tiny shells that I had discovered were all over in the sand.
PACIFIC BEACH
MAR 23 2002

Pacific Beach

Supplies

Patterned vellum: Autumn Leaves
Sand patterned paper: Wübie Prints
Letter stamps: Plaid Enterprises
Stamping ink: ColorBox, Clearsnap
Metal studs: Westrim Crafts
Circle punch: Family Treasures
Computer fonts: CK Penman, "The Best of Creative Lettering" CD Vol. 4, *Creating Keepsakes*; John Handy, WordPerfect
Other: Shell charm, date stamp, shells, sandpaper and twine

♥ **I Love It!:** *Placing white cardstock behind this particular patterned vellum on the bottom half of the layout highlights the pattern, while placing blue cardstock behind the top half mutes it. This creates a scene of sand and sky for the background of this beach layout.*

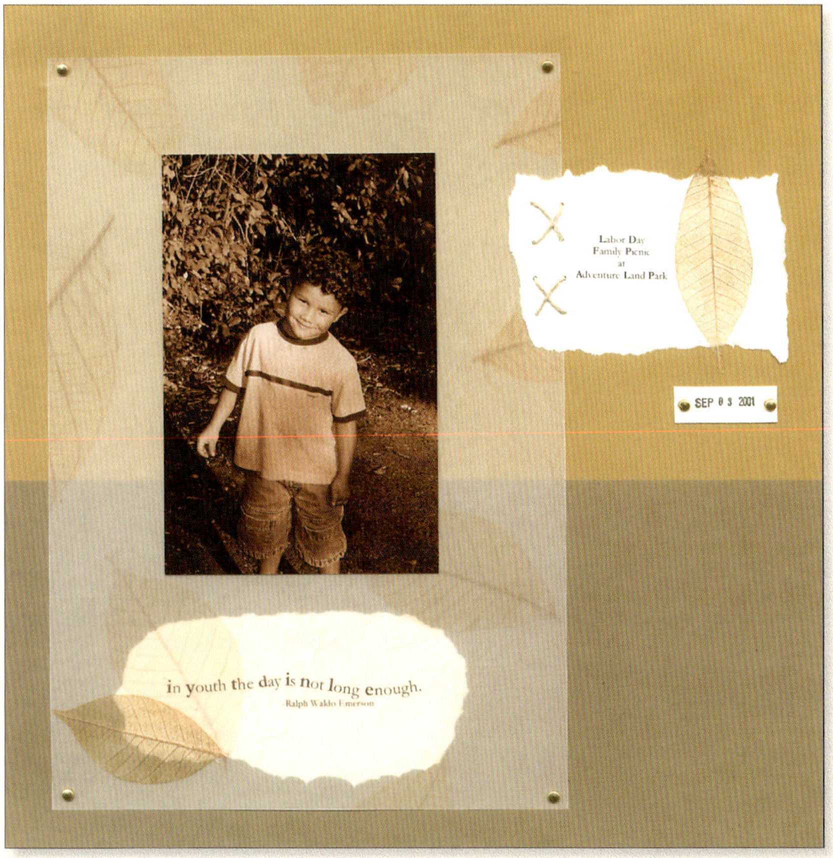
Labor Day
Family Picnic
at
Adventure Land Park
SEP 03 2001
in youth the day is not long enough.
Ralph Waldo Emerson

In Youth …

Supplies

Patterned vellum: WorldWin
Skeletonized leaf: Black Ink
Brads: Making Memories
Computer font: Garamond, Microsoft Word
Other: Date stamp and twine

♥ **I Love It!:** *Printing the quote below the photograph on white cardstock would have pulled attention away from the photo, but the quote wasn't visible enough printed on vellum. Muting the white cardstock by placing it underneath the vellum, then printing the quote onto the vellum, subtly highlights the quote—the perfect compromise!*

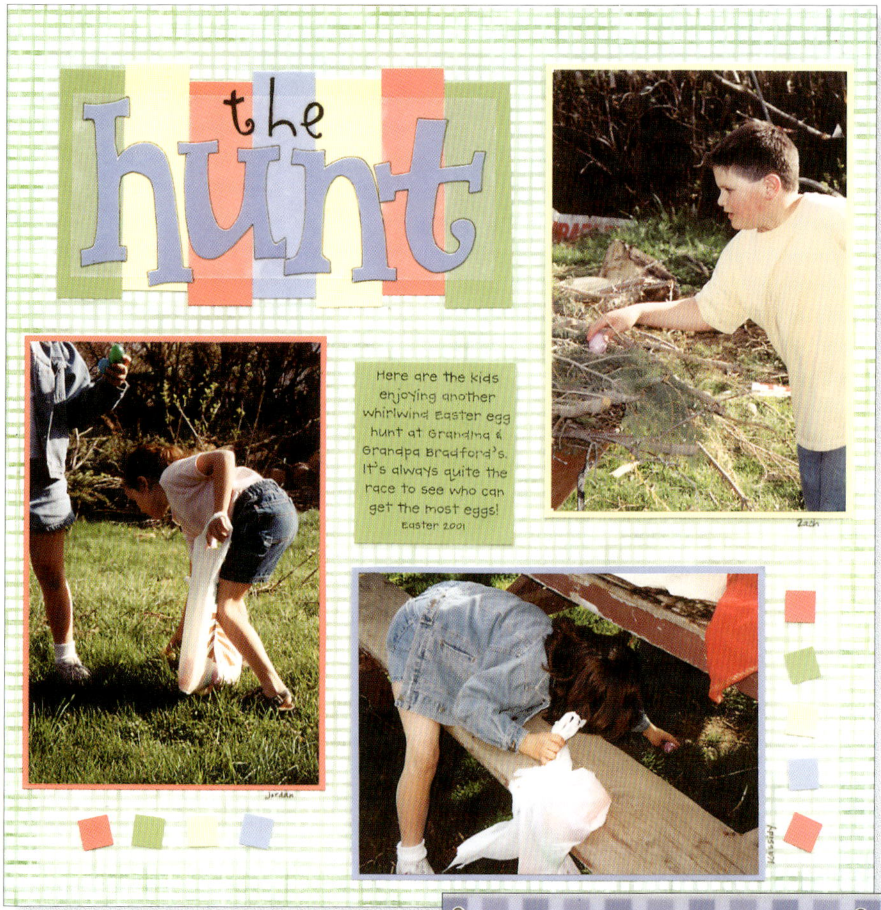
the hunt
Here are the kids enjoying another whirlwind Easter egg hunt at Grandma & Grandpa Bradford's. It's always quite the race to see who can get the most eggs!
Easter 2001
Zach

The Hunt

Supplies

Patterned paper, solid paper and vellum: Colorbök
Letter stickers: David Walker, Colorbök
Square Punch: EK Success
Computer font: CK Handprint, "The Best of Creative Lettering" CD Combo, *Creating Keepsakes*
Lettering template: Party, ScrapPagerz

♥ **I Love It!:** *The checked pattern on this paper is perfect for a spring egg hunt page. To make sure it doesn't compete with the photographs, trim a piece of vellum slightly smaller than the patterned paper and center it on the page. This creates a slightly muted area to mount your photographs on while leaving a darker border around the edge of the page.*

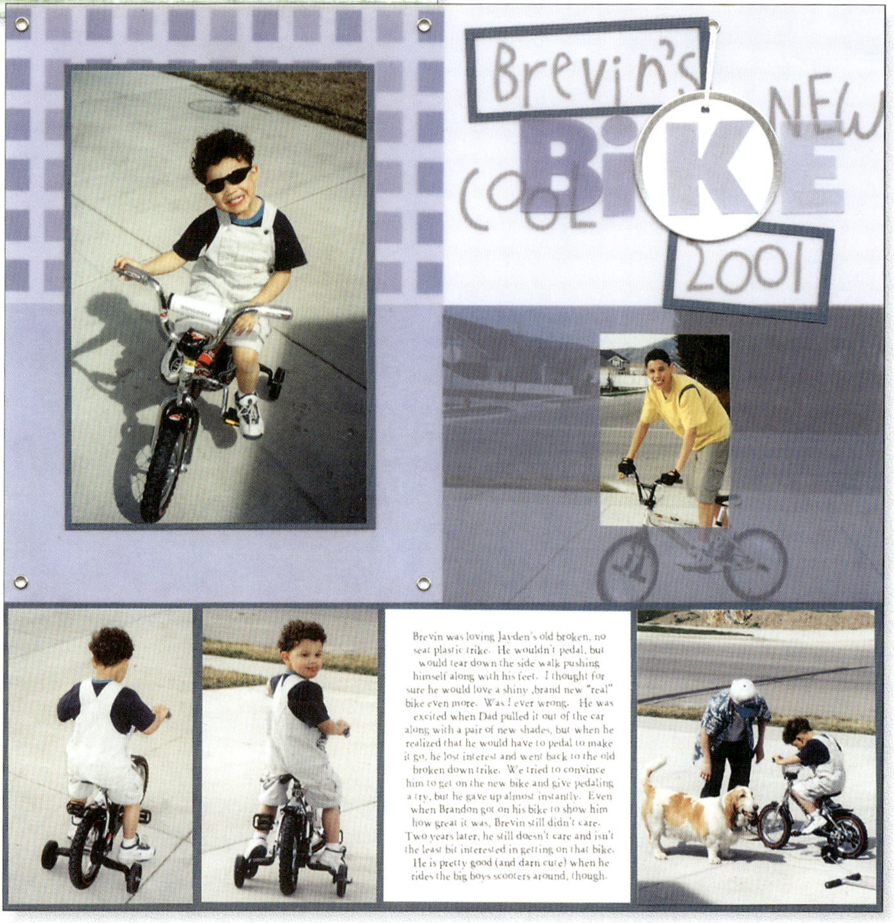
Brevin's
NEW
BIKE
COOL
2001
Brevin was loving Jayden's old broken, no seat plastic trike. He wouldn't pedal, but would tear down the side walk pushing himself along with his feet. I thought for sure he would love a shiny ,brand new "real" bike even more. Was I ever wrong. He was excited when Dad pulled it out of the car along with a pair of new shades, but when he realized that he would have to pedal to make it go, he lost interest and went back to the old broken down trike. We tried to convince him to get on the new bike and give pedaling a try, but he gave up almost instantly. Even when Brandon got on his bike to show him how great it was, Brevin still didn't care. Two years later, he still doesn't care and isn't the least bit interested in getting on that bike. He is pretty good (and darn cute) when he rides the big boys scooters around, though.

Brevin's New Bike

Supplies

Vellum: American Crafts
Letter stickers: Colorbök
Letter die cuts: Sizzix
Tag and eyelets: Making Memories
Computer font: CK Stenography, "Fresh Fonts" CD, *Creating Keepsakes*

♥ **I Love It!:** *On this page, vellum helps you find the most important element in the photograph. For this technique, cut a piece of vellum the same size as your photograph, then cut a shape out of the vellum—experiment with squares, rectangles, circles or ovals—and place it over the subject you want to highlight. The rest of the photograph is still slightly visible, but there's no question what the focus is!*

tip 8

reveal interesting page elements in an innovative way.

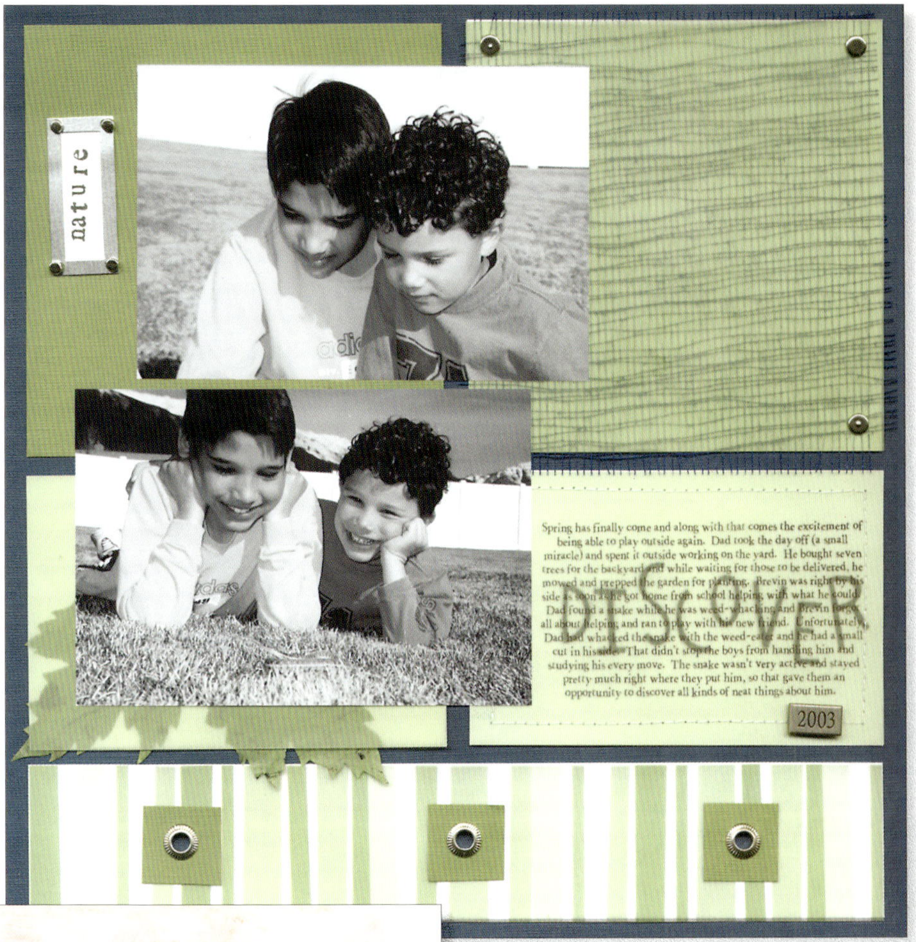
nature
2003

Discover

Supplies
Vellum: American Crafts
Letter stickers: Sue Dreamer, Colorbök
Letter stamps: PSX Design
Stamping ink: ColorBox, Clearsnap
Metal accents: Making Memories
Leaves: Black Ink
Mesh: Magenta
Square punch: Family Treasures
Computer font: CK Stenography, "Fresh Fonts" CD, *Creating Keepsakes*

♥ **I Love It!:** *By subtly revealing the words and other items behind the vellum, the accents on this page illustrate the layout's theme of discovery.*

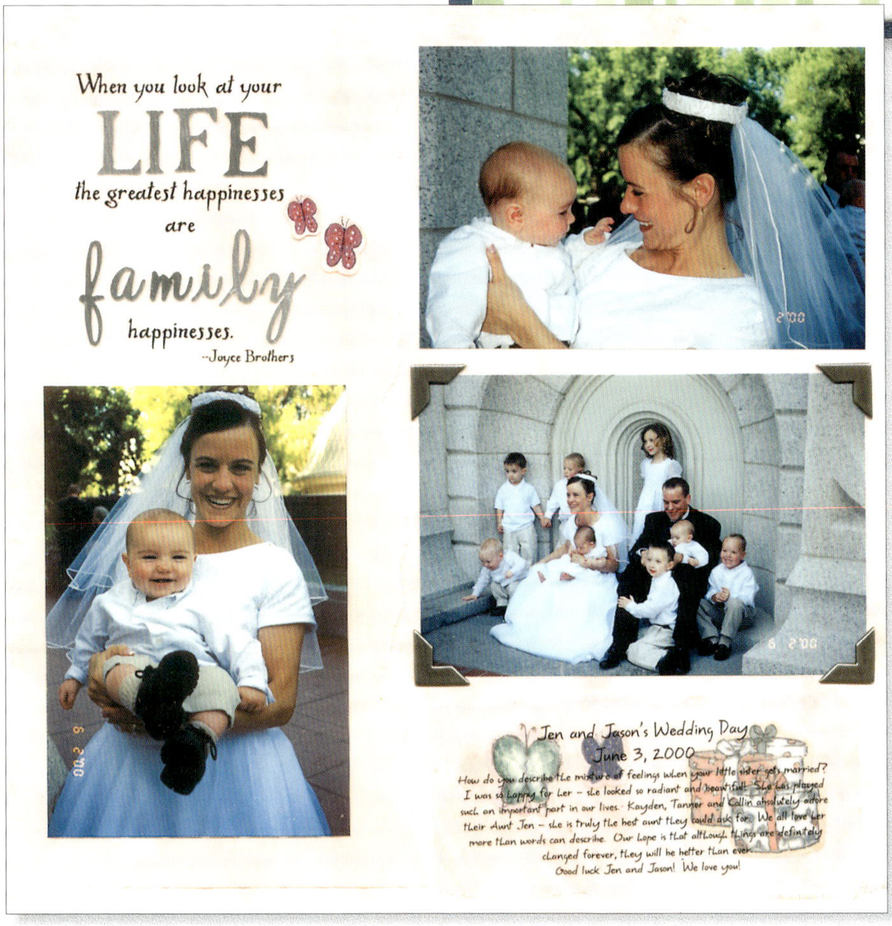
When you look at your
LIFE
the greatest happinesses
are
family
happinesses.
-Joyce Brothers
Jen and Jason's Wedding Day
June 3, 2000
How do you describe the mixture of feelings when your little sister gets married?
I was so happy for her - she looked so radiant and beautiful! She has played
such an important part in our lives. Kayden, Tanner and Callin absolutely adore
their Aunt Jen - she is truly the best aunt they could ask for. We all love her
more than words can describe. Our hope is that although things are definitely
changed forever, they will be better than ever.
Good luck Jen and Jason! We love you!

Family Happinesses

Supplies
Patterned paper: Flavia, Colorbök
Embossed vellum: Lasting Impressions for Paper
Vellum: Provo Craft
Stickers: Colorbök
Metal accents: Making Memories
Computer fonts: CK Artisan, Becky Higgins' "Creative Clips & Fonts" CD; CK Inky, "Fresh Fonts" CD, *Creating Keepsakes*

♥ **I Love It!:** *Create a small sticker collage to layer your journaling over—with vellum, the background will show through while maintaining the visibility of the smaller journaling.*

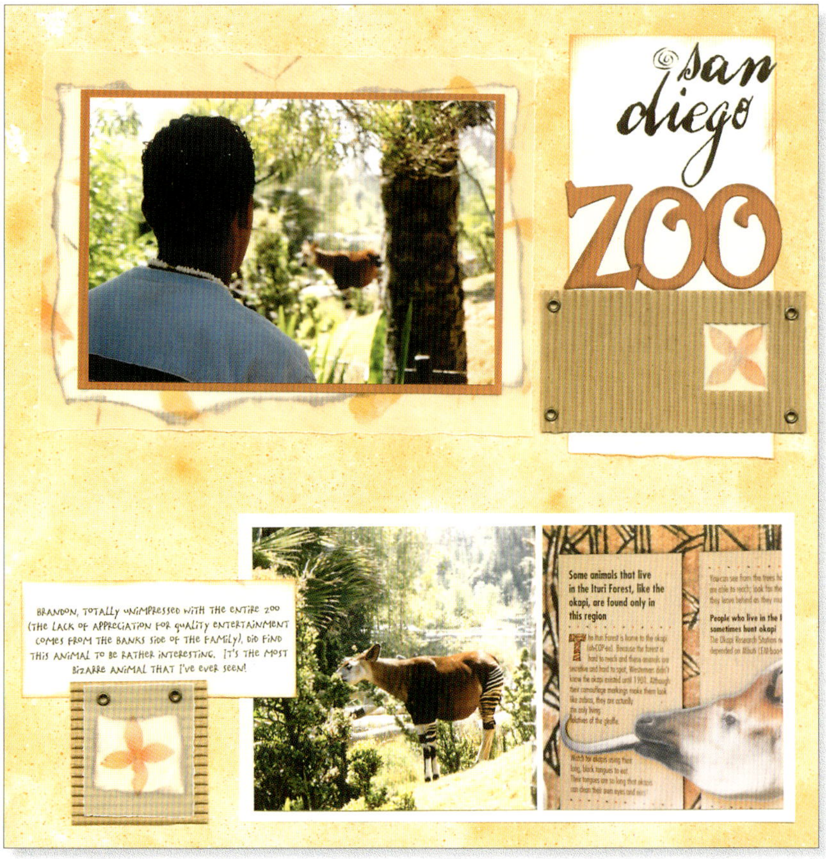
san diego
ZOO
Brandon, totally unimpressed with the entire zoo (the lack of appreciation for quality entertainment comes from the Banks side of the family), did find this animal to be rather interesting. It's the most bizarre animal that I've ever seen!
Some animals that live in the Ituri Forest, like the okapi, are found only in this region

San Diego Zoo

Supplies
Patterned paper: Provo Craft
Patterned vellum: WorldWin
Letter stickers: Flavia, Colorbök
Letter die cuts: Sizzix
Stamping ink: ColorBox, Clearsnap
Computer font: Scrap Sloppy, Inspire Graphics
Eyelets: Making Memories
Chalk: Stampin' Up!

♥ **I Love It!:** *The flower accent cut from patterned vellum in the top-right corner of this layout wasn't scaled correctly for the title block. To solve the problem, a strip was cut from corrugated paper, creating a block that was scaled correctly for the title block. Then, a small window was cut in the corrugated paper to reveal the flower.*

It's a Guy Thing

Supplies
Patterned papers: Provo Craft
Letter stickers: Sue Dreamer, Colorbök
Metal Accent: Making Memories
Mesh: Magenta
Computer font: CK Penman, "The Best of Creative Lettering" CD Vol. 3, *Creating Keepsakes*

♥ **I Love It!:** *Make album viewers feel like they're being let in on a little secret by pulling one corner of your layout up to reveal another pattern. Back the corner with a third pattern to add interest and variety. Anchor the lifted corner to the page with a decorative accent. To keep the fold raised, use thin pop dots under the fold.*

Same Idea, Slightly Different: *Instead of pulling one corner up and anchoring it to your layout to reveal the patterned paper beneath, try tearing a corner of your layout to reveal a different patterned paper below. Once you've torn the edge, fold it back slightly and sew it into place.*

My Maternal Grandma

Supplies
Patterned papers, letter stickers, die-cut flowers and decorative tag: Tim Coffey, K & Company
Computer fonts: DJ Fancy, "Fontastic!" CD, D.J. Inkers; CB Wednesday, package unknown, Chatterbox

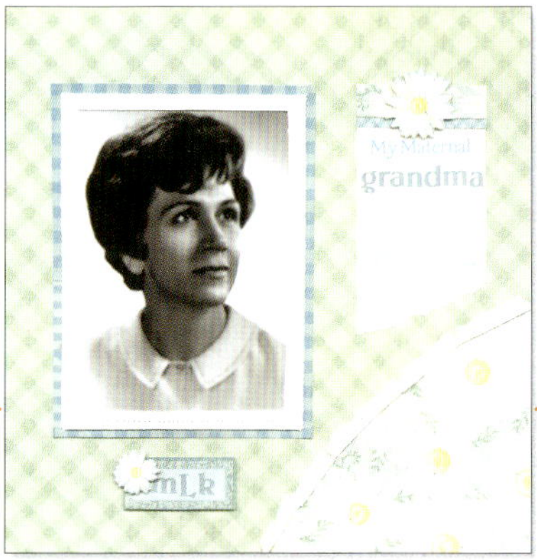
My Maternal
grandma
mlk

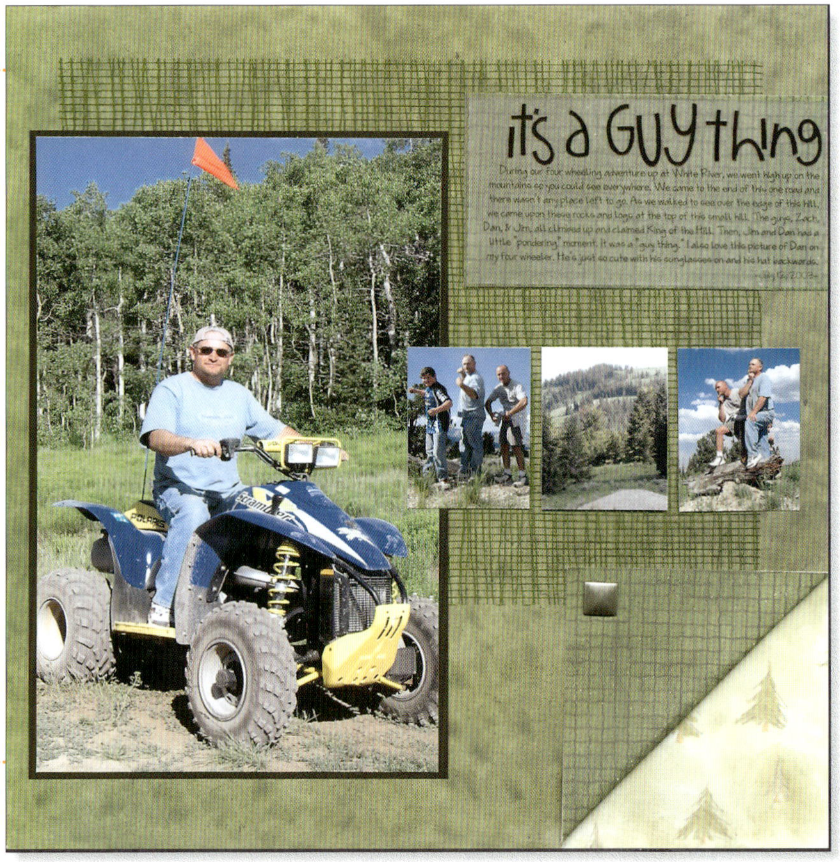
it's a GUY thing

tip 9
add texture and tactile elements to your pages.

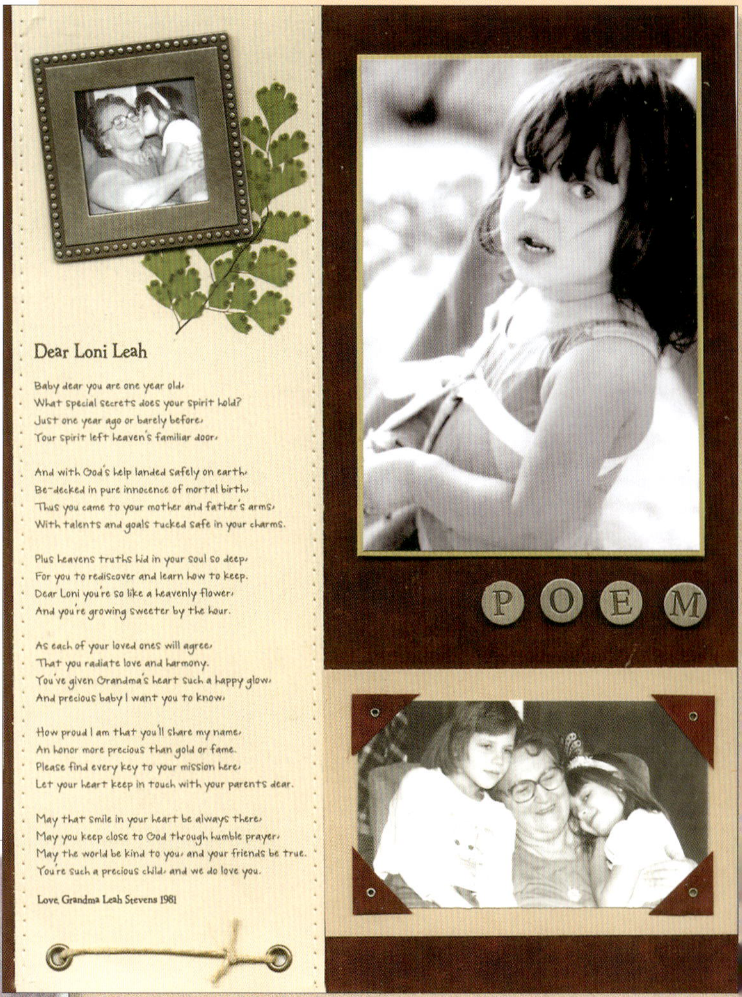
Dear Loni Leah
Baby dear you are one year old.
What special secrets does your spirit hold?
Just one year ago or barely before,
Your spirit left heaven's familiar door.
And with God's help landed safely on earth,
Be-decked in pure innocence of mortal birth.
Thus you came to your mother and father's arms,
With talents and goals tucked safe in your charms.
Plus heavens truths hid in your soul so deep,
For you to rediscover and learn how to keep.
Dear Loni you're so like a heavenly flower,
And you're growing sweeter by the hour.
As each of your loved ones will agree,
That you radiate love and harmony.
You've given Grandma's heart such a happy glow,
And precious baby I want you to know,
How proud I am that you'll share my name,
An honor more precious than gold or fame.
Please find every key to your mission here,
Let your heart keep in touch with your parents dear.
May that smile in your heart be always there,
May you keep close to God through humble prayer,
May the world be kind to you, and your friends be true.
You're such a precious child, and we do love you.
Love, Grandma Leah Stevens 1981
POEM

Poem

Supplies
Suede paper: K & Company
Metal accents: Making Memories
Computer fonts: CK Jot, "The Art of Creative Lettering" CD; CK Constitution, "Fresh Fonts" CD, *Creating Keepsakes*
Pressed leaf: Nature's Pressed
Other: Twine

♥ **I Love It!:** *Pressed foliage adds earthy texture to your layouts. Use a spray adhesive from the craft store for best results when adhering delicate pressed foliage.*

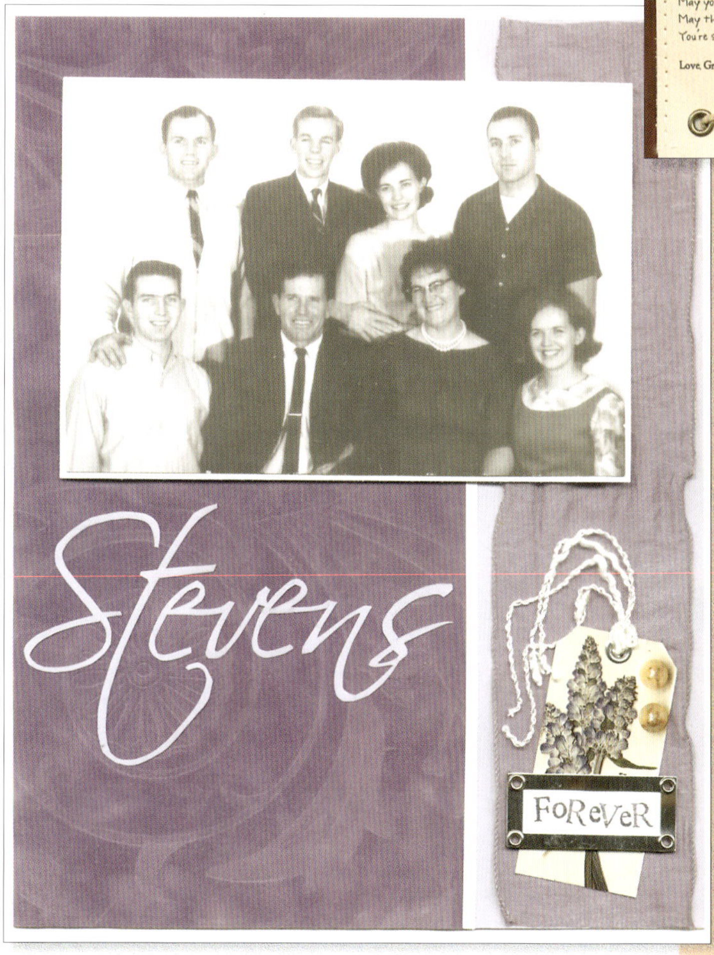
Stevens
FoReVeR

Stevens

Supplies
Embossed suede paper: K & Company
Tag: Fresh Cuts, EK Success
Bookplate and eyelets: Making Memories
Computer font: Scriptina, downloaded from the Internet
Letter stamps: PSX Design
Stamping ink: ColorBox, Clearsnap
Other: 3-D foam adhesive, ribbon and fibers

♥ **I Love It!:** *The contrast between the soft, slightly blurry suede paper and the wrinkled, shiny ribbon beside it adds so much visual interest to this page! Watch for other products that will create contrasting textures on your layouts.*

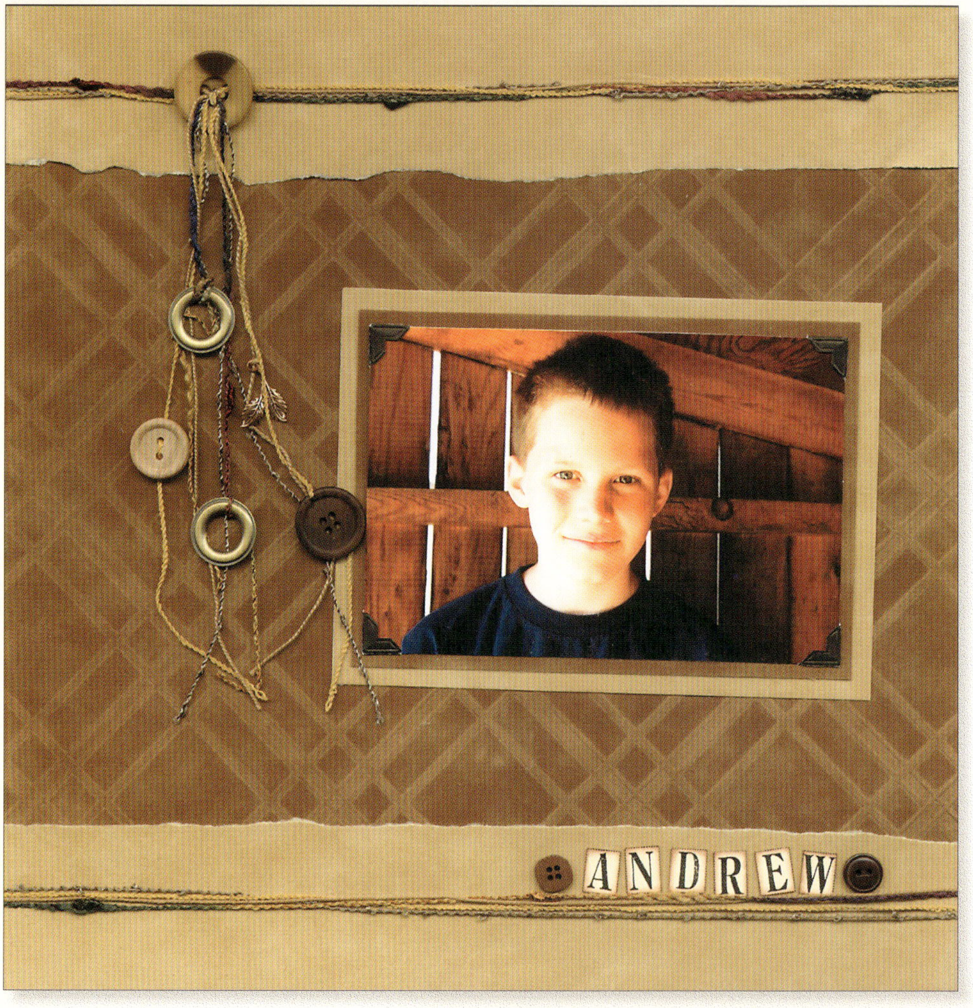
ANDREW

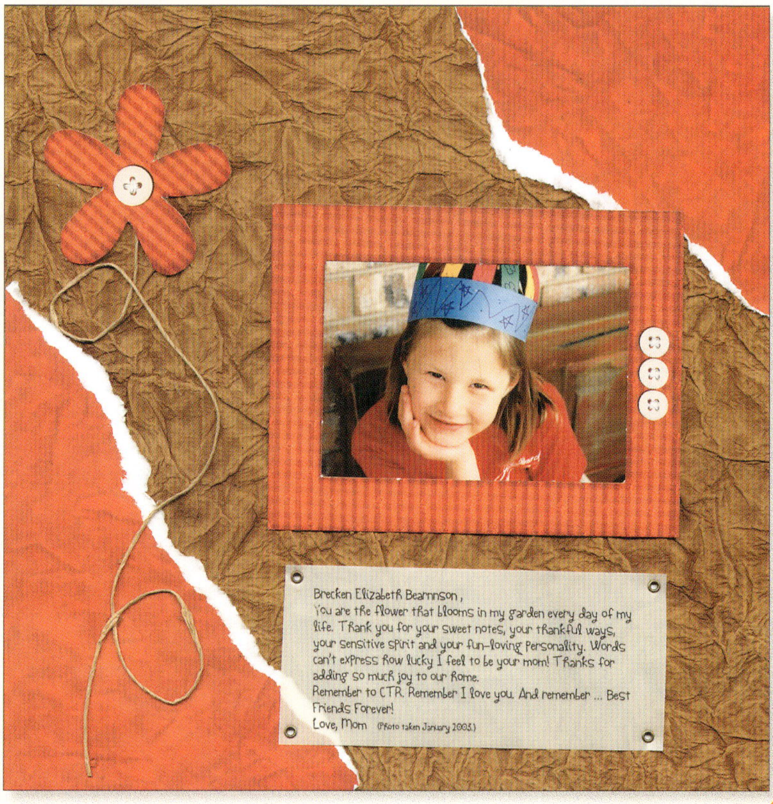
Brecken Elizabeth Bearnson,
You are the flower that blooms in my garden every day of my life. Thank you for your sweet notes, your thankful ways, your sensitive spirit and your fun-loving personality. Words can't express how lucky I feel to be your mom! Thanks for adding so much joy to our home.
Remember to CTR. Remember I love you. And remember ... Best Friends Forever!
Love, Mom (Photo taken January 2003)

Andrew

Supplies
Suede and embossed papers: K & Company
Fibers: On The Surface
Other: Buttons, leaf charm, metal rings and letter accents

♥ **I Love It!:** *Matching textures in your photos with items on your layout is a fun way to create unity. But, contrasting textures in your photos with textures on your layout is another way to create interest. Mix a photograph with a rustic wood pattern in the background with the soft look of suede paper, or mix a dressy heritage photograph with the mottled texture of corkboard. The different textures will create a tactile dimension on your layout.*

Brecken Elizabeth Bearnson

Supplies
Patterned and crumpled papers: Provo Craft
Frame and flower accent: My Mind's Eye
Vellum: Autumn Leaves
Eyelets: Making Memories
Computer font: CK Fresh, "Fresh Fonts" CD, *Creating Keepsakes*
Other: Twine
Page idea: This layout is based on the layout "You Are the Flower" by Angelia Wigginton on pg. 13 of *A Simple Guide to Designing Scrapbooks.*

♥ **I Love It!:** *The red patterned paper on this layout is smooth, but the pattern looks like crumpled paper. Pairing this paper with an actual textured paper creates an interesting illusion for the eye.*

tip 10

lighten your layout with the sparkle of glitter.

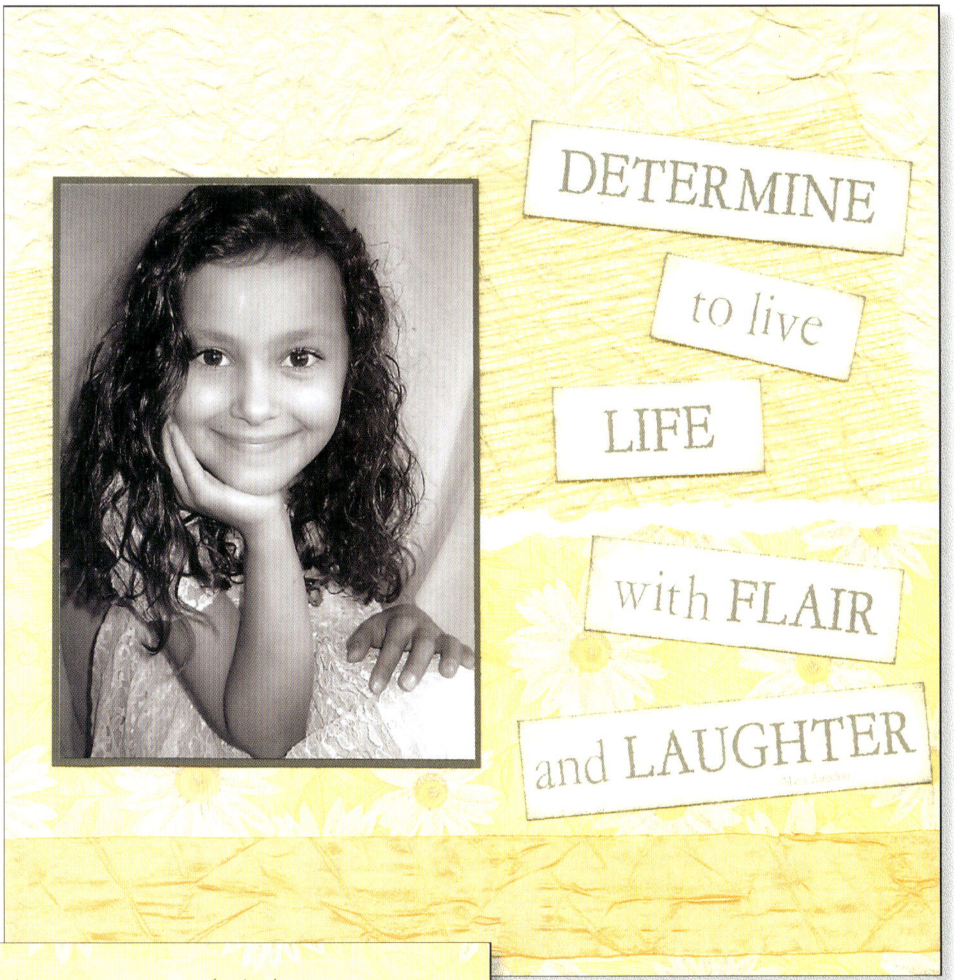
DETERMINE
to live
LIFE
with FLAIR
and LAUGHTER

Flair and Laughter

Supplies
Crumpled paper: Provo Craft
Patterned paper: K & Company
Mesh: Magenta
Computer font: CK Extra, "Fresh Fonts" CD, *Creating Keepsakes*
Stamping ink: ColorBox, Clearsnap
Other: Ribbon

♥ **I Love This!:** *The sparkle from the glitter paper draws attention to the light in the photo subject's eyes. Use glitter paper to repeat sparkle already seen in a photograph or to illustrate the theme of the layout.*

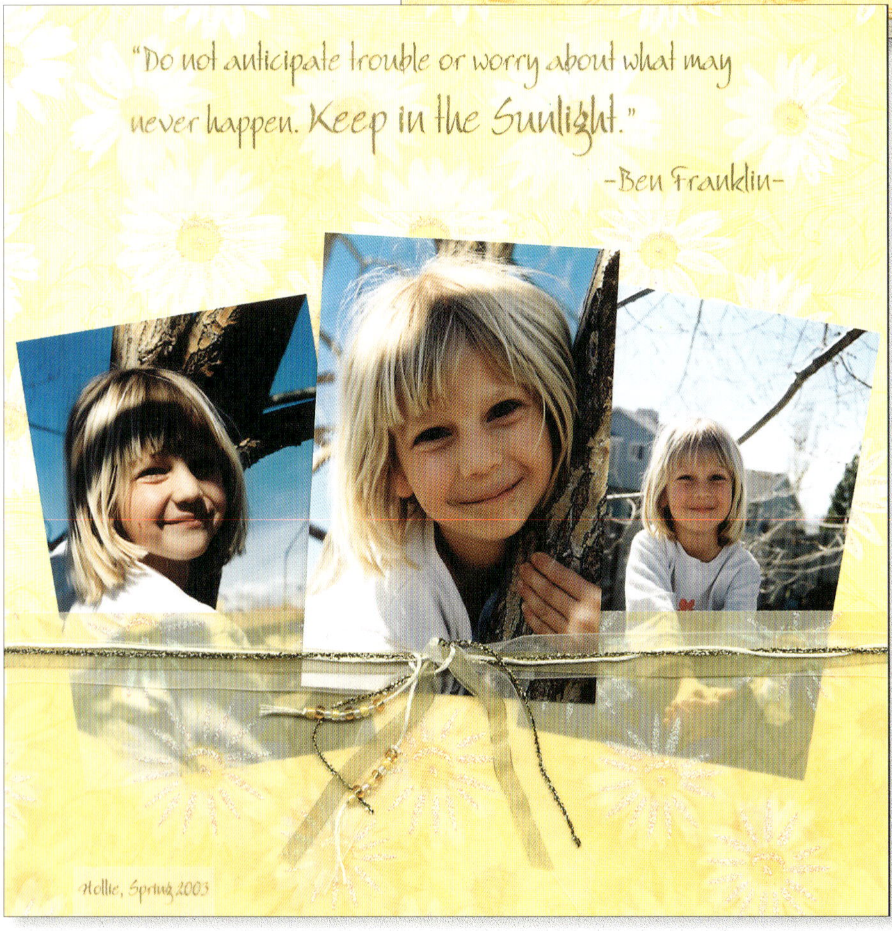
"Do not anticipate trouble or worry about what may never happen. Keep in the Sunlight."
-Ben Franklin-

Keep in the Sunlight

Supplies
Patterned papers and vellum: K & Company
Computer font: Unknown
Other: Ribbon, fibers and beads

♥ **I Love It!:** *The casual arrangement of the photos and the ribbon and bow overlapping them create a mental image of a bouquet of flowers. The beads threaded onto the fibers mimic the sparkle of the glitter.*

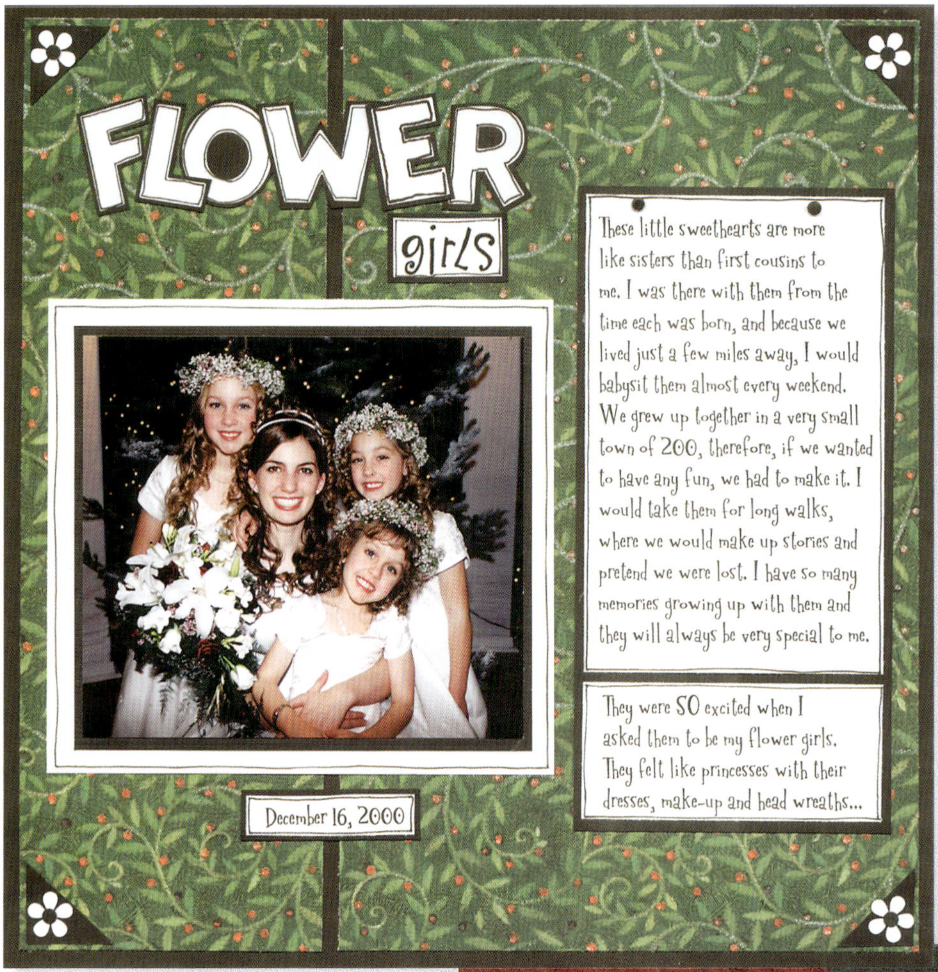
FLOWER
girls
These little sweethearts are more like sisters than first cousins to me. I was there with them from the time each was born, and because we lived just a few miles away, I would babysit them almost every weekend. We grew up together in a very small town of 200, therefore, if we wanted to have any fun, we had to make it. I would take them for long walks, where we would make up stories and pretend we were lost. I have so many memories growing up with them and they will always be very special to me.
They were SO excited when I asked them to be my flower girls. They felt like princesses with their dresses, make-up and head wreaths...
December 16, 2000

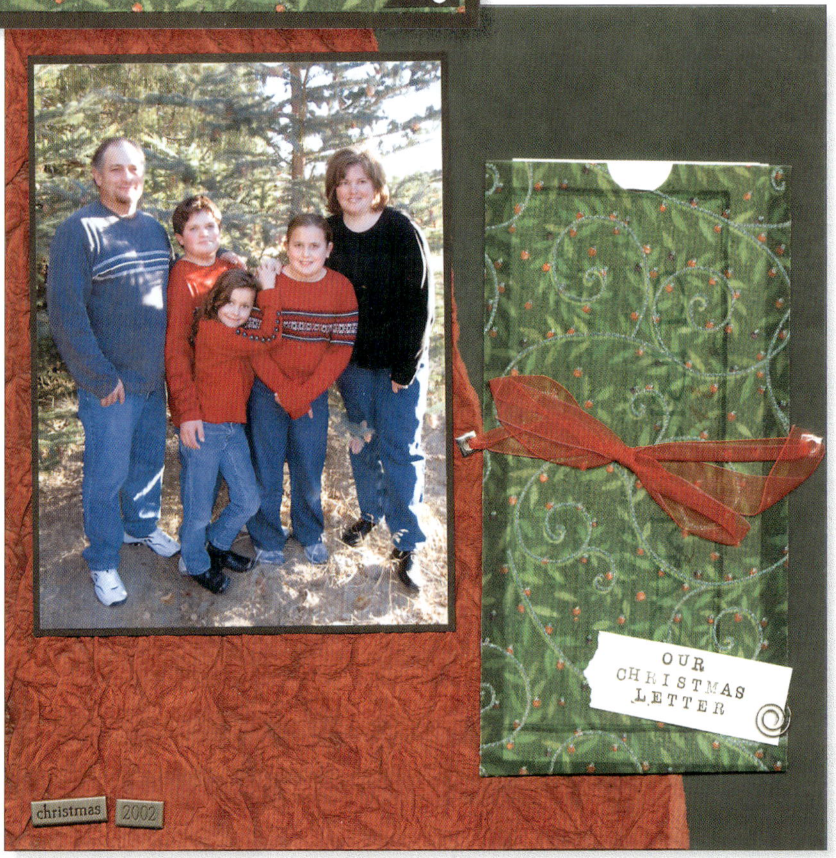
OUR CHRISTMAS LETTER
christmas
2002

Flower Girls

Supplies
Patterned paper: K & Company
Lettering template: Block Upper, EK Success
Letter stickers: David Walker, Colorbök
Computer font: Unknown
Brads: Making Memories
Pen: Zig Writer, EK Success
Other: Flower and circle punches

♥ **I Love It!:** *The sparkle in the glitter paper draws attention to the Christmas lights in the photograph. Notice the visual interest the slightly off-center break in patterned paper adds to the overall layout.*

Our Christmas Letter

Supplies
Crumpled paper: Provo Craft
Patterned paper: K & Company
Metal accents and letter stamps: Making Memories
Circle punch: Marvy Uchida
Other: Ribbon

♥ **I Love It!:** *If glitter paper seems too dominant to use as a background for your layout, use your imagination! A few simple folds created this beautiful envelope, which holds a family Christmas letter.*

tips

lisa's lessons on paper

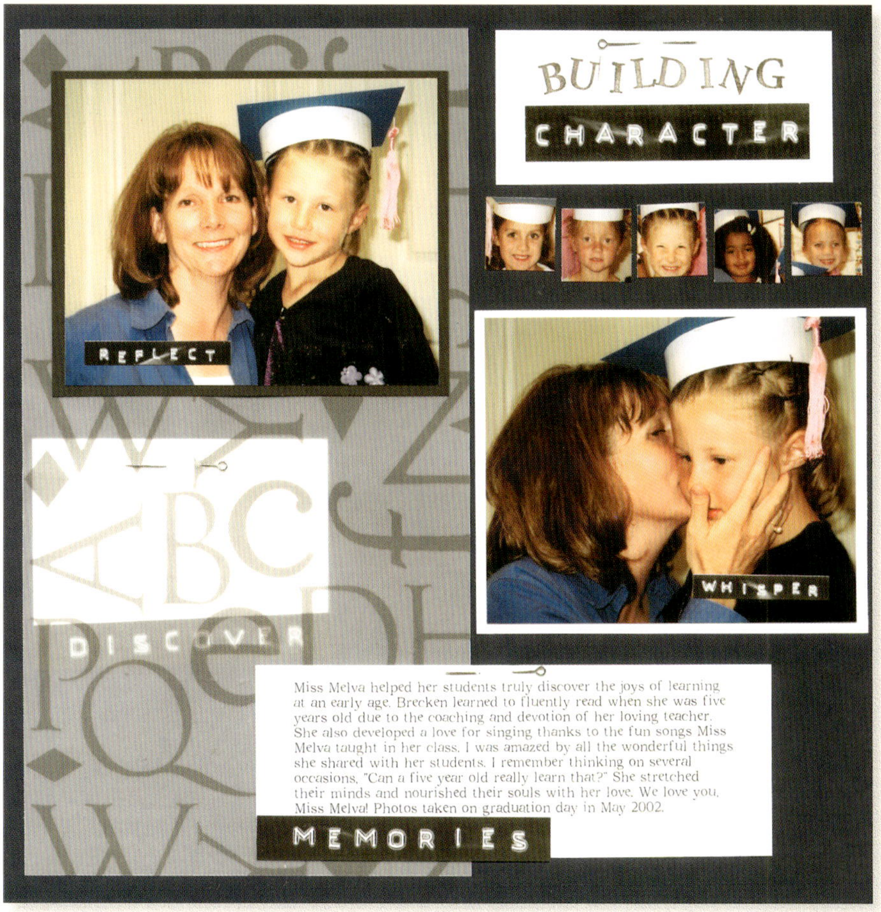
BUILDING
CHARACTER
REFLECT
ABC
DISCOVER
WHISPER
Miss Melva helped her students truly discover the joys of learning at an early age. Brecken learned to fluently read when she was five years old due to the coaching and devotion of her loving teacher. She also developed a love for singing thanks to the fun songs Miss Melva taught in her class. I was amazed by all the wonderful things she shared with her students. I remember thinking on several occasions, "Can a five year old really learn that?" She stretched their minds and nourished their souls with her love. We love you, Miss Melva! Photos taken on graduation day in May 2002.
MEMORIES

Vellum has to be one of my all-time favorite scrapbooking supplies. Here are two great tips for scrapbooking with vellum:

- Only use vellum if you have some type of paper, texture or accent underneath a portion of it to take advantage of its sheerness. On the layout above, I cut a white rectangle of cardstock and placed it behind the portion of the patterned vellum with the letters "A," "B" and "C." I also placed a word sticker behind the background, knowing it would show through enough to be readable but still be subtle.
- Solve the problem of "distracting adhesive"—adhesive that shows through the vellum and unintentionally draws the eye away from the subject of the page—by placing adhesive squares on portions of the vellum that will be underneath page elements, such as photographs or journaling blocks.

Three more favorite tips from this page:

- My set of square punches is my best friend! I love using them for a variety of things on my pages but especially as a quick-and-easy photo cropper. I love the row of carefully punched photographs under the title on this layout—all those sweet faces are clearly visible because of the effective cropping.
- I'm always on the lookout for innovative ways to put a new twist on an old classic, and these straight pins caught my eye. Instead of just adhering the page title and journaling block to my layout, I stuck a pin through the tops of the blocks to add a little variety to the page. I've learned that a little something different here and there goes a long way in making your albums interesting and fun.
- I actually had taken two more photographs of this event, both of Brecken and her class sitting in two rows. Although I didn't end up using them on the layout because they didn't quite match the theme and look I was striving to create, I still wanted to keep them with the layout so she could refer to the photographs later. I simply attached each photograph neatly to the back of the layout. The two photos aren't visible to casual viewers of our family albums, but Brecken knows they're there!

Building Character

Supplies
Vellum: NRN Designs
Label-maker stickers: Pebbles Inc.
Letter stamps: PSX Design
Stamping ink: Stampin' Up!
Straight pins: Making Memories
Computer font: CK Newsprint, "Fresh Fonts" CD, *Creating Keepsakes*

lisa says:

"Accents are what scrapbooking is all about! The decorations you carefully choose and artfully place on your layouts *illustrate* your theme, *highlight* your photographs and please the eye. With the thousands of products available to scrapbookers today, ideas for using and customizing accents are in great *demand."*

ACCENTS

ch.2

all about accents

ACCENT *n.*
an emphasized detail or area

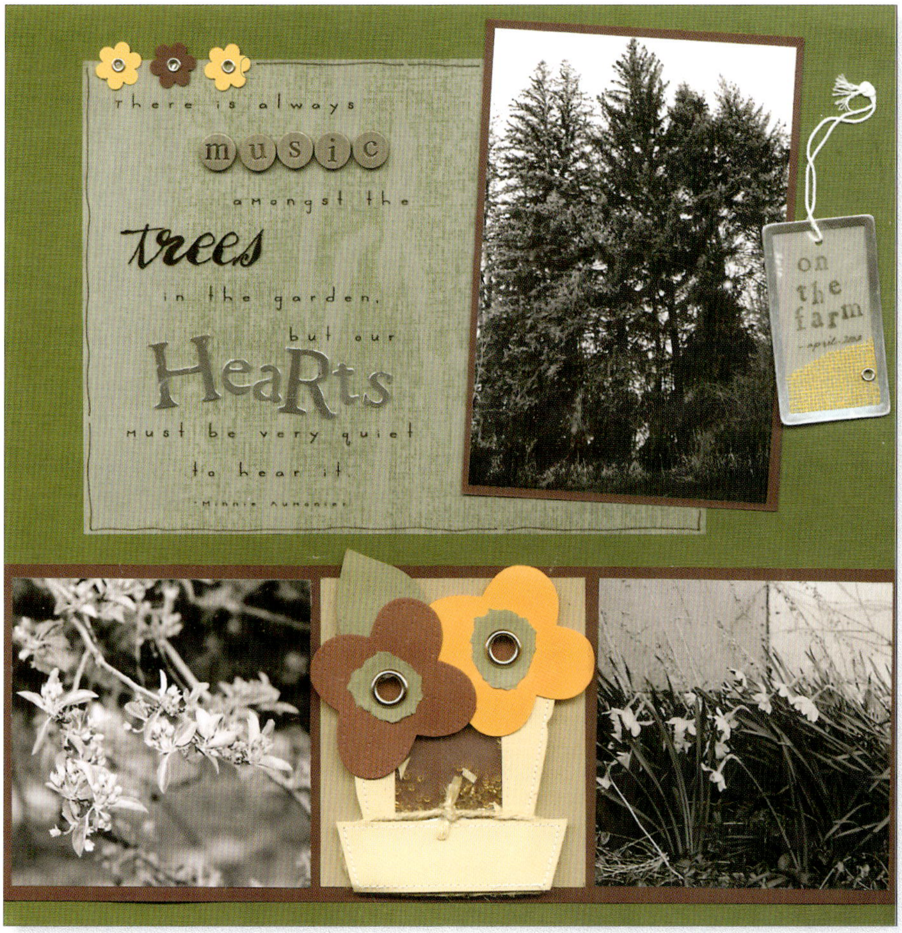
There is always
music
amongst the
trees
in the garden,
but our
HeaRts
must be very quiet
to hear it.
on
the
farm

On the Farm

Supplies
Vellum: Autumn Leaves
Letter stickers: Flavia, Colorbök
Shaker box accent: EK Success
Tag and metal accents: Making Memories
Mesh: Magenta
Letter stamps: PSX Design
Stamping ink: Brilliance, Tsukineko
Flower punch: All Night Media
Computer font: 2Peas Think Small, downloaded from *www.twopeasinabucket.com*

♥ **I Love It!:** *Create a unified layout by making custom accents that match your store-bought accents. To echo the look of the pre-made shaker box at the bottom center of this layout, three flowers with eyelet centers in the same colors as the shaker box were placed along the top of the journaling block.*

tip 1

silhouette pre-made accents to add to their versatility.

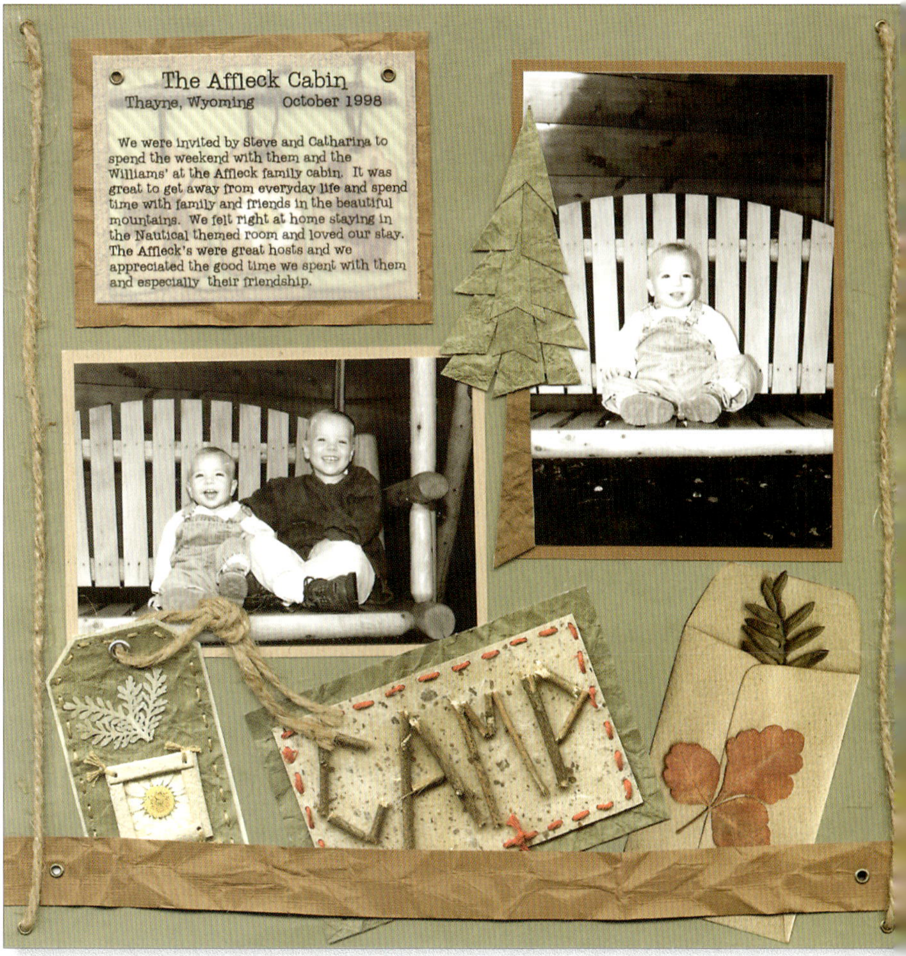
The Affleck Cabin
Thayne, Wyoming October 1998
We were invited by Steve and Catharina to spend the weekend with them and the Williams' at the Affleck family cabin. It was great to get away from everyday life and spend time with family and friends in the beautiful mountains. We felt right at home staying in the Nautical themed room and loved our stay. The Affleck's were great hosts and we appreciated the good time we spent with them and especially their friendship.
CAMP

The Affleck Cabin

Supplies
Preprinted accents: Fresh Cuts, EK Success
Computer font: CK Stenography, "Fresh Fonts" CD, *Creating Keepsakes*
Eyelets: Making Memories
Other: Jute

♥ **I Love It!:** *Closely silhouetted, tall accents are great for decorating photo mats. I love how this slender pine tree subtly draws the eye to the photograph without dominating the layout.*

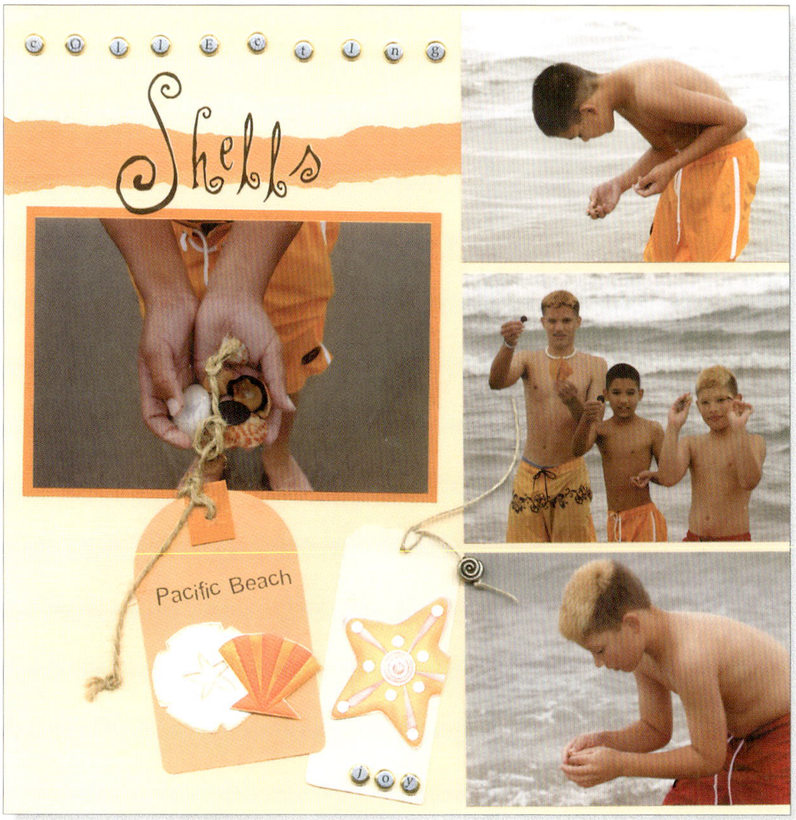
collecting
Shells
Pacific Beach
joy

Collecting Shells

Supplies
Preprinted accents: Embossible Designs, We R Memory Keepers
Letter stickers: Sonnets, Creative Imaginations
Letter brads: Creative Imaginations
Computer font: CK Elusive, "Fresh Fonts" CD, *Creating Keepsakes*
Other: Twine, jute and spiral bead

♥ **I Love It!:** *These silhouetted accents look great elevated slightly on 3-D foam adhesive and folded around the edge of the tag.*

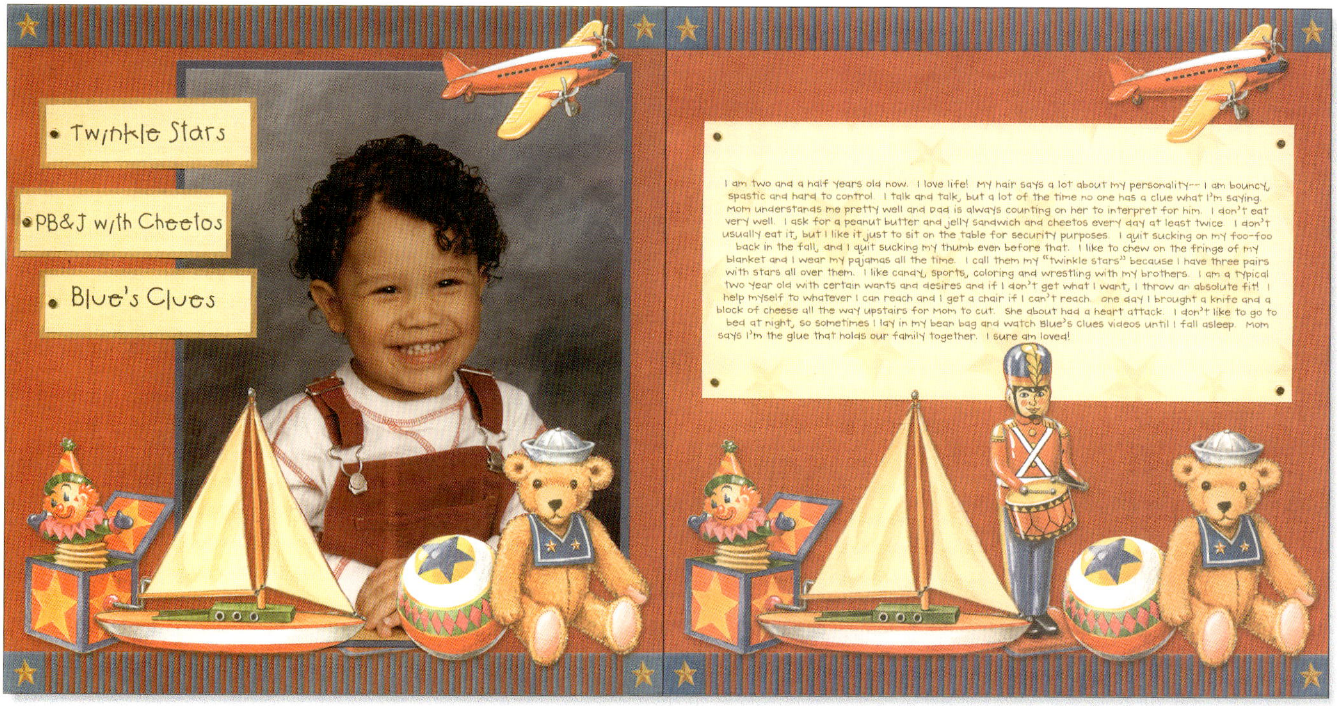
• Twinkle Stars
• PB&J with Cheetos
• Blue's Clues
I am two and a half years old now. I love life! My hair says a lot about my personality-- I am bouncy, spastic and hard to control. I talk and talk, but a lot of the time no one has a clue what I'm saying. Mom understands me pretty well and Dad is always counting on her to interpret for him. I don't eat very well. I ask for a peanut butter and jelly sandwich and cheetos every day at least twice. I don't usually eat it, but I like it just to sit on the table for security purposes. I quit sucking on my foo-foo back in the fall, and I quit sucking my thumb even before that. I like to chew on the fringe of my blanket and I wear my pajamas all the time. I call them my "twinkle stars" because I have three pairs with stars all over them. I like candy, sports, coloring and wrestling with my brothers. I am a typical two year old with certain wants and desires and if I don't get what I want, I throw an absolute fit! I help myself to whatever I can reach and I get a chair if I can't reach. one day I brought a knife and a block of cheese all the way upstairs for Mom to cut. She about had a heart attack. I don't like to go to bed at night, so sometimes I lay in my bean bag and watch Blue's Clues videos until I fall asleep. Mom says I'm the glue that holds our family together. I sure am loved!

Brevin at 2½

Supplies

Patterned paper: K & Company
Computer fonts: DJ Crayon, package unknown, D.J. Inkers; CK Handprint, "The Best of Creative Lettering" CD Combo, *Creating Keepsakes*
Brads: Making Memories

♥ **I Love It!:** *Imitate the look of silhouetted accents using preprinted papers with picture borders. Using a craft knife, cut along the edges of the pictures and overlap them onto your photographs and journaling. This quick technique creates an advanced-looking result!*

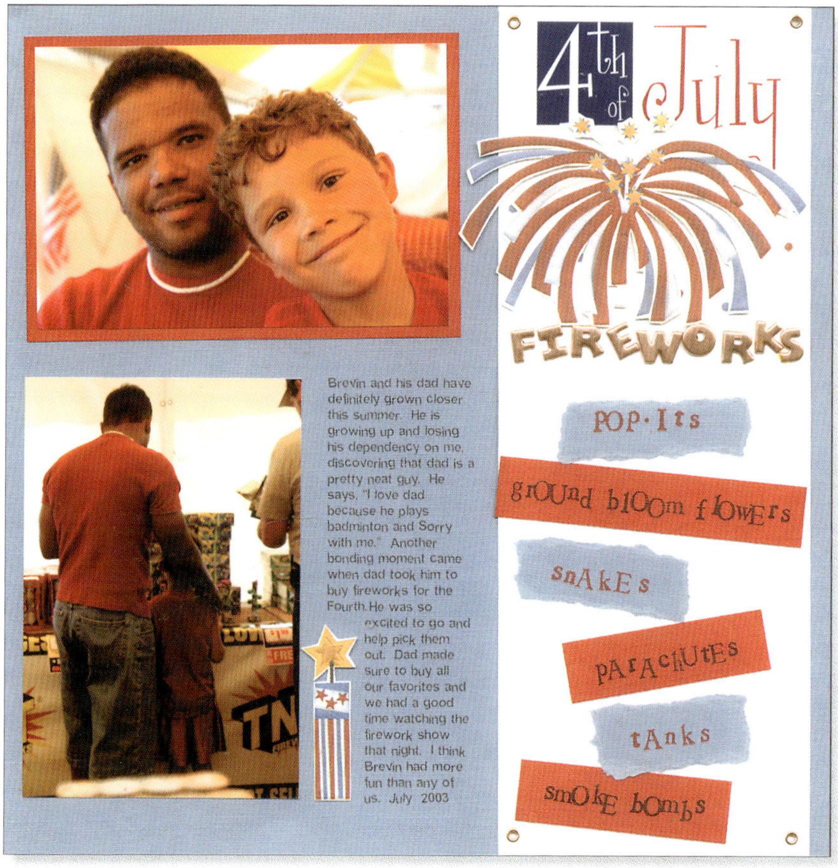
4th of July
FIREWORKS
Brevin and his dad have definitely grown closer this summer. He is growing up and losing his dependency on me, discovering that dad is a pretty neat guy. He says, "I love dad because he plays badminton and Sorry with me." Another bonding moment came when dad took him to buy fireworks for the Fourth. He was so excited to go and help pick them out. Dad made sure to buy all our favorites and we had a good time watching the firework show that night. I think Brevin had more fun than any of us. July 2003
POP·Its
grOUnd blOOm flOWErs
snAkEs
PArAchUtEs
tAnks
smOkE bOmbs

4th of July

Supplies

Preprinted accents: Embossible Designs, We R Memory Keepers
Sticker: Phrase Café, EK Success
Letter brads: Provo Craft
Eyelets: Making Memories
Letter stamps: PSX Design
Stamping ink: ColorBox, Clearsnap
Computer font: CK Elusive, "Fresh Fonts" CD, *Creating Keepsakes*

♥ **I Love It!:** *Silhouetting this fireworks accent allowed it to overlap the title slightly without interfering with the title's readability.*

tip 2

align accents to create unique borders.

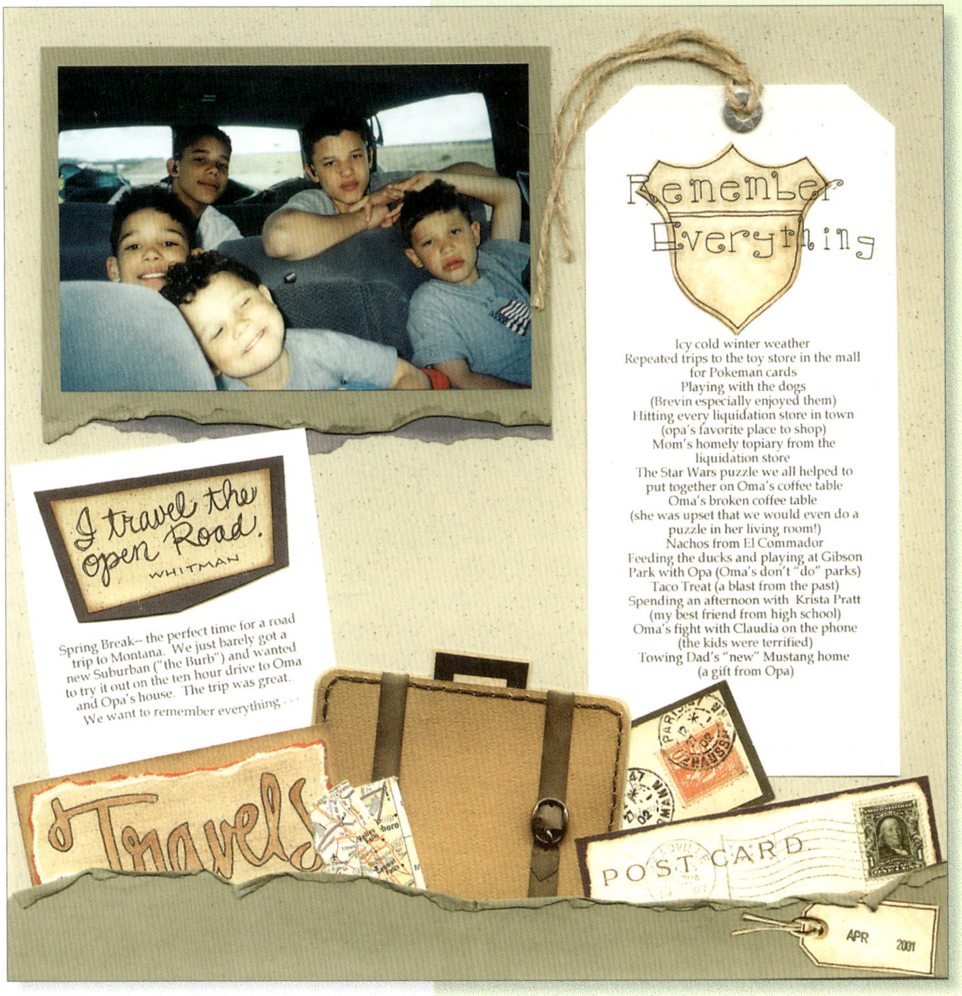

Remember Everything
Icy cold winter weather
Repeated trips to the toy store in the mall for Pokeman cards
Playing with the dogs
(Brevin especially enjoyed them)
Hitting every liquidation store in town
(opa's favorite place to shop)
Mom's homely topiary from the liquidation store
The Star Wars puzzle we all helped to put together on Oma's coffee table
Oma's broken coffee table
(she was upset that we would even do a puzzle in her living room!)
Nachos from El Commador
Feeding the ducks and playing at Gibson Park with Opa (Oma's don't "do" parks)
Taco Treat (a blast from the past)
Spending an afternoon with Krista Pratt
(my best friend from high school)
Oma's fight with Claudia on the phone
(the kids were terrified)
Towing Dad's "new" Mustang home
(a gift from Opa)
I travel the open Road.
WHITMAN
Spring Break-- the perfect time for a road trip to Montana. We just barely got a new Suburban ("the Burb") and wanted to try it out on the ten hour drive to Oma and Opa's house. The trip was great. We want to remember everything . . .
Travels
POST CARD
APR 2001

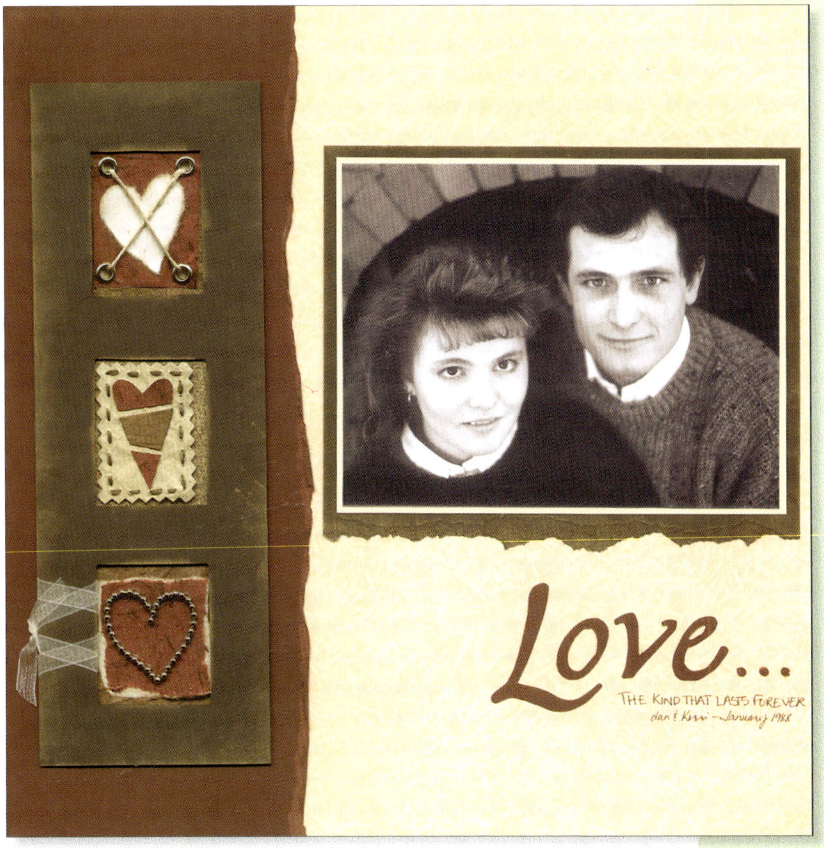

Love...
THE KIND THAT LASTS FOREVER

Remember Everything

Supplies

Preprinted accents: Fresh Cuts, EK Success
Letter stickers: Provo Craft
Computer font: Garamond, Microsoft Word
Other: Washer and jute

♥ **I Love It!:** *Slip preprinted accents underneath a torn border of cardstock, overlapping them at different angles, to create a natural-looking border for your layout.*

Love ...

Supplies

Patterned paper: Liz King
Preprinted accents: Fresh Cuts, EK Success
Metallic stamping ink: ColorBox, Clearsnap
Pen: Zig Writer, EK Success
Other: Ribbon

♥ **I Love It!:** *Frame your preprinted accent border with a 3-D cardstock frame. Cut a length of cardstock, then cut rectangles at even intervals to reveal the accents. Ink the edges with metallic stamping ink, then wrap a ribbon around the bottom corner as a finishing touch.*

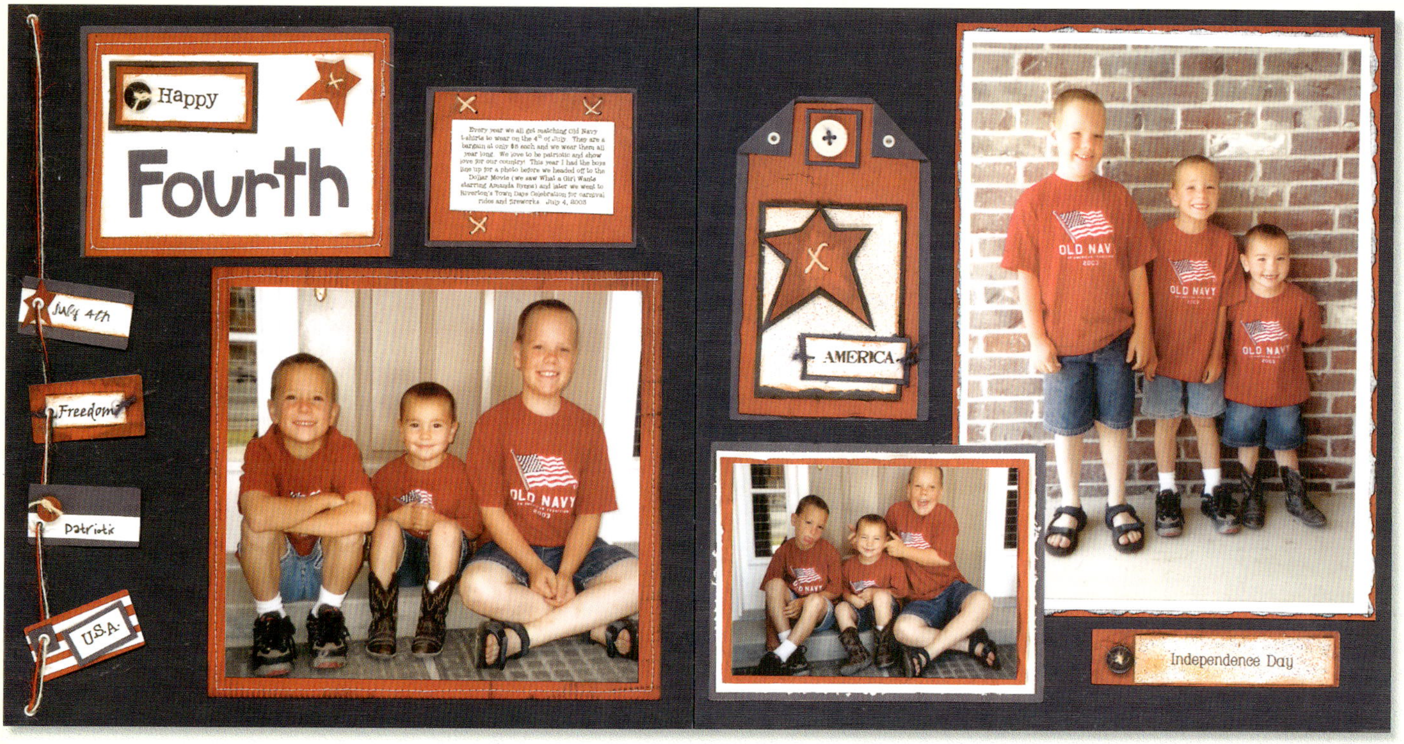
Happy
Fourth
Every year we all get matching Old Navy t-shirts to wear on the 4th of July. They are a bargain at only $5 each and we wear them all year long. We love to be patriotic and show love for our country! This year I had the boys line up for a photo before we headed off to the Dollar Movie (we saw What a Girl Wants starring Amanda Bynes) and later we went to Riverton's Town Days Celebration for carnival rides and fireworks. July 4, 2003
July 4th
Freedom
Patriotic
U.S.A.
AMERICA
Independence Day

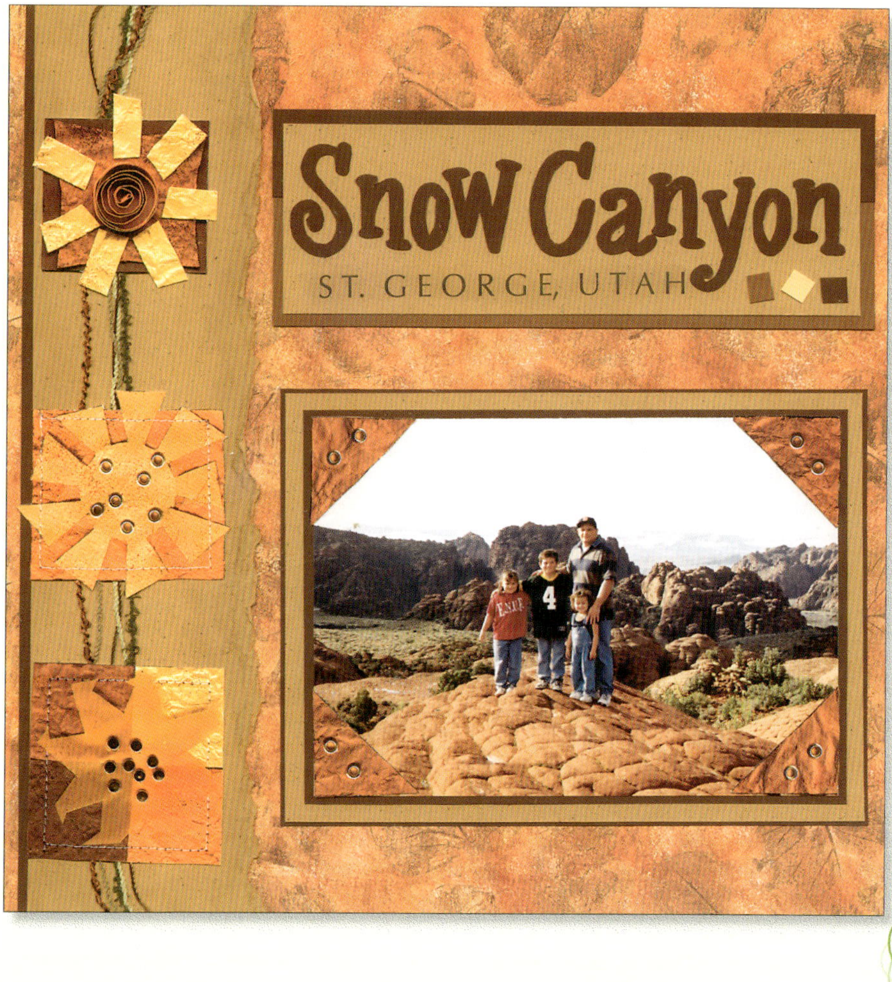
Snow Canyon
ST. GEORGE, UTAH

Happy Fourth

Supplies

Preprinted accents: Mats & More, My Mind's Eye
Stamping ink: Stampin' Up!
Eyelets: Making Memories
Computer font: CK Stenography, "Fresh Fonts" CD, *Creating Keepsakes*
Other: Twine

♥ **I Love It!:** *The photo mat on the second page was created with a paper trimmer. To re-create it, cut the paper, but don't press down completely on the blade. Tear away the edges, then ink the rough edge lightly.*

Snow Canyon

Supplies

Patterned paper: Scrap-Ease
Preprinted accents: Fresh Cuts, EK Success
Computer font: Whipper Basic, Whipper Snapper Designs
Fibers: On The Surface

♥ **I Love It!:** *Connect the silhouetted accents you've arranged in a border by laying them over several strands of fibers.*

tip 3

hang accents from other page elements.

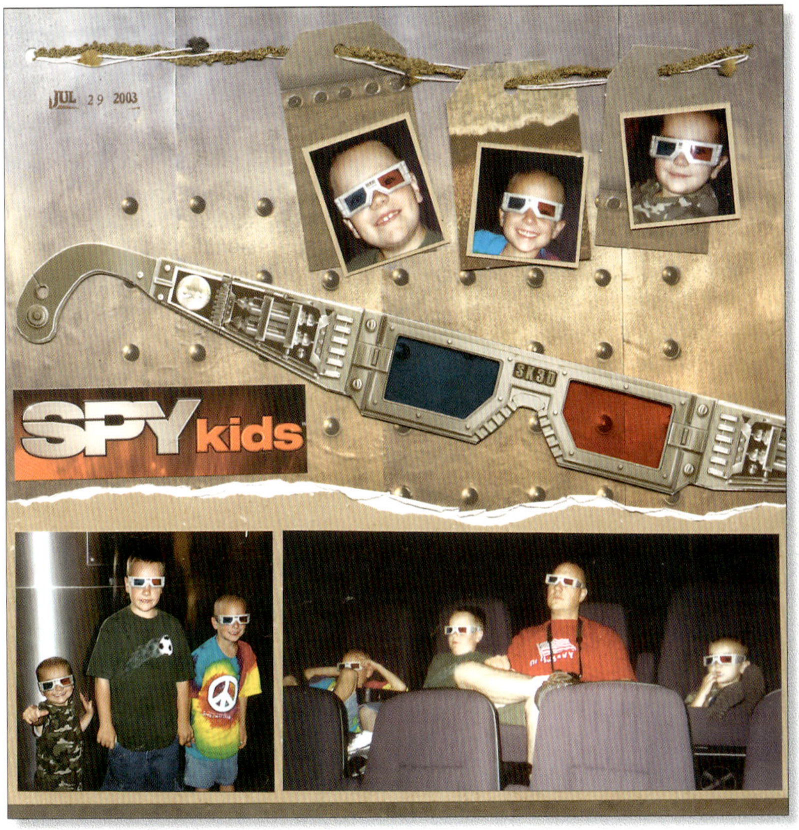

JUL 29 2003
SPY kids

Spy Kids

Supplies

Patterned paper and preprinted tags: Paper Loft
Date stamp: Making Memories
Other: Fibers and 3-D glasses

♥ **I Love It!:** *Thread fibers along the top of your layout, then hang a grouping of tag accents from the fibers. For added whimsy, don't place the matted photographs squarely on the tags—tilt them and let the edges hang slightly off the tags.*

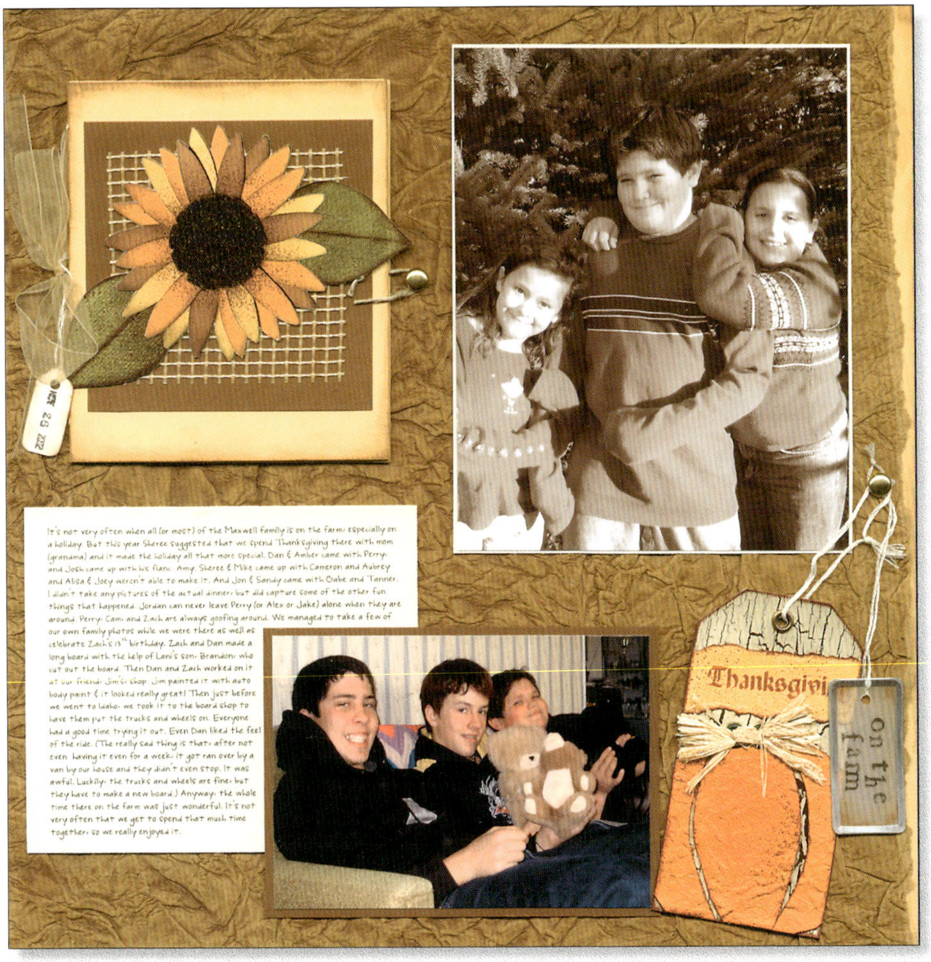

It's not very often when all (or most) of the Maxwell family is on the farm, especially on a holiday. But this year Sheree suggested that we spend Thanksgiving there with mom (grandma) and it made the holiday all that more special. Dan & Amber came with Perry, and Josh came up with his fianc Amy. Sheree & Mike came up with Cameron and Aubrey and Alisa & Joey weren't able to make it. And Jon & Sandy came with Gabe and Tanner. I didn't take any pictures of the actual dinner, but did capture some of the other fun things that happened. Jordan can never leave Perry (or Alex or Jake) alone when they are around. Perry, Cam, and Zach are always goofing around. We managed to take a few of our own family photos while we were there as well as celebrate Zach's 13th birthday. Zach and Dan made a long board with the help of Lani's son, Brandon, who cut out the board. Then Dan and Zach worked on it at our friend, Jim's, shop. Jim painted it with auto body paint & it looked really great! Then just before we went to Idaho, we took it to the board shop to have them put the trucks and wheels on. Everyone had a good time trying it out. Even Dan liked the feel of the ride. (The really sad thing is that, after not even having it even for a week, it got ran over by a van by our house and they didn't even stop. It was awful. Luckily, the trucks and wheels are fine, but they have to make a new board.) Anyway, the whole time there on the farm was just wonderful. It's not very often that we get to spend that much time together, so we really enjoyed it.
Thanksgivi
on the farm

Thanksgiving on the Farm

Supplies

Crumpled paper: Provo Craft
Preprinted accents: Fresh Cuts, EK Success
Small Tag: Avery
Vellum tag: Making Memories
Mesh: Magic Mesh
Letter stamps: PSX Design
Stamping ink: Brilliance (black), Tsukineko; ColorBox (brown), Clearsnap
Computer font: CK Jot, "The Art of Creative Lettering" CD, *Creating Keepsakes*
Other: Brad and ribbon

♥ **I Love It!:** *Tags and fibers are a natural combination, so why not take it one step further and tie the fibers to a brad or decorative eyelet? This creates the illusion that the tag is actually hanging on the layout.*

♥ **I Love It!:** *Creating the mini-album on this page raised the photo count from two to eight without adding clutter.*

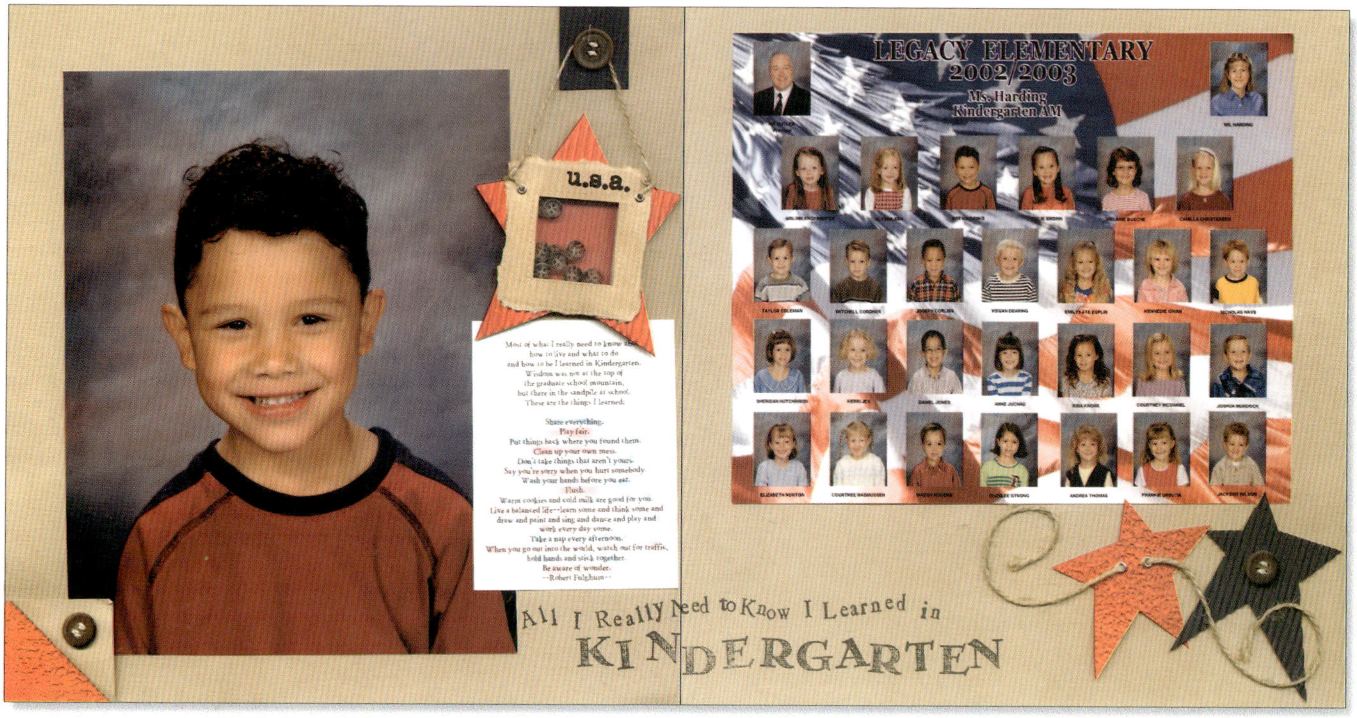

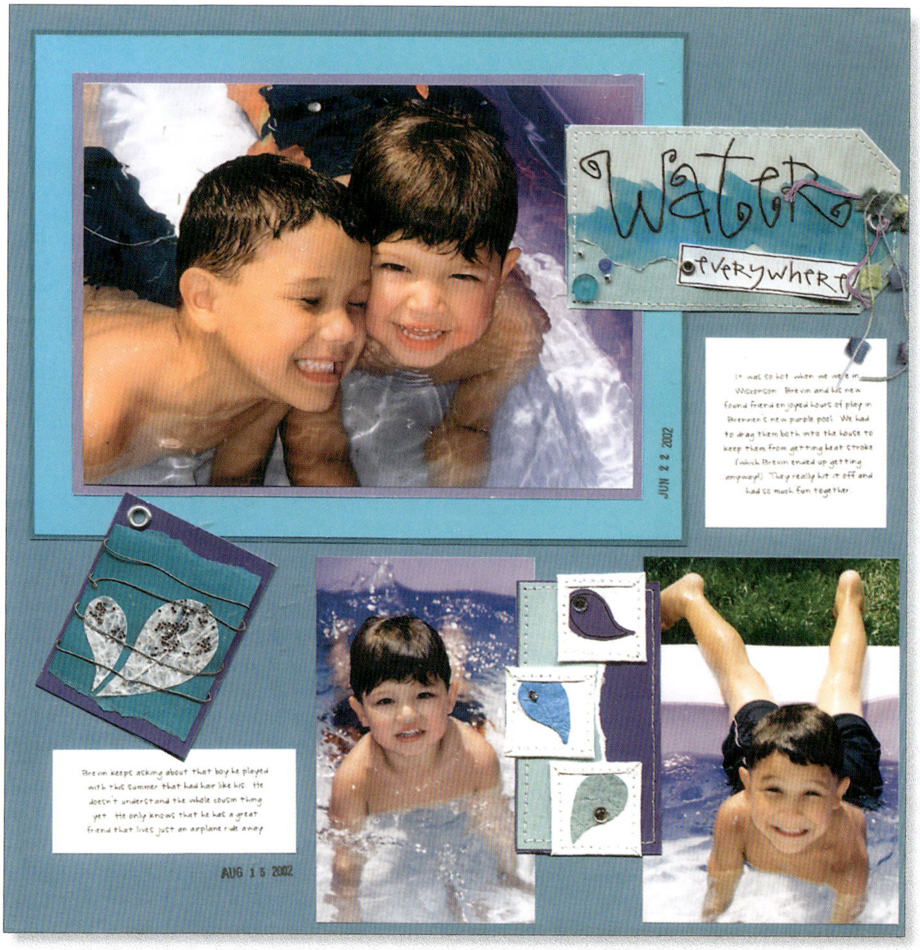

Kindergarten

Supplies
Textured paper: Provo Craft
Letter stamps: PSX Design (small), Barnes and Noble (large)
Star template: Close To My Heart
Chalks: Stampin' Up!
Eyelets: Making Memories
Computer font: CK Constitution, "Fresh Fonts" CD, *Creating Keepsakes*
Other: Buttons and jute

♥ **I Love It!:** *Add color to a blah-looking journaling block with chalks. Choose colors from your layout, then, alternating colors, highlight key words in the journaling, important phrases or items in a list.*

Water Everywhere

Supplies
Preprinted accents: Fresh Cuts, EK Success
Computer font: CK Jot, "The Art of Creative Lettering" CD, *Creating Keepsakes*
Eyelet: Making Memories
Fibers: Adornaments, EK Success

♥ **I Love It!:** *Hang a preprinted accent from a photo mat or journaling block with a simple eyelet. On a layout where everything else is place squarely on the layout, the angle of the hanging accent will add variety and interest to the page.*

tip 4

piece together a collage of photos and accents.

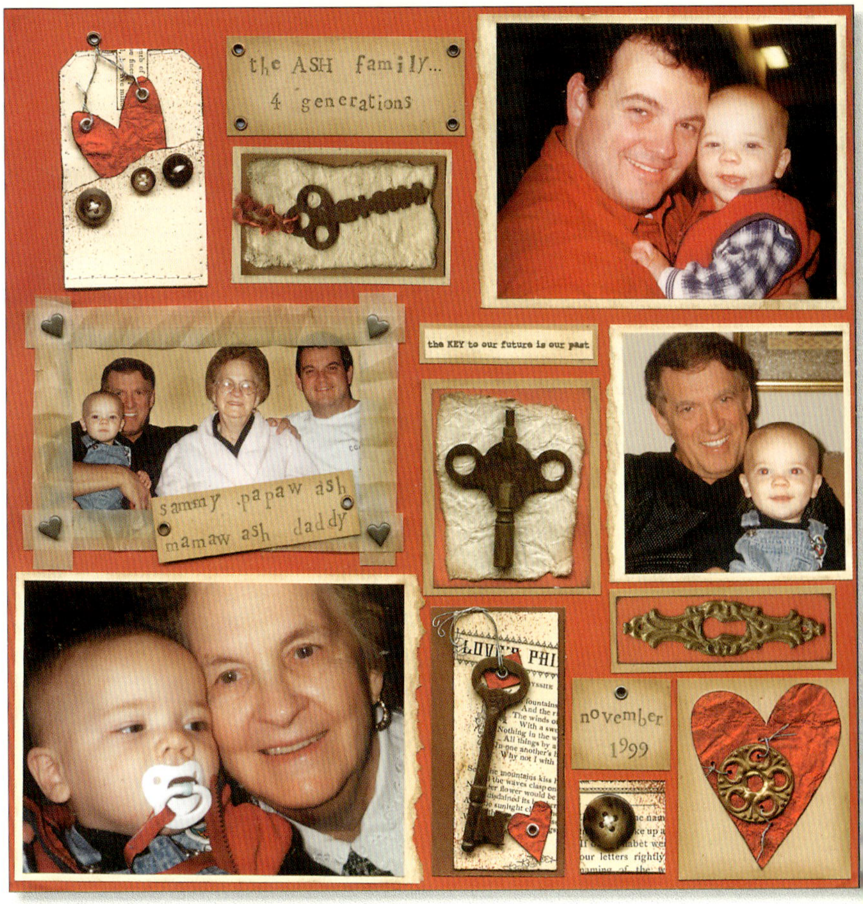

The Ash Family

Supplies

Vellum: WorldWin
Preprinted accents: Fresh Cuts, EK Success
Letter stamps: Hero Arts
Stamping ink: ColorBox, Clearsnap
Computer font: CK Typewriter, "Fresh Fonts" CD, *Creating Keepsakes*
Heart eyelets: Colorbök
Eyelets: Making Memories

♥ **I Love It!:** *Use brown chalk to "age" new-looking scrapbook supplies. The cardstock elements on this page were aged to match the preprinted accents.*

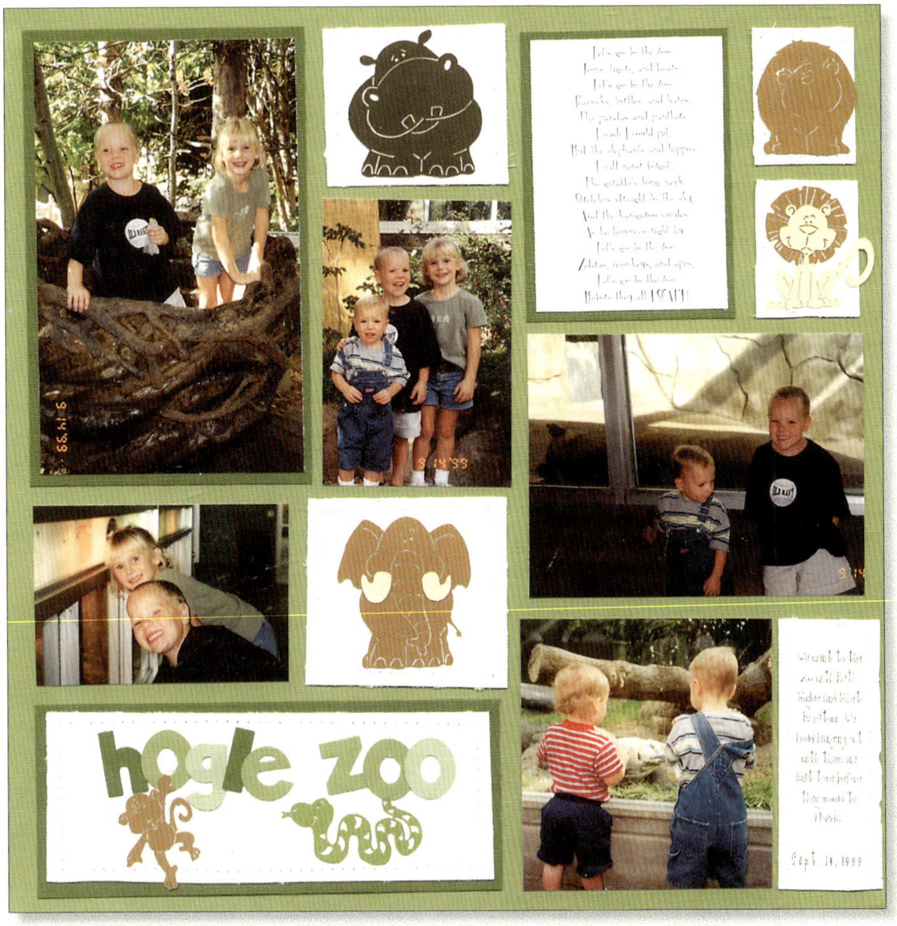

Hogle Zoo

Supplies

Laser die cuts: Laser Layouts, Provo Craft
Letter punches: EK Success
Computer font: Girls Are Weird, downloaded from the Internet
Preprinted poem: Tiny Tales, My Mind's Eye

♥ **I Love It!:** *Create this fun, crumpled cardstock look by wetting your cardstock with a spray bottle, crumpling the paper, smoothing it out, then ironing it on a low setting.*

♥ **I Love It!:** *Watch for opportunities to combine accents and other page elements, such as the monkey accent and the "o" in the title. These combinations add a touch of authenticity to your layout.*

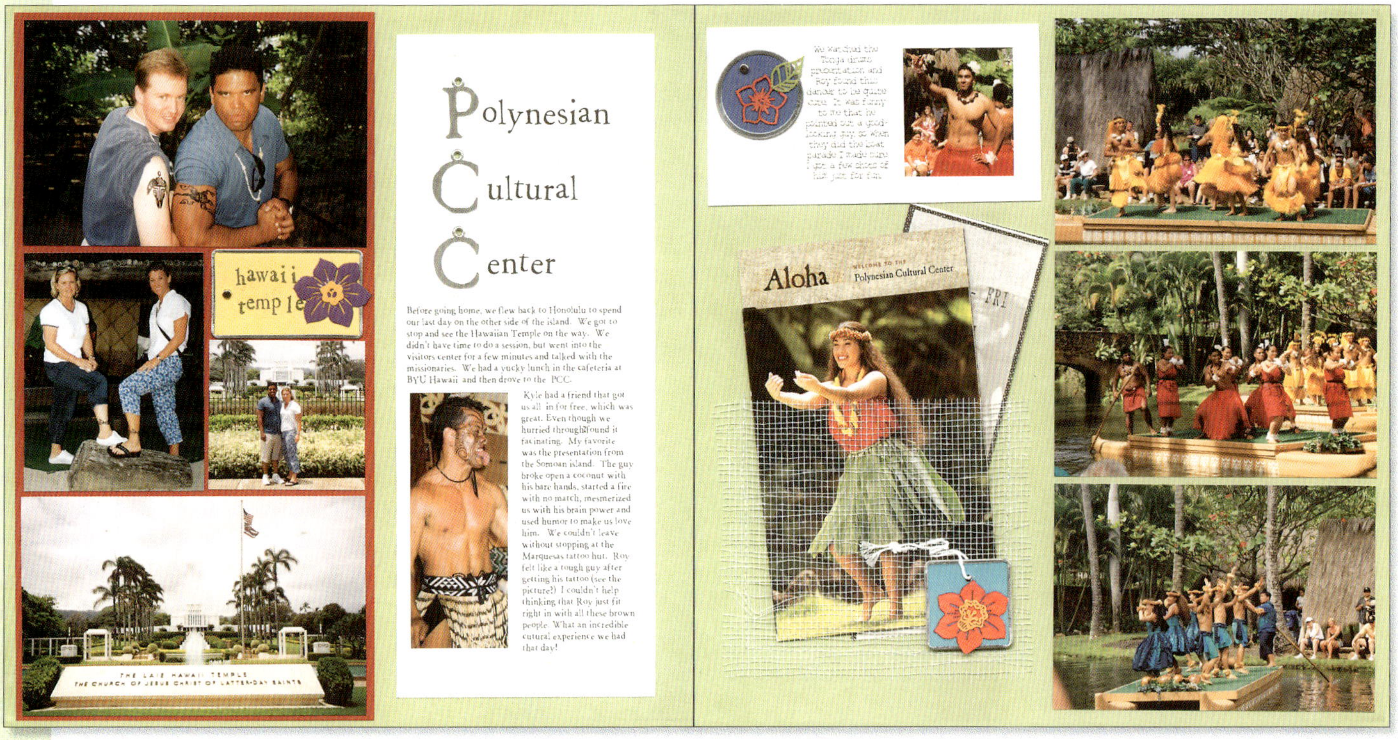
hawaii temple
Polynesian Cultural Center
Before going home, we flew back to Honolulu to spend our last day on the other side of the island. We got to stop and see the Hawaiian Temple on the way. We didn't have time to do a session, but went into the visitors center for a few minutes and talked with the missionaries. We had a yucky lunch in the cafeteria at BYU Hawaii and then drove to the PCC.
Kyle had a friend that got us all in for free, which was great. Even though we hurried through, I found it facinating. My favorite was the presentation from the Somoan island. The guy broke open a coconut with his bare hands, started a fire with no match, mesmerized us with his brain power and used humor to make us love him. We couldn't leave without stopping at the Marquesas tattoo hut. Roy felt like a tough guy after getting his tattoo (see the picture?) I couldn't help thinking that Roy just fit right in with all these brown people. What an incredible cutural experience we had that day!
Aloha
Polynesian Cultural Center

Polynesian Cultural Center

Supplies
Laser die cuts: Laser Layouts, Provo Craft
Metal-rimmed tags, metal letters, brads and eyelets: Making Memories
Mesh: Magic Mesh
Computer font: CK Constitution, "Fresh Fonts" CD, *Creating Keepsakes*

♥ **I Love It!:** *Create a fun pocket for photos or memorabilia by sewing a square or rectangle of mesh on your layout. The contents are still visible through the see-through mesh!*

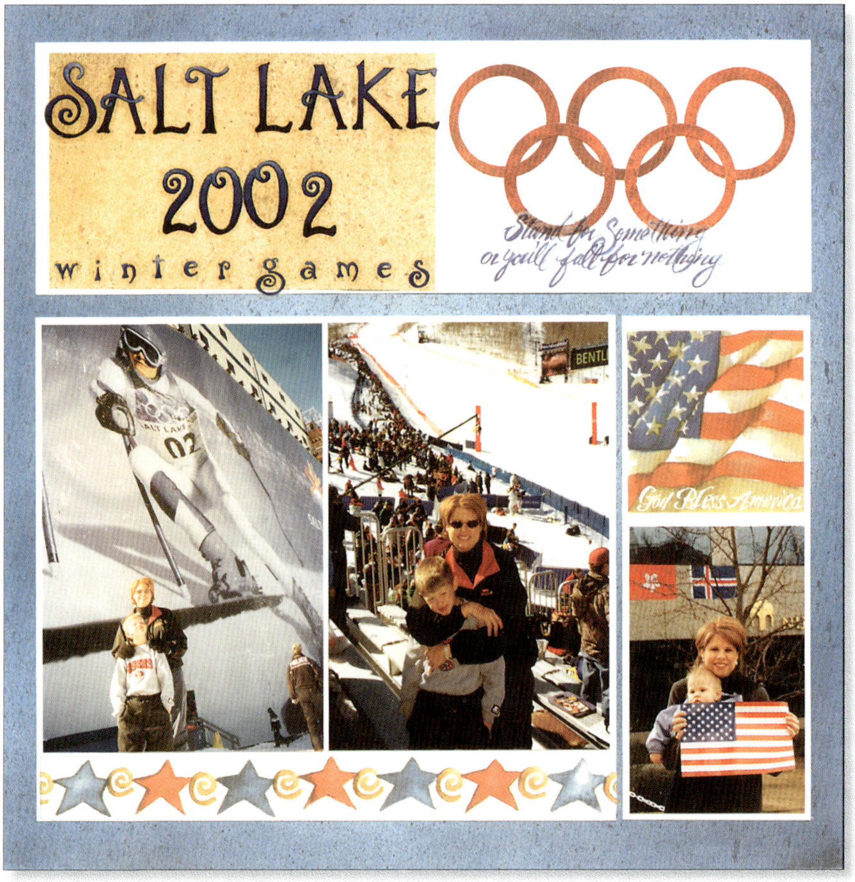
SALT LAKE
2002
winter games
Stand for Something or you'll fall for nothing
God Bless America

Salt Lake 2002

Supplies
Patterned paper and stickers: Provo Craft

♥ **I Love It!:** *Make collaging page elements easy by trimming a piece of neutral cardstock to the size you want the finished collage to be. Leaving backs on stickers and trimming preprinted accents to size, arrange the page elements until the collage is correctly spaced and arranged. Then adhere the items to the cardstock.*

tip 5

combine

accents with vellum or transparency paper.

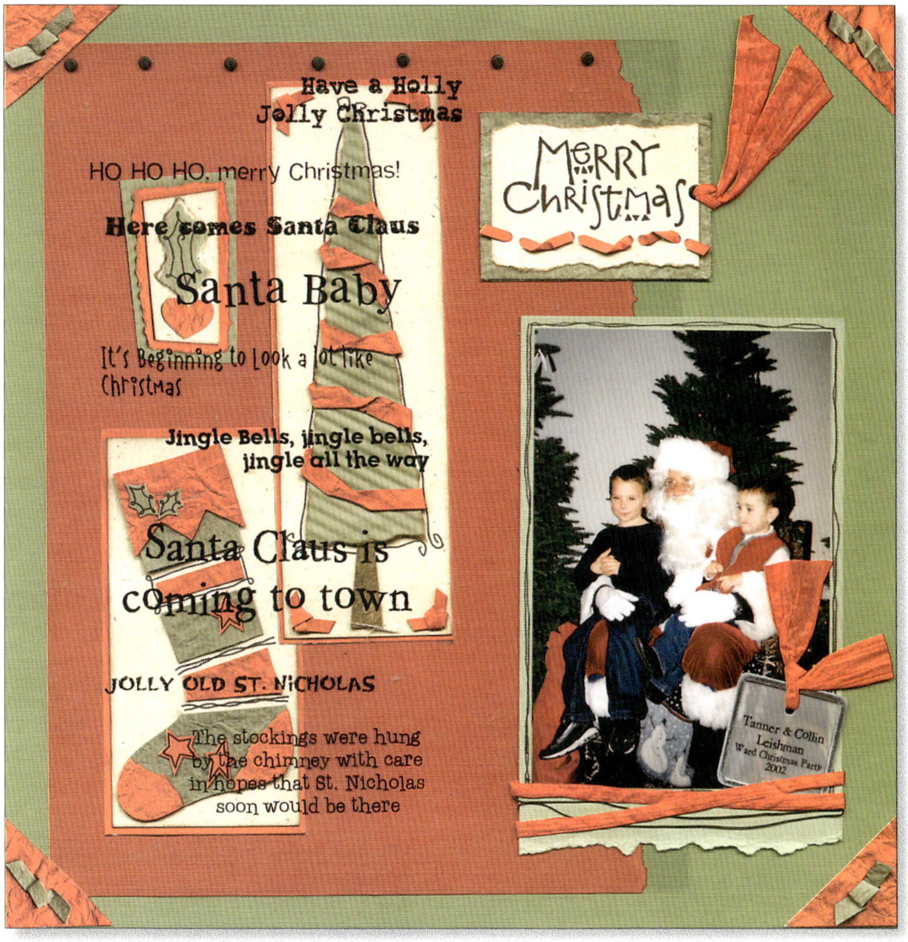

Have a Holly Jolly Christmas
MERRY CHRISTMAS
HO HO HO, merry Christmas!
Here comes Santa Claus
Santa Baby
It's Beginning to Look a lot like Christmas
Jingle Bells, jingle bells, jingle all the way
Santa Claus is coming to town
JOLLY OLD ST. NICHOLAS
The stockings were hung by the chimney with care in hopes that St. Nicholas soon would be there
Tanner & Collin Leishman
Ward Christmas Party
2002

Merry Christmas

Supplies
Preprinted accents: Fresh Cuts, EK Success
Metal-rimmed tag: Making Memories
Craft wire: Artista
Brads and eyelet: Impress Rubber Stamps
Computer fonts: CK Typewriter, CK Elusive, CK Lumpy, CK Twilight, CK Porridge, CK Tipsy, CK Constitution, CK Shiver and CK Stenography, "Fresh Fonts" CD, *Creating Keepsakes*
Other: Paper ribbon and transparency paper

♥ **I Love It!:** *Type journaling in fun, bold computer fonts and print them on transparency paper. Then, arrange preprinted accents behind the transparency paper to highlight the text. Adhere the accents to the background, then attach the transparency paper with brads or eyelets.*

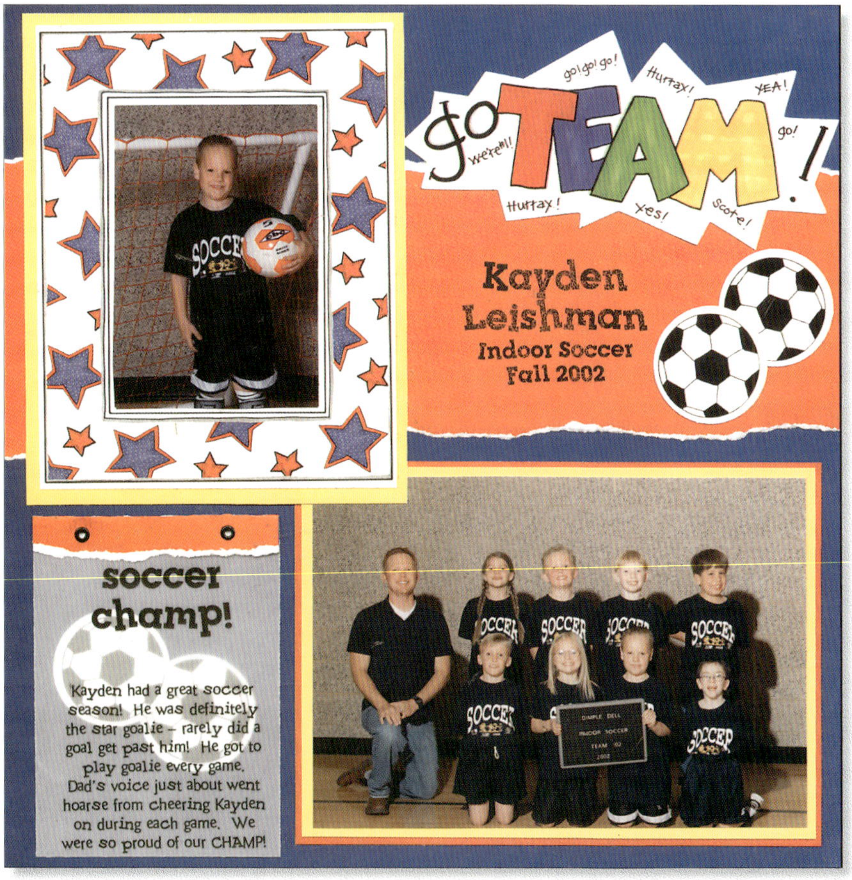

go TEAM!
go! go! go!
Hurray!
YEA!
we're #1!
go!
Hurray!
Yes!
Score!
Kayden Leishman
Indoor Soccer
Fall 2002
soccer champ!
Kayden had a great soccer season! He was definitely the star goalie - rarely did a goal get past him! He got to play goalie every game. Dad's voice just about went hoarse from cheering Kayden on during each game. We were so proud of our CHAMP!

Soccer Champ!

Supplies
Preprinted frame, title and accents: My Mind's Eye
Eyelets: Making Memories
Computer fonts: Unknown

♥ **I Love It!:** *Mimic the look of a legal pad on your journaling block by folding a narrow piece of cardstock over the top, then tearing the edge. Fasten the cardstock to the journaling block with eyelets or brads.*

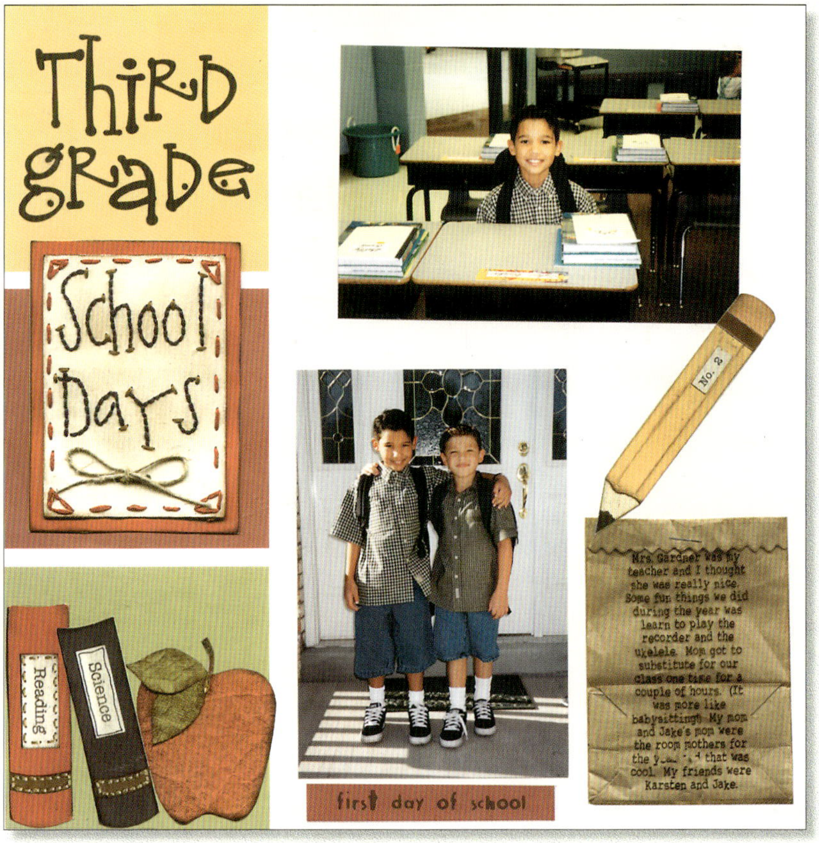
Third grade
School Days
No. 2
Reading
Science
Mrs. Gardner was my teacher and I thought she was really nice. Some fun things we did during the year was learn to play the recorder and the ukelele. Mom got to substitute for our class one time for a couple of hours. (It was more like babysitting!) My mom and Jake's mom were the room mothers for the y that was cool. My friends were Karsten and Jake.
first day of school

Third Grade

Supplies

Patterned paper: SEI
Preprinted accents: Fresh Cuts, EK Success
Letter stickers: Source unknown
Computer fonts: Unknown
Other: Transparency paper and staple

♥ **I Love It!:** *Create the illusion of journaling on a preprinted accent by printing your journaling on transparency paper, then stapling or attaching it to the preprinted accent.*

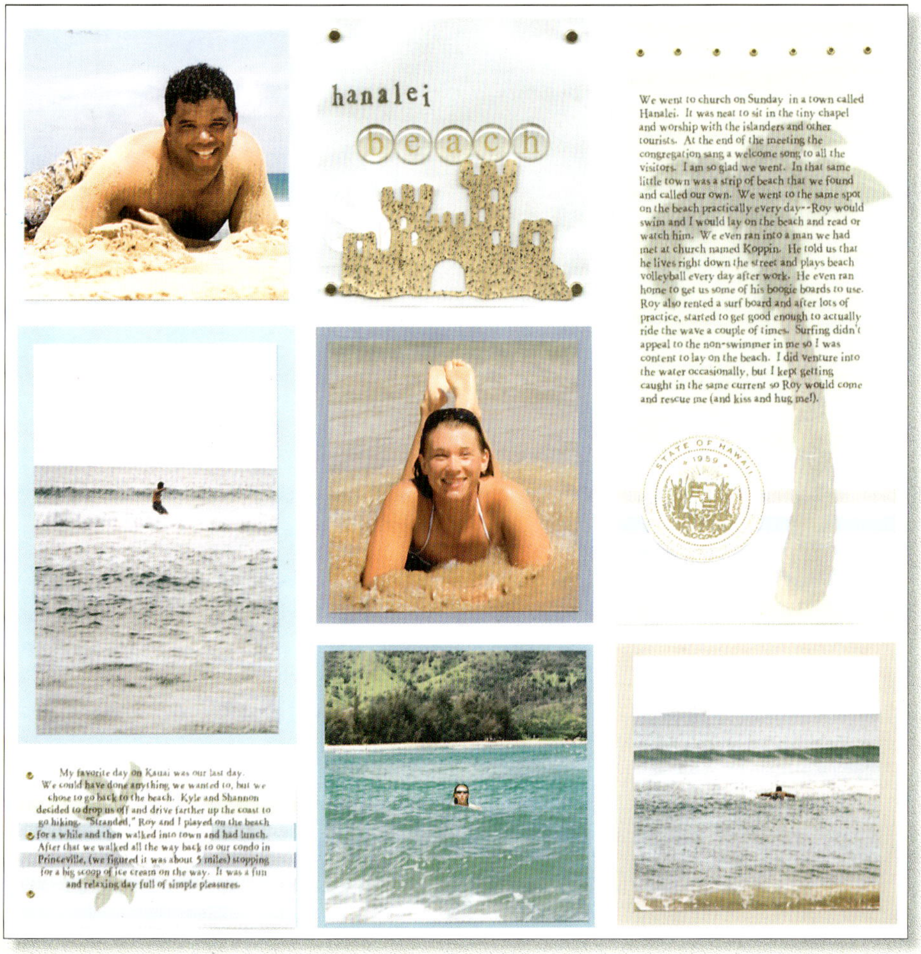
hanalei
beach
We went to church on Sunday in a town called Hanalei. It was neat to sit in the tiny chapel and worship with the islanders and other tourists. At the end of the meeting the congregation sang a welcome song to all the visitors. I am so glad we went. In that same little town was a strip of beach that we found and called our own. We went to the same spot on the beach practically every day--Roy would swim and I would lay on the beach and read or watch him. We even ran into a man we had met at church named Koppin. He told us that he lives right down the street and plays beach volleyball every day after work. He even ran home to get us some of his boogie boards to use. Roy also rented a surf board and after lots of practice, started to get good enough to actually ride the wave a couple of times. Surfing didn't appeal to the non-swimmer in me so I was content to lay on the beach. I did venture into the water occasionally, but I kept getting caught in the same current so Roy would come and rescue me (and kiss and hug me!).
STATE OF HAWAII
1959
My favorite day on Kauai was our last day. We could have done anything we wanted to, but we chose to go back to the beach. Kyle and Shannon decided to drop us off and drive farther up the coast to go hiking. "Stranded," Roy and I played on the beach for a while and then walked into town and had lunch. After that we walked all the way back to our condo in Princeville, (we figured it was about 5 miles) stopping for a big scoop of ice cream on the way. It was a fun and relaxing day full of simple pleasures.

Hanalei Beach

Supplies

Patterned paper: SEI
Laser die cuts: Laser Layouts, Provo Craft
Letter pebbles: Making Memories
Computer font: CK Constitution, "Fresh Fonts" CD, *Creating Keepsakes*
Eyelets: Making Memories

♥ **I Love It!:** *Layering heavy-weight vellum over laser die cuts creates a shadow effect that adds interest to an otherwise plain journaling block. Add even more interest by adhering the die cut to a piece of patterned paper before covering it with vellum.*

tip 6

add action to your layouts with shaker boxes.

Pumpkin Walk Accent

Supplies

Shaker-box accent: EK Success
Laser die cut fence: Deluxe Cuts
Computer fonts: CK Wired and CK Twilight, "Fresh Fonts" CD, *Creating Keepsakes*
Eyelets: Making Memories
Embossing powder: Stamp-n-Stuff, Stampendous!
Other: Twine

♥ **I Love It!:** *Instead of journaling in straight lines every time, try using the WordArt feature in Microsoft Word, which allows you to create special effects with the fonts you already have on your computer.*

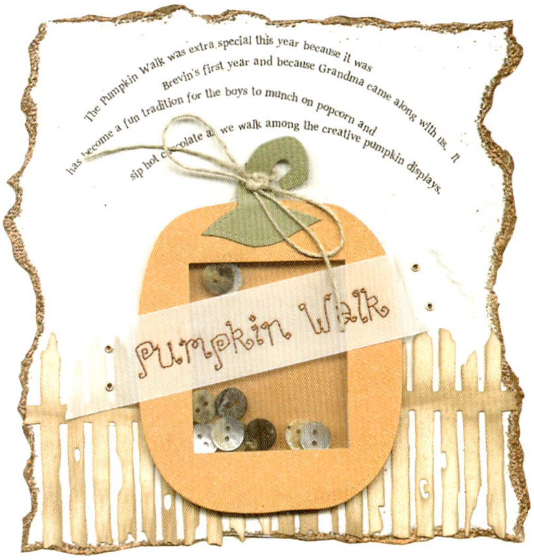
The Pumpkin Walk was extra special this year because it was
Brevin's first year and because Grandma came along with us. It
has become a fun tradition for the boys to munch on popcorn and
sip hot
we walk among the creative pumpkin displays.
Pumpkin Walk

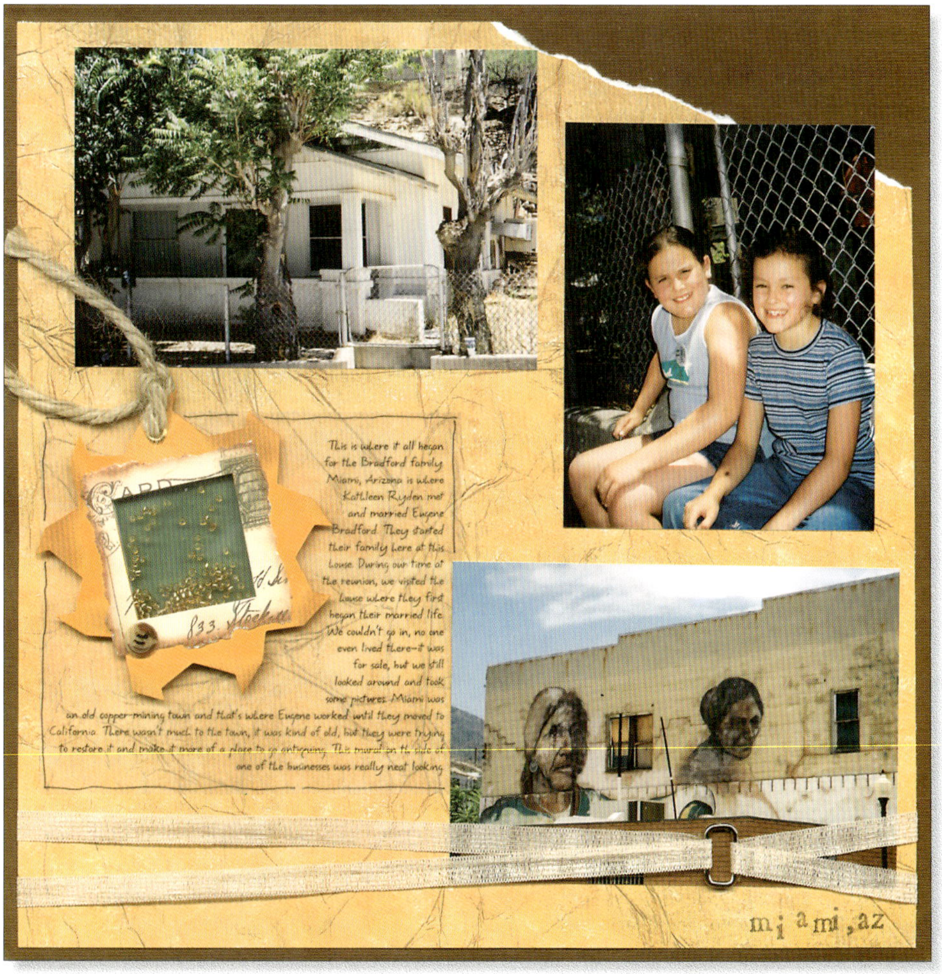
This is where it all began for the Bradford family. Miami, Arizona is where Kathleen Ryden met and married Eugene Bradford. They started their family here at this house. During our time at the reunion, we visted the house where they first began their married life. We couldn't go in, no one even lived there—it was for sale, but we still looked around and took some pictures. Miami was an old copper-mining town and that's where Eugene worked until they moved to California. There wasn't much to the town, it was kind of old, but they were trying to restore it and make it more of a place to go antiquing. This mural on the side of one of the businesses was really neat looking.
mi ami, az

Miami, AZ

Supplies

Patterned paper: Scrap-Ease
Shaker box accent: EK Success
Fibers: Adornaments, EK Success
Letter stamps: PSX Design
Stamping ink: Brilliance, Tsukineko
Computer font: CK Artisan, "Fresh Fonts" CD, *Creating Keepsakes*
Pen: Pigma Micron, Sakura
Metal rectangle ring: 7 Gypsies
Other: Jute and ribbon

♥ **I Love It!:** *Head to your local fabric store to find innovative materials to include on your pages. Many sewing items make perfect borders and accents!*

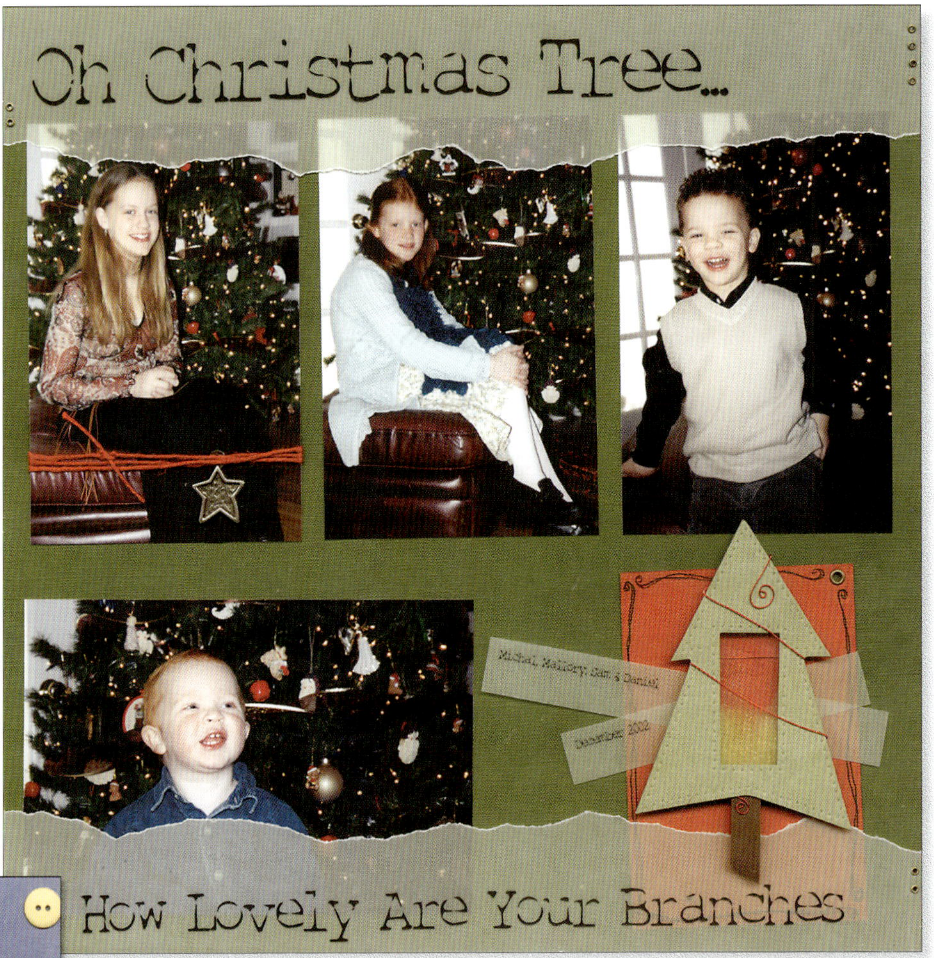
Oh Christmas Tree...
Michal, Mallory, Sam & Daniel
December 2002
How Lovely Are Your Branches

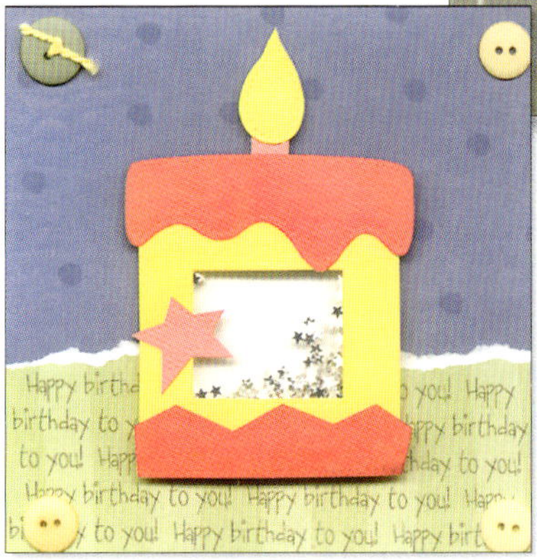

Happy Birthday Card

Supplies
Patterned papers: Lasting Impressions for Paper
Shaker box accent: EK Success
Computer font: CK Eclectic, "Fresh Fonts" CD, *Creating Keepsakes*
Buttons: Making Memories
Embroidery floss: DMC

♥ **I Love It!:** *The visual appeal of shaker boxes makes them perfect for a variety of projects. Create this simple yet adorable birthday card and accent it with a twinkling shaker box.*

Oh, Christmas Tree

Supplies
Vellum: Autumn Leaves
Shaker box accent: EK Success
Eyelets and metal star charm: Making Memories
Computer font: CK Gutenburg, "Fresh Fonts" CD, *Creating Keepsakes*
Pen: Zig Writer, EK Success
Other: Red hemp fiber

♥ **I Love It!:** *Attach strips of vellum with brief details, such as names and dates, underneath a shaker box.*

♥ **I Love It!:** *Try attaching random numbers of tiny eyelets to the edges of vellum borders on your page. Instead of using three eyelets on each edge, for example, mix it up a bit and use two on one edge, four on another and three on another. This random placement actually creates a pleasing effect on your layout.*

tip 7
customize pre-made accents to create a variety of looks.

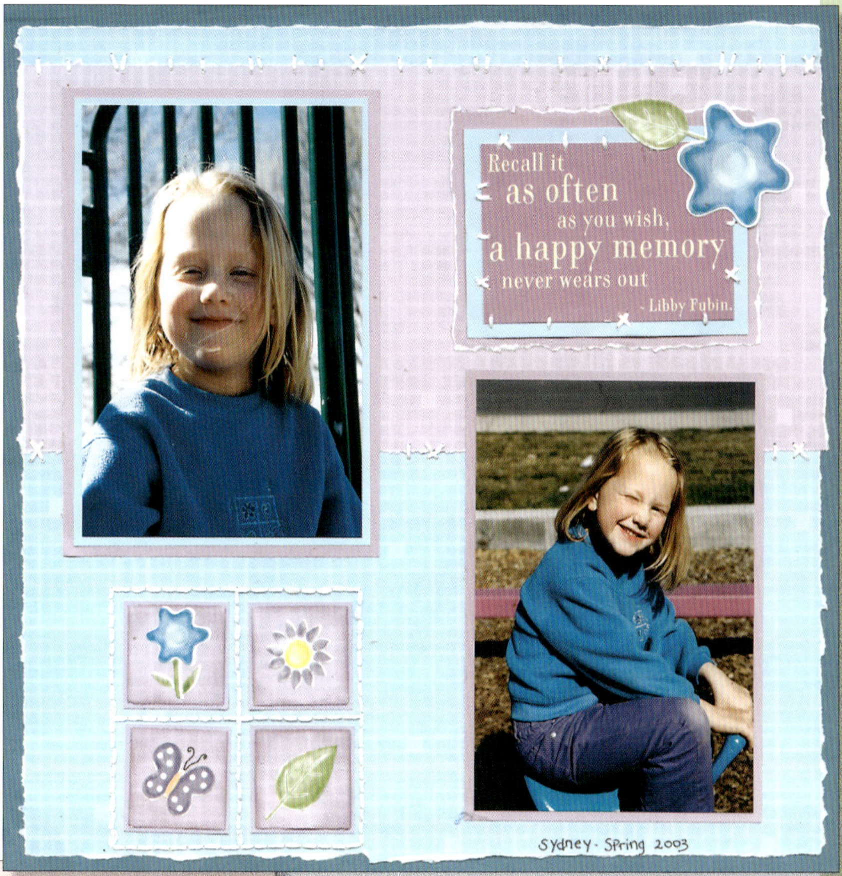

Recall it
as often
as you wish,
a happy memory
never wears out
- Libby Fubin.
Sydney - Spring 2003

Happy Memory

Supplies
Patterned paper and stickers: Colorbök
Embroidery floss: DMC
Pen: Zig Writer, EK Success

♥ **I Love It!:** *Add a handmade look and feel to preprinted accents by stitching on and around them.*

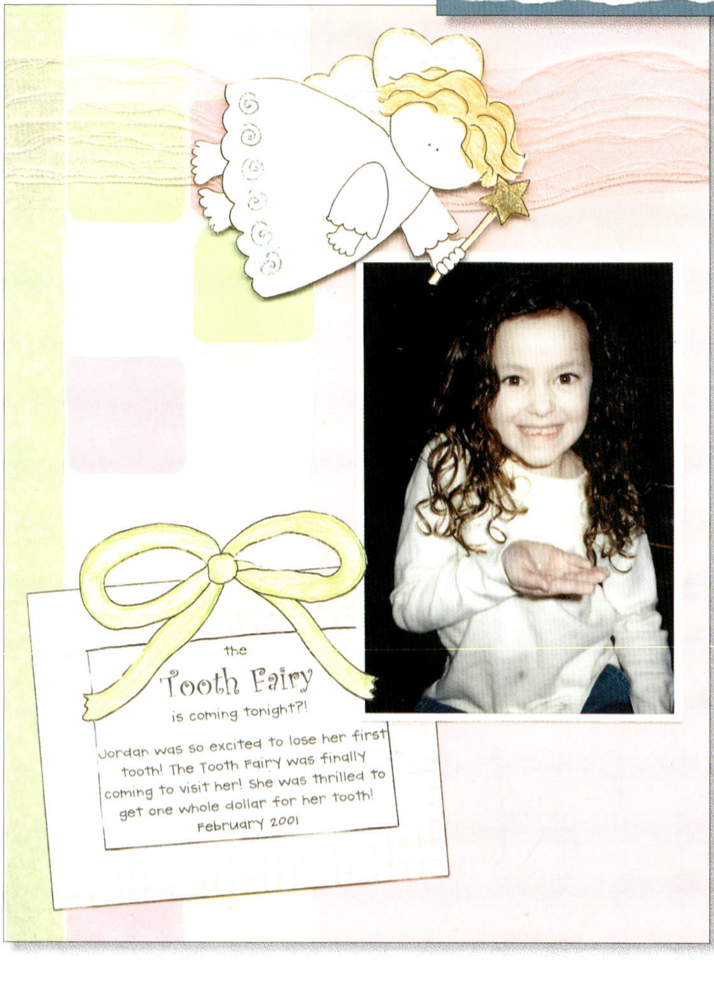

the
Tooth Fairy
is coming tonight?!
Jordan was so excited to lose her first tooth! The Tooth Fairy was finally coming to visit her! She was thrilled to get one whole dollar for her tooth!
February 2001

The Tooth Fairy

Supplies
Patterned papers: Paper Adventures (pastel squares), Keeping Memories Alive (green speckle)
Preprinted frame and accent: My Mind's Eye
Computer font: CK Handprint, "The Best of Creative Lettering" CD Combo, *Creating Keepsakes*
Glitter: Stampa Rosa
Other: Ribbon

♥ **I Love It!:** *Add some sparkle to preprinted accents with glitter.*

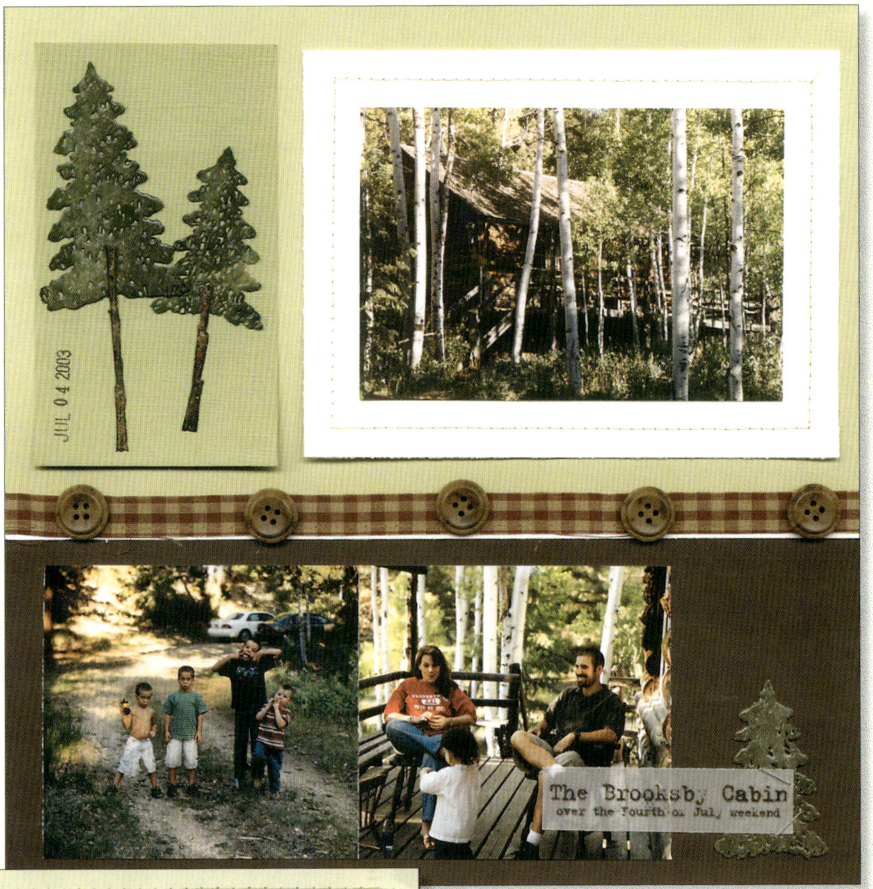
JUL 04 2003
The Brooksby Cabin
over the Fourth of July weekend

The Brooksby Cabin

Supplies
Vellum: WorldWin
Laser die cuts: Laser Layouts, Provo Craft
Computer font: Maszyna Plus, downloaded from the Internet
Embossing powder: Suze Weinberg
Other: Date stamp, buttons and ribbon

♥ **I Love It!:** *Before coating a cardstock die cut with embossing powder, try inking it with different shades of one color. The embossing enamel will form a glassy covering that will help visually blend the colors, creating a variegated accent for your layout.*

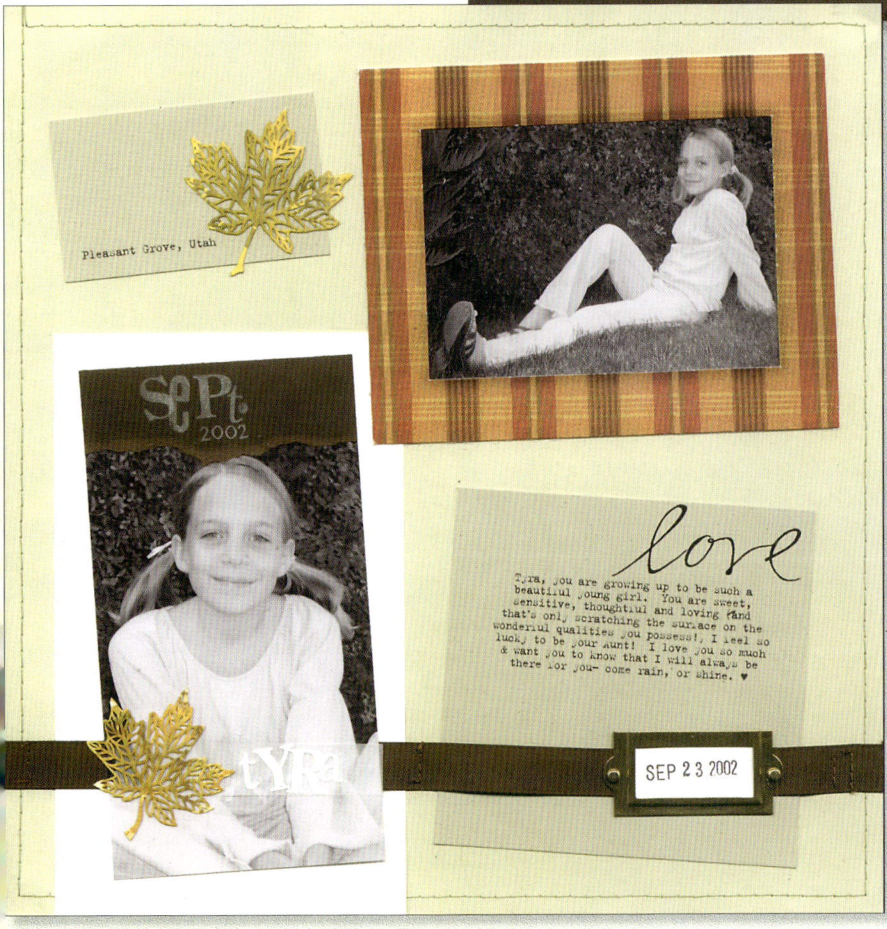
Pleasant Grove, Utah
Sept 2002
tyra
love
Tyra, you are growing up to be such a beautiful young girl. You are sweet, sensitive, thoughtful and loving (and that's only scratching the surface on the wonderful qualities you possess!). I feel so lucky to be your Aunt! I love you so much & want you to know that I will always be there for you- come rain, or shine. ♥
SEP 23 2002

Tyra

Supplies
Preprinted frame: My Mind's Eye
Laser die cuts: Laser Layouts, Provo Craft
Computer font: Last Words, downloaded from the Internet
Letter stamps: The Missing Link Stamp Co.
Stamping ink: Ranger Industries
Embossing powder: Ranger Industries
Rub-on words: Making Memories
Other: Date stamp and bookplate

♥ **I Love It!:** *Change the look of cardstock die cuts by coating them with ultra-thick embossing enamel. Try using coordinating colors of embossing enamel to create a mottled look.*

tip 8

tie accents with twine, ribbon or fibers.

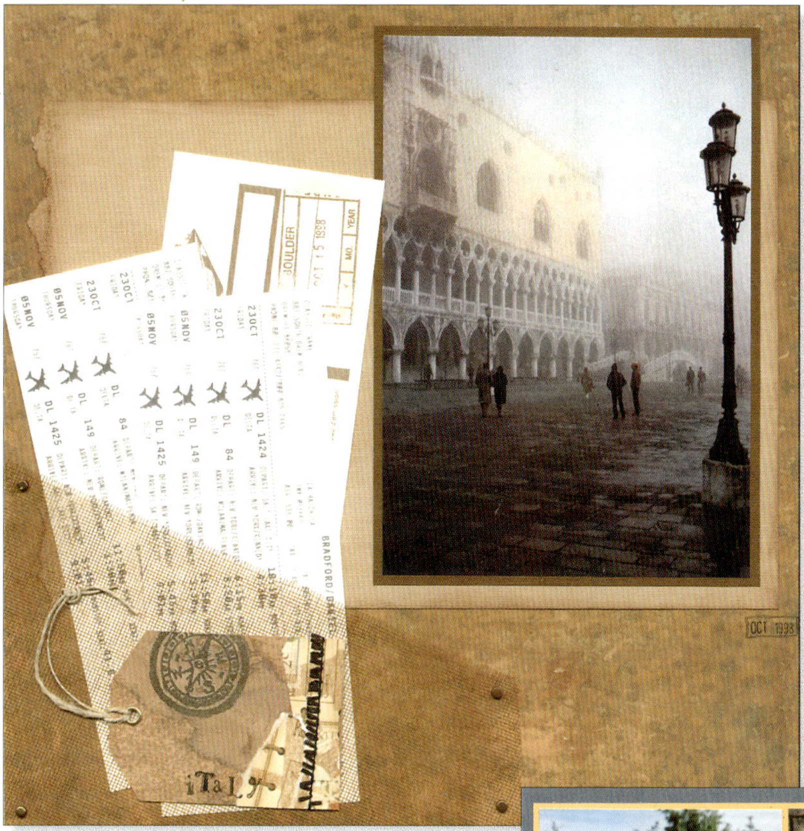
iTaLy
BRADFORD/DANVERS
OCT 1998

Italy

Supplies

Patterned paper: Karen Foster Design
Preprinted tag: Paper Loft
Mesh: Magenta
Letter and compass stamps: PSX Design
Stamping ink: Brilliance, Tsukineko
Pen: Pigma Micron, Sakura
Brads: Making Memories
Eyelet: Prym-Dritz
Other: Jute

♥ **I Love It!:** *Get creative with preprinted tags by using them as a base for additional embellishments. Layer them with coordinating papers, stamps, accents or fibers to create new looks.*

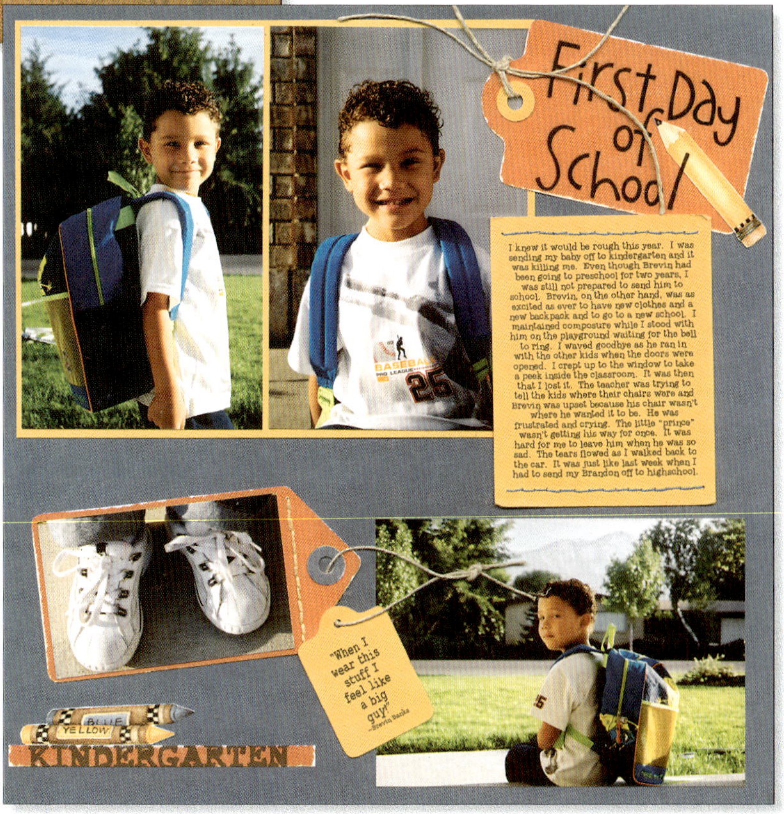
First Day of School
I knew it would be rough this year. I was sending my baby off to kindergarten and it was killing me. Even though Brevin had been going to preschool for two years, I was still not prepared to send him to school. Brevin, on the other hand, was as excited as ever to have new clothes and a new backpack and to go to a new school. I maintained composure while I stood with him on the playground waiting for the bell to ring. I waved goodbye as he ran in with the other kids when the doors were opened. I crept up to the window to take a peek inside the classroom. It was then that I lost it. The teacher was trying to tell the kids where their chairs were and Brevin was upset because his chair wasn't where he wanted it to be. He was frustrated and crying. The little "prince" wasn't getting his way for once. It was hard for me to leave him when he was so sad. The tears flowed as I walked back to the car. It was just like last week when I had to send my Brandon off to highschool.
"When I wear this stuff I feel like a big guy!"
—Brevin Backs
BLUE
YELLOW
KINDERGARTEN

First Day of School

Supplies

Tags: Coluzzle, Provo Craft
Stickers: Debbie Mumm, Creative Imaginations
Letter stickers: Sue Dreamer, Colorbök
Embroidery floss: Making Memories
Computer fonts: CK Stenography and CK Typewriter, "Fresh Fonts" CD, *Creating Keepsakes*
Circle punch: Family Treasures

♥ **I Love It!:** *Type endearing quotes from family members on miniature tags and attach them to larger tags with jute or twine.*

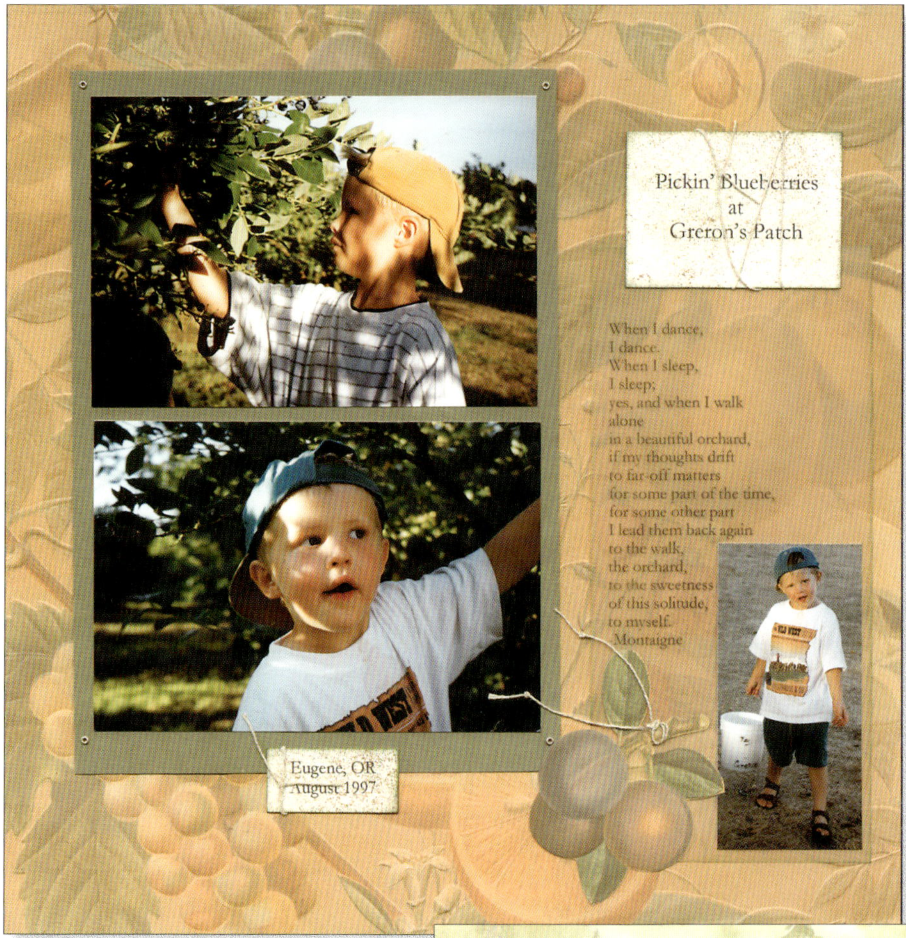
Pickin' Blueberries
at
Greron's Patch
When I dance,
I dance.
When I sleep,
I sleep;
yes, and when I walk
alone
in a beautiful orchard,
if my thoughts drift
to far-off matters
for some part of the time,
for some other part
I lead them back again
to the walk,
the orchard,
to the sweetness
of this solitude,
to myself.
Montaigne
Eugene, OR
August 1997

Pickin' Blueberries

Supplies
Embossed paper, vellum and stickers: K & Company
Computer font: Garamond, Microsoft Word
Eyelets: Making Memories
Ink spritzer: Color Workshop

♥ **I Love It!:** *Tying twine or fibers onto tags is a given, but what about tying twine around other accents to add a 3-D quality to a layout? Knot the ends of a piece of twine or ribbon, then wrap it around a narrow part of the accent for a fresh, new look.*

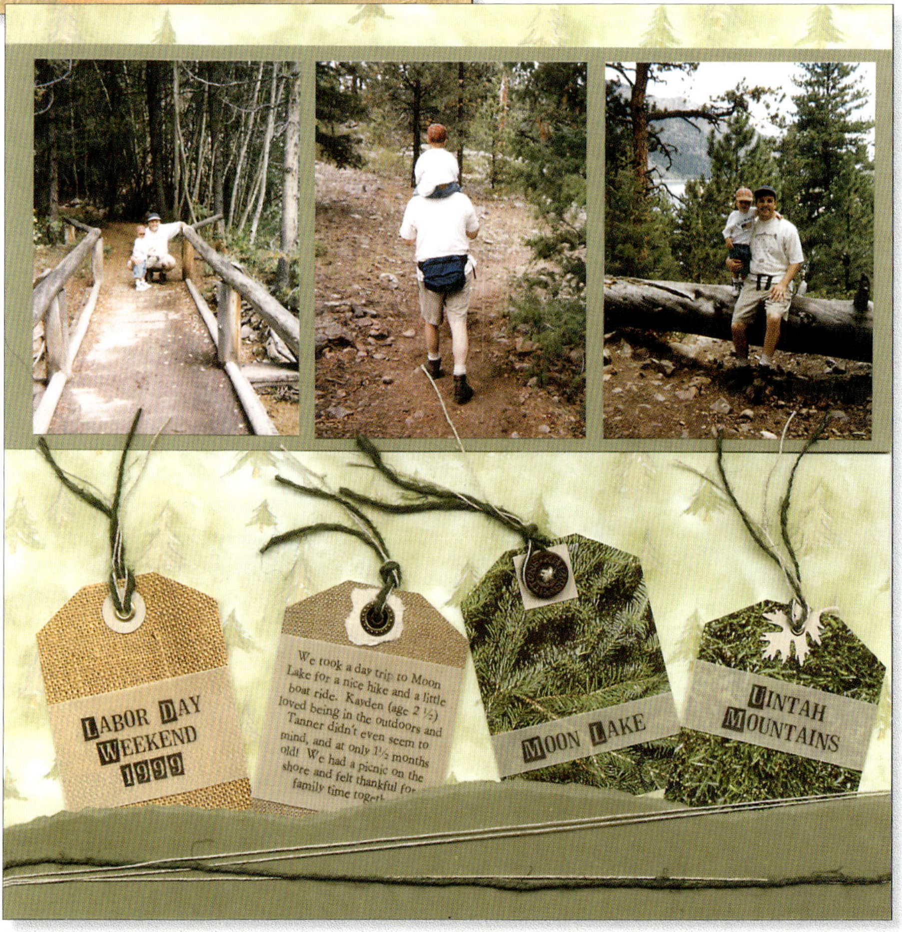
Labor Day Weekend 1999
We took a day trip to Moon Lake for a nice hike and a little boat ride. Kayden (age 2 ½) loved being in the outdoors and Tanner didn't even seem to mind, and at only 1½ months old! We had a picnic on the shore and felt thankful for family time
Moon Lake
Uintah Mountains

Labor Day Weekend 1999

Supplies
Patterned paper: Provo Craft
Vellum: Autumn Leaves
Preprinted tags: Paper Loft
Leaf punch: McGill
Computer fonts: CK Wanted and CK Constitution, "Fresh Fonts" CD, *Creating Keepsakes*
Eyelets: Making Memories
Rivets: Chatterbox
Other: Hemp, twine and button

♥ **I Love It!:** *Finishing tags with eyelets, rivets, buttons or brads is truly an art in itself. This page is a great example of the endless variations you can create. Combine fibers in different thicknesses, colors and textures to tie to your tags.*

tip 9
print information onto pre-made accents.

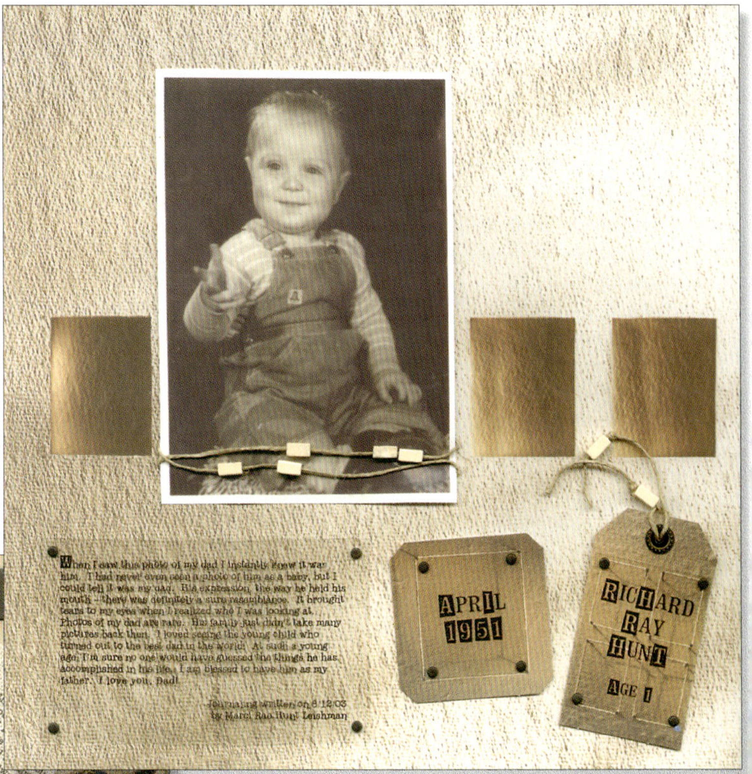

When I saw this photo of my dad I instantly knew it was him. I had never even seen a photo of him as a baby, but I could tell it was my dad. His expression, the way he held his mouth – there was definitely a sure resemblance. It brought tears to my eyes when I realized who I was looking at. Photos of my dad are rare. His family just didn't take many pictures back then. I loved seeing the young child who turned out to the best dad in the world. At such a young age, I'm sure no one would have guessed the things he has accomplished in his life. I am blessed to have him as my father. I love you, Dad!
APRIL 1951
RICHARD RAY HUNT
AGE 1

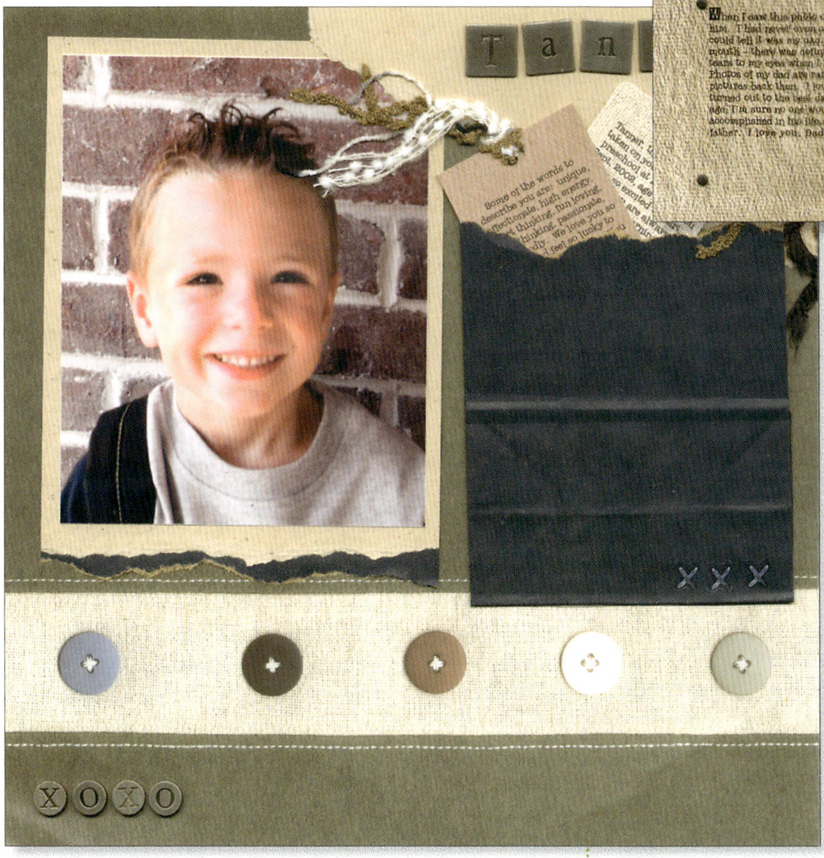

XOXO

Richard Ray Hunt

Supplies

Patterned paper and preprinted tags: Paper Loft
Rivets: Chatterbox
Computer fonts: CK Wanted and CK Stenography, "Fresh Fonts" CD, *Creating Keepsakes*
Other: Brads, hemp, wooden beads and transparency paper

♥ **I Love It!:** *Use transparency paper to create the illusion that you've printed onto odd-sized paper or preprinted accents. Simply size your journaling, print it onto the transparency paper and attach the transparency to the accent or paper using brads, eyelets or a clear adhesive.*

Tanner

Supplies

Patterned paper, stickers and tags: SEI
Metal letters and fibers: Making Memories
Paper bag accent: DMD, Inc.
Computer font: CK Stenography, "Fresh Fonts" CD, *Creating Keepsakes*

♥ **I Love It!:** *Send pre-made tags and accents through your printer to create journaling or titles. Here's how: Format the text to the size of the tag or accent and print onto regular paper. Double-check the formatting, then carefully tape the accent or tag over the printed text on the paper. Run the paper back through the printer so the text will print onto the tag or accent.*

Same Idea, Slightly Different: *This layout uses the exact same idea of printing on tags and tucking them into a paper bag accent but shows a smaller version.*

Boots

Supplies

Patterned paper and preprinted tags: Paper Loft
Paper bag accent: DMD, Inc.
Letter stamps: Barnes and Noble
Stamping ink: Tsukineko
Rivets: Chatterbox
Chalk: Craf-T Products
Computer font: CK Corral, "Fresh Fonts" CD, *Creating Keepsakes*
Other: Jute and brads

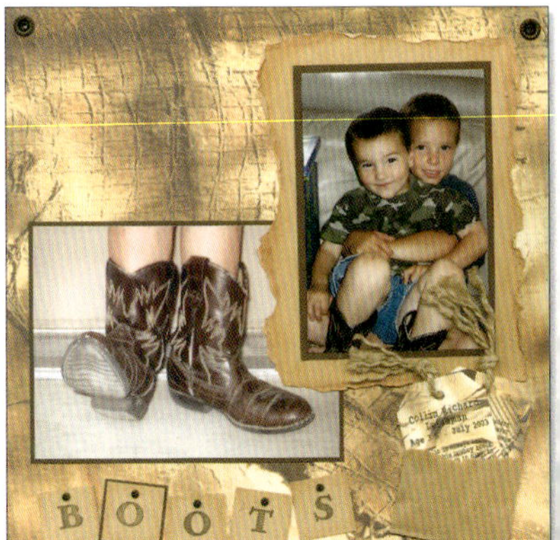

BOOTS

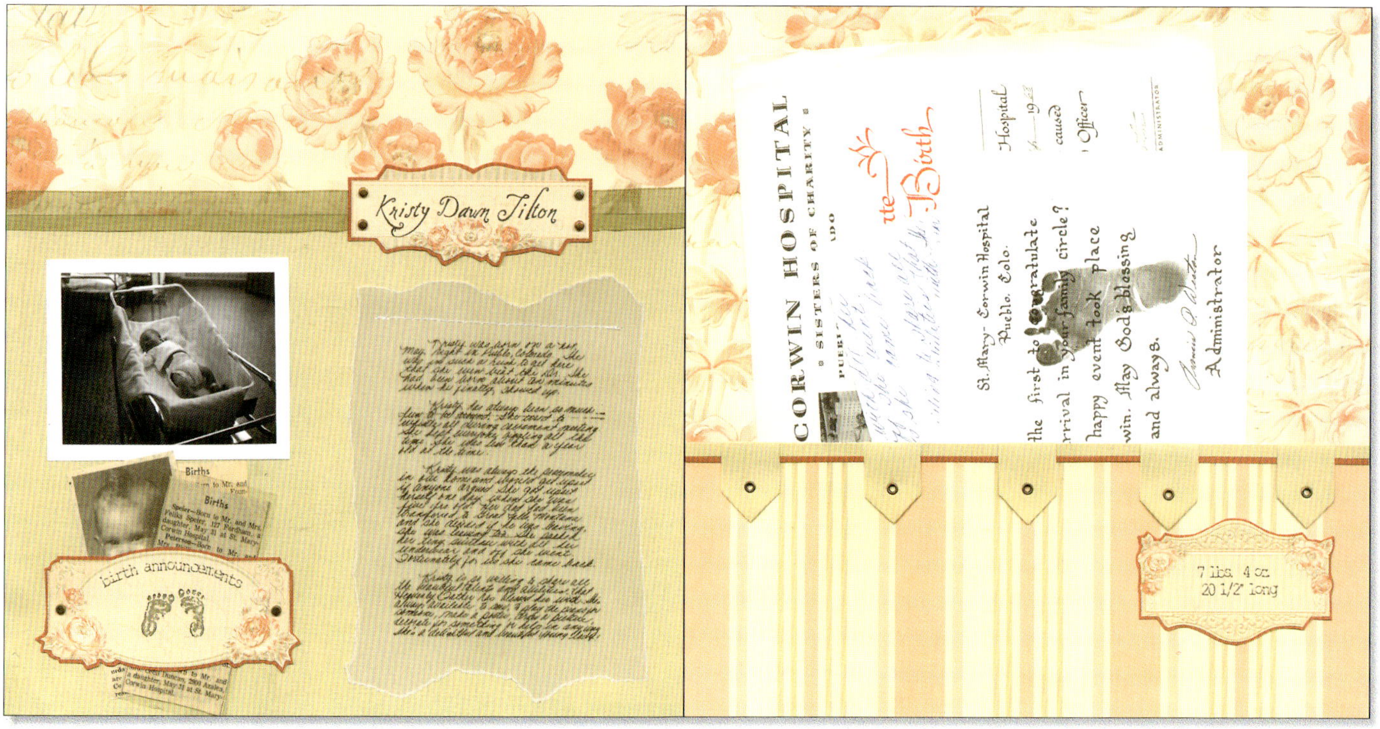
Kristy Dawn Tilton
birth announcements
Births
7 lbs. 4 oz.
20 1/2" long

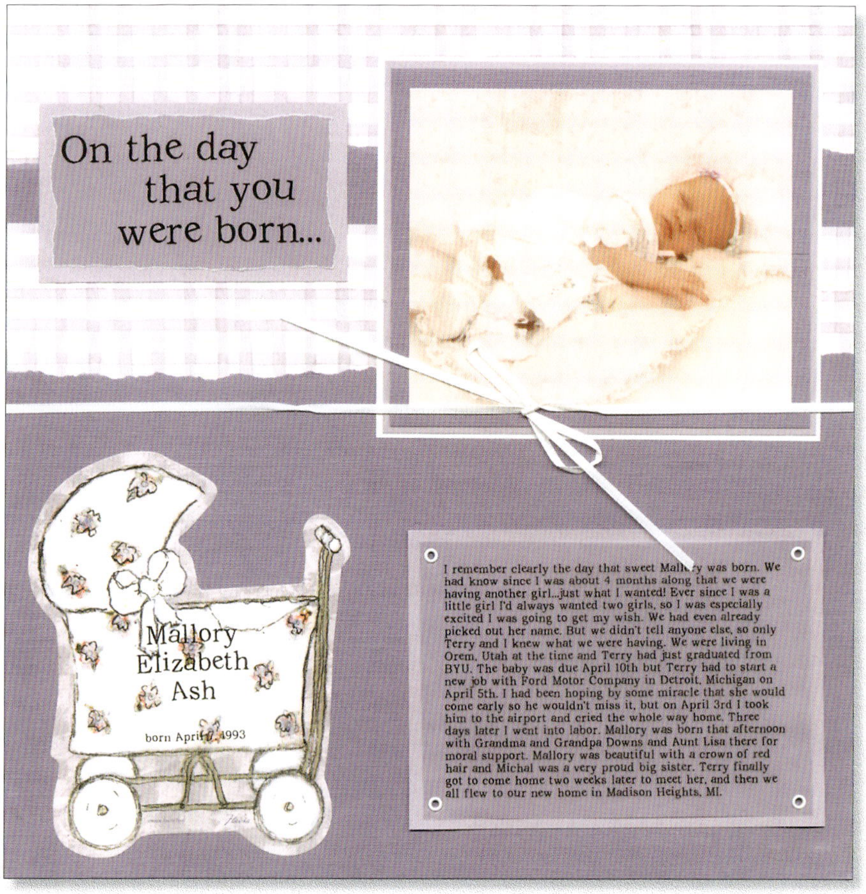
On the day that you were born...
Mallory Elizabeth Ash
I remember clearly the day that sweet Mall y was born. We had know since I was about 4 months along that we were having another girl...just what I wanted! Ever since I was a little girl I'd always wanted two girls, so I was especially excited I was going to get my wish. We had even already picked out her name. But we didn't tell anyone else, so only Terry and I knew what we were having. We were living in Orem, Utah at the time and Terry had just graduated from BYU. The baby was due April 10th but Terry had to start a new job with Ford Motor Company in Detroit, Michigan on April 5th. I had been hoping by some miracle that she would come early so he wouldn't miss it, but on April 3rd I took him to the airport and cried the whole way home. Three days later I went into labor. Mallory was born that afternoon with Grandma and Grandpa Downs and Aunt Lisa there for moral support. Mallory was beautiful with a crown of red hair and Michal was a very proud big sister. Terry finally got to come home two weeks later to meet her, and then we all flew to our new home in Madison Heights, MI.

Kristy Dawn Tilton

Supplies
Patterned paper and stickers: K & Company
Computer fonts: CK Gettysburg and CK Elegant, "Fresh Fonts" CD, *Creating Keepsakes*
Eyelets and brads: Making Memories
Other: Ribbon

♥ **I Love It!:** *Use tags to hold small memorabilia items on your page.*

The Day That You Were Born

Supplies
Patterned paper and preprinted accent: Flavia, Colorbök
Vellum: Colorbök
Computer font: CK Newsprint, "Fresh Fonts" CD, *Creating Keepsakes*
Eyelets: Making Memories
Other: Ribbon

♥ **I Love It!:** *Larger preprinted accents make perfect announcements, invitations, cards and page titles.*

tip 10

wrap text printed onto vellum around preprinted accents.

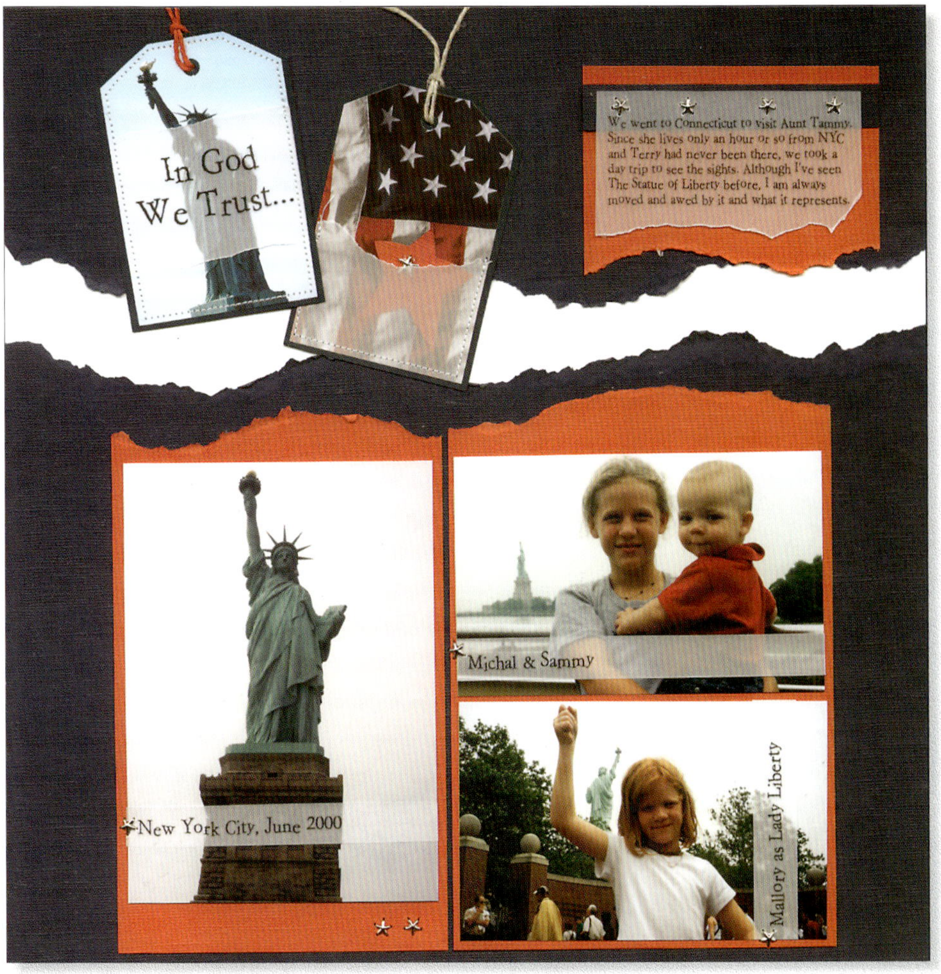

In God We Trust...
We went to Connecticut to visit Aunt Tammy. Since she lives only an hour or so from NYC and Terry had never been there, we took a day trip to see the sights. Although I've seen The Statue of Liberty before, I am always moved and awed by it and what it represents.
Michal & Sammy
New York City, June 2000
Mallory as Lady Liberty

In God We Trust

Supplies

Preprinted tags: Paper Loft
Vellum: WorldWin
Metal star nailheads: Scrapworks
Star punch: Emagination Crafts
Computer font: CK Constitution, "Fresh Fonts" CD, *Creating Keepsakes*
Other: Hemp

♥ **I Love It!:** *Stitch vellum onto a tag to create a pocket, or simply stitch a strip of vellum with the title of your layout onto a printed tag.*

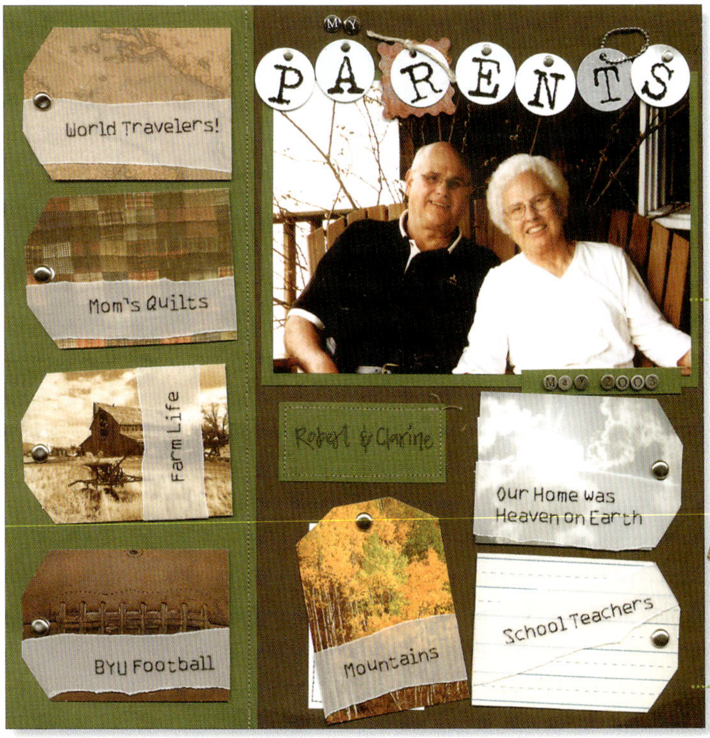

MY
PARENTS
World Travelers!
Mom's Quilts
Farm Life
BYU Football
Robert & Clarine
Our Home was Heaven on Earth
Mountains
School Teachers

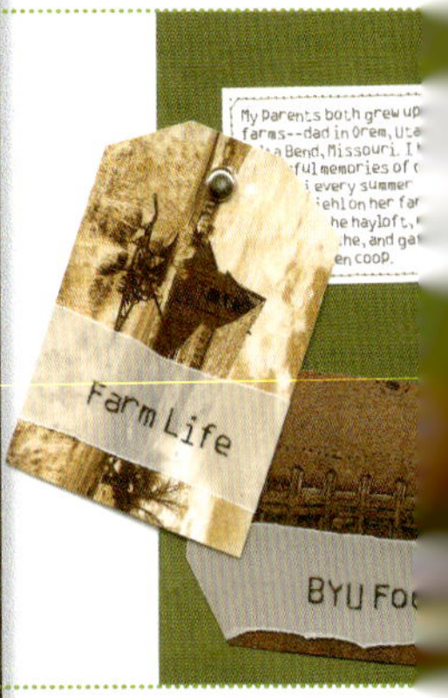

Farm Life

My Parents

Supplies

Preprinted tags: Paper Loft
Letter brads: Creative Imaginations
Metal accents: Making Memories
Computer font: CK Carbon Copy, "Fresh Fonts" CD, *Creating Keepsakes*

♥ **I Love It!:** *Attach tags to your layout with brads so they can be moved to reveal journaling blocks underneath. Be sure to type headings for each journaling block, print the headings on vellum and wrap the vellum around each tag.*

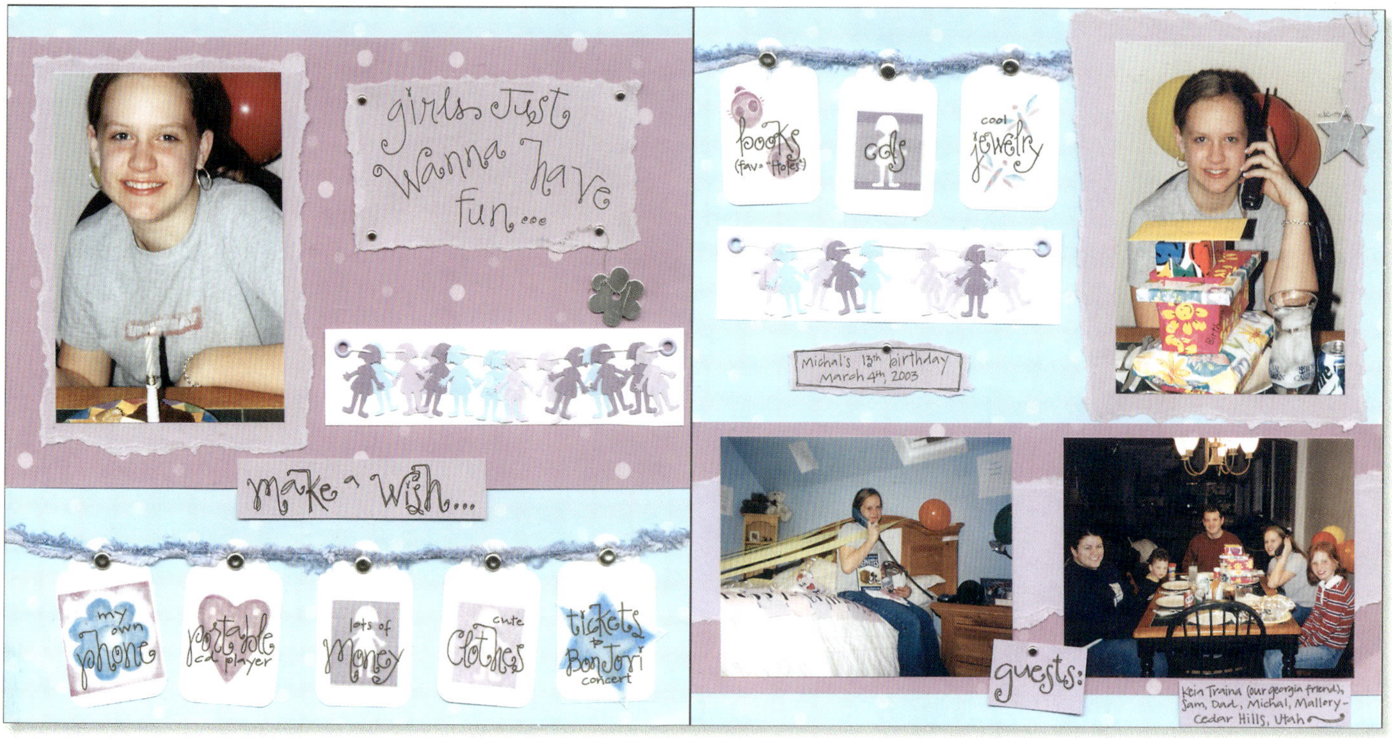
girls Just wanna have fun...
make a wish...
my own phone
portable cd player
lots of money
cute clothes
tickets to Bon Jovi concert
books (fav. "Potter")
cds
cool jewelry
Michal's 13th birthday March 4th 2003
guests:
Kein Traina (our georgia friend), Sam, Dad, Michal, Mallory - Cedar Hills, Utah

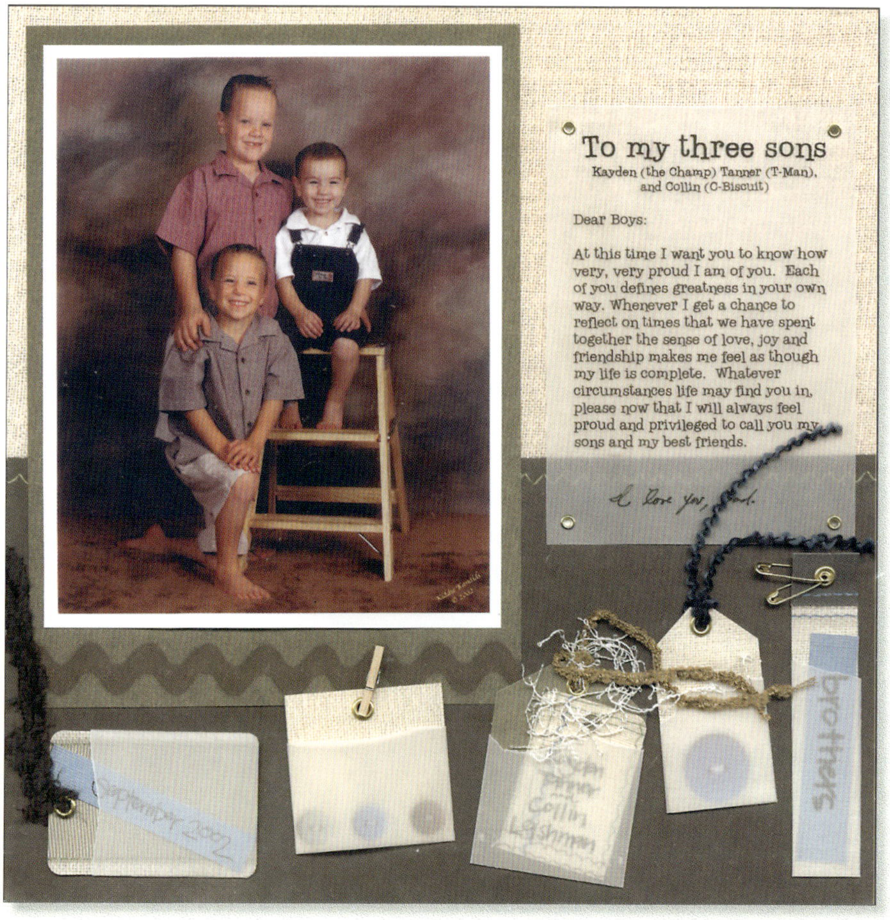
To my three sons
Kayden (the Champ) Tanner (T-Man), and Collin (C-Biscuit)
Dear Boys:
At this time I want you to know how very, very proud I am of you. Each of you defines greatness in your own way. Whenever I get a chance to reflect on times that we have spent together the sense of love, joy and friendship makes me feel as though my life is complete. Whatever circumstances life may find you in, please now that I will always feel proud and privileged to call you my sons and my best friends.
brothers

Girls Just Wanna Have Fun

Supplies

Patterned papers, brads, fibers and metal charms: Colorbök
Craft wire: Making Memories
Paper doll punch: McGill
Pen: Zig Writer, EK Success

I Love It!: *Create an adorable border for your page by punching paper dolls from various colors of cardstock and threading them onto embroidery floss. Lay the paper doll chain on a cardstock background and thread the floss through an eyelet on each end of the cardstock. This idea was first seen in* Scrapbooking Life's Little Treasures *by Rebecca Sower.*

To My Three Sons

Supplies

Patterned paper and preprinted tags: SEI
Vellum: Provo Craft
Small eyelets: Making Memories
Large eyelets: Impress Rubber Stamps
Computer font: CK Stenography, "Fresh Fonts" CD, *Creating Keepsakes*
Pen: Zig Writer, EK Success
Other: Mini-clothespins, safety pins and fibers

Love It!: *Create a tag border by folding mini-vellum envelopes for each tag, then adhering the envelopes in a row along the bottom of your layout. Be sure to embellish each tag in a fun, new way!*

lisa's lessons on accents

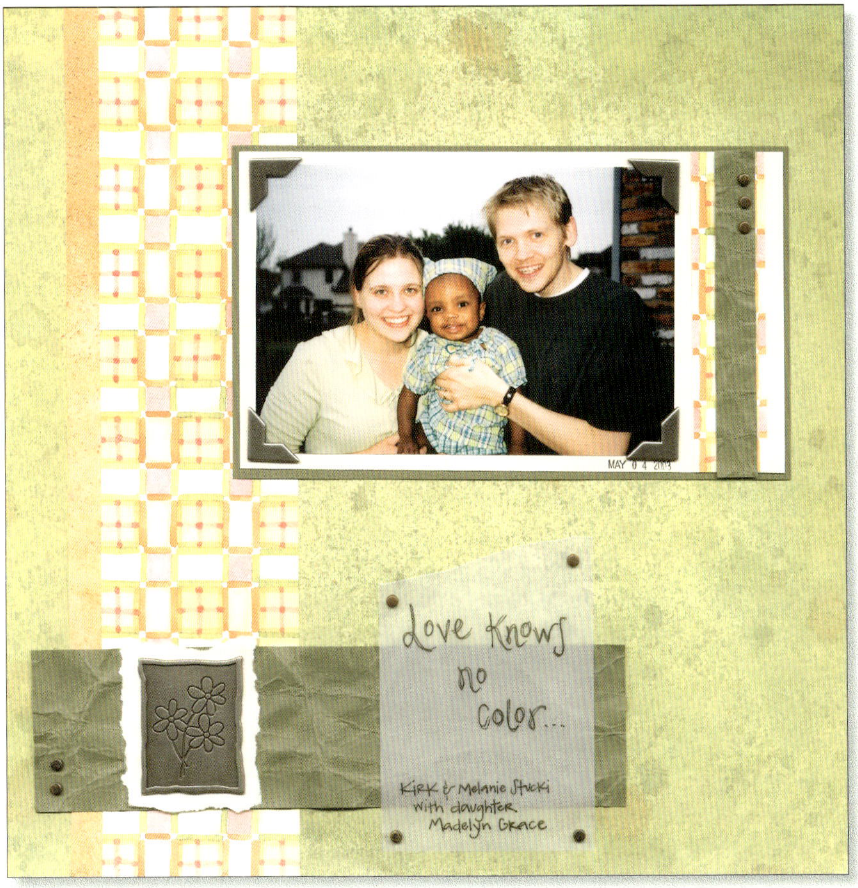

I'm a huge believer in pre-made accents. Here are my two favorite tips for using accents effectively:

- Maintain a consistent feel in the accents you choose. On the layout above, I selected the metal flower accent first because I loved its simplicity and sweetness. To incorporate metal somewhere else on the page, I chose matching metal photo corners. While reviewing the layout, I realized brads would be the perfect finishing touch, but instead of choosing shiny silver or perfectly painted brads, I found brads in the same matte silver-toned metal as the accent and photo corners. Try to maintain this kind of consistency no matter what kind of accents you choose to include on your layout.
- Less is more. Gone are the days when every inch of your layout had to be covered with decorations. A few carefully placed accents leave pages looking understatedly beautiful. Correctly placed white space actually lets your brain relax enough to enjoy the beauty of the page.

Three more favorite tips from this page:

- Don't get stuck thinking that page elements like brads or photo corners are purely functional. On this layout not all the brads were used for their fastening capabilities, but I loved the way their subtle presence really seemed to complete the design of the page, so I used them anyway.
- Do a "final check" of your layout before you chalk up another finished page for your album. After arranging the items on the page the way I wanted them, I decided the green cardstock looked "too new" against the more casual patterned papers. Simply crumpling the cardstock and smoothing it out again created the more comfortable "lived in" look I was after.
- Consider how well your accents stand out against the paper they're placed on. These metal accents have a slight greenish tone to them, so when I placed them directly on the green cardstock they seemed to blend right in—not the effect I was after. Matting the accent and photograph on cream-colored cardstock gave the metal better visibility and lightened up my layout as well.

Love Knows No Color

Supplies
Patterned papers and vellum: Provo Craft
Metal accents: Making Memories
Brads: Boxer Scrapbook Productions
Pen: Zig Writer, EK Success
Other: Date stamp

lisa says:

"Stickers are the non-artist's best friend! They allow you to include amazing *artwork* on your layouts with incredible *ease.* From playful or whimsical to formal or masculine, I always make sure to have a wide *assortment* of stickers at my fingertips when I'm creating layouts. The greatest thing about stickers is their versatility—just because you've used them once doesn't mean you can't use them *again!"*

STICKERS

ch. 3

stuck on stickers

STICKER *n. a slip of paper with an adhesive back that can be fastened to a surface*

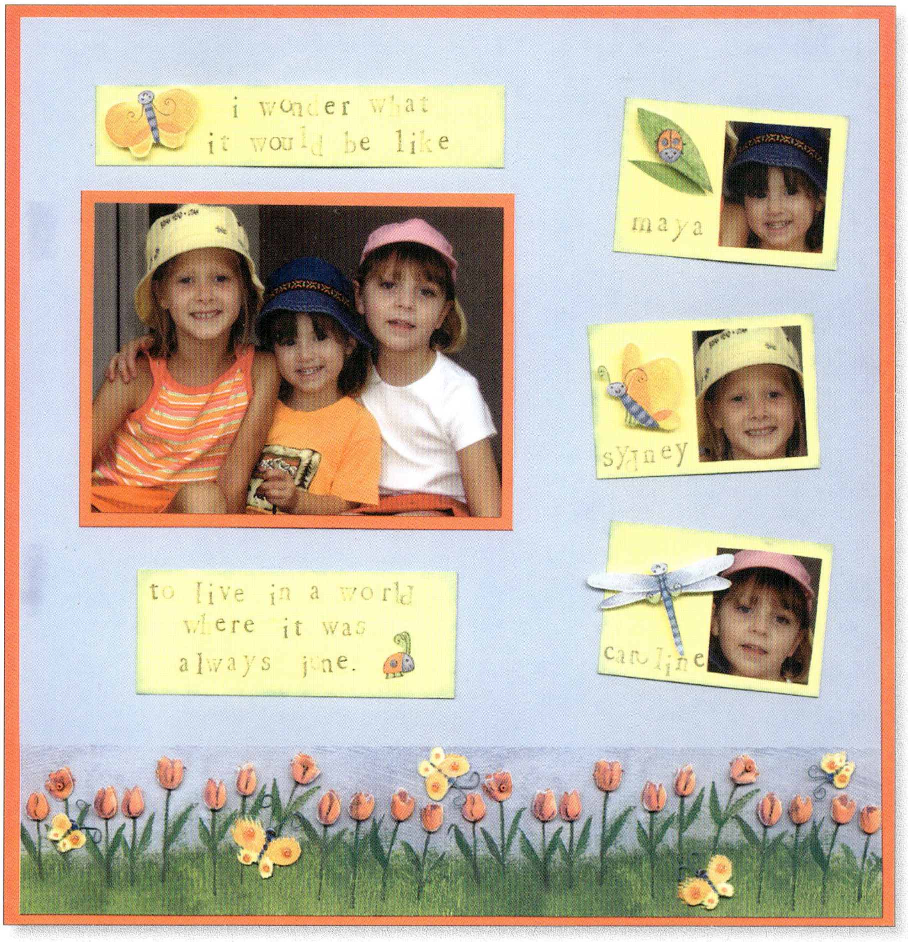
i wonder what
it would be like
maya
sydney
to live in a world
where it was
always june.
caroline

Always June

Supplies
Stickers and 3-D sticker border: Tim Coffey, K & Company
Letter stamps: PSX Design
Stamping ink: ColorBox, Clearsnap
Chalks: Stampin' Up!

♥ **I Love It!:** *Really make your pages "pop" by raising stickers on 3-D foam adhesive. I love the ladybug sticker on this layout—one part of the leaf is raised while the other is flat, creating a fun, dimensional look.*

tip 1

create subtle visual triangles with stickers.

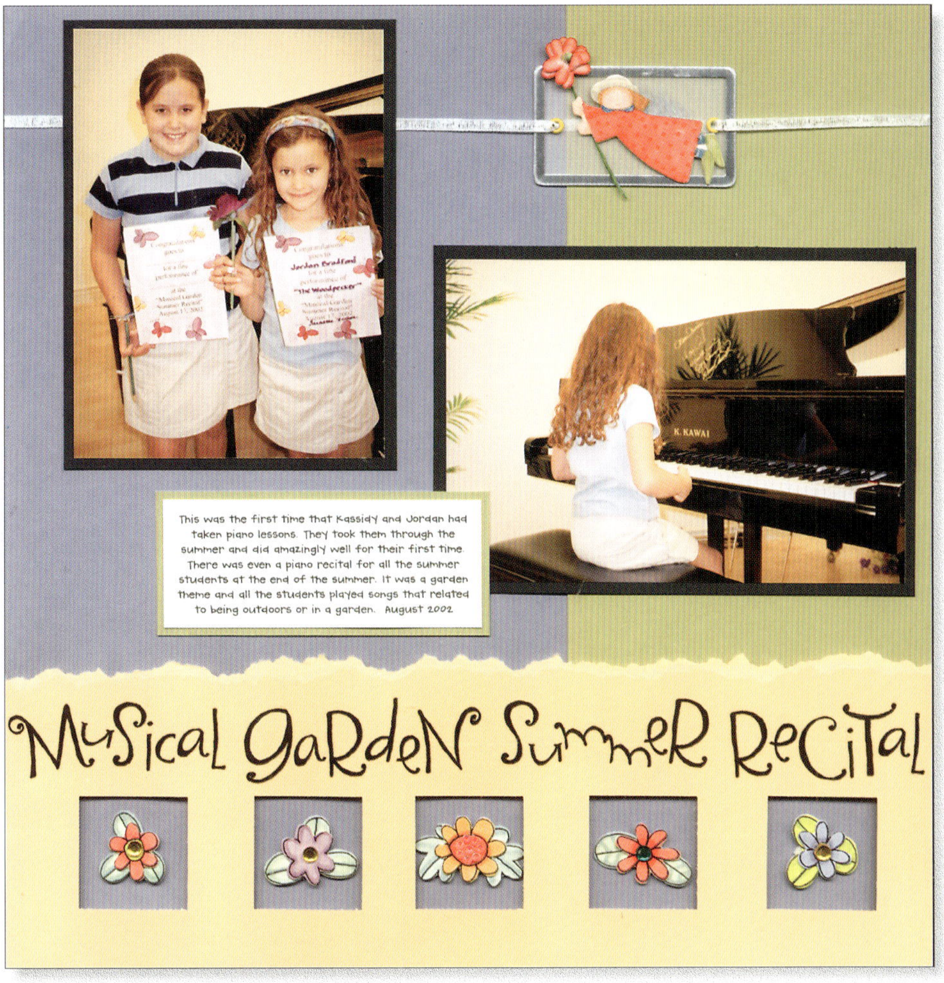
This was the first time that Kassidy and Jordan had taken piano lessons. They took them through the summer and did amazingly well for their first time. There was even a piano recital for all the summer students at the end of the summer. It was a garden theme and all the students played songs that related to being outdoors or in a garden. August 2002
K. KAWAI
Musical Garden Summer Recital

Musical Garden Summer Recital

Supplies
Stickers: Sue Dreamer, Colorbök
Letter stickers: David Walker, Colorbök
Metal-rimmed tag: Making Memories
Eyelets: Doodlebug Design
Computer font: CK Handprint, "The Best of Creative Lettering" CD Vol. 4, *Creating Keepsakes*
Other: 3-D foam adhesive and ribbon

♥ **I Love It!:** *Believe it or not, the eye subconsciously recognizes "visual triangles" and finds them pleasing. Drawing imaginary lines from the angel sticker above the photograph to each end of the line of stickers along the bottom of the layout creates a visual triangle on this layout.*

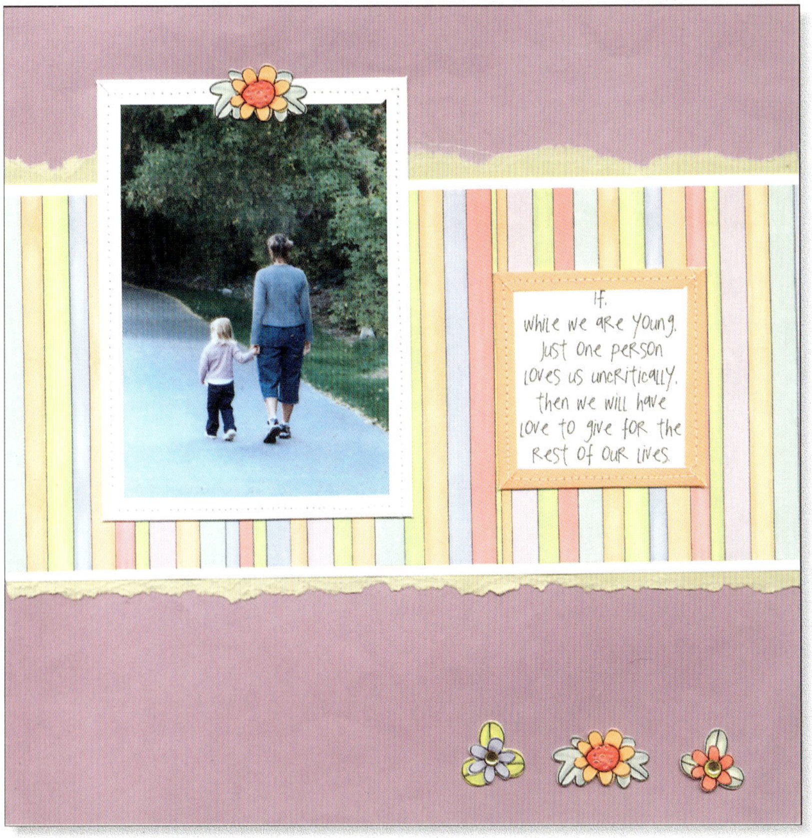
If
while we are young,
just one person
loves us uncritically,
then we will have
love to give for the
rest of our lives.

Loving Uncritically

Supplies
Patterned paper: Colorbök
Stickers: Sue Dreamer, Colorbök

♥ **I Love It!:** *Can you find the visual triangle? Draw imaginary lines from the sticker on the photo mat to the end stickers along the bottom of the layout. Notice that directly in the path of those imaginary lines lie the most important page elements: the photograph and the journaling block.*

♥ **I Love It!:** *Create this sewn photo mat by placing your photograph in the center of a larger rectangle of cardstock and folding up the edges around it. Then slice the corners into diagonals and sew the cardstock to the edges of the photograph.*

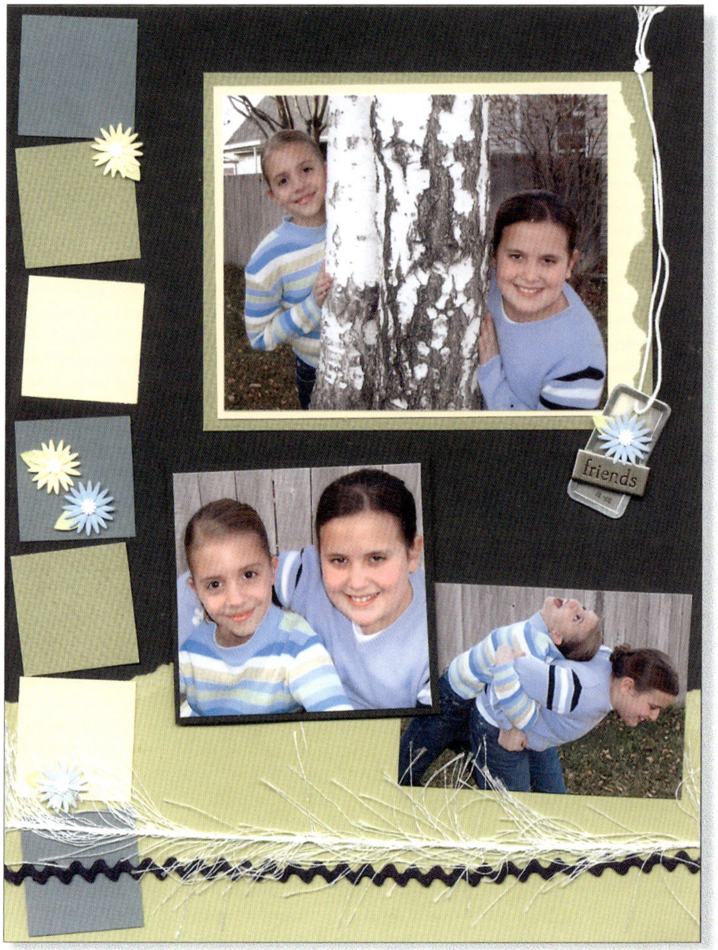

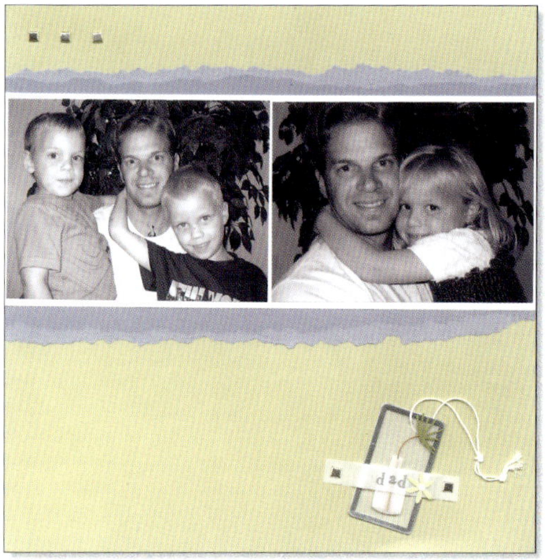

Same Idea, Slightly Different: *This beautiful tag accent follows the same design as the one at left but replaces the metal word accent with a strip of vellum fastened across the tag with two square-shaped brads.*

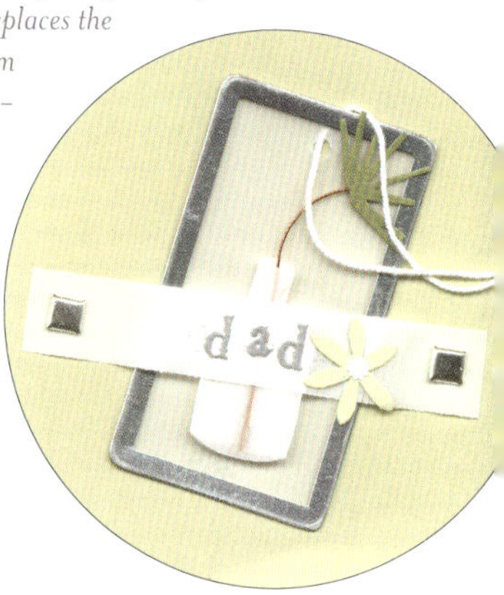

Dad

Supplies
Vellum: WorldWin
Metal-rimmed tag: Making Memories
Sticker: Jolee's Boutique, EK Success
Letter stamps: PSX Design
Stamping ink: ColorBox, Clearsnap
Embossing powder: Stamp-n-Stuff, Stampendous!
Other: Square-shaped brads

Friends

Supplies
Stickers: Jolee's Boutique, EK Success
Metal-rimmed tag and "Friends" metal accent: Making Memories
Fibers: Adornaments (white), EK Success; Memory Lane Paper Company (blue)

♥ **I Love It!:** *We turned the visual triangle on its side for this one. The imaginary lines go from the sticker tag to the top and bottom flower stickers on the border along the side of the layout.*

♥ **I Love It!:** *Simple squares cut from coordinating colors create a wonderful border along the side of this page. Don't try to complicate things—remember that simplicity is usually the best policy!*

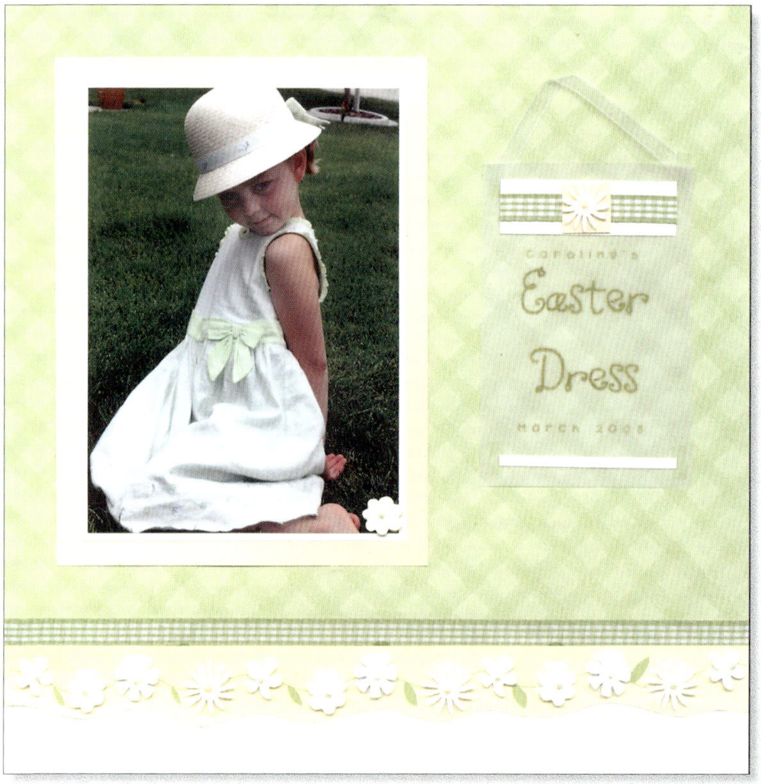

Easter Dress

Supplies
Patterned paper and stickers: Tim Coffey, K & Company
Vellum: WorldWin
Computer fonts: 2Peas Spread Sunshine, downloaded from *www.twopeasinabucket.com*; BH Frilly, package unknown
Other: Ribbon

♥ **I Love It!:** *Customize a sticker border by running a length of coordinating ribbon or patterned paper along the top. Be sure to incorporate the ribbon or patterned paper into other sticker accents you create for the rest of the page.*

tip 2

attach stickers to borders to create a new look.

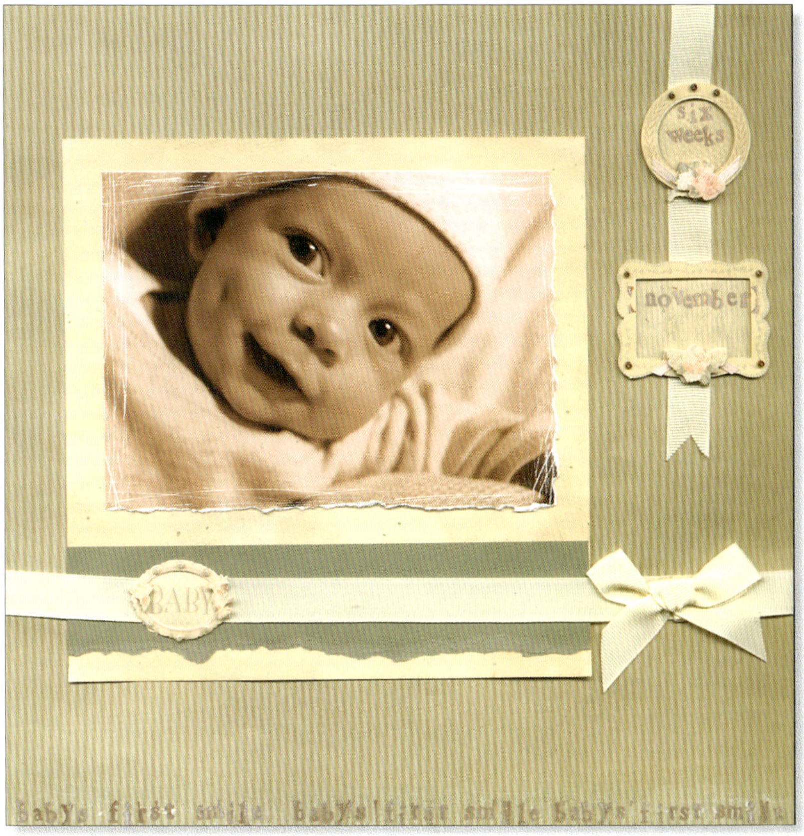

Six Weeks

Supplies

Patterned paper and stickers: K & Company
Letter stamps: PSX Design
Stamping ink: ColorBox, Clearsnap
Other: Ribbon

♥ **I Love It!:** *The photograph on this page was printed on regular photo paper. Two edges of the photograph were torn, then the edges were aged slightly with steel wool.*

♥ **I Love It!:** *Create a simple ribbon border for your page, tie a bow off to one side, then balance the border by attaching a matching 3-D sticker to the other side.*

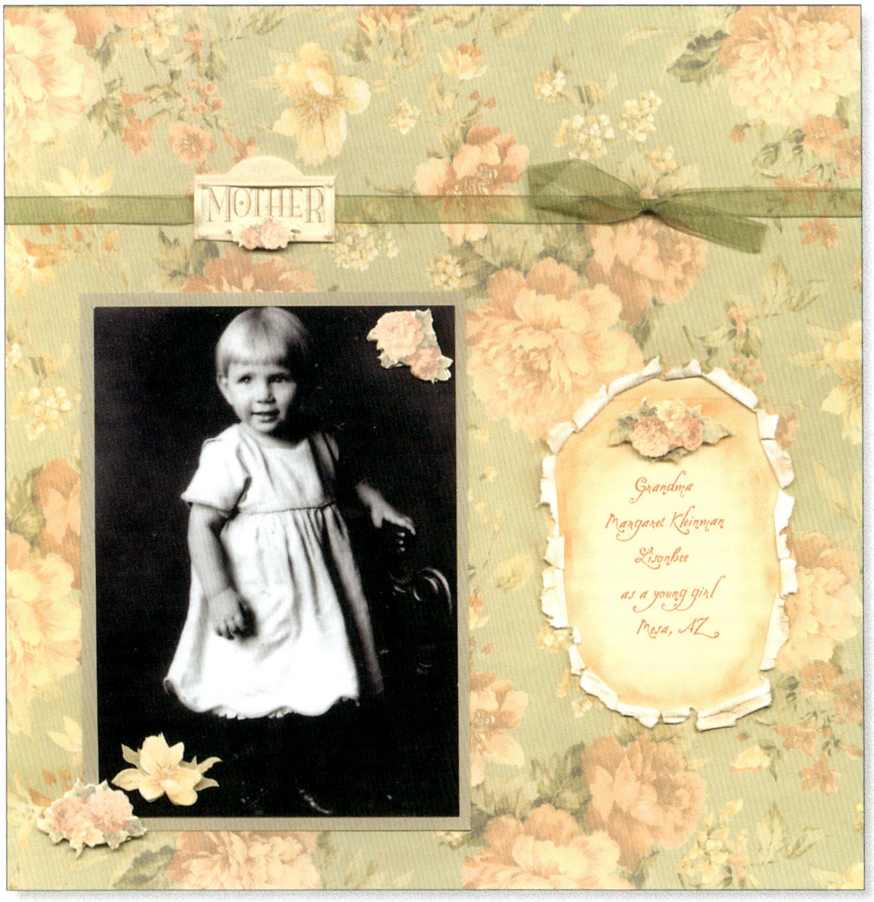

Grandma as a Young Girl

Supplies

Patterned paper and stickers: K & Company
Computer font: CK Elegant, "Fresh Fonts" CD, *Creating Keepsakes*
Other: Ribbon

♥ **I Love It!:** *Instead of always cropping dead space from your photos, take advantage of a dark background to really make your 3-D stickers stand out. Generally, clusters of two or three (like this triangle made from three stickers) are most pleasing to the eye.*

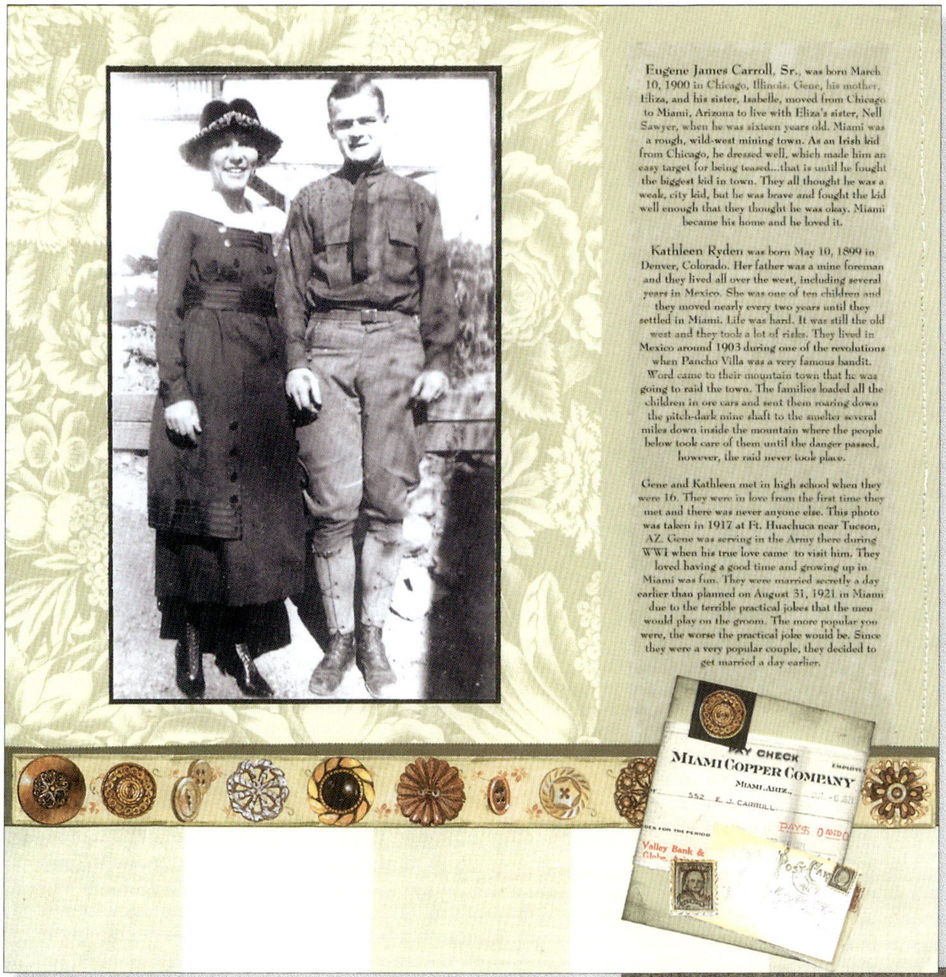
Eugene James Carroll, Sr., was born March 10, 1900 in Chicago, Illinois. Gene, his mother, Eliza, and his sister, Isabelle, moved from Chicago to Miami, Arizona to live with Eliza's sister, Nell Sawyer, when he was sixteen years old. Miami was a rough, wild-west mining town. As an Irish kid from Chicago, he dressed well, which made him an easy target for being teased...that is until he fought the biggest kid in town. They all thought he was a weak, city kid, but he was brave and fought the kid well enough that they thought he was okay. Miami became his home and he loved it.
Kathleen Ryden was born May 10, 1899 in Denver, Colorado. Her father was a mine foreman and they lived all over the west, including several years in Mexico. She was one of ten children and they moved nearly every two years until they settled in Miami. Life was hard. It was still the old west and they took a lot of risks. They lived in Mexico around 1903 during one of the revolutions when Pancho Villa was a very famous bandit. Word came to their mountain town that he was going to raid the town. The families loaded all the children in ore cars and sent them roaring down the pitch-dark mine shaft to the smelter several miles down inside the mountain where the people below took care of them until the danger passed, however, the raid never took place.
Gene and Kathleen met in high school when they were 16. They were in love from the first time they met and there was never anyone else. This photo was taken in 1917 at Ft. Huachuca near Tucson, AZ. Gene was serving in the Army there during WWI when his true love came to visit him. They loved having a good time and growing up in Miami was fun. They were married secretly a day earlier than planned on August 31, 1921 in Miami due to the terrible practical jokes that the men would play on the groom. The more popular you were, the worse the practical joke would be. Since they were a very popular couple, they decided to get married a day earlier.
PAY CHECK
MIAMI COPPER COMPANY
MIAMI, ARIZ.

Eugene James Carroll

Supplies
Patterned paper: Anna Griffin
Vellum: Autumn Leaves
Stickers: Colorbök
Stamping ink: Brilliance, Tsukineko
Computer font: Bernhard Modern BT, Microsoft Word

♥ I Love It!: *Take advantage of coordinating stickers and sticker borders. Place a sticker border over a matching piece of ribbon, then create an accent that incorporates a small photograph or memorabilia item (like this photocopy of a first paycheck) and stickers that coordinate with the sticker border. This layout looks so "put together"!*

School Days

Supplies
Patterned paper: Rocky Mountain Scrapbook Co.
Stickers: Nostalgiques, EK Success
Metal-rimmed tag: Making Memories
Photo corners: Canson
Computer font: Baskerville Old Face, Microsoft Word
Antiquing gel: Delta Technical Coatings
Other: Transparency paper

♥ I Love It!: *Cut the center out of a metal-rimmed tag, then use the metal frame to highlight the important person in a school or group photograph. This metal frame was aged to match the mood of the heritage photograph.*

♥ I Love It!: *This charming sticker accent and border were created by adhering the sticker border along the bottom of the page and adhering the calendar sticker to the left side of the border. Then, the journaling was printed on clear transparency paper, brown antiquing gel was applied to the underside of the transparency, and the transparency was adhered over the calendar sticker.*

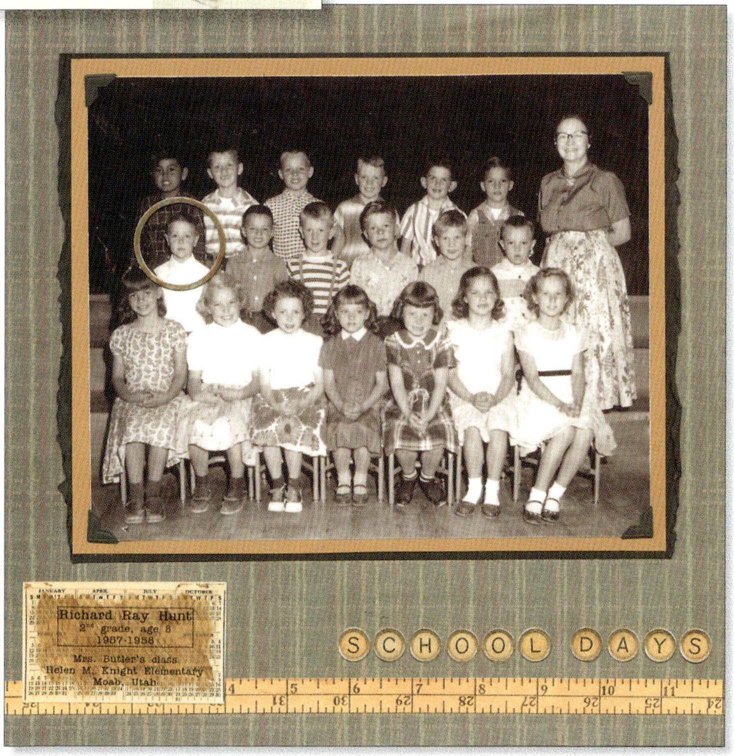
Richard Ray Hunt
2nd grade, age 8
1957-1958
Mrs. Butler's class
Helen M. Knight Elementary
Moab, Utah
SCHOOL DAYS

tip 3

frame stickers with a simple, decorative mat.

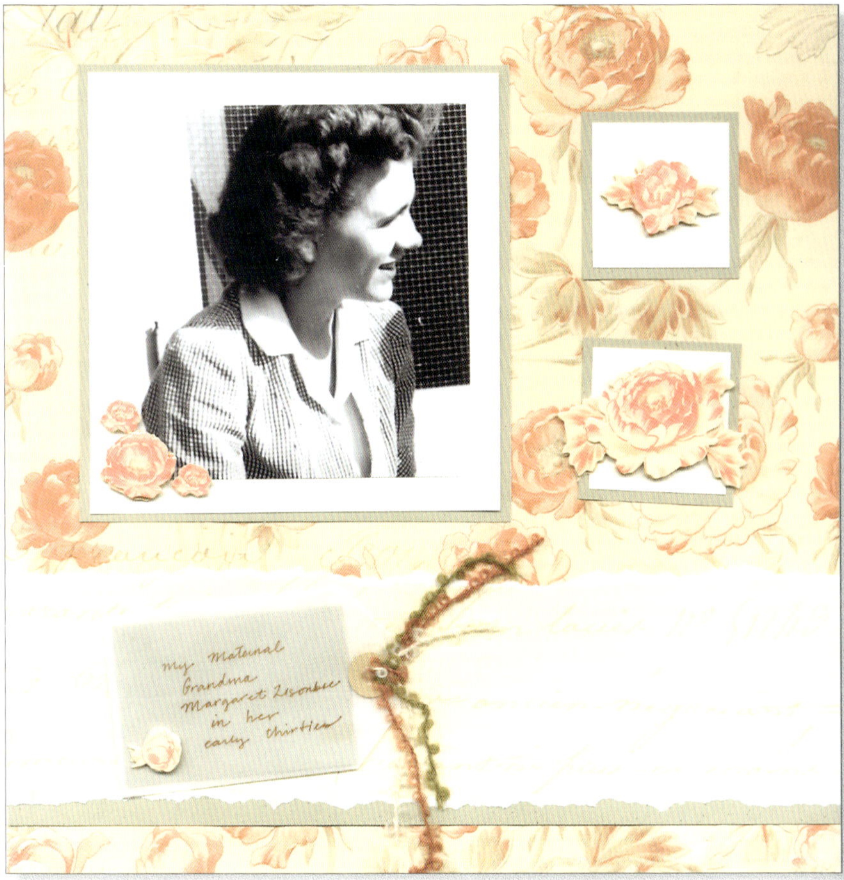
my Maternal Grandma Margaret
in her early thirties

My Maternal Grandma

Supplies
Patterned paper and stickers: K & Company
Vellum: WorldWin
Pen: Zig Writer, EK Success
Other: Fibers

♥ **I Love It!:** *Let a sticker, especially a 3-D sticker, extend past the cardstock mat you create for it. This creates a natural-looking accent without a lot of extra white space.*

Remembering Yesterday

Supplies
Patterned paper, letter stickers, preprinted accents, vellum and stickers: K & Company
Eyelets: Making Memories
Computer font: Silver Script Regular, downloaded from the Internet
Other: String

♥ **I Love It!:** *Frames aren't only for photographs—these adorable sticker frames make the perfect border for matching sticker accents. Hang the resulting accents with mini-eyelets and different lengths of string from the journaling block.*

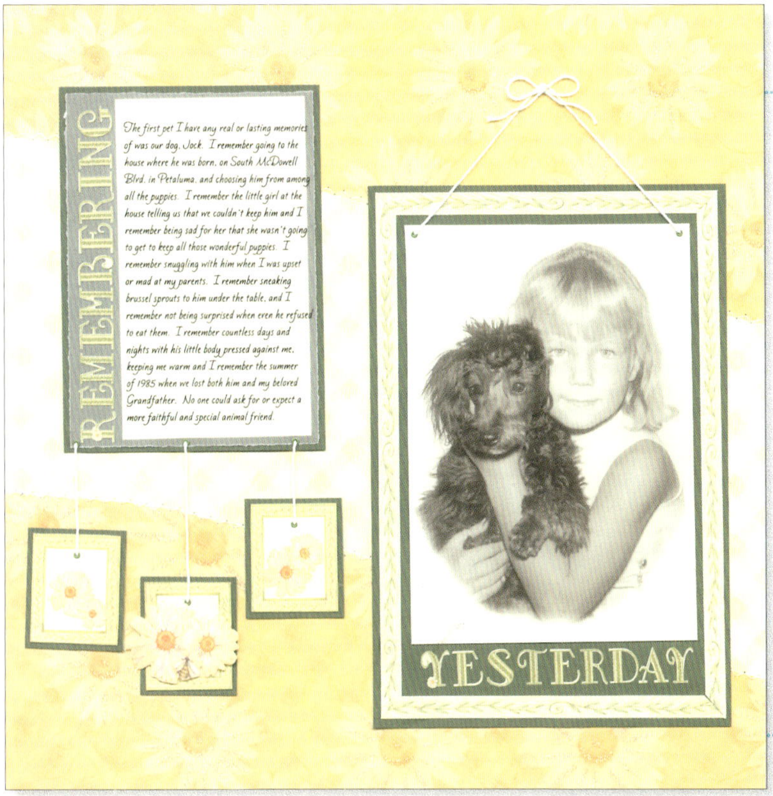
REMEMBERING
The first pet I have any real or lasting memories of was our dog, Jock. I remember going to the house where he was born, on South McDowell Blvd. in Petaluma, and choosing him from among all the puppies. I remember the little girl at the house telling us that we couldn't keep him and I remember being sad for her that she wasn't going to get to keep all those wonderful puppies. I remember snuggling with him when I was upset or mad at my parents. I remember sneaking brussel sprouts to him under the table, and I remember not being surprised when even he refused to eat them. I remember countless days and nights with his little body pressed against me, keeping me warm and I remember the summer of 1985 when we lost both him and my beloved Grandfather. No one could ask for or expect a more faithful and special animal friend.
YESTERDAY

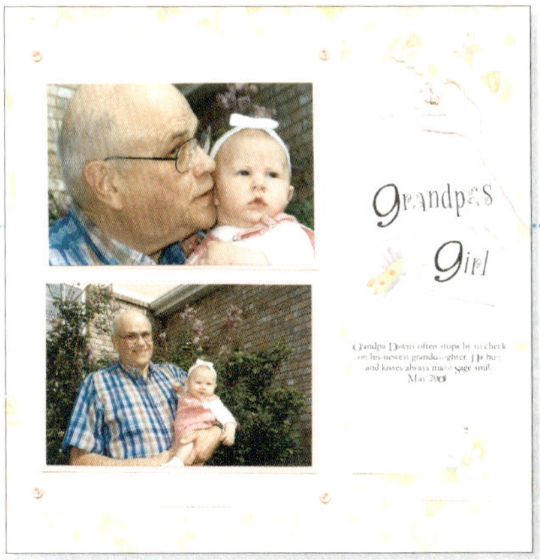
Grandpa's Girl

Same Idea, Slightly Different: *These stickers were also matted with a simple cardstock double mat. Then an eyelet was added and sheer ribbon was tied to the top for a sweet finishing touch.*

Grandpa's Girl

Supplies
Patterned paper and stickers: K & Company
Letters stickers: me & my
BIG ideas and Colorbök ("G")
Eyelet: Doodlebug Design
Square punch: Family Treasures
Computer font: Garamond, Microsoft Word
Other: Fibers and mini-buttons

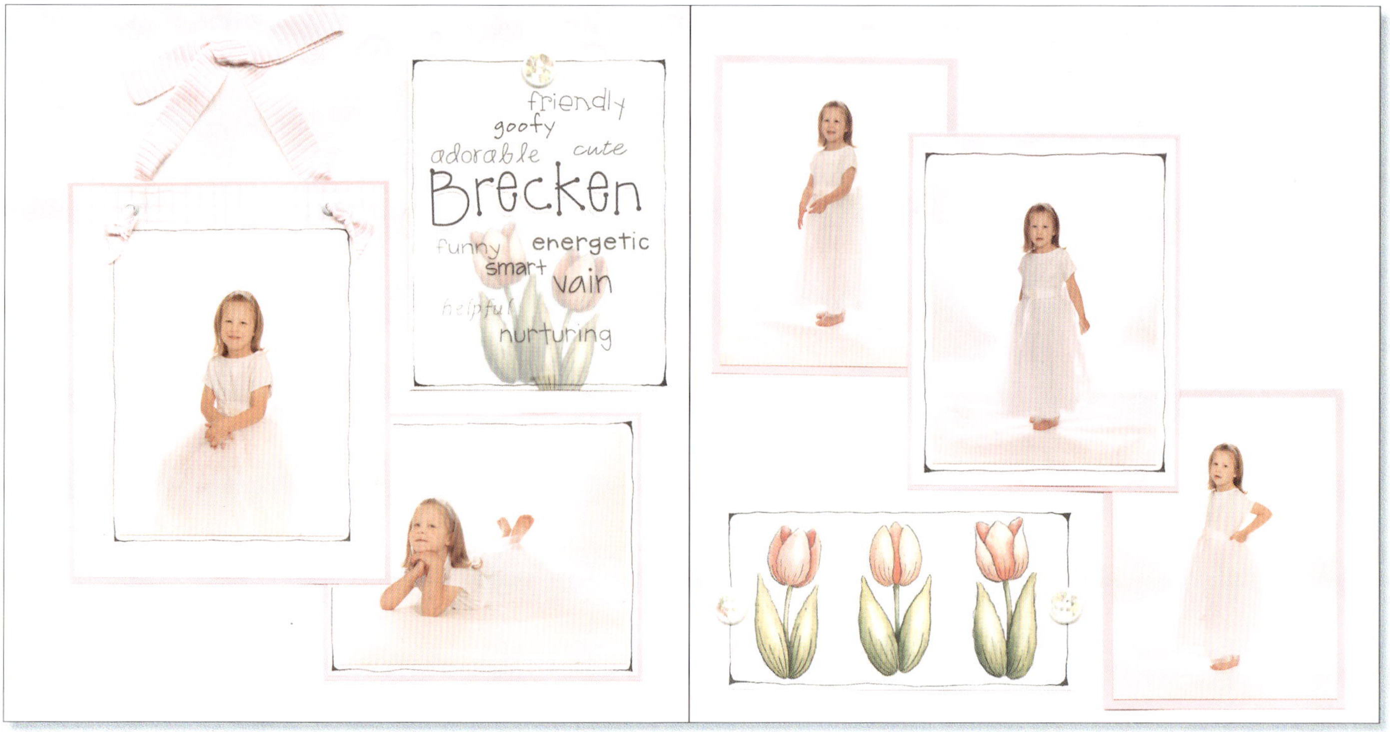
friendly
goofy
adorable
cute
Brecken
funny
energetic
smart
vain
helpful
nurturing

Brecken

Supplies
Patterned papers and stickers: Provo Craft
Vellum: Autumn Leaves
Computer fonts: CK Script and CK Print, "The Best of Creative Lettering" CD Vol. 1; CK Journaling, "The Best of Creative Lettering" CD Vol. 2; CK Toggle, "The Best of Creative Lettering" CD Vol. 3; CK Penman, "The Best of Creative Lettering" CD Vol. 4; CK Handprint, "The Best of Creative Lettering" CD Combo; CK Fun, CK Sketch, CK Pretty and CK Italic, "The Art of Creative Lettering" CD, *Creating Keepsakes*
Pen: Zig Writer, EK Success
Other: Buttons, ribbon, eyelets

♥ **I Love It!:** *Mat your stickers on white cardstock, then pen a simple border around the edge of the cardstock. Create a matching pen border around your photographs to complete the look.*

♥ **I Love It!:** *Keep on the lookout for patterned or printed buttons. They add a subtle, decorative touch to your pages.*

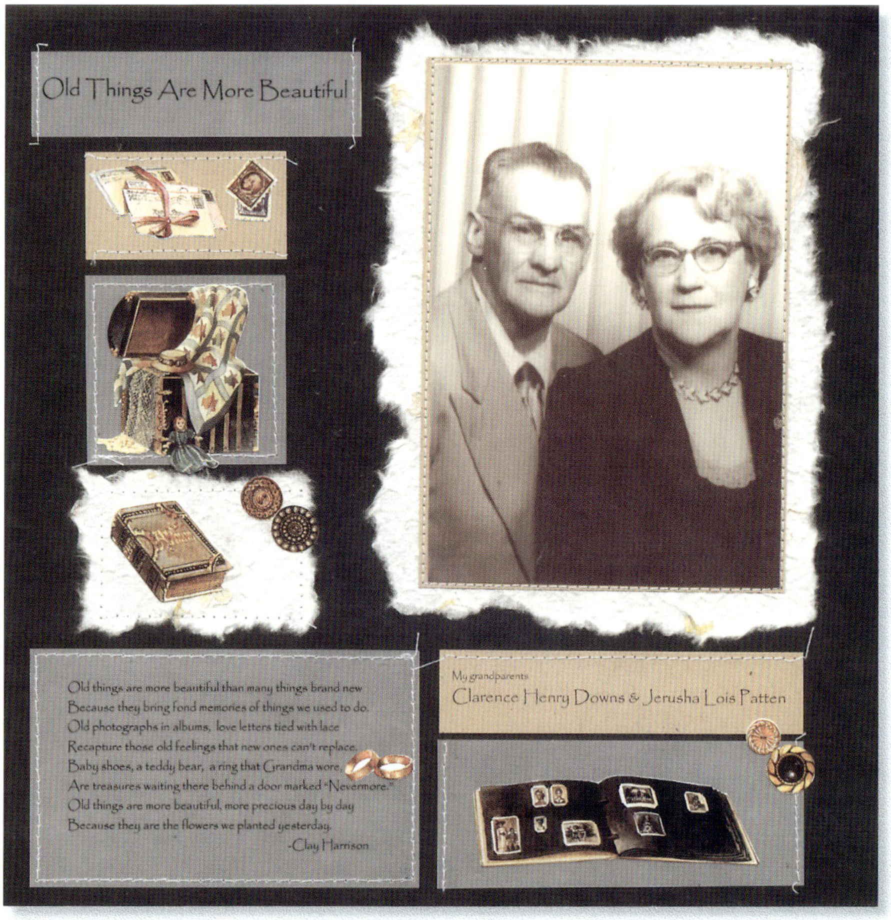
Old Things Are More Beautiful
Old things are more beautiful than many things brand new
Because they bring fond memories of things we used to do.
Old photographs in albums, love letters tied with lace
Recapture those old feelings that new ones can't replace.
Baby shoes, a teddy bear, a ring that Grandma wore,
Are treasures waiting there behind a door marked "Nevermore."
Old things are more beautiful, more precious day by day
Because they are the flowers we planted yesterday.
-Clay Harrison
My grandparents
Clarence Henry Downs & Jerusha Lois Patten

Old Things Are More Beautiful

Supplies
Computer font: Papyrus, Microsoft Word
Stickers: Colorbök
Other: Handmade paper

♥ **I Love It!:** *Arrange stickers on cardstock rectangles in coordinating colors, then sew a simple border around each rectangle to create a fast and easy frame for your sticker accents. Notice how the poem beautifully complements the stickers.*

tip 4

frame stickers using pre-made tags.

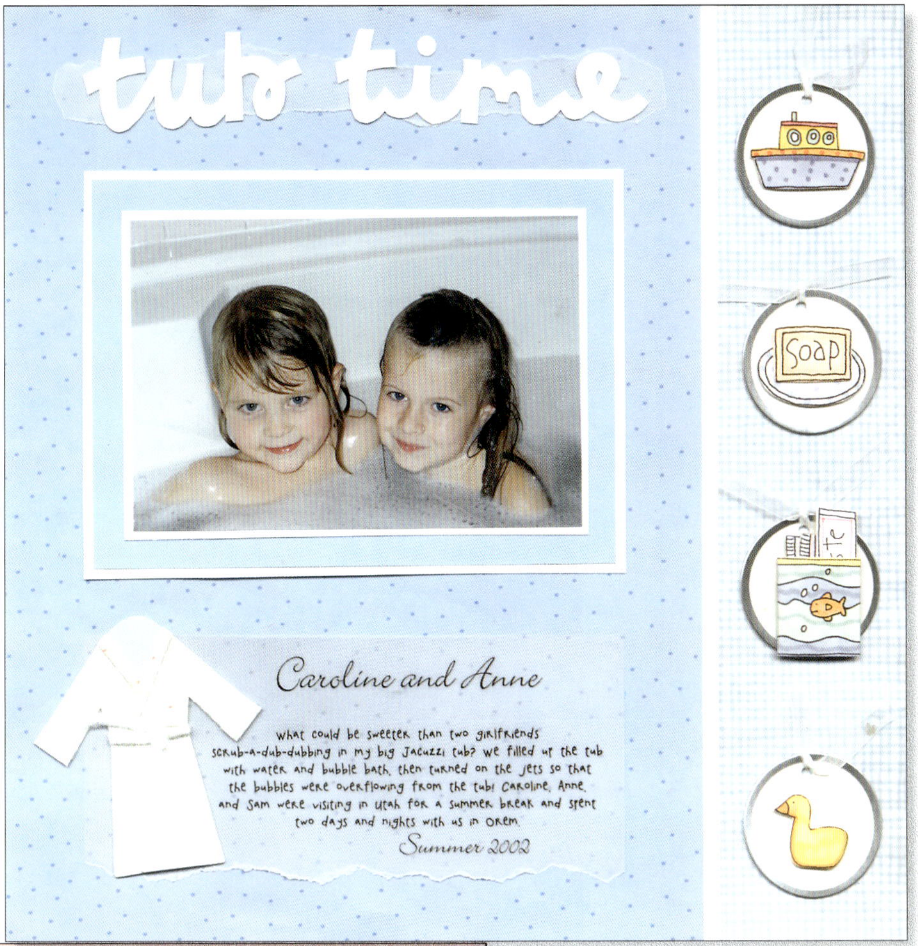

tub time
Soap
Caroline and Anne
What could be sweeter than two girlfriends scrub-a-dub-dubbing in my big Jacuzzi tub? We filled up the tub with water and bubble bath, then turned on the jets so that the bubbles were overflowing from the tub! Caroline, Anne, and Sam were visiting in Utah for a summer break and spent two days and nights with us in Orem.
Summer 2002

Tub Time

Supplies

Patterned paper and stickers: Sue Dreamer, Colorbök
Vellum: WorldWin
Computer font: 2Peas Chicken Shack, downloaded from *www.two-peasinabucket.com*; Bickley Script LET, Macromedia
Lettering template: Whimsy Lower, EK Success
Other: Ribbon and metal-rimmed tags

♥ **I Love It!:** *Layer a wide strip of patterned paper that coordinates with the background paper along one edge of your layout, then run a series of sticker-accented tags tied with ribbon along the strip for a quick-but-cute border.*

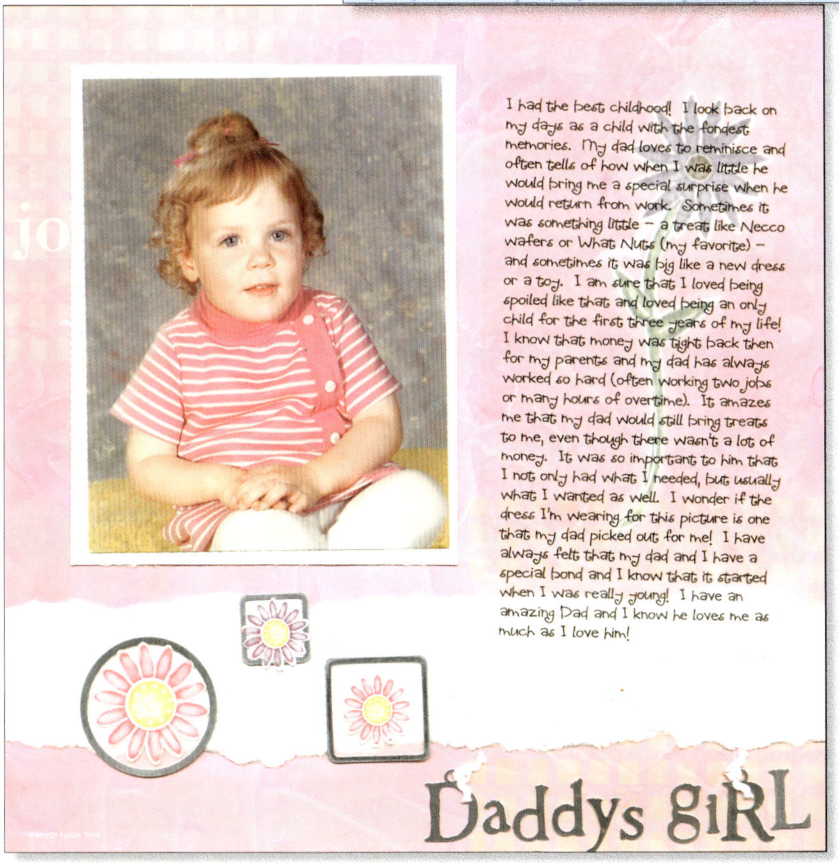

I had the best childhood! I look back on my days as a child with the fondest memories. My dad loves to reminisce and often tells of how when I was little he would bring me a special surprise when he would return from work. Sometimes it was something little – a treat like Necco wafers or What Nuts (my favorite) – and sometimes it was big like a new dress or a toy. I am sure that I loved being spoiled like that and loved being an only child for the first three years of my life! I know that money was tight back then for my parents and my dad has always worked so hard (often working two jobs or many hours of overtime). It amazes me that my dad would still bring treats to me, even though there wasn't a lot of money. It was so important to him that I not only had what I needed, but usually what I wanted as well. I wonder if the dress I'm wearing for this picture is one that my dad picked out for me! I have always felt that my dad and I have a special bond and I know that it started when I was really young! I have an amazing Dad and I know he loves me as much as I love him!
Daddys girl

Daddy's Girl

Supplies

Patterned paper and stickers: Flavia, Colorbök
Vellum: Provo Craft
Metal-rimmed tags and metal letters: Making Memories
Computer font: CK Daydream, Becky Higgins' "Creative Clips & Fonts" CD, *Creating Keepsakes*
Other: Fibers

♥ **I Love It!:** *Combine different sizes and shapes of tags, then add stickers in the centers of the tags. Group the tag accents in odd numbers for the most visual impact.*

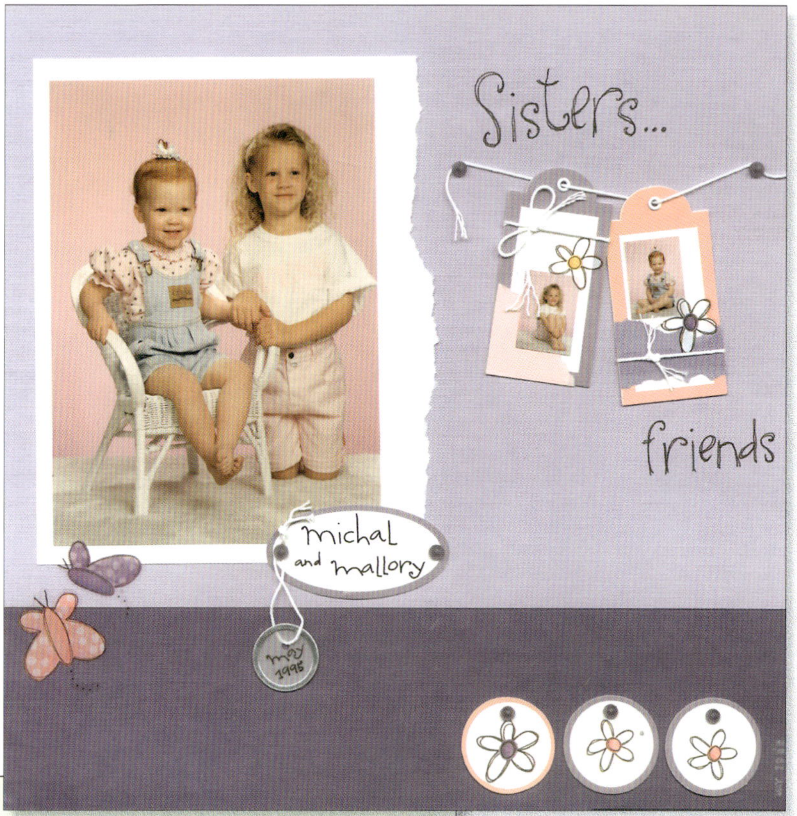
Sisters...
friends
michal and mallory
may 1995

Sisters ... Friends

Supplies
Stickers and eyelets: All My Memories
Metal-rimmed tag: Making Memories
Cardstock tags and nailhead rivets: Chatterbox
Pen: Zig Writer, EK Success
Other: String

♥ **I Love It!:** *Use tiny proofs or index prints to accent tags. They're the perfect size and would probably go unused otherwise!*

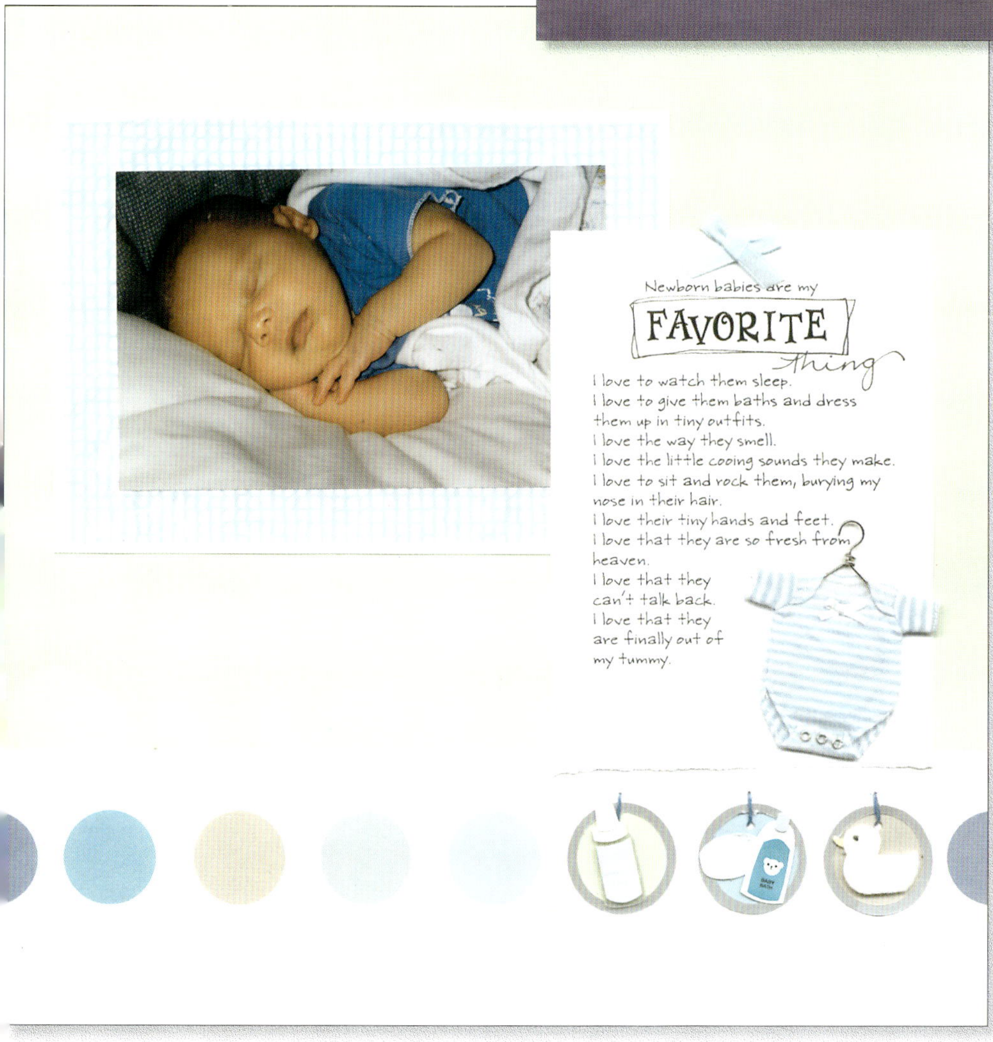
Newborn babies are my
FAVORITE
thing
I love to watch them sleep.
I love to give them baths and dress them up in tiny outfits.
I love the way they smell.
I love the little cooing sounds they make.
I love to sit and rock them, burying my nose in their hair.
I love their tiny hands and feet.
I love that they are so fresh from heaven.
I love that they can't talk back.
I love that they are finally out of my tummy.

Favorite Thing

Supplies
Patterned paper: SEI
Stickers: Jolee's Boutique, EK Success
Letter stickers: Provo Craft
Fibers: Making Memories
Computer font: CK Sketch, "Fresh Fonts" CD, *Creating Keepsakes*
Other: Metallic paper, textured paper and ribbon bow

♥ **I Love It!:** *If you haven't gotten into the metal craze yet, create your own mock metal-rimmed tag. This page shows you how to use preprinted papers that use geometric shapes similar to those used for tags. Simply use a circle or square punch (depending on the pattern printed on your paper) to create a "metal" rim out of metallic paper, then adhere the rim to the shape.*

tip 5
create your own adorable tag accents using stickers.

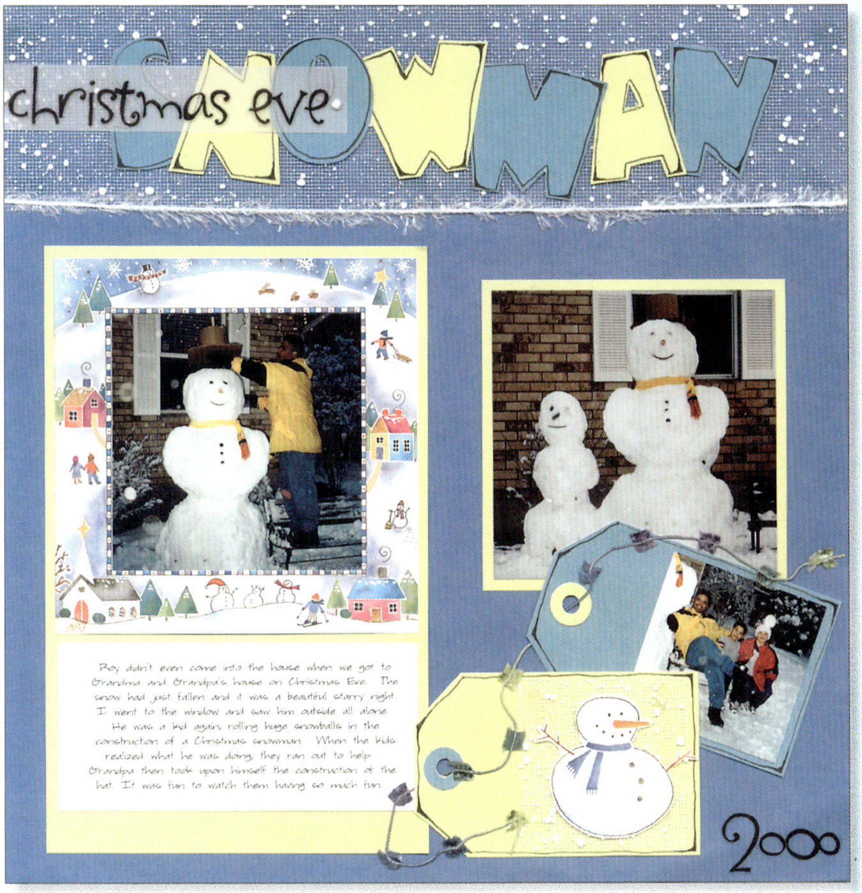
christmas eve
SNOWMAN
Roy didn't even come into the house when we got to Grandma and Grandpa's house on Christmas Eve. The snow had just fallen and it was a beautiful starry night. I went to the window and saw him outside all alone. He was a kid again, rolling huge snowballs in the construction of a Christmas snowman. When the kids realized what he was doing, they ran out to help. Grandpa then took upon himself the construction of the hat. It was fun to watch them having so much fun.
2000

Christmas Eve Snowman

Supplies
Sticker frame and stickers: Colorbök
Letter stickers: David Walker, Colorbök
Mesh: Magenta
Fibers: Adornaments, EK Success
Circle punches: Family Treasures
Computer font: Scrap Casual, "Lettering Delights" CD, Inspire Graphics

♥ I Love It!: *Use a large lettering template or computer font for one word of your title. Create the rest of your title on a strip of vellum using smaller stickers or fonts, then overlap the vellum over part of the larger word for a playful effect.*

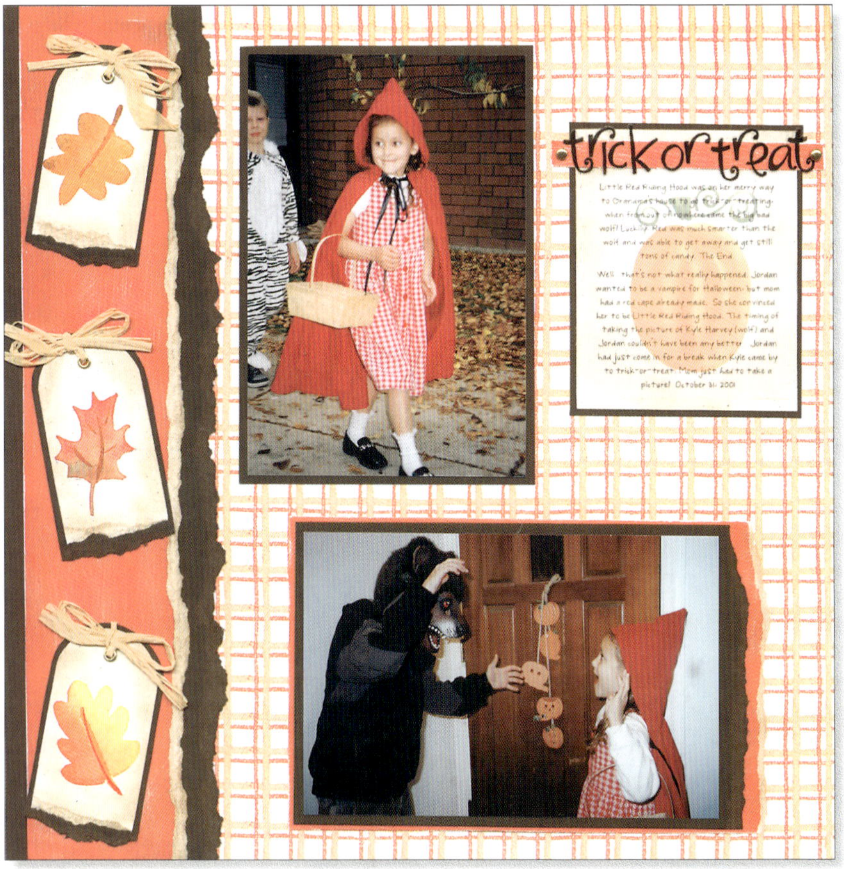
trick or treat
Little Red Riding Hood was on her merry way to Grandma's house to go trick-or-treating. when from out of nowhere came the big bad wolf! Luckily Red was much smarter than the wolf and was able to get away and get still tons of candy. The End
Well that's not what really happened. Jordan wanted to be a vampire for Halloween, but mom had a red cape already made. So she convinced her to be Little Red Riding Hood. The timing of taking the picture of Kyle Harvey (wolf) and Jordan couldn't have been any better. Jordan had just come in for a break when Kyle came by to trick-or-treat. Mom just had to take a picture! October 31, 2001

Trick or Treat

Supplies
Patterned paper and stickers: Kathy Davis, Colorbök
Letter stickers: David Walker, Colorbök
Computer font: CK Jot, "The Art of Creative Lettering" CD, *Creating Keepsakes*
Eyelets: Making Memories
Chalks: Craf-T Products
Other: Raffia

♥ I Love It!: *The fall season evokes such rustic, cozy images—why not duplicate the same feeling on a layout? Aging paper with sandpaper, chalking tags with brown chalk, tearing edges and using raffia are all great techniques for creating rustic layouts for your albums.*

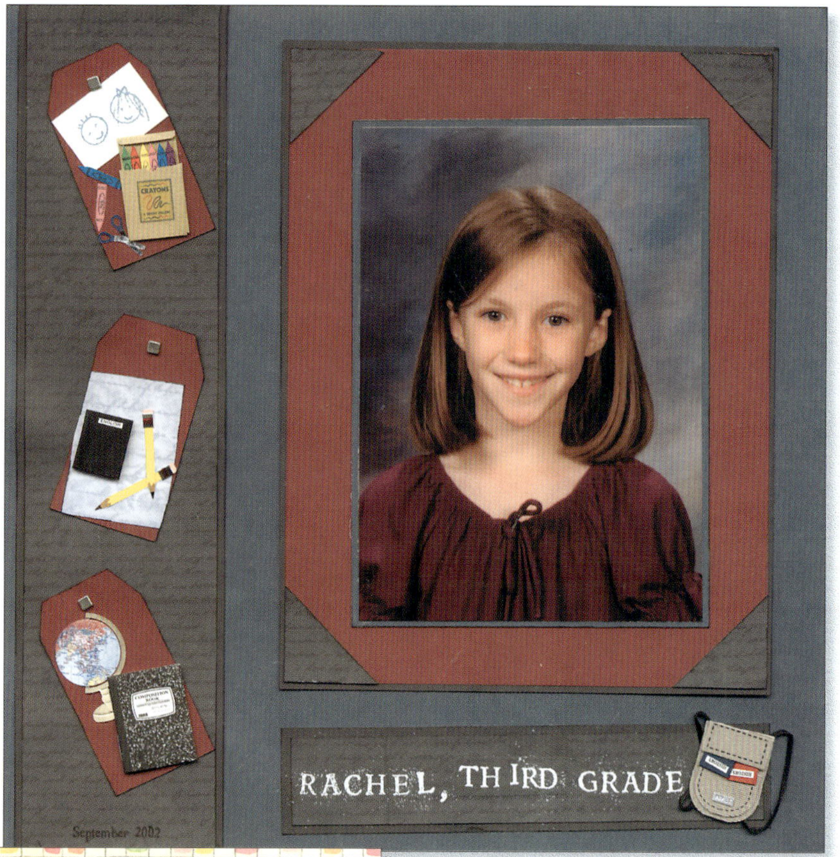

Rachel, Third Grade

Supplies
Patterned paper: Source unknown
Stickers: Jolee's Boutique, EK Success
Letter stamps: Source unknown
Stamping ink: ColorBox, Clearsnap
Other: Square brads

♥ I Love It!: *Collage stickers with the same theme onto tags for quick and easy accents.*

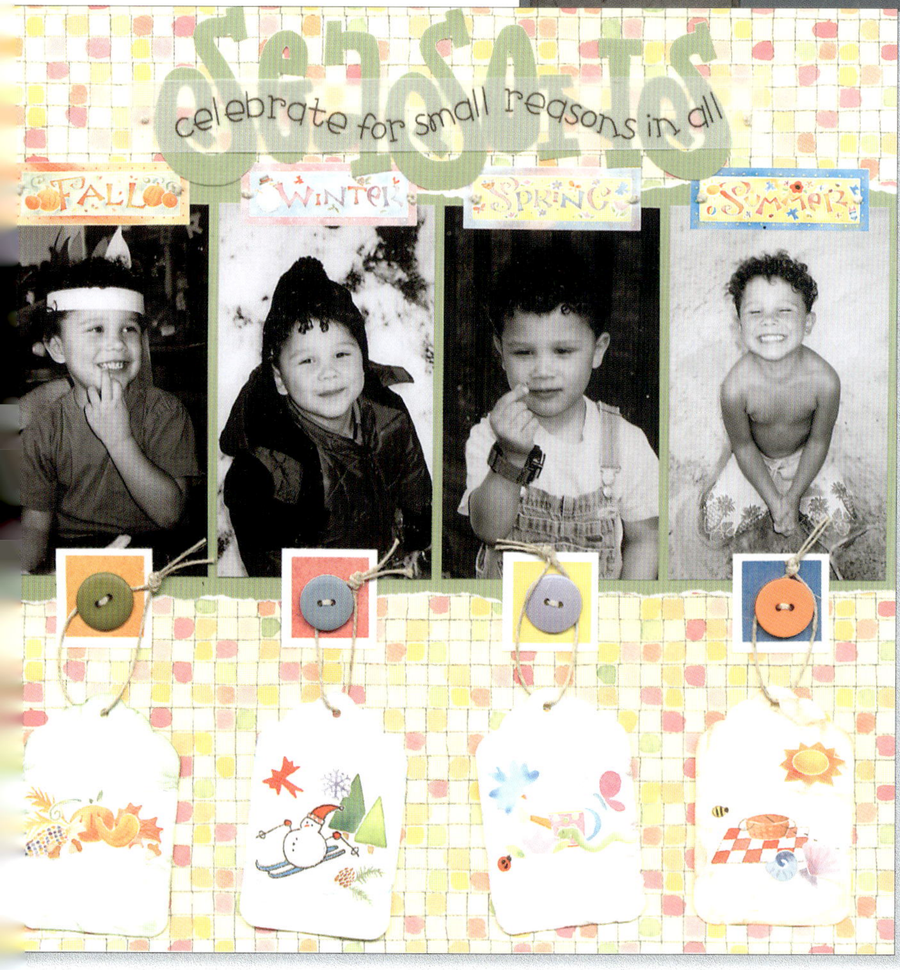

Seasons

Supplies
Patterned paper, vellum and stickers: Colorbök
Chalks: Stampin' Up!
Computer fonts: CK Fun, "The Art of Creative Lettering" CD, *Creating Keepsakes*; DJ Dude, package unknown, D.J. Inkers
Other: Buttons and twine

♥ I Love It!: *Arrange stickers that come in sets (several stickers related to the same theme) into scenes. Remember to ground stickers by placing them as if they were resting on a physical object (like the ground, a table, etc.).*

♥ I Love It!: *Because the colors on this layout are vivid, the photographs were changed to black and white. The darkness of the photographs helps them stand out against the brighter colors of the layout.*

tip 6

use innovative products and techniques to frame stickers.

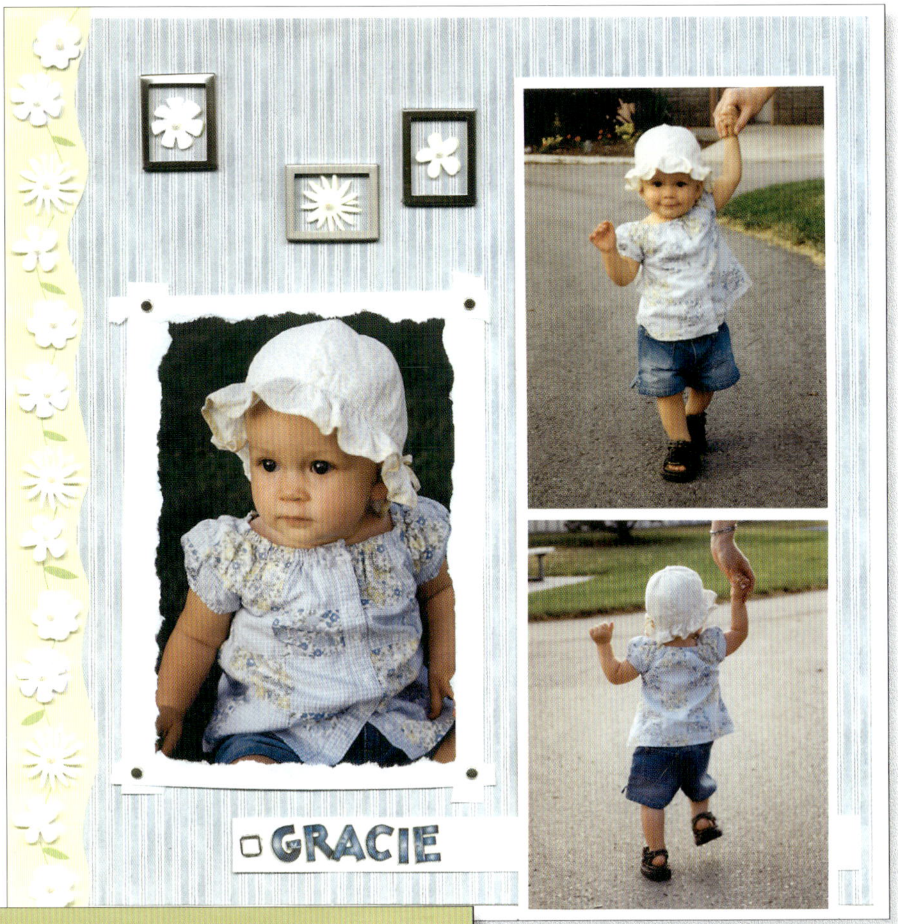

GRACIE

Gracie

Supplies

Patterned paper, stickers and border: K & Company
Metal frames: Scrapworks
Letter stickers: Beary Patch
Brads: Making Memories

♥ **I Love It!:** *This adorable photo frame is simple to reproduce. Tear two strips of cardstock, leaving one long edge on each strip straight. Cut the strips just longer than the length or width of your photograph and arrange around the photo, leaving the straight edge out and the torn edge inside. Fasten each corner with brads, eyelets or adhesive. Try using this technique to frame stickers as well.*

♥ **I Love It!:** *Cut portions of the border to use as individual framed accents.*

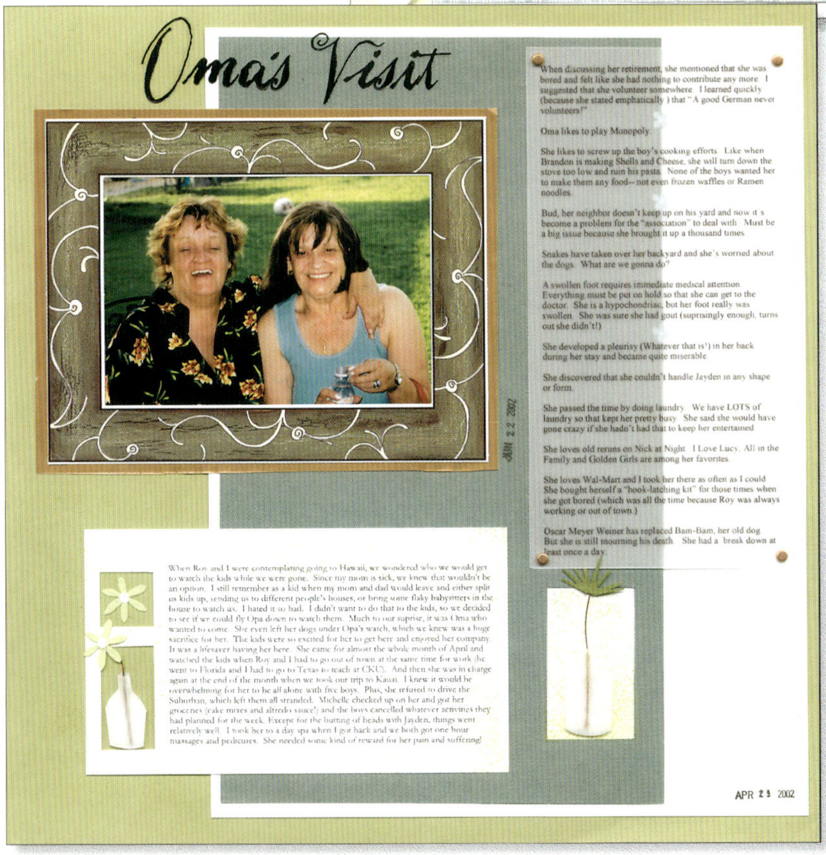

Oma's Visit
When discussing her retirement, she mentioned that she was bored and felt like she had nothing to contribute any more. I suggested that she volunteer somewhere. I learned quickly (because she stated emphatically) that "A good German never volunteers!"
Oma likes to play Monopoly.
She likes to screw up the boy's cooking efforts. Like when Brandon is making Shells and Cheese, she will turn down the stove too low and ruin his pasta. None of the boys wanted her to make them any food-- not even frozen waffles or Ramen noodles.
Bud, her neighbor doesn't keep up on his yard and now it's become a problem for the "association" to deal with. Must be a big issue because she brought it up a thousand times.
Snakes have taken over her backyard and she's worried about the dogs. What are we gonna do?
A swollen foot requires immediate medical attention. Everything must be put on hold so that she can get to the doctor. She is a hypochondriac, but her foot really was swollen. She was sure she had gout (suprisingly enough, turns out she didn't!)
She developed a pleurisy (Whatever that is!) in her back during her stay and became quite miserable.
She discovered that she couldn't handle Jayden in any shape or form.
She passed the time by doing laundry. We have LOTS of laundry so that kept her pretty busy. She said she would have gone crazy if she hadn't had that to keep her entertained.
She loves old reruns on Nick at Night. I Love Lucy, All in the Family and Golden Girls are among her favorites.
She loves Wal-Mart and I took her there as often as I could. She bought herself a "hook-latching kit" for those times when she got bored (which was all the time because Roy was always working or out of town.)
Oscar Meyer Weiner has replaced Bam-Bam, her old dog. But she is still mourning his death. She had a break down at least once a day.
JAN 22 2002
APR 23 2002

Oma's Visit

Supplies

Preprinted frame: My Mind's Eye
Vellum: Provo Craft
Letter stickers: Flavia, Colorbök
Stickers: Jolee's Boutique, EK Success
Computer font: Times New Roman, Microsoft Word
Ink spritzer: Color Works
Other: Date stamp and copper brads

♥ **I Love It!:** *Instead of matting stickers on cardstock, create this fun, "reverse-mat." Decide where on your layout you want the stickers to be placed. Then, using a craft knife, cut squares or rectangles out of the cardstock and back the area with cardstock in a different shade or color. To finish, place the stickers into the cut-out areas.*

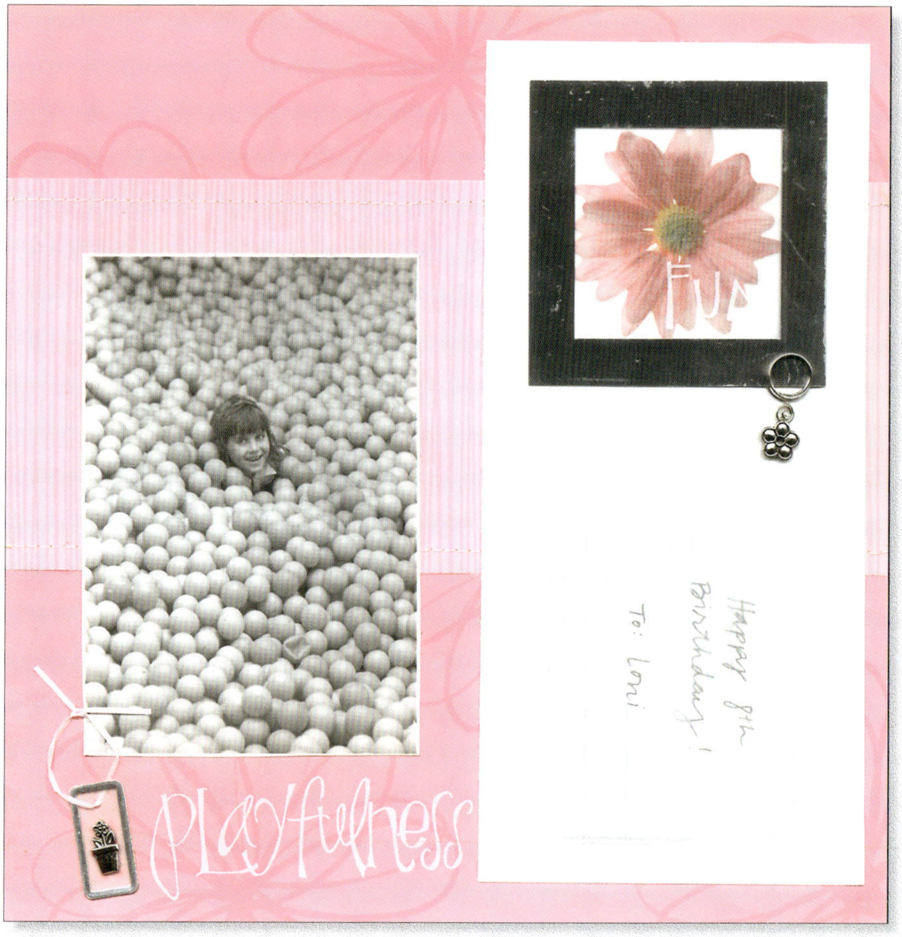
FUN
Happy 8th Birthday!
To: Lori
Playfulness

Playfulness

Supplies

Patterned paper: KI Memories
Flower sticker: Remember When
Vellum: Colorbök
Metal frame, metal-rimmed tag and rub-on words: Making Memories
Spiral paper clip: 7 Gypsies
Charms: Buttons Galore

♥ I Love It!: *Some scrapbooking products intended for use with photographs are great to use with stickers or accents, too! Keep your eyes open for metal frames, preprinted frames, cardstock frames or other products you can combine with stickers in fresh, new ways.*

♥ I Love It!: *When you want to include your thoughts and feelings, but fear having too many words on your layout will detract from the design, slip a piece of paper into a vellum envelope where the text is hidden but available.*

Happiness

Supplies

Patterned papers: Tim Coffey (pastels), K & Company; 7 Gypsies (dictionary print)
Stickers: Tim Coffey, K & Company
Slide holders: Scrapworks
Computer font: CK Constitution, "Fresh Fonts" CD, *Creating Keepsakes*
Other: Acrylic paint, ribbon and staples

♥ I Love It!: *Don't forget, you can frame your stickers and put stickers on your frames! These fun slide holder accents are dressed to perfection with pastel flower stickers.*

♥ I Love It!: *The aged look of the slide holders was created with acrylic paints. First, coat the slide holder with green paint, then lightly brush white paint over the green, using a coarse paint brush. If the white paint comes off the brush too heavily, wait until the paint dries and gently sand some of the paint off with sandpaper.*

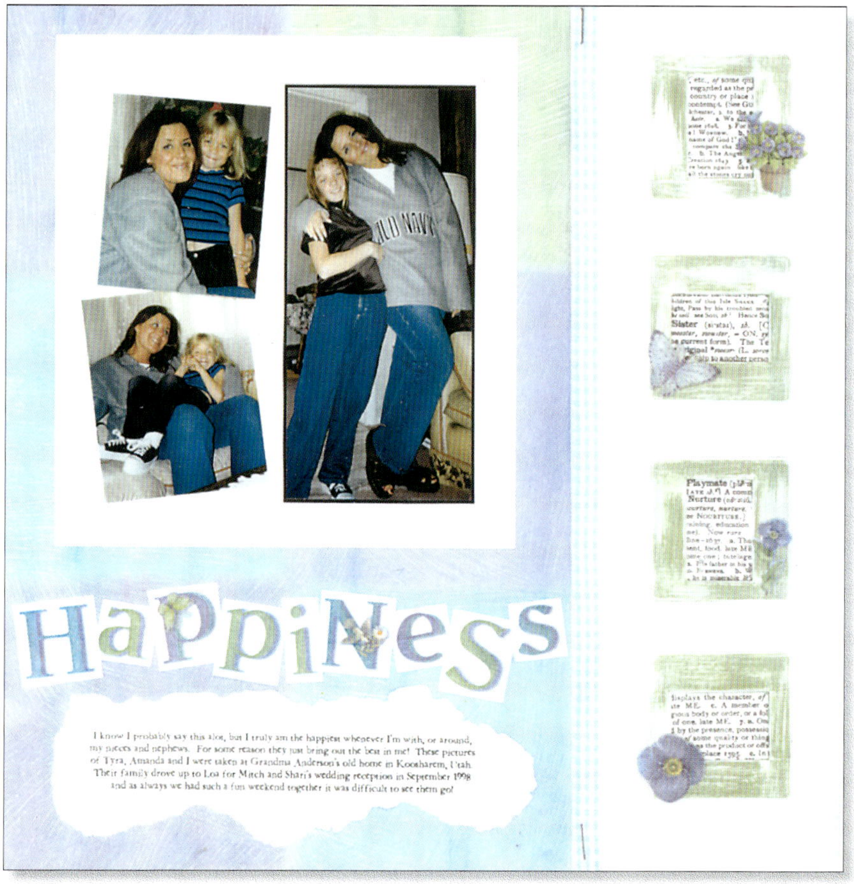
HaPPiNess
I know I probably say this alot, but I truly am the happiest whenever I'm with, or around, my nieces and nephews. For some reason they just bring out the best in me! These pictures of Tyra, Amanda and I were taken at Grandma Anderson's old home in Koosharem, Utah. Their family drove up to Loa for Mitch and Shari's wedding reception in September 1998 and as always we had such a fun weekend together it was difficult to see them go!

tip 7

take advantage of clear stickers by creating interesting backgrounds.

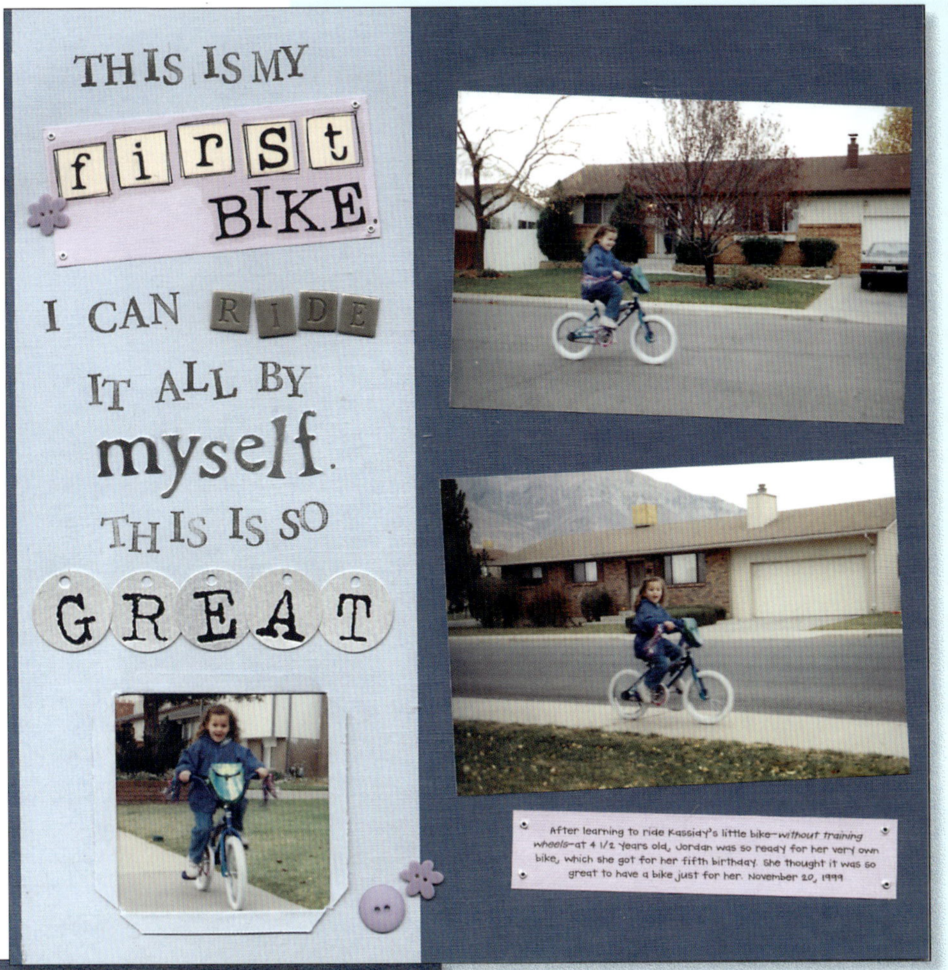
THIS IS MY
first
BIKE.
I CAN RIDE
IT ALL BY
myself.
THIS IS SO
GREAT
After learning to ride Kassidy's little bike—*without training wheels*—at 4 1/2 years old, Jordan was so ready for her very own bike, which she got for her fifth birthday. She thought it was so great to have a bike just for her. November 20, 1999

First Bike

Supplies
Sticker: Phrase Café, EK Success
Metal accents: Making Memories
Letter stamps: The Missing Link Stamp Co.
Stamping ink: Fabrico, Tsukineko
Buttons: Making Memories

♥ I Love It!: *Simply placing a clear title sticker on a different color of cardstock gives it enough emphasis to stand out from the rest of the layout.*

♥ I Love It!: *The cut and folded photo mat at the bottom left of the layout is a creative way to showcase a photograph. Cut a square or rectangle out of cardstock, make small diagonal cuts in each corner, fold back the flaps and trim the edges off to form diagonal edges.*

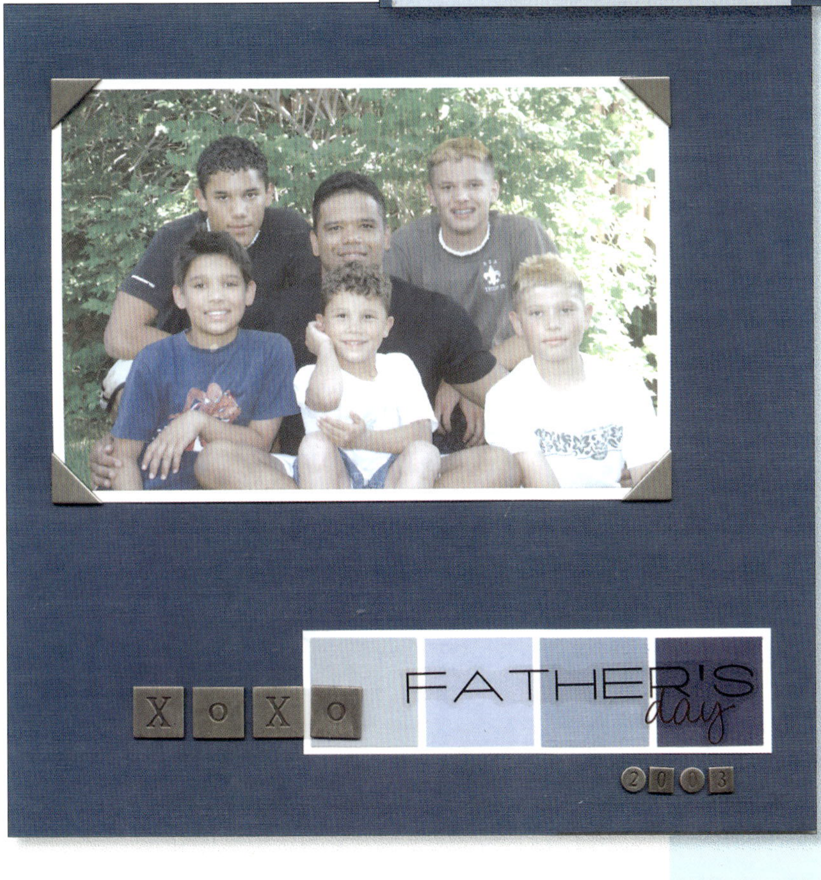
XOXO
FATHER'S day
2003

Father's Day

Supplies
Sticker: Phrase Café, EK Success
Metal accents: Making Memories

♥ I Love It!: *A simple color-blocked strip of shades of blue provides an attractive backdrop for this clear title sticker.*

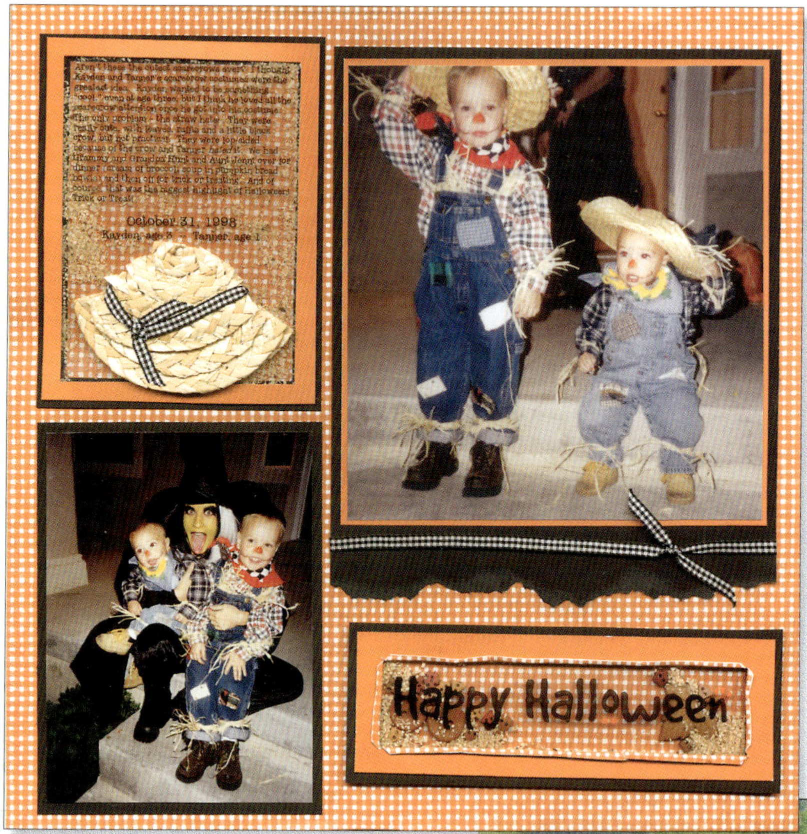

Happy Halloween

Supplies

Patterned cardstock: Source unknown
Sticker: Phrase Café, EK Success
Computer font: CK Stenography, "Fresh Fonts" CD, *Creating Keepsakes*
Other: Buttons, ribbon, transparency paper and straw hat accent

♥ **I Love It!:** *Use clear title stickers to accent a shaker box for your layout. To create a shaker box, cut two rectangles of clear transparency paper. Line one rectangle with 3-D foam tape, fill the middle with the items of your choice, and place the second rectangle onto the 3-D foam tape (all edges should be sealed). Create a decorative frame to place over the top of the shaker box to hide the foam tape.*

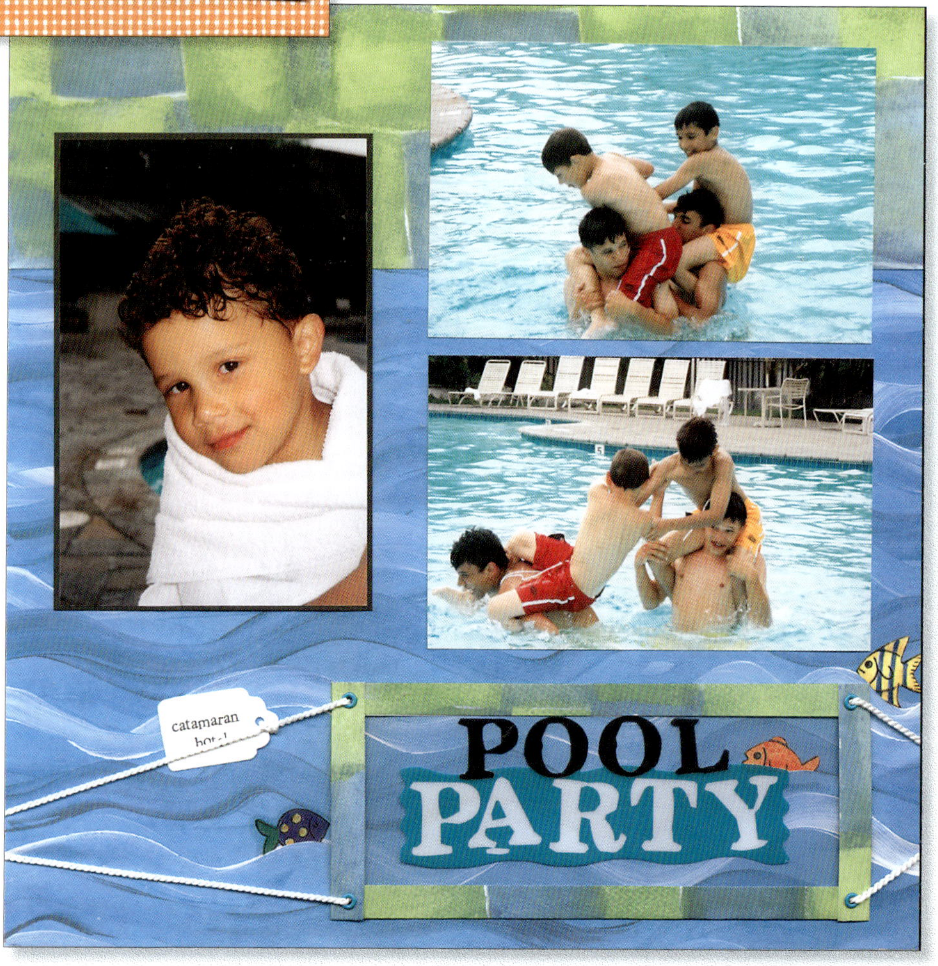

Pool Party

Supplies

Patterned papers: Karen Foster Design
Stickers: me & my BIG ideas (fish); Phrase Café (title), EK Success
Computer font: CK Stenography, "Fresh Fonts" CD, *Creating Keepsakes*
Eyelets: Doodlebug Design
Other: Tag, twine and transparency paper

♥ **I Love It!:** *Here's how to create this adorable title block:*

1. *Cut slits in the patterned paper using a craft knife, following the lines of the waves on the paper.*
2. *Insert fish stickers into the slits and adhere to the page.*
3. *Place the title sticker on a piece of clear transparency paper. Trim the title block to the correct size for your layout.*
4. *Fold strips of patterned paper over each edge of the title block to create a border.*
5. *Fasten each corner of the title block with an eyelet, and adhere the accent to your layout.*

tip 8

enhance the beauty of writing on your page by adding stickers.

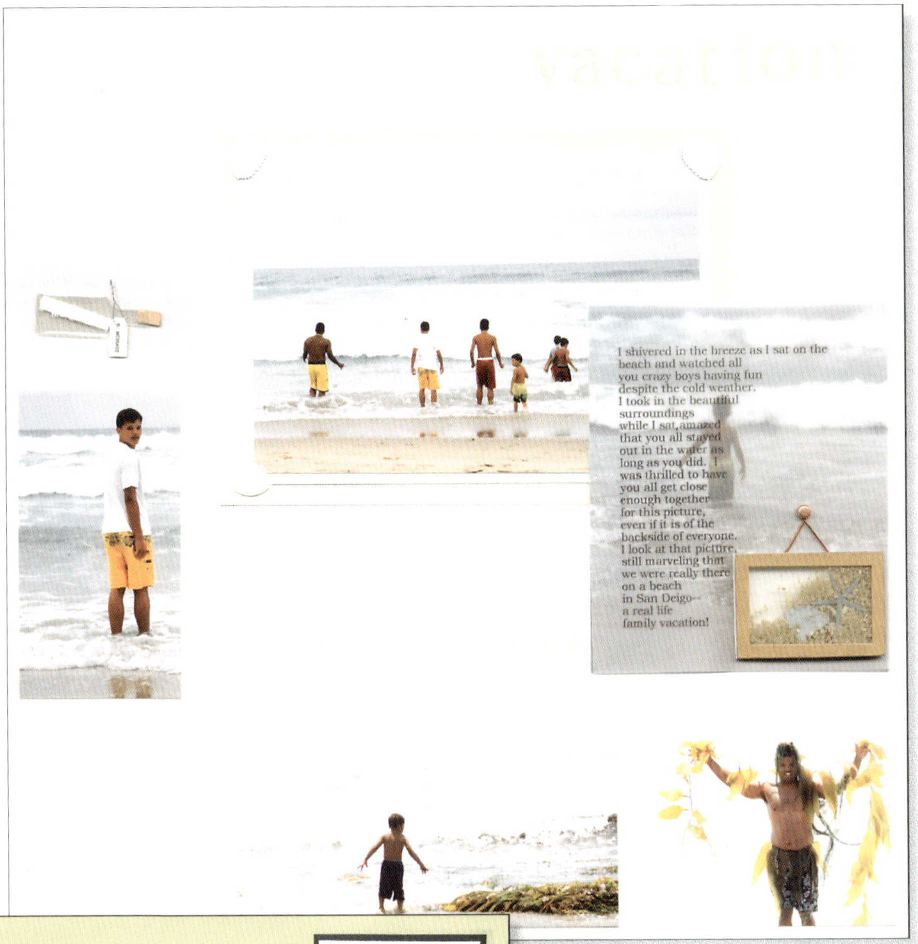

vacation
I shivered in the breeze as I sat on the beach and watched all you crazy boys having fun despite the cold weather. I took in the beautiful surroundings while I sat, amazed that you all stayed out in the water as long as you did. I was thrilled to have you all get close enough together for this picture, even if it is of the backside of everyone. I look at that picture, still marveling that we were really there on a beach in San Deigo-- a real life family vacation!

Vacation

Supplies

Patterned paper and letter stickers: SEI
Vellum: Provo Craft
Stickers: Jolee's Boutique, EK Success
Computer font: Times New Roman, Microsoft Word

♥ **I Love It!:** *Journaling doesn't always have to be written on plain cardstock. The understated beauty of the journaling block on this layout is easy to duplicate. Choose a photograph that's not too busy to serve as the backdrop for your journaling. Type the journaling and print it onto vellum. Fill blank space by placing a 3-D sticker in the bottom corner of the journaling block.*

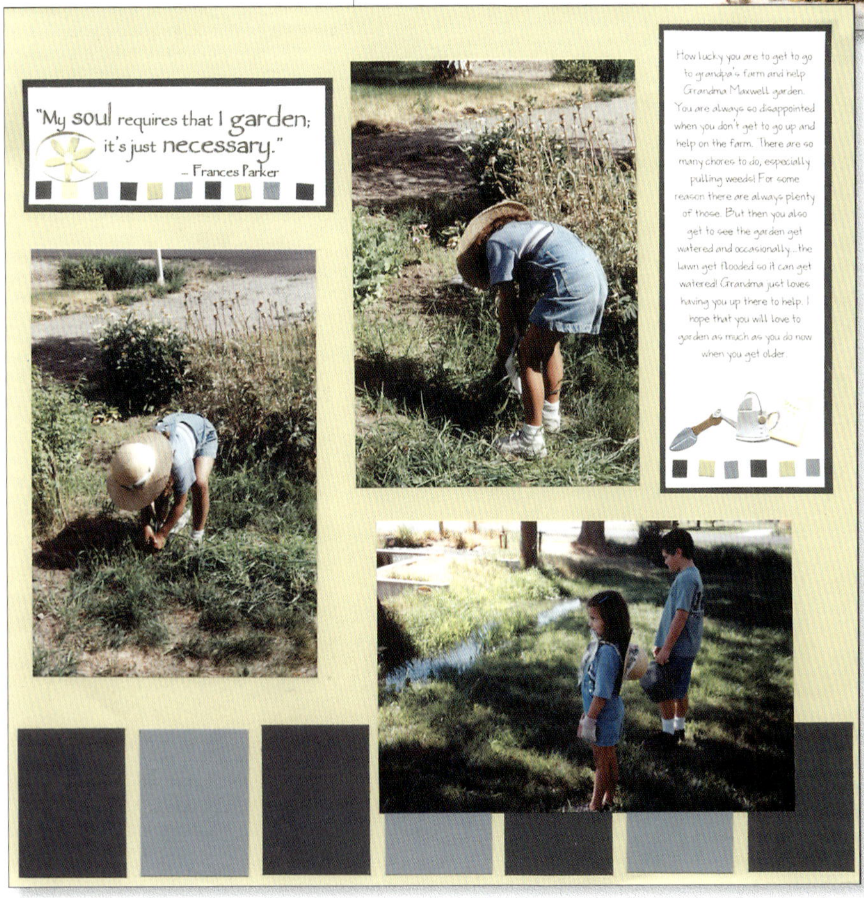

"My soul requires that I garden; it's just necessary."
– Frances Parker
How lucky you are to get to go to grandpa's farm and help Grandma Maxwell garden. You are always so disappointed when you don't get to go up and help on the farm. There are so many chores to do, especially pulling weeds! For some reason there are always plenty of those. But then you also get to see the garden get watered and occasionally...the lawn get flooded so it can get watered! Grandma just loves having you up there to help. I hope that you will love to garden as much as you do now when you get older.

Gardening

Supplies

Stickers: Jolee's Boutique, EK Success
Pebble accents: Making Memories
Computer font: CK Penman, "The Best of Creative Lettering" CD Vol. 3, *Creating Keepsakes*

♥ **I Love It!:** *Accent an otherwise plain journaling block by creating a mini-scene with stickers of a related theme. Repeat any borders or unique design elements from the layout along the bottom of the journaling block to unify the design.*

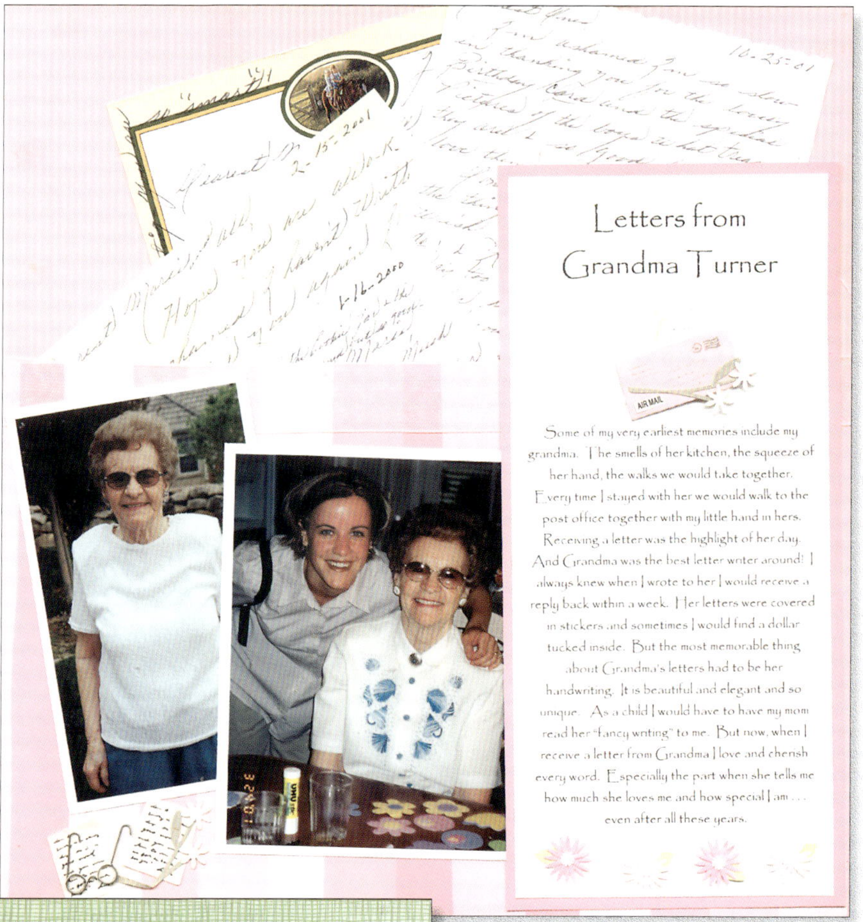

Letters from
Grandma Turner
AIR MAIL
Some of my very earliest memories include my grandma. The smells of her kitchen, the squeeze of her hand, the walks we would take together. Every time I stayed with her we would walk to the post office together with my little hand in hers. Receiving a letter was the highlight of her day. And Grandma was the best letter writer around! I always knew when I wrote to her I would receive a reply back within a week. Her letters were covered in stickers and sometimes I would find a dollar tucked inside. But the most memorable thing about Grandma's letters had to be her handwriting. It is beautiful and elegant and so unique. As a child I would have to have my mom read her "fancy writing" to me. But now, when I receive a letter from Grandma I love and cherish every word. Especially the part when she tells me how much she loves me and how special I am . . . even after all these years.

Letters from Grandma Turner

Supplies
Patterned paper and vellum: Colorbök
Stickers: Jolee's Boutique, EK Success
Computer font: Papyrus, Microsoft Word
Ribbon: Stampin' Up!

♥ I Love It!: *Combine your title block and journaling block into one, but leave space between the title and journaling. Add a sticker accent that communicates the theme of your layout to enhance the artistic quality of your design. Finish the title and journaling block off with a simple border of matching stickers.*

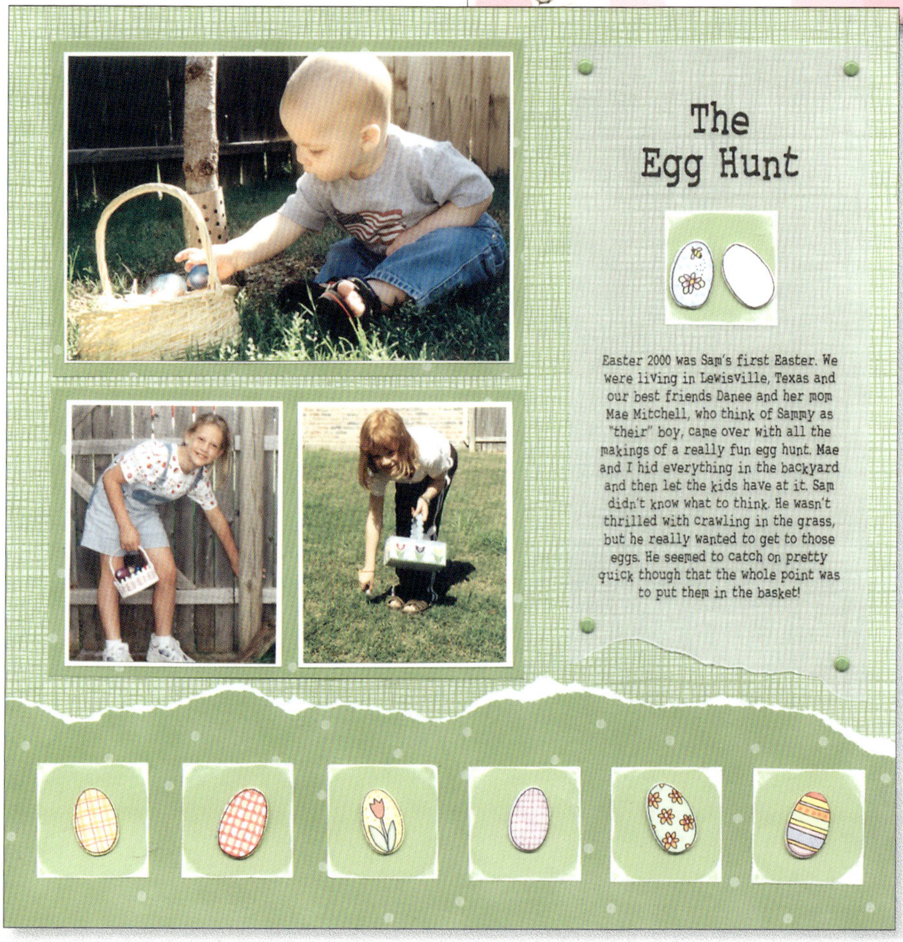

The
Egg Hunt
Easter 2000 was Sam's first Easter. We were living in Lewisville, Texas and our best friends Danee and her mom Mae Mitchell, who think of Sammy as "their" boy, came over with all the makings of a really fun egg hunt. Mae and I hid everything in the backyard and then let the kids have at it. Sam didn't know what to think. He wasn't thrilled with crawling in the grass, but he really wanted to get to those eggs. He seemed to catch on pretty quick though that the whole point was to put them in the basket!

The Egg Hunt

Supplies
Patterned paper: Making Memories
Vellum: Colorbök
Stickers: Sue Dreamer, Colorbök
Computer font: Unknown
Brads: Doodlebug Design

♥ I Love It!: *Paper that's printed a solid color on one side and is white on the other is great for aging. To re-create the boxes on this layout, use sandpaper to wear away the colored edges of the paper before adhering stickers to each block. Then, repeat the accents found in the border by including a sticker block between the title and journaling.*

tip 9

fill in the blanks in journaling blocks with sticker words and accents.

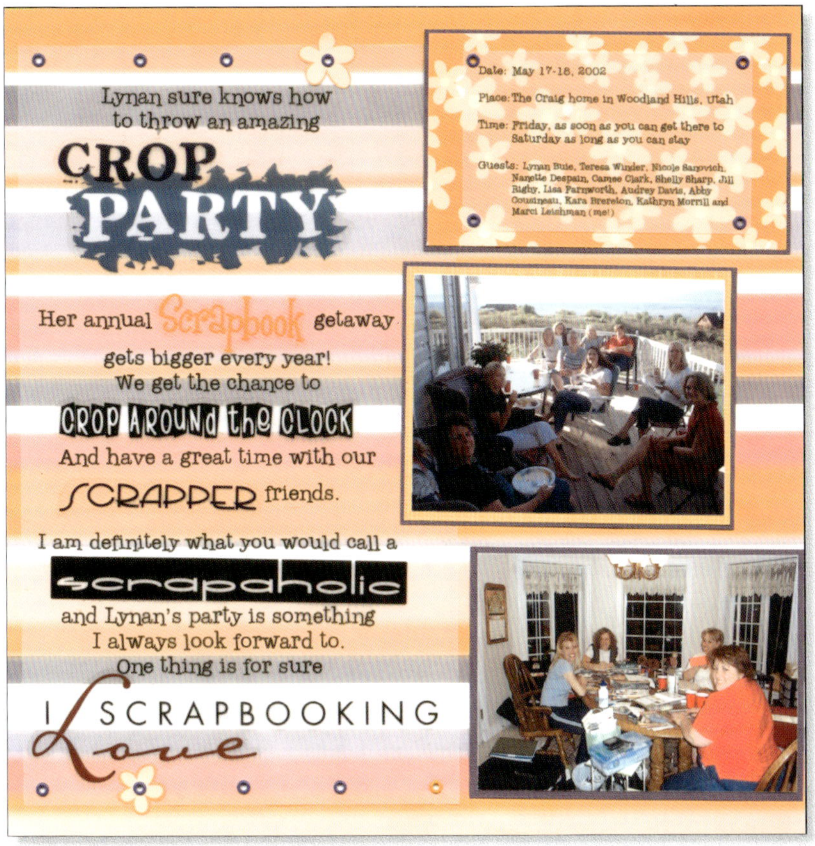
Date: May 17-18, 2002
Place: The Craig home in Woodland Hills, Utah
Time: Friday, as soon as you can get there to Saturday as long as you can stay
Guests: Lynan Buie, Teresa Winder, Nicole Sanovich, Nanette Despain, Camee Clark, Shelly Sharp, Jill Rigby, Lisa Farnworth, Audrey Davis, Abby Cousineau, Kara Brereton, Kathryn Morrill and Marci Leishman (me!)
Lynan sure knows how to throw an amazing
CROP PARTY
Her annual Scrapbook getaway gets bigger every year!
We get the chance to
CROP AROUND the CLOCK
And have a great time with our
SCRAPPER friends.
I am definitely what you would call a
scrapaholic
and Lynan's party is something I always look forward to.
One thing is for sure
I Love SCRAPBOOKING

Crop Party

Supplies

Patterned paper: Chatterbox
Vellum: Colorbök
Stickers: Phrase Café, EK Success
Eyelets: Stampin' Up!
Computer font: CK Stenography, "Fresh Fonts" CD, *Creating Keepsakes*

♥ I Love It!: *To format this fun journaling block, type your journaling, leaving space for the sticker phrases, then print it on regular paper. Holding the paper up to a window or another light source, check to make sure each sticker fits in the allotted space. Make any needed adjustments to the spacing before printing the final journaling block on vellum.*

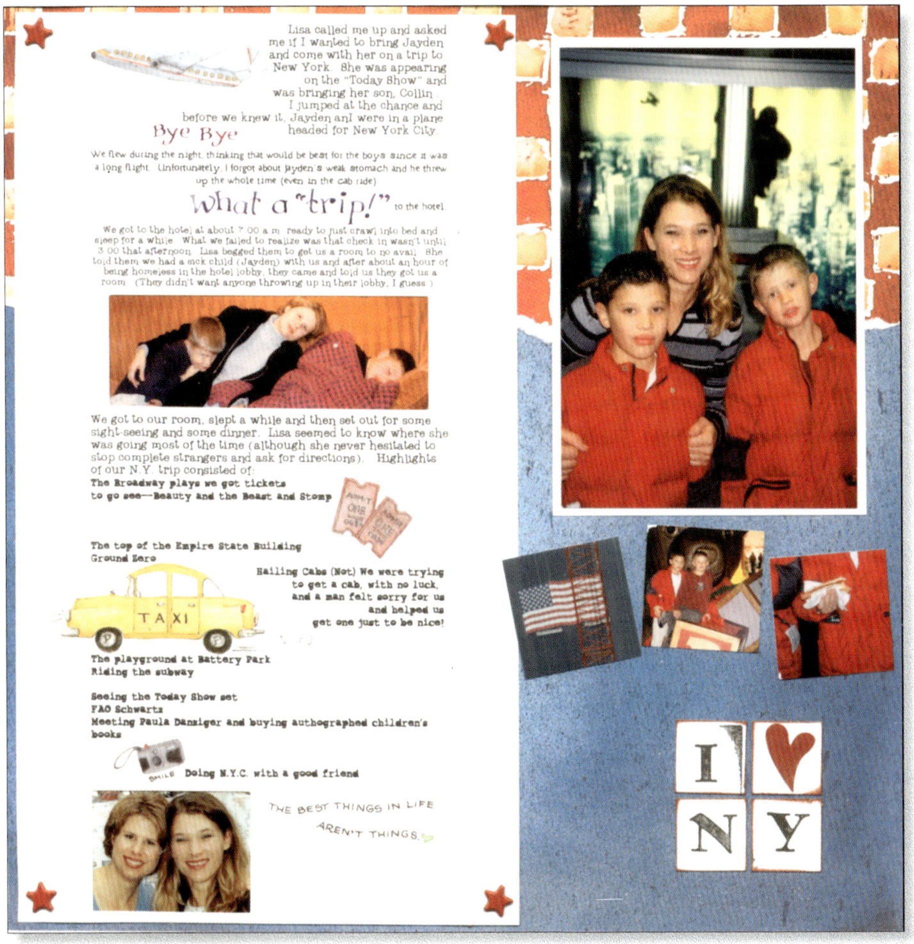
Lisa called me up and asked me if I wanted to bring Jayden and come with her on a trip to New York. She was appearing on the "Today Show" and was bringing her son, Collin. I jumped at the chance and before we knew it, Jayden and I were in a plane headed for New York City.
Bye Bye
We flew during the night, thinking that would be best for the boys since it was a long flight. Unfortunately, I forgot about Jayden's weak stomach and he threw up the whole time (even in the cab ride)
What a "trip!" to the hotel.
We got to the hotel at about 7:00 a.m. ready to just crawl into bed and sleep for a while. What we failed to realize was that check in wasn't until 3:00 that afternoon. Lisa begged them to get us a room to no avail. She told them we had a sick child (Jayden) with us and after about an hour of being homeless in the hotel lobby, they came and told us they got us a room. (They didn't want anyone throwing up in their lobby, I guess.)
We got to our room, slept a while and then set out for some sight-seeing and some dinner. Lisa seemed to know where she was going most of the time (although she never hesitated to stop complete strangers and ask for directions). Highlights of our N.Y. trip consisted of:
The Broadway plays we got tickets to go see---Beauty and the Beast and Stomp
The top of the Empire State Building
Ground Zero
Hailing Cabs (Not) We were trying to get a cab, with no luck, and a man felt sorry for us and helped us get one just to be nice!
TAXI
The playground at Battery Park
Riding the subway
Seeing the Today Show set
FAO Schwartz
Meeting Paula Danziger and buying authographed children's books
SMILE
Doing N.Y.C. with a good friend
THE BEST THINGS IN LIFE AREN'T THINGS.
I ♥ NY

I Love NY

Supplies

Patterned paper: Provo Craft
Stickers: Susan Branch, Colorbök
Computer fonts: CK Stenography and CK Typewriter, "Fresh Fonts" CD, *Creating Keepsakes*
Letter stamps: Barnes and Noble
Stamping ink: ColorBox, Clearsnap
Heart punch: Posh Impressions
Star brads: Provo Craft

♥ I Love It!: *Crop your photographs into small squares to emphasize specific aspects or memories from your trip, like the American flag flying or hot dogs from Central Park.*

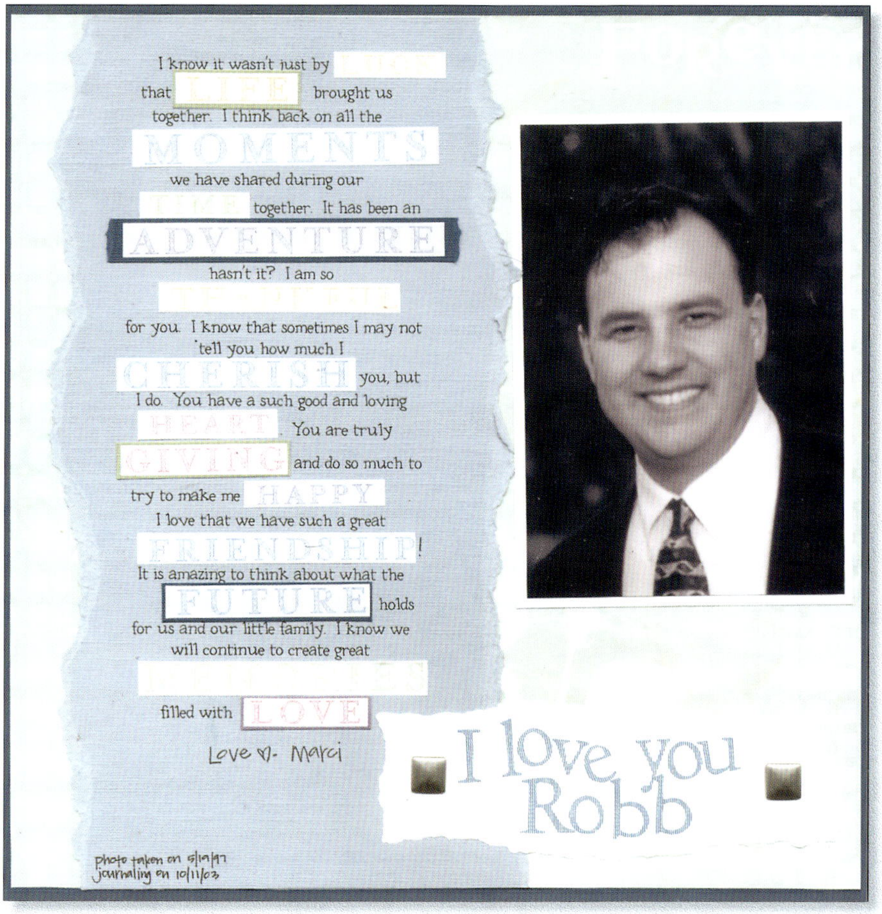
I know it wasn't just by
that LIFE brought us together. I think back on all the
MOMENTS
we have shared during our
together. It has been an
ADVENTURE
hasn't it? I am so
for you. I know that sometimes I may not tell you how much I
CHERISH you, but
I do. You have a such good and loving
HEART. You are truly
GIVING and do so much to
try to make me HAPPY.
I love that we have such a great
FRIENDSHIP!
It is amazing to think about what the
FUTURE holds
for us and our little family. I know we will continue to create great
filled with LOVE
Love - Marci
I love you Robb
photo taken on 5/19/97
journaling on 10/11/03

I Love You, Robb

Supplies
Patterned paper and stickers: Flavia, Colorbök
Pen: Zig Writer, EK Success
Other: Metal square accents

♥ I Love It!: *Want a little hint on how to save time when creating word collages with stickers? Position the words you'll be substituting stickers for on the ends of the lines. As long as the lines of text are different lengths and the word stickers vary in size, it won't be obvious that every word is on the end. To add emphasis, mat certain important word stickers on cardstock before incorporating them into the journaling.*

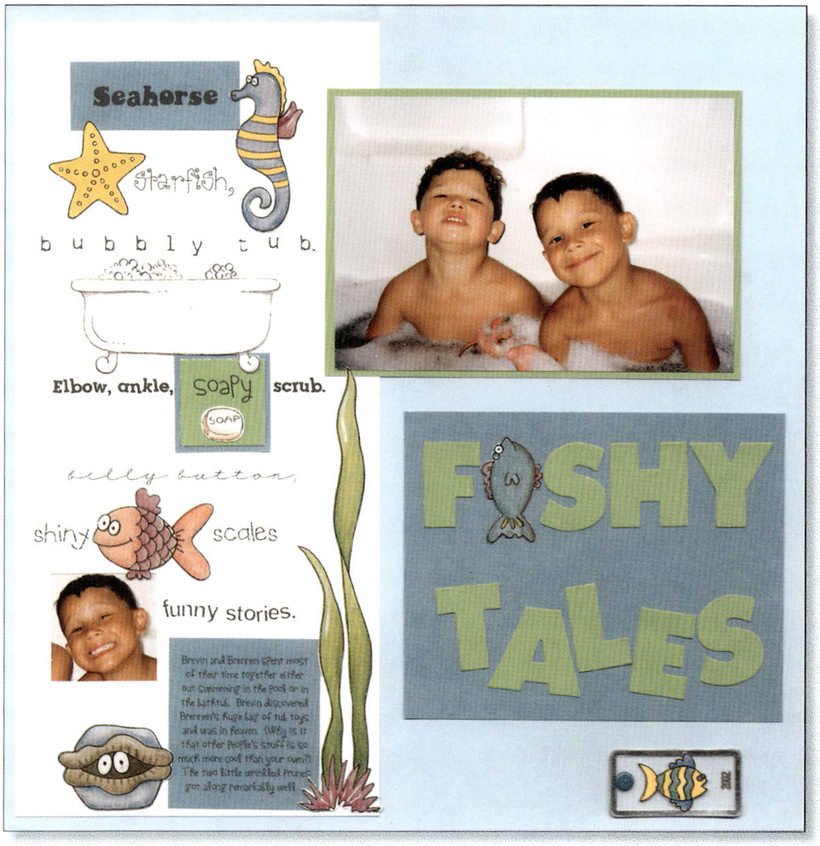
Seahorse
starfish,
b u b b l y t u b.
Elbow, ankle, soapy scrub.
SOAP
belly button,
shiny
scales
funny stories.
FISHY TALES
2002

Fishy Tales

Supplies
Stickers: Provo Craft
Letter die cuts: Sizzix
Metal-rimmed tag and colored brad: Making Memories
Computer fonts: CK Lumpy, CK Wired, CK Cursive, CK Tipsy, CK Carbon Copy, CK Squiggle, CK Elusive and CK Fresh, "Fresh Fonts" CD, *Creating Keepsakes*

♥ I Love It!: *Once you've got the hang of mixing word or phrase stickers into your journaling block, try your hand at this technique: Type each line of your journaling block in a different computer font, leaving space for sticker accents. This technique, reminiscent of storybooks, is especially fun on children's pages.*

tip 10

alter the look of stickers to suit your needs.

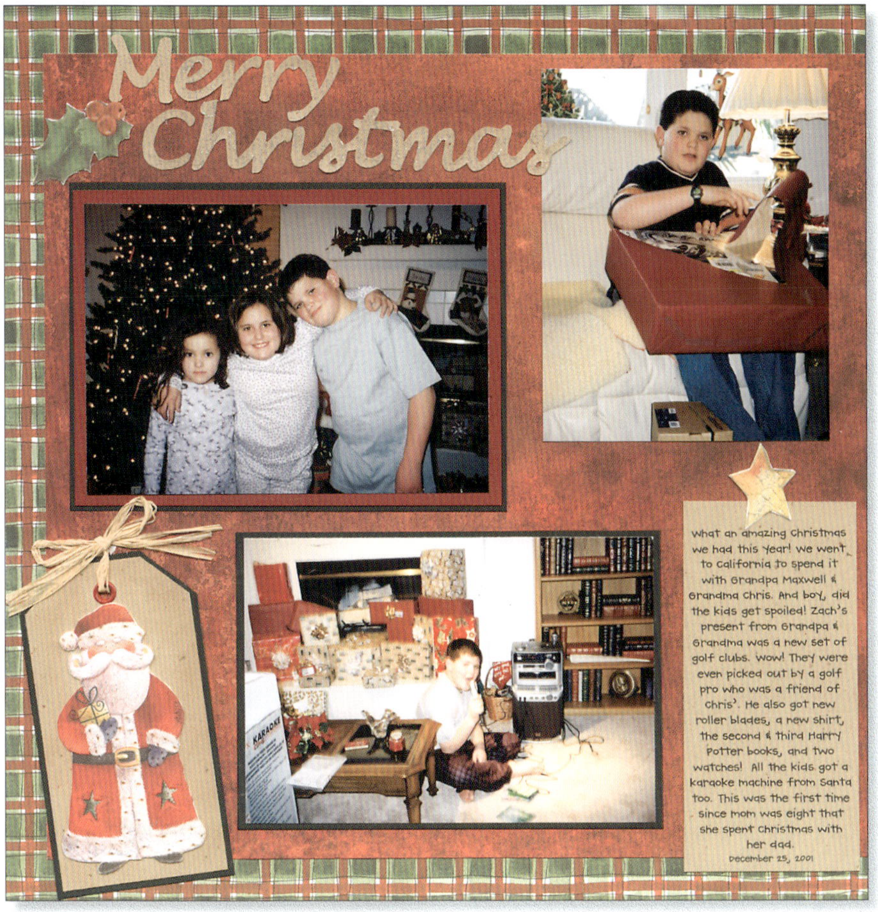

Merry Christmas
what an amazing Christmas we had this year! we went to California to spend it with Grandpa Maxwell & Grandma Chris. And boy, did the kids get spoiled! Zach's present from Grandpa & Grandma was a new set of golf clubs. Wow! They were even picked out by a golf pro who was a friend of Chris'. He also got new roller blades, a new shirt, the second & third Harry Potter books, and two watches! All the kids got a karaoke machine from Santa too. This was the first time since mom was eight that she spent Christmas with her dad.
December 25, 2001

Merry Christmas

Supplies
Patterned papers: Provo Craft
Stickers: K & Company
Glitter: PSX Design
Computer fonts: CAC Leslie, downloaded from the Internet; CK Handprint, "The Best of Creative Lettering" CD Combo, *Creating Keepsakes*
Other: Eyelets and raffia

♥ I Love It!: *Glitter adds a magical feel to almost anything. Added to the stickers on this layout, it communicates the magic of Christmas.*

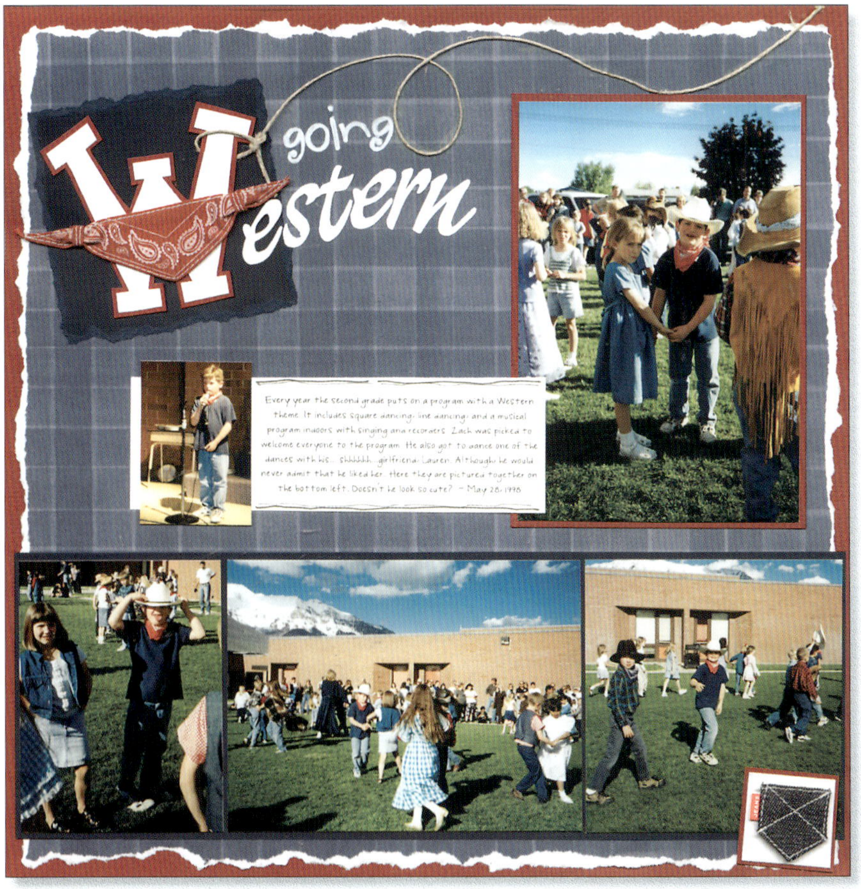

going Western
Every year the second grade puts on a program with a Western theme. It includes square dancing, line dancing, and a musical program indoors with singing and recorders. Zach was picked to welcome everyone to the program. He also got to dance one of the dances with his... shhhhhh... girlfriend, Lauren. Although he would never admit that he liked her. Here they are pictured together on the bottom left. Doesn't he look so cute? ~ May 28, 1998

Going Western

Supplies
Patterned paper: All My Memories
Stickers: Jolee's Boutique, EK Success
Letter stickers: David Walker, Colorbök
Computer font: CK Jot, "The Art of Creative Lettering" CD, *Creating Keepsakes*
Pen: Zig Opaque Writer, EK Success
Other: Jute

♥ I Love It!: *The letter stickers on this layout (the word "Going") were originally black. To make them match the layout more closely, they were traced over with a white opaque pen.*

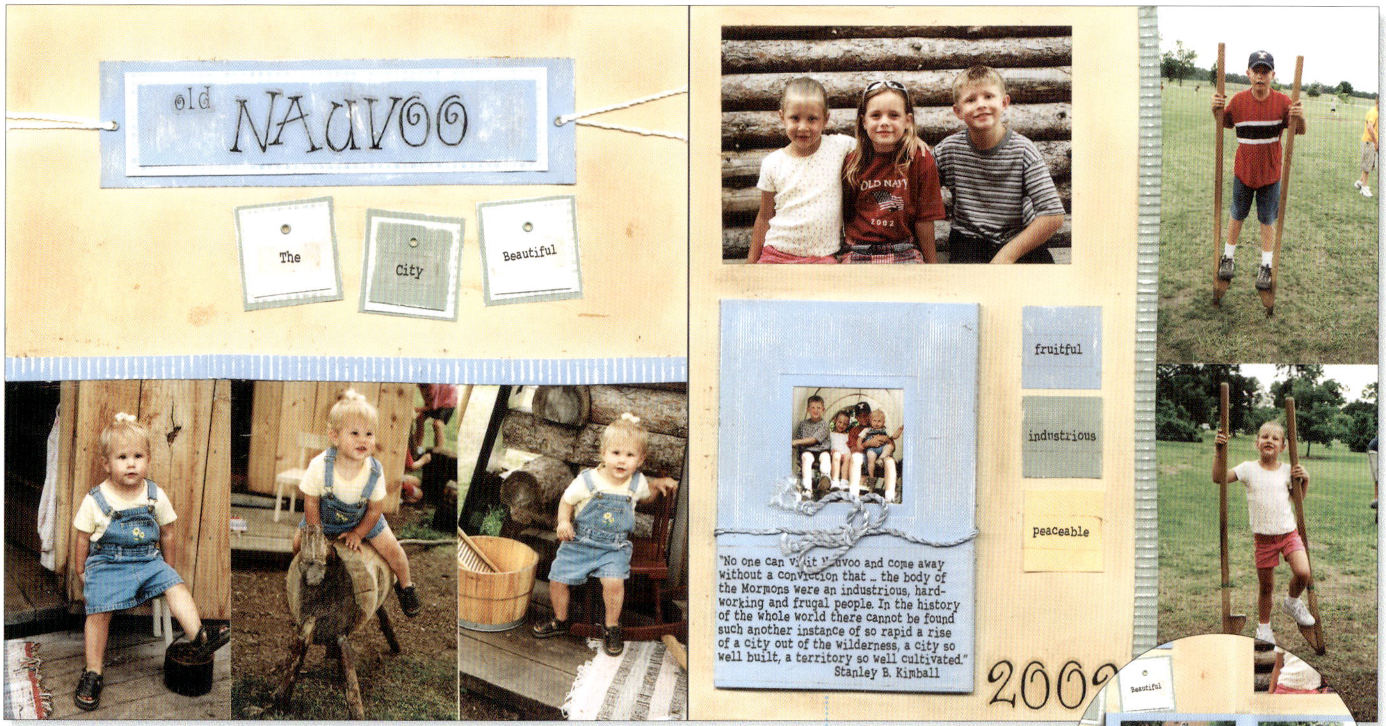
old NAUVOO
The
City
Beautiful
fruitful
industrious
peaceable
"No one can vi it uvoo and come away without a conv tion that … the body of the Mormons were an industrious, hard-working and frugal people. In the history of the whole world there cannot be found such another instance of so rapid a rise of a city out of the wilderness, a city so well built, a territory so well cultivated."
Stanley B. Kimball
200

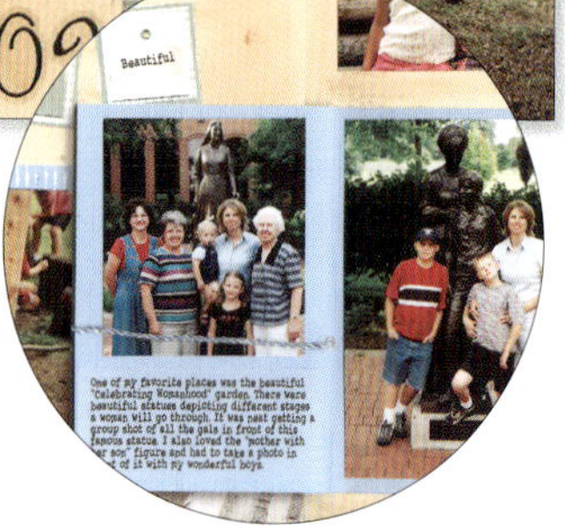
Beautiful

Old Nauvoo

Supplies

Pre-cut title block, squares and corrugated strips: Déjà Views
Letter stickers: Provo Craft
Computer font: Unknown
Mini-album: Déjà Views
Eyelets: Doodlebug Design
Twine: Déjà Views

♥ **I Love It!:** *This entire layout (except the photographs) was aged with sandpaper, then brushed with brown chalk to create a more rustic feel.*

♥ **I Love It!:** *Including the mini-album on the layout increased the photo count from seven to 15!*

Christmas Traditions

Supplies

Patterned paper: Carolee's Creations
Stickers: Colorbök
Craft wire: Making Memories
Computer font: Scrap Casual, "Lettering Delights" CD, Inspire Graphics
Other: Date stamp

♥ **I Love It!:** *Use sandpaper or a coarse nail file to age stickers that look "too perfect" for your layout.*

♥ **I Love It!:** *The journaling for this layout was cleverly written in recipe format on cards along the bottom of the layout.*

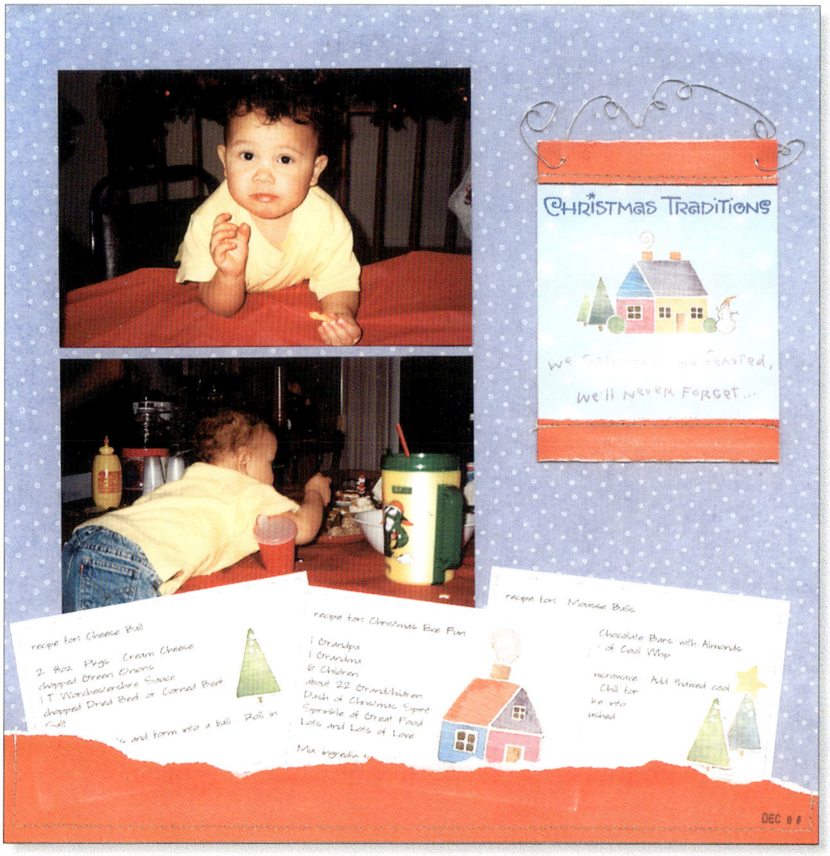
CHRISTMAS TRADITIONS
we'll never forget...
recipe for: Cheese Ball
recipe for: Christmas Eve Fun
1 Grandpa
1 Grandma
6 Children
Lots and Lots of Love

lisa's lessons on stickers

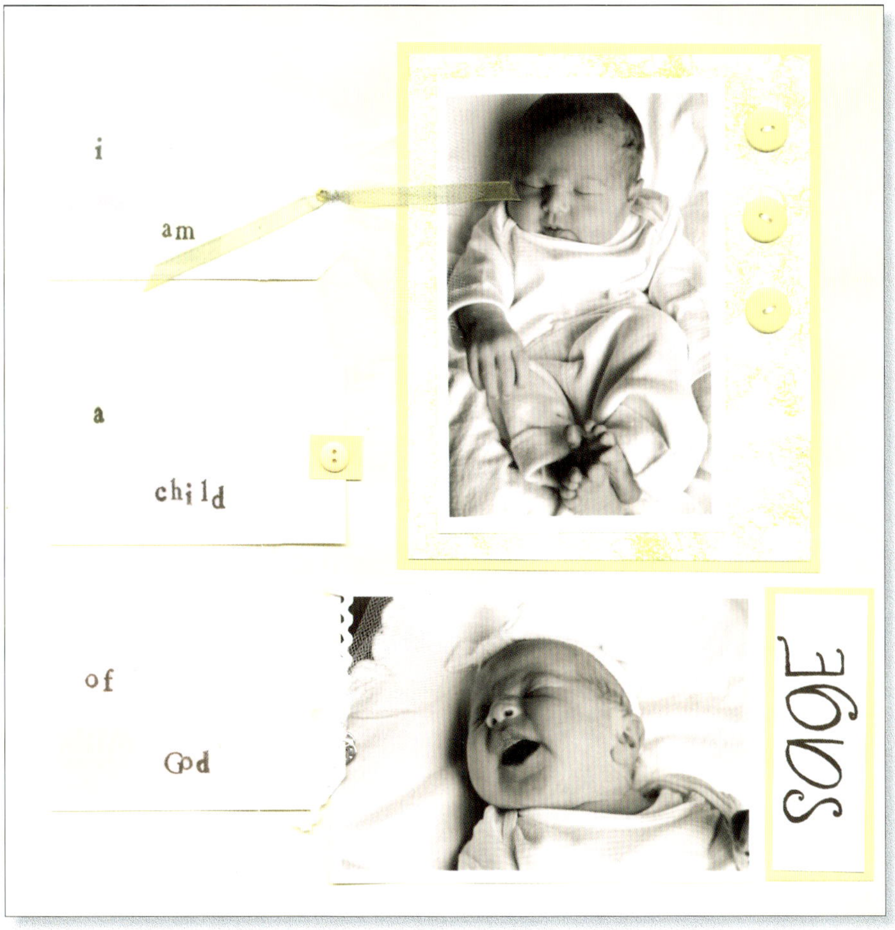

i
am
a
child
of
God
sage

I love the ever-growing assortment of stickers available to scrapbookers. Here are my two favorite tips to remember when using stickers on scrapbook pages:

- If you're not sure exactly where you want to place a sticker on a layout, sprinkle the back of it with baby powder. Baby powder instantly takes the "stickiness" out of the sticker, allowing you to move it to find the best location. When you're ready to adhere the sticker to your layout, simply use an adhesive square.
- Don't panic if your sticker gets stuck where you don't want it! The miracle product *un-du*® removes stickers from layouts without harming the sticker or your photographs (even some inks go unharmed, but be sure to test first!).

Three more favorite tips from this page:

- I knew the look I wanted for the photo mat for the focal-point photograph on this layout, but I couldn't find a patterned paper that matched the mental picture I had. Instead of giving up, I grabbed an ink pad and created the look myself with the perfect shade of green and a sponge. Before you give up on your creative ideas, kick your brain into problem-solving mode and see if you can come up with an innovative solution yourself.
- Don't allow yourself to get stuck in a rut with your stickers. Have the confidence to try new things—the pastel square stickers under the vellum were intended for a different purpose, but when I looked at them, I realized they would make the perfect background for my stamped subtitle.
- I love the look of tags on my layouts. You know what I love even more? When the top of each tag on a layout is "finished" in a different way. Ribbon, buttons, charms and tulle were all used to finish the tags on this layout, and the possibilities for even more creativity here are limitless. Remember, variety is the spice of life!

Sage

Supplies
Vellum: Provo Craft
Stickers and letter stickers: Colorbök
Letter stamps: PSX Design
Stamping ink: Stampin' Up!
Buttons: Making Memories

lisa says:

"Pre-made frames make scrapbooking so much easier! They're a *fast* and easy way to make sure the *focus* stays on your photographs, and you don't have to worry about measuring and cutting photo mats. You can find *pre-made* frames in colorful, youthful patterns or beautiful, *sophisticated* designs—you can even find pre-made frames in metal! Take advantage of this *timesaving* scrapbooking tool whenever you can."

FRAMES

ch 4

fantastic frames

FRAME *n.*
an enclosing border

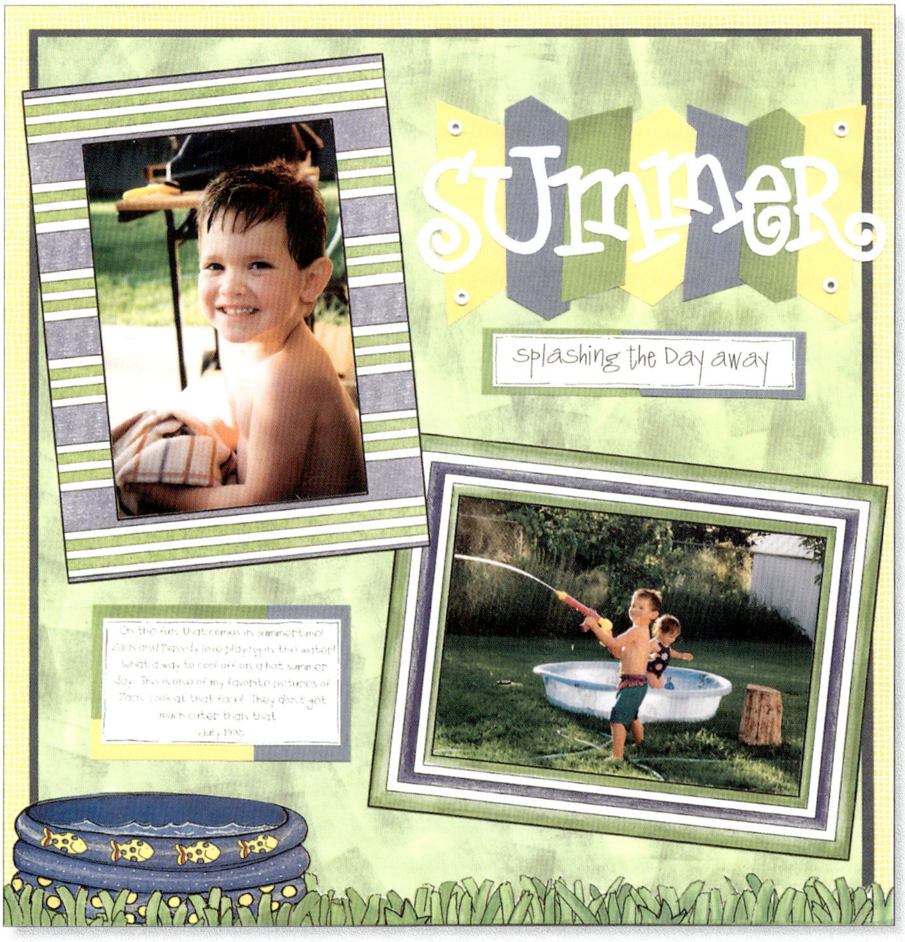

Summer

Supplies
Patterned papers: Provo Craft (yellow), The Honey Tree (green)
Frames and border: My Mind's Eye
Computer fonts: Love Letters, downloaded from the Internet; CK Fun, "The Art of Creative Lettering" CD, *Creating Keepsakes*
Eyelets: Doodlebug Design

♥ **I Love It!:** *Speed up your scrapbooking with pre-made frames! Take your photos with you to the scrapbook store and find frames that complement your photographs well. Then, use the colors in the frames to choose the background papers and other accents you'll include on your page.*

tip 1

mat pre-made frames to create different looks.

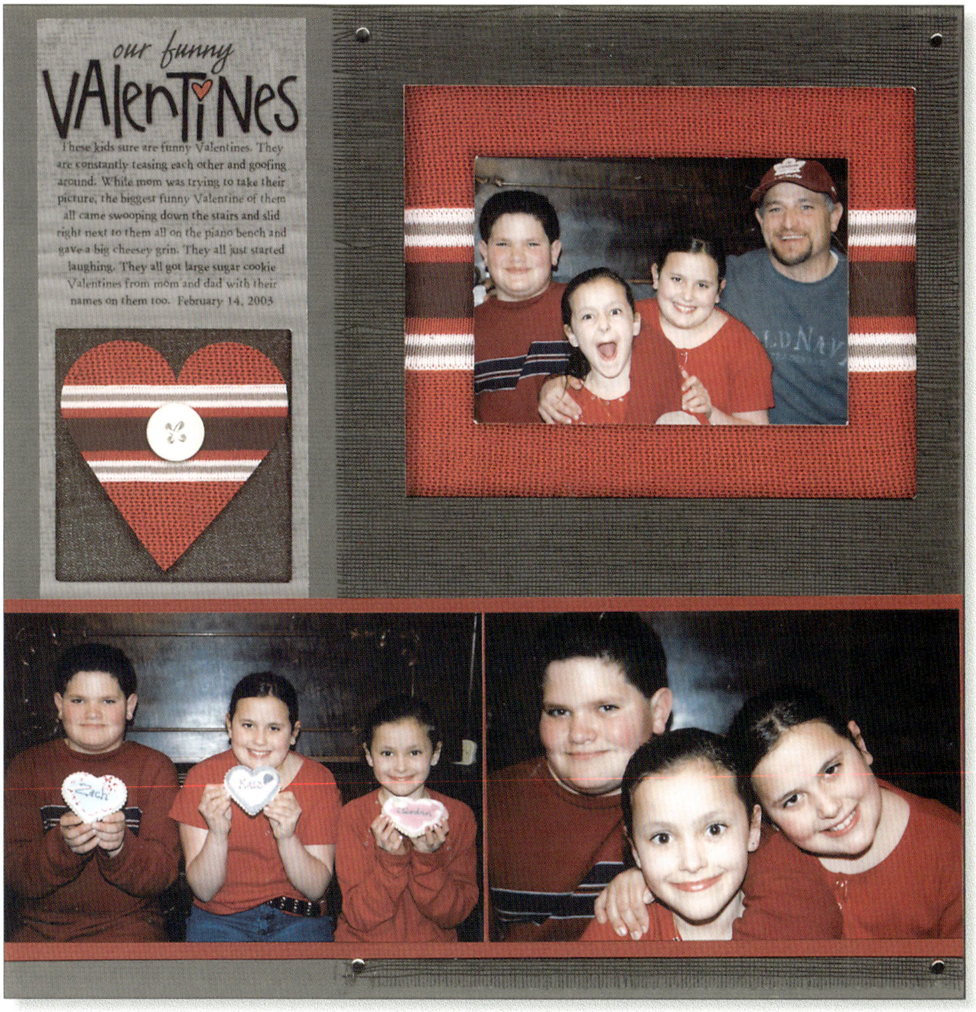
our funny
VAlenTiNes
These kids sure are funny Valentines. They are constantly teasing each other and goofing around. While mom was trying to take their picture, the biggest funny Valentine of them all came swooping down the stairs and slid right next to them all on the piano bench and gave a big cheesey grin. They all just started laughing. They all got large sugar cookie Valentines from mom and dad with their names on them too. February 14, 2003

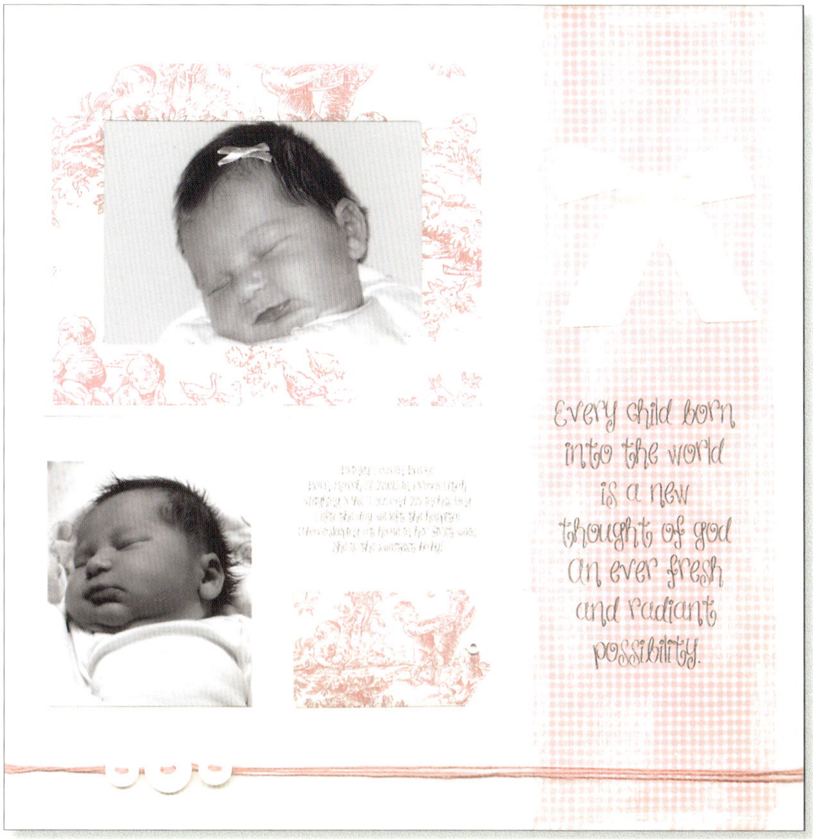
Every child born into the world is a new thought of god an ever fresh and radiant possibility.

Our Funny Valentines

Supplies

Vellum: WorldWin
Preprinted frame and die cut: My Mind's Eye
Computer fonts: CAC Leslie, downloaded from the Internet; P22 Garamouche, Impress Rubber Stamps
Letter stickers: Sue Dreamer, Colorbök
Mesh: Magenta
Other: Brads

♥ **I Love It!:** *This preprinted frame was matted with mesh to mimic its knitted texture.*

Brinley Lauren Burke

Supplies

Patterned paper: O'Scrap!, Imaginations!
Preprinted frame, tag and bow: My Mind's Eye
Computer font: 2Peas Beautiful, downloaded from *www.twopeasinabucket.com*
Eyelets and buttons: Making Memories
Fibers: May Arts

♥ **I Love It!:** *The patterned toile frame seemed to blend into the light-pink background, so the frame was matted with crisp white cardstock to bring more attention to the focal-point photograph.*

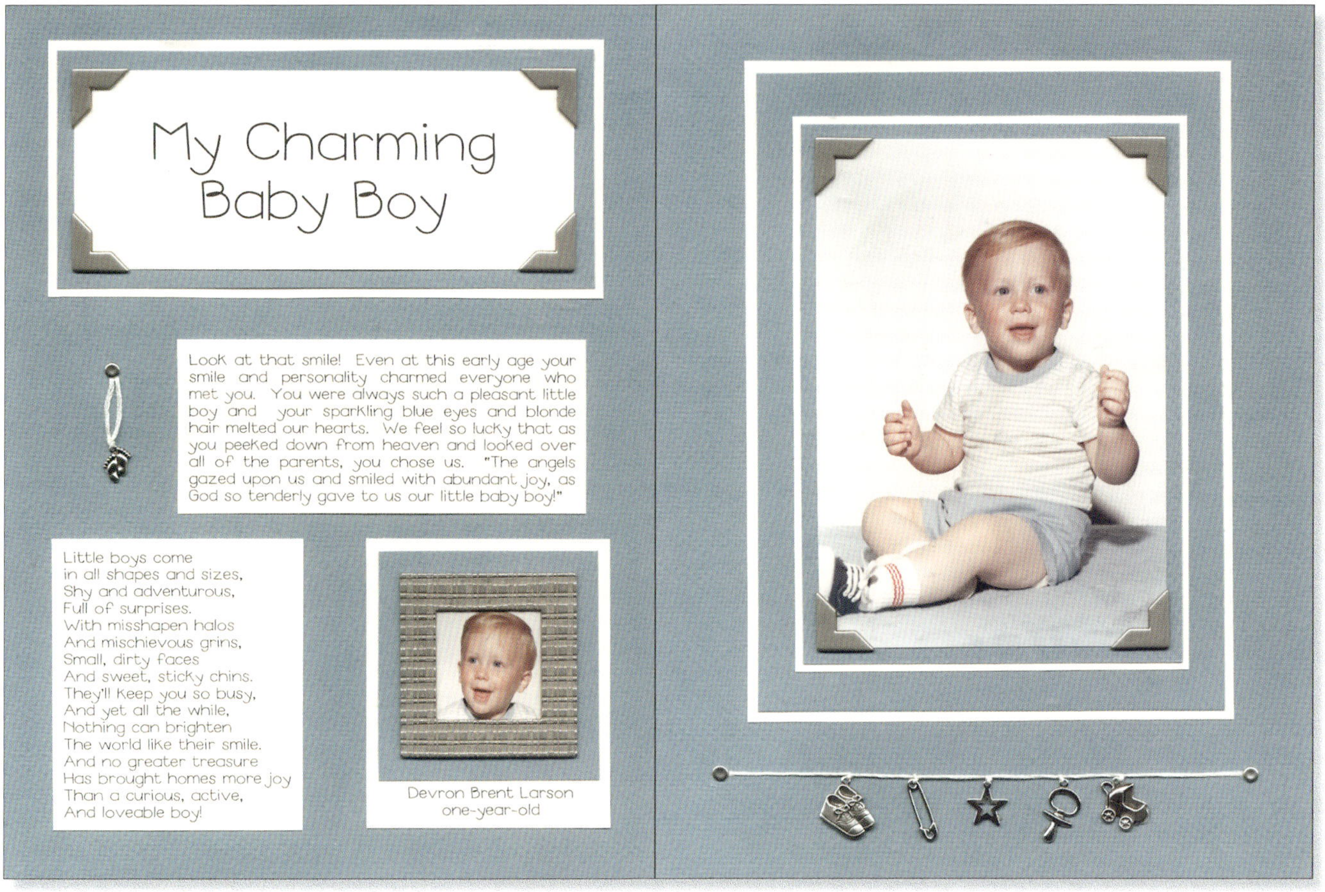
My Charming
Baby Boy
Look at that smile! Even at this early age your smile and personality charmed everyone who met you. You were always such a pleasant little boy and your sparkling blue eyes and blonde hair melted our hearts. We feel so lucky that as you peeked down from heaven and looked over all of the parents, you chose us. "The angels gazed upon us and smiled with abundant joy, as God so tenderly gave to us our little baby boy!"
Little boys come
in all shapes and sizes,
Shy and adventurous,
Full of surprises.
With misshapen halos
And mischievous grins,
Small, dirty faces
And sweet, sticky chins.
They'll keep you so busy,
And yet all the while,
Nothing can brighten
The world like their smile.
And no greater treasure
Has brought homes more joy
Than a curious, active,
And loveable boy!
Devron Brent Larson
one-year-old

My Charming Baby Boy

Supplies

Metal frame and photo corners: Making Memories
Metal charms: Buttons Galore
Computer font: CK Handprint, "The Best of Creative Lettering" CD Combo, *Creating Keepsakes*
Other: Eyelets and string

♥ **I Love It!:** *The off-white cardstock on this layout naturally draws the eye, so the photo and metal frame were double matted to draw more attention to the photo.*

Dinosaur Dig

Supplies

Patterned paper: Provo Craft
Computer fonts: CK Handprint, "The Best of Creative Lettering" CD Combo, *Creating Keepsakes*; Roughedge and Garamond, WordPerfect
Preprinted frame, die cuts and title: My Mind's Eye
Metal-rimmed tags and colored snaps: Making Memories
Ink spritzer: Color Workshop
Mesh: Magenta

♥ **I Love It!:** *Although preprinted frames are generally placed over photographs, this frame was used to mat a journaling block—the cardstock journaling block was placed over the preprinted frame with a thin border showing.*

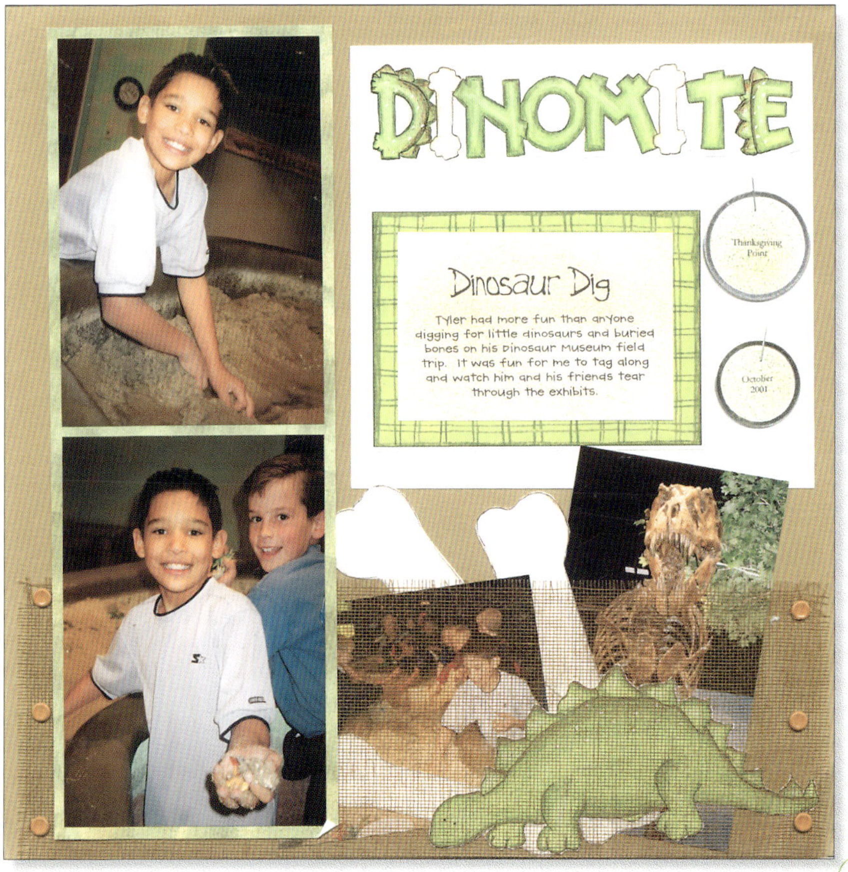
DINOMITE
Dinosaur Dig
Tyler had more fun than anyone digging for little dinosaurs and buried bones on his Dinosaur Museum field trip. It was fun for me to tag along and watch him and his friends tear through the exhibits.
Thanksgiving Point
October 2001

tip 2

use coordinating preprinted frames for quick scrapbooking.

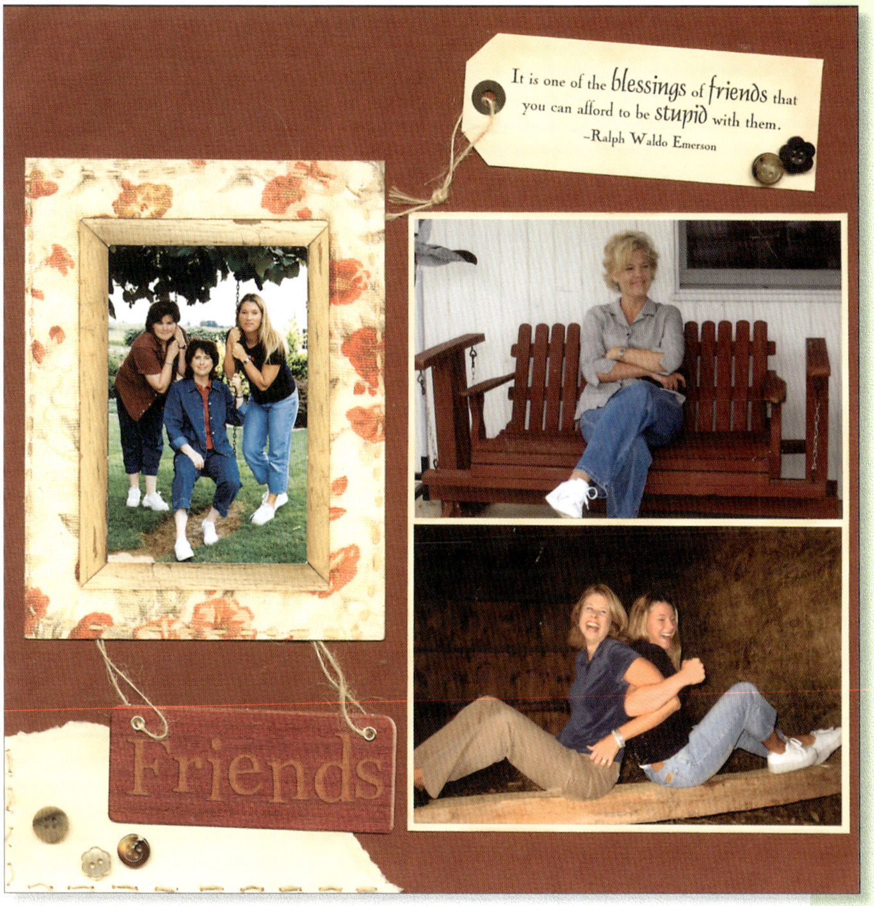

Friends

Supplies

Preprinted frames and accent: My Mind's Eye
Eyelets: Making Memories
Computer fonts: Bernhard Modern BT and Dauphin, WordPerfect
Chalk: Craf-T Products
Other: Buttons and jute

♥ **I Love It!:** *The two coordinating frames on this layout were layered to create a "double matted" look. It looks like a real photo frame!*

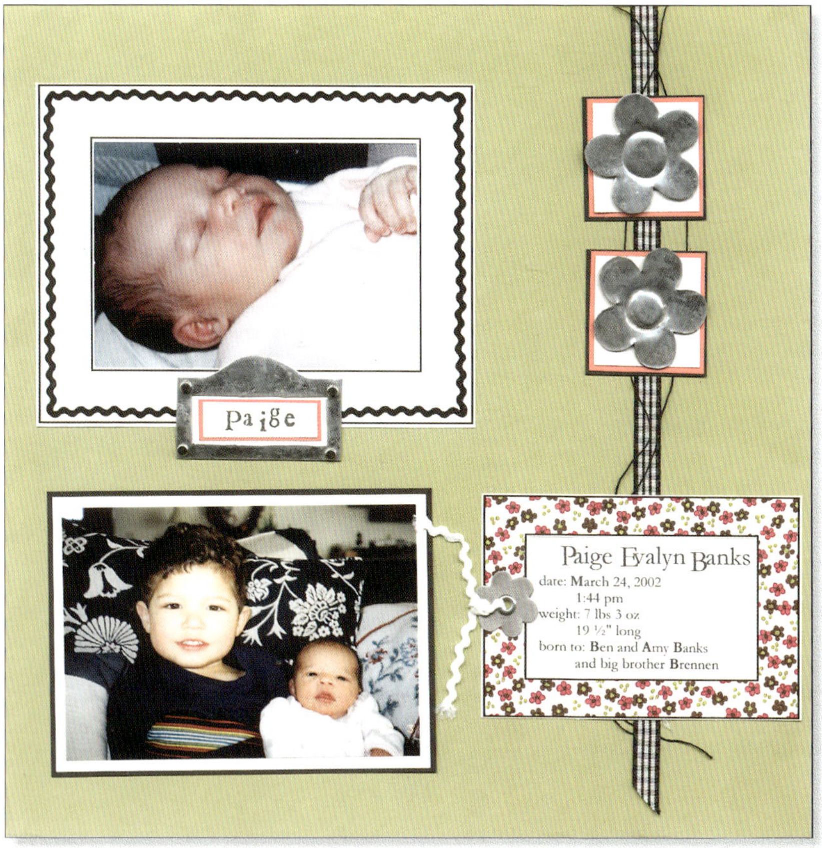

Paige Evalyn Banks

Supplies

Preprinted frames: My Mind's Eye
Metal accents: Provo Craft
Letter stamps: PSX Design
Stamping ink: ColorBox, Clearsnap
Computer font: Garamond, Microsoft Word
Brads: Making Memories
Other: Rickrack and ribbon

♥ **I Love It!:** *Preprinted frames make quick and easy invitations, announcements and cards—for your layouts or for sending through the mail!*

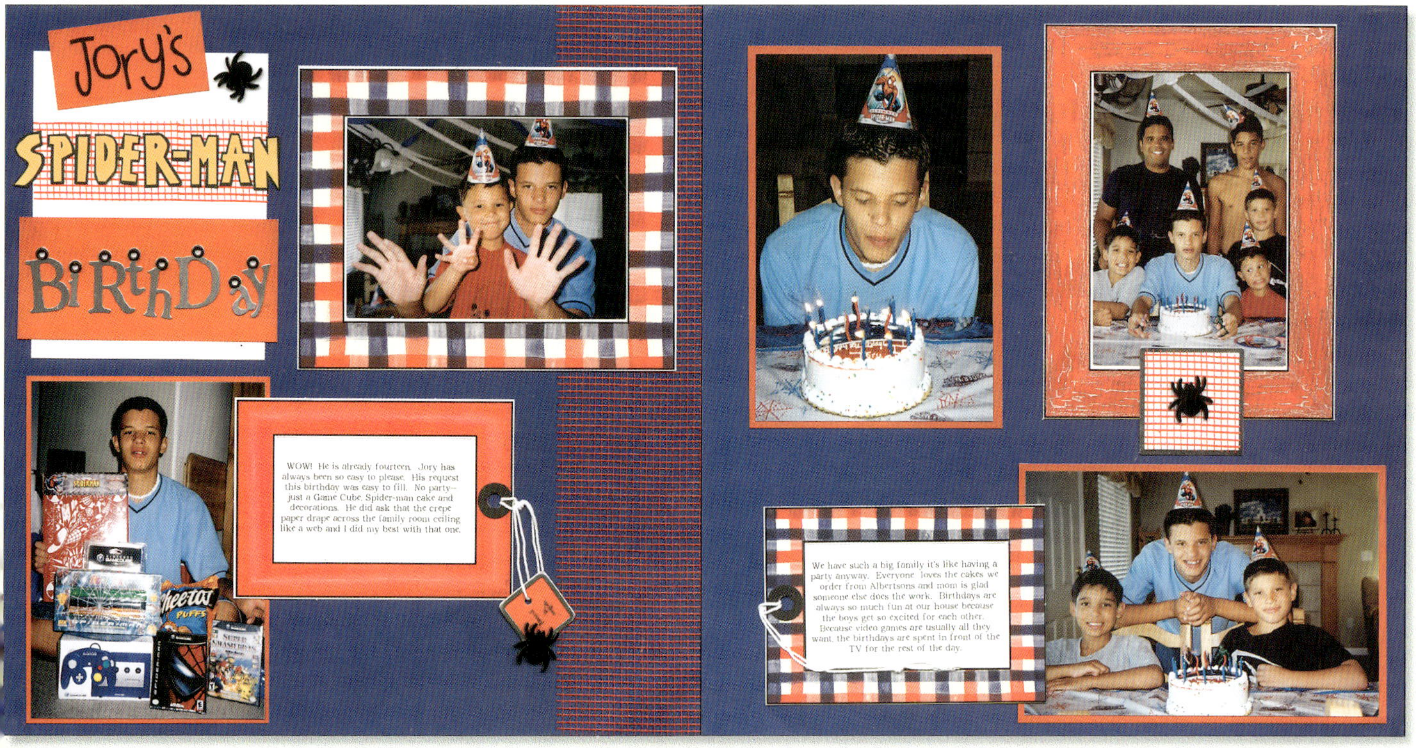

Jory's
SPIDER-MAN
BiRthDay
WOW! He is already fourteen. Jory has always been so easy to please. His request this birthday was easy to fill. No party–just a Game Cube, Spider-man cake and decorations. He did ask that the crepe paper drape across the family room ceiling like a web and I did my best with that one.
14
We have such a big family it's like having a party anyway. Everyone loves the cakes we order from Albertsons and mom is glad someone else does the work. Birthdays are always so much fun at our house because the boys get so excited for each other. Because video games are usually all they want, the birthdays are spent in front of the TV for the rest of the day.

Jory's Spiderman Birthday

Supplies
Preprinted frames: My Mind's Eye
Computer font: CK Newsprint, "Fresh Fonts" CD, *Creating Keepsakes*
Letter stickers: Sue Dreamer, Colorbök
Metal letter charms, metal-rimmed tags and eyelets: Making Memories
Letter stamps: PSX Design
Buttons: Buttons Galore
Mesh: Magenta

♥ **I Love It!:** *With just black cardstock, a circle punch and some string, the smaller frames on this page were transformed into tags.*

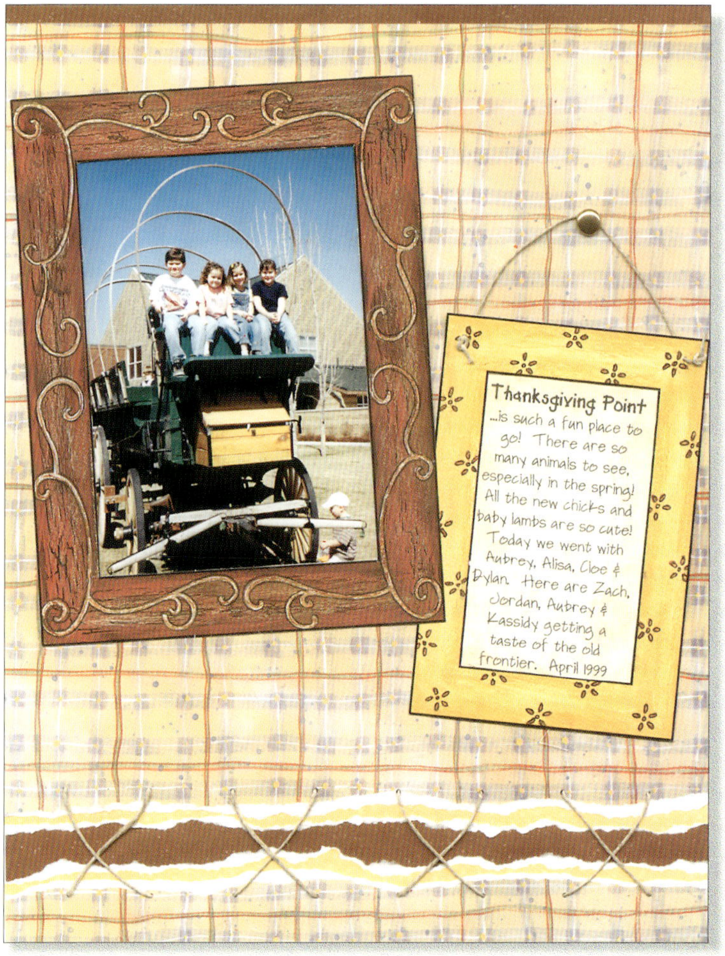

Thanksgiving Point
...is such a fun place to go! There are so many animals to see, especially in the spring! All the new chicks and baby lambs are so cute! Today we went with Aubrey, Alisa, Cloe & Dylan. Here are Zach, Jordan, Aubrey & Kassidy getting a taste of the old frontier. April 1999

Thanksgiving Point

Supplies
Patterned papers: Rocky Mountain Paper Co. (plaid), Keeping Memories Alive (yellow and brown)
Preprinted frames: My Mind's Eye
Computer fonts: PC Beach, "Little Images" Hugware CD and PC Chopsticks, "Headliners" Hugware CD, Provo Craft
Other: Brads and jute

♥ **I Love It!:** *Preprinted frames aren't just for photographs! Use them to frame journaling, memorabilia or accents.*

tip 3
embellish
preprinted frames with coordinating preprinted accents.

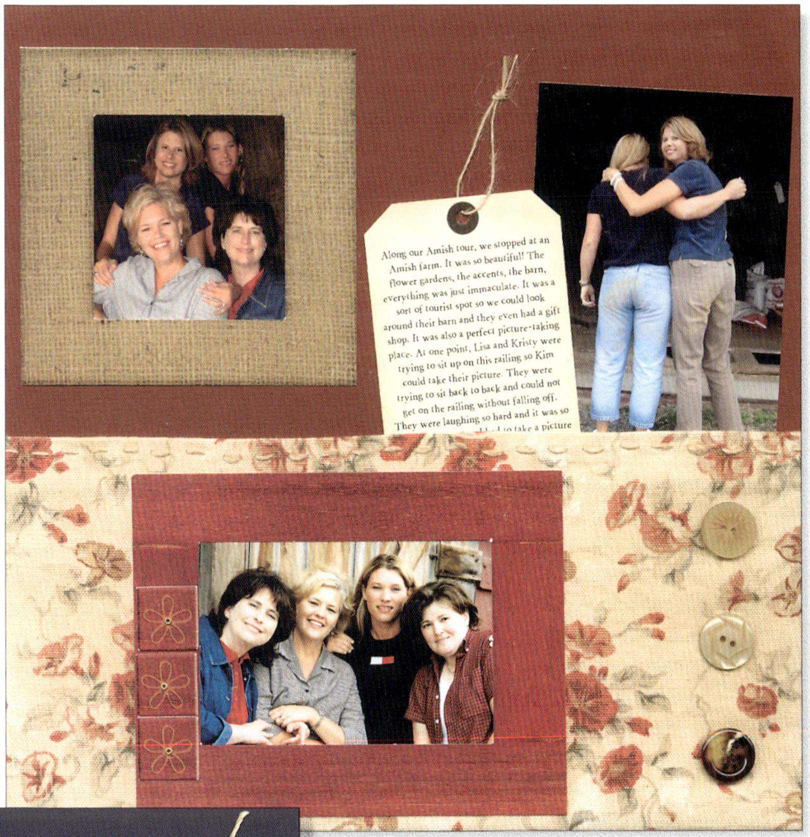
Along our Amish tour, we stopped at an Amish farm. It was so beautiful! The flower gardens, the accents, the barn, everything was just immaculate. It was a sort of tourist spot so we could look around their barn and they even had a gift shop. It was also a perfect picture-taking place. At one point, Lisa and Kristy were trying to sit up on this railing so Kim could take their picture. They were trying to sit back to back and could not get on the railing without falling off. They were laughing so hard and it was so

Friends

Supplies
Preprinted frames and flower accents: My Mind's Eye
Computer font: P22 Garamouche, Impress Rubber Stamps
Other: Buttons, jute and fabric

♥ **I Love It!:** *The matching flower accent squares were attached in a row along the side of the preprinted frame with tiny eyelets.*

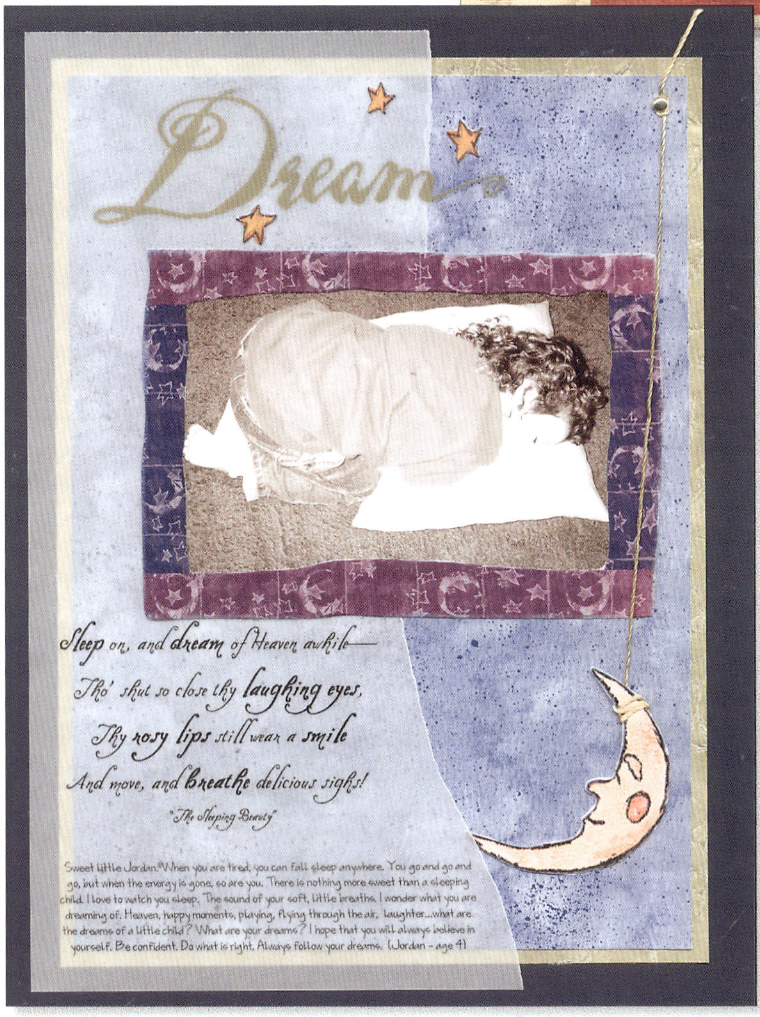
Dream
Sleep on, and dream of Heaven awhile—
Tho' shut so close thy laughing eyes,
Thy rosy lips still wear a smile
And move, and breathe delicious sighs!
"The Sleeping Beauty"
Sweet little Jordan. When you are tired, you can fall sleep anywhere. You go and go and go, but when the energy is gone, so are you. There is nothing more sweet than a sleeping child. I love to watch you sleep. The sound of your soft, little breaths. I wonder what you are dreaming of. Heaven, happy moments, playing, flying through the air, laughter...what are the dreams of a little child? What are your dreams? I hope that you will always believe in yourself. Be confident. Do what is right. Always follow your dreams. (Jordan - age 4)

Dream

Supplies
Patterned paper: Over The Moon Press
Vellum: Autumn Leaves
Preprinted frame, accents and letter stickers: Colorbök
Computer fonts: CK Penman, "The Best of Creative Lettering" CD Vol. 4; CK Elegant, "Fresh Fonts" CD, *Creating Keepsakes*
Fiber: On The Surface
Other: Brad

♥ **I Love It!:** *The moon accent was wrapped with a piece of fiber and hung from a brad to accent the frame.*

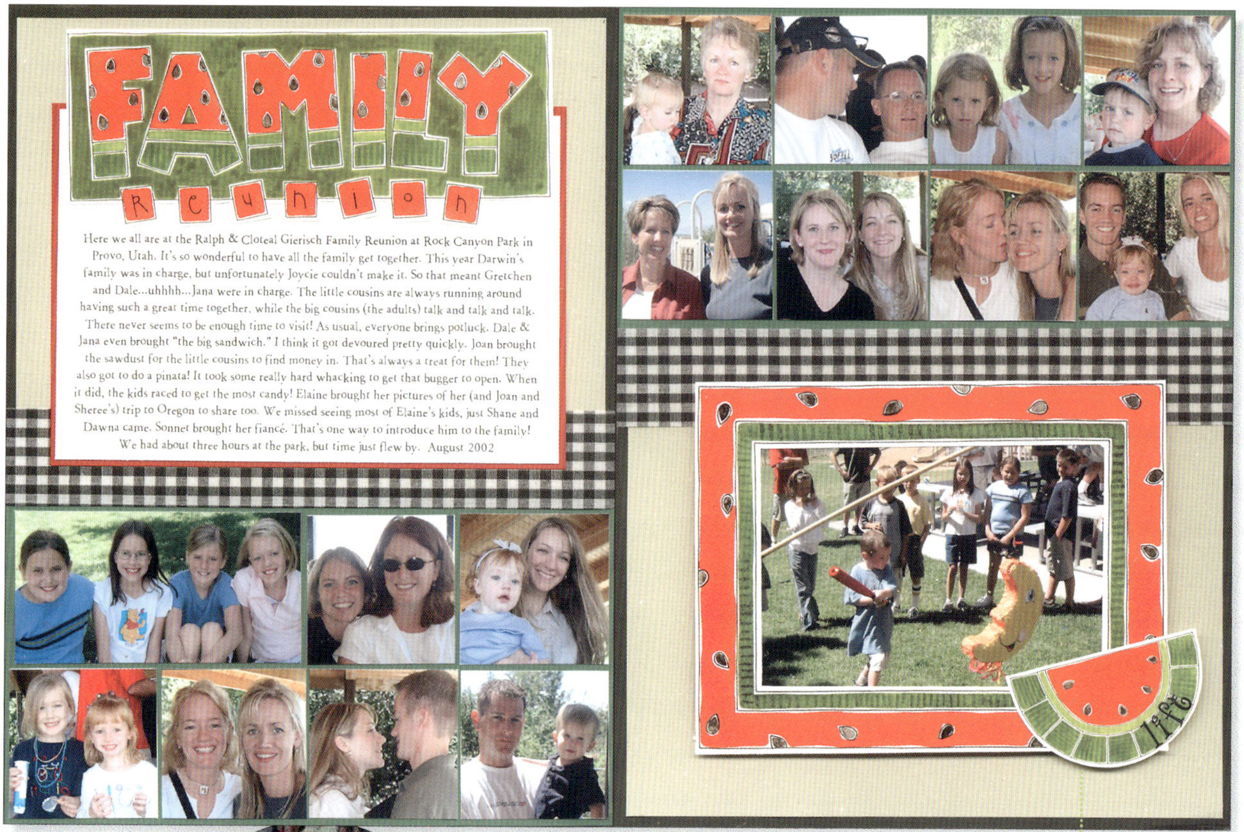
FAMILY
Reunion
Here we all are at the Ralph & Cloteal Gierisch Family Reunion at Rock Canyon Park in Provo, Utah. It's so wonderful to have all the family get together. This year Darwin's family was in charge, but unfortunately Joycie couldn't make it. So that meant Gretchen and Dale...uhhhh...Jana were in charge. The little cousins are always running around having such a great time together, while the big cousins (the adults) talk and talk and talk. There never seems to be enough time to visit! As usual, everyone brings potluck. Dale & Jana even brought "the big sandwich." I think it got devoured pretty quickly. Joan brought the sawdust for the little cousins to find money in. That's always a treat for them! They also got to do a pinata! It took some really hard whacking to get that bugger to open. When it did, the kids raced to get the most candy! Elaine brought her pictures of her (and Joan and Sheree's) trip to Oregon to share too. We missed seeing most of Elaine's kids, just Shane and Dawna came. Sonnet brought her fiancé. That's one way to introduce him to the family! We had about three hours at the park, but time just flew by. August 2002
lift

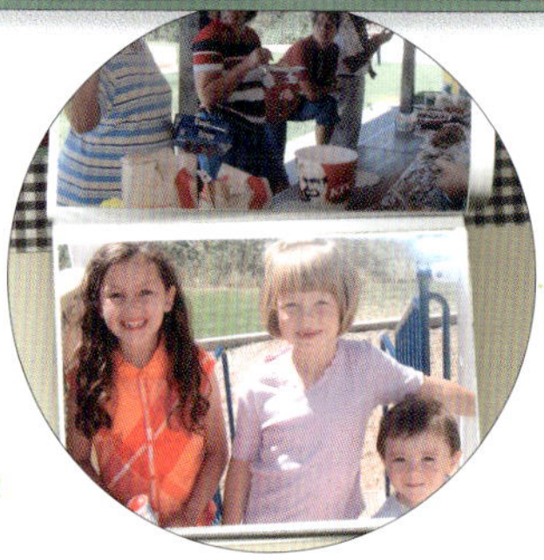

Family Reunion

Supplies

Preprinted frame, title and accent: My Mind's Eye
Letter stickers: Provo Craft
Computer font: Garamouche, Impress Rubber Stamps
Photo flip book: Zippity DooDad
Other: Ribbon

♥ **I Love It!:** *This preprinted frame was attached to a mini-album, which increased the photo count from an impressive 15 to an astounding 25!*

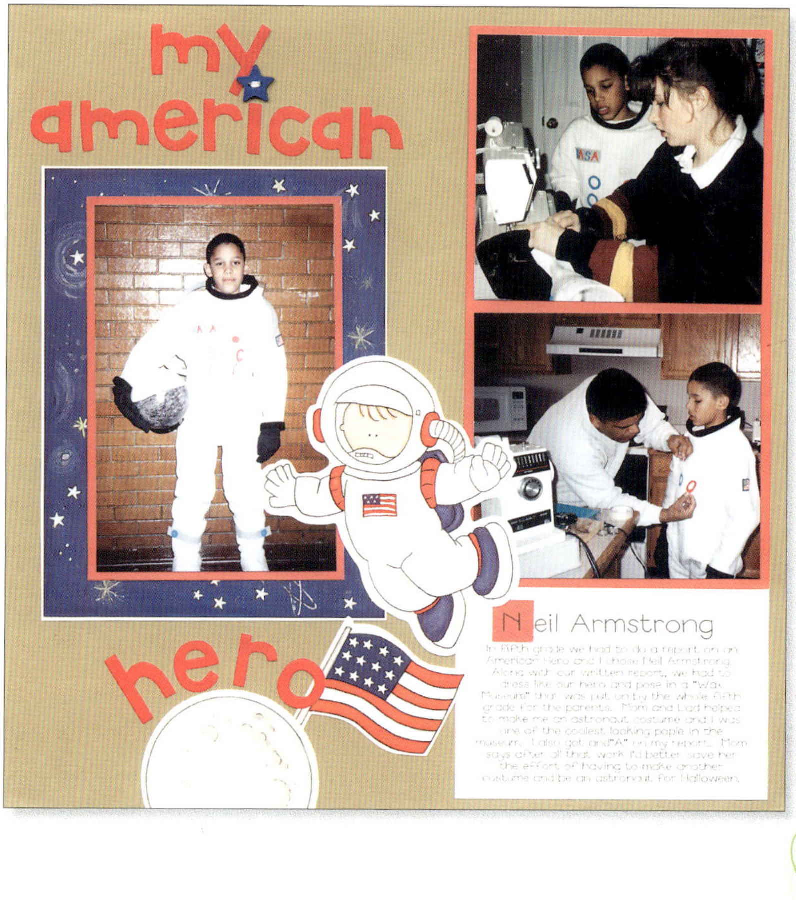
my american
hero
Neil Armstrong
In fifth grade we had to do a report on an American Hero and I chose Neil Armstrong. Along with our written report, we had to dress like our hero and pose in a "Wax Museum" that was put on by the whole fifth grade for the parents. Mom and Dad helped to make me an astronaut costume and I was one of the coolest looking pople in the museum. I also got and"A" on my report. Mom says after all that work I'd better save her the effort of having to make another costume and be an astronaut for Halloween.

My American Hero

Supplies

Preprinted frame, accents and letter stickers: My Mind's Eye
Computer font: CK Primary, "The Art of Creative Lettering" CD, *Creating Keepsakes*
Buttons: Buttons Galore

♥ **I Love It!:** *This preprinted frame was placed under a matted photograph instead of over it for a fresh, new look.*

♥ **I Love It!:** *Instead of randomly placing the astronaut, moon and flag accents around the layout, a scene was created showing the astronaut landing on the moon.*

tip 4

customize preprinted frames by adding your own special touches.

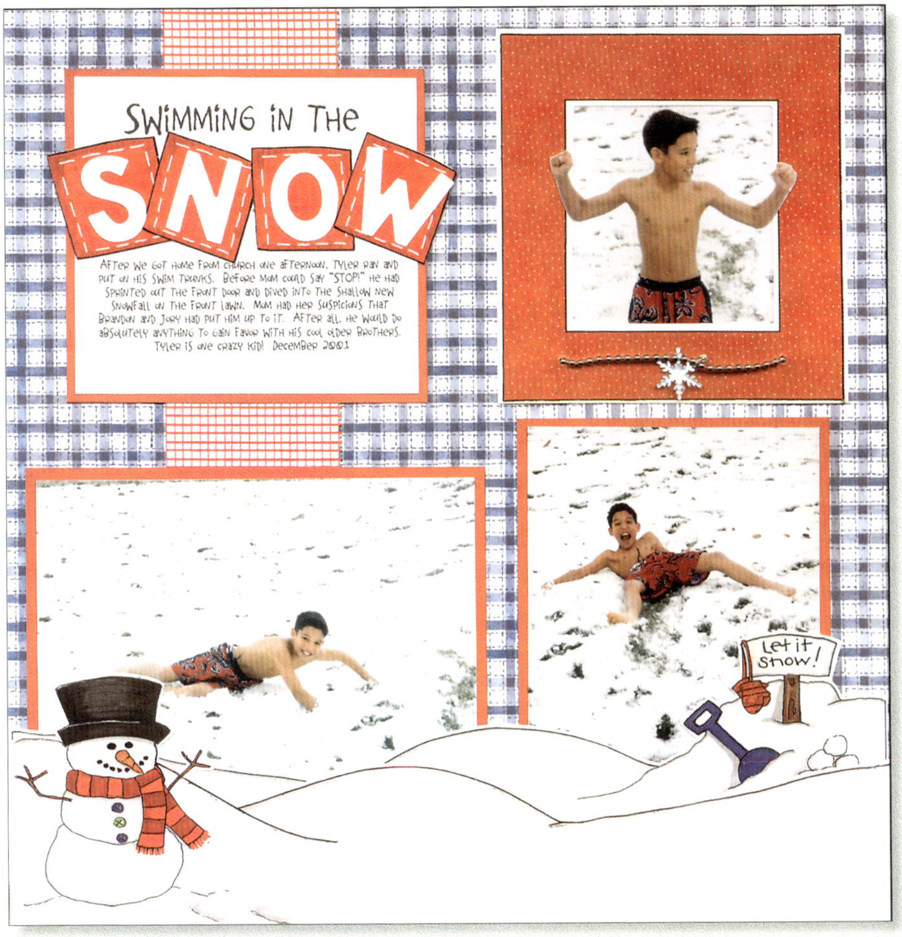
Swimming in the
SNOW
After we got home from church one afternoon, Tyler ran and put on his swim trunks. Before Mom could say "STOP!" he had sprinted out the front door and dived into the shallow new snowfall on the front lawn. Mom had her suspicions that Brandon and Jory had put him up to it. After all, he would do absolutely anything to gain favor with his cool older brothers. Tyler is one crazy kid! December 2001
let it snow!

Swimming in the Snow

Supplies
Patterned paper: Colorbök
Preprinted frame, border, title blocks and letter stickers: My Mind's Eye
Computer font: Scrap Brother, "Lettering Delights" CD, Inspire Graphics
Mesh: Magic Mesh
Bead chain: Westrim Crafts
Other: Snowflake charm

♥ **I Love It!:** *This frame was customized with a simple beaded chain and snowflake charm. Try the same idea using jute, embroidery floss or wire.*

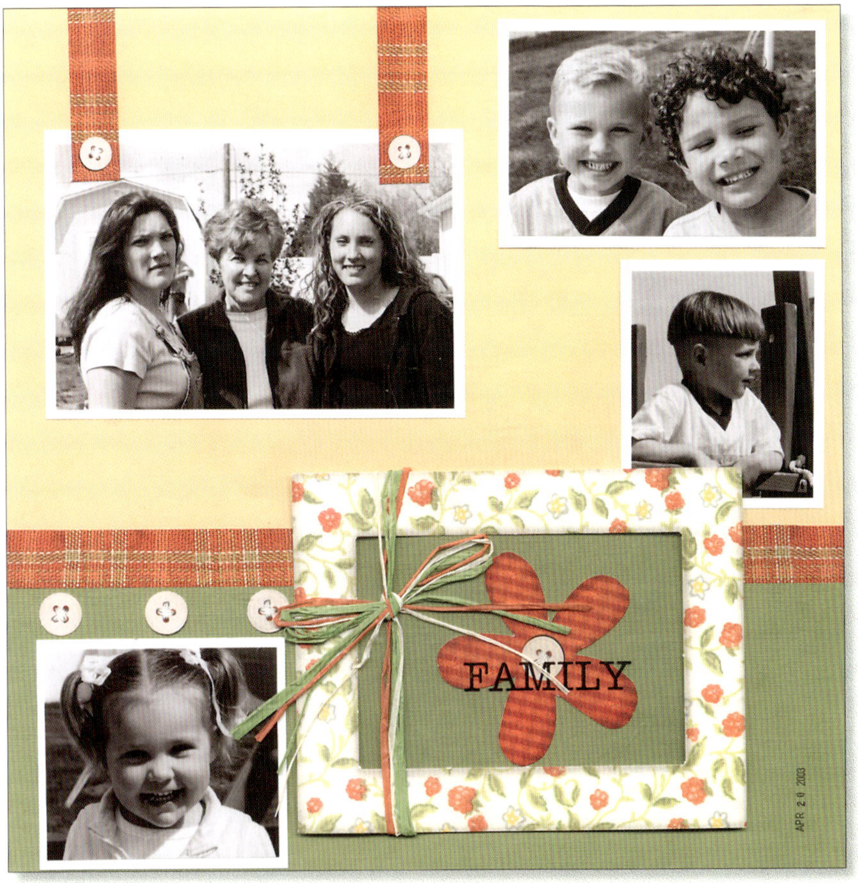
FAMILY
APR 20 2003

Family

Supplies
Patterned paper: SEI
Preprinted frame and accents: My Mind's Eye
Computer font: AmerType, WordPerfect
Other: Transparency paper, date stamp and raffia

♥ **I Love It!:** *The preprinted frame on this page actually serves as the title block. The word "Family" was printed onto clear transparency paper and attached to the frame. The flower accent was adhered to a rectangle of green cardstock, which was then glued under the transparency paper. The adhesive was placed around the edges of the green cardstock, which are covered by the frame.*

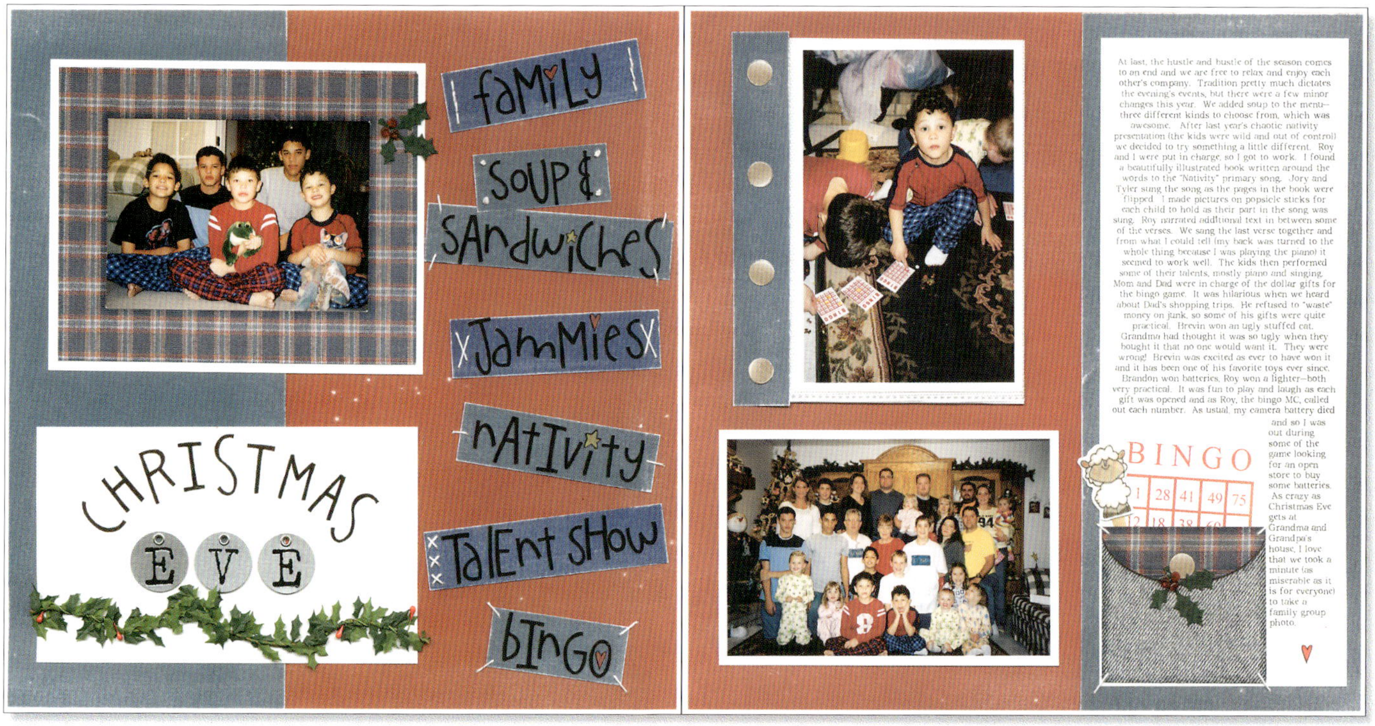

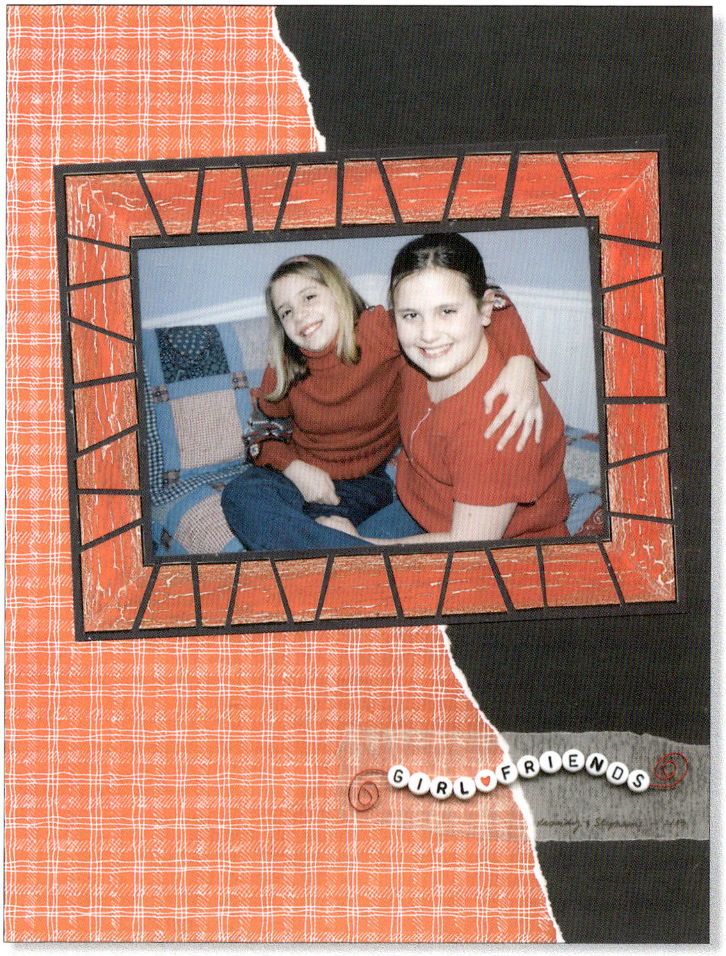

Christmas Eve

Supplies

Preprinted frame and accent: My Mind's Eye
Stickers: Provo Craft
Letter stickers: Sue Dreamer, Colorbök
Metal letter tags and eyelets: Making Memories
Holly punch: Family Treasures
Computer font: CK Newsprint, "Fresh Fonts" CD, *Creating Keepsakes*
Other: Mini-album, beads and embroidery floss

♥ **I Love It!:** *The mini-album on this layout increased the photo count from three to six!*

♥ **I Love It!:** *Take advantage of accents that are large enough to act as pockets on your layout. I love the bingo card and Popsicle-stick puppet peeking out of this pocket accent.*

Girlfriends

Supplies

Patterned paper: Provo Craft
Vellum: Autumn Leaves
Preprinted frame: My Mind's Eye
Craft wire: Artistic Wire Ltd.
Letter beads: Westrim Crafts
Pen: Pigma Micron, Sakura

♥ **I Love It!:** *This preprinted frame was randomly cut into pieces, then pieced back together on a block of cardstock to create a mosaic look.*

tip 5

decorate

preprinted frames with studs, brads, eyelets, buttons or charms.

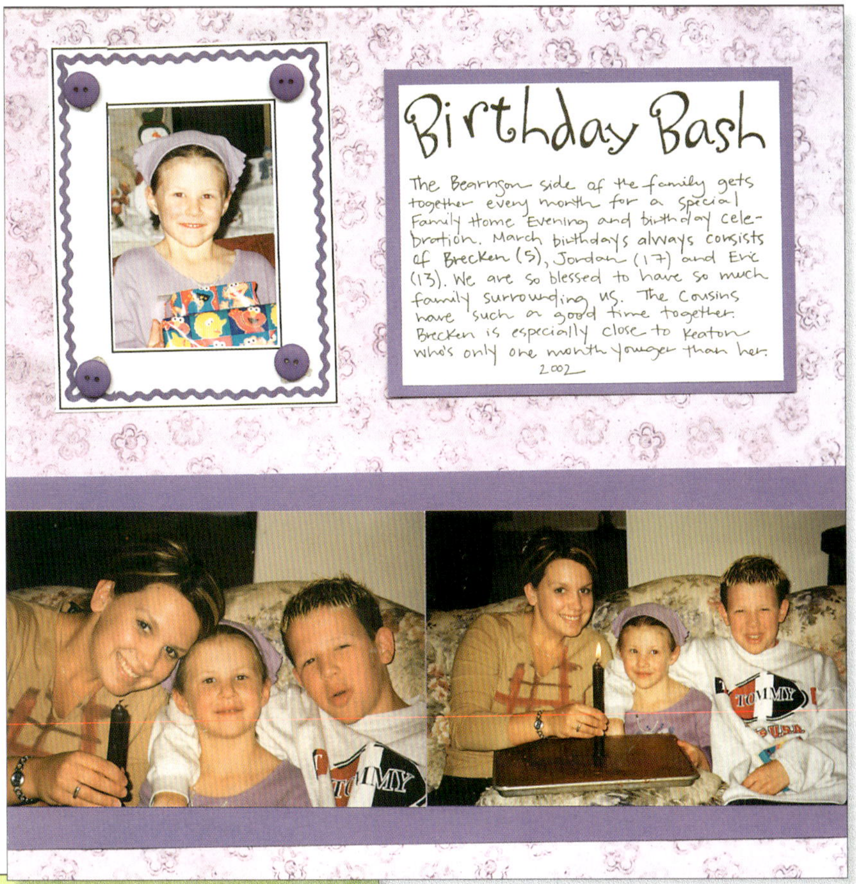
Birthday Bash
The Bearnson side of the family gets together every month for a special Family Home Evening and birthday celebration. March birthdays always consists of Brecken (5), Jordan (17) and Eric (13). We are so blessed to have so much family surrounding us. The Cousins have such a good time together. Brecken is especially close to Keaton who's only one month younger than her.
2002
TOMMY
TOMMY

Birthday Bash

Supplies
Patterned paper: Provo Craft
Preprinted frame: My Mind's Eye
Letter stickers: David Walker, Colorbök
Pen: American Crafts

♥ **I Love It!:** *The preprinted frame was too large for the cropped photo, so it was trimmed to a smaller size. Simply cut the shorter edge from the frame (following the inside line), slide it to the desired size (making sure the pattern matches up), trim the extra edges and adhere the frame back together. This is a great way to get rid of unwanted elements in the background of a photograph.*

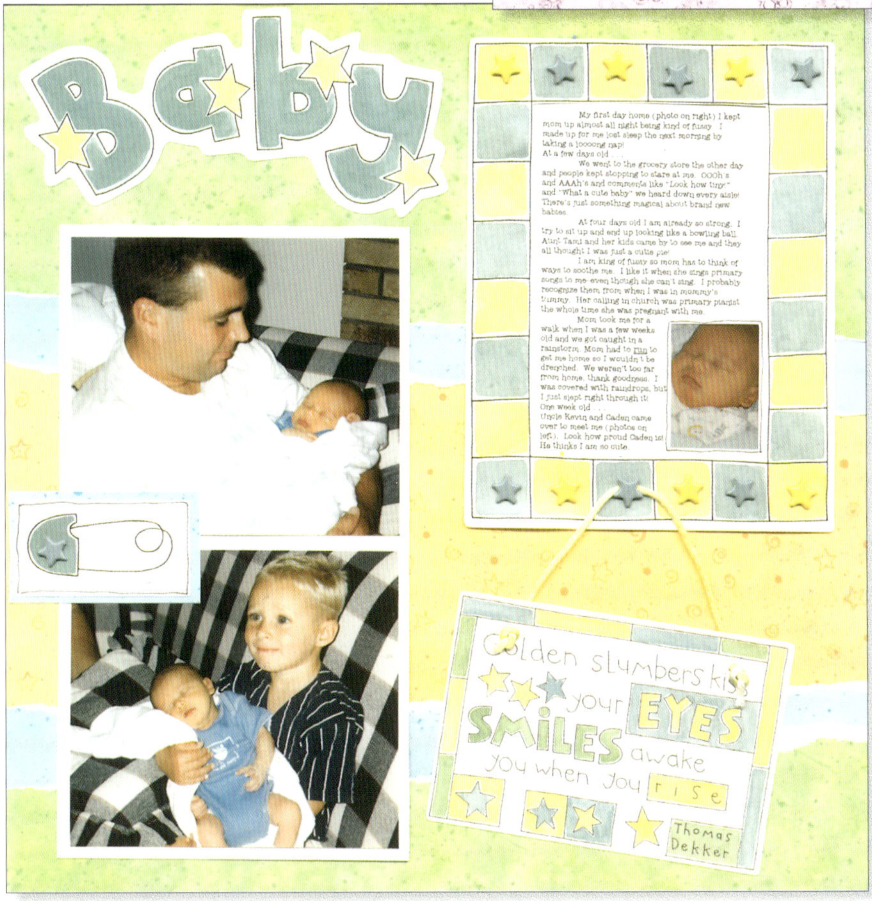
Baby
My first day home (photo on right) I kept mom up almost all night being kind of fussy. I made up for me lost sleep the next morning by taking a loooong nap!
At a few days old . . .
We went to the grocery store the other day and people kept stopping to stare at me. OOOh's and AAAh's and comments like "Look how tiny!" and "What a cute baby" we heard down every aisle! There's just something magical about brand new babies.
At four days old I am already so strong. I try to sit up and end up looking like a bowling ball. Aunt Tami and her kids came by to see me and they all thought I was just a cutie pie!
I am king of fussy so mom has to think of ways to soothe me. I like it when she sings primary songs to me-even though she can't sing. I probably recognize them from when I was in mommy's tummy. Her calling in church was primary pianist the whole time she was pregnant with me.
Mom took me for a walk when I was a few weeks old and we got caught in a rainstorm. Mom had to run to get me home so I wouldn't be drenched. We weren't too far from home, thank goodness. I was covered with raindrops, but I just slept right through it!
One week old . . .
Uncle Kevin and Caden came over to meet me (photos on left). Look how proud Caden is! He thinks I am so cute.
Golden slumbers kiss your EYES SMILES awake you when you rise
Thomas Dekker

Baby

Supplies
Patterned papers and star brads: Provo Craft
Preprinted frame, title, accent and quote: My Mind's Eye
Computer font: CK Stenography, "Fresh Fonts" CD, *Creating Keepsakes*
Other: Nylon string

♥ **I Love It!:** *Brads, eyelets and studs come in so many different shapes, there's sure to be one to match the theme of your page. These star brads line the top and bottom of the preprinted frame and decorate the head of the safety-pin accent.*

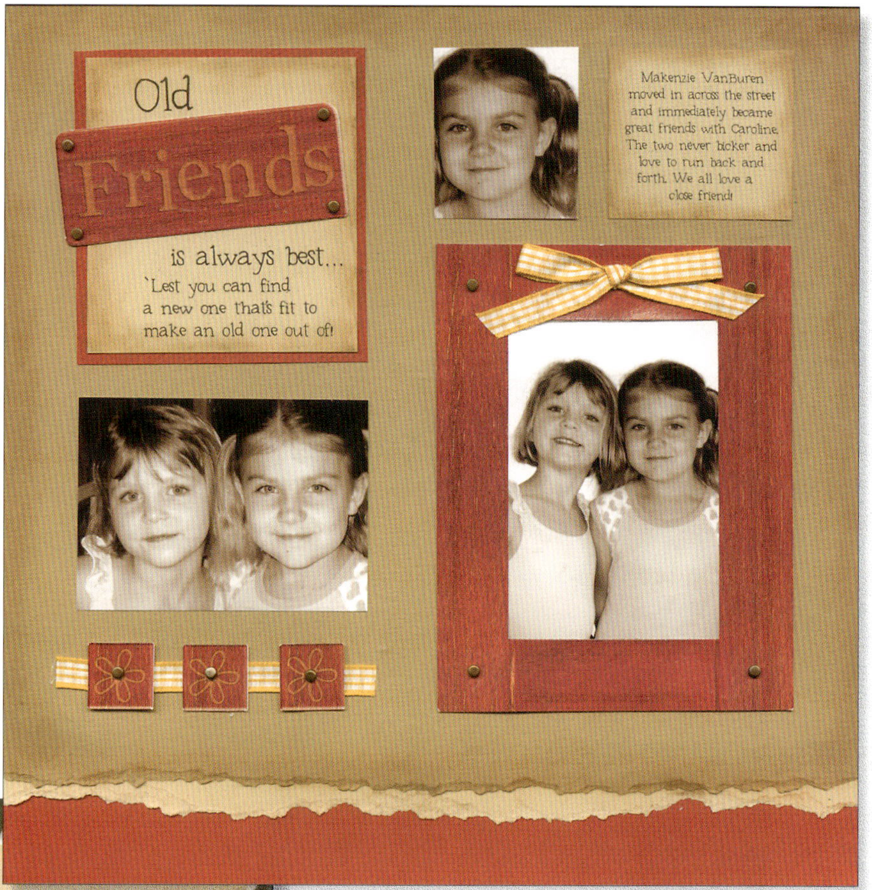
Old
Friends
is always best...
`Lest you can find
a new one that's fit to
make an old one out of!
Makenzie VanBuren moved in across the street and immediately became great friends with Caroline. The two never bicker and love to run back and forth. We all love a close friend!

Old Friends

Supplies
Preprinted frames: My Mind's Eye
Computer font: BH Traditional, package unknown
Brads: Memory Lane Paper Company
Ribbon: May Arts

♥ **I Love It!:** *Brads make the perfect centers for these rustic-looking flower accents, but they looked a bit out of place with the rest of the layout. Incorporating the brads onto the "Friends" title accent and in the four corners of the preprinted frame makes them look like they belong. The ribbon bow adds a feminine touch to the rustic frame.*

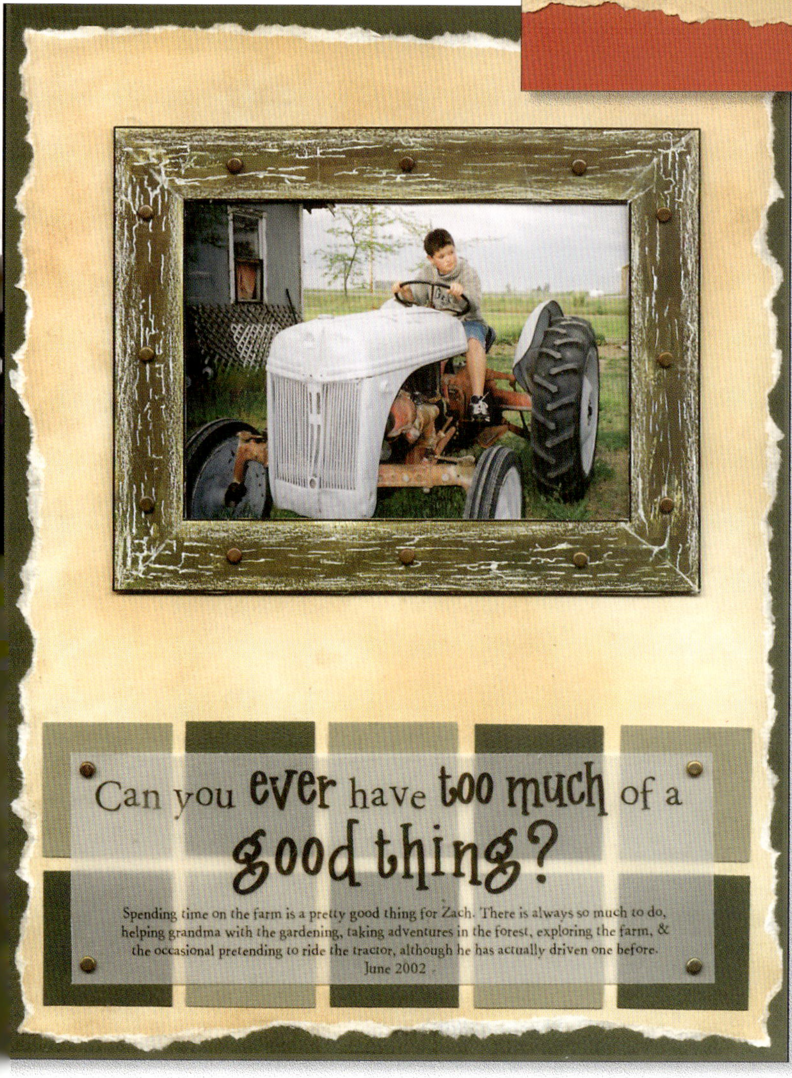
Can you ever have too much of a
good thing?
Spending time on the farm is a pretty good thing for Zach. There is always so much to do, helping grandma with the gardening, taking adventures in the forest, exploring the farm, & the occasional pretending to ride the tractor, although he has actually driven one before.
June 2002

A Good Thing

Supplies
Vellum: WorldWin
Preprinted frame: My Mind's Eye
Computer fonts: Whipper Basic, Whipper Snapper Designs; P22 Garamouche, Impress Rubber Stamps
Other: Brads and 3-D foam adhesive

♥ **I Love It!:** *Aged copper brads placed at even intervals around the preprinted frame add to the rustic look of this layout. The brads were incorporated again in the four corners of the journaling block for a unified look.*

tip 6

create a window using preprinted frames.

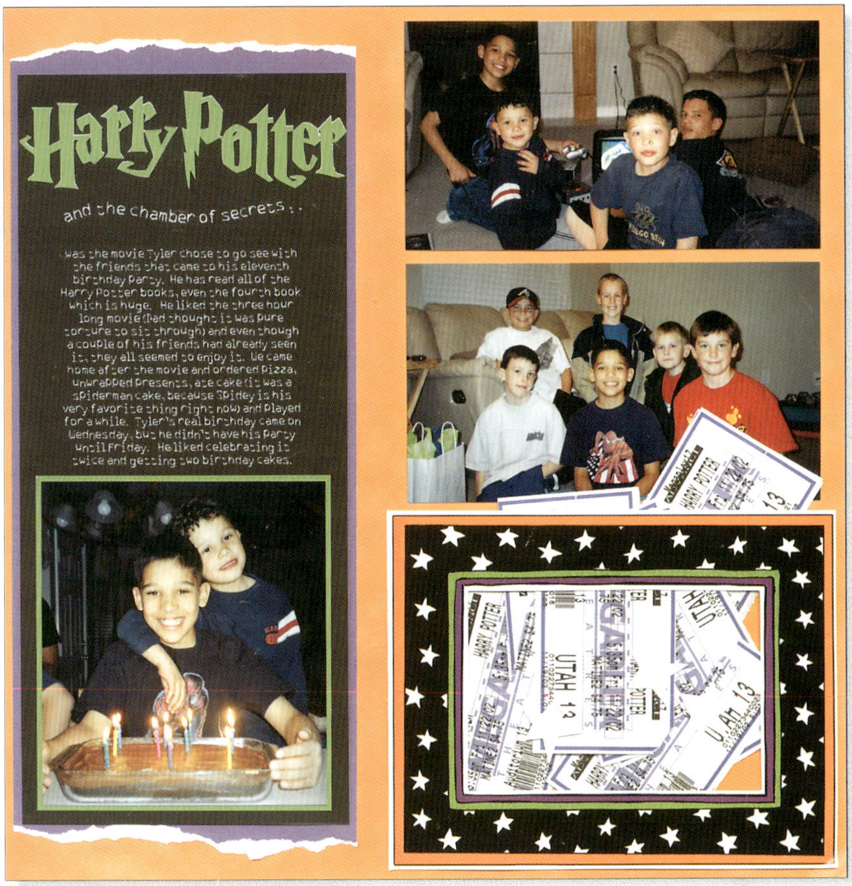

Harry Potter
and the chamber of secrets . . .
was the movie Tyler chose to go see with the friends that came to his eleventh birthday party. He has read all of the Harry Potter books, even the fourth book which is huge. He liked the three hour long movie (Dad thought it was pure torture to sit through) and even though a couple of his friends had already seen it, they all seemed to enjoy it. We came home after the movie and ordered pizza, unwrapped presents, ate cake (it was a spiderman cake, because Spidey is his very favorite thing right now) and played for a while. Tyler's real birthday came on Wednesday, but he didn't have his party until Friday. He liked celebrating it twice and getting two birthday cakes.

Harry Potter

Supplies

Preprinted frame: My Mind's Eye
Computer font: CK Carbon Copy, "Fresh Fonts" CD, *Creating Keepsakes*
Star punch: Posh Impressions
Other: Transparency paper

♥ **I Love It!:** *The Harry Potter title was created by scanning the title from a book jacket, enlarging it, printing it backward and cutting it out with a craft knife.*

♥ **I Love It!:** *Wondering how to print white text on black paper? In your word-processing program, change the text color to white, then select black as the fill color.*

♥ **I Love It!:** *This preprinted frame was turned into a pocket to hold movie ticket stubs. Simply place a sheet of transparency paper behind the frame, adhere the edges of the frame to the page and slip your memorabilia inside.*

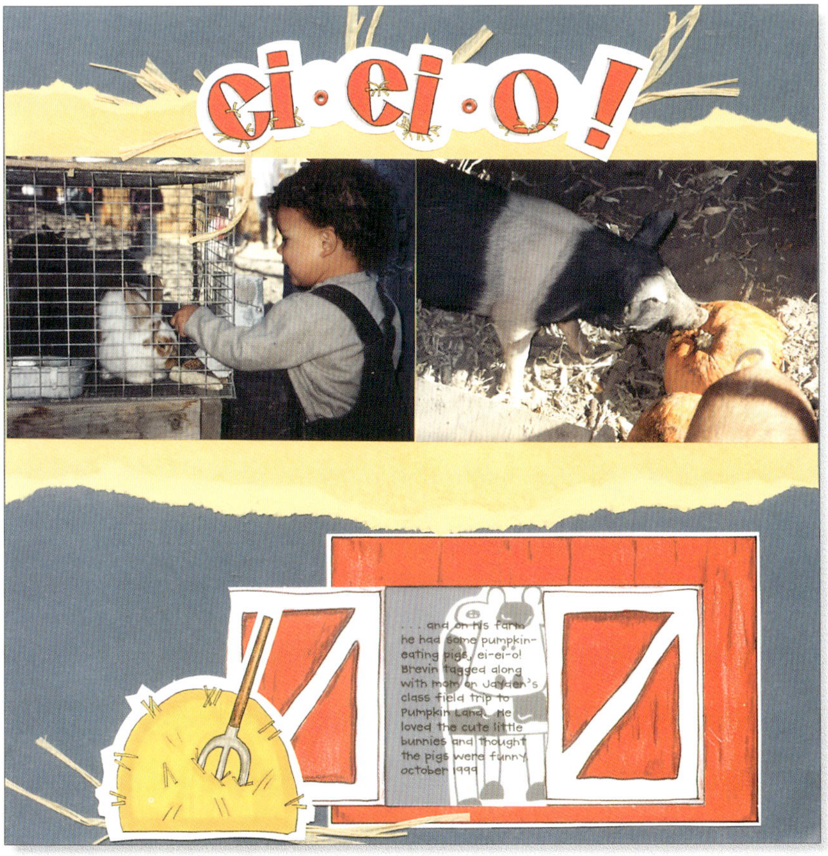

ei-ei-o!
. . . and on his farm he had some pumpkin-eating pigs, ei-ei-o! Brevin tagged along with mom on Jayden's class field trip to Pumpkin Land. He loved the cute little bunnies and thought the pigs were funny. october 1999

EI-EI-O!

Supplies

Preprinted frame, title and accents: My Mind's Eye
Vellum: Provo Craft
Computer font: CK Handprint, "The Best of Creative Lettering" CD Combo, *Creating Keepsakes*
Eyelets: Doodlebug Design
Other: Raffia

♥ **I Love It!:** *This frame with barn door accents opens to reveal a cow accent peeking through the journaling.*

♥ **I Love It!:** *Eyelets were set over drawn dots on the preprinted title to create a custom look.*

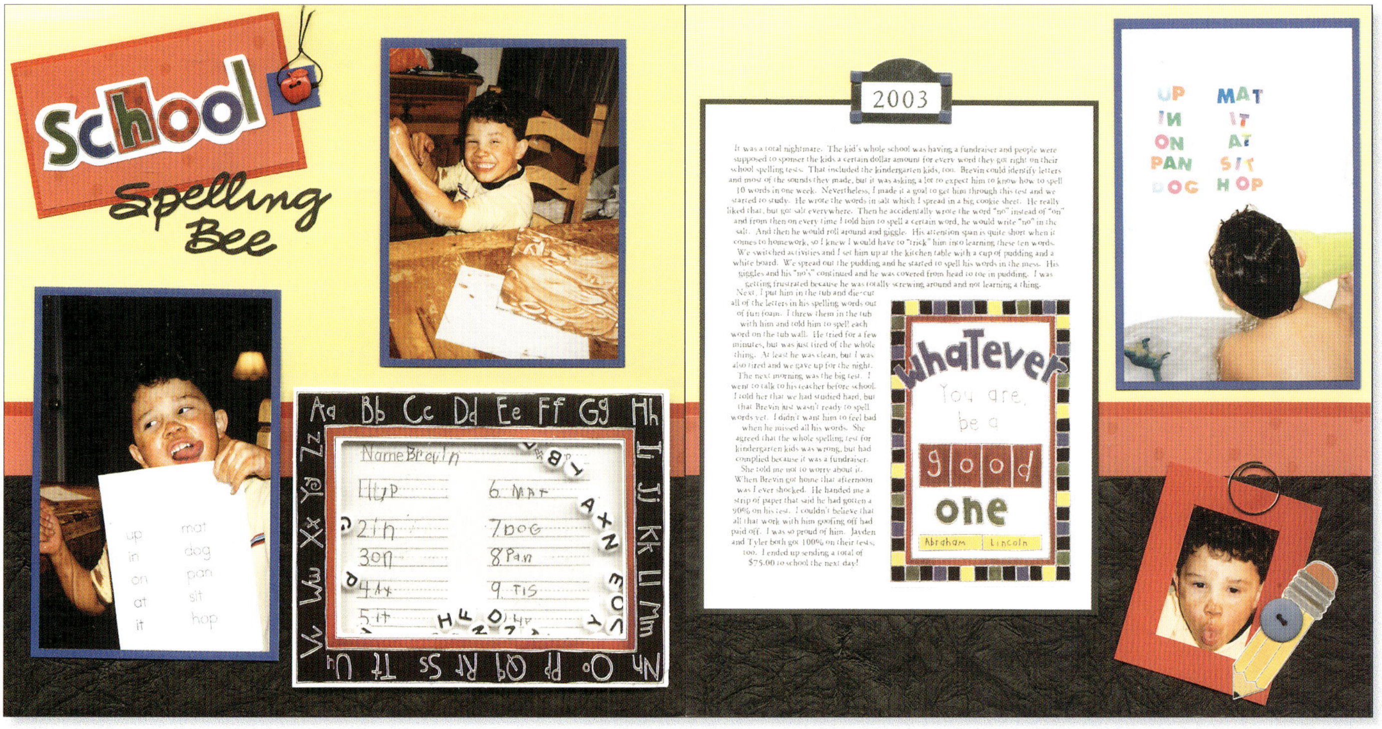
School
Spelling Bee
2003
It was a total nightmare. The kid's whole school was having a fundraiser and people were supposed to sponser the kids a certain dollar amount for every word they got right on their school spelling tests. That included the kindergarten kids, too. Brevin could identify letters and most of the sounds they made, but it was asking a lot to expect him to know how to spell 10 words in one week. Nevertheless, I made it a goal to get him through this test and we started to study. He wrote the words in salt which I spread in a big cookie sheet. He really liked that, but got salt everywhere. Then he accidentally wrote the word "no" instead of "on" and from then on every time I told him to spell a certain word, he would write "no" in the salt. And then he would roll around and giggle. His attention span is quite short when it comes to homework, so I knew I would have to "trick" him into learning these ten words. We switched activities and I set him up at the kitchen table with a cup of pudding and a white board. We spread out the pudding and he started to spell his words in the mess. His giggles and his "no's" continued and he was covered from head to toe in pudding. I was getting frustrated because he was totally screwing around and not learning a thing.
Next, I put him in the tub and die-cut all of the letters in his spelling words out of fun foam. I threw them in the tub with him and told him to spell each word on the tub wall. He tried for a few minutes, but was just tired of the whole thing. At least he was clean, but I was also tired and we gave up for the night.
The next morning was the big test. I went to talk to his teacher before school. I told her that we had studied hard, but that Brevin just wasn't ready to spell words yet. I didn't want him to feel bad when he missed all his words. She agreed that the whole spelling test for kindergarten kids was wrong, but had complied because it was a fundraiser. She told me not to worry about it. When Brevin got home that afternoon was I ever shocked. He handed me a strip of paper that said he had gotten a 90% on his test. I couldn't believe that all that work with him goofing off had paid off. I was so proud of him. Jayden and Tyler both got 100% on their tests, too. I ended up sending a total of $75.00 to school the next day!
whatever
You are,
be a
good
one
Abraham Lincoln
UP
IN
ON
PAN
DOG
MAT
IT
AT
SIT
HOP

School Spelling Bee

Supplies

Crumpled paper: Provo Craft
Patterned paper: Lasting Impressions for Paper
Preprinted frame, quote, accent and title: My Mind's Eye
Computer fonts: CK Script, "The Best of Creative Lettering" CD Vol. 1, *Creating Keepsakes*; P22 Garamouche, Impress Rubber Stamps
Bookplate: Making Memories
Buttons: Buttons Galore (apple), Making Memories (blue)
Brads: Provo Craft
Other: Letter beads, spiral paper clip and transparency paper

♥ **I Love It!:** *This frame was transformed into a shaker box accent. Clear transparency paper was adhered behind the frame. An actual spelling test was scanned and sized to provide the backdrop for the shaker box. 3-D foam tape was placed all the way around the edges of the spelling test backdrop, letter beads were placed inside, and the frame was placed on the 3-D foam tape, sealing all edges.*

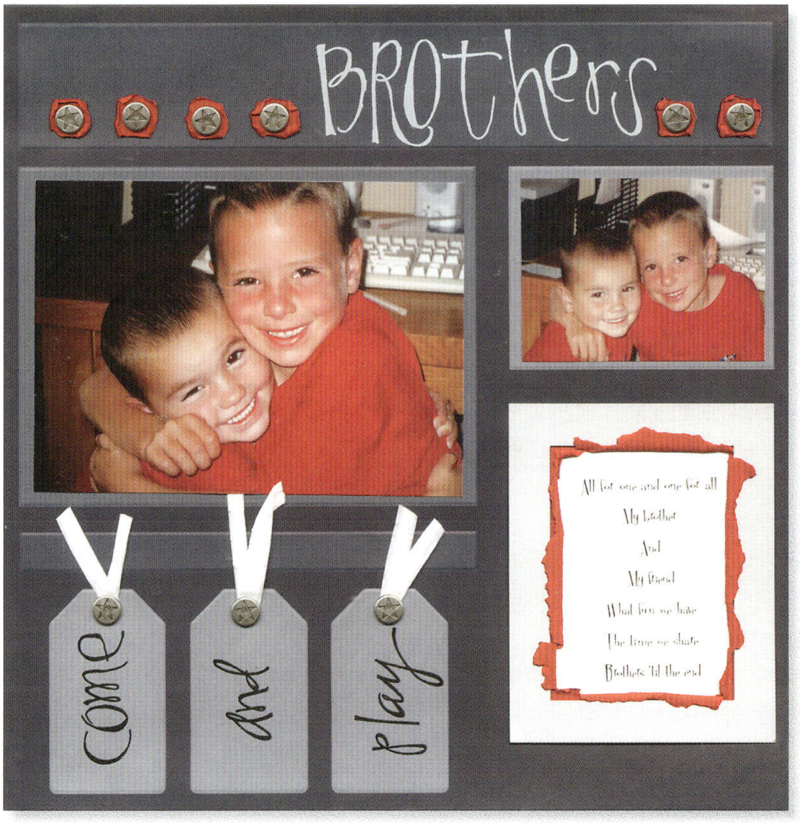
Brothers
All for one and one for all
My brother
And
My friend
What fun we have
The time we share
Brothers 'til the end
come
And
play

Brothers

Supplies

Pre-formatted paper: All My Memories
Preprinted poem: Tiny Tales, My Mind's Eye
Metal frame, rub-on words and star studs: Making Memories
Other: White paper ribbon

♥ **I Love It!:** *To create this adorable frame accent, the frame was placed on red cardstock. The center of the cardstock was torn around the edges of the frame, leaving a slight border. The border was then folded up around the edges of the frame.*

tip 7

arrange frames in a row to accent your pages.

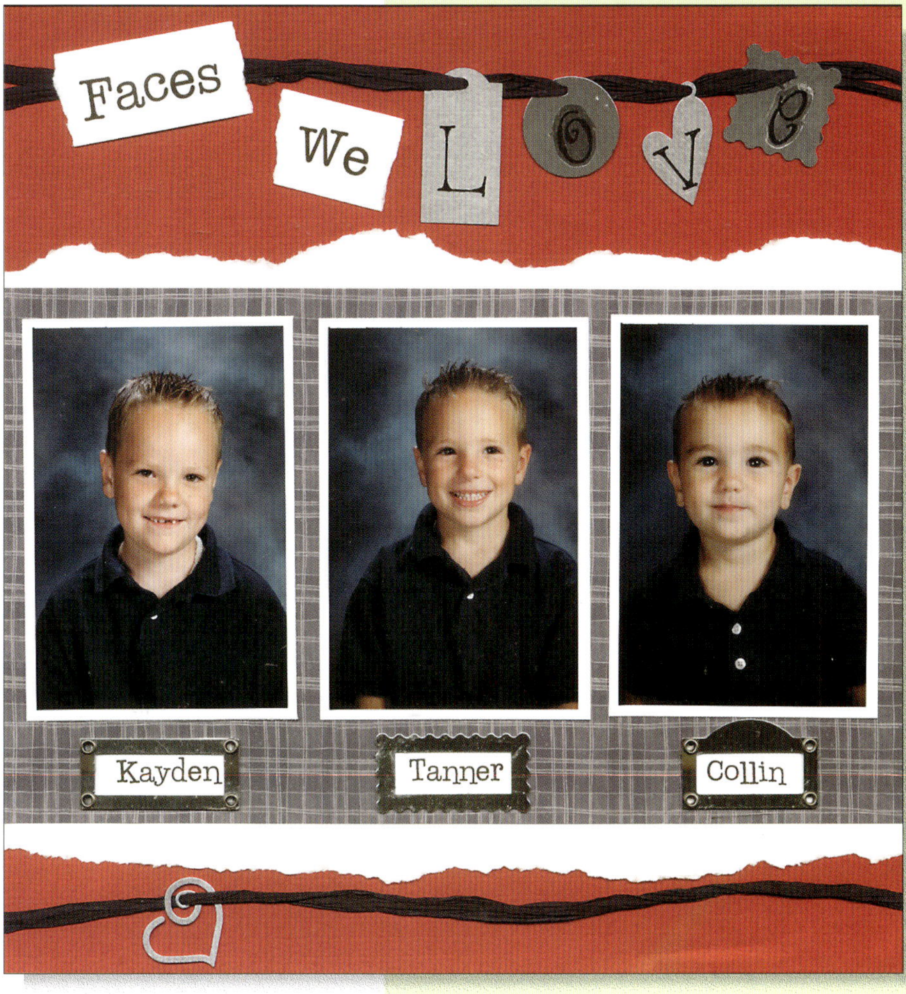
Faces
We
LOVE
Kayden
Tanner
Collin

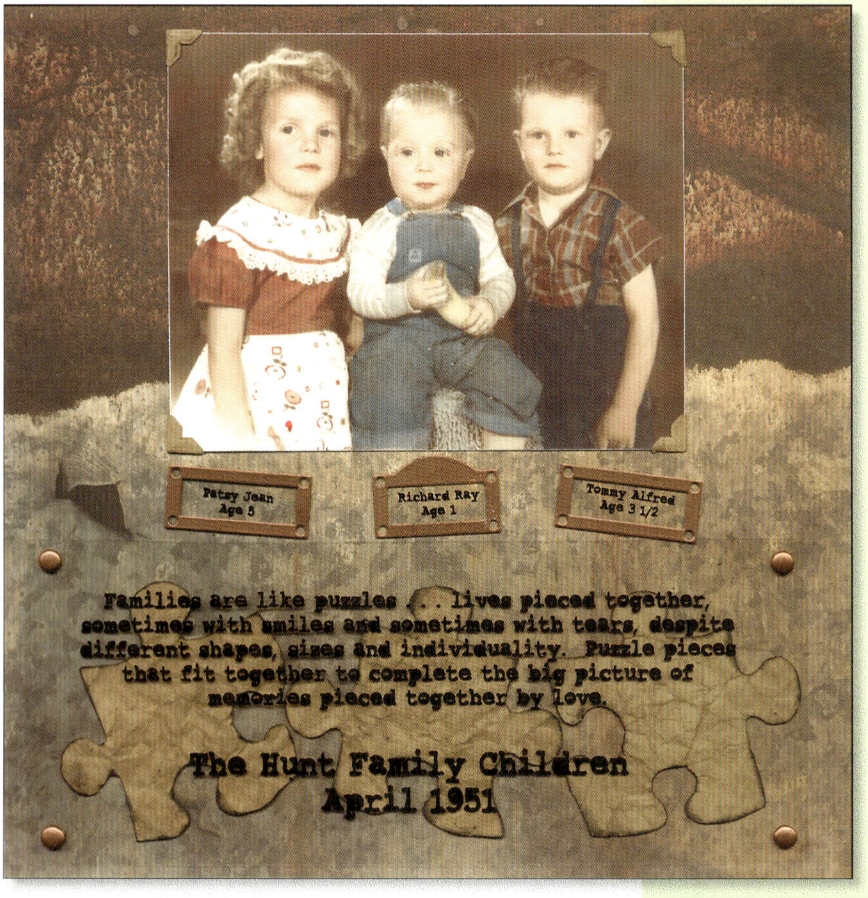
Patsy Jean
Age 5
Richard Ray
Age 1
Tommy Alfred
Age 3 1/2
Families are like puzzles . . . lives pieced together, sometimes with smiles and sometimes with tears, despite different shapes, sizes and individuality. Puzzle pieces that fit together to complete the big picture of memories pieced together by love.
The Hunt Family Children
April 1951

Faces We Love

Supplies

Patterned paper: Keeping Memories Alive
Letter stickers: Provo Craft
Metal tags, heart accent, eyelets and bookplates: Making Memories
Computer font: CK Stenography, "Fresh Fonts" CD, *Creating Keepsakes*
Other: Colored raffia

♥ **I Love It!:** *These adorable metal bookplate frames are perfect for including each child's name under his or her photograph. Mix and match different styles of bookplates for a less-formal page.*

Hunt Family Children

Supplies

Patterned paper: Paper Loft
Bookplates: Making Memories
Computer font: CK Typewriter, "Fresh Fonts" CD, *Creating Keepsakes*
Embossing Powder: Magic Dust
Other: Brads, transparency paper and photo corners

♥ **I Love It!:** *Although these metal bookplates and brads were originally silver, they didn't match the colors of the layout. They were each coated with embossing ink, dipped in copper embossing powder, and heat embossed so they would match the color scheme.*

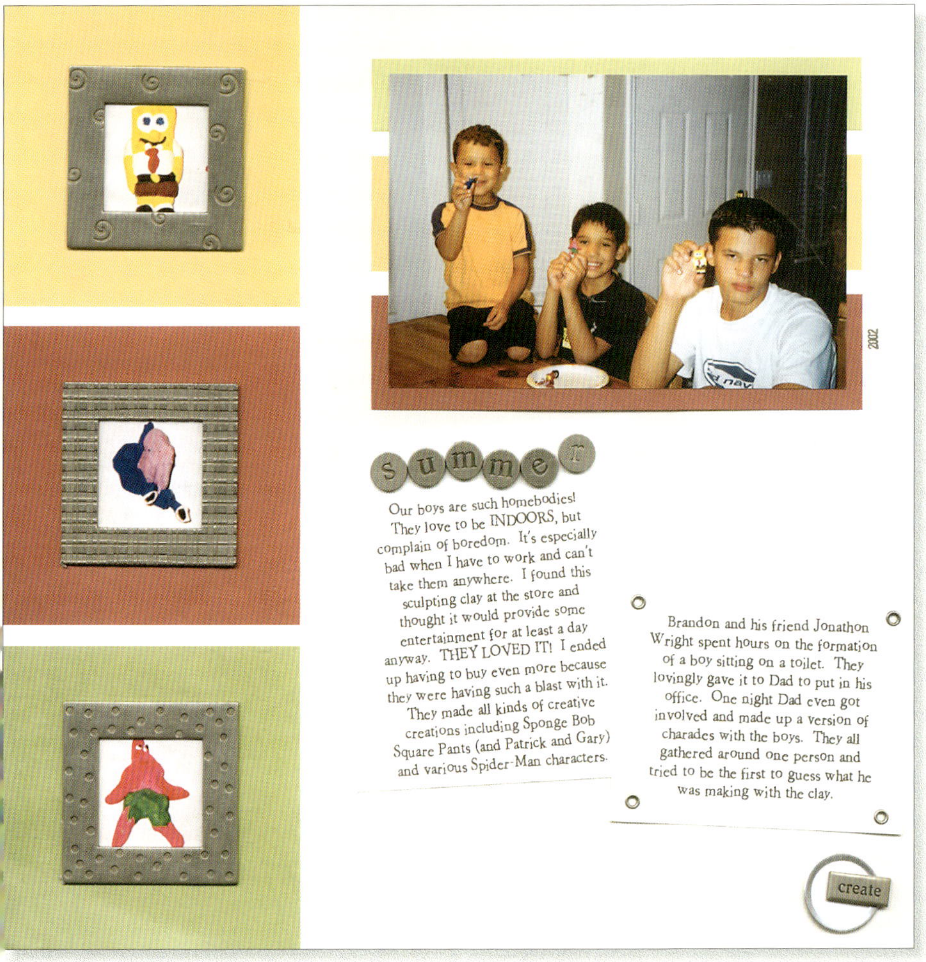
2002
summer
Our boys are such homebodies! They love to be INDOORS, but complain of boredom. It's especially bad when I have to work and can't take them anywhere. I found this sculpting clay at the store and thought it would provide some entertainment for at least a day anyway. THEY LOVED IT! I ended up having to buy even more because they were having such a blast with it. They made all kinds of creative creations including Sponge Bob Square Pants (and Patrick and Gary) and various Spider-Man characters.
Brandon and his friend Jonathon Wright spent hours on the formation of a boy sitting on a toilet. They lovingly gave it to Dad to put in his office. One night Dad even got involved and made up a version of charades with the boys. They all gathered around one person and tried to be the first to guess what he was making with the clay.
create

Summer

Supplies

Patterned paper: SEI
Metal accents and metal-rimmed tag: Making Memories
Computer font: CK Constitution, "Fresh Fonts" CD, *Creating Keepsakes*
Other: Date stamp

♥ **I Love It!:** *These metal frames, lined up in a row down the side of the page, showcase photographs of art projects.*

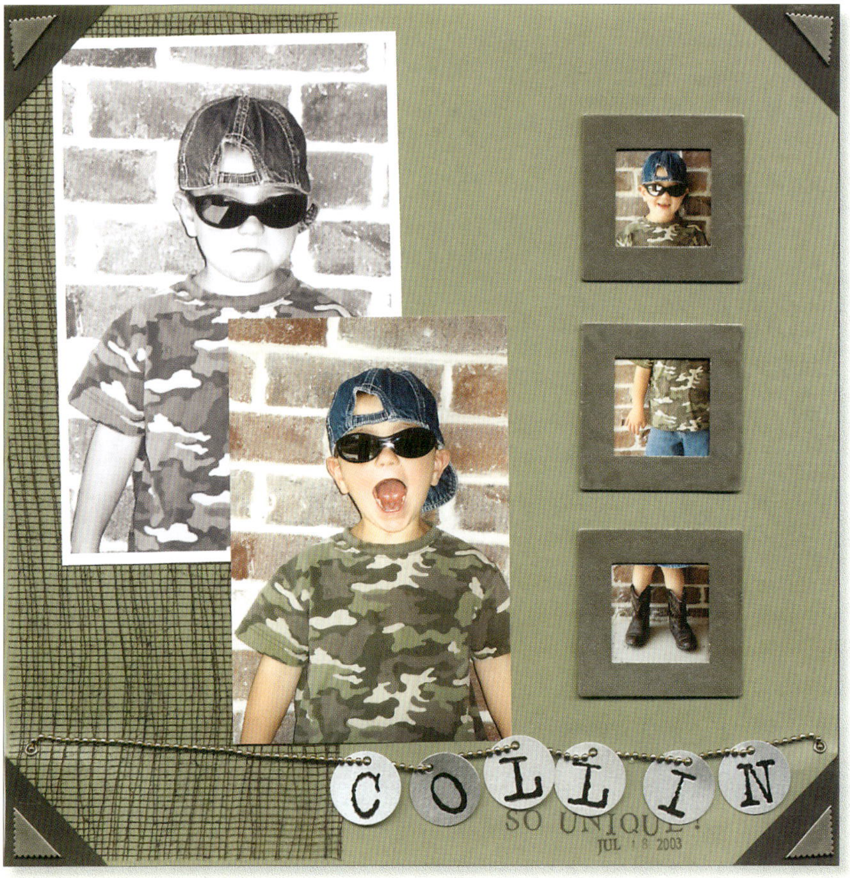
COLLIN
SO UNIQUE!

Collin

Supplies

Metal accents: Making Memories
Mesh: Magenta
Beaded chain: Westrim Crafts
Letter stamps: PSX Design
Stamping ink: ColorBox, Clearsnap
Other: Date stamp

♥ **I Love It!:** *These metal frames actually had different patterns on them. To make them match each other and coordinate better with the page, they were turned over. What you're looking at is actually the back of each frame!*

tip 8

integrate pre-made frames into another page element.

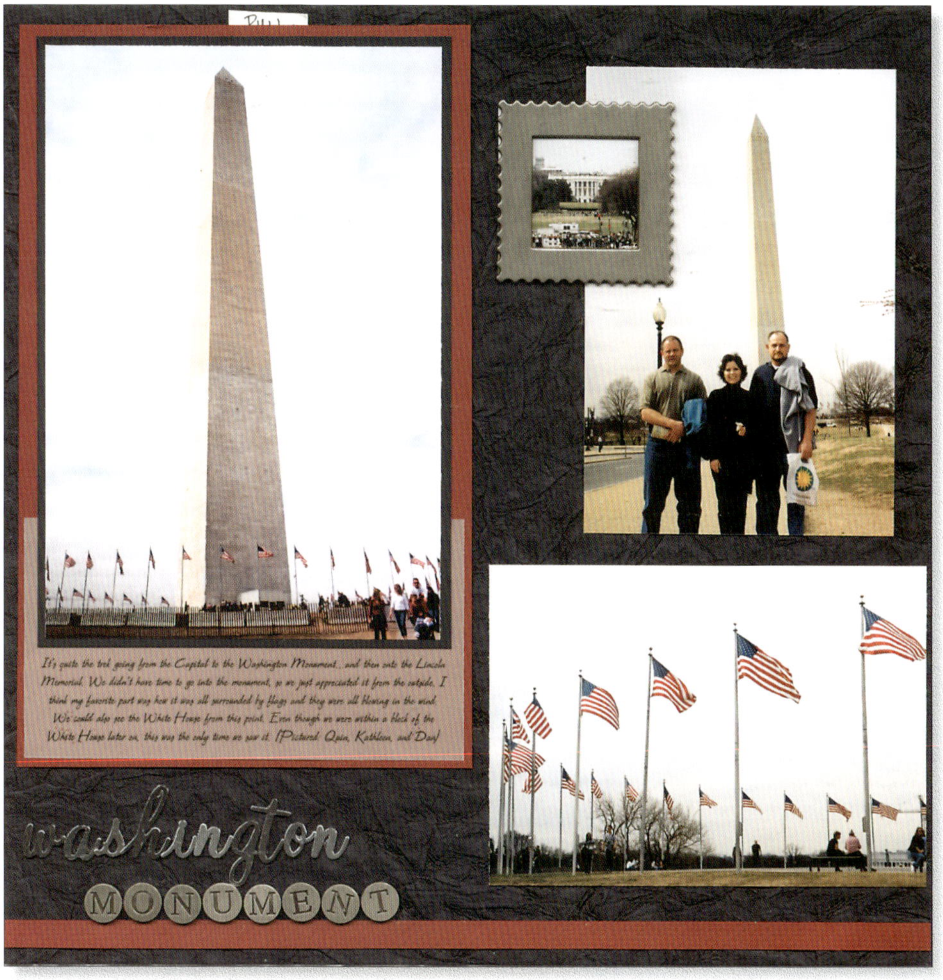
It's quite the trek going from the Capitol to the Washington Monument...and then onto the Lincoln Memorial. We didn't have time to go into the monument, so we just appreciated it from the outside. I think my favorite part was how it was all surrounded by flags and they were all blowing in the wind. We could also see the White House from this point. Even though we were within a block of the White House later on, this was the only time we saw it. (Pictured: Quin, Kathleen, and Dan)
washington
MONUMENT

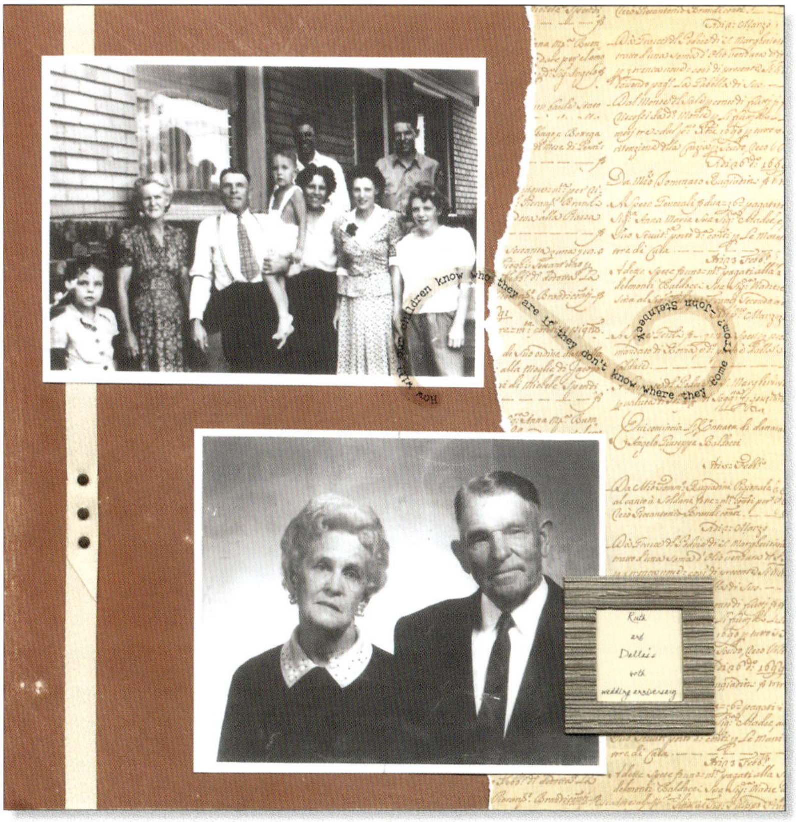

Washington Monument

Supplies
Crumpled paper: Provo Craft
Metal accents: Making Memories
Computer font: CAC Leslie, downloaded from the Internet

♥ **I Love It!:** *If you have a photograph with a far-away subject you just have to include on your layout, draw attention to it by cropping the photo closely around the subject, then placing it in a metal frame. The metal will help the smaller photograph stand out against the larger photographs.*

Wedding Anniversary

Supplies
Patterned papers: Design Originals
Quote sticker: Phrase Café, EK Success
Metal frame, ribbon and brads: Making Memories

♥ **I Love It!:** *Don't want your title to steal the show? Typing the title in a nice font, placing it in a metal frame and overlapping it slightly onto a photograph will make it visible but not dominant on your layout.*

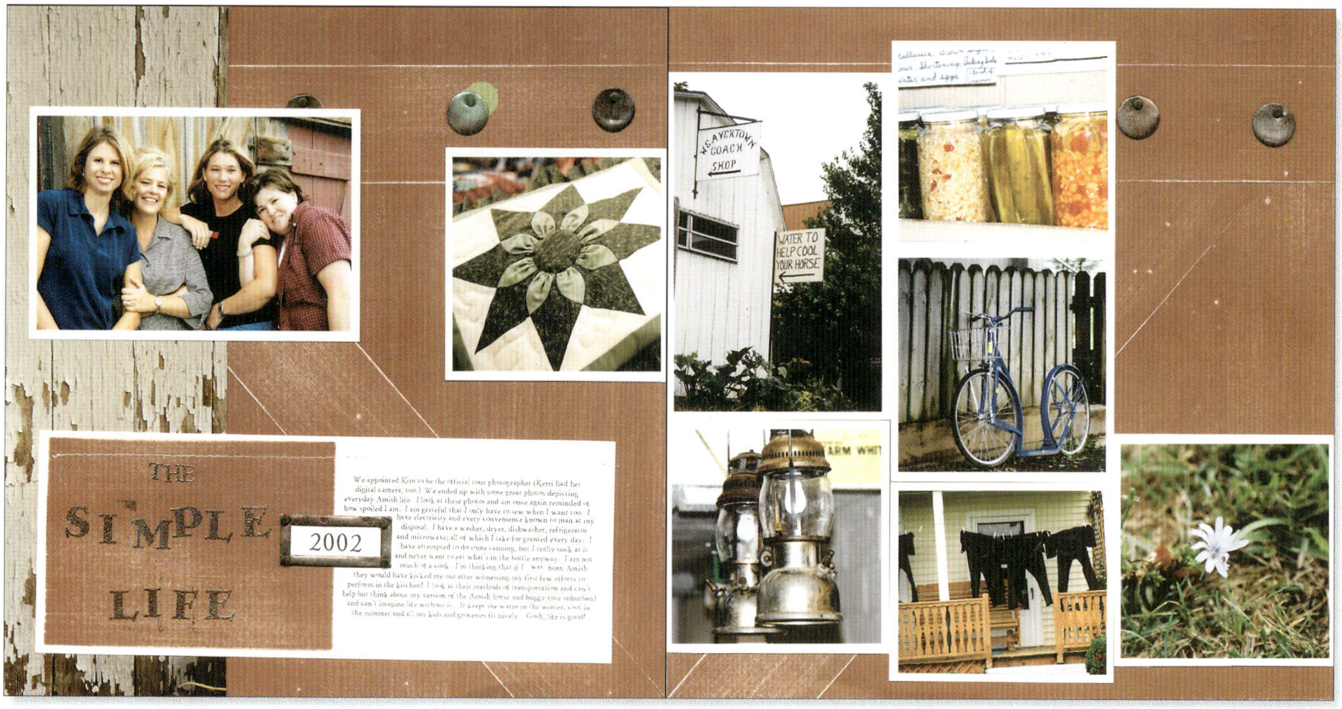
THE SIMPLE LIFE
2002
WATER TO HELP COOL YOUR HORSE

The Simple Life

Supplies
Patterned paper: Provo Craft
Photographic border: Shotz by Danelle Johnson, Creative Imaginations
Bookplate, charms and brads: Making Memories
Letter stamps: Barnes and Noble
Stamping ink: ColorBox, Clearsnap
Embossing powder: Stamp-n-Stuff, Stampendous!
Computer font: CK Constitution, "Fresh Fonts" CD, *Creating Keepsakes*

♥ **I Love It!:** *I love asking my photo developer to leave a thin, white border around my photographs. Create a uniform look when cropping your photographs by cutting thin strips of white cardstock to replace any white edges you may have trimmed from them.*

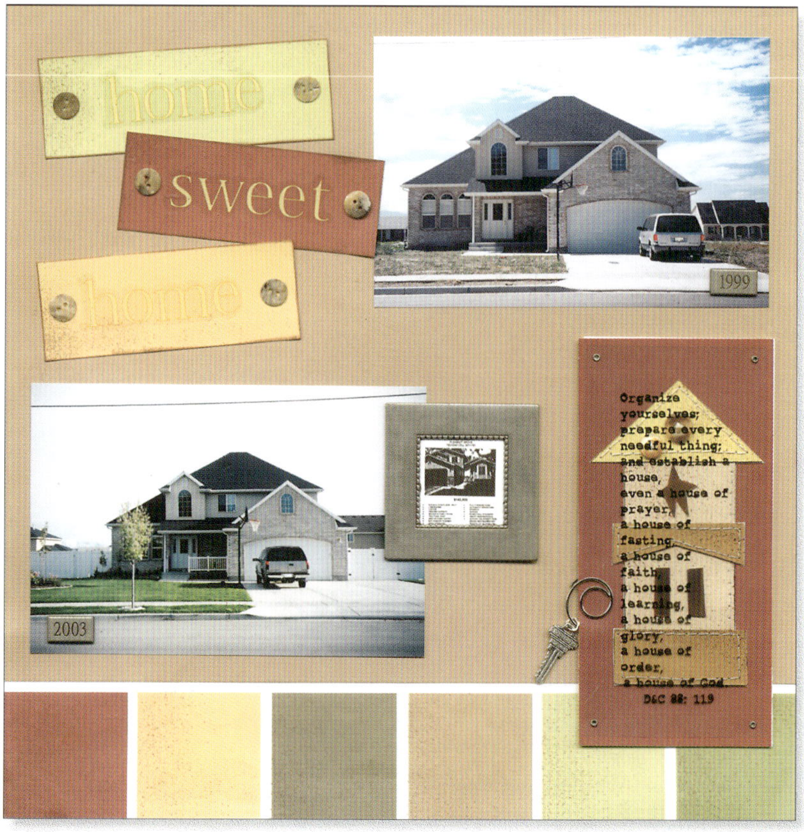
home
sweet
home
1999
2003
Organize yourselves; prepare every needful thing; and establish a house, even a house of prayer, a house of fasting, a house of faith, a house of learning, a house of glory, a house of order, a house of God.
D&C 88: 119

Home Sweet Home

Supplies
Patterned paper and stickers: SEI
Preprinted accent: Fresh Cuts, EK Success
Metal accents: Making Memories
Key charm: Lasting Impressions for Paper
Computer fonts: CK Typewriter and CK Newsprint, "Fresh Fonts" CD, *Creating Keepsakes*
Ink spritzer: Color Workshop
Other: Spiral paper clip and buttons

♥ **I Love It!:** *The metal frame on this layout holds a small printout of the house listing.*

♥ **I Love It!:** *Underneath the house accent is an accordion-folded piece of cardstock that contains journaling and information about the house.*

tips

lisa's lessons on frames

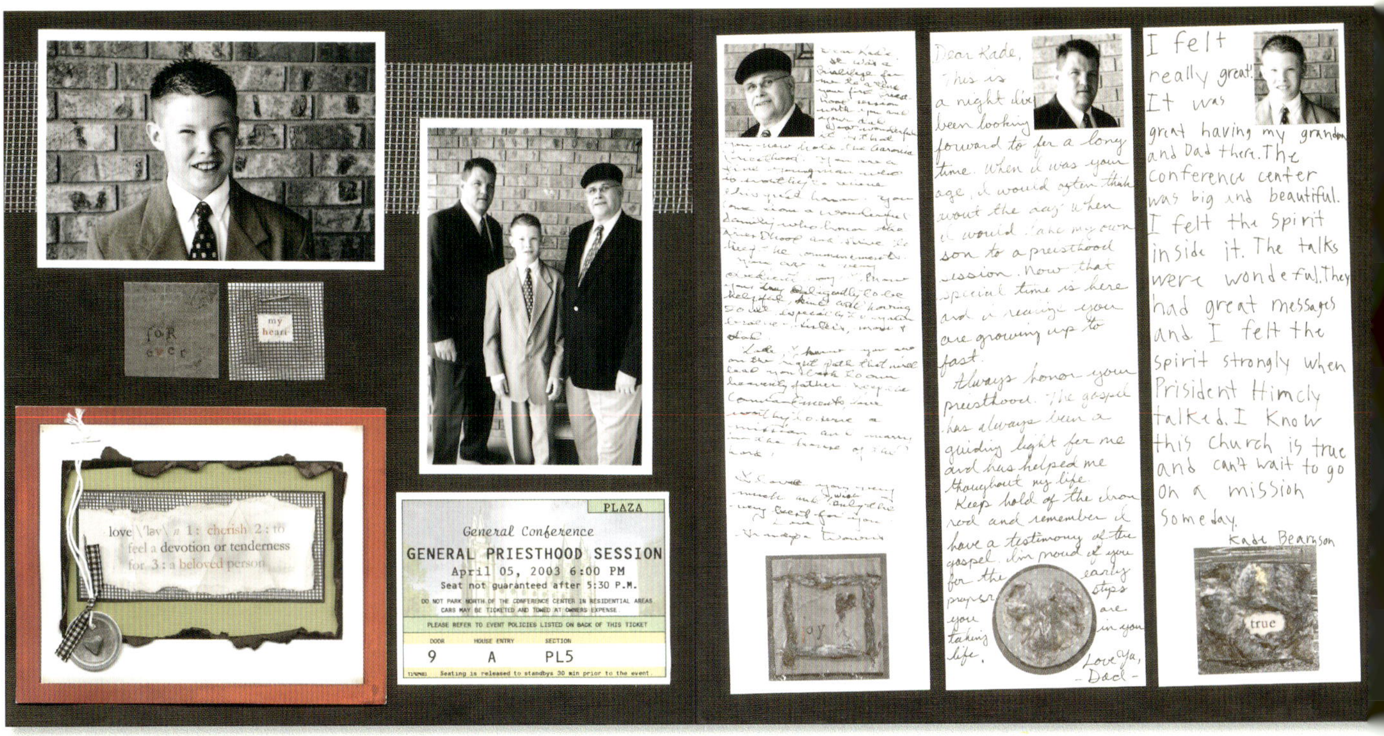

Take advantage of pre-made frames as a great way to draw attention to important page elements without spending a lot of time. Here are two tips to keep in mind when using pre-made frames:

- Pre-made frames aren't just for photographs! Use them to frame quotes, titles, definitions, accents, memorabilia or other items on your page.
- Just because a frame is pre-made doesn't mean you have to use it as is. Customizing frames to make them perfect for the individual layout you're creating can be quick, easy and very rewarding. For example, the ripped cardstock frame placed inside the pre-made frame on the layout above was a simple way to create a more "artsy" feel that matched the rest of the layout.

Three more favorite tips from this page:

- Using pop dots under pre-made frames, or other pre-made products, gives depth and dimension to layouts. Make sure the raised element is an important part of the page, as it will naturally draw the eye.
- Let family members write in their own handwriting on your pages. Even if their handwriting looks like "chicken scratch," you'll come to love the precious memories it will invoke for years to come.
- Don't ever hesitate to dedicate a full page—yes, even if you scrapbook in the 12" x 12" format!—to journaling. Photographs are important, but even more important are the memories you want to preserve for yourself and your family. Sometimes words, a lot of words, are the only way to capture the whole memory.

General Session

Supplies
Preprinted frame: My Mind's Eye
Stickers: Memories Complete
Metal-rimmed tag and heart brad: Making Memories
Mesh: Magic Mesh
Pen: Zig Writer, EK Success
Other: Ribbon

lisa says:

"I love taking advantage of all the preprinted, and often coordinating, titles and borders out there! They're a *quick* way to put a *finishing* touch on your layouts. Here are some great ideas for making the most of these *versatile,* convenient products."

TITLES & BORDERS

ch. 5

terrific titles & borders

TITLE *n.* *a descriptive or general heading*

BORDER *n. a plain or decorative margin around printed matter*

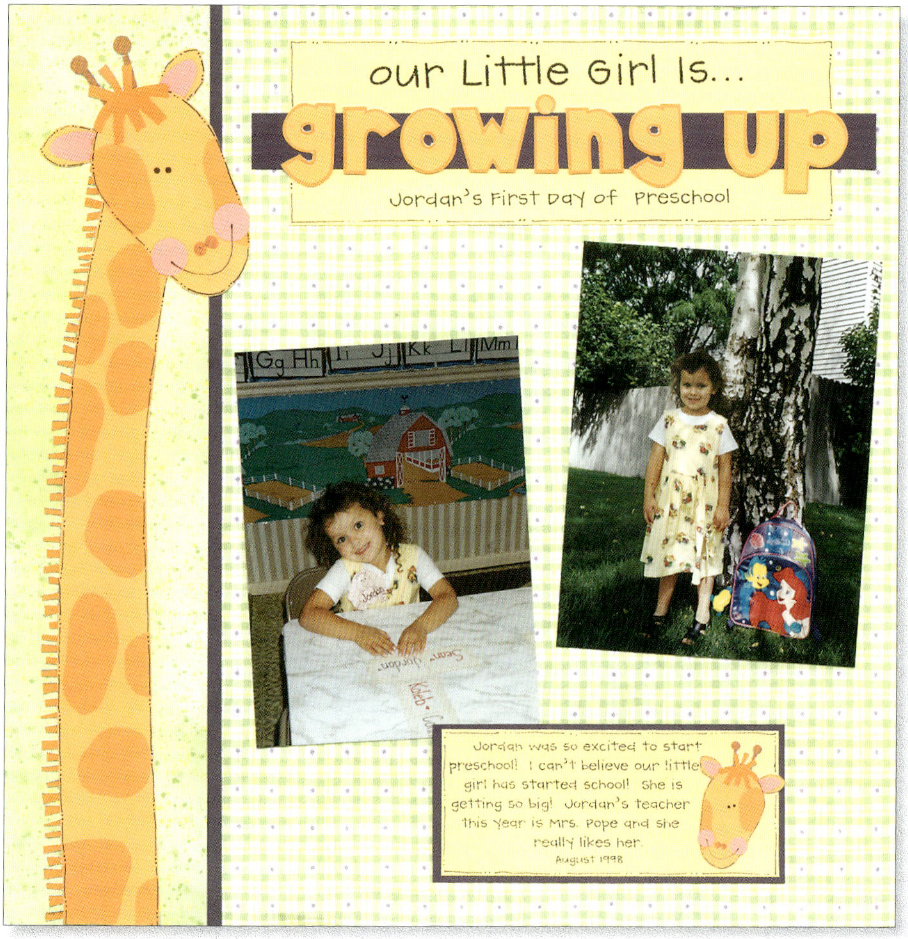

our Little Girl is...
growing up
Jordan's First Day of Preschool
Jordan was so excited to start preschool! I can't believe our little girl has started school! She is getting so big! Jordan's teacher this year is Mrs. Pope and she really likes her.
August 1998

Growing Up

Supplies
Patterned papers: Doodlebug Design (plaid), Provo Craft (speckle)
Title and giraffe border: EK Success
Computer font: CK Handprint, "The Best of Creative Lettering" CD Combo, *Creating Keepsakes*
Pen: Zig Writer, EK Success

♥ I Love It!: *To create a sense of unity on the page, the dot-and-line border around the preprinted giraffe accent was repeated around the title and journaling blocks.*

tip 1

trim preprinted titles into new shapes to suit your layout.

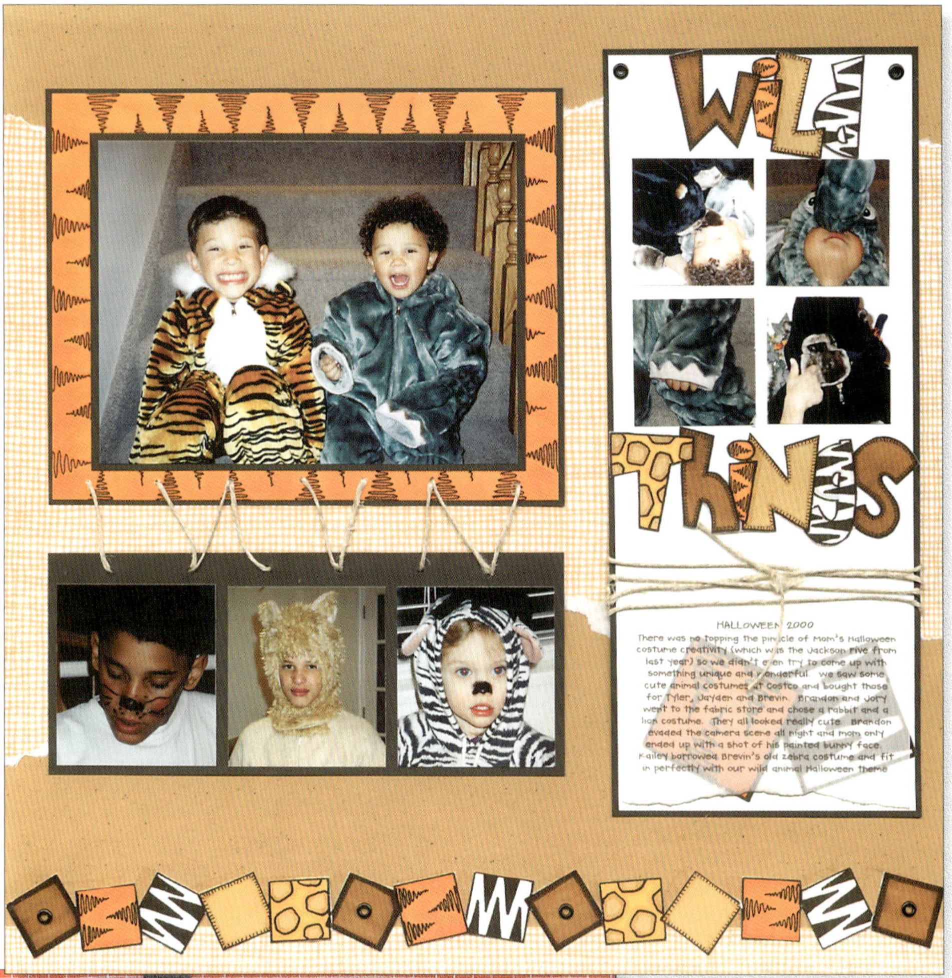

Wild Things
HALLOWEEN 2000
There was no topping the pinnacle of Mom's Halloween costume creativity (which was the Jackson Five from last year) so we didn't even try to come up with something unique and wonderful. We saw some cute animal costumes at Costco and bought those for Tyler, Jayden and Brevin. Brandon and Jory went to the fabric store and chose a rabbit and a lion costume. They all looked really cute. Brandon evaded the camera scene all night and mom only ended up with a shot of his painted bunny face. Kailey borrowed Brevin's old zebra costume and fit in perfectly with our wild animal Halloween theme

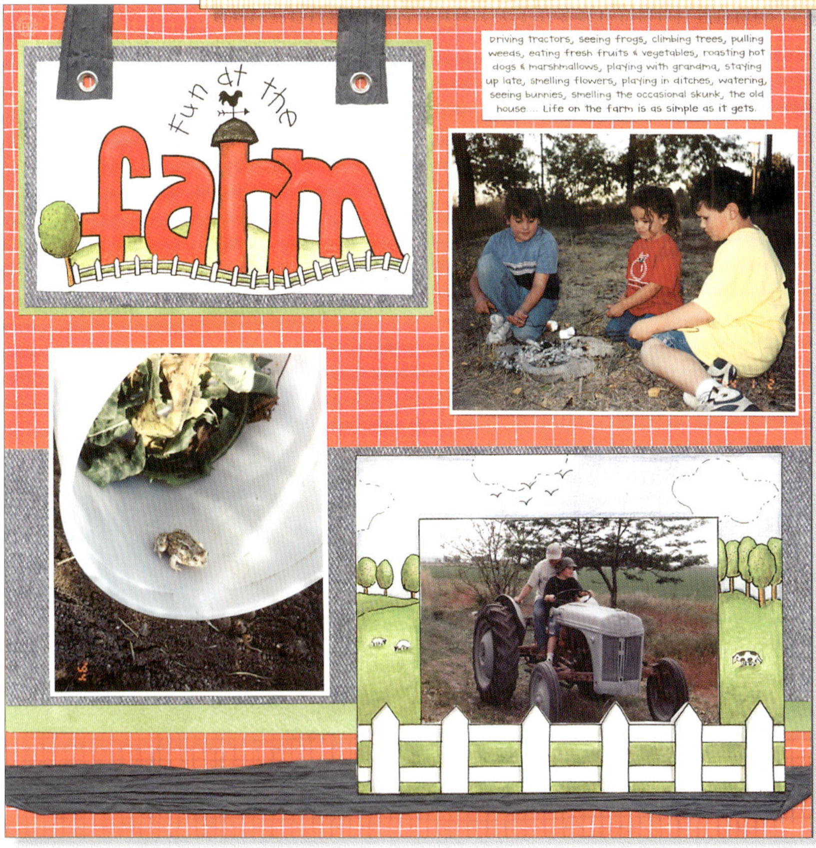

fun at the farm
Driving tractors, seeing frogs, climbing trees, pulling weeds, eating fresh fruits & vegetables, roasting hot dogs & marshmallows, playing with grandma, staying up late, smelling flowers, playing in ditches, watering, seeing bunnies, smelling the occasional skunk, the old house... Life on the farm is as simple as it gets.

Wild Things

Supplies

Patterned paper: Cock-A-Doodle Design
Preprinted frame, title and border: Cock-A-Doodle Design
Computer font: CK Journaling, "The Best of Creative Lettering" CD Vol. 2, *Creating Keepsakes*
Other: Eyelets and jute

♥ I Love It!: *This preprinted title was silhouetted from its white background so the words could be used separately on the layout.*

Fun at the Farm

Supplies

Patterned papers: Doodlebug Design (plaid), Provo Craft (denim and green)
Preprinted frame and title: My Mind's Eye
Computer font: CK Handprint, "The Best of Creative Lettering" CD Combo, *Creating Keepsakes*
Other: Eyelets and raffia

♥ I Love It!: *This title was triple matted and hung from the top of the layout with two strips of raffia and eyelets.*

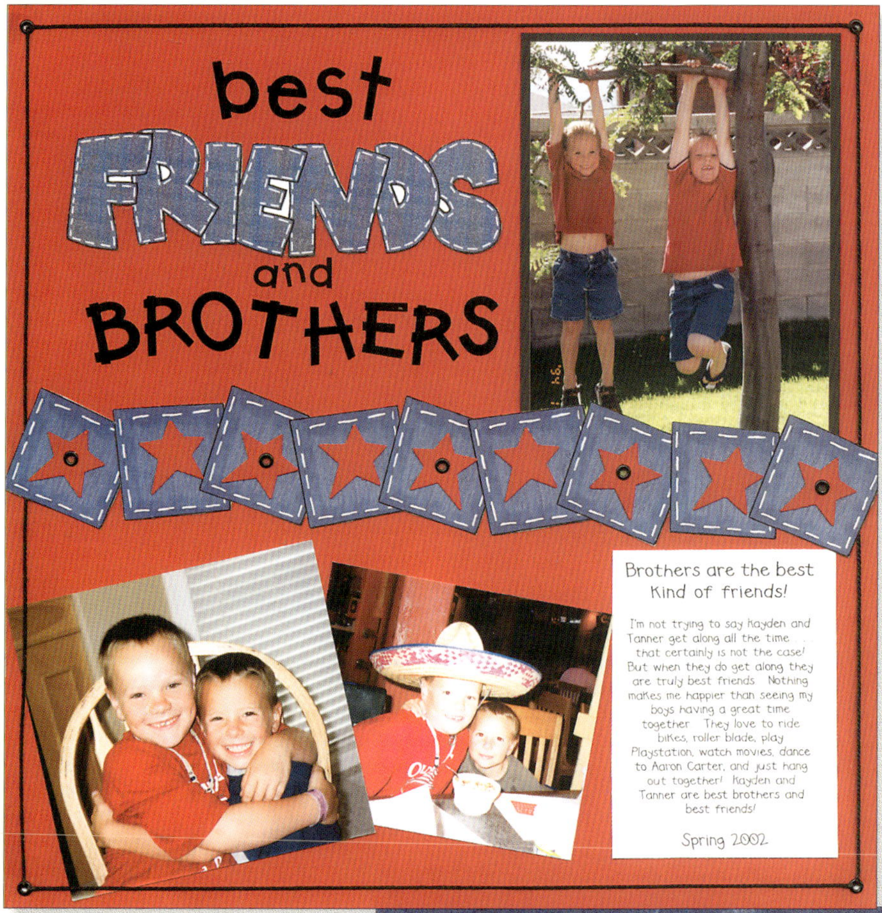
best
FRIENDS
and
BROTHERS
Brothers are the best Kind of friends!
I'm not trying to say Kayden and Tanner get along all the time . . . that certainly is not the case! But when they do get along they are truly best friends. Nothing makes me happier than seeing my boys having a great time together. They love to ride bikes, roller blade, play Playstation, watch movies, dance to Aaron Carter, and just hang out together! Kayden and Tanner are best brothers and best friends!
Spring 2002

Best Friends and Brothers

Supplies

Preprinted title and border: My Mind's Eye
Letter stickers: Stickopotamus, EK Success
Computer font: Unknown
Eyelets: Making Memories
Star punch: Posh Impressions
Other: Embroidery floss

♥ **I Love It!:** *Instead of matting the entire design with cardstock to create a thin border around the page, embroidery floss was threaded through eyelets in each corner of the page to create a visual frame.*

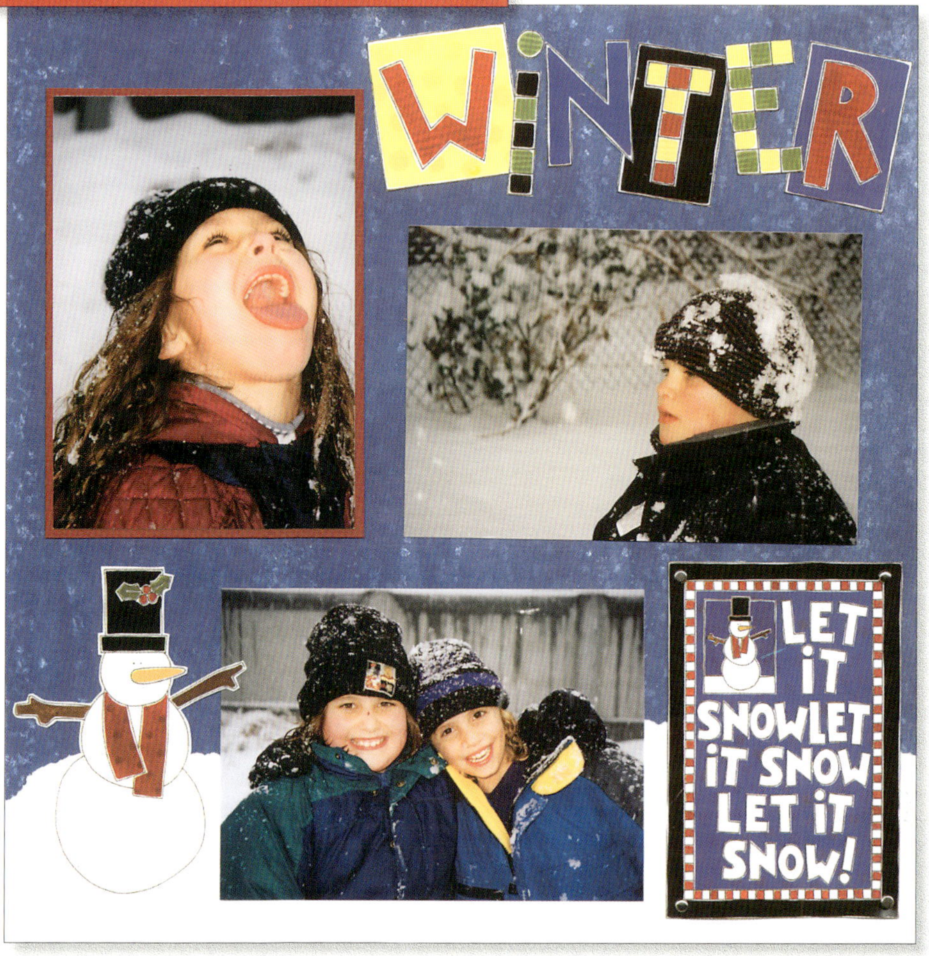
WINTER
LET IT SNOW LET IT SNOW LET IT SNOW!

Winter

Supplies

Patterned paper: Karen Foster Design
Preprinted title, quote and accent: My Mind's Eye
Other: Brads

♥ **I Love It!:** *Each letter was trimmed from the white background so the letters could be tilted and overlapped on this layout.*

tip 2

layer pre-made borders to add dimension to your pages.

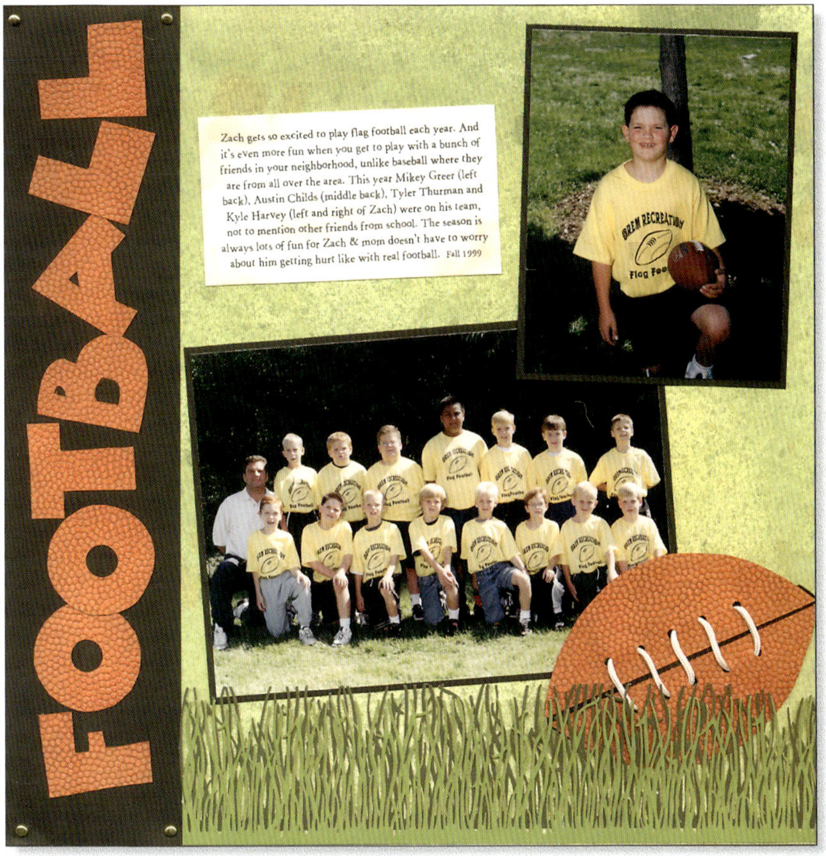
FOOTBALL
Zach gets so excited to play flag football each year. And it's even more fun when you get to play with a bunch of friends in your neighborhood, unlike baseball where they are from all over the area. This year Mikey Greer (left back), Austin Childs (middle back), Tyler Thurman and Kyle Harvey (left and right of Zach) were on his team, not to mention other friends from school. The season is always lots of fun for Zach & mom doesn't have to worry about him getting hurt like with real football. Fall 1999

Football

Supplies

Patterned paper, lettering template and laser-cut grass border: Provo Craft
Textured paper: Freckle Press
Computer font: P22 Garamouche, Impress Rubber Stamps
Chalks: Craf-T Products
Other: Cord

♥ I Love It!: *This cool grass border was created with two of the same laser-cut grass borders in different shades of green. The grass borders come in two different colors so they can be layered and staggered for variation in the blades of grass.*

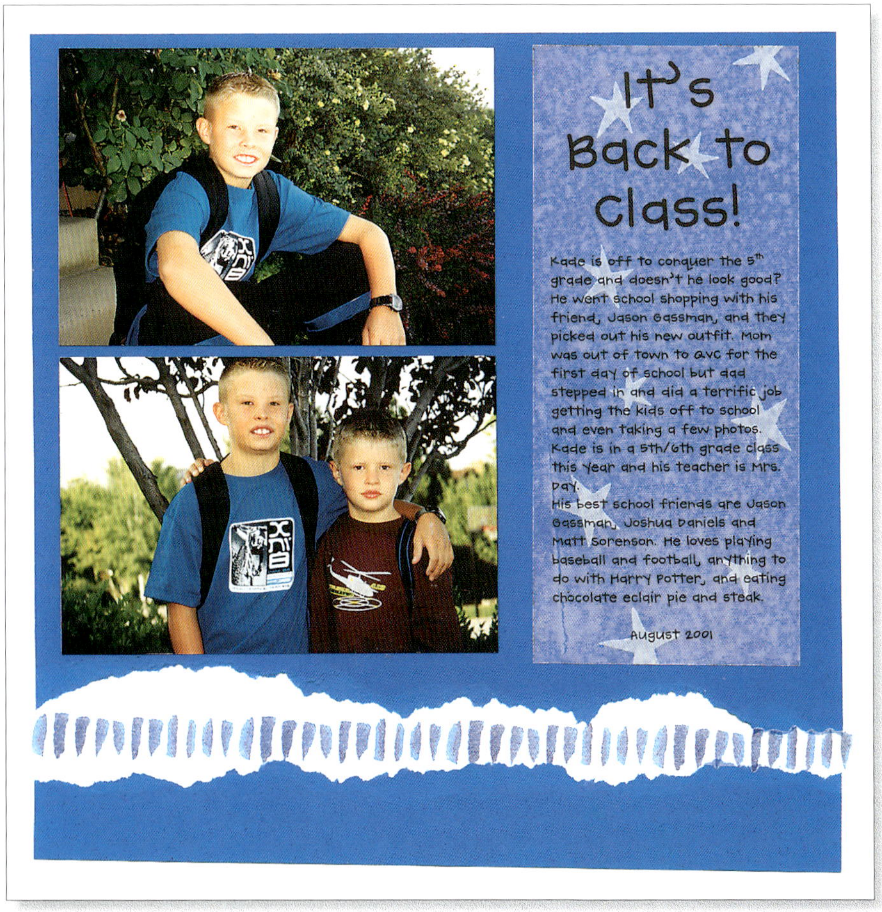
It's Back to Class!
Kade is off to conquer the 5th grade and doesn't he look good? He went school shopping with his friend, Jason Gassman, and they picked out his new outfit. Mom was out of town to QVC for the first day of school but dad stepped in and did a terrific job getting the kids off to school and even taking a few photos. Kade is in a 5th/6th grade class this year and his teacher is Mrs. Day.
His best school friends are Jason Gassman, Joshua Daniels and Matt Sorenson. He loves playing baseball and football, anything to do with Harry Potter, and eating chocolate eclair pie and steak.
August 2001

It's Back to Class

Supplies

Patterned vellum: Printworks
Preprinted border: Printworks
Computer font: CK Handprint, "The Best of Creative Lettering" CD Combo, *Creating Keepsakes*

♥ I Love It!: *Instead of layering this border on top of the background, the blue background cardstock was actually torn away in a strip to allow the border to be placed on the white background below.*

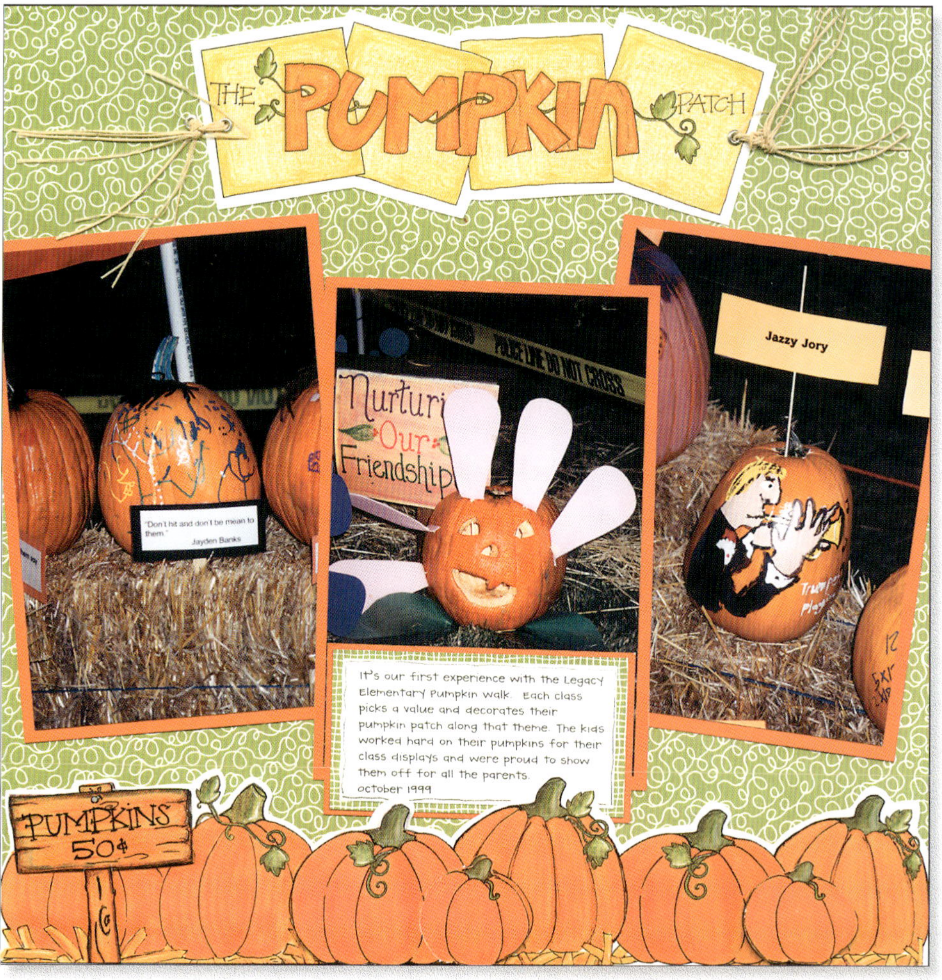
THE PUMPKIN PATCH
Jazzy Jory
It's our first experience with the Legacy Elementary Pumpkin walk. Each class picks a value and decorates their pumpkin patch along that theme. The kids worked hard on their pumpkins for their class displays and were proud to show them off for all the parents.
October 1999
PUMPKINS
50¢

The Pumpkin Patch

Supplies
Patterned papers: Provo Craft
Preprinted title and border: My Mind's Eye
Computer font: CK Handprint, "The Best of Creative Lettering" CD Combo, *Creating Keepsakes*
Other: 3-D foam adhesive, eyelets and raffia

♥ I Love It!: *This border was created by using two identical borders. The first border was placed along the bottom of the page. Then, the pumpkin sign and three pumpkins were cut from the second border and adhered to the first border using 3-D foam adhesive to add dimension.*

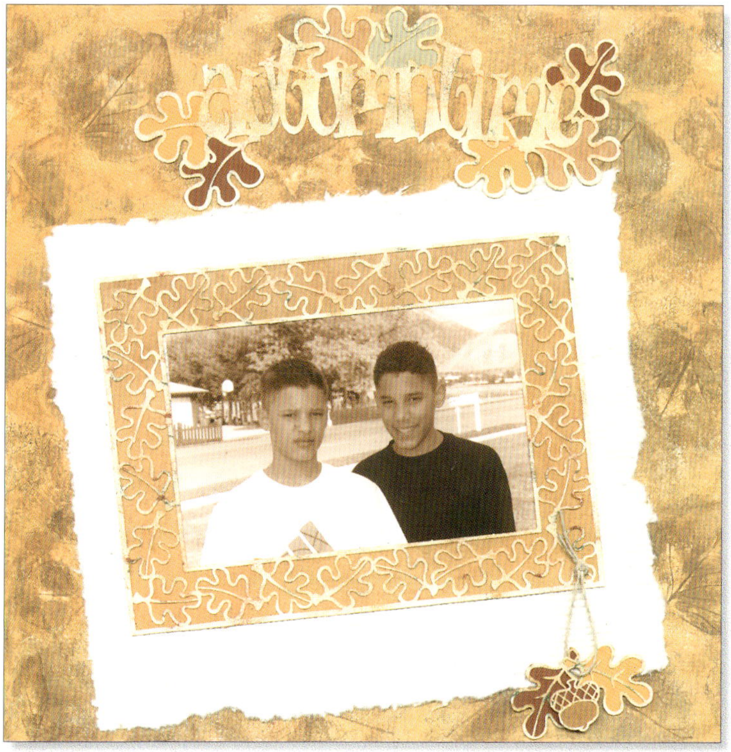

Autumn Time

Supplies
Patterned paper: Scrap-Ease
Laser-cut title, frame and accent: Laser Layouts, Provo Craft
Ink spritzer: Color Workshop

♥ I Love It!: *Different colors of cardstock were placed behind each laser-cut leaf on the title and accent to help the leaves stand out against the background.*

tip 3

extend preprinted titles and accents to fit the width of your page.

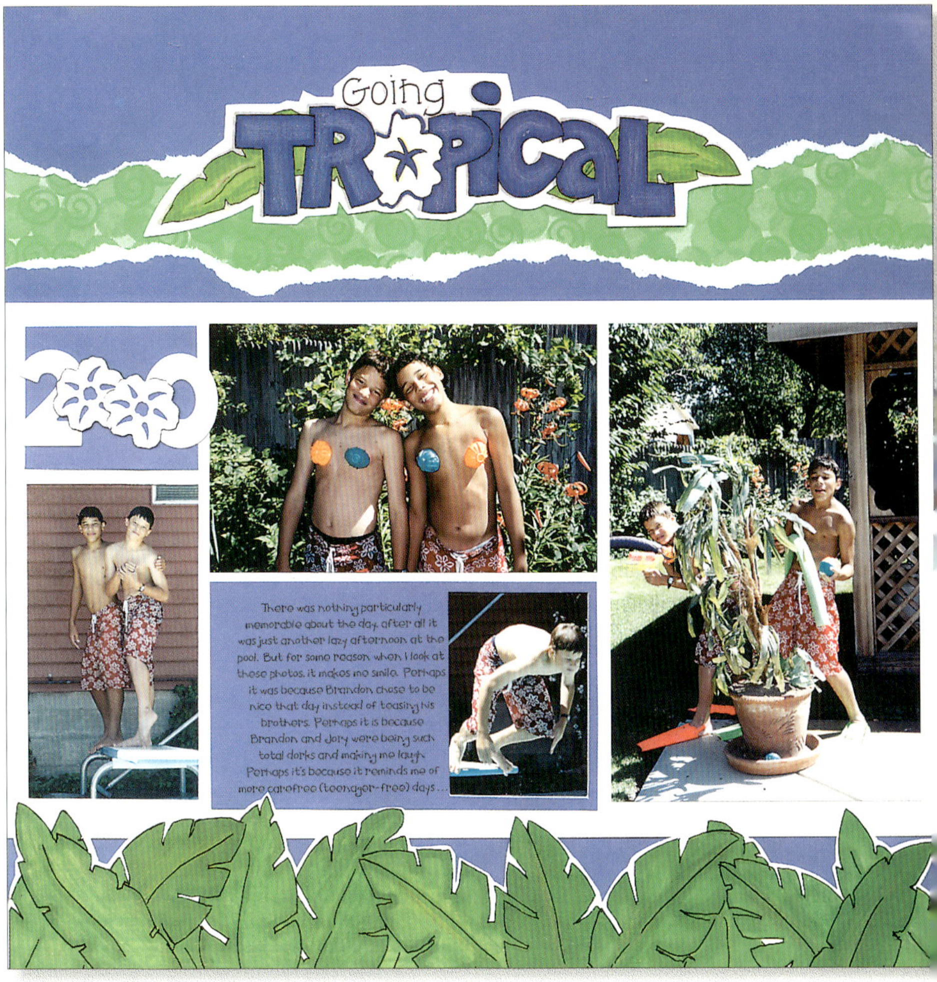
Going
TROPICAL
There was nothing particularly memorable about the day. after all it was just another lazy afternoon at the pool. But for some reason when I look at these photos, it makes me smile. Perhaps it was because Brandon chose to be nice that day instead of teasing his brothers. Perhaps it is because Brandon and Jory were being such total dorks and making me laugh. Perhaps it's because it reminds me of more carefree (teenager-free) days...

Going Tropical

Supplies

Patterned paper: Provo Craft
Preprinted title and border: My Mind's Eye
Number punches: EK Success
Flower punch: Family Treasures
Computer font: CK Fun, "The Art of Creative Lettering" CD, *Creating Keepsakes*

♥ I Love It!: *Keep an eye out for products that match the preprinted titles and borders you purchase (for example, the flower punch on this page matches the flower in the preprinted title). This flower punch is a perfect substitute for the two middle zeros in "2000."*

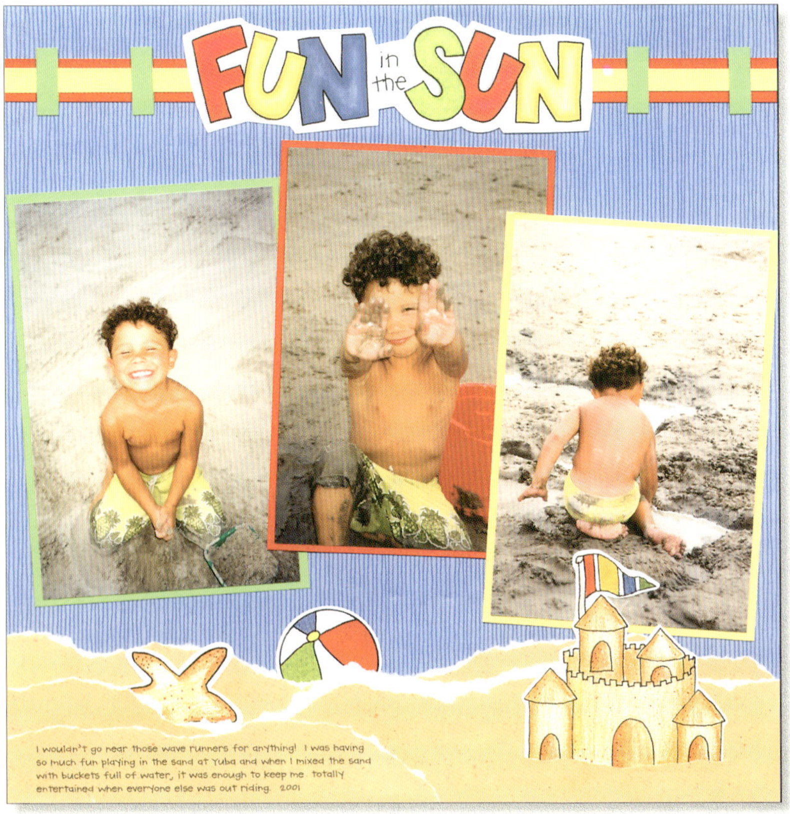
FUN in the SUN
I wouldn't go near those wave runners for anything! I was having so much fun playing in the sand at Yuba and when I mixed the sand with buckets full of water, it was enough to keep me totally entertained when everyone else was out riding. 2001

Fun in the Sun

Supplies

Patterned paper: Doodlebug Design
Preprinted title and accents: My Mind's Eye
Computer font: CK Handprint, "The Best of Creative Lettering" CD Combo, *Creating Keepsakes*

♥ I Love It!: *This beach border was created by tearing different lengths of sand patterned paper and overlapping them along the bottom of the page. Beach-themed accents were then tucked in between the layers of sand patterned paper.*

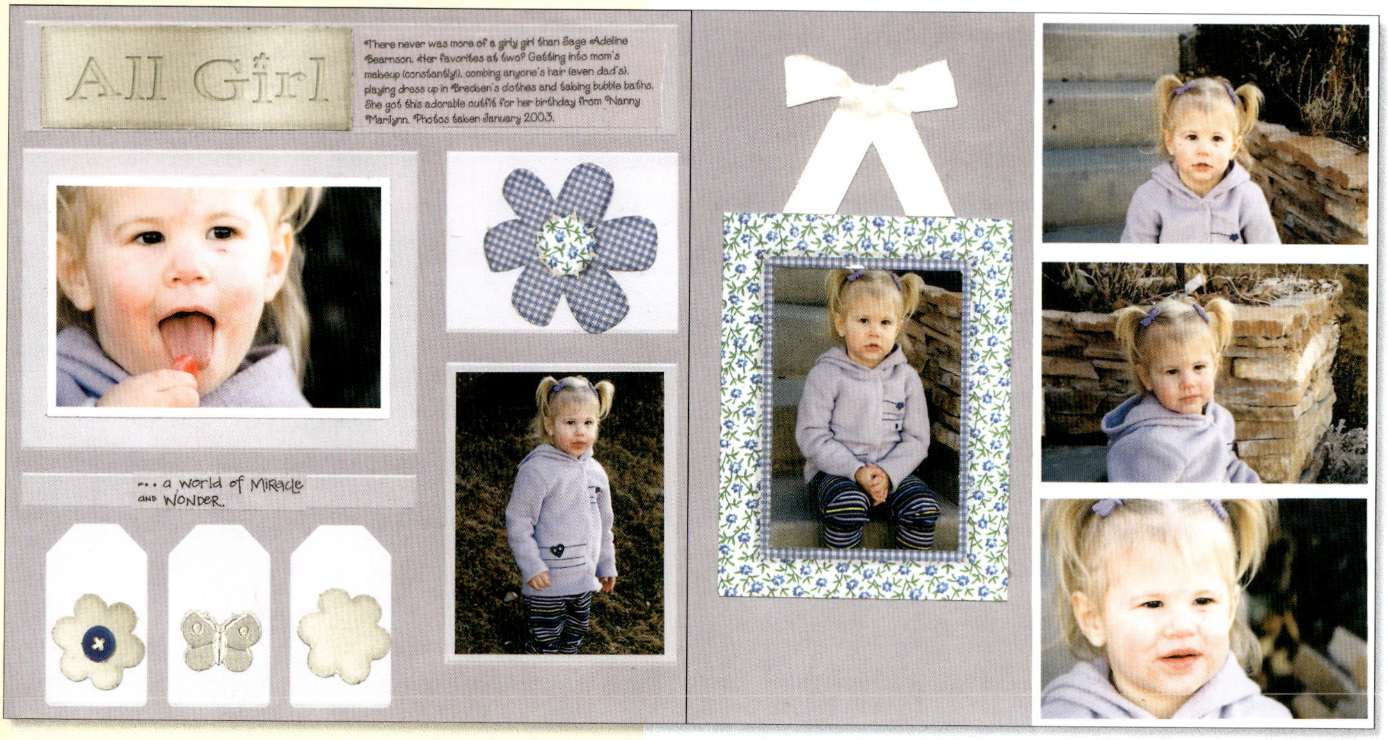
All Girl
There never was more of a girly girl than Sage Adeline Bearnson. Her favorites at two? Getting into mom's makeup (constantly!), combing anyone's hair (even dad's), playing dress up in Brecken's clothes and taking bubble baths. She got this adorable outfit for her birthday from Nanny Marilynn. Photos taken January 2003.
... a world of Miracle and Wonder

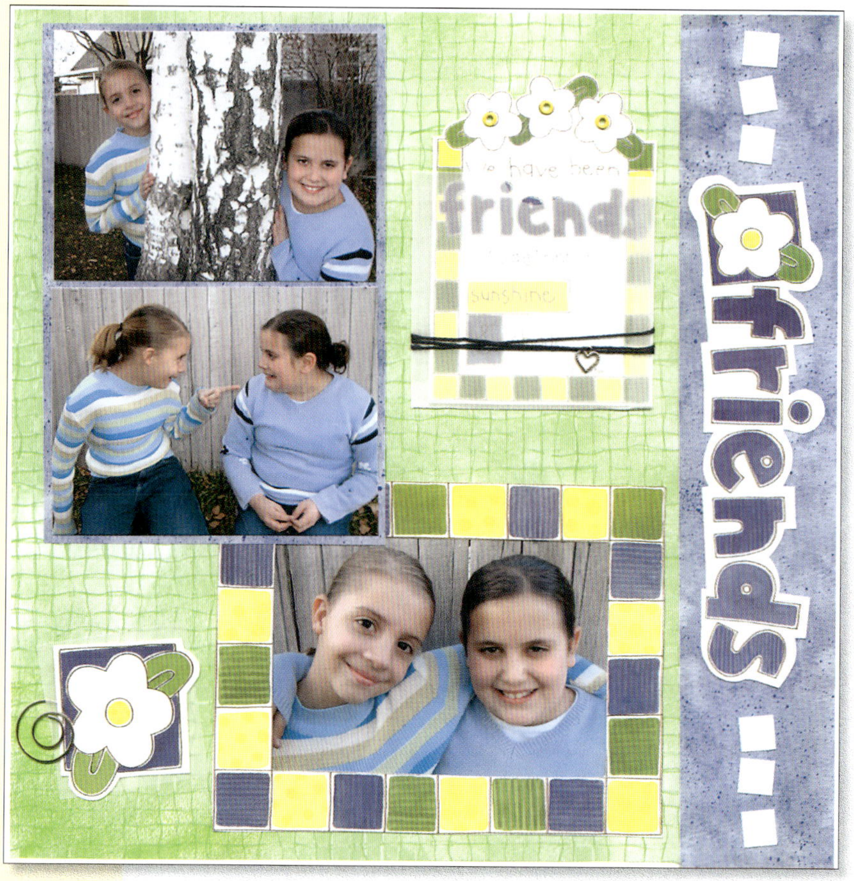
friends
friends

All Girl

Supplies

Pre-formatted paper: All My Memories
Preprinted title, frame and accents: My Mind's Eye
Vellum: Provo Craft
Computer font: CK Curly, "The Best of Creative Lettering" CD Combo, *Creating Keepsakes*

♥ I Love It!: *Combining the preprinted title and journaling onto one strip saves space and allows them to span the entire layout.*

Friends

Supplies

Patterned papers and vellum: Provo Craft
Preprinted title, frame, quote and accent: My Mind's Eye
Heart charm: American Tag Co.
Eyelets: Making Memories
Other: Embroidery floss and spiral paper clip

♥ I Love It!: *This quote accent was slipped into a handmade vellum envelope decorated with fibers and a tiny heart charm.*

tip 4

overlap photos onto preprinted borders for a unique, put-together look.

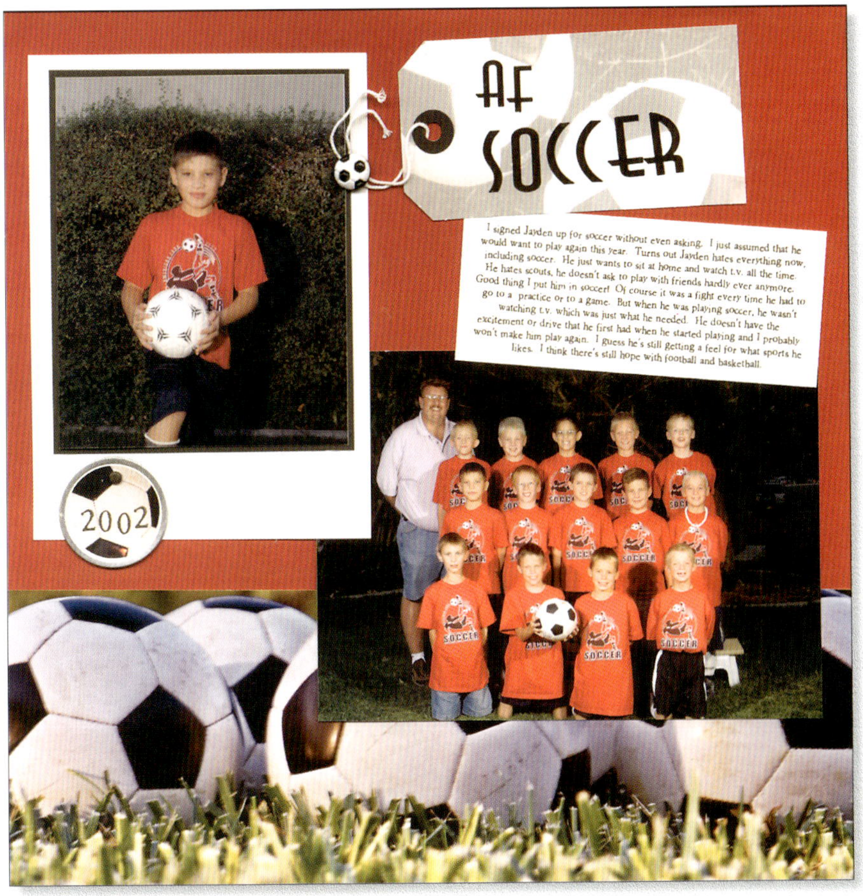

AF SOCCER
I signed Jayden up for soccer without even asking. I just assumed that he would want to play again this year. Turns out Jayden hates everything now, including soccer. He just wants to sit at home and watch t.v. all the time. He hates scouts, he doesn't ask to play with friends hardly ever anymore. Good thing I put him in soccer! Of course it was a fight every time he had to go to a practice or to a game. But when he was playing soccer, he wasn't watching t.v. which was just what he needed. He doesn't have the excitement or drive that he first had when he started playing and I probably won't make him play again. I guess he's still getting a feel for what sports he likes. I think there's still hope with football and basketball.
2002

AF Soccer

Supplies

Photographic border and tag: Shotz by Danelle Johnson, Creative Imaginations
Metal-rimmed tag: Making Memories
Soccer ball button: Buttons Galore
Letter stickers: Creative Imaginations
Letter stamps: PSX Design
Stamping ink: ColorBox, Clearsnap
Computer font: CK Constitution, "Fresh Fonts" CD, *Creating Keepsakes*

♥ I Love It!: *The metal-rimmed tag makes a perfect "frame" for the soccer ball accent with the date hand-stamped on it.*

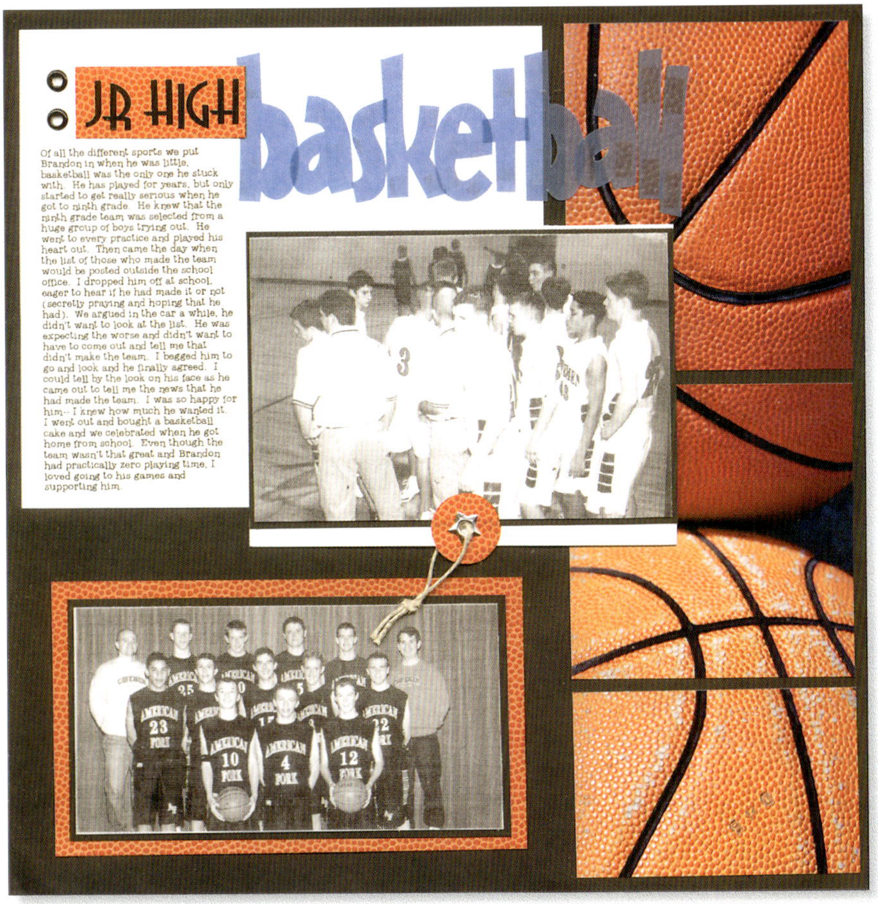

JR HIGH
basketball
Of all the different sports we put Brandon in when he was little, basketball was the only one he stuck with. He has played for years, but only started to get really serious when he got to ninth grade. He knew that the ninth grade team was selected from a huge group of boys trying out. He went to every practice and played his heart out. Then came the day when the list of those who made the team would be posted outside the school office. I dropped him off at school, eager to hear if he had made it or not (secretly praying and hoping that he had). We argued in the car a while, he didn't want to look at the list. He was expecting the worse and didn't want to have to come out and tell me that didn't make the team. I begged him to go and look and he finally agreed. I could tell by the look on his face as he came out to tell me the news that he had made the team. I was so happy for him-- I knew how much he wanted it. I went out and bought a basketball cake and we celebrated when he got home from school. Even though the team wasn't that great and Brandon had practically zero playing time, I loved going to his games and supporting him.

Basketball

Supplies

Textured paper: Freckle Press
Vellum: Autumn Leaves
Photographic border: Shotz by Danelle Johnson, Creative Imaginations
Letter stickers: Creative Imaginations
Lettering template: Lucky, Déjà Views
Computer font: CK Stenography, "Fresh Fonts" CD, *Creating Keepsakes*
Eyelets: Making Memories
Other: Jute

♥ I Love It!: *The main photograph on this page lifts to reveal additional journaling.*

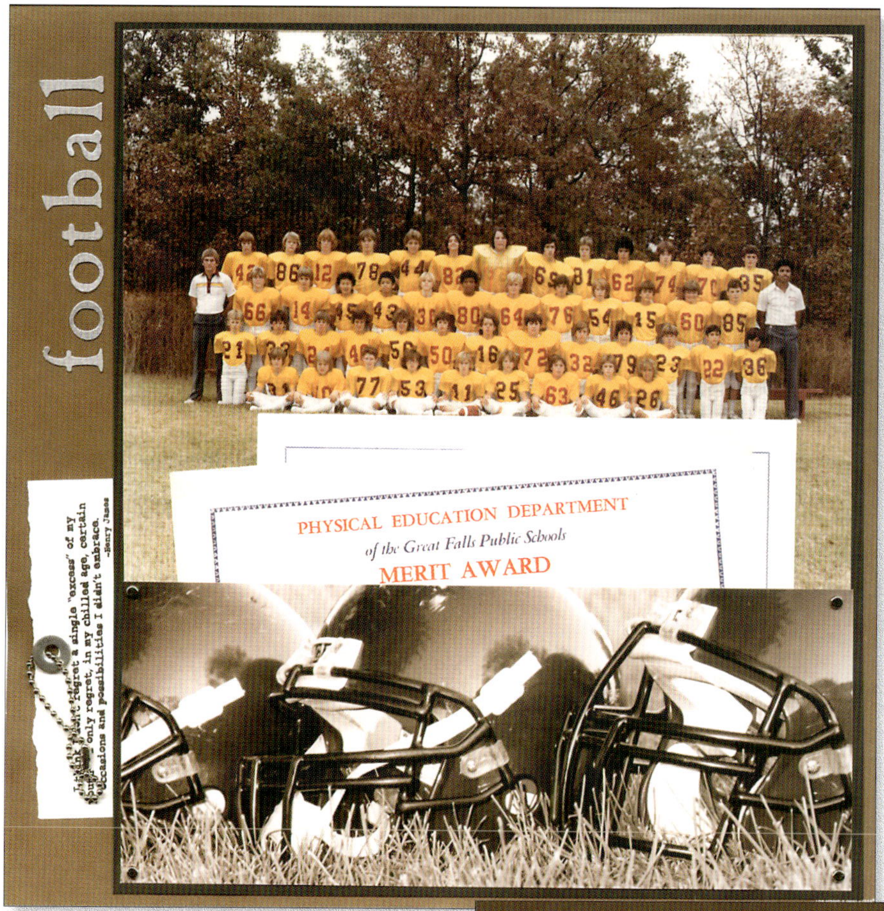

Football

Supplies
Photographic border: Shotz by Danelle Johnson, Creative Imaginations
Beaded chain: Westrim Crafts
Brads and metal letter charms: Making Memories
Computer font: CK Typewriter, "Fresh Fonts" CD, *Creating Keepsakes*
Other: Metal washer

♥ **I Love It!:** *The photographic border was attached to the bottom of a team photograph to create a pocket, which holds certificates and memorabilia. The quote to the left of the border slides out to reveal additional journaling.*

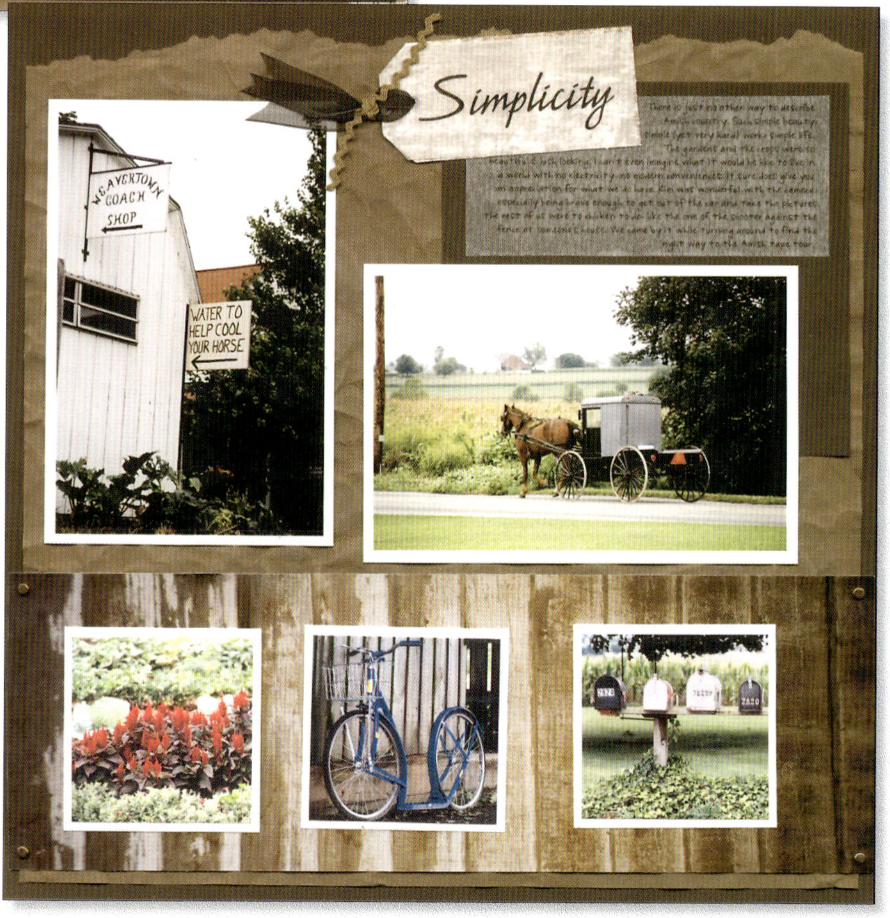

Simplicity

Supplies
Photographic border and tag: Shotz by Danelle Johnson, Creative Imaginations
Vellum: Provo Craft
Computer fonts: CAC Leslie, downloaded from the Internet; CK Jot, "The Art of Creative Lettering" CD, *Creating Keepsakes*
Brads: Making Memories
Other: Ribbon and rickrack

♥ **I Love It!:** *The texture in the photographic border is a perfect background for the country-scene photographs. To make sure the photographs stood out from the background, they were matted with bright-white cardstock.*

tip 5

hang accents from titles or borders to connect and unify your layout.

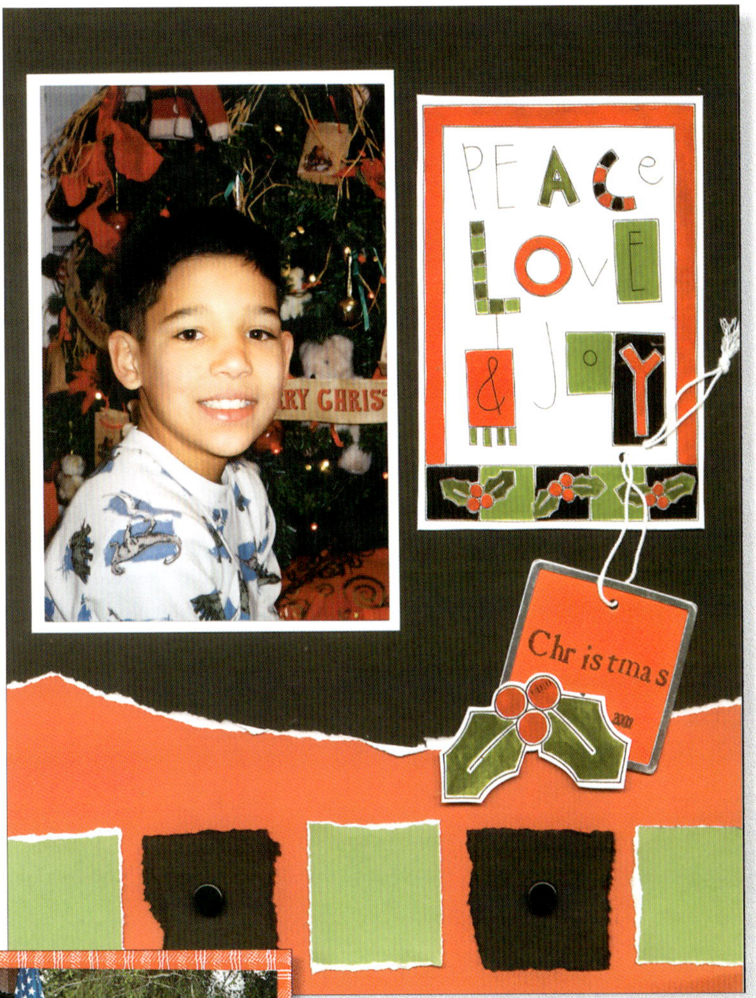

Christmas 2001

Supplies
Preprinted quote and accent: My Mind's Eye
Metal-rimmed tag: Making Memories
Letter stamps: PSX Design
Stamping ink: ColorBox, Clearsnap
Other: Brads

♥ I Love It!: *Every once in a while, try using a black background for your scrapbook pages. Black will make your photographs look more vivid, plus, colors placed against black stand out beautifully.*

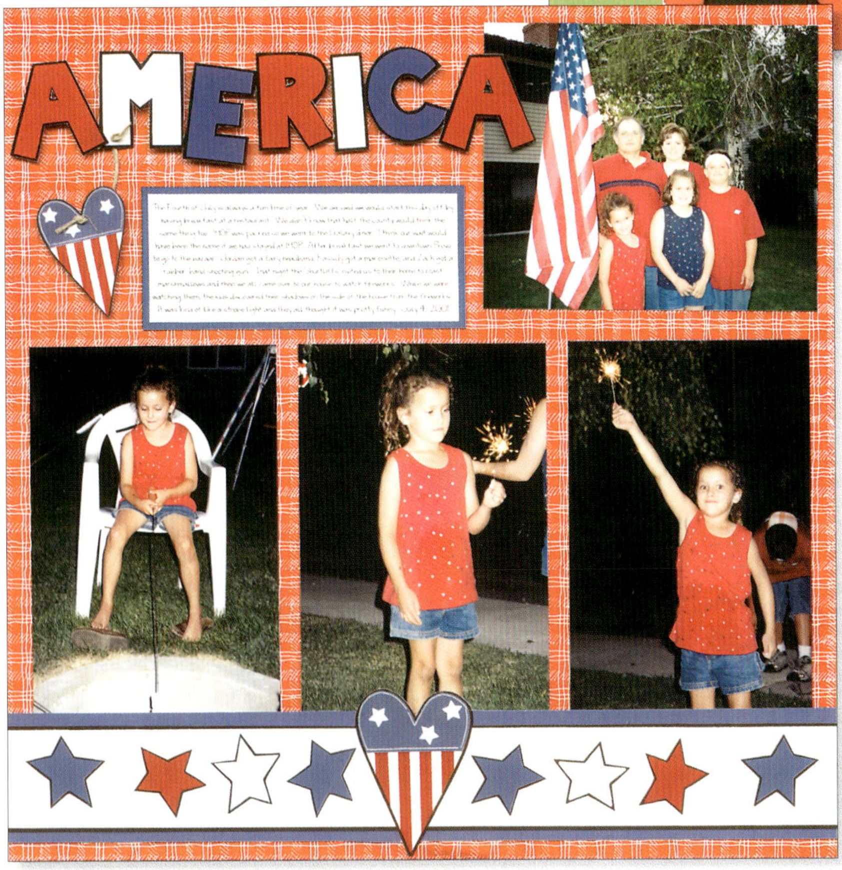

America

Supplies
Patterned paper: Provo Craft
Preprinted title, border and accent: EK Success
Computer font: CK Penman, "The Best of Creative Lettering" CD Vol. 4, *Creating Keepsakes*
Other: Jute

♥ I Love It!: *Don't hesitate to overlap a letter or two from your title onto a photograph if necessary, as long as the letters don't cover up important parts of the photo.*

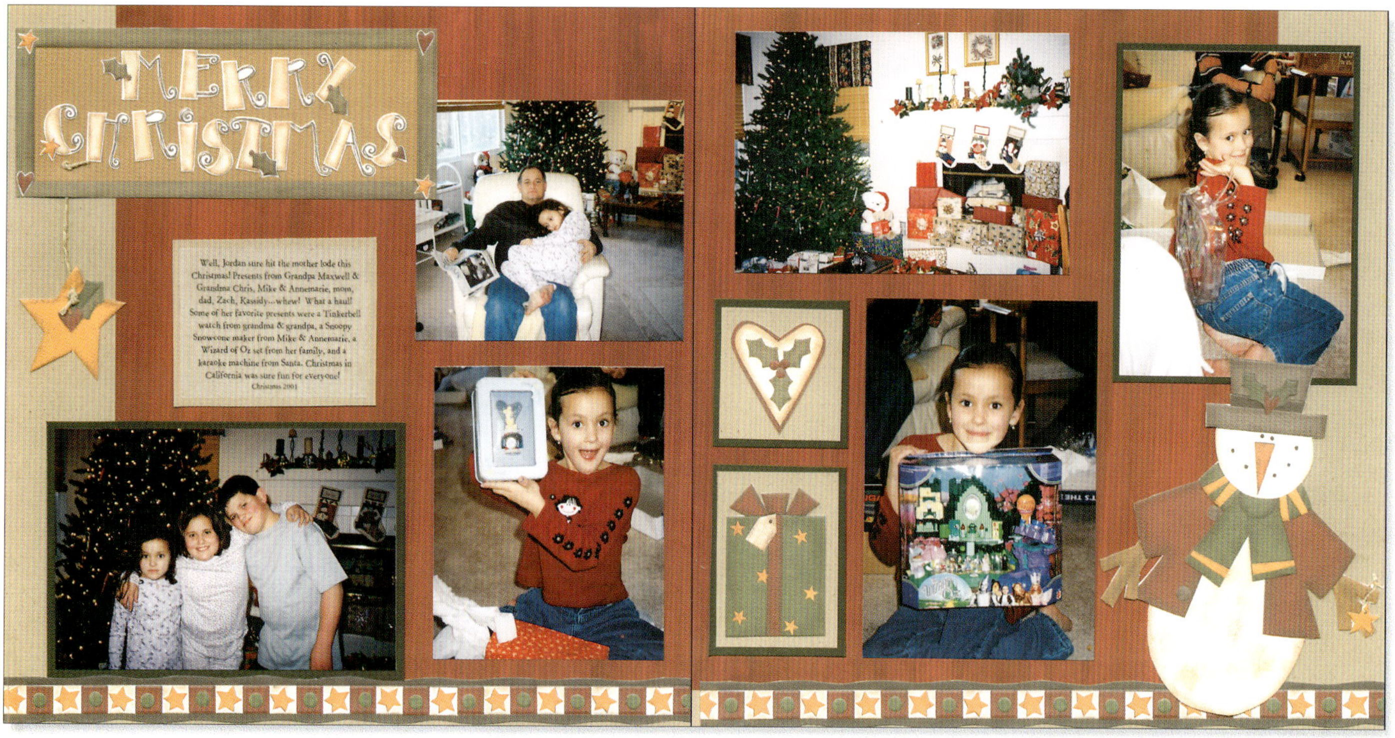
MERRY CHRISTMAS
Well, Jordan sure hit the mother lode this Christmas! Presents from Grandpa Maxwell & Grandma Chris, Mike & Annemarie, mom, dad, Zach, Kassidy...whew! What a haul! Some of her favorite presents were a Tinkerbell watch from grandma & grandpa, a Snoopy Snowcone maker from Mike & Annemarie, a Wizard of Oz set from her family, and a karaoke machine from Santa. Christmas in California was sure fun for everyone!
Christmas 2001

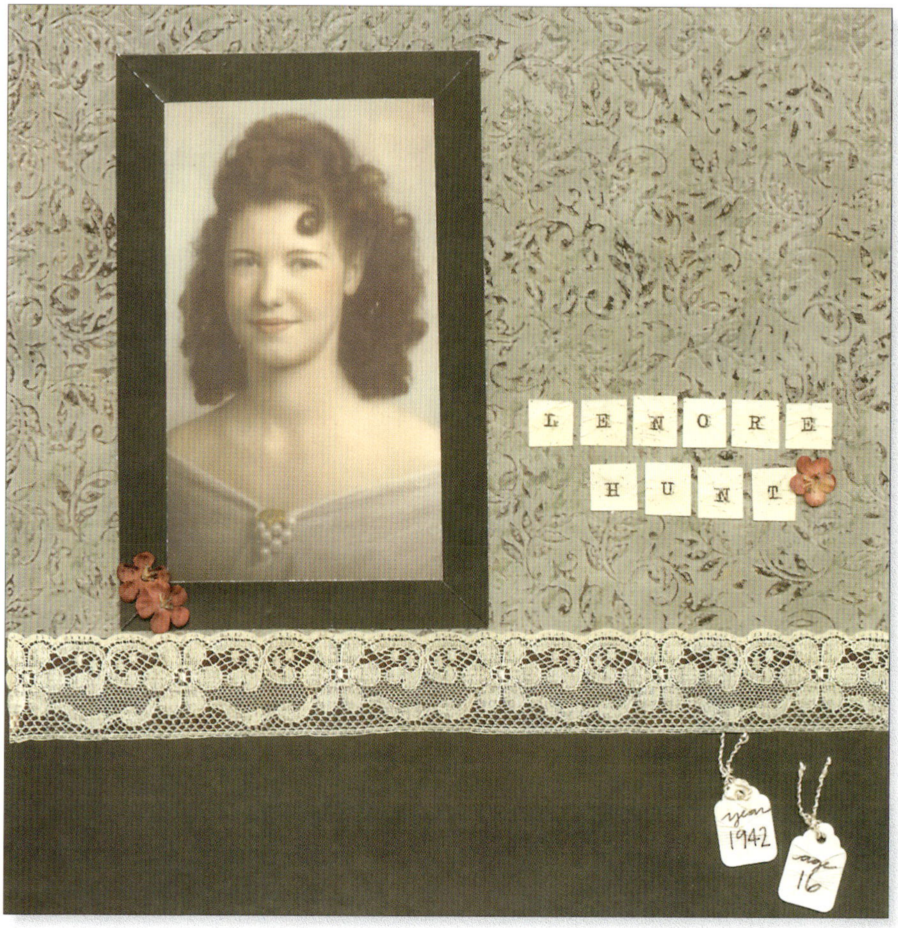
LENORE
HUNT
year 1942
age 16

Merry Christmas

Supplies
Patterned paper: Magenta
Preprinted title, borders and accents: Embossible Designs, We R Memory Keepers
Computer font: P22 Garamouche, Impress Rubber Stamps
Other: Jute

♥ I Love It!: *When using materials such as ribbon or raffia to hang accents on your layout, pay attention to the style of accents you're using. For example, these embossed accents look very casual and slightly country. Sheer white ribbon would have seemed too dressy, but textured jute matches the accents perfectly.*

Lenore Hunt

Supplies
Patterned paper: Source unknown
Preprinted border and letter stickers: Nostalgiques, EK Success
Other: Silk flowers, mini-tags, fibers and embossing enamel

♥ I Love It!: *The mini-tags were coated with clear ultra-thick embossing enamel and cracked to mimic the "cracked glass" look of the letter stickers.*

tip 6

merge a preprinted title or border with another page element.

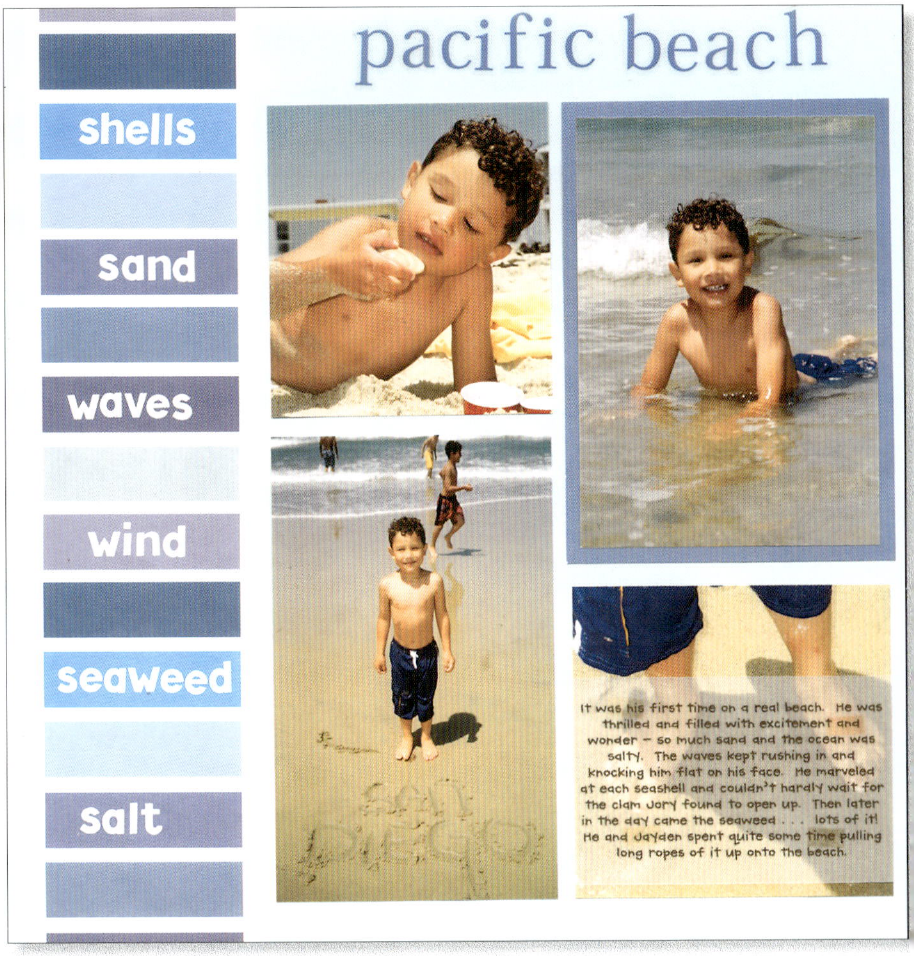
pacific beach
shells
sand
waves
wind
seaweed
salt
It was his first time on a real beach. He was thrilled and filled with excitement and wonder – so much sand and the ocean was salty. The waves kept rushing in and knocking him flat on his face. He marveled at each seashell and couldn't hardly wait for the clam Jory found to open up. Then later in the day came the seaweed . . . lots of it! He and Jayden spent quite some time pulling long ropes of it up onto the beach.

Pacific Beach

Supplies
Patterned paper: SEI
Vellum: WorldWin
Letter stickers: SEI (blue), Making Memories (white)
Computer font: CK Handprint, "The Best of Creative Lettering" CD Combo, *Creating Keepsakes*

♥ I Love It!: *Take advantage of papers with borders printed on them. This border was combined with key words about a day at the beach.*

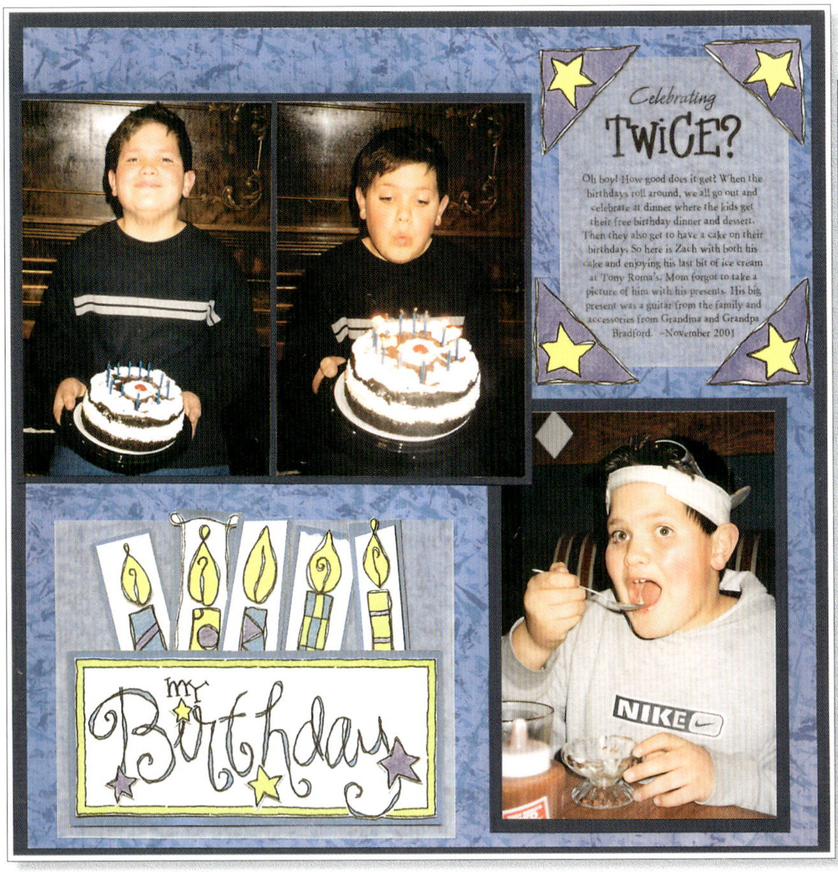
Celebrating
TWICE?
Oh boy! How good does it get? When the birthdays roll around, we all go out and celebrate at dinner where the kids get their free birthday dinner and dessert. Then they also get to have a cake on their birthday. So here is Zach with both his cake and enjoying his last bit of ice cream at Tony Roma's. Mom forgot to take a picture of him with his presents. His big present was a guitar from the family and accessories from Grandma and Grandpa Bradford. –November 2001
my Birthday
NIKE

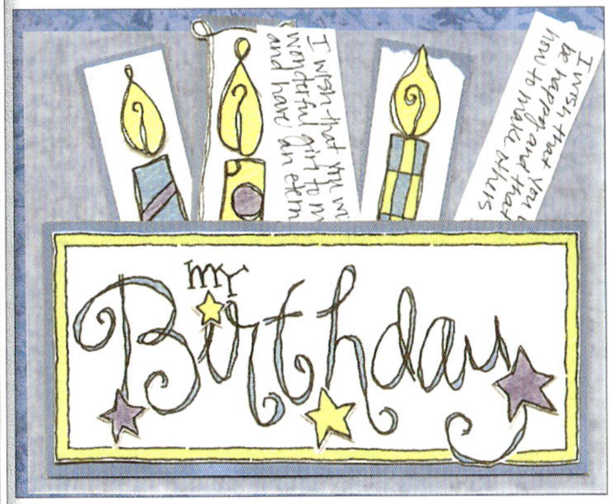
my Birthday

Celebrating Twice?

Supplies
Patterned paper: Source unknown
Vellum: Provo Craft
Preprinted title and accents: Fresh Cuts, EK Success
Computer fonts: CAC Leslie, downloaded from the Internet; Whipper Basic, Whipper Snapper Designs; P22 Garamouche, Impress Rubber Stamps

♥ I Love It!: *The candle accents were trimmed and slipped behind the title block. Journaling was included on the back of each candle.*

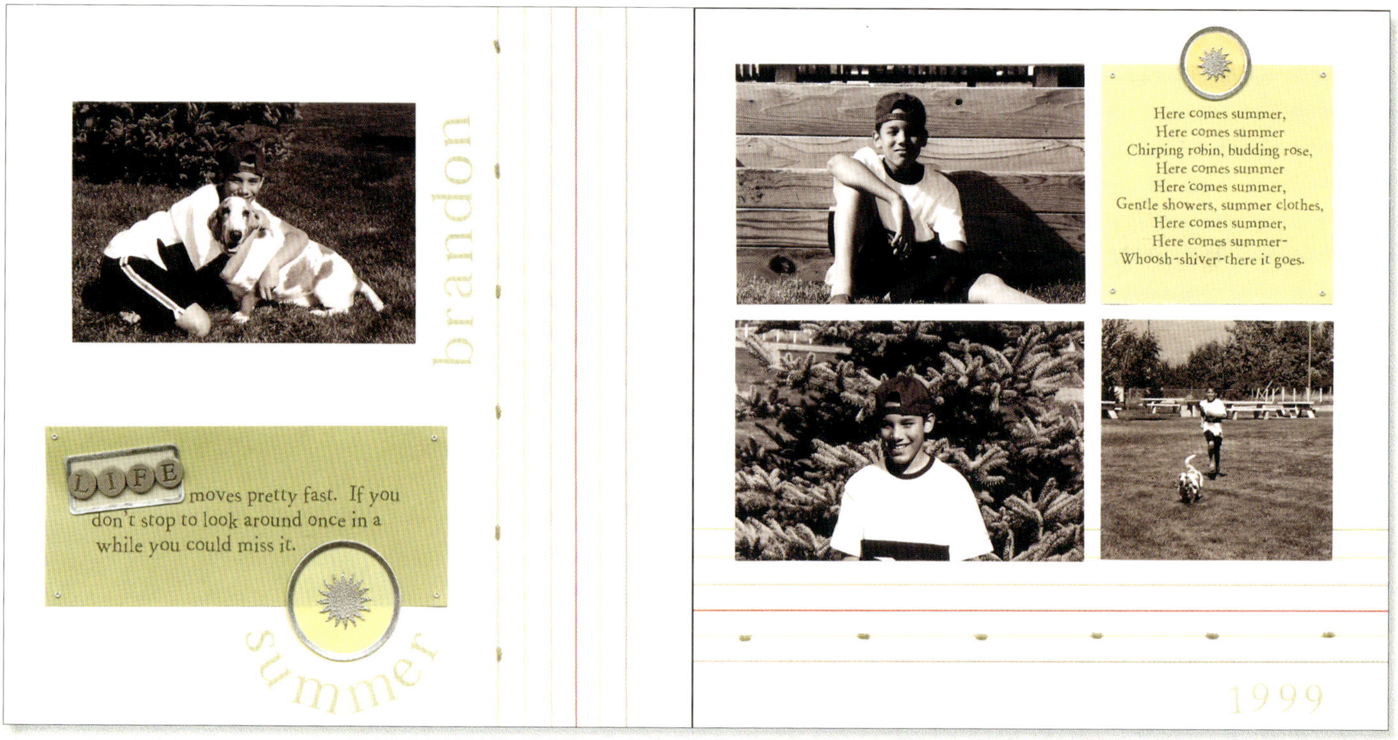
brandon
LIFE moves pretty fast. If you don't stop to look around once in a while you could miss it.
summer
Here comes summer,
Here comes summer
Chirping robin, budding rose,
Here comes summer
Here comes summer,
Gentle showers, summer clothes,
Here comes summer,
Here comes summer-
Whoosh-shiver-there it goes.
1999

Summer

Supplies
Patterned paper and letter stickers: SEI
Metal accents and metal-rimmed tags: Making Memories
Sun punch: Family Treasures
Computer font: CK Newsprint, "Fresh Fonts" CD, *Creating Keepsakes*
Beads: Westrim Crafts
Other: Wire

♥ I Love It!: *Tiny beads were threaded onto wire and attached to the border's green stripe at even intervals.*

I Love You

Supplies
Preprinted title and border: Embossible Designs, We R Memory Keepers
Pen: Zig Writer, EK Success
Other: Brads

♥ I Love It!: *The preprinted title acts as a cover for the mini-book on the layout, which includes a letter and accent.*

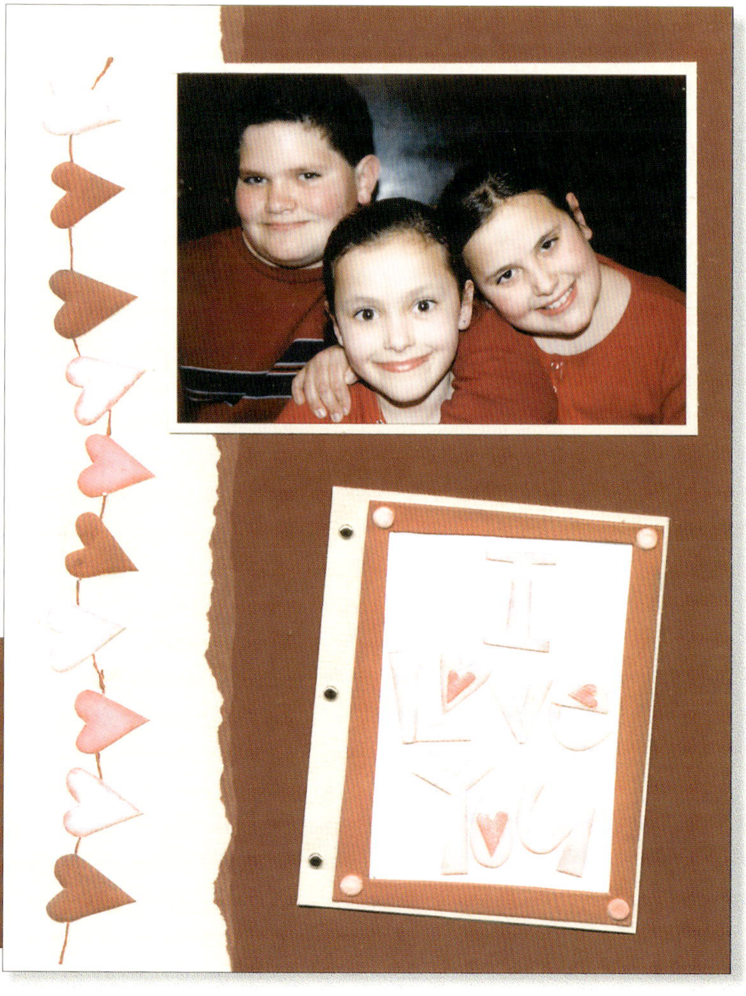
I Love You

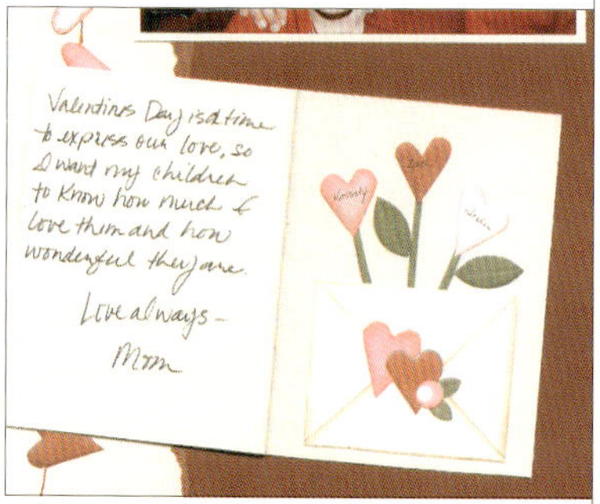
Valentine's Day is a time to express our love, so I want my children to know how much I love them and how wonderful they are.
Love always -
Mom

tips

lisa's lessons on titles & borders

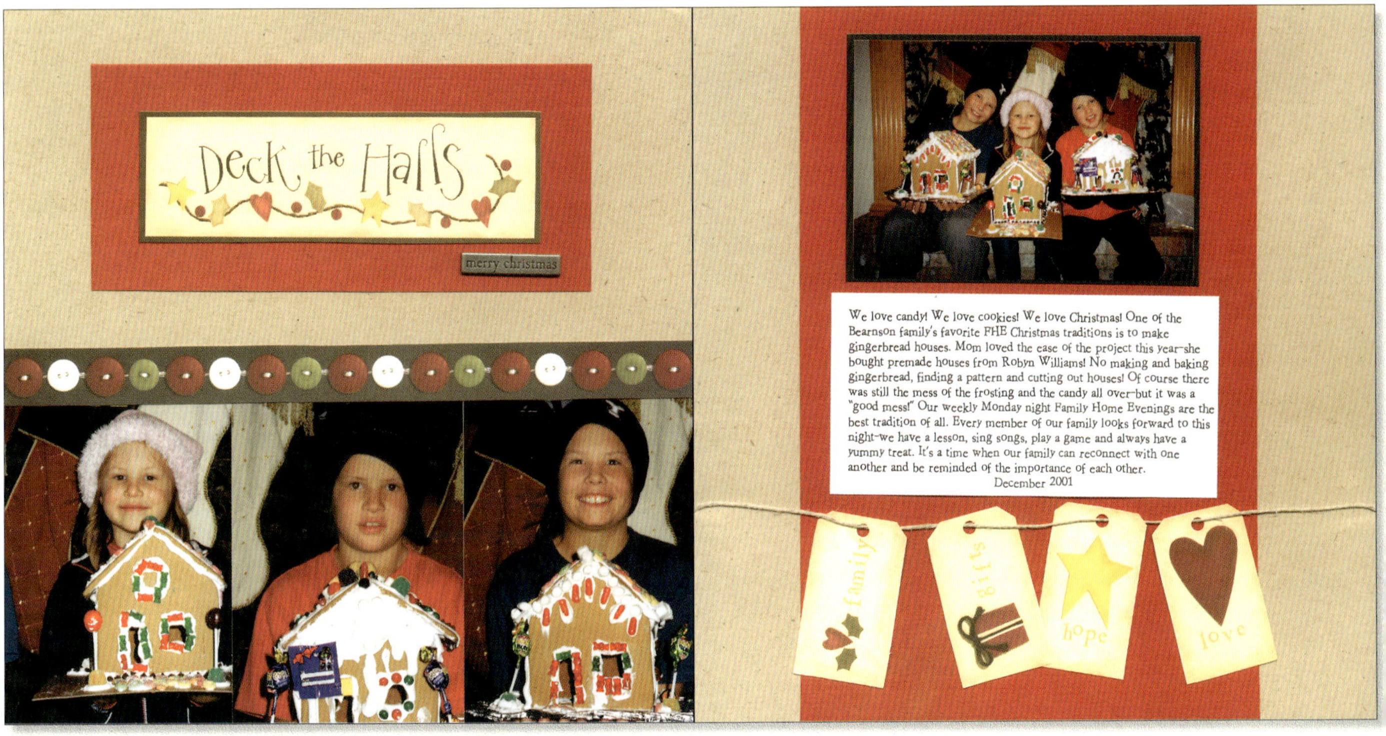

Deck the Halls
merry christmas
We love candy! We love cookies! We love Christmas! One of the Bearnson family's favorite FHE Christmas traditions is to make gingerbread houses. Mom loved the ease of the project this year-she bought premade houses from Robyn Williams! No making and baking gingerbread, finding a pattern and cutting out houses! Of course there was still the mess of the frosting and the candy all over-but it was a "good mess!" Our weekly Monday night Family Home Evenings are the best tradition of all. Every member of our family looks forward to this night-we have a lesson, sing songs, play a game and always have a yummy treat. It's a time when our family can reconnect with one another and be reminded of the importance of each other.
December 2001
family
gifts
hope
love

Pre-made titles and borders are lifesavers when you're stumped for creative ideas or in a hurry to complete a record number of layouts. Here are my favorite tips to remember when using pre-made titles and borders:

- Borders don't always have to be on the edge of your page. They can provide a smooth transition between two different patterns of background paper, separate a title from the rest of the layout, or highlight a row of photographs. Remember, borders can be cut, folded, torn and silhouetted to create new looks for your pages.
- Many pre-made titles are written by, you guessed it, professional writers. That means they're often clever, cute and all those other things you're looking for in a title. Instead of feeling guilty that you didn't come up with the phrase yourself, take advantage of these adorable titles, then customize your own layout by creating a subtitle or including journaling that gives more personal information. With the perfectly worded title and your favorite memories included, you'll have created the quintessential page!

Three more favorite tips from this layout:

- Have you ever noticed a layout that looked "too centered"? I loved the look of the red strip of cardstock down the second page of this layout, but I worried that it made the page look a bit too perfect to be pleasing. The problem was easily solved when I affixed a metal word accent to the bottom-right corner of the title—that tiny detail provided just enough variety to keep the layout attractive and natural.
- Most photo developers' standard print size is 4" x 6". This is incredibly handy for 12" x 12" scrapbookers, because that means three photographs placed side by side reach the entire length or width of a page. No photo mats needed!
- Don't be obsessive about matching the exact colors found in pre-made titles or borders. Although you want the colors you select to coordinate with your pre-made materials, usually there's a little room for variation. On the layout above, I used a true red even though the border and accents are more of a burgundy. Trust your eye above all else—if it looks good to *you*, it's okay to use on *your* layouts!

Deck the Halls

Supplies
Preprinted title, border and accents: O'Scrap!, Imaginations!
Metal accent: Making Memories
Computer font: CK Constitution, "Fresh Fonts" CD, *Creating Keepsakes*
Other: Twine

lisa says:

"Letter stickers, metal alphabets, word accents and other word-oriented products have really revolutionized scrapbooking!

Writing and journaling is a *necessary* part of your scrapbook pages, but it doesn't have to be boring thanks to these great products. Turn the *text* you're including in your albums into art with these *great* ideas."

LETTERS
& WORDS

love those letters & words

ch. 6

LETTER *n. a symbol representing a speech sound and constituting a unit of an alphabet*

WORD *n. a written or printed character or combination of characters representing a spoken word*

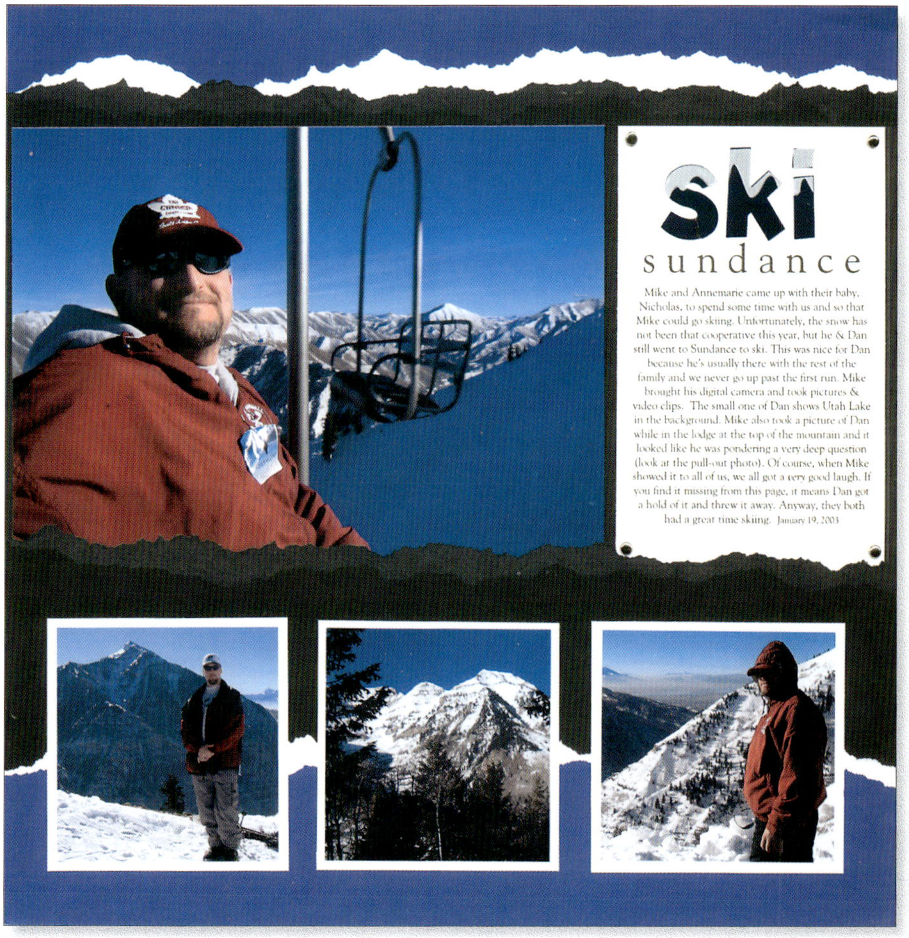

Ski
sundance
Mike and Annemarie came up with their baby, Nicholas, to spend some time with us and so that Mike could go skiing. Unfortunately, the snow has not been that cooperative this year, but he & Dan still went to Sundance to ski. This was nice for Dan because he's usually there with the rest of the family and we never go up past the first run. Mike brought his digital camera and took pictures & video clips. The small one of Dan shows Utah Lake in the background. Mike also took a picture of Dan while in the lodge at the top of the mountain and it looked like he was pondering a very deep question (look at the pull-out photo). Of course, when Mike showed it to all of us, we all got a very good laugh. If you find it missing from this page, it means Dan got a hold of it and threw it away. Anyway, they both had a great time skiing. January 19, 2003

Ski

Supplies

Letter stickers and overlays: Making Memories
Computer font: Goudy Old Style BT, WordPerfect
Brads: Making Memories

♥ **I Love It!:** *This layout is such a great example of drawing the colors of your layout from your photographs. When you're lucky enough to have your photographs capture such gorgeous colors, make sure you emphasize them on your layout for the maximum effect.*

tip 1

highlight important words or phrases.

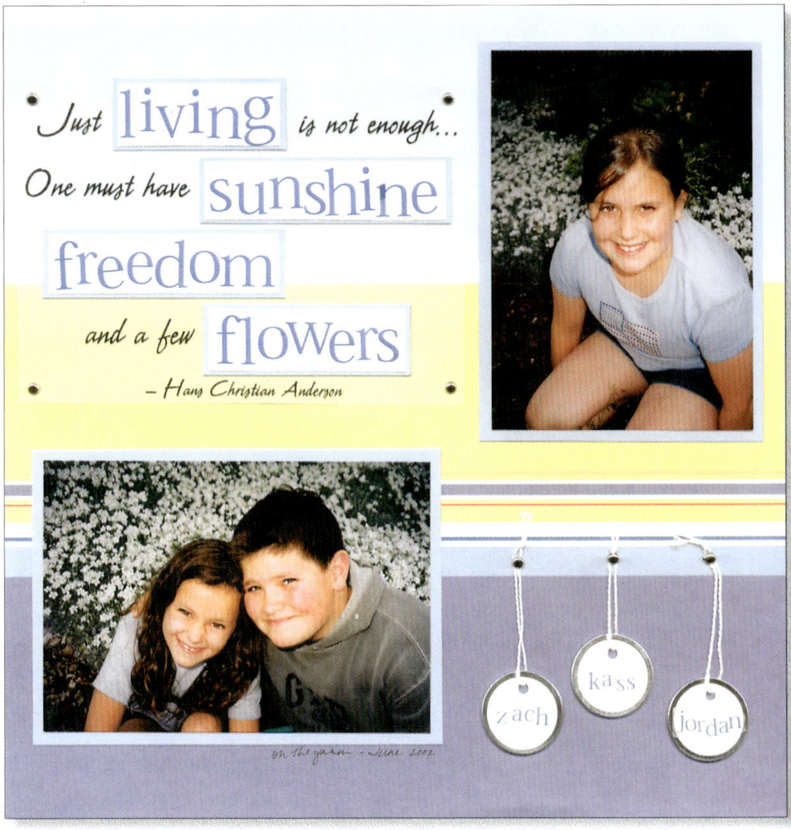
Just living is not enough...
One must have sunshine
freedom
and a few flowers
– Hans Christian Anderson
zach
kass
jordan

Sunshine, Freedom and Flowers

Supplies

Patterned paper and letter stickers: SEI
Vellum: Provo Craft
Computer font: CAC Leslie, downloaded from the Internet
Metal-rimmed tags: Avery
Pen: Zig Writer, EK Success
Other: Brads

♥ **I Love It!:** *Highlight meaningful words in a favorite quote or in your journaling by inserting matted blocks with the words spelled out in letter stickers. At a quick glance, viewers know the theme of the page and are drawn into the quote, wanting to read more.*

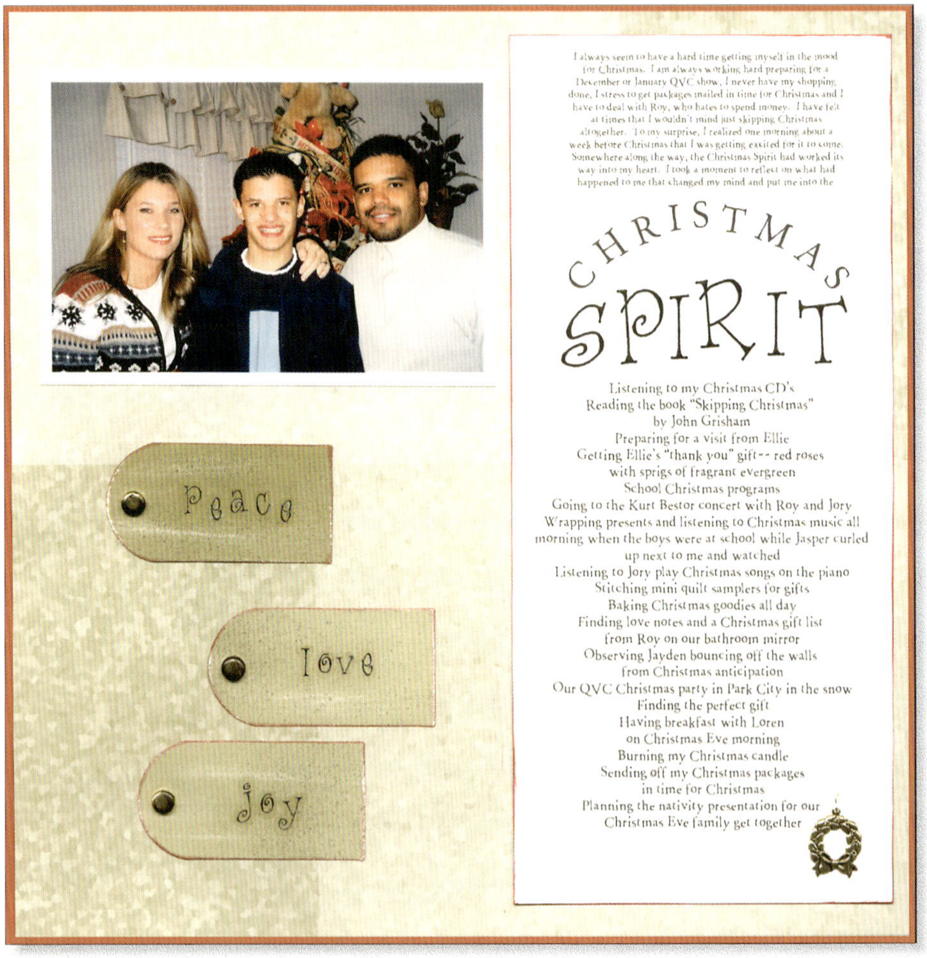
I always seem to have a hard time getting myself in the mood for Christmas. I am always working hard preparing for a December or January QVC show, I never have my shopping done, I stress to get packages mailed in time for Christmas and I have to deal with Roy, who hates to spend money. I have felt at times that I wouldn't mind just skipping Christmas altogether. To my surprise, I realized one morning about a week before Christmas that I was getting excited for it to come. Somewhere along the way, the Christmas Spirit had worked its way into my heart. I took a moment to reflect on what had happened to me that changed my mind and put me into the
CHRISTMAS
SPIRIT
Listening to my Christmas CD's
Reading the book "Skipping Christmas" by John Grisham
Preparing for a visit from Ellie
Getting Ellie's "thank you" gift-- red roses with sprigs of fragrant evergreen
School Christmas programs
Going to the Kurt Bestor concert with Roy and Jory
Wrapping presents and listening to Christmas music all morning when the boys were at school while Jasper curled up next to me and watched
Listening to Jory play Christmas songs on the piano
Stitching mini quilt samplers for gifts
Baking Christmas goodies all day
Finding love notes and a Christmas gift list from Roy on our bathroom mirror
Observing Jayden bouncing off the walls from Christmas anticipation
Our QVC Christmas party in Park City in the snow
Finding the perfect gift
Having breakfast with Loren on Christmas Eve morning
Burning my Christmas candle
Sending off my Christmas packages in time for Christmas
Planning the nativity presentation for our Christmas Eve family get together
peace
love
joy

Christmas Spirit

Supplies

Patterned paper: Paper Loft
Letter stickers: Provo Craft
Tags: Sizzix
Computer font: P22 Garamouche, Impress Rubber Stamps
Ink spritzer: Color Workshop
Other: Charm and brads

♥ **I Love It!:** *Titles don't always have to come before the journaling. The title of this layout, "Christmas Spirit," is actually part of the journaling text, but it's set apart because of its larger size and different font style.*

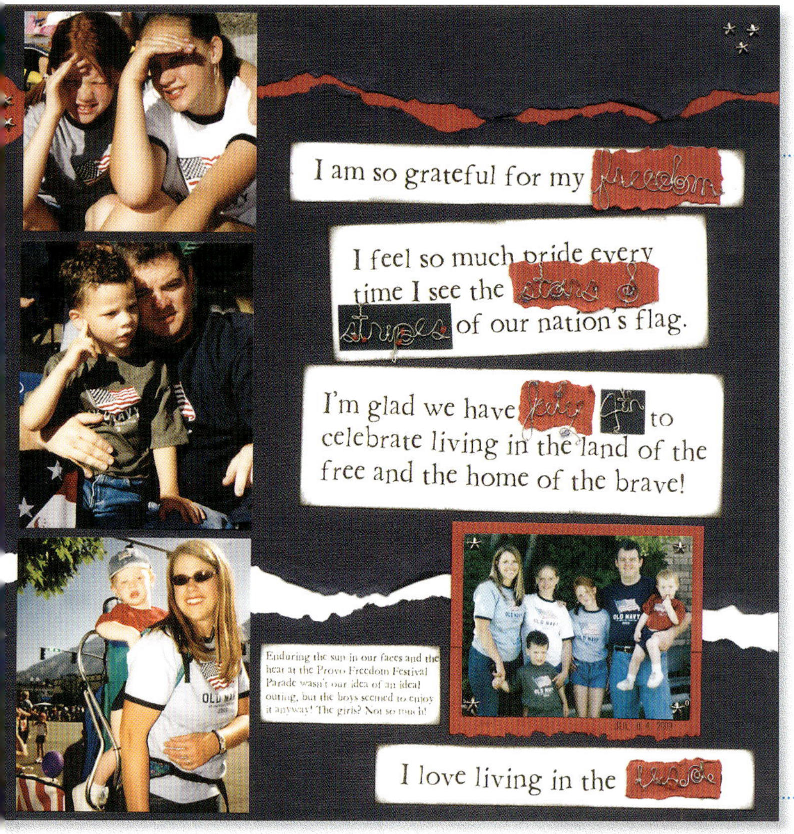
I am so grateful for my freedom
I feel so much pride every time I see the stars & stripes of our nation's flag.
I'm glad we have july 4th to celebrate living in the land of the free and the home of the brave!
Enduring the sun in our faces and the heat at the Provo Freedom Festival Parade wasn't our idea of an ideal outing, but the boys seemed to enjoy it anyway! The girls? Not so much!
I love living in the

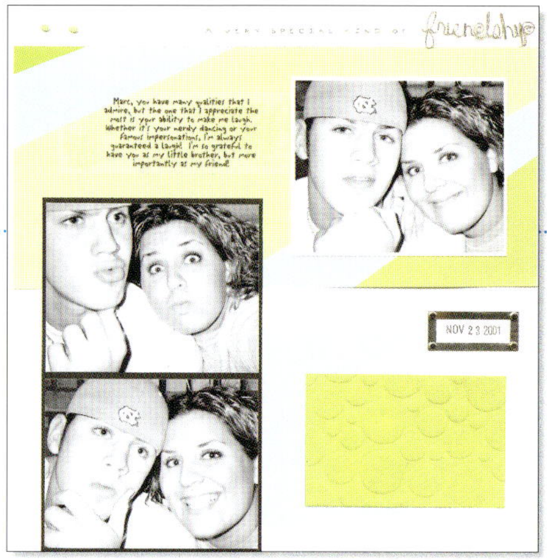
friendship
NOV 23 2001

Same Idea, Slightly Different: *This attractive layout shows the same product in a new way—instead of matting the wire word, it's placed at the end of a phrase directly onto the cardstock background.*

Friendship

Supplies

Patterned paper: NRN Designs
Vellum: Paper Adventures
Wire words and bookplate: Making Memories
Brads: Doodlebug Design
Computer font: 2Peas Think Small, downloaded from *www.twopeasinabucket.com*
Other: Date stamp and textured paper

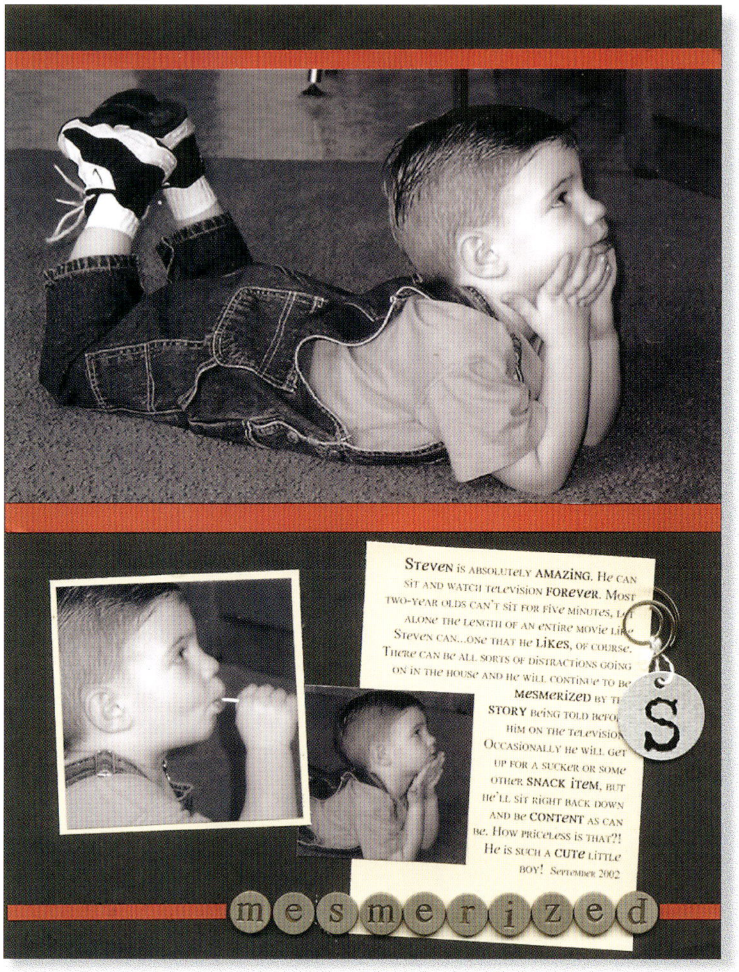
mesmerized
S

Freedom

Supplies

Wire words: Making Memories
Metal star studs: Scrapworks
Computer font: CK Fraternity, Becky Higgins' "Creative Clips & Fonts" CD, *Creating Keepsakes*
Stamping ink: ColorBox, Clearsnap

♥ **I Love It!:** *Word accents exist for many mainstream holidays and themes—take advantage of them when you can! On this layout, each wire word is backed with red or blue cardstock to make them more readable against the white cardstock.*

Mesmerized

Supplies

Metal letters: Making Memories
Computer font: CK Chemistry, "Fresh Fonts" CD, *Creating Keepsakes*
Other: Spiral paper clip

♥ **I Love It!:** *Choose one word that sums up how you feel about the photographs you're scrapbooking or the experience you're recording, then highlight that word on your layout with special letter accents.*

tip 2

create a visual headline for your layout with alphabet and word products.

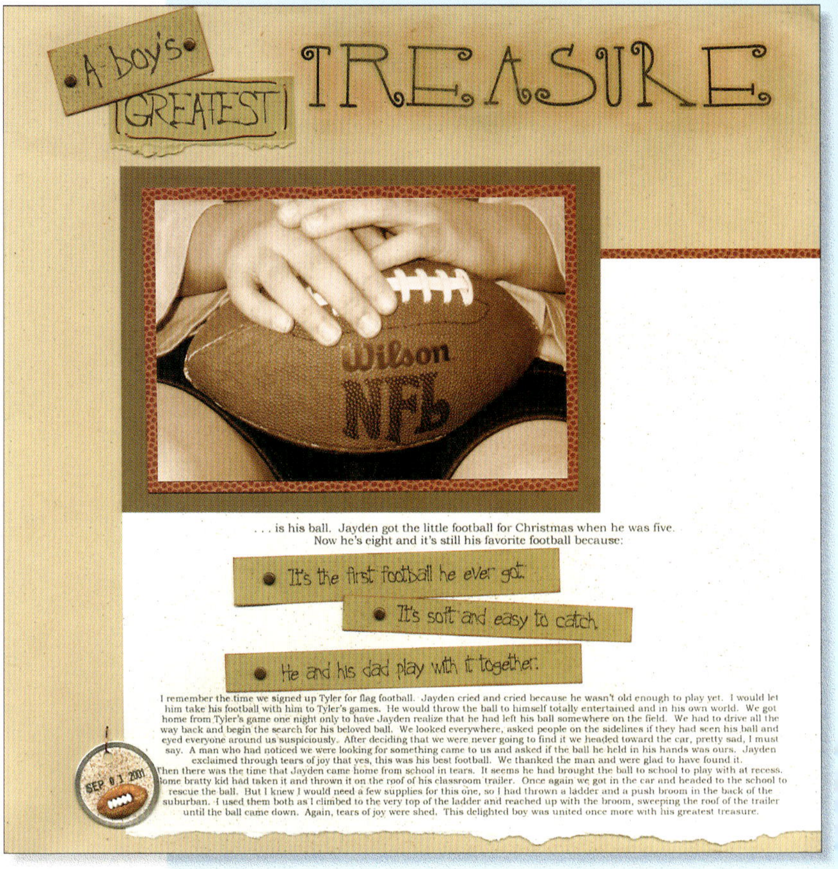
A boy's GREATEST TREASURE
. . . is his ball. Jayden got the little football for Christmas when he was five. Now he's eight and it's still his favorite football because:
It's the first football he ever got.
It's soft and easy to catch.
He and his dad play with it together.
I remember the time we signed up Tyler for flag football. Jayden cried and cried because he wasn't old enough to play yet. I would let him take his football with him to Tyler's games. He would throw the ball to himself totally entertained and in his own world. We got home from Tyler's game one night only to have Jayden realize that he had left his ball somewhere on the field. We had to drive all the way back and begin the search for his beloved ball. We looked everywhere, asked people on the sidelines if they had seen his ball and eyed everyone around us suspiciously. After deciding that we were never going to find it we headed toward the car, pretty sad, I must say. A man who had noticed we were looking for something came to us and asked if the ball he held in his hands was ours. Jayden exclaimed through tears of joy that yes, this was his best football. We thanked the man and were glad to have found it.
Then there was the time that Jayden came home from school in tears. It seems he had brought the ball to school to play with at recess. Some bratty kid had taken it and thrown it on the roof of his classroom trailer. Once again we got in the car and headed to the school to rescue the ball. But I knew I would need a few supplies for this one, so I had thrown a ladder and a push broom in the back of the suburban. I used them both as I climbed to the very top of the ladder and reached up with the broom, sweeping the roof of the trailer until the ball came down. Again, tears of joy were shed. This delighted boy was united once more with his greatest treasure.

A Boy's Greatest Treasure

Supplies

Textured paper: Freckle Press
Letter stickers: Provo Craft
Computer fonts: Roughedge and Garamond, WordPerfect
Metal-rimmed tag, wire and brads: Making Memories
Football button: Buttons Galore
Ink spritzer: Color Workshop
Other: Date stamp

♥ **I Love It!:** *This is a great photograph! I love the way it makes the viewer pause and study the way the fingers are resting on the ball, the way the ball fits right into the boy's lap. These elements would have been lost had the photo been a full-body shot of a boy holding a football. Choosing to print the photo in sepia tones adds a timeless, classic feeling—as if the photo could have been taken last year or in 1940! (The idea for this photograph came from p. 100 of The 2001 Scrapbook Hall of Fame.)*

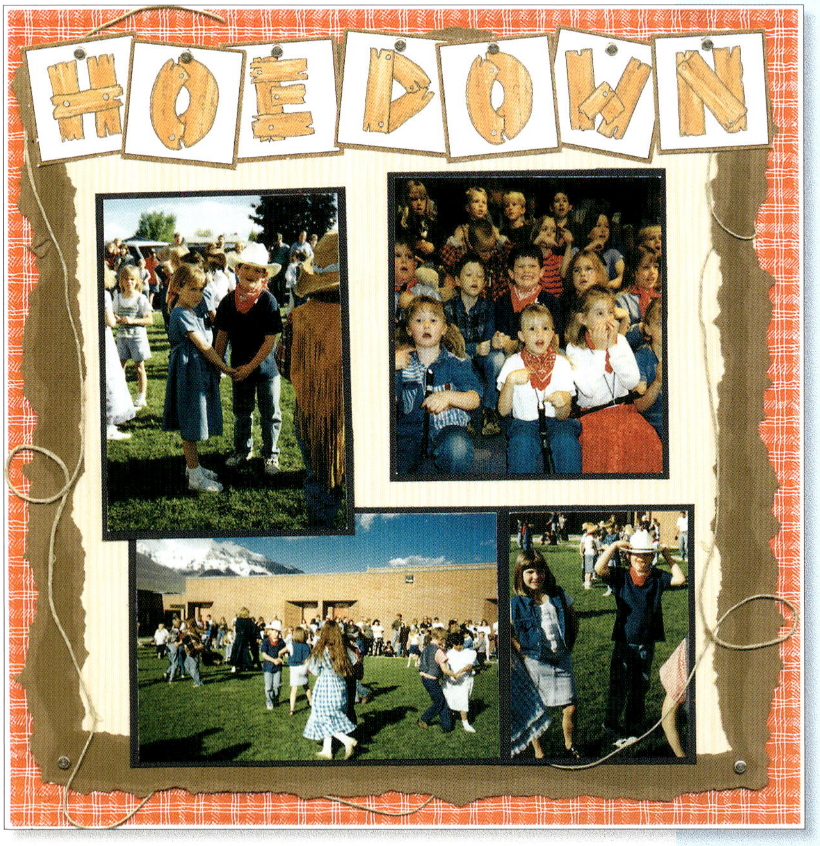
HOEDOWN

Hoedown

Supplies

Patterned papers: Provo Craft (red), Keeping Memories Alive (tan)
Letter squares: My Mind's Eye
Metal studs: Westrim Crafts
Other: Jute

♥ **I Love It!:** *Wrapping jute around the border of the page was incredibly easy, but it's such a great accent for the layout. The loops and lengths of jute bring to mind lassos and cow-boys—and the jute follows the rustic theme of the letter squares perfectly!*

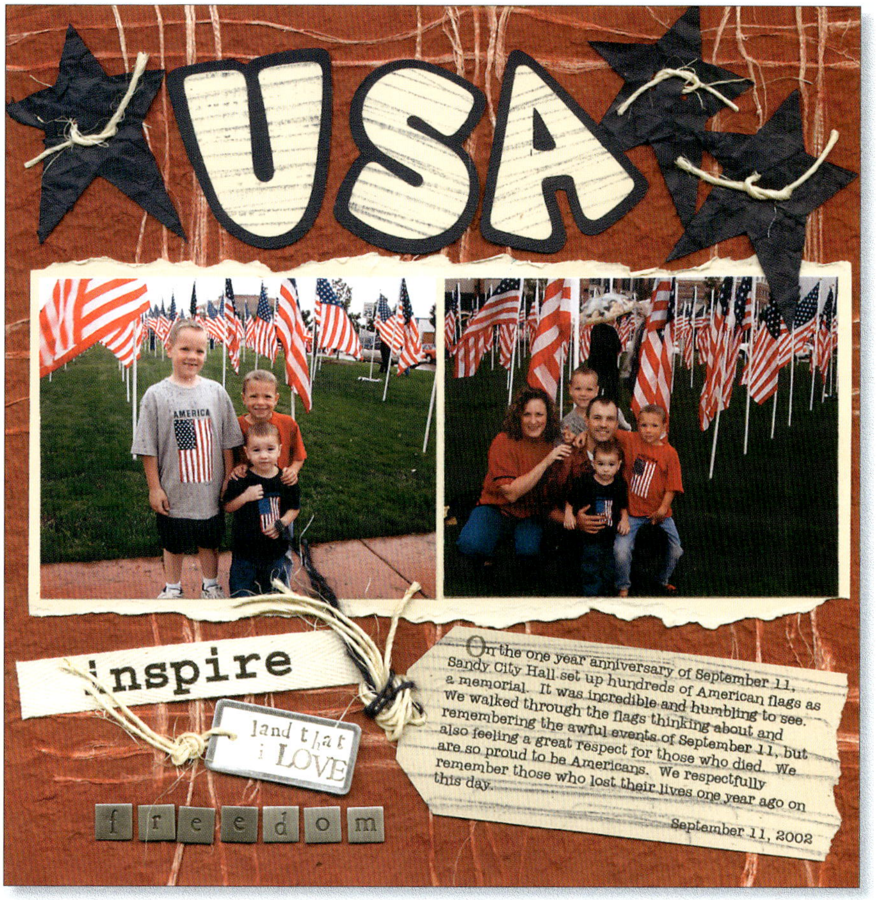
USA
inspire
land that i LOVE
freedom
On the one year anniversary of September 11, Sandy City Hall set up hundreds of American flags as a memorial. It was incredible and humbling to see. We walked through the flags thinking about and remembering the awful events of September 11, but also feeling a great respect for those who died. We are so proud to be Americans. We respectfully remember those who lost their lives one year ago on this day.
September 11, 2002

USA

Supplies
Lettering and star template: Coluzzle, Provo Craft
Canvas printed ribbon: 7 Gypsies
Metal-rimmed tag and metal letters: Making Memories
Letter stamps: Hero Arts ("Land That I"), PSX Design ("Love")
Stamping ink: Ranger Industries
Computer font: CK Stenography, "Fresh Fonts" CD, *Creating Keepsakes*
Other: Rope, hemp and textured paper

♥ **I Love It!:** *The line pattern on the "USA" title and tag were created by repeatedly pressing the edge of a stamp pad down the letters and tag.*

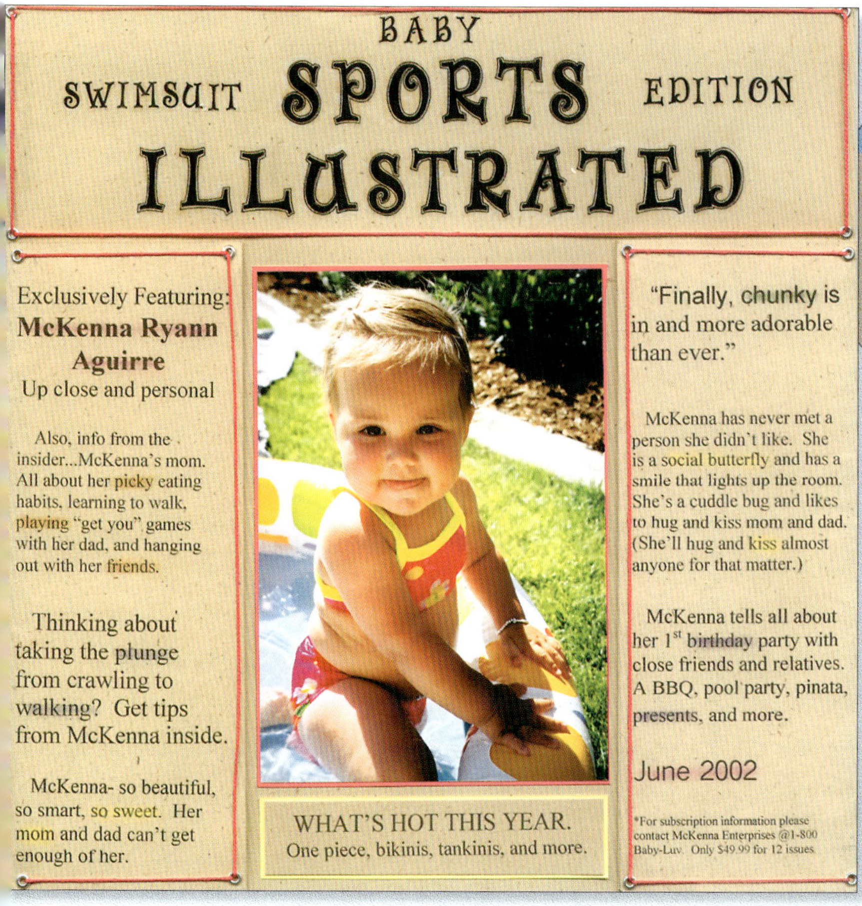
BABY
SWIMSUIT SPORTS EDITION
ILLUSTRATED
Exclusively Featuring:
McKenna Ryann Aguirre
Up close and personal
Also, info from the insider...McKenna's mom. All about her picky eating habits, learning to walk, playing "get you" games with her dad, and hanging out with her friends.
Thinking about taking the plunge from crawling to walking? Get tips from McKenna inside.
McKenna- so beautiful, so smart, so sweet. Her mom and dad can't get enough of her.
WHAT'S HOT THIS YEAR.
One piece, bikinis, tankinis, and more.
"Finally, chunky is in and more adorable than ever."
McKenna has never met a person she didn't like. She is a social butterfly and has a smile that lights up the room. She's a cuddle bug and likes to hug and kiss mom and dad. (She'll hug and kiss almost anyone for that matter.)
McKenna tells all about her 1st birthday party with close friends and relatives. A BBQ, pool party, pinata, presents, and more.
June 2002
*For subscription information please contact McKenna Enterprises @1-800 Baby-Luv. Only $49.99 for 12 issues.

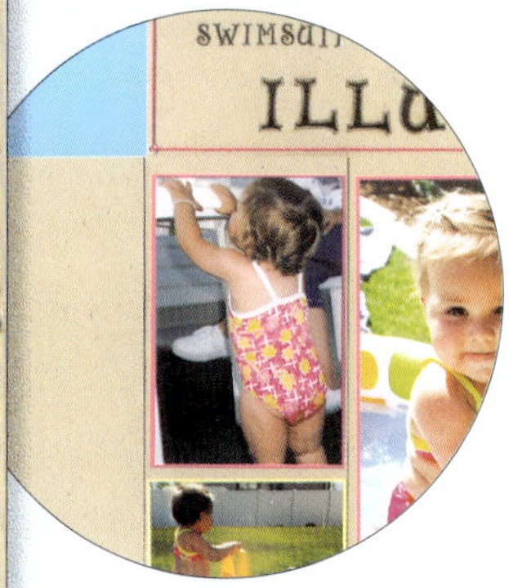

Baby Swimsuit Edition

Supplies
Letter stickers: Provo Craft
Computer font: Times New Roman, Microsoft Word
Eyelets: Doodlebug Design
Embroidery floss: DMC
Chalks: Craf-T Products

♥ **I Love It!:** *The side columns of text open to reveal several more photographs of the baby in her swimsuit. What a playful way to scrapbook your photographs!*

tip 3
shadow letters to add depth and interest.

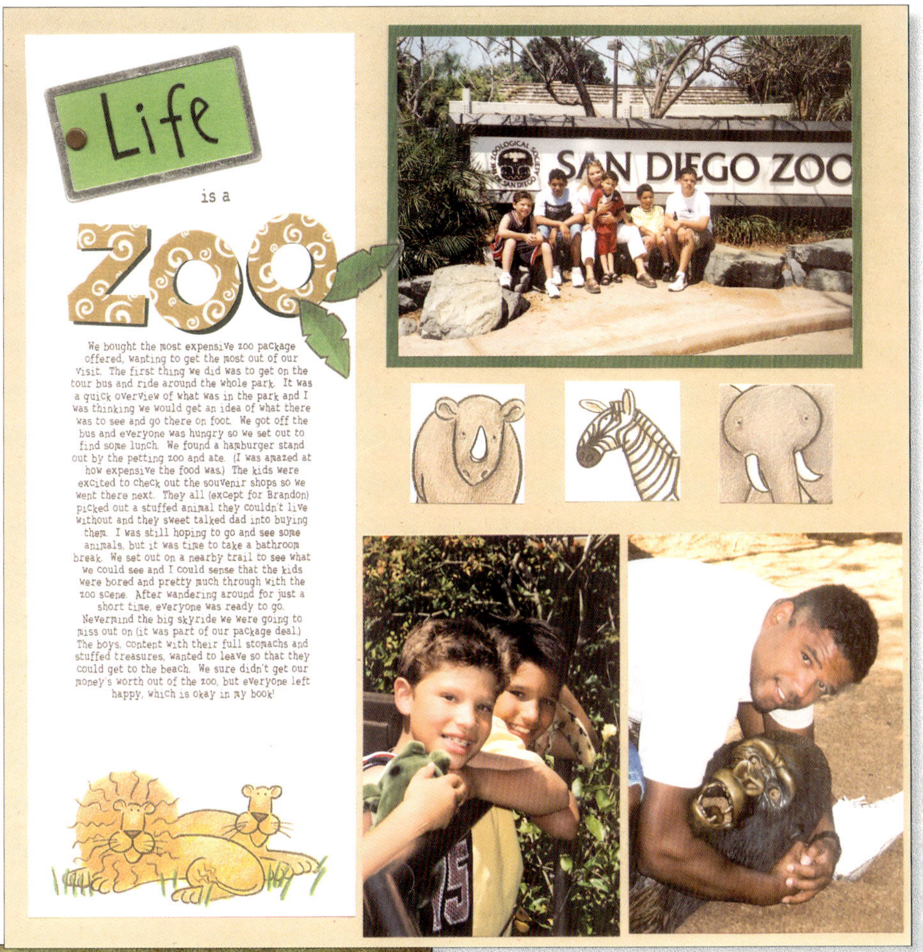

Life
is a
ZOO
We bought the most expensive zoo package offered, wanting to get the most out of our visit. The first thing we did was to get on the tour bus and ride around the whole park. It was a quick overview of what was in the park and I was thinking we would get an idea of what there was to see and go there on foot. We got off the bus and everyone was hungry so we set out to find some lunch. We found a hamburger stand out by the petting zoo and ate. (I was amazed at how expensive the food was.) The kids were excited to check out the souvenir shops so we went there next. They all (except for Brandon) picked out a stuffed animal they couldn't live without and they sweet talked dad into buying them. I was still hoping to go and see some animals, but it was time to take a bathroom break. We set out on a nearby trail to see what we could see and I could sense that the kids were bored and pretty much through with the zoo scene. After wandering around for just a short time, everyone was ready to go. Nevermind the big skyride we were going to miss out on (it was part of our package deal.) The boys, content with their full stomachs and stuffed treasures, wanted to leave so that they could get to the beach. We sure didn't get our money's worth out of the zoo, but everyone left happy, which is okay in my book!
SAN DIEGO ZOO

Life is a Zoo

Supplies
Letter stickers: Making Memories
Metal-rimmed tag: Making Memories
Stickers: Me & My Big Ideas
Computer Font: CK Stenography, "Fresh Fonts" CD, *Creating Keepsakes*

♥ **I Love It!:** *These swirl letter stickers were shadowed with the same-style letter stickers in black.*

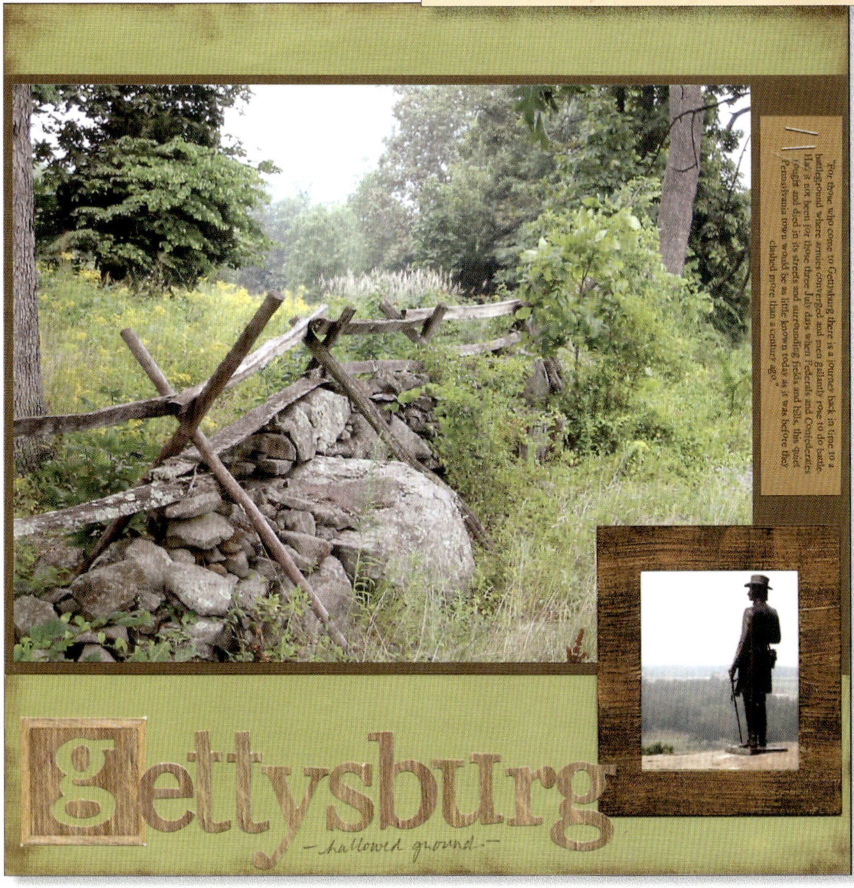

gettysburg
-hallowed ground-

Gettysburg

Supplies
Letter punch-outs: My Mind's Eye
Metal frame: Making Memories
Computer font: CK Constitution, "Fresh Fonts" CD, *Creating Keepsakes*
Stamping ink: StazOn, Tsukineko

♥ **I Love It!:** *The frame on this layout used to be silver! It was painted, then stamped with permanent ink to create a wood-grain look.*

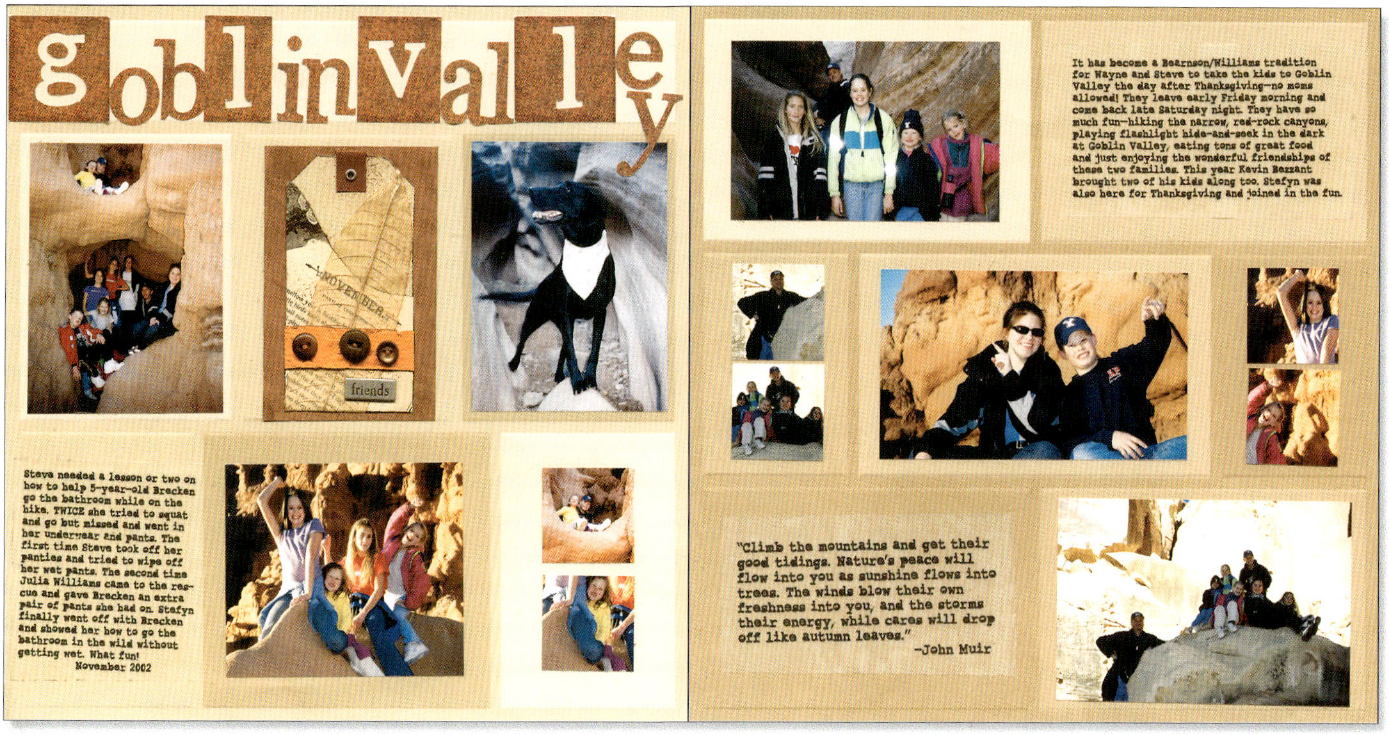
goblin valley
It has become a Bearnson/Williams tradition for Wayne and Steve to take the kids to Goblin Valley the day after Thanksgiving—no moms allowed! They leave early Friday morning and come back late Saturday night. They have so much fun—hiking the narrow, red-rock canyons, playing flashlight hide-and-seek in the dark at Goblin Valley, eating tons of great food and just enjoying the wonderful friendships of these two families. This year Kevin Bezzant brought two of his kids along too. Stefyn was also here for Thanksgiving and joined in the fun.
friends
Steve needed a lesson or two on how to help 5-year-old Brecken go the bathroom while on the hike. TWICE she tried to squat and go but missed and went in her underwear and pants. The first time Steve took off her panties and tried to wipe off her wet pants. The second time Julia Williams came to the rescue and gave Brecken an extra pair of pants she had on. Stefyn finally went off with Brecken and showed her how to go the bathroom in the wild without getting wet. What fun!
November 2002
"Climb the mountains and get their good tidings. Nature's peace will flow into you as sunshine flows into trees. The winds blow their own freshness into you, and the storms their energy, while cares will drop off like autumn leaves."
-John Muir

Goblin Valley

Supplies

Pre-formatted paper: All My Memories
Vellum: WorldWin
Letter punch-outs: My Mind's Eye
Preprinted tag: Fresh Cuts, EK Success
Metal word accent: Making Memories
Computer font: CK Typewriter, "Fresh Fonts" CD, *Creating Keepsakes*

♥ **I Love It!:** *This patterned paper has embossed and shaded areas already marked for a title, accents and photographs. It saves tons of time and creative energy when you want to finish pages fast.*

♥ **I Love It!:** *These punch-out letters end up having a "positive-space" piece (the punched-out letter) and a "negative-space" piece (the piece of paper the letter was punched out of). Mixing the two adds an interesting effect and gives you double the product for your money!*

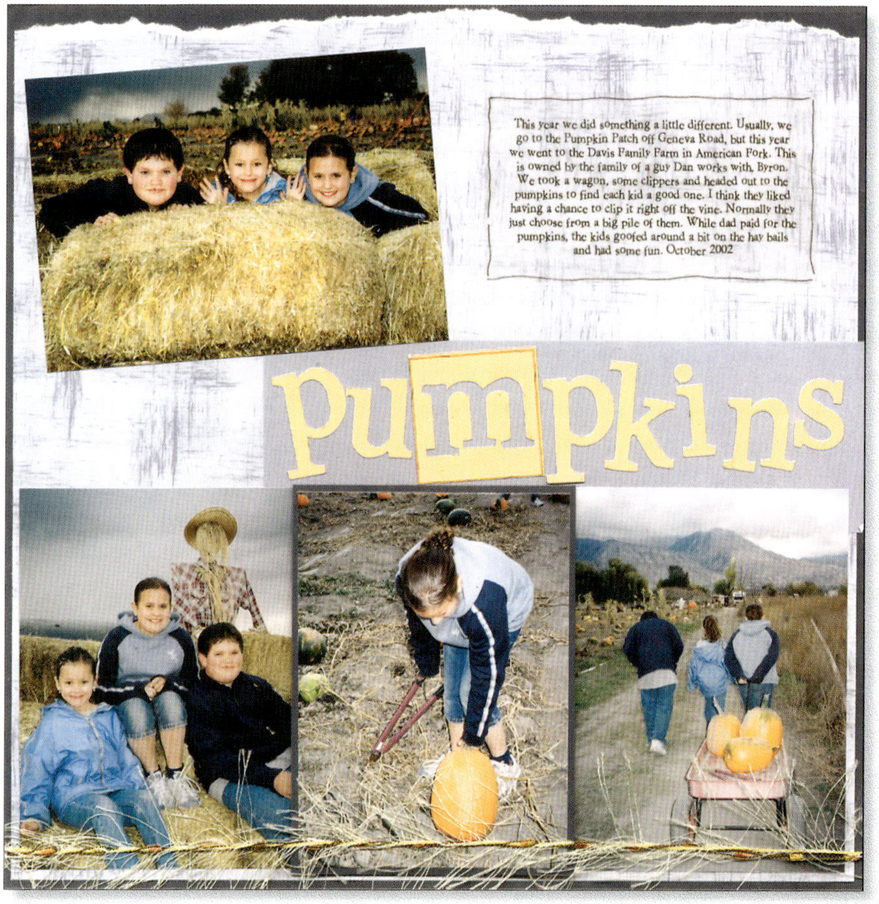
This year we did something a little different. Usually, we go to the Pumpkin Patch off Geneva Road, but this year we went to the Davis Family Farm in American Fork. This is owned by the family of a guy Dan works with, Byron. We took a wagon, some clippers and headed out to the pumpkins to find each kid a good one. I think they liked having a chance to clip it right off the vine. Normally they just choose from a big pile of them. While dad paid for the pumpkins, the kids goofed around a bit on the hay bails and had some fun. October 2002
pumpkins

Pumpkins

Supplies

Patterned paper: Mustard Moon
Letter punch-outs: My Mind's Eye
Computer font: CK Constitution, "Fresh Fonts" CD, *Creating Keepsakes*
Fibers: Adornaments, EK Success
Pen: Pigma Micron, Sakura
Other: 3-D foam adhesive

♥ **I Love It!:** *Wondering why this color scheme works so well? Orange and blue are complementary colors on the color wheel, so they naturally look great together. Be sure to use complementary colors in matching shades and intensities.*

tip 4
illustrate the theme of your page with your choice of letter or word accents.

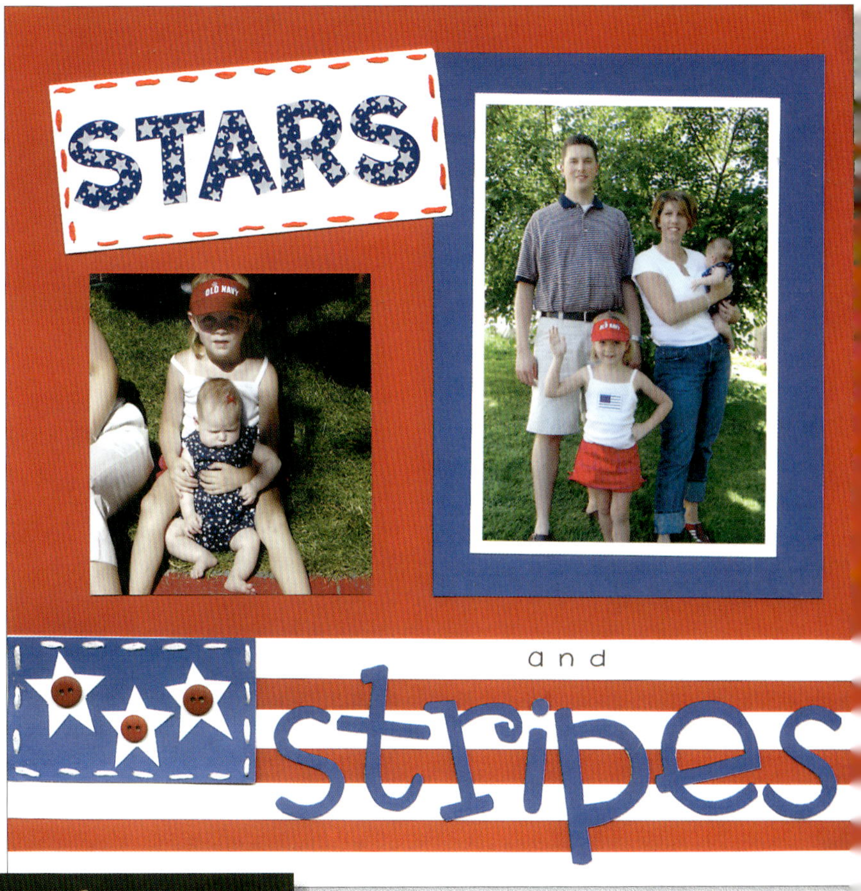

Stars and Stripes

Supplies
Letter stickers and overlays: Making Memories
Computer fonts: 2Peas Spread Sunshine, downloaded from *www.twopeasinabucket.com*; CK Fun, "The Art of Creative Lettering" CD, *Creating Keepsakes*
Buttons: Theresa's Hand Dyed Buttons
Embroidery floss: DMC

♥ **I Love It!:** *Basic, even stitching done with an embroidery needle and floss around title or journaling blocks creates a handmade, crafty look in just minutes.*

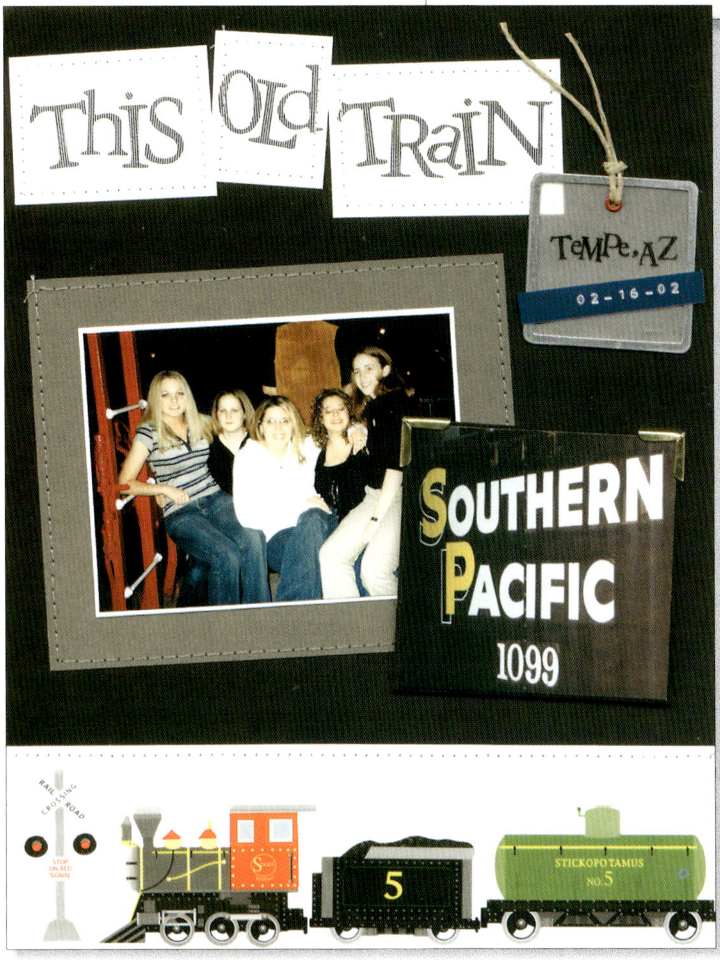

This Old Train

Supplies
Letter stickers and overlays: Flavia, ColorBök
Metal-rimmed tag: Making Memories
Train stickers: Stickopotamus by EK Success
Letter stamps: PSX Design
Stamping ink: ColorBox, Clearsnap
Other: Jute and label

♥ **I Love It!:** *The striped pattern of these letter stickers is reminiscent of an old-fashioned railroad. Take advantage of "matching" sticker sets—they often make quick-and-easy but still quite impressive borders on your layouts.*

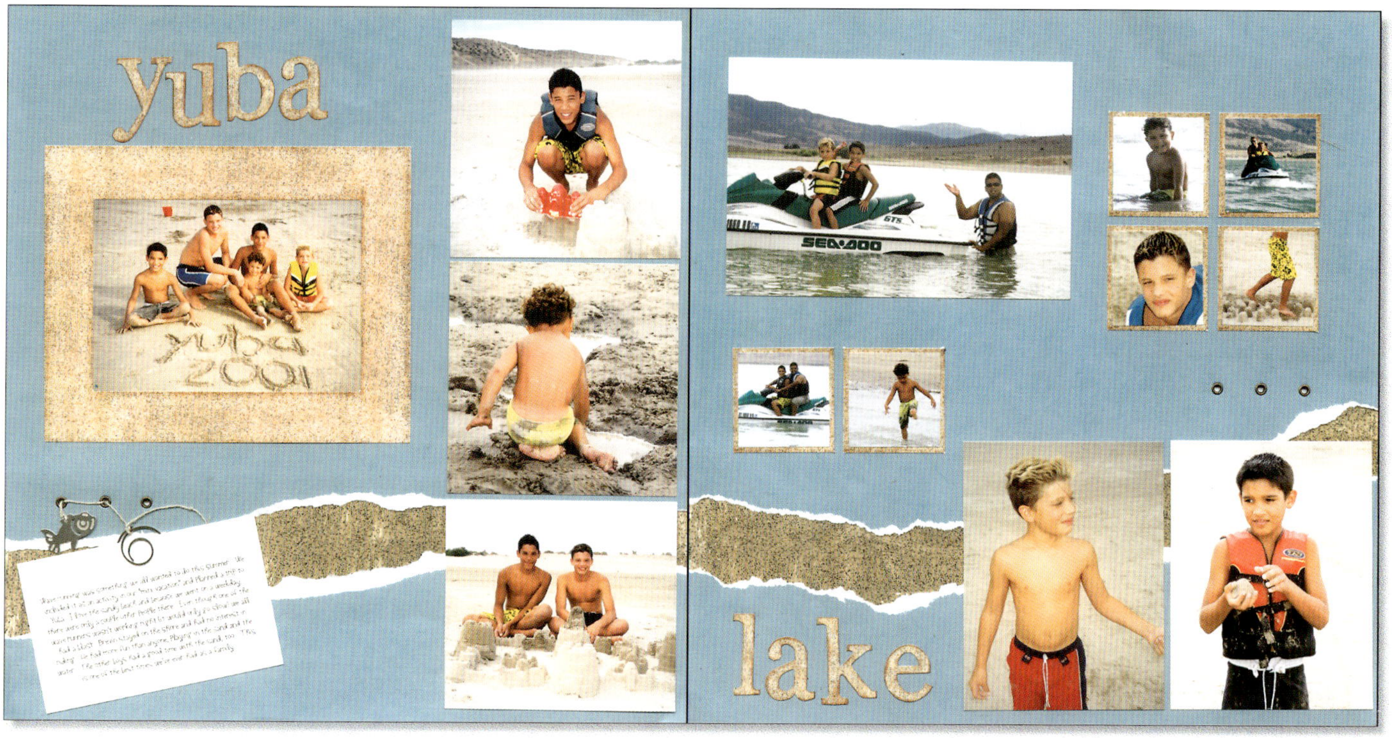
yuba
yuba 2001
SEA-DOO
lake

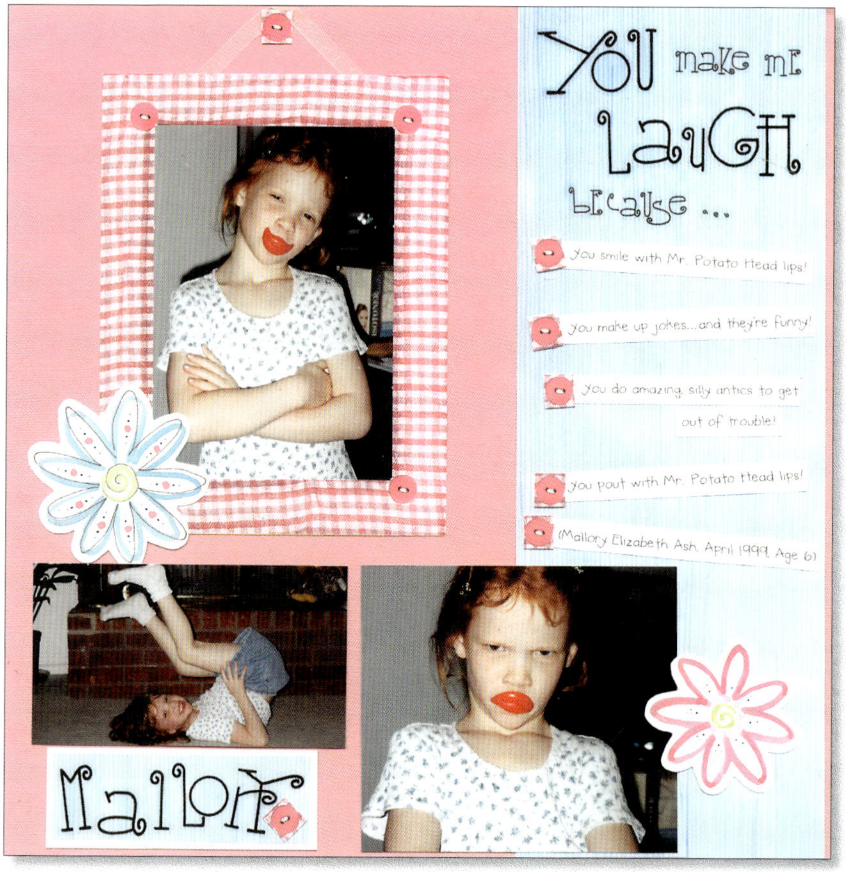
You make me
Laugh
because ...
You smile with Mr. Potato Head lips!
You make up jokes...and they're funny!
You do amazing, silly antics to get out of trouble!
You pout with Mr. Potato Head lips!
(Mallory Elizabeth Ash, April 1999, Age 6)
Mallory

Yuba Lake

Supplies
Letter punch-outs and preprinted frame: My Mind's Eye
Fish charm: Charmed I'm Sure
Eyelets: Making Memories
Stamping ink: ColorBox, Clearsnap
Computer font: CK Fresh, "Fresh Fonts" CD, *Creating Keepsakes*
Other: String and spiral paper clip

♥ **I Love It!:** *Once the letters were punched out of their frames (they come in perforated blocks), the frames were used to mat the smaller photographs on this layout.*

You Make Me Laugh

Supplies
Patterned paper and letter stickers: Provo Craft
Preprinted frame and accents: My Mind's Eye
Computer font: CK Toggle, "The Best of Creative Lettering" CD Vol. 3, *Creating Keepsakes*

♥ **I Love It!:** *These lighthearted, whimsical letter stickers graphically represent the comical theme of the layout.*

tip 5

transform letters and words into accents.

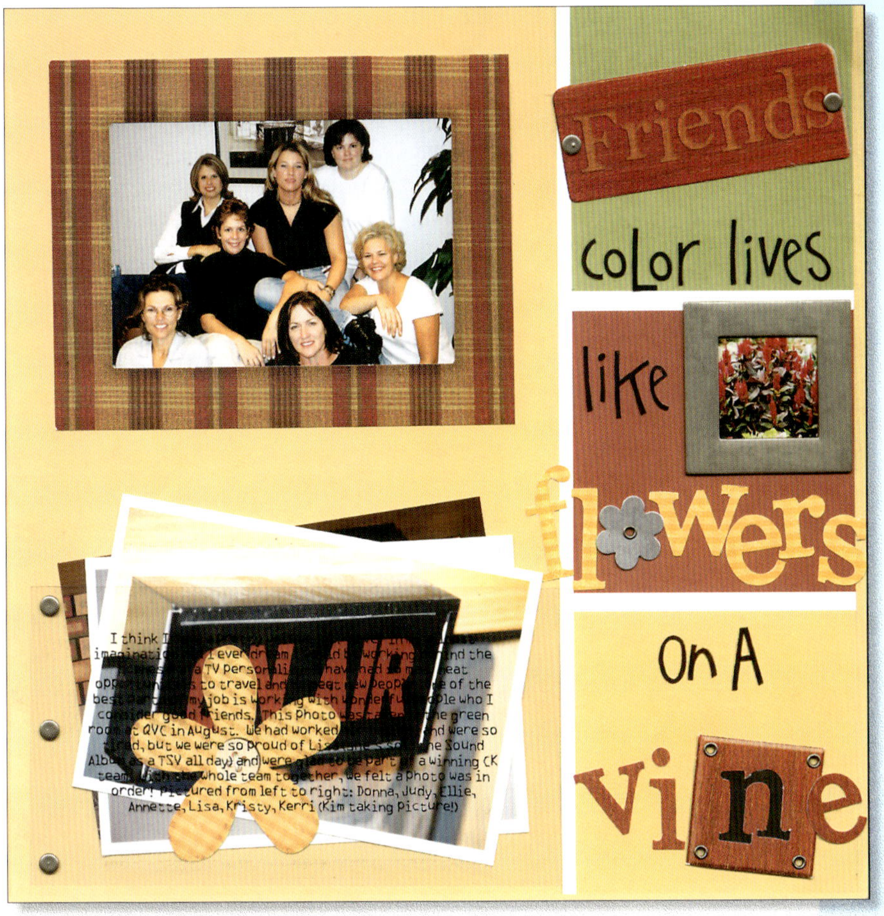
Friends
color lives
like
flowers
on a
vine

Friends Color Lives

Supplies

Patterned paper: SEI
Preprinted frame, word, letter punch-outs and accents: My Mind's Eye
Letter stickers: Sue Dreamer, Colorbök
Metal accents, eyelets and snaps: Making Memories
Computer font: CK Carbon Copy, "Fresh Fonts" CD, *Creating Keepsakes*
Other: Transparency paper

♥ **I Love It!:** *The journaling for this layout was printed on clear transparency paper, which was then attached on three edges to create a pocket. The pocket holds three photographs.*

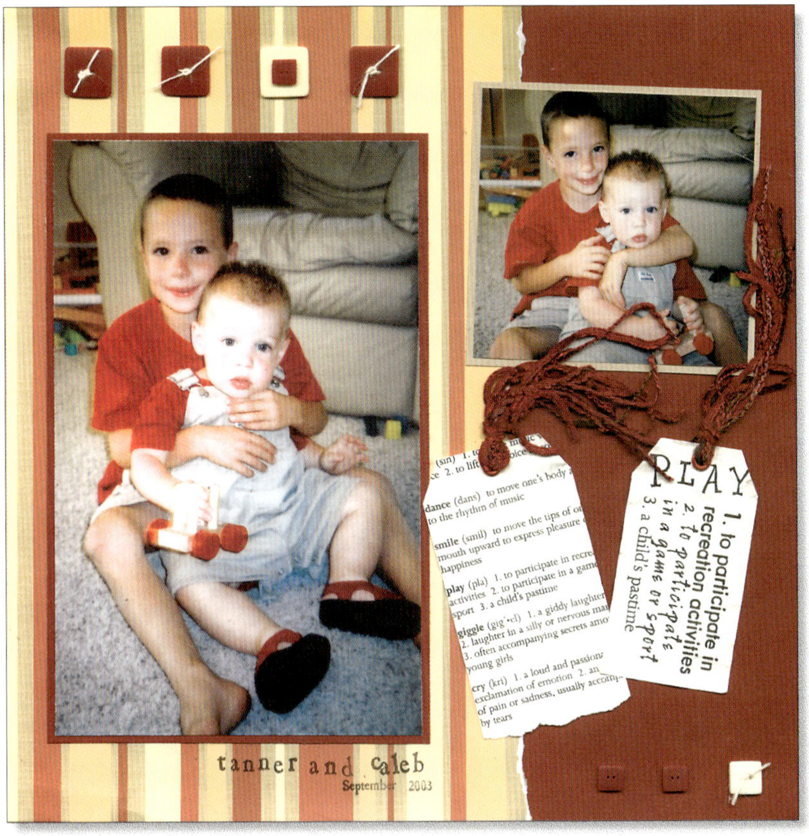
PLAY
1. to participate in recreation activities
2. to participate in a game or sport
3. a child's pastime
tanner and caleb
September 2003

Tanner and Caleb

Supplies

Patterned paper: Chatterbox
Definition accents, buttons and date stamp: Making Memories
Letter stamps: PSX Design
Stamping ink: ColorBox, Clearsnap
Fibers: On The Surface
Eyelet: Impress Rubber Stamps

♥ **I Love It!:** *The definition accents were trimmed and torn into tags to accent the layout.*

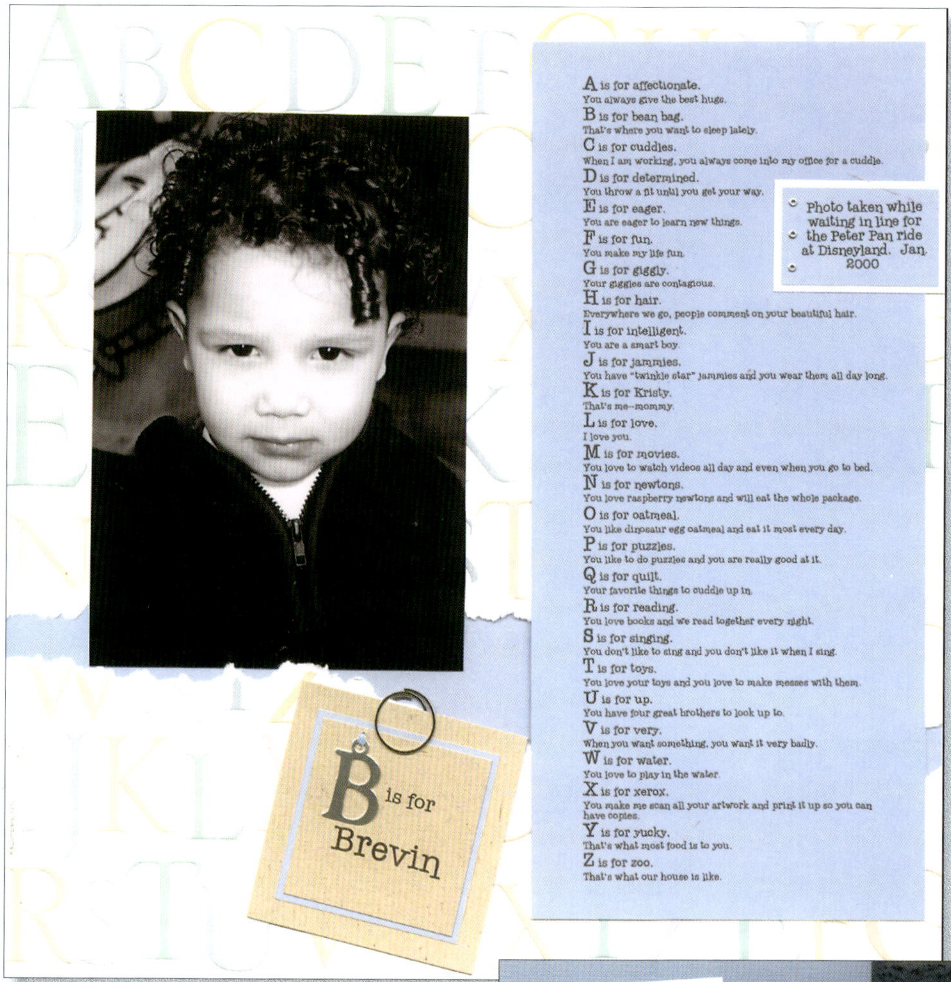
A is for affectionate.
You always give the best hugs.
B is for bean bag.
That's where you want to sleep lately.
C is for cuddles.
When I am working, you always come into my office for a cuddle.
D is for determined.
You throw a fit until you get your way.
E is for eager.
You are eager to learn new things.
F is for fun.
You make my life fun.
G is for giggly.
Your giggles are contagious.
H is for hair.
Everywhere we go, people comment on your beautiful hair.
I is for intelligent.
You are a smart boy.
J is for jammies.
You have "twinkle star" jammies and you wear them all day long.
K is for Kristy.
That's me—mommy.
L is for love.
I love you.
M is for movies.
You love to watch videos all day and even when you go to bed.
N is for newtons.
You love raspberry newtons and will eat the whole package.
O is for oatmeal.
You like dinosaur egg oatmeal and eat it most every day.
P is for puzzles.
You like to do puzzles and you are really good at it.
Q is for quilt.
Your favorite things to cuddle up in.
R is for reading.
You love books and we read together every night.
S is for singing.
You don't like to sing and you don't like it when I sing.
T is for toys.
You love your toys and you love to make messes with them.
U is for up.
You have four great brothers to look up to.
V is for very.
When you want something, you want it very badly.
W is for water.
You love to play in the water.
X is for xerox.
You make me scan all your artwork and print it up so you can have copies.
Y is for yucky.
That's what most food is to you.
Z is for zoo.
That's what our house is like.
Photo taken while waiting in line for the Peter Pan ride at Disneyland. Jan. 2000
B is for Brevin

B Is for Brevin

Supplies
Embossed cardstock: K & Company
Metal letter charm and eyelets: Making Memories
Computer font: CK Stenography, "Fresh Fonts" CD, *Creating Keepsakes*
Other: Spiral paper clip and embroidery floss

♥ **I Love It!:** *When you're struggling to express in words exactly how you feel, use this "alphabet journaling" technique: Starting with "A," think of a word that relates to the subject of your layout for every letter of the alphabet. Be sure to include a brief explanation of each word and how it relates to your theme.*

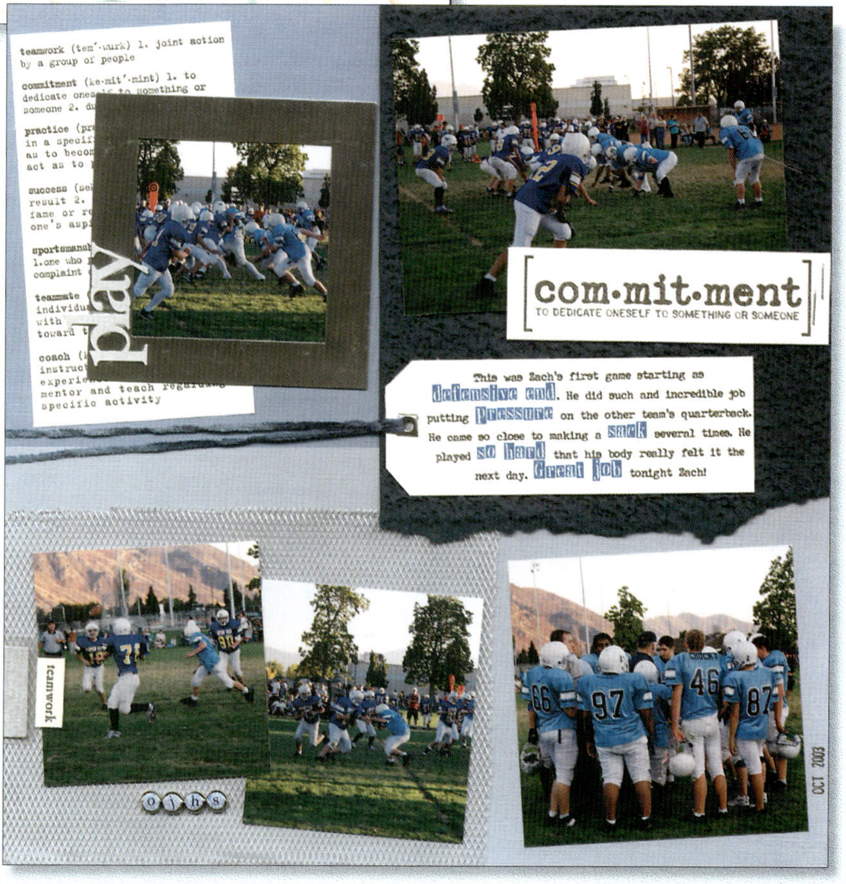
teamwork
play
com·mit·ment
TO DEDICATE ONESELF TO SOMETHING OR SOMEONE
This was Zach's first game starting as defensive end. He did such and incredible job putting pressure on the other team's quarterback. He came so close to making a sack several times. He played so hard that his body really felt it the next day. Great job tonight Zach!
teamwork
ojhs
OCT 2003

Commitment

Supplies
Textured paper: Provo Craft
Preprinted words, definitions and metal accents: Making Memories
Letter brads: Creative Imaginations
Fibers: On The Surface
Computer fonts: CK Typewriter, "Fresh Fonts" CD, *Creating Keepsakes*; 2Peas Gift, downloaded from *www.twopeasinabucket.com*
Other: Metal screening, plastic index tab and date stamp

♥ **I Love It!:** *The metal word "play" was glued with liquid adhesive to the metal frame to create a subtle accent that looks like it was already a part of the frame.*

tip 6
combine different styles and sizes of fonts.

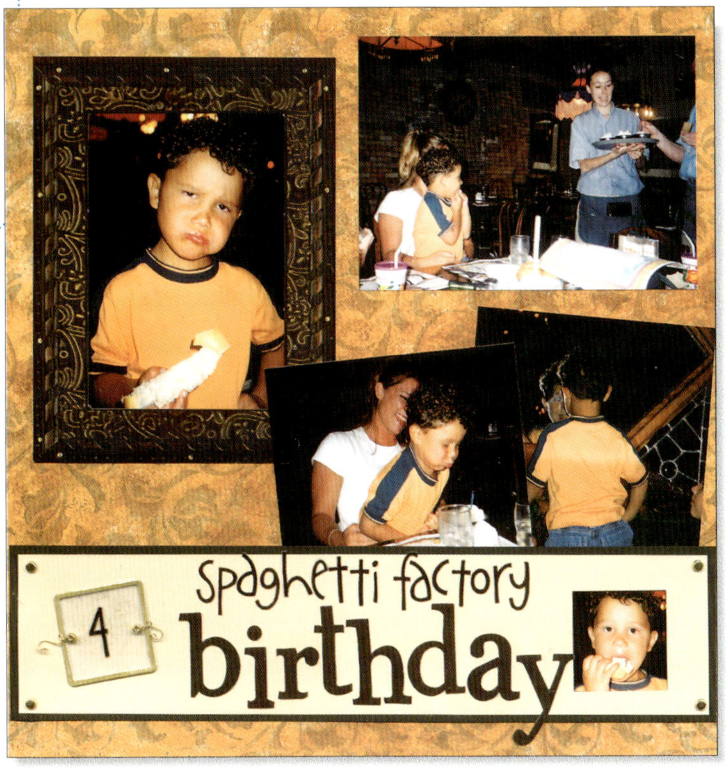

spaghetti factory
4
birthday

Spaghetti Factory Birthday

Supplies
Patterned paper: Scrap-Ease
Preprinted frame and letter punch-outs: My Mind's Eye
Letter stickers: Sue Dreamer, Colorbök
Metal-rimmed tag and brads: Making Memories
Other: Wire and beads

♥ **I Love It!:** *Your focal-point photograph doesn't always have to show a perfect subject with a perfect smile. I love the personality that shows through in the framed photograph on this layout!*

The Sound of Music

Supplies
Textured cardstock: NRN Designs
Metal letter accents: Making Memories
Preprinted poem: Tiny Tales, My Mind's Eye
Other: Mulberry paper, fibers and wire

♥ **I Love It!:** *Once you've introduced metal onto your layout using metal letter accents, maintain a consistent feel by creating simple wire accents to match.*

♥ **I Love It!:** *A color copy of a certificate of completion is included on the back of this page for future reference.*

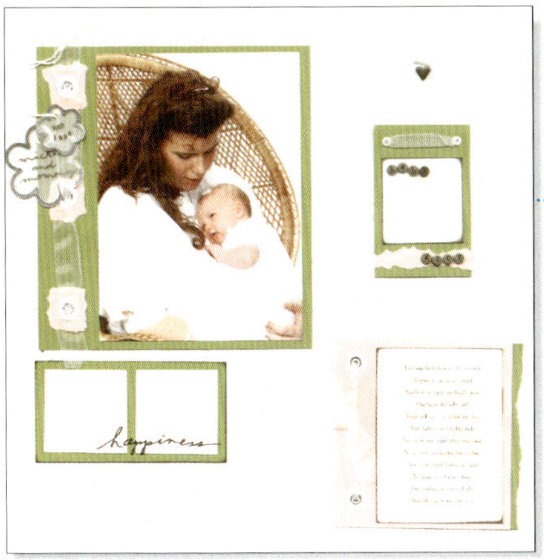

happiness

Same Idea, Slightly Different: *These matte metal letter accents are so versatile: they were used on the graphic, geometric page at right and on this sweet, feminine tag on the page above.*

Baby Girl

Supplies
Metal letter accents: Making Memories
Rubber stamps and stamping ink: Rubber Stampede
Preprinted poem: Tiny Tales, My Mind's Eye
Eyelets: Doodlebug Design
Other: Ribbon

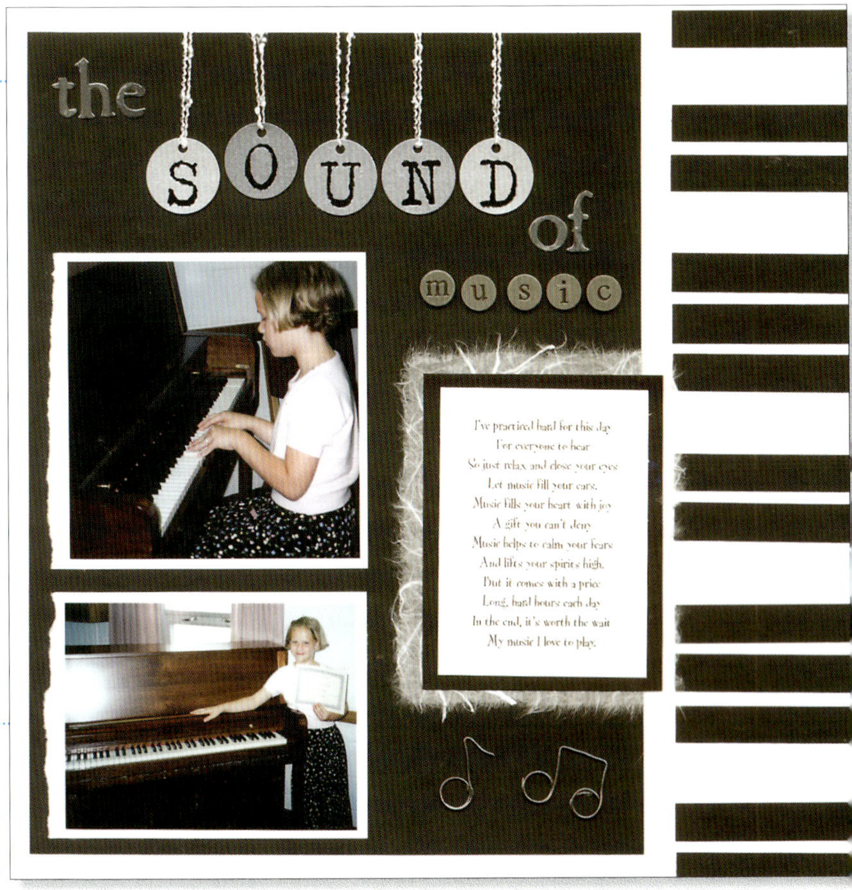

the
SOUND
of
music
I've practiced hard for this day
For everyone to hear
So just relax and close your eyes
Let music fill your ears.
Music fills your heart with joy
A gift you can't deny
Music helps to calm your fears
And lifts your spirits high.
But it comes with a price
Long, hard hours each day
In the end, it's worth the wait
My music I love to play.

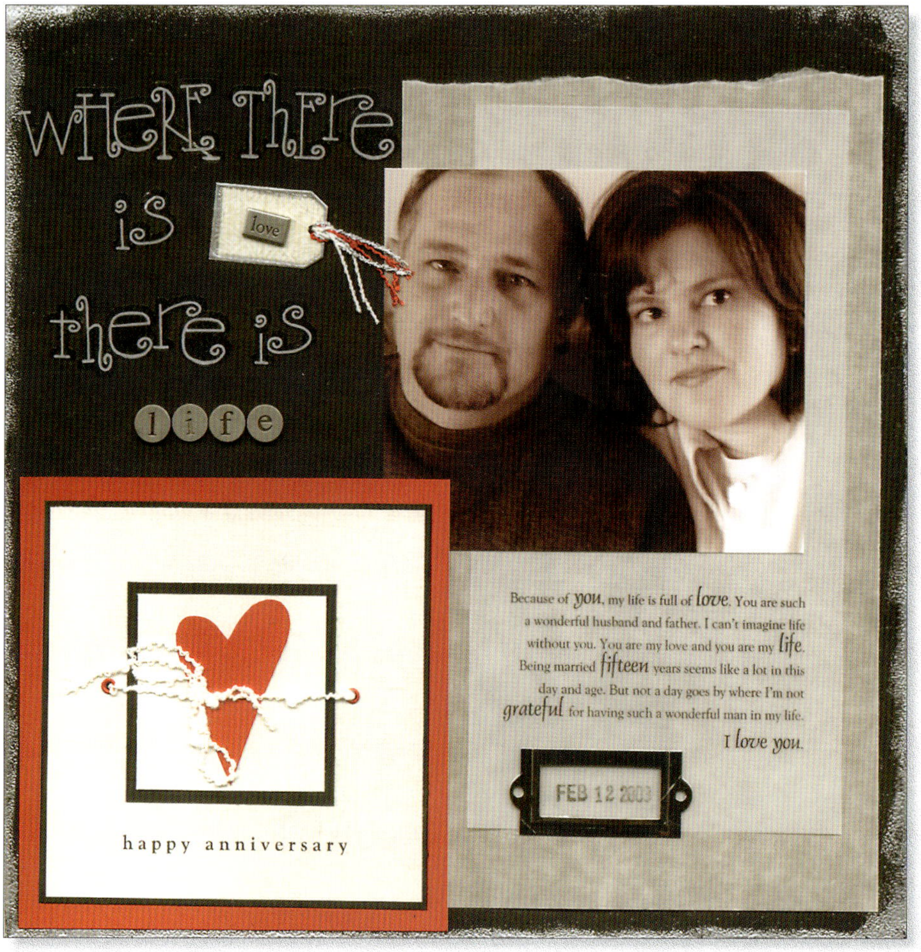
where there is
love
there is life
Because of you, my life is full of love. You are such a wonderful husband and father. I can't imagine life without you. You are my love and you are my life. Being married fifteen years seems like a lot in this day and age. But not a day goes by where I'm not grateful for having such a wonderful man in my life.
I love you.
FEB 12 2003
happy anniversary

Where There Is Love

Supplies
Vellum: WorldWin
Letter stickers: Provo Craft
Metal letter and word accents: Making Memories
Bookplate: Magic Scraps
Fibers: On The Surface
Embossing powder: Stamp-n-Stuff, Stampendous!
Heart template: Coluzzle, Provo Craft
Computer fonts: Dauphin and Times New Roman, WordPerfect
Other: Date stamp and eyelets
Card idea from Creative Cards *by Becky Higgins*

I Love It!: *Duplicate the look of metal-rimmed tags on tags you create by hand. Here's how: Carefully moisten the edges of the tag with embossing ink, then coat the inked edges with metallic embossing powder and heat-emboss until raised. Embellish as desired.*

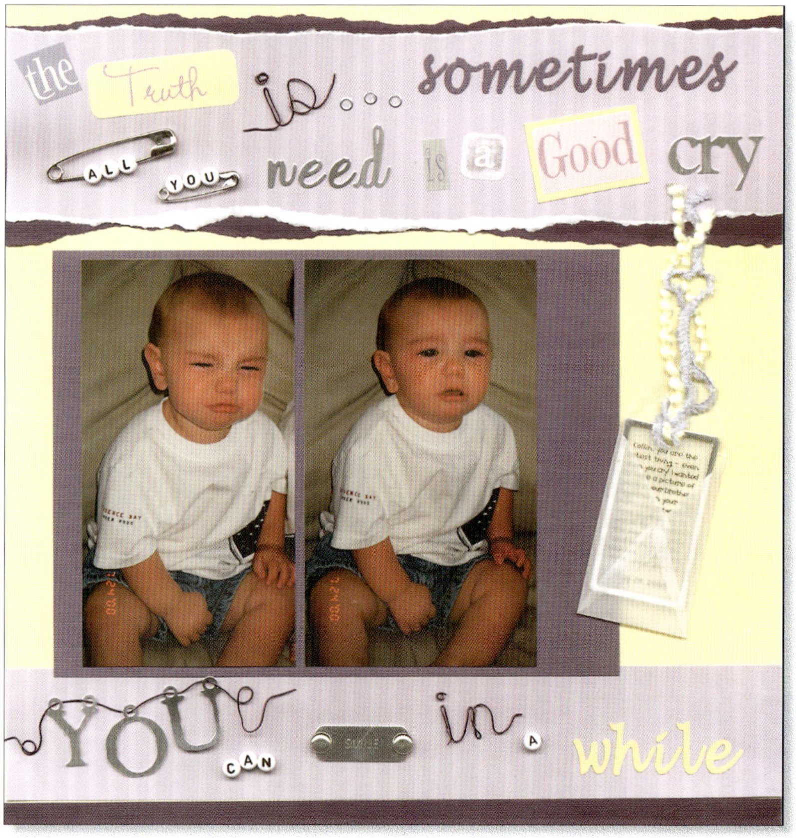
the Truth is... sometimes
ALL YOU need is a Good cry
YOU CAN in a while

The Truth Is ...

Supplies
Patterned paper, word stickers, vellum envelope, fibers, metal word tags, brads and washers: Colorbök
Letter sticker: Sonnets by Sharon Soneff, Creative Imaginations
Metal letter accents and metal-rimmed tag: Making Memories
Craft wire: Artista
Letter die cuts: QuicKutz
Computer font: CK Fun, "The Art of Creative Lettering" CD, *Creating Keepsakes*
Other: Letter beads and safety pins

I Love It!: *Let your title serve as a design element as well when you create an artistic word collage like this one. Use small needle-nose pliers to bend wire into tight curves and spirals.*

ip 7

mix and match different styles and sizes of fonts in the same word.

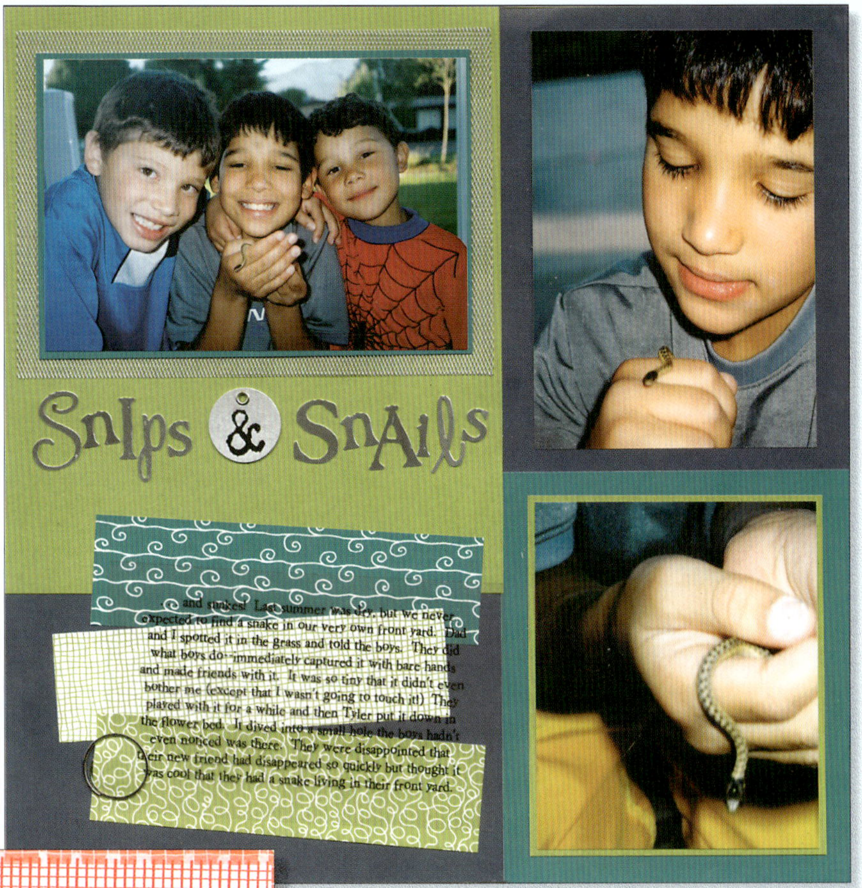

Snips & Snails
and snakes! Last summer was dry, but we never expected to find a snake in our very own front yard. Dad and I spotted it in the grass and told the boys. They did what boys do - immediately captured it with bare hands and made friends with it. It was so tiny that it didn't even bother me (except that I wasn't going to touch it!) They played with it for a while and then Tyler put it down in the flower bed. It dived into a small hole the boys hadn't even noticed was there. They were disappointed that their new friend had disappeared so quickly but thought it was cool that they had a snake living in their front yard.

Snips & Snails

Supplies
Patterned papers: Provo Craft
Metal letter accents: Making Memories
Computer font: CK Constitution, "Fresh Fonts" CD, *Creating Keepsakes*
Other: Wire screen, transparency paper and spiral paper clip

♥ **I Love It!:** *Try mixing and matching cursive and print fonts in your titles and journaling.*

♥ **I Love It!:** *The wire screening is the perfect photo mat for these outdoor, all-boy photographs.*

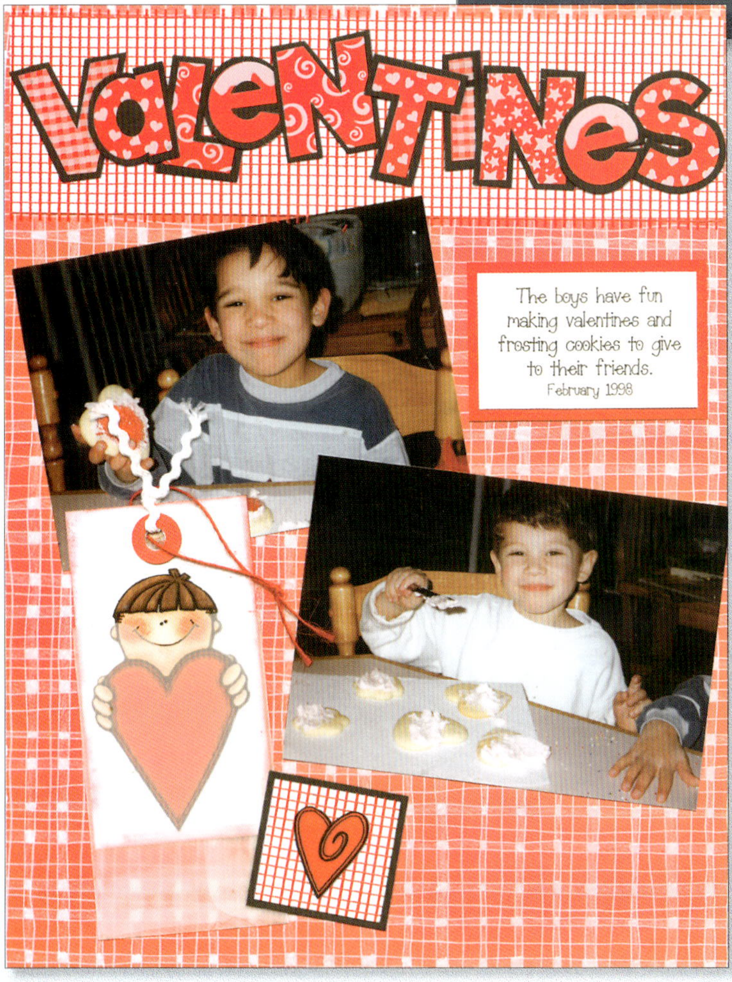

Valentines
The boys have fun making valentines and frosting cookies to give to their friends.
February 1998

Valentines

Supplies
Patterned paper: Source unknown
Letter stickers and overlays: Making Memories
Preprinted accents: Cock-A-Doodle Design
Mesh: Magic Mesh
Computer font: Scrap Heart, "Lettering Delights" CD, Inspire Graphics
Chalks: Craf-T Products
Other: Vellum envelope and fibers

♥ **I Love It!:** *When product allows, mix and match different patterns, colors and sizes of letter stickers to suit the mood of your layout.*

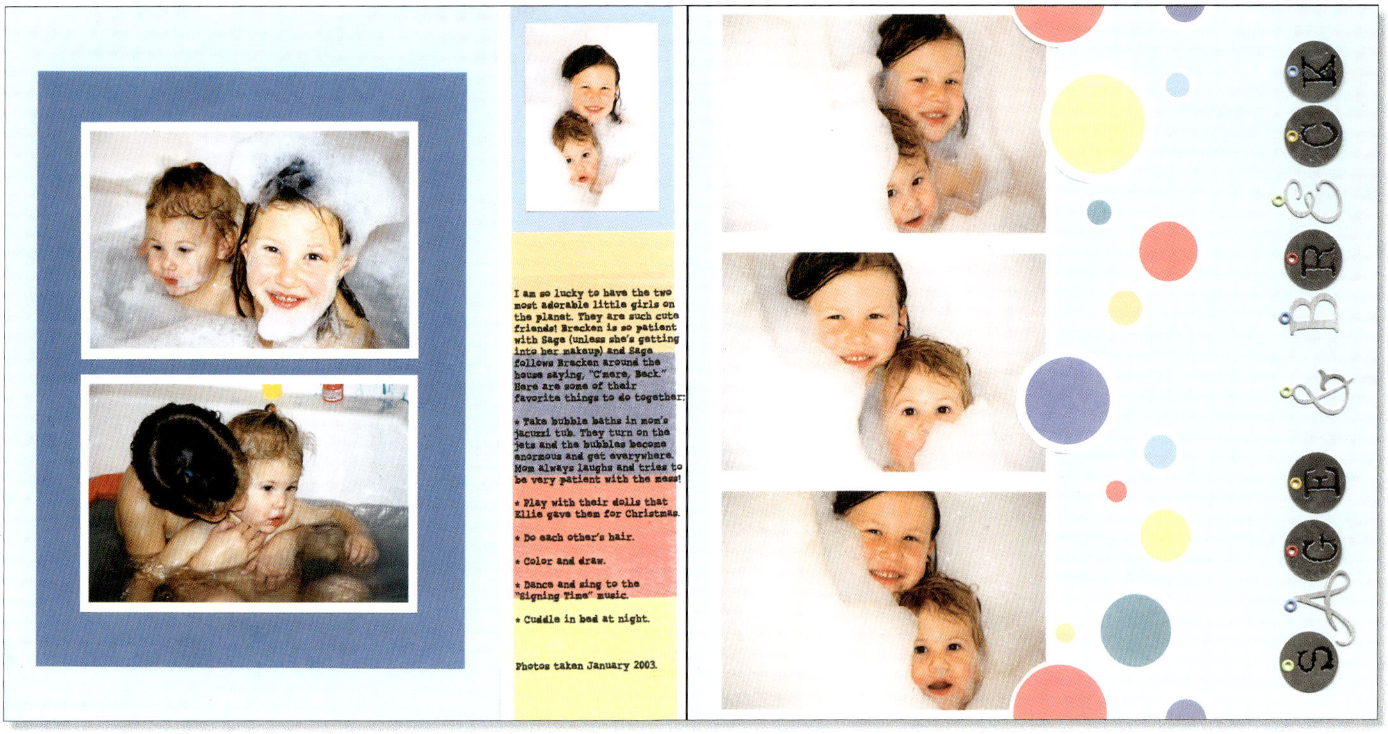
I am so lucky to have the two most adorable little girls on the planet. They are such cute friends! Bracken is so patient with Sage (unless she's getting into her makeup) and Sage follows Bracken around the house saying, "C'mere, Back." Here are some of their favorite things to do together:
* Take bubble baths in mom's jacuzzi tub. They turn on the jets and the bubbles become enormous and get everywhere. Mom always laughs and tries to be very patient with the mess!
* Play with their dolls that Ellie gave them for Christmas.
* Do each other's hair.
* Color and draw.
* Dance and sing to the "Signing Time" music.
* Cuddle in bed at night.
Photos taken January 2003.
SAGE & BRECK

Sage & Breck

Supplies
Patterned paper: SEI
Vellum: Colorbök
Metal letter accents and eyelets: Making Memories
Computer font: CK Typewriter, "Fresh Fonts" CD, *Creating Keepsakes*

♥ **I Love It!:** *Parts of the patterned paper were slit with a craft knife so the photographs could be slipped underneath the circles in the pattern.*

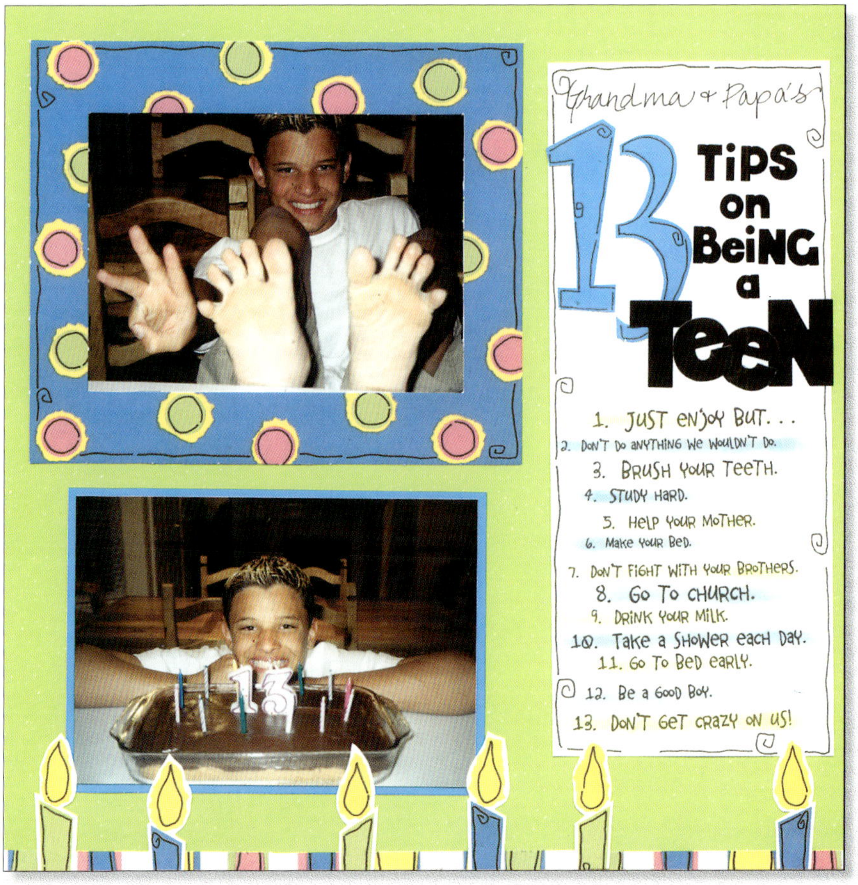
Grandma & Papa's
13 Tips on Being a Teen
1. Just enjoy but...
2. Don't do anything we wouldn't do.
3. Brush your teeth.
4. Study hard.
5. Help your mother.
6. Make your bed.
7. Don't fight with your brothers.
8. Go to church.
9. Drink your milk.
10. Take a shower each day.
11. Go to bed early.
12. Be a good boy.
13. Don't get crazy on us!

Grandma's 13 Tips

Supplies
Patterned paper: Making Memories
Preprinted frame and accents: Nankong
Letter stickers: Provo Craft
Lettering template: Whimsy, Déjà Views
Computer font: Scrap Brother, "Lettering Delights" CD, Inspire Graphics
Chalks: Stampin' Up!
Pen: Zig Writer, EK Success

♥ **I Love It!:** *Mix and match upper- and lowercase letters in the same font style for a fun twist.*

♥ **I Love It!:** *Graphically represent your child's age in a photograph by having the child hold up the appropriate number of fingers (and toes, if necessary!).*

tip 8

create one-word titles for maximum impact on your layouts.

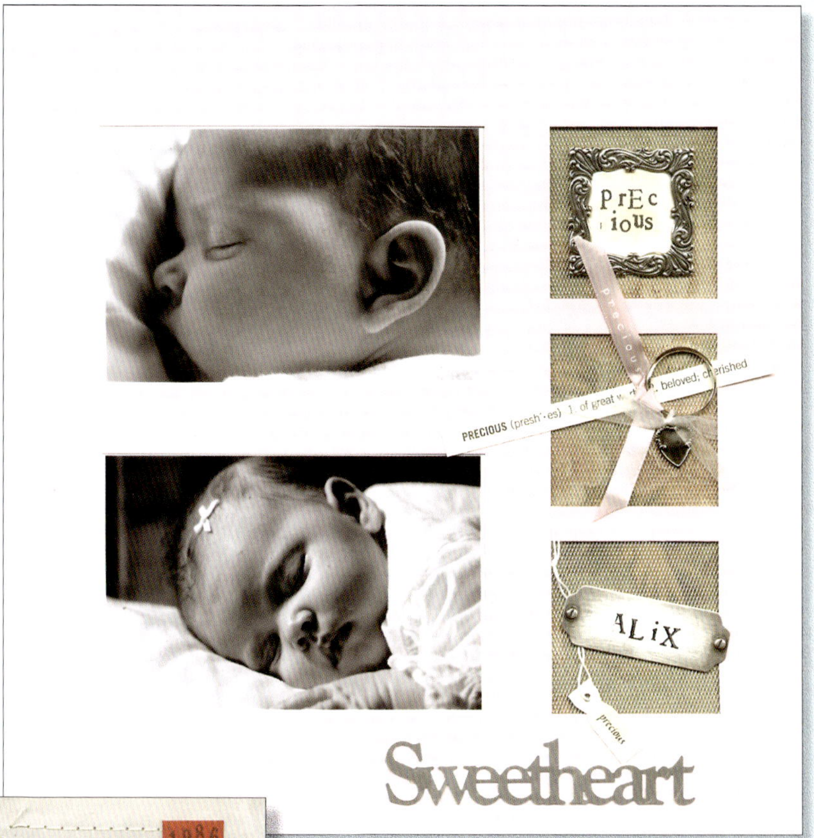

PrEc
ious
PRECIOUS (presh'·es) 1. of great w... beloved; cherished
precious
ALiX
Sweetheart

Sweetheart

Supplies
Preformatted cardstock, metal word accent, definition and printed ribbon: Making Memories
Patterned paper: Daisy D's (behind metal screening)
Charm: Buttons Galore
Metal frame and nameplate: Once Upon a Charm
Chalk: Stampin' Up!
Letter stamps: PSX Design
Stamping ink: ColorBox, Clearsnap

♥ **I Love It!:** *These photographs were printed with a thin white border, which provides a matted effect with the pre-cut windows in the cardstock.*

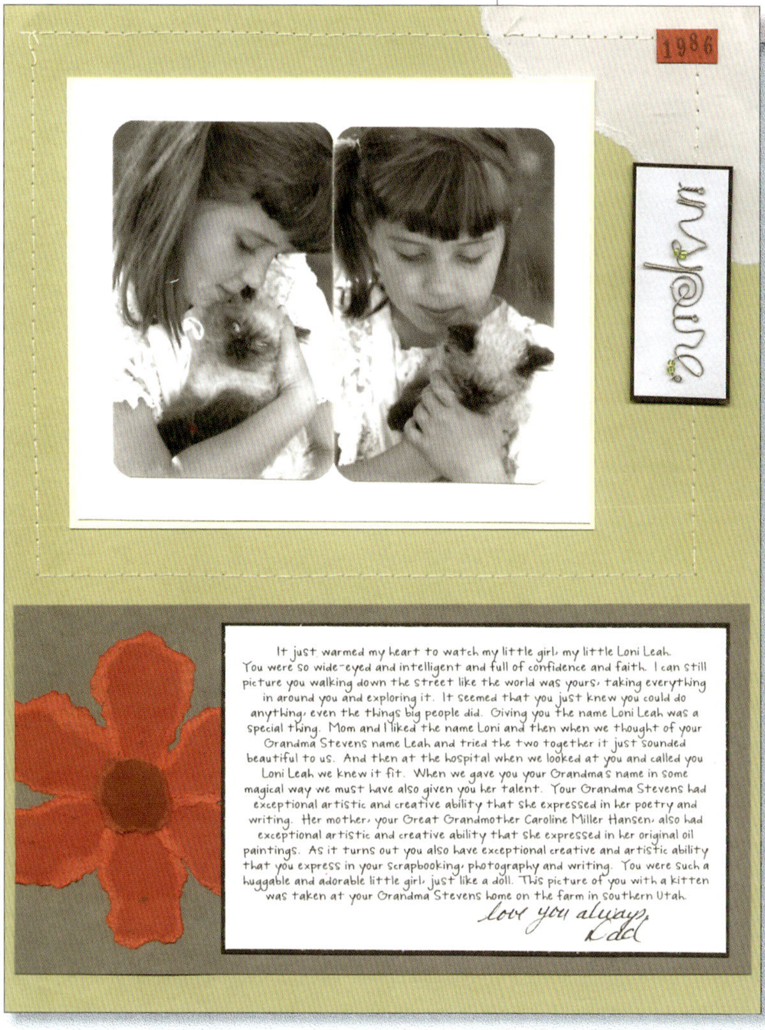

1986
inspire
It just warmed my heart to watch my little girl, my little Loni Leah. You were so wide-eyed and intelligent and full of confidence and faith. I can still picture you walking down the street like the world was yours, taking everything in around you and exploring it. It seemed that you just knew you could do anything, even the things big people did. Giving you the name Loni Leah was a special thing. Mom and I liked the name Loni and then when we thought of your Grandma Stevens name Leah and tried the two together it just sounded beautiful to us. And then at the hospital when we looked at you and called you Loni Leah we knew it fit. When we gave you your Grandma's name in some magical way we must have also given you her talent. Your Grandma Stevens had exceptional artistic and creative ability that she expressed in her poetry and writing. Her mother, your Great Grandmother Caroline Miller Hansen, also had exceptional artistic and creative ability that she expressed in her original oil paintings. As it turns out you also have exceptional creative and artistic ability that you express in your scrapbooking, photography and writing. You were such a huggable and adorable little girl, just like a doll. This picture of you with a kitten was taken at your Grandma Stevens home on the farm in southern Utah.
love you always,
Dad

Inspire

Supplies
Wire word accent: Making Memories
Computer font: CK Jot, "The Art of Creative Lettering" CD, *Creating Keepsakes*

♥ **I Love It!:** *So much scrapbooking is done by moms. Did you notice that the letter on this layout was written by a dad? Remember to include the perspectives and feelings of all your family members or loved ones in your albums.*

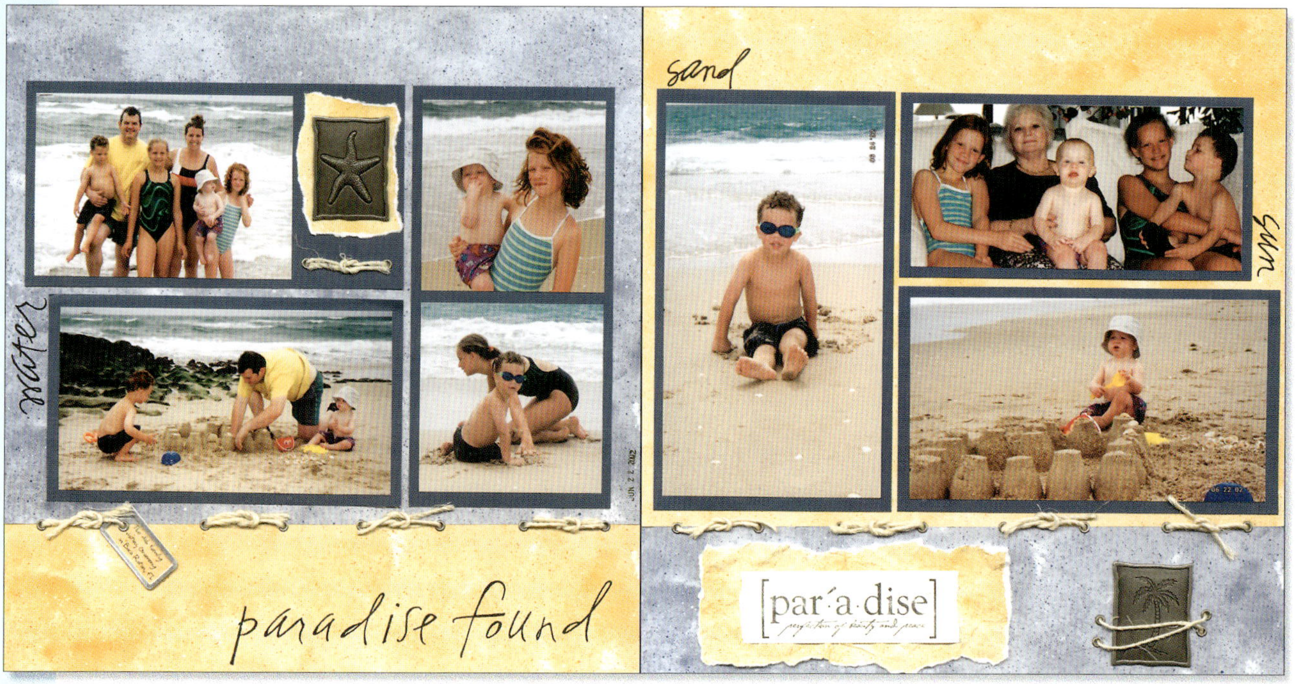
sand
sun
water
paradise found
[par'a·dise]

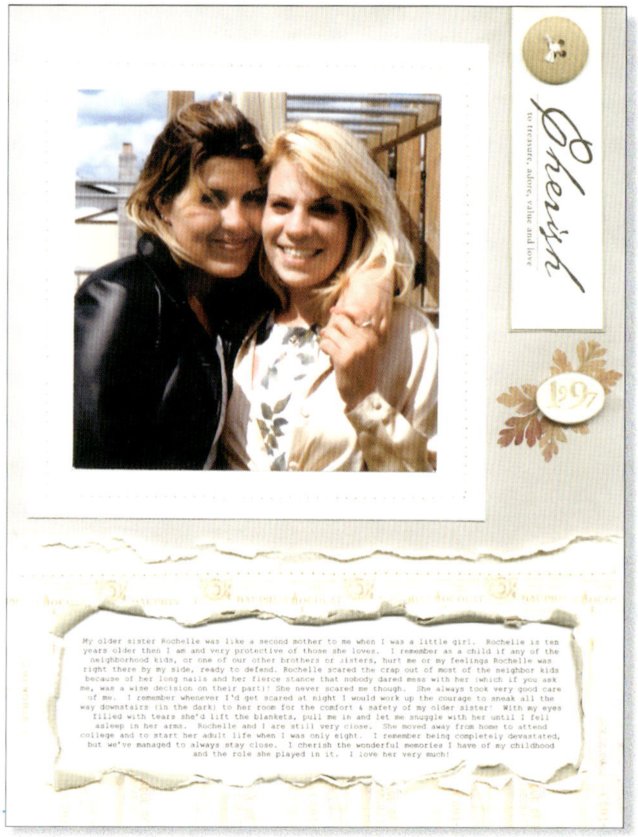
Cherish
to treasure, adore, value and love
1997
My older sister Rochelle was like a second mother to me when I was a little girl. Rochelle is ten years older then I am and very protective of those she loves. I remember as a child if any of the neighborhood kids, or one of our other brothers or sisters, hurt me or my feelings Rochelle was right there by my side, ready to defend. Rochelle scared the crap out of most of the neighbor kids because of her long nails and her fierce stance that nobody dared mess with her (which if you ask me, was a wise decision on their part)! She never scared me though. She always took very good care of me. I remember whenever I'd get scared at night I would work up the courage to sneak all the way downstairs (in the dark) to her room for the comfort & safety of my older sister! With my eyes filled with tears she'd lift the blankets, pull me in and let me snuggle with her until I fell asleep in her arms. Rochelle and I are still very close. She moved away from home to attend college and to start her adult life when I was only eight. I remember being completely devastated, but we've managed to always stay close. I cherish the wonderful memories I have of my childhood and the role she played in it. I love her very much!

Paradise

Supplies
Patterned paper: Provo Craft
Definition accents, rub-on words, metal accents and metal-rimmed tag: Making Memories
Eyelets: Doodlebug Design
Computer font: CK Artisan, "Fresh Fonts" CD, *Creating Keepsakes*
Other: Jute, date stamp and transparency paper

♥ **I Love It!:** *The vellum center of the metal-rimmed tag was removed and replaced with clear transparency paper with journaling printed on it.*

Cherish

Supplies
Patterned paper: 7 Gypsies
Preprinted word accent, definition and pebble accent: Making Memories
Number stamps: PSX Design
Stamping ink: ColorBox, Clearsnap
Pressed leaf: Nature's Pressed
Computer font: Linenstroke, downloaded from the Internet
Other: Button, twine and 3-D foam tape

♥ **I Love It!:** *The beautiful page pebble accent on this layout was adhered with 3-D foam tape to raise it slightly above the pressed leaf, adding dimension.*

Same Idea, Slightly Different: *If paper accents are looking too crisp and new for your layouts, try dyeing them with walnut ink. The blotchy, distinctive color evokes images of the past.*

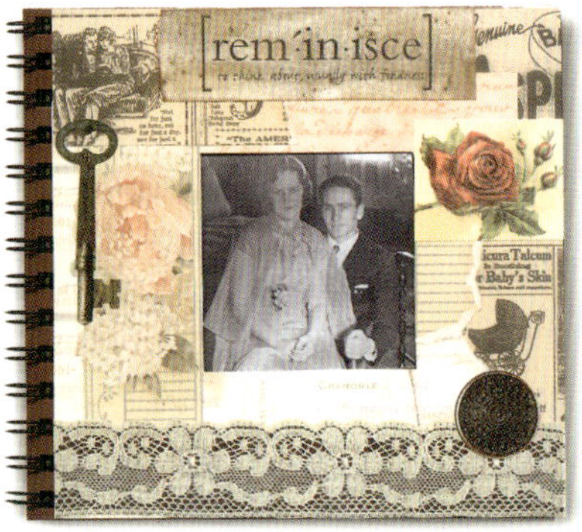
[rem'in·isce]

Reminisce Album

Supplies
Patterned papers: Rusty Pickle (newspaper), 7 Gypsies (all others)
Stickers: Nostalgiques, EK Success
Floral border: K & Company
Definition accent: Making Memories
Walnut ink: Anima Designs

tip 9

define key words or themes on your layout for an artistic effect.

Friendship

Supplies

Patterned papers: Design Originals (dictionary), K & Company (striped)
Definition accent and eyelet: Making Memories
Fabric label and train ephemera: me & my BIG ideas
Pearl snap: Prym-Dritz
Paper photo corners: Kolo
Metal photo corners: 7 Gypsies
Number stamps: Stampington and Company
Stamping ink: Ranger Industries
Computer font: Maszyna Plus, downloaded from the Internet
Other: Twine, wood buttons, compass, ribbon and staples

♥ **I Love It!:** *The bright red of the embroidery floss and fabric label add just enough of a splash of color to enliven the layout but not so much that they detract from the focal point.*

♥ **I Love It!:** *Looking for a quick, casual adhesive? Try something you're guaranteed to already have—a stapler! That's right, stapling accents, photographs and journaling to your layouts is a fun trend in scrapbooking right now, and it couldn't be easier!*

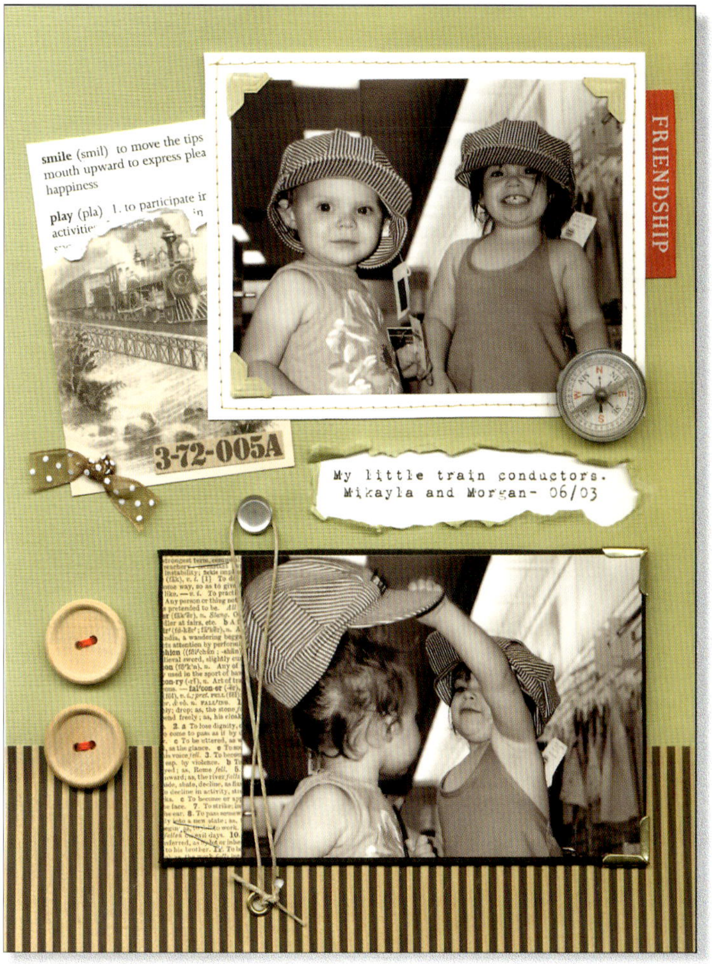
FRIENDSHIP
3-72-005A
My little train conductors.
Mikayla and Morgan- 06/03

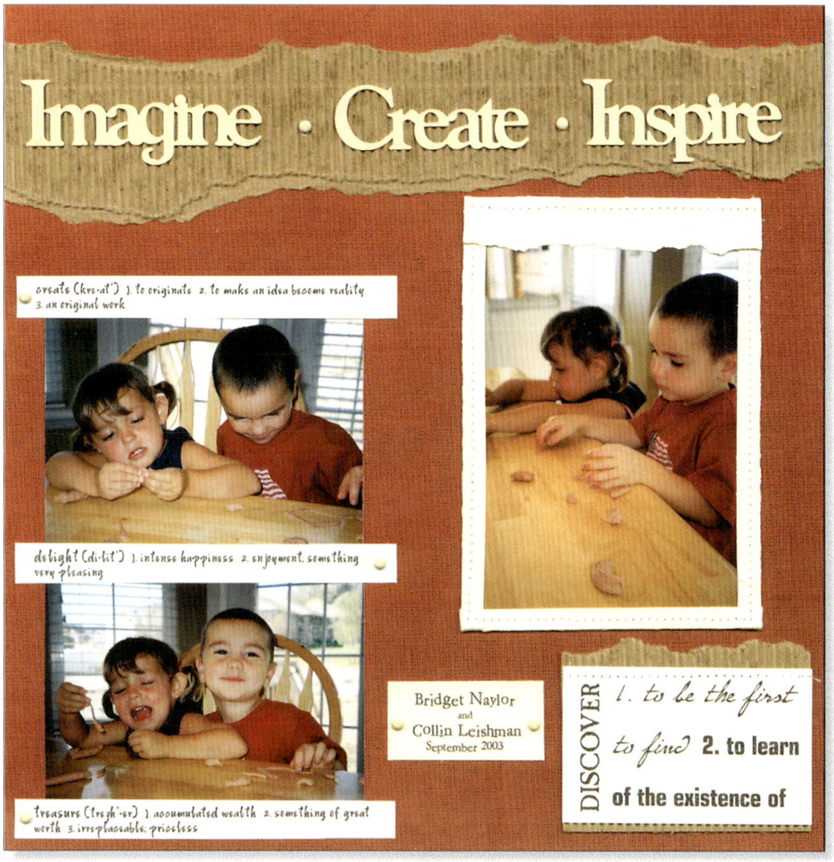
Imagine · Create · Inspire
create (kre-at') 1. to originate 2. to make an idea become reality 3. an original work
delight (di-lit') 1. intense happiness 2. enjoyment, something very pleasing
treasure (trezh'-er) 1. accumulated wealth 2. something of great worth 3. irreplaceable, priceless
Bridget Naylor
and
Collin Leishman
September 2003
DISCOVER
1. to be the first to find 2. to learn of the existence of

Imagine, Create, Inspire

Supplies

Patterned paper: K & Company
Corrugated paper: DMD, Inc.
Definition accents, metal words and brads: Making Memories
Computer font: CK Constitution, "Fresh Fonts" CD, *Creating Keepsakes*

♥ **I Love It!:** *The metal word accents and brads were painted with acrylic paints to match the colors of the layout.*

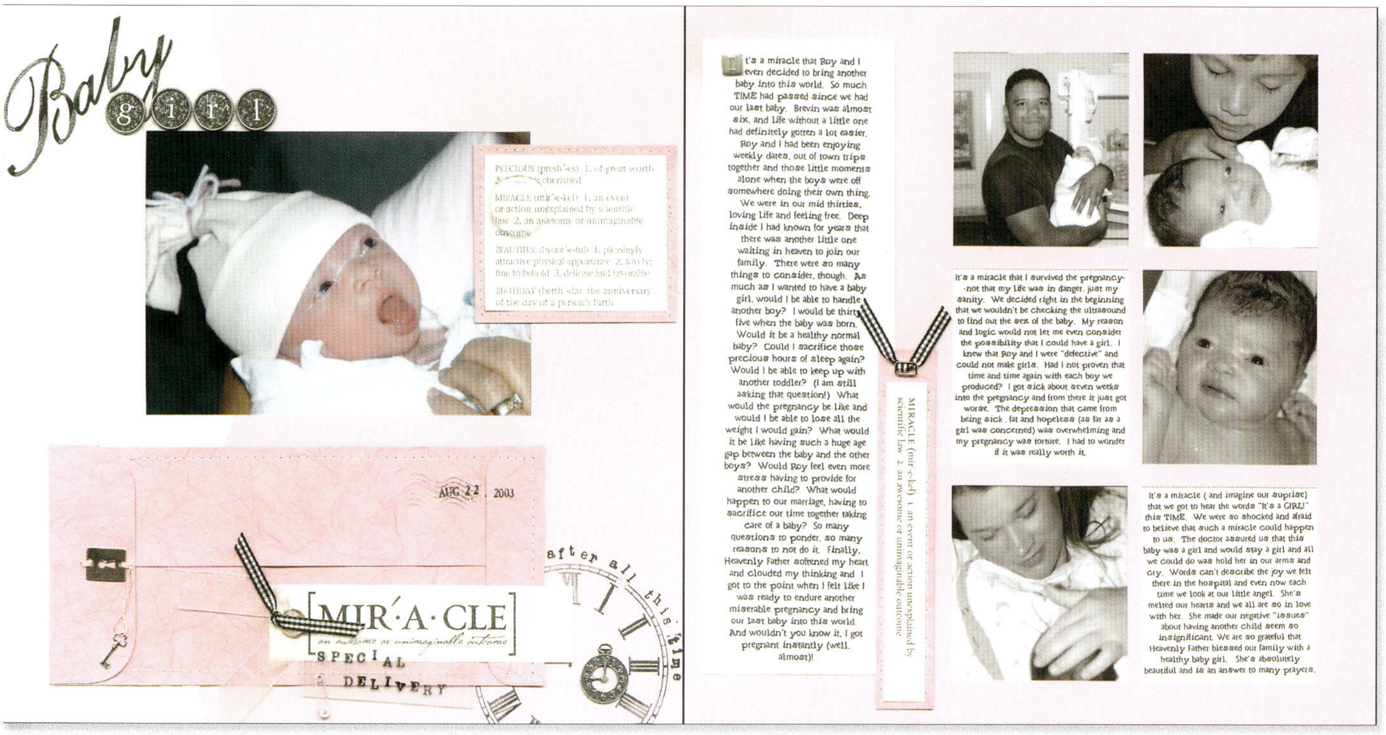
Baby girl
AUG 22 . 2003
MIR'A·CLE
an awesome or unimaginable outcome
SPECIAL DELIVERY
after all this time
It's a miracle that Roy and I even decided to bring another baby into this world. So much TIME had passed since we had our last baby. Brevin was almost six, and life without a little one had definitely gotten a lot easier. Roy and I had been enjoying weekly dates, out of town trips together and those little moments alone when the boys were off somewhere doing their own thing. We were in our mid thirties, loving life and feeling free. Deep inside I had known for years that there was another little one waiting in heaven to join our family. There were so many things to consider, though. As much as I wanted to have a baby girl, would I be able to handle another boy? I would be thirty five when the baby was born. Would it be a healthy normal baby? Could I sacrifice those precious hours of sleep again? Would I be able to keep up with another toddler? (I am still asking that question!) What would the pregnancy be like and would I be able to lose all the weight I would gain? What would it be like having such a huge age gap between the baby and the other boys? Would Roy feel even more stress having to provide for another child? What would happen to our marriage, having to sacrifice our time together taking care of a baby? So many questions to ponder, so many reasons to not do it. Finally, Heavenly Father softened my heart and clouded my thinking and I got to the point when I felt like I was ready to endure another miserable pregnancy and bring our last baby into this world. And wouldn't you know it, I got pregnant instantly (well, almost)!
MIRACLE (mir'e·kel) 1. an event or action unexplained by scientific law 2. an awesome or unimaginable outcome
It's a miracle that I survived the pregnancy--not that my life was in danger, just my sanity. We decided right in the beginning that we wouldn't be checking the ultrasound to find out the sex of the baby. My reason and logic would not let me even consider the possibility that I could have a girl. I knew that Roy and I were "defective" and could not make girls. Had I not proven that time and time again with each boy we produced? I got sick about seven weeks into the pregnancy and from there it just got worse. The depression that came from being sick, fat and hopeless (as far as a girl was concerned) was overwhelming and my pregnancy was torture. I had to wonder if it was really worth it.
It's a miracle (and imagine our suprise) that we got to hear the words "It's a GIRL!" this TIME. We were so shocked and afraid to believe that such a miracle could happen to us. The doctor assured us that this baby was a girl and would stay a girl and all we could do was hold her in our arms and cry. Words can't describe the joy we felt there in the hospital and even now each time we look at our little angel. She's melted our hearts and we all are so in love with her. She made our negative "issues" about having another child seem so insignificant. We are so grateful that Heavenly Father blessed our family with a healthy baby girl. She's absolutely beautiful and is an answer to many prayers.

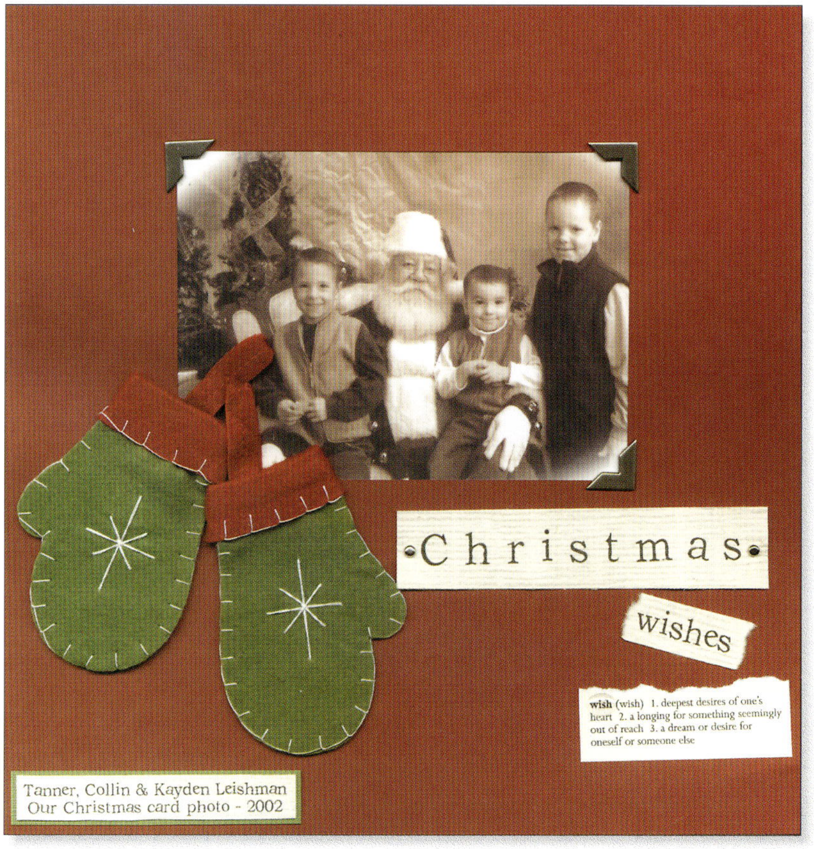
Christmas
wishes
wish (wish) 1. deepest desires of one's heart 2. a longing for something seemingly out of reach 3. a dream or desire for oneself or someone else
Tanner, Collin & Kayden Leishman
Our Christmas card photo - 2002

Baby Girl

Supplies
Preformatted cardstock, preprinted word and definition accents: Making Memories
Embossed cardstock: K & Company
Metal letters ("Girl"): Hot Off The Press
Computer fonts: English Vivace BT, WordPerfect; CK Evolution, "Fresh Fonts" CD, *Creating Keepsakes*
Rubber stamps: Stampington and Company (postage mark), Stampers Anonymous (clock), Making Memories (letters)
Stamping ink: ColorBox, Clearsnap
Embossing powder: Magic Dust
Watch crystal: Scrapworks
Microscope slide: Foofala
Charms: Once Upon a Charm
Safety pin: Li'l Davis Designs
Metal "I": All My Memories
Other: Ribbon, embroidery floss and date stamp

♥ **I Love It!:** *Alternating photographs and journaling in precut square photo mats ensures you'll have room to tell the whole story—in words and photos!*

Christmas Wishes

Supplies
Preformatted cardstock, definitions, page pebble, metal photo corners and brads: Making Memories
Computer font: CK Newsprint, "Fresh Fonts" CD, *Creating Keepsakes*

♥ **I Love It!:** *The adorable mitten accents on this layout are actually gift tags purchased at a local store. Keeping those eyes peeled for scrapbooking materials sure paid off on this layout!*

lisa's lessons on letters & words

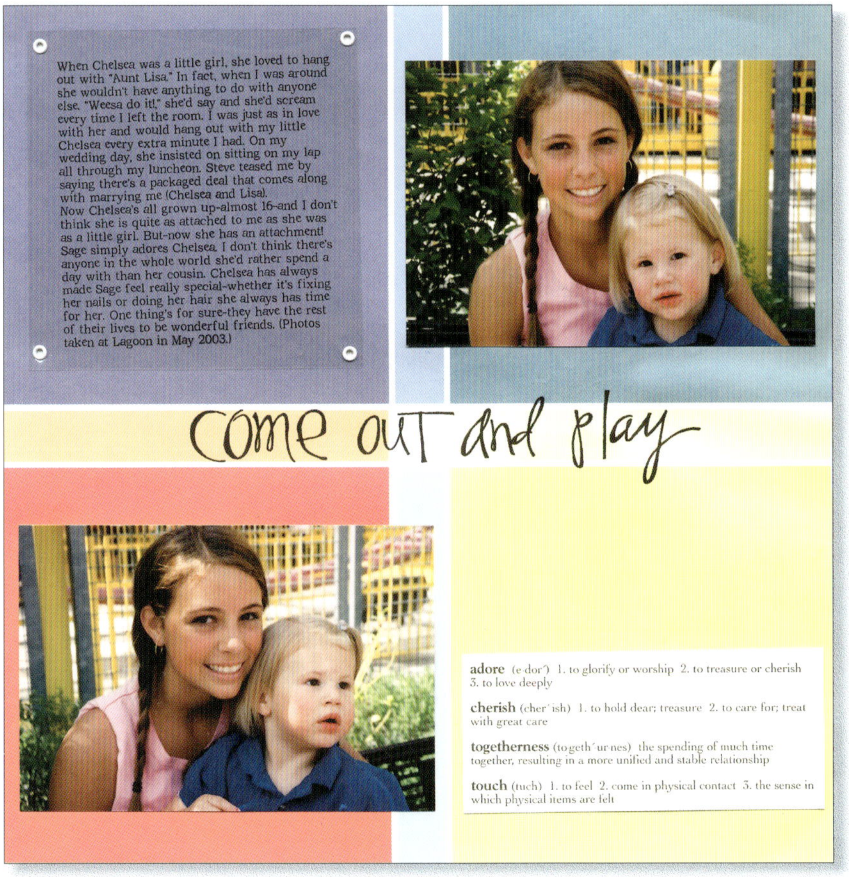

When Chelsea was a little girl, she loved to hang out with "Aunt Lisa." In fact, when I was around she wouldn't have anything to do with anyone else. "Weesa do it!," she'd say and she'd scream every time I left the room. I was just as in love with her and would hang out with my little Chelsea every extra minute I had. On my wedding day, she insisted on sitting on my lap all through my luncheon. Steve teased me by saying there's a packaged deal that comes along with marrying me (Chelsea and Lisa).
Now Chelsea's all grown up-almost 16-and I don't think she is quite as attached to me as she was as a little girl. But-now she has an attachment! Sage simply adores Chelsea. I don't think there's anyone in the whole world she'd rather spend a day with than her cousin. Chelsea has always made Sage feel really special-whether it's fixing her nails or doing her hair she always has time for her. One thing's for sure-they have the rest of their lives to be wonderful friends. (Photos taken at Lagoon in May 2003.)
come out and play
adore (e·dor´) 1. to glorify or worship 2. to treasure or cherish 3. to love deeply
cherish (cher´ish) 1. to hold dear; treasure 2. to care for; treat with great care
togetherness (to·geth´ur·nes) the spending of much time together, resulting in a more unified and stable relationship
touch (tuch) 1. to feel 2. come in physical contact 3. the sense in which physical items are felt

I admit it, I'm sometimes guilty of "handwriting envy." Lucky for me, there are plenty of products in the scrapbooking world that let me create perfect titles, journaling and word accents. Here are two of my favorite tips for using pre-made letter and word products:

- Writing on my layouts can really stress me out, but the thousands of computer fonts, letter stickers, alphabet charms and other products introduce the fun back into recording memories. Take a lighthearted approach to using these products on your pages. Try new and interesting combinations, or find a product that exactly matches the mood or subject of your layout. Most of all, remember that your handwriting, good or bad, is part of who you are. Be sure to include it on a page here and there along with these wonderful products.
- Allow yourself to create a layout now and then with no embellishments besides a great-looking title. Choose simple yet effective words for your titles to allow the photographs to take center stage.

Three more favorite tips from this page:

- Many patterned papers have designs that make title placement easy. Take advantage of printed lines (straight or wavy), boxes or areas that are the perfect size for a page title.
- Remember principles of balance when using preprinted papers. After typing my journaling for this layout, I realized that printing the journaling on white cardstock would cover almost the entire purple box on the paper. The journaling would have dominated the entire layout. Instead, I printed the journaling on transparency paper so the color would be visible and proportionate to the yellow square in the opposite corner.
- Allow elements to overlap. My first instinct was to crop my photographs into squares to fit neatly into the printed design on the paper. Luckily I caught myself and laid the photographs on the paper before cutting to see what it would look like! Now the photographs overlap onto another printed section, but the layout design follows a clear "Z" shape, leading the eye along the layout in a pleasing and effective way.

Come Out and Play

Supplies
Patterned paper: SEI
Rub-on words, definition accent and eyelets: Making Memories
Computer font: CK Constitution, "Fresh Fonts" CD, *Creating Keepsakes*
Other: Transparency paper

lisa says:

"No longer is scrapbooking only about paper and stickers. Scrapbookers today are *stretching* their creativity beyond the borders of traditional *materials* and incorporating anything and *everything* that strikes them on their pages. From buttons and fibers to metal screening and eyelets, this chapter will show you that *anything* is possible on your pages!"

MIXED MEDIA

mad about mixed media

MIXED *adj. made up of or involving items of more than one kind*

MEDIA *n. a medium of cultivation, conveyance or expression*

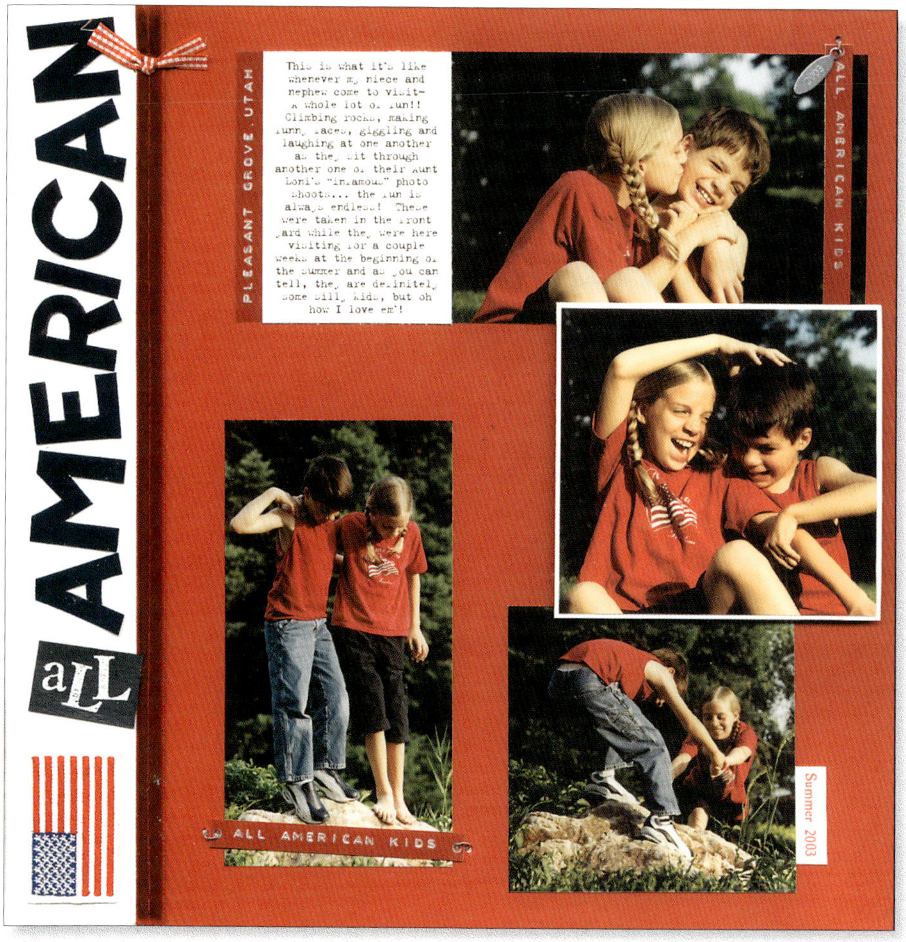
aLL AMERICAN
PLEASANT GROVE, UTAH
This is what it's like whenever my niece and nephew come to visit- a whole lot of fun!! Climbing rocks, making funny faces, giggling and laughing at one another as they sit through another one of their Aunt Loni's "infamous" photo shoots... the fun is always endless! These were taken in the front yard while they were here visiting for a couple weeks at the beginning of the summer and as you can tell, they are definitely some silly kids, but oh how I love em'!
2003
ALL AMERICAN KIDS
ALL AMERICAN KIDS
Summer 2003

All-American Kids

Supplies
Letter stickers: Making Memories
Letter stamps: The Missing Link Stamp Co.
Stamping ink: ColorBox, Clearsnap
Computer font: Last Words, downloaded from the Internet
Date stamp, metal date tag and jump rings: Making Memories
Other: Label maker, 3-D foam adhesive, gingham ribbon, velvet ribbon and flag appliqué

♥ **I Love It!:** *Label makers aren't just for file folders and plastic boxes anymore! Printed labels look great on scrapbook pages. On this layout, the labels were attached across the photographs with jump rings.*

tip **1**

adhere tricky materials to your pages.

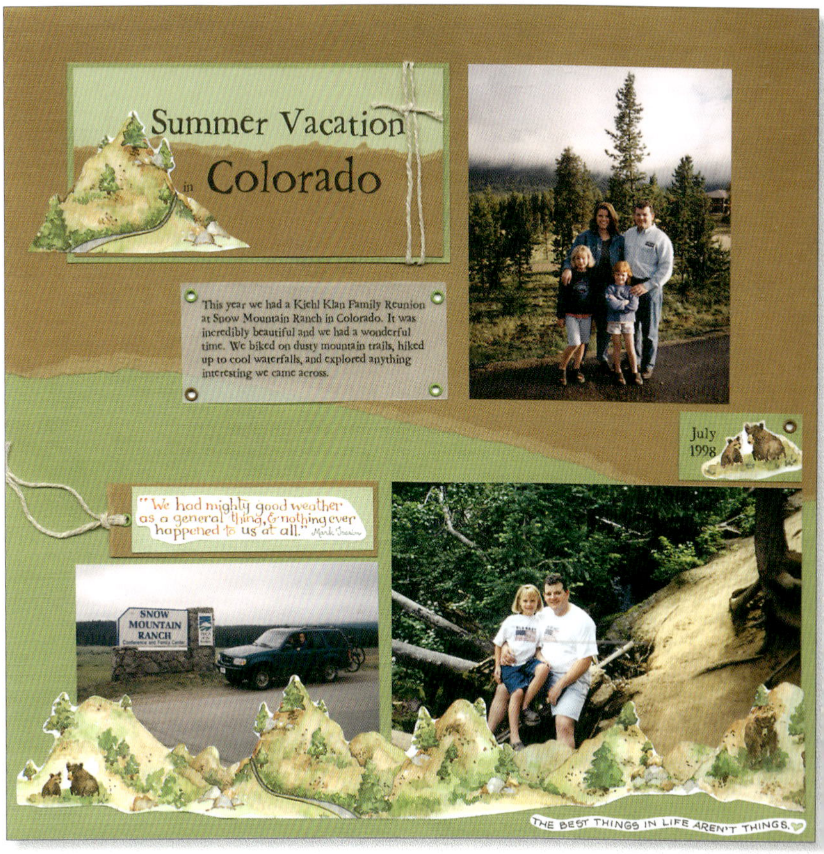

Summer Vacation in Colorado
This year we had a Kiehl Klan Family Reunion at Snow Mountain Ranch in Colorado. It was incredibly beautiful and we had a wonderful time. We biked on dusty mountain trails, hiked up to cool waterfalls, and explored anything interesting we came across.
July 1998
"We had mighty good weather as a general thing, & nothing ever happened to us at all." Mark Twain
SNOW MOUNTAIN RANCH
THE BEST THINGS IN LIFE AREN'T THINGS.

Summer Vacation

Supplies
Stickers: Colorbök
Vellum: Paper Adventures
Computer font: CK Fraternity, Becky Higgins' "Creative Clips & Fonts" CD, *Creating Keepsakes*
Eyelets: Making Memories
Other: Jute

♥ **I Love It!:** *Vellum can be a problem to adhere to layouts—it's hard to find adhesives that stick well without wrinkling or showing through the vellum. A quick and easy solution? Use eyelets, rivets or brads to adhere each corner to your layout. This works well with clear transparency paper, as well.*

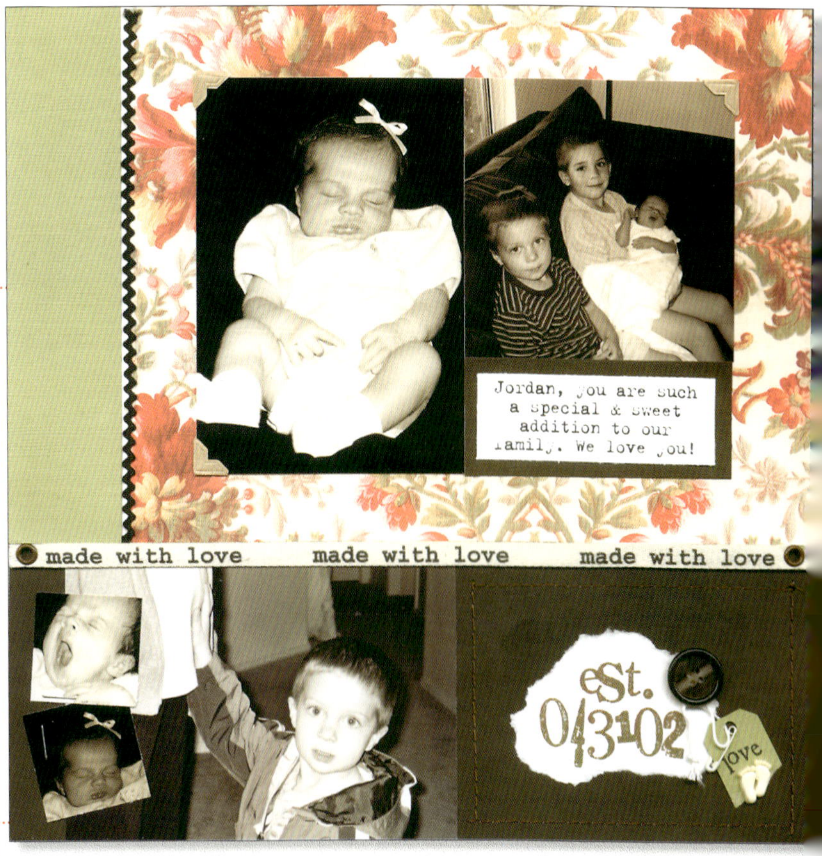

Jordan, you are such a special & sweet addition to our family. We love you!
made with love made with love made with love
est. 043102
love

Made with Love

Supplies
Patterned paper: Anna Griffin
Printed twill tape: 7 Gypsies
Computer font: Linenstroke, downloaded from the Internet
Number stamps: Postmodern Design
Stamping ink: ColorBox, Clearsnap
Feet button: Buttons Galore
Eyelets: Prym-Dritz
Photo corners: Kolo
Safety pin: Li'l Davis Designs
Other: Button and rickrack

♥ **I Love It!:** *Use rivets, eyelets, brads or buttons to adhere ribbon to your layout—tape doesn't always stick well, and most liquid adhesives will show through the ribbon.*

Same Idea, Slightly Different: *Rubber-stamping words on ribbon looks great on layouts, but regular stamping inks can bleed or take too long to dry. For the best results, look for stamping ink formulated especially for stamping on fabrics.*

Mount Vernon

Supplies
Patterned paper: Karen Foster Design
Preprinted frame, leaf accent and pocket: My Mind's Eye
Letter stamps: The Missing Link Stamp Co.
Stamping ink: Fabrico, Tsukineko
Mesh: Magenta
Rivets: Chatterbox
Eyelets: Making Memories

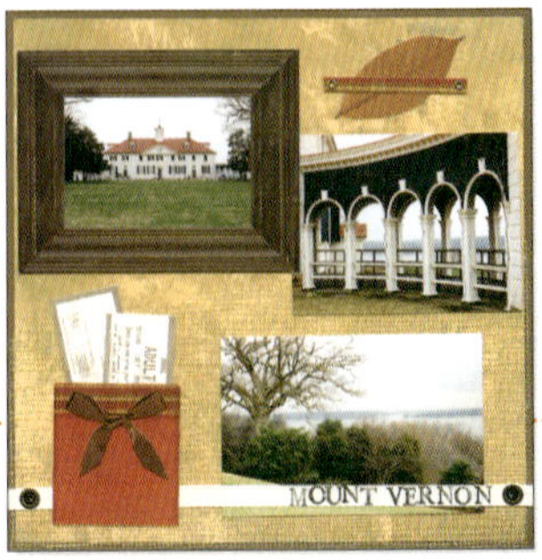

MOUNT VERNON

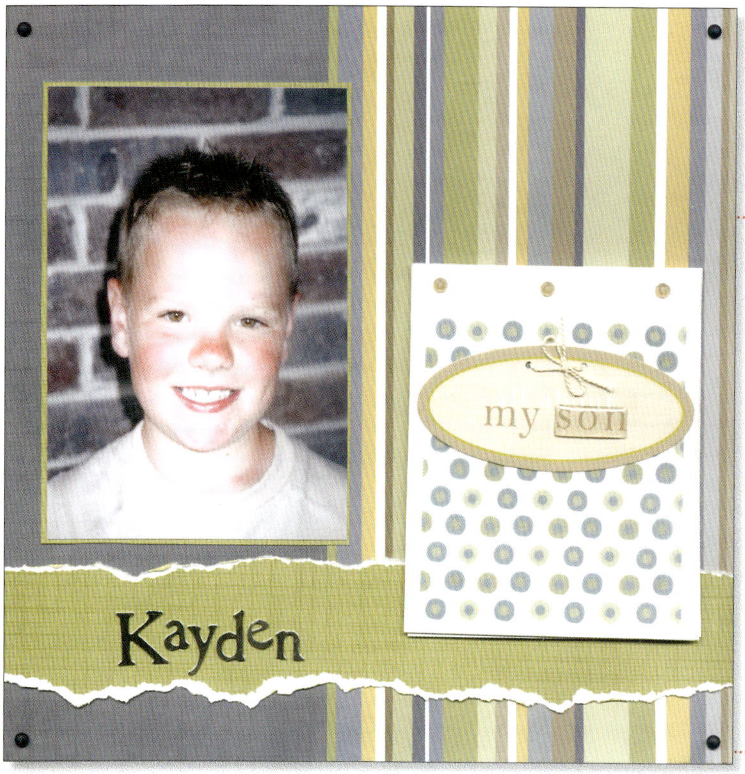
my son
Kayden

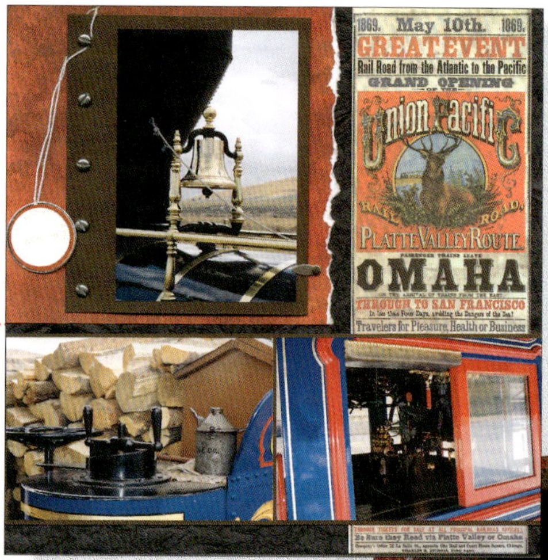
1869. May 10th. 1869.
GREAT EVENT
Rail Road from the Atlantic to the Pacific
GRAND OPENING
Union Pacific
RAIL ROAD.
PLATTE VALLEY ROUTE
OMAHA
THROUGH TO SAN FRANCISCO
Travelers for Pleasure, Health or Business

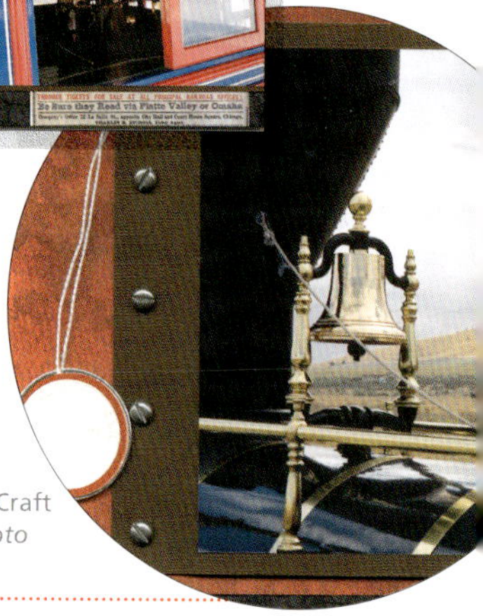

Same Idea, Slightly Different: *This mini-album was bound with a row of rivets that look like the heads of screws. A photo anchor was used to keep the book closed on the layout.*

Trains

Supplies
Patterned and crumpled papers: Provo Craft
Metal-rimmed tag, screw rivets and photo anchor: Making Memories

All About My Son

Supplies
Patterned papers, vellum, colored rivets and preprinted title tag: Chatterbox
Pebble accent and metal letter charms: Making Memories
Computer font: CK Stenography, "Fresh Fonts" CD, *Creating Keepsakes*
Other: String

♥ **I Love It!:** *The mini-album on this layout was created simply by riveting several sheets of cardstock together. The booklet contains information about the subject of the layout.*

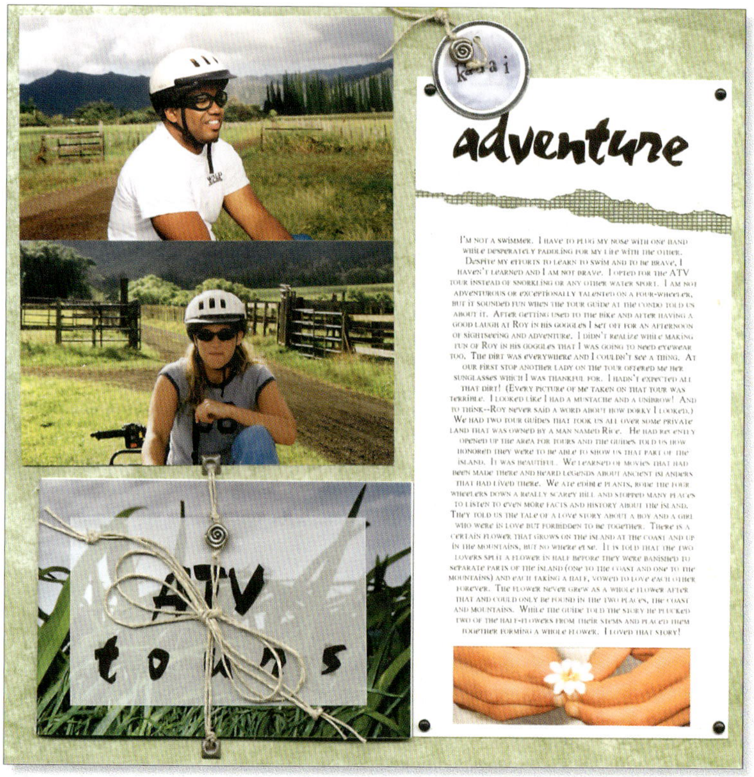
Kauai
adventure
I'm not a swimmer. I have to plug my nose with one hand while desperately paddling for my life with the other. Despite my efforts to learn to swim and to be brave, I haven't learned and I am not brave. I opted for the ATV tour instead of snorkling or any other water sport. I am not adventurous or exceptionally talented on a four-wheeler, but it sounded fun when the tour guide at the condo told us about it. After getting used to the bike and after having a good laugh at Roy in his goggles I set off for an afternoon of sightseeing and adventure. I didn't realize while making fun of Roy in his goggles that I was going to need eyewear too. The dirt was everywhere and I couldn't see a thing. At our first stop another lady on the tour offered me her sunglasses which I was thankful for. I hadn't expected all that dirt! (Every picture of me taken on that tour was terrible. I looked like I had a mustache and a unibrow! And to think--Roy never said a word about how dorky I looked.) We had two tour guides that took us all over some private land that was owned by a man named Rice. He had recently opened up the area for tours and the guides told us how honored they were to be able to show us that part of the island. It was beautiful. We learned of movies that had been made there and heard legends about ancient islanders that had lived there. We ate edible plants, rode the four wheelers down a really scarey hill and stopped many places to listen to even more facts and history about the island. They told us the tale of a love story about a boy and a girl who were in love but forbidden to be together. There is a certain flower that grows on the island at the coast and up in the mountains, but no where else. It is told that the two lovers split a flower in half before they were banished to separate parts of the island (one to the coast and one to the mountains) and each taking a half, vowed to love each other forever. The flower never grew as a whole flower after that and could only be found in the two places, the coast and mountains. While the guide told the story he plucked two of the half-flowers from their stems and placed them together forming a whole flower. I loved that story!
ATV

Kauai Adventure

Supplies
Patterned paper: Provo Craft
Letter stickers: Creative Imaginations
Photographic border: Shotz by Danelle Johnson, Creative Imaginations
Mesh: Magic Mesh
Letter stamps: PSX Design
Stamping ink: ColorBox, Clearsnap
Computer font: CK Chemistry, "Fresh Fonts" CD, *Creating Keepsakes*
Eyelets and brads: Making Memories
Ink spritzer: Color Workshop
Other: Twine, spiral beads and tag

♥ **I Love It!:** *This mini-album cover is actually a preprinted photographic border folded in half. Strips of white cardstock that are the same length as the border were placed on top of the underside of the border. A straight line was stitched vertically through the center of the strips to bind the mini-album together. The strips were then folded in half along the sewn line.*

♥ **I Love It!:** *Because of the thickness of this book, it would have been hard to adhere to the layout. Instead, square eyelets were set in the background paper just above and below the mini-album, and jute was threaded through the eyelets and tied around the album to hold it in place.*

tip 2
embellish your layouts with themed products.

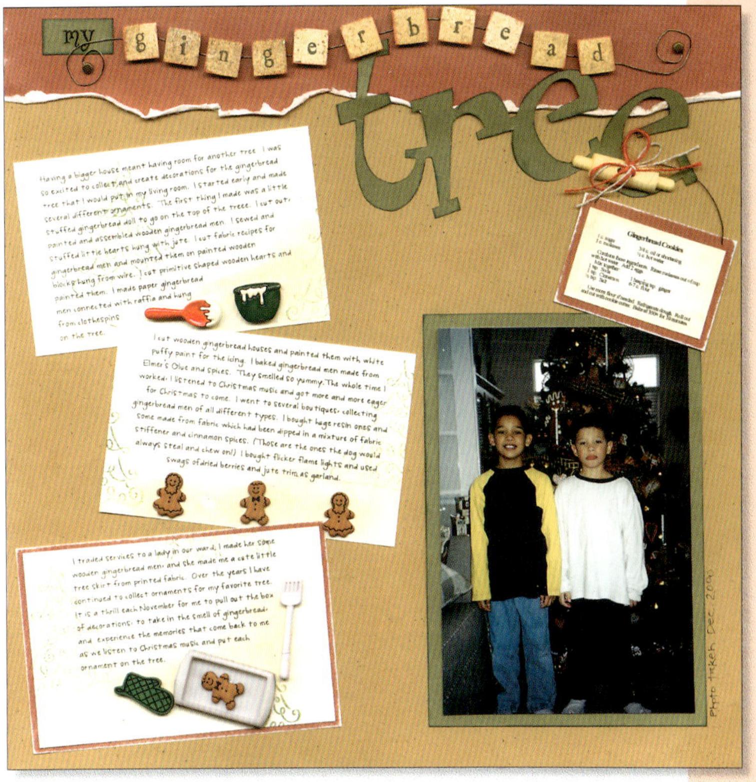
my gingerbread tree

My Gingerbread Tree

Supplies
Patterned paper and letter stickers: Provo Craft
Rubber stamps and stamping ink: Stampin' Up!
Letter stamps: PSX Design
Computer fonts: Garamond, Microsoft Word; CK Jot, "The Art of Creative Lettering" CD, *Creating Keepsakes*
Lettering template: Whimsy, Déjà Views
Buttons: Buttons Galore
Craft wire: Artistic Wire Ltd.
Brads: Making Memories

♥ **I Love It!:** *Include a favorite recipe on your cooking lay-outs to share family traditions with future generations.*

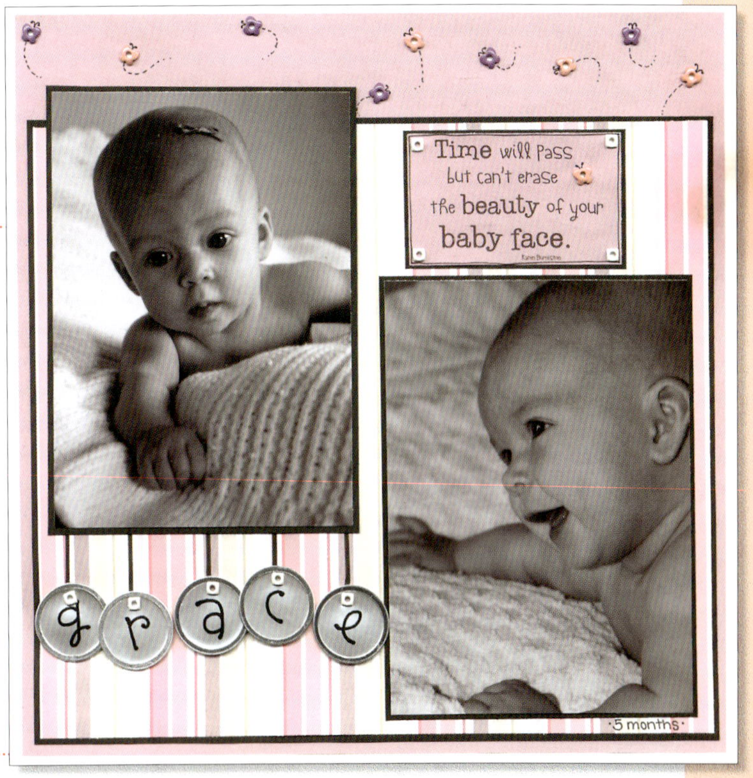
Time will pass
but can't erase
the beauty of your
baby face.
grace
5 months

Grace

Supplies
Patterned paper: Chatterbox
Metal-rimmed tags: Avery
Eyelets: Buttons Galore
Computer fonts: CK Stenography and CK Fresh, "Fresh Fonts" CD, *Creating Keepsakes*
Pen: Zig Writer, EK Success

♥ **I Love It!:** *Dotted lines to show movement and tiny antennae were added to the butterfly eyelets to create a cute border.*

Same Idea, Slightly Different: *Three butterfly eyelets embellish extra space on this label border.*

Happy Birthday Card

Supplies
Patterned paper: Chatterbox
Butterfly eyelets: Buttons Galore
Other: Date stamp, bookplate, plastic flower and label maker

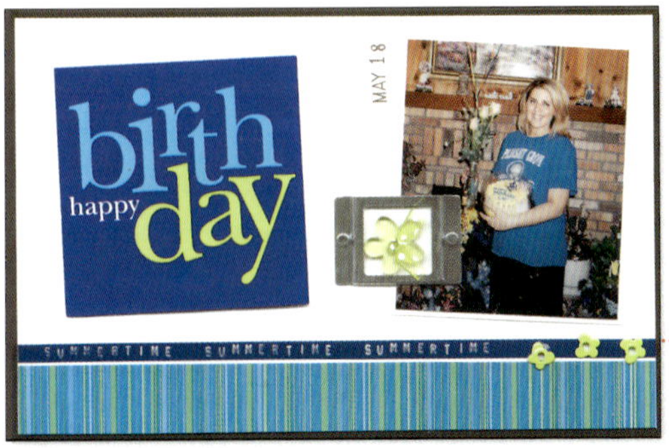
happy birthday
MAY 18
SUMMERTIME SUMMERTIME SUMMERTIME

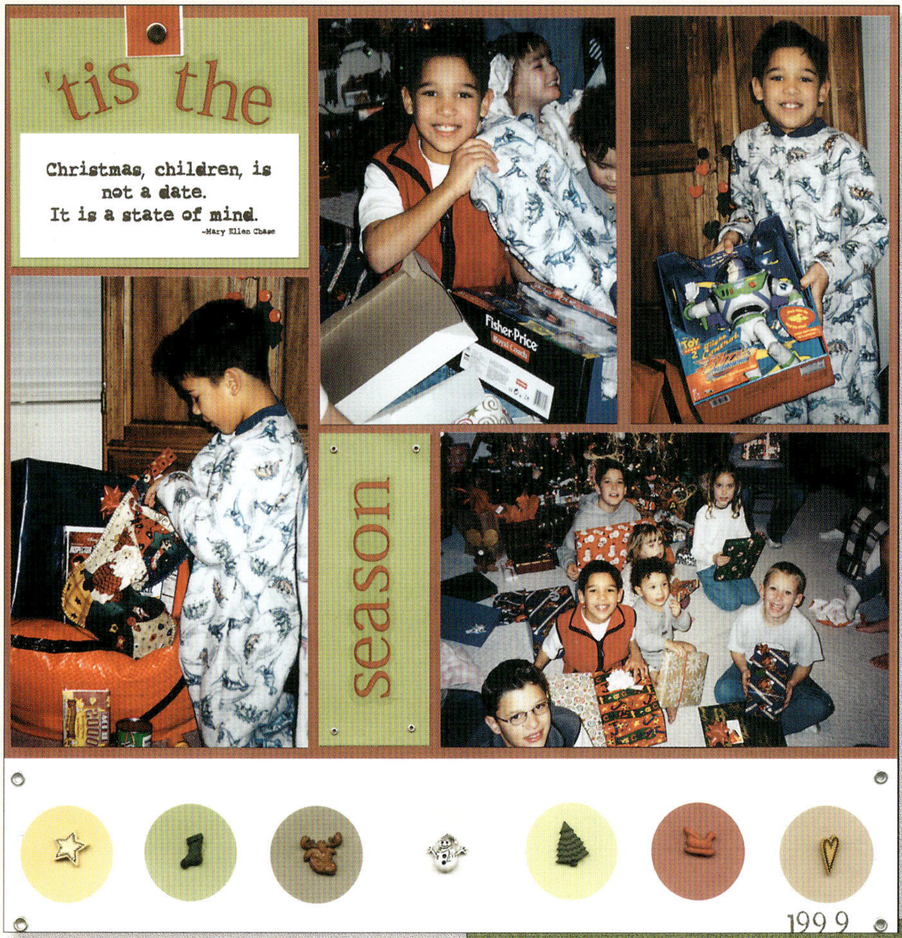

'Tis the Season

Supplies
Patterned paper and letter stickers: SEI
Letter stamps: PSX Design
Stamping ink: ColorBox, Clearsnap
Computer font: CK Typewriter, "Fresh Fonts" CD, *Creating Keepsakes*
Snap and eyelets: Making Memories
Buttons: Buttons Galore

♥ **I Love It!:** *The graphic patterns on preprinted papers make perfect spots for tiny accents, like these holiday buttons. The buttons were placed inside circles of the same color on the paper for a monochromatic effect.*

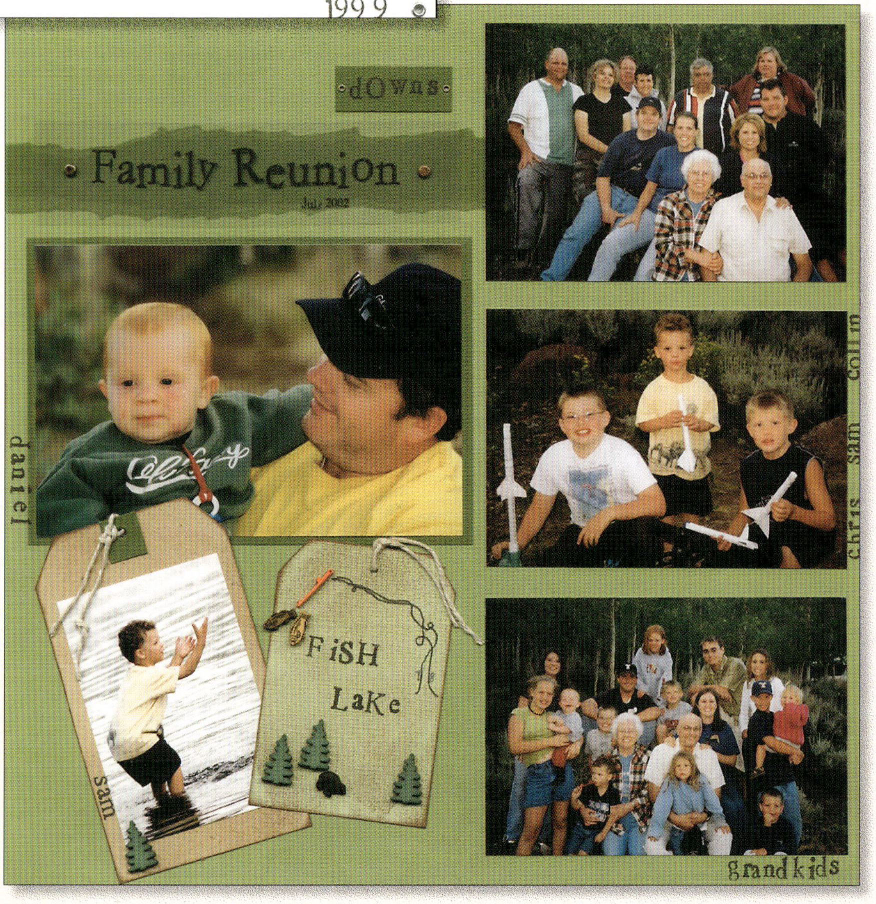

Downs Family Reunion

Supplies
Buttons: Buttons Galore
Computer font: CK Constitution, "Fresh Fonts" CD, *Creating Keepsakes*
Brads and eyelets: Making Memories
Letter stamps: PSX Design
Stamping ink: Stampin' Up!
Other: Jute and transparency paper

♥ **I Love It!:** *These tiny, themed buttons are a simple yet effective way to accent this layout without overwhelming the photographs.*

tip 3

anchor items physically and visually to your pages.

Friends

Supplies
Letter stamps: The Missing Link Stamp Co.
Stamping ink: Ranger Industries
Embossing powder: Adirondack, Ranger Industries
Metal flower accent: Woohoo Wowies
Rivets: Chatterbox
Pen: Zig Writer, EK Success
Chalks: Craf-T Products
Other: Fibers

♥ **I Love It!:** *Without the rivets holding the title strips to the layout, they would have appeared to be "floating." The rivets ground the title strips by showing clearly that they are connected to the layout.*

♥ **I Love It!:** *Want to include some information on your page but without the obvious journaling block? Choose a pen a shade or two darker than your background color and neatly write your journaling around the edge of the layout.*

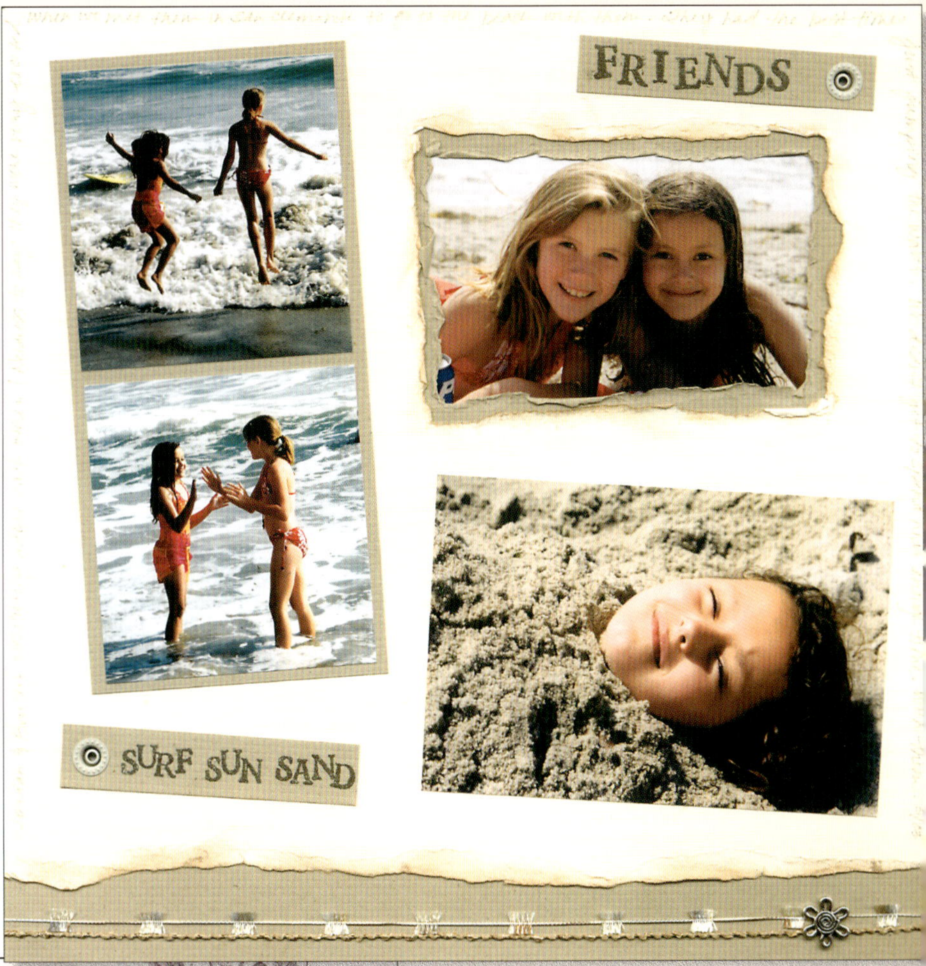

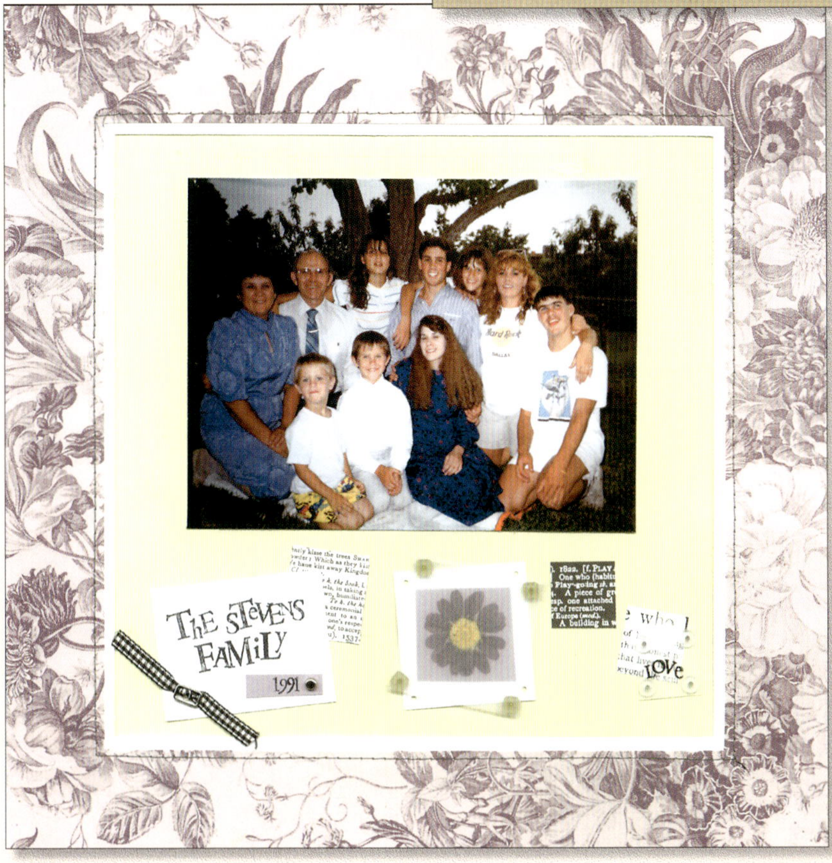

The Stevens Family

Supplies
Patterned papers: Anna Griffin (floral), 7 Gypsies (dictionary)
Rivets and clear plastic "windows": Chatterbox
Pressed flower: Nature's Pressed
Concho: Scrapworks
Letter stamps: PSX Design and Hero Arts
Stamping ink: ColorBox, Clearsnap
Other: Gingham ribbon

♥ **I Love It!:** *These clear plastic "window" accents were placed crookedly over pressed flower and dictionary-paper accents and attached to the layout with nailheads. It's a great reminder that things don't always have to be lined up squarely on your layouts to look great.*

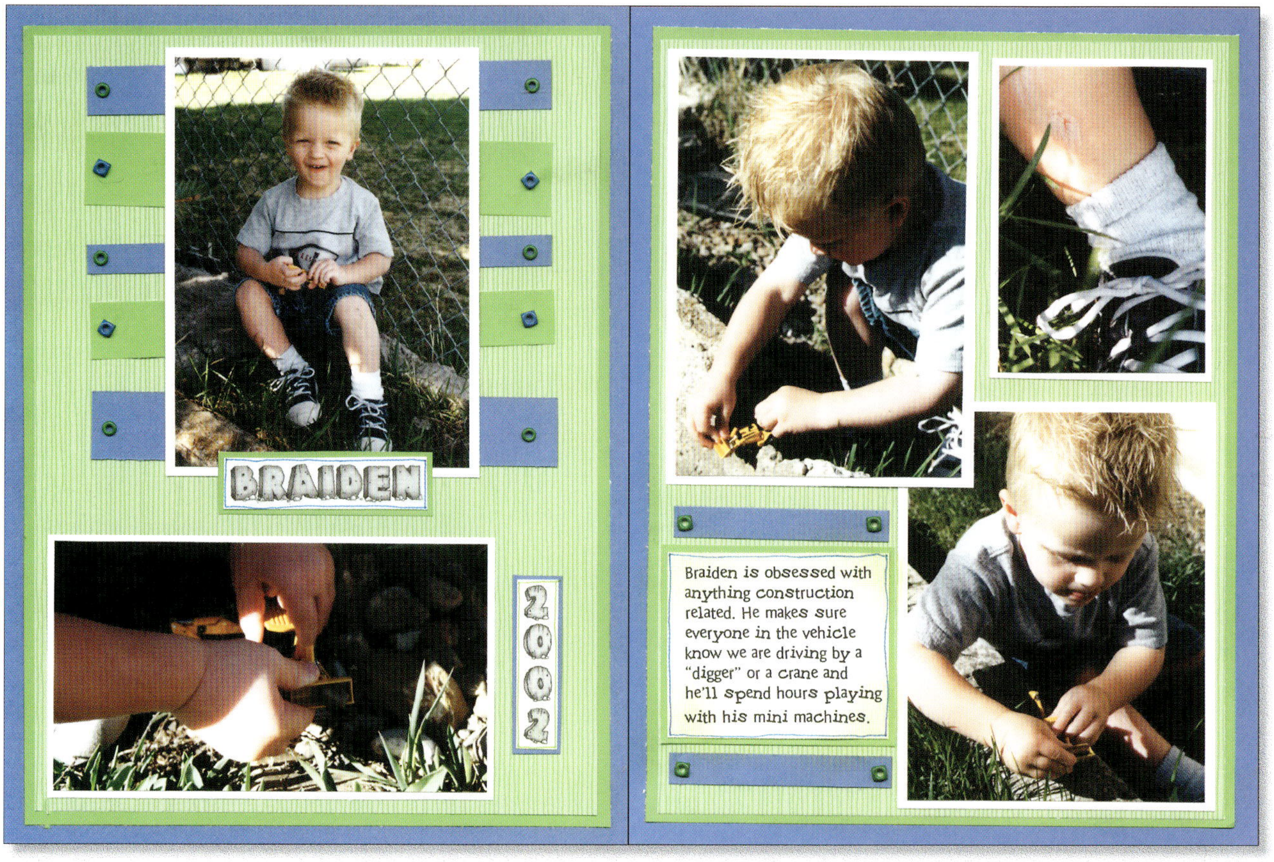
BRAIDEN
2002
Braiden is obsessed with anything construction related. He makes sure everyone in the vehicle know we are driving by a "digger" or a crane and he'll spend hours playing with his mini machines.

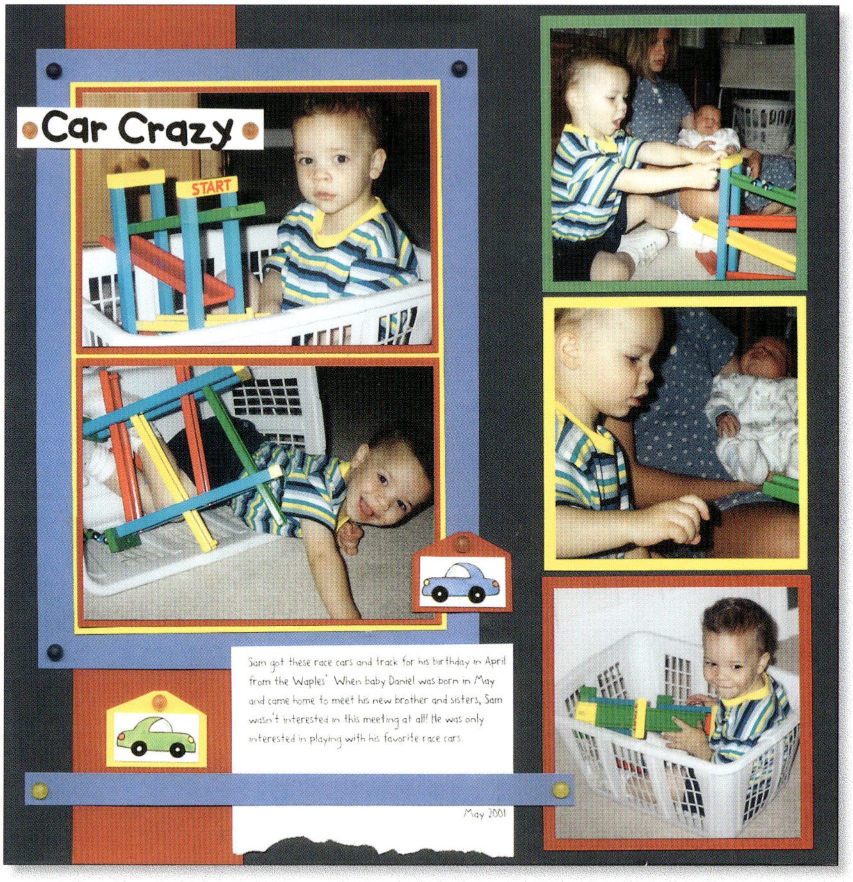
Car Crazy
START
Sam got these race cars and track for his birthday in April from the Waples' When baby Daniel was born in May and came home to meet his new brother and sisters, Sam wasn't interested in this meeting at all! He was only interested in playing with his favorite race cars.
May 2001

Braiden

Supplies
Patterned paper: Making Memories
Letter stickers: Source unknown
Eyelets: Buttons Galore
Computer font: CK Evolution, "Fresh Fonts" CD, *Creating Keepsakes*
Pens: Zig Writer, EK Success

♥ **I Love It!:** *The alternating blue and green strips, anchored to the layout with circle and square eyelets behind the focal-point photograph, are a playful way to draw the eye to the most important element of the layout.*

Car Crazy

Supplies
Stickers: Source unknown
Rivets: Chatterbox
Computer font: Scrap Brother, "Lettering Delights" CD, Inspire Graphics

♥ **I Love It!:** *This layout is a great example of the power of color. Besides cardstock, this layout uses three supplies, but it's far from boring! When your subject and theme permit, incorporate bright colors on your layouts to communicate fun and vibrance.*

tip 4

hang elements from or with mixed-media items on your layouts.

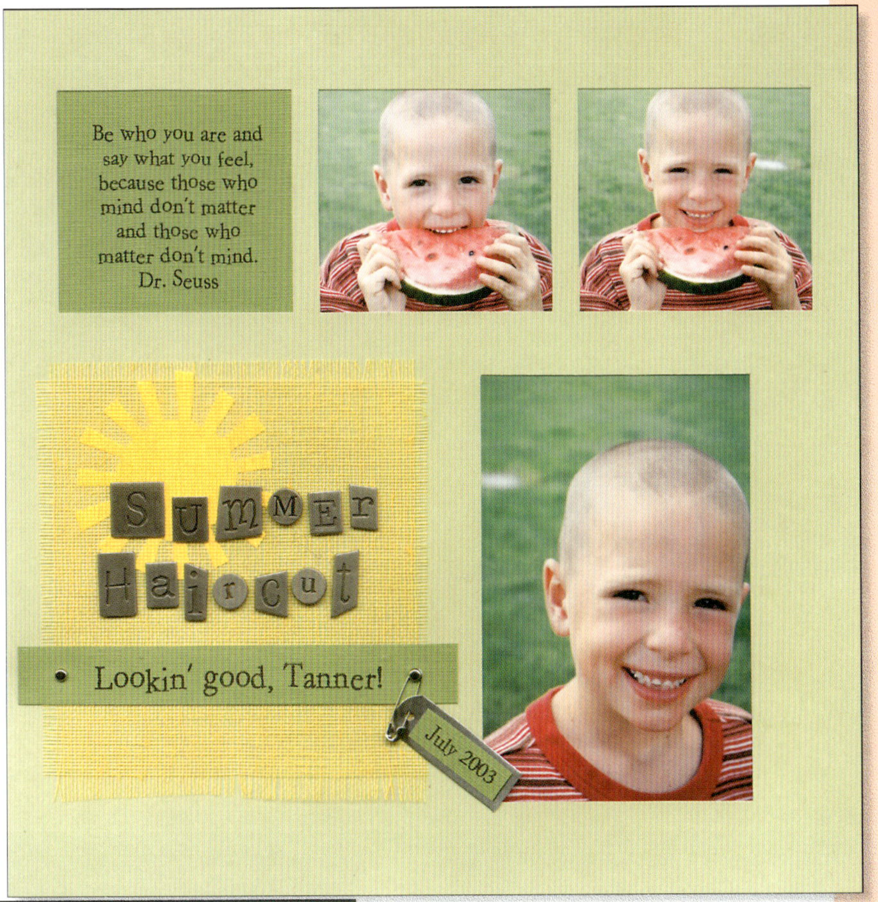

Be who you are and say what you feel, because those who mind don't matter and those who matter don't mind. Dr. Seuss
Summer Haircut
Lookin' good, Tanner!
July 2003

Summer Haircut

Supplies

Pre-formatted cardstock: Making Memories
Metal letter accents, metal tag and brads: Making Memories
Sun die cut: Ellison
Mesh: Magenta
Computer font: CK Constitution, "Fresh Fonts" CD, *Creating Keepsakes*
Other: Safety pin

♥ **I Love It!:** *Instead of hanging tags with fibers, use a common safety pin for a fun variation.*

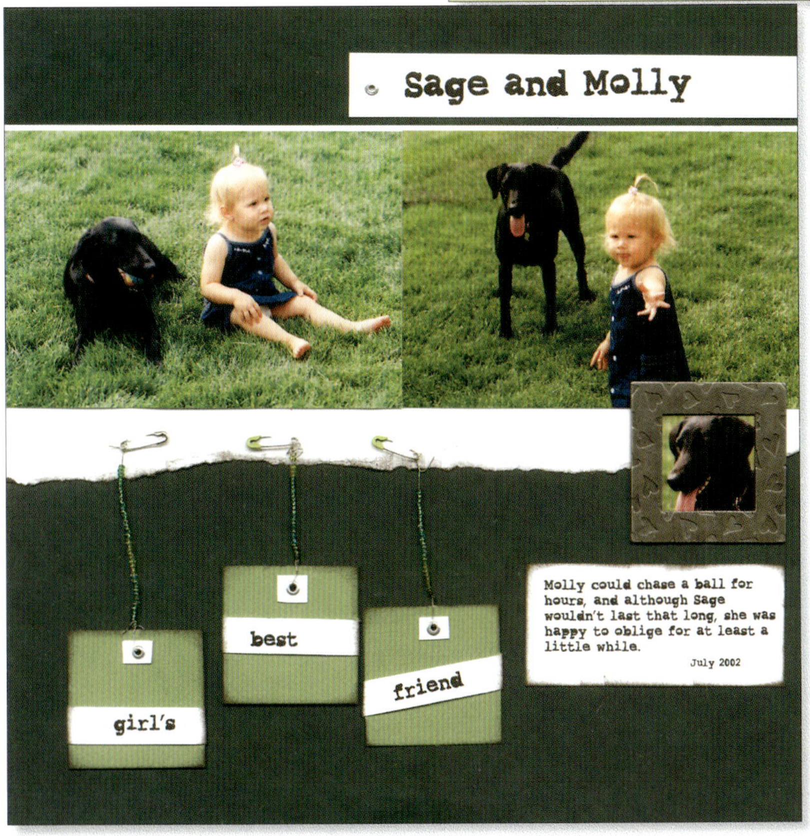

Sage and Molly
Molly could chase a ball for hours, and although Sage wouldn't last that long, she was happy to oblige for at least a little while.
July 2002
girl's
best
friend

Sage and Molly

Supplies

Patterned cardstock: The Crafter's Workshop
Computer font: CK Typewriter, "Fresh Fonts" CD, *Creating Keepsakes*
Metal frame and safety pins: Making Memories
Eyelets: Doodlebug Design
Stamping ink: ColorBox, Clearsnap
Beads: Westrim Crafts
Craft wire: Artistic Wire Ltd.

♥ **I Love It!:** *Drop journaling blocks with key words from your photo mat with beaded wire for a playful yet functional accent on your pages.*

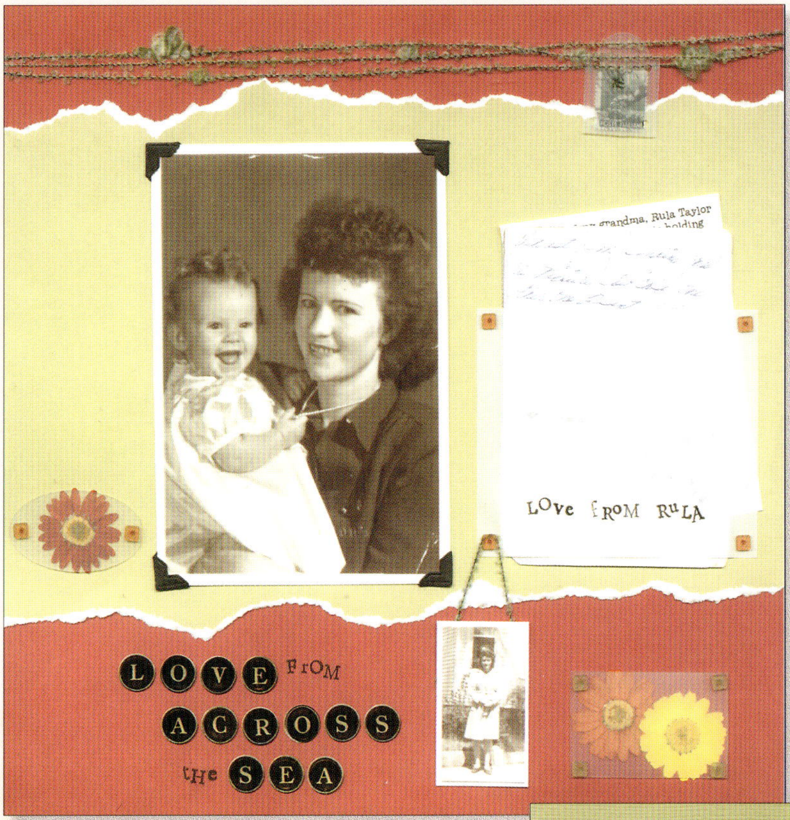

Love from Across the Sea

Supplies
Vellum: Provo Craft
Letter stickers: Nostalgiques, EK Success
Rivets and clear plastic "window" accents: Chatterbox
Letter stamps: Hero Arts
Stamping ink: ColorBox, Clearsnap
Computer font: CK Stenography, "Fresh Fonts" CD, *Creating Keepsakes*
Photo corners: Canson
Other: Fibers, pressed flowers and stamp

♥ **I Love It!:** *Many heritage photographs are smaller than the sizes we see today. Draw attention to smaller photographs by hanging them from your journaling block or focal-point photograph.*

♥ **I Love It!:** *The back of this original heritage photograph contains handwritten information. To preserve both the handwriting and the information, the back of the photograph was color-copied and slipped into a pocket with additional journaling.*

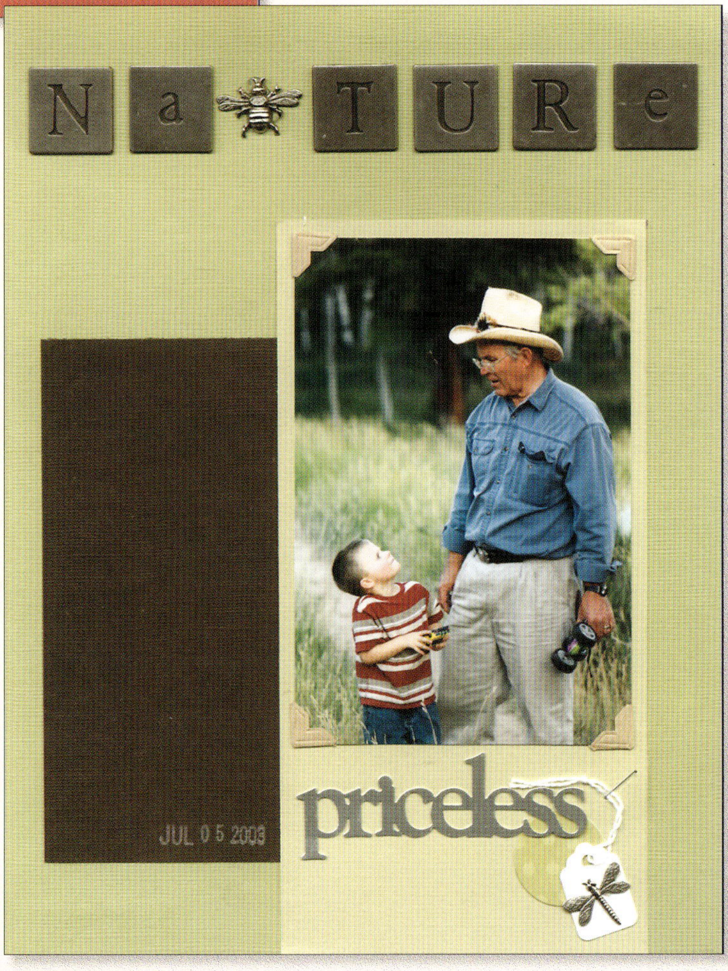

Nature

Supplies
Patterned circle accent: KI Memories
Metal letters and word: Making Memories
Charms: Buttons Galore
Photo corners: Kolo
Other: Mini-tag and date stamp

♥ **I Love It!:** *A beautiful bee charm separates the title word "Nature" into syllables.*

♥ **I Love It!:** *A simple staple holds a dragonfly charm affixed to a mini-tag on the layout.*

tip 5
frame important items on your layout with fibers.

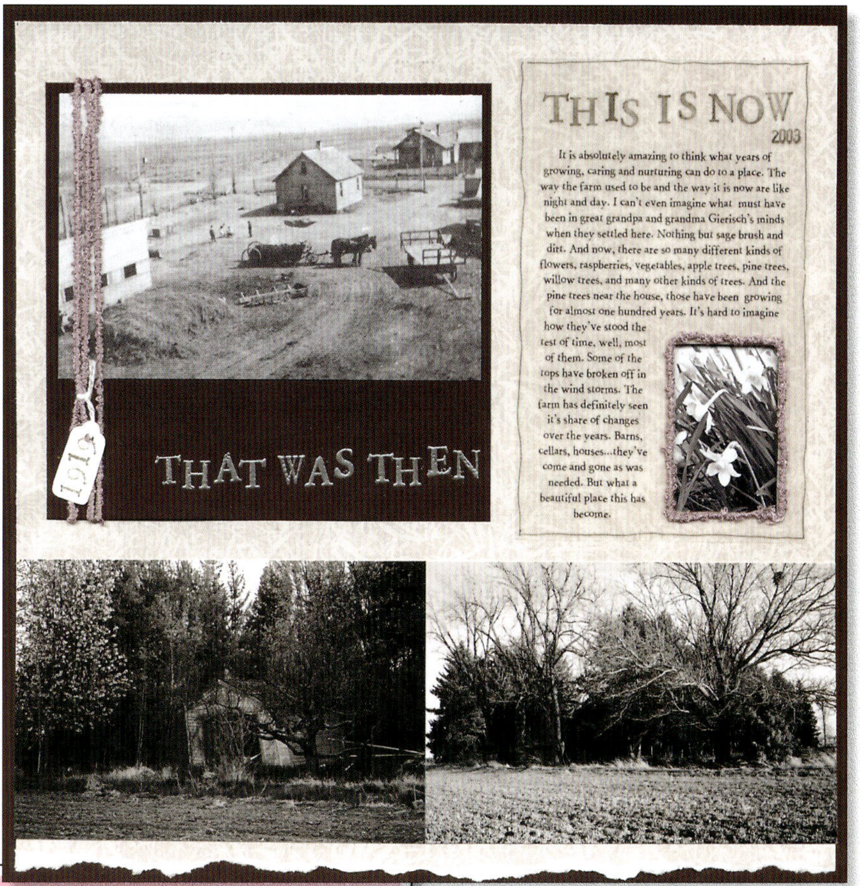
THIS IS NOW
2003
It is absolutely amazing to think what years of growing, caring and nurturing can do to a place. The way the farm used to be and the way it is now are like night and day. I can't even imagine what must have been in great grandpa and grandma Gierisch's minds when they settled here. Nothing but sage brush and dirt. And now, there are so many different kinds of flowers, raspberries, vegetables, apple trees, pine trees, willow trees, and many other kinds of trees. And the pine trees near the house, those have been growing for almost one hundred years. It's hard to imagine how they've stood the test of time, well, most of them. Some of the tops have broken off in the wind storms. The farm has definitely seen it's share of changes over the years. Barns, cellars, houses...they've come and gone as was needed. But what a beautiful place this has become.
1919
THAT WAS THEN

That Was Then

Supplies
Patterned paper: Liz King
Vellum: Provo Craft
Letter stamps: The Missing Link Stamp Co.
Stamping ink: Brilliance, Tsukineko
Silver embossing powder: Stamp-n-Stuff, Stampendous!
Computer font: P22 Garamouche, Impress Rubber Stamps
Pen: Pigma Micron, Sakura
Fibers: Adornaments, EK Success
Other: Mini-tag and date stamp

♥ **I Love It!:** *A small window was cut in the journaling block with a craft knife so a photo could be seen through it. Fibers were wrapped around the photograph to create a "frame."*

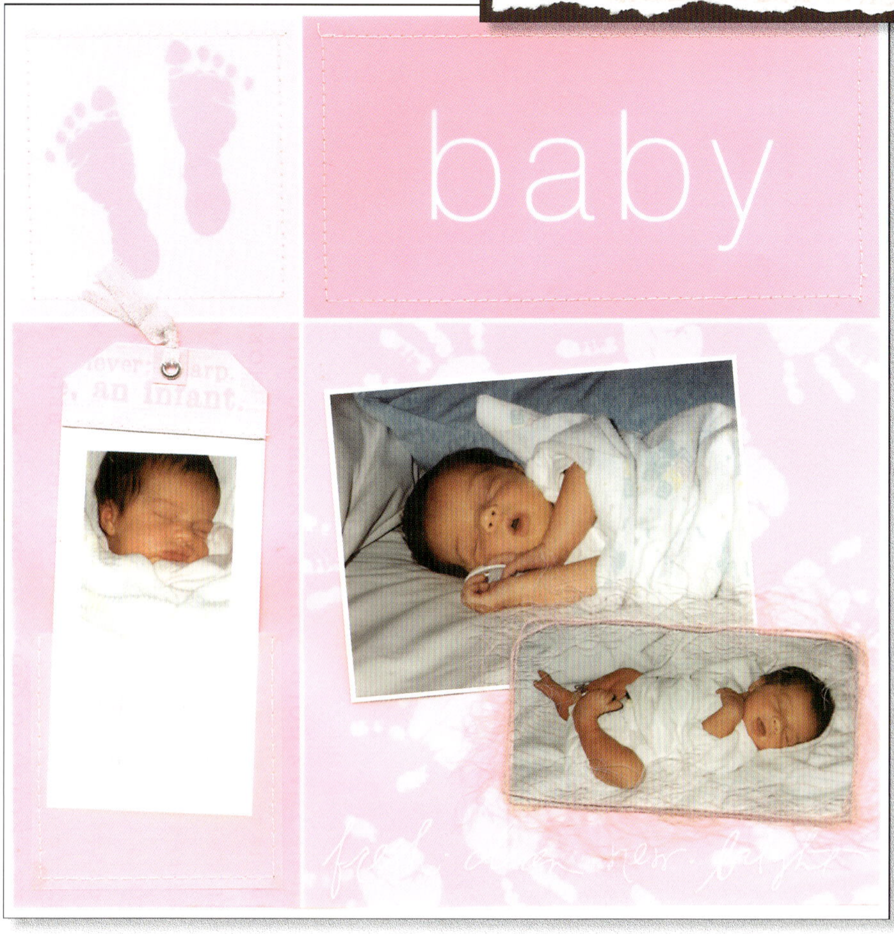
baby

Baby

Supplies
Patterned paper: American Crafts
Letter stamps: PSX Design
Stamping ink: ColorBox, Clearsnap
Rub-on words: Making Memories
Fibers: Adornaments, EK Success

♥ **I Love It!:** *A fuzzy pink fiber was wrapped around the smaller photograph of the baby, evoking the feeling of soft baby blankets and clothes.*

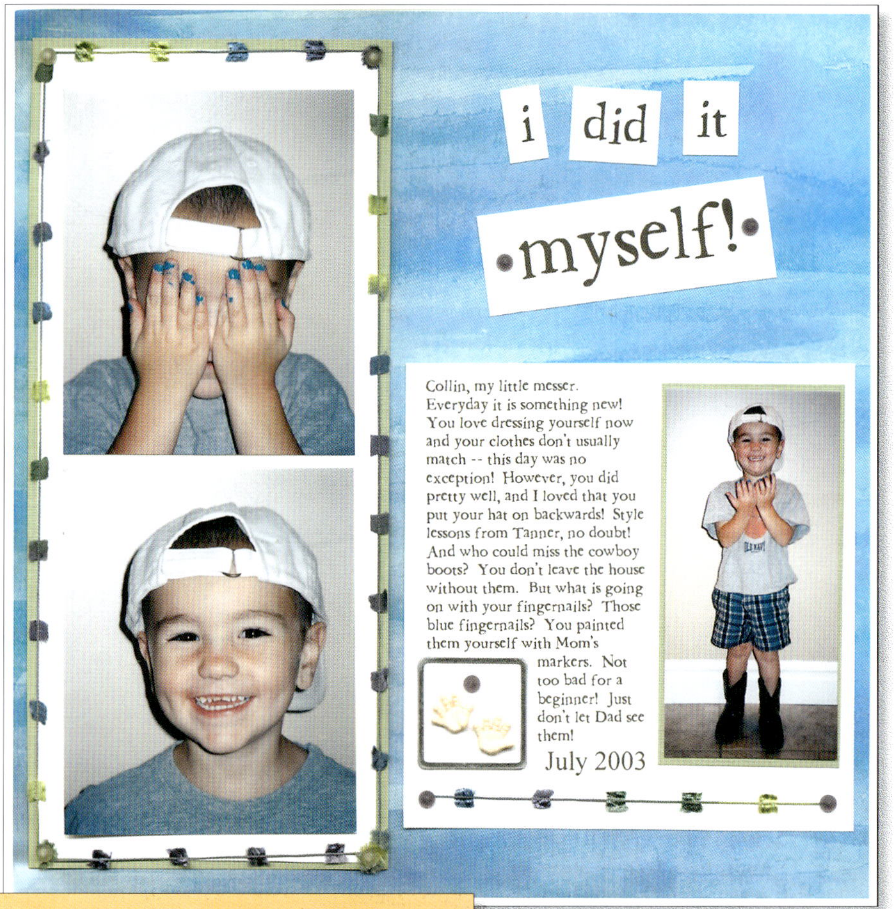

i did it
myself!
Collin, my little messer.
Everyday it is something new!
You love dressing yourself now
and your clothes don't usually
match -- this day was no
exception! However, you did
pretty well, and I loved that you
put your hat on backwards! Style
lessons from Tanner, no doubt!
And who could miss the cowboy
boots? You don't leave the house
without them. But what is going
on with your fingernails? Those
blue fingernails? You painted
them yourself with Mom's
markers. Not
too bad for a
beginner! Just
don't let Dad see
them!
July 2003

I Did It Myself!

Supplies

Patterned paper: NRN Designs
Metal-rimmed tag: Making Memories
Computer font: CK Fraternity, Becky Higgins' "Creative Clips & Fonts" CD, *Creating Keepsakes*
Nails: Chatterbox
Fibers: Adornaments, EK Success
Buttons: Buttons Galore

♥ **I Love It!:** *Place nails in the four corners of the photograph you'd like to outline with fibers or ribbon, then wrap the ribbon around the outside of the rivets. You'll get a straight, clean edge every time!*

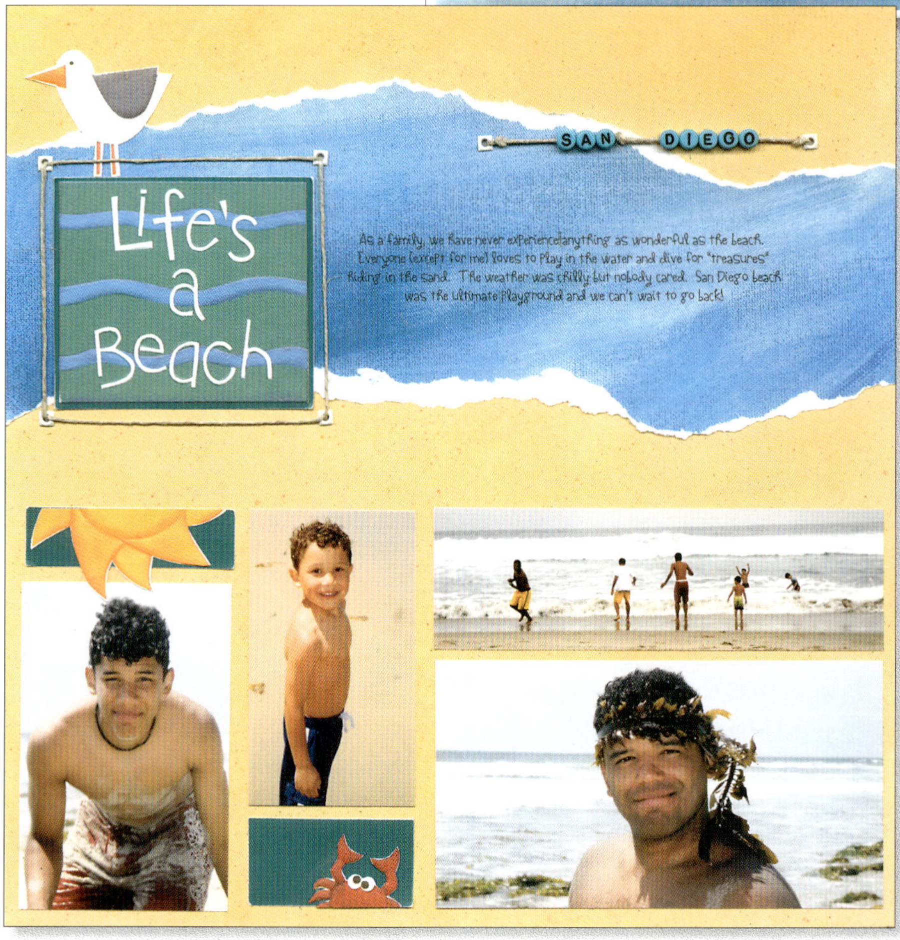

SAN DIEGO
Life's a Beach
As a family, we have never experienced anything as wonderful as the beach.
Everyone (except for me) loves to play in the water and dive for "treasures"
hiding in the sand. The weather was chilly but nobody cared. San Diego beach
was the ultimate playground and we can't wait to go back!

Life's a Beach!

Supplies

Patterned papers: Karen Foster Design
Preprinted accents: Embossible Designs, We R Memory Keepers
Eyelets: Buttons Galore
Computer font: CK Fresh, "Fresh Fonts" CD, *Creating Keepsakes*
Other: Letter beads and jute

♥ **I Love It!:** *Thread jute, ribbon or wire through eyelets set at the four corners of an item for a quick and easy frame.*

♥ **I Love It!:** *String beads spelling important dates, locations or names onto jute or other fibers for a unique embellishment.*

tip 6
connect
page elements
together.

United States Air Force

Supplies
Embossed suede paper: K & Company
Letter stamps: PSX Design and Hero Arts
Stamping ink: Ranger Industries
Computer font: Linenstroke, downloaded from the Internet
Other: Buttons, twine and envelope

♥ **I Love It!:** *Create this artistic button and twine envelope clasp to hold special memorabilia and documents. Sew one button to the flap of the envelope, and one below the flap (remember not to sew through both layers of the envelope, or it will be unusable). Wrap a thread of jute around the buttons to hold the envelope closed.*

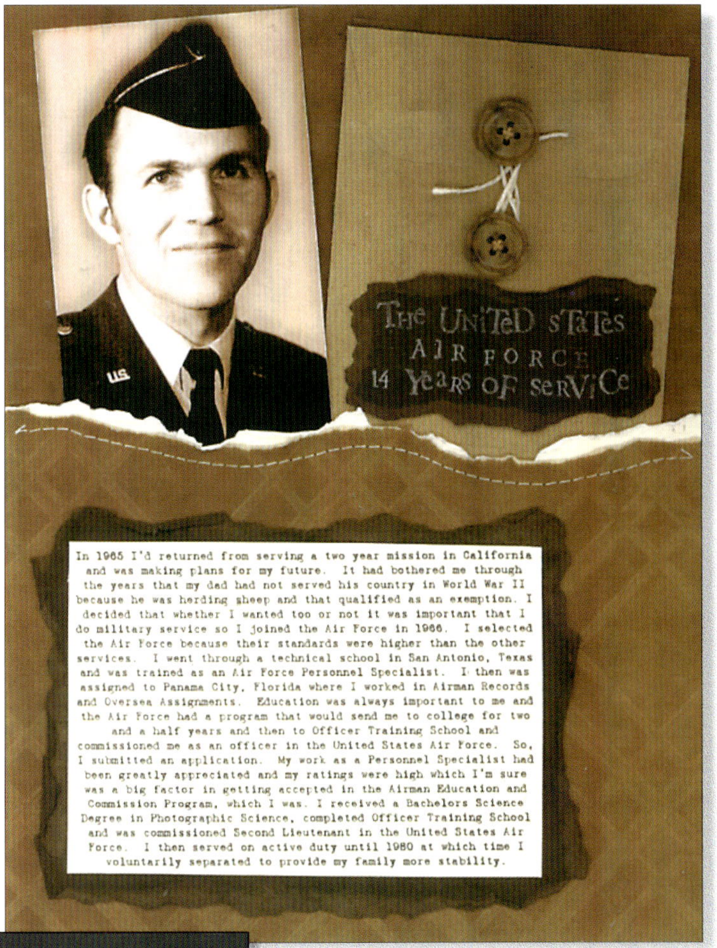

The UNiTeD sTaTes
AIR FORCE
14 Years oF serViCe
In 1965 I'd returned from serving a two year mission in California and was making plans for my future. It had bothered me through the years that my dad had not served his country in World War II because he was herding sheep and that qualified as an exemption. I decided that whether I wanted too or not it was important that I do military service so I joined the Air Force in 1966. I selected the Air Force because their standards were higher than the other services. I went through a technical school in San Antonio, Texas and was trained as an Air Force Personnel Specialist. I then was assigned to Panama City, Florida where I worked in Airman Records and Oversea Assignments. Education was always important to me and the Air Force had a program that would send me to college for two and a half years and then to Officer Training School and commissioned me as an officer in the United States Air Force. So, I submitted an application. My work as a Personnel Specialist had been greatly appreciated and my ratings were high which I'm sure was a big factor in getting accepted in the Airman Education and Commission Program, which I was. I received a Bachelors Science Degree in Photographic Science, completed Officer Training School and was commissioned Second Lieutenant in the United States Air Force. I then served on active duty until 1980 at which time I voluntarily separated to provide my family more stability.

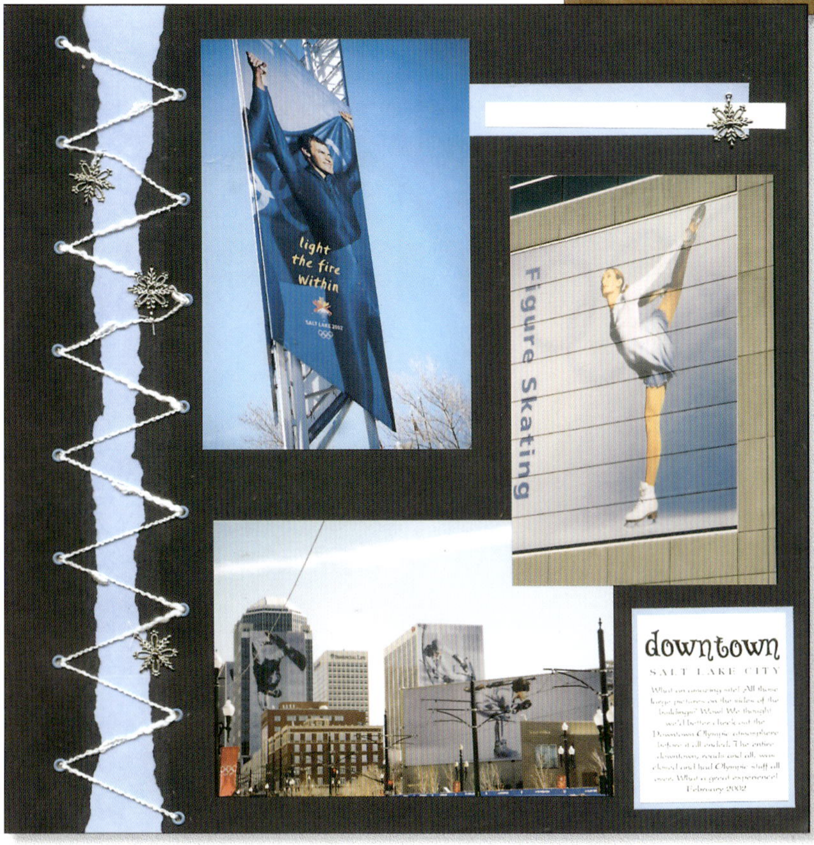

light the fire within
Figure Skating
downtown
SALT LAKE CITY

Downtown Salt Lake City

Supplies
Letter stickers: Provo Craft
Eyelets: Making Memories
Fibers: On The Surface
Snowflake charms: American Tag Co.
Computer font: President, Microsoft Word

♥ **I Love It!:** *Tear a strip from your background paper and place a coordinating color beneath. Set eyelets in a zigzag pattern on each side of the tear, then lace fibers through the eyelets to create this "shoelace" pattern border. For additional fun, lace charms randomly on the fiber as you thread the fiber through the eyelets.*

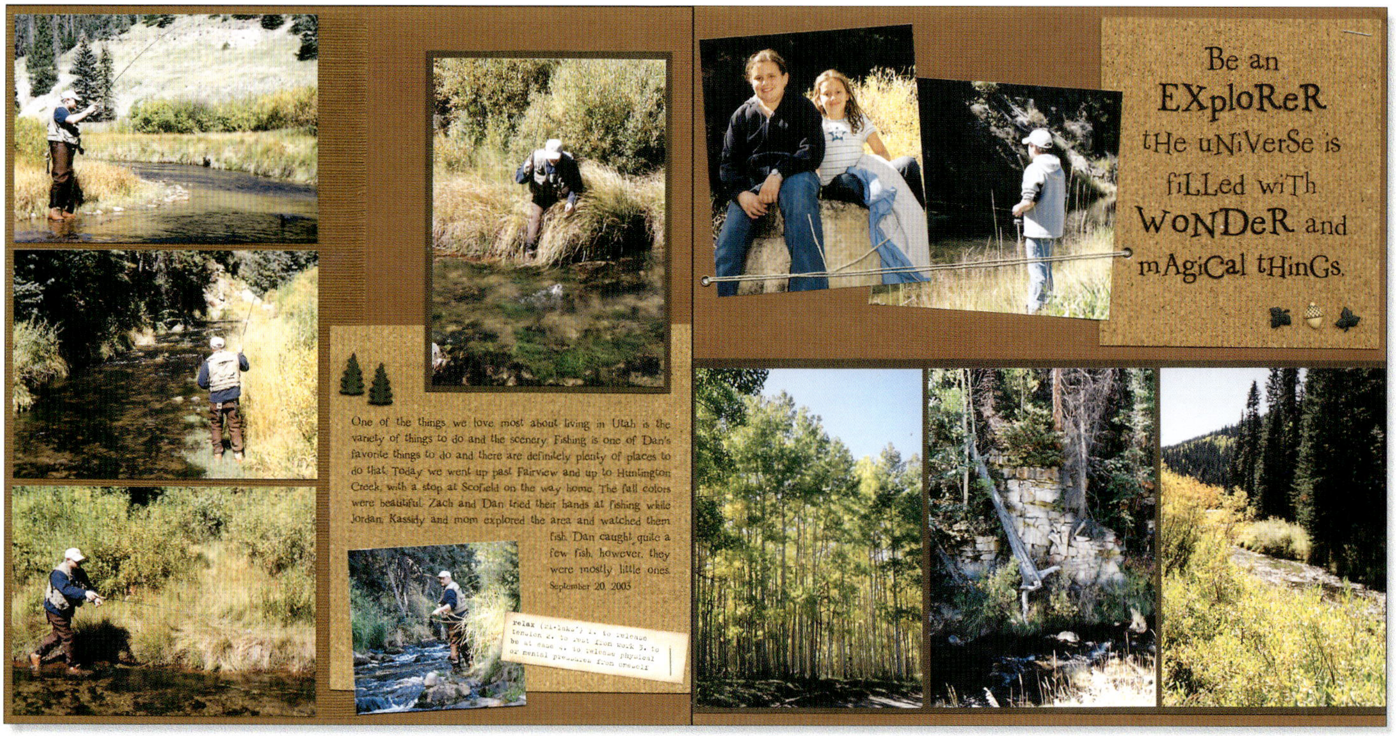
One of the things we love most about living in Utah is the variety of things to do and the scenery. Fishing is one of Dan's favorite things to do and there are definitely plenty of places to do that. Today we went up past Fairview and up to Huntington Creek, with a stop at Scofield on the way home. The fall colors were beautiful. Zach and Dan tried their hands at fishing while Jordan, Kassidy and mom explored the area and watched them fish. Dan caught quite a few fish, however, they were mostly little ones.
September 20, 2003
relax
Be an
EXploReR
tHe uNiVerSe is
fiLLed wiTh
WONDeR and
mAgiCal tHinGs.

Be an Explorer

Supplies
Computer font: 2Peas Flea Market by Sharon Soneff, downloaded from *www.twopeasinabucket.com*
Definition accent and eyelets: Making Memories
Mesh: Magenta
Buttons: Buttons Galore
Stamping ink: StazOn, Tsukineko
Other: Cork paper, staples, jute and transparency paper

♥ **I Love It!:** *Cork paper, available at craft stores, is the perfect texture and color for outdoor or nature photographs.*

♥ **I Love It!:** *Jute was threaded through two eyelets to "hold" two photographs onto the layout.*

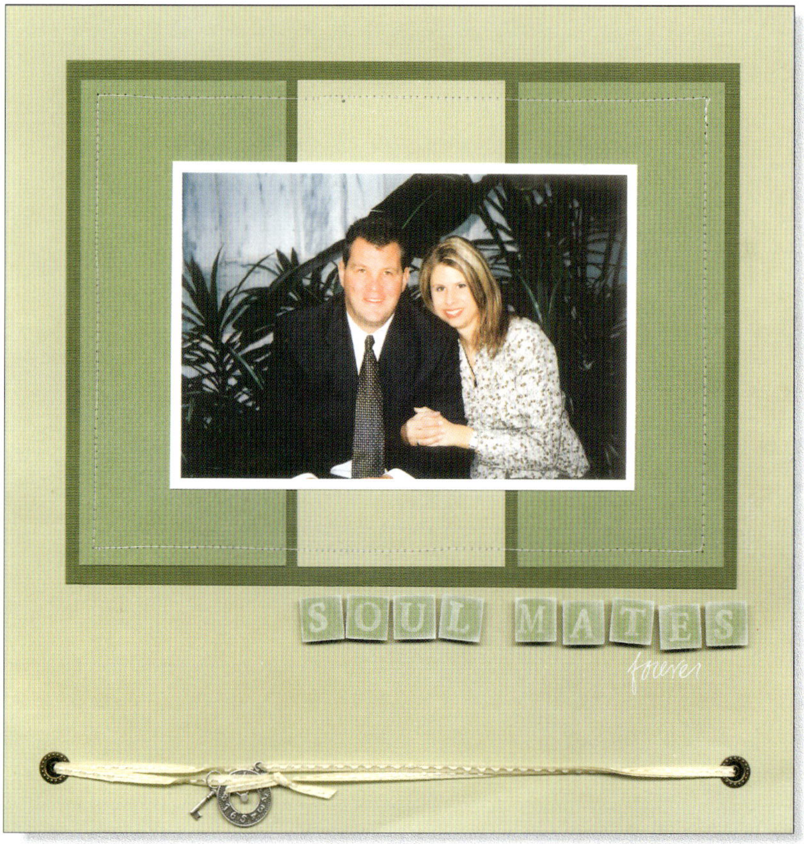
SOUL MATES
forever

Soul Mates Forever

Supplies
Letter stamps: PSX Design
Stamping ink: ColorBox, Clearsnap
Rivets: Chatterbox
Rub-on word and fibers: Making Memories
Charms: Once Upon a Charm
Square punch: Family Treasures
Other: Date stamp, jump rings, 3-D foam adhesive

♥ **I Love It!:** *Each rubber-stamped letter was cut into a square and adhered to the layout with 3-D foam adhesive to add dimension.*

♥ **I Love It!:** *The color scheme of this layout is so soothing! I love the color-blocked photo mat in shades of green with the stitched border.*

tip 7

add finishing touches to pre-made embellishments.

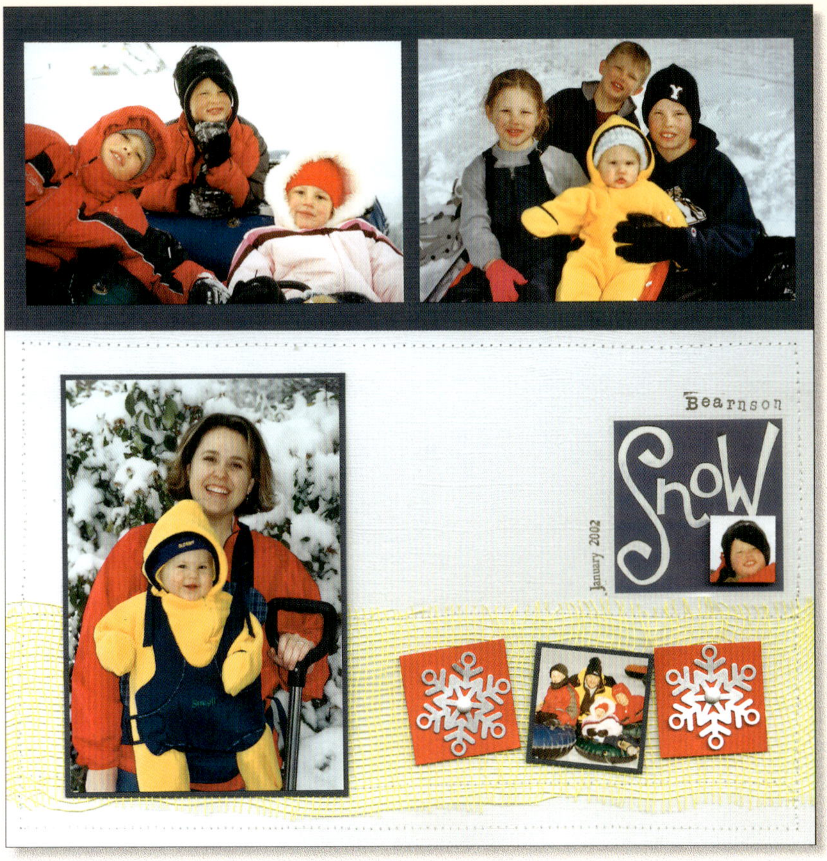
Bearnson
Snow
January 2002

Snow

Supplies

"Snow" title: Pebbles Inc.
Metal accents: Making Memories
Nails: Chatterbox
Date stamp: Making Memories
Mesh: Magic Mesh

♥ **I Love It!:** *Use different-colored rivets, brads or eyelets as the centers of snowflakes, flowers or other accents.*

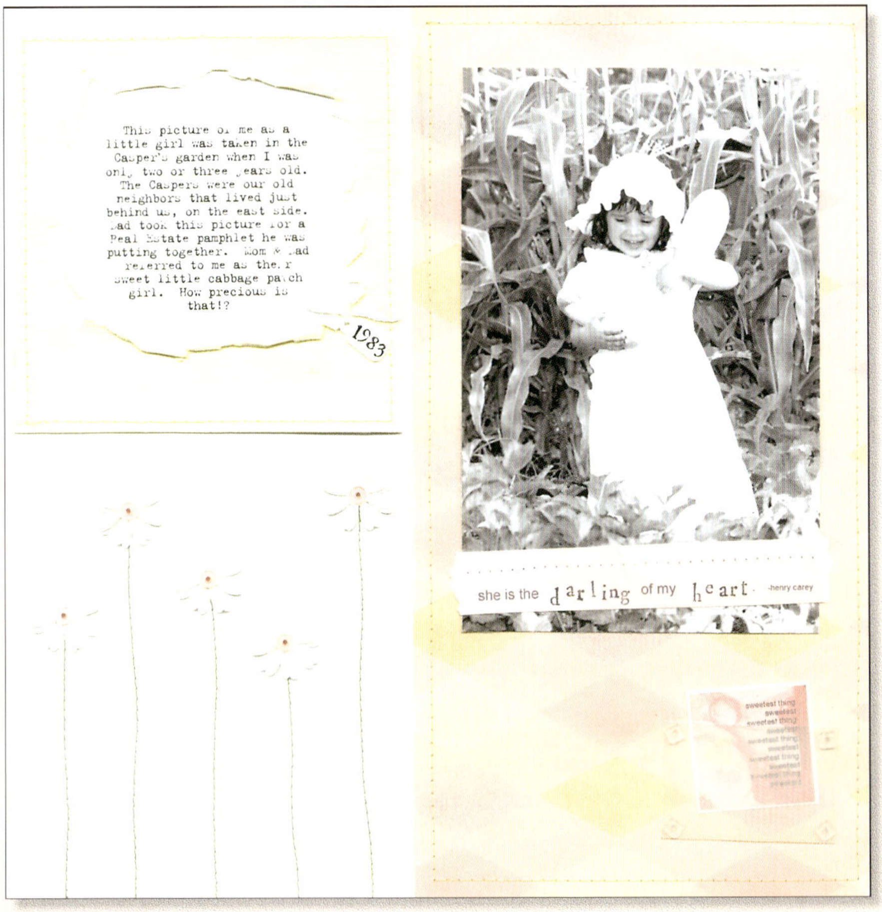
This picture of me as a little girl was taken in the Casper's garden when I was only two or three years old. The Caspers were our old neighbors that lived just behind us, on the east side. Dad took this picture for a Real Estate pamphlet he was putting together. Mom & Dad referred to me as their sweet little cabbage patch girl. How precious is that!?
1983
she is the darling of my heart -henry carey

Darling of My Heart

Supplies

Patterned paper: K & Company
Sticker: Complete Stickers
Nails and clear plastic "window" accents: Chatterbox
Number stamps: Hero Arts
Stamping ink: ColorBox, Clearsnap
Embossing powder: Suze Weinberg
Daisy punch: Family Treasures
Computer font: Last Words, downloaded from the Internet
Other: Mini-tag

♥ **I Love It!:** *The stems of these layered daisy punches were stitched with a sewing machine. The daisy punches were sprinkled with embossing powder and heat-embossed to create a slight shine.*

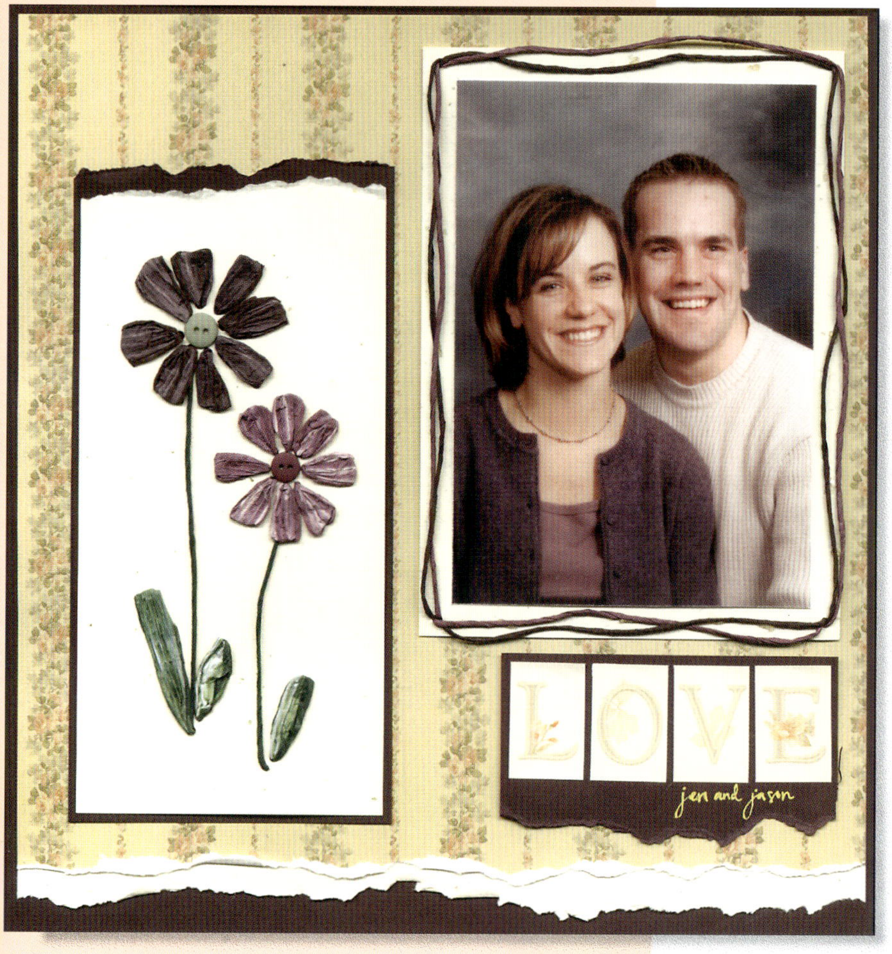

Love

Supplies
Patterned paper and letter stickers: K & Company
Paper ribbon and buttons: Making Memories
Pen: American Crafts

♥ **I Love It!:** *These beautiful flowers were created with paper ribbon. The ribbon comes wound into a cord, which can be pulled open to reveal the color variations seen in the petals of the flowers. The same paper ribbon was used as a border around the main photograph.*

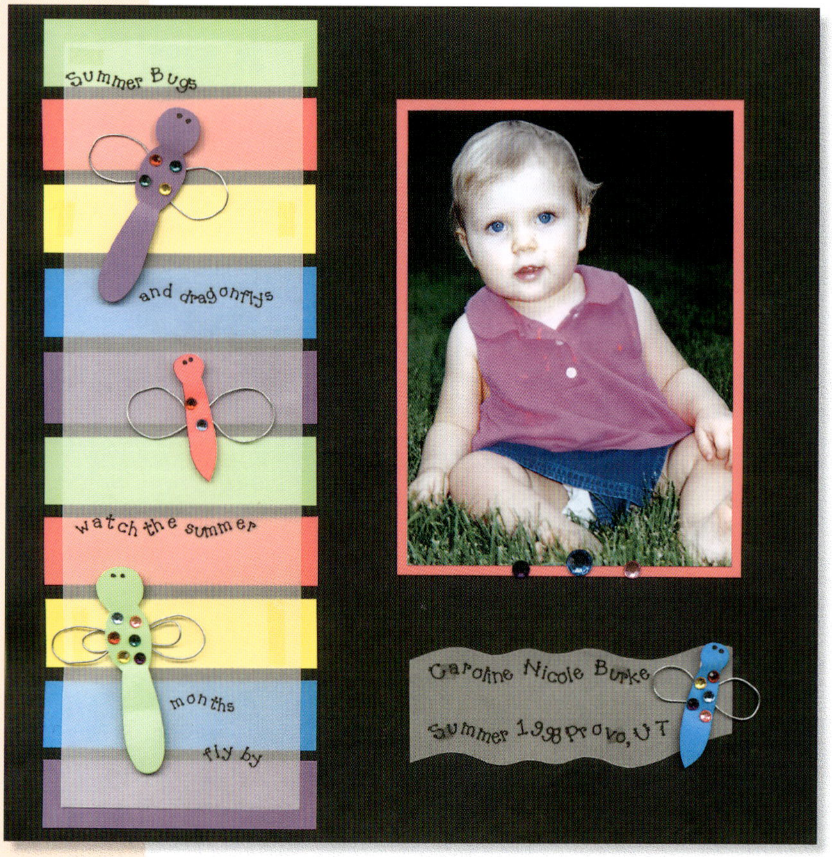

Summer Bugs

Supplies
Computer font: DJ Doodlers, "Fontastic" CD, D.J. Inkers
Journaling software: Journaling Genie, Chatterbox
Bug template: ScrapPagerz
Craft wire: Provo Craft
Other: Plastic craft gems

♥ **I Love It!:** *Instead of being created completely out of cardstock, these dragonflies were adorned with wire wings and beautiful gemstone markings.*

tip 8

represent key themes on your pages with mixed-media items.

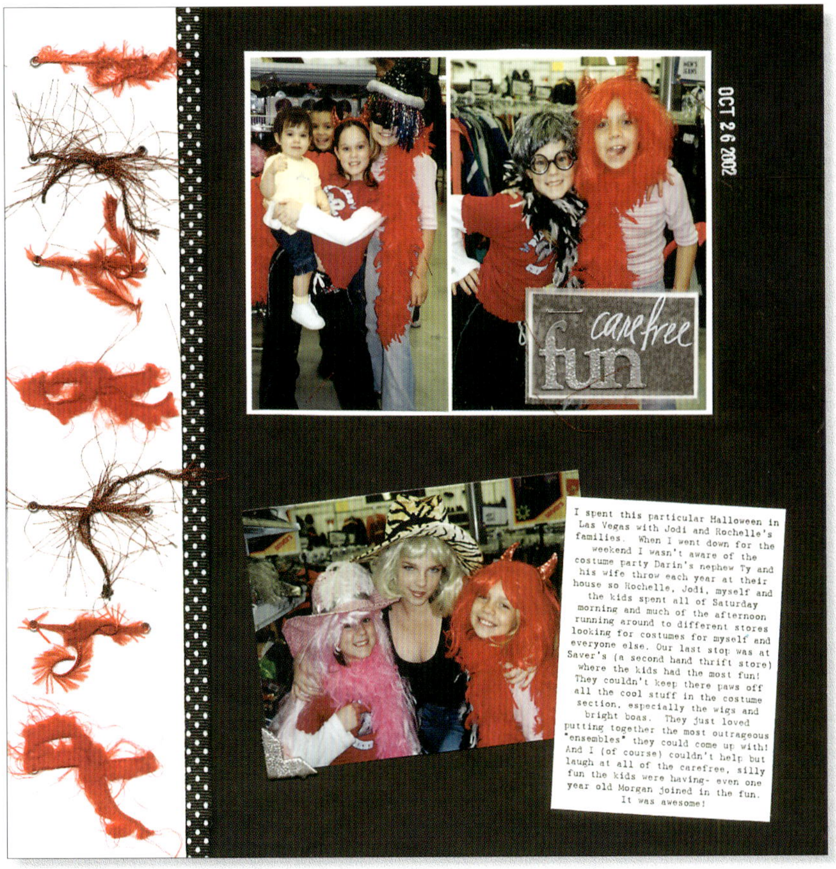

OCT 26 2002
carefree
fun
I spent this particular Halloween in Las Vegas with Jodi and Rochelle's families. When I went down for the weekend I wasn't aware of the costume party Darin's nephew Ty and his wife throw each year at their house so Rochelle, Jodi, myself and the kids spent all of Saturday morning and much of the afternoon running around to different stores looking for costumes for myself and everyone else. Our last stop was at Saver's (a second hand thrift store) where the kids had the most fun! They couldn't keep there paws off all the cool stuff in the costume section, especially the wigs and bright boas. They just loved putting together the most outrageous "ensembles" they could come up with! And I (of course) couldn't help but laugh at all of the carefree, silly fun the kids were having- even one year old Morgan joined in the fun. It was awesome!

Carefree Fun

Supplies

Fibers: Adornaments, EK Success
Rub-on word, metal word, photo corner and eyelets: Making Memories
Vellum: Provo Craft
Computer font: Linenstroke, downloaded from the Internet
Embossing powder: Adirondack, Ranger Industries
Other: Ribbon and glitter

♥ **I Love It!:** *The fibers on this border look feathery, just like the feather boa in the photographs.*

♥ **I Love It!:** *The title block was created by placing vellum over a rectangle of black cardstock matted on white cardstock.*

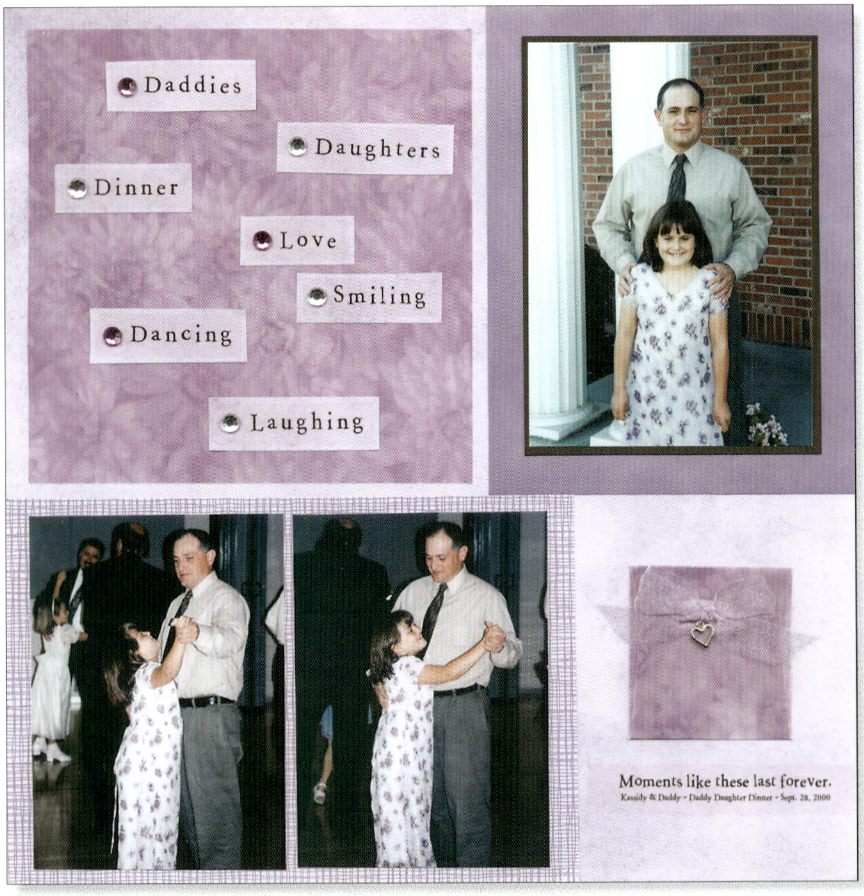

Daddies
Daughters
Dinner
Love
Smiling
Dancing
Laughing
Moments like these last forever.

Daddies and Daughters

Supplies

Patterned papers: Making Memories
Patterned vellum: Autumn Leaves
Plastic craft gems: Westrim Crafts
Heart charm: American Tag Co.
Computer font: P22 Garamouche, Impress Rubber Stamps
Envelope template: Coluzzle, Provo Craft
Other: Ribbon

♥ **I Love It!:** *Although it's unspoken symbolism, I love that the gems on this layout represent "treasured" moments spent between a daddy and his daughter.*

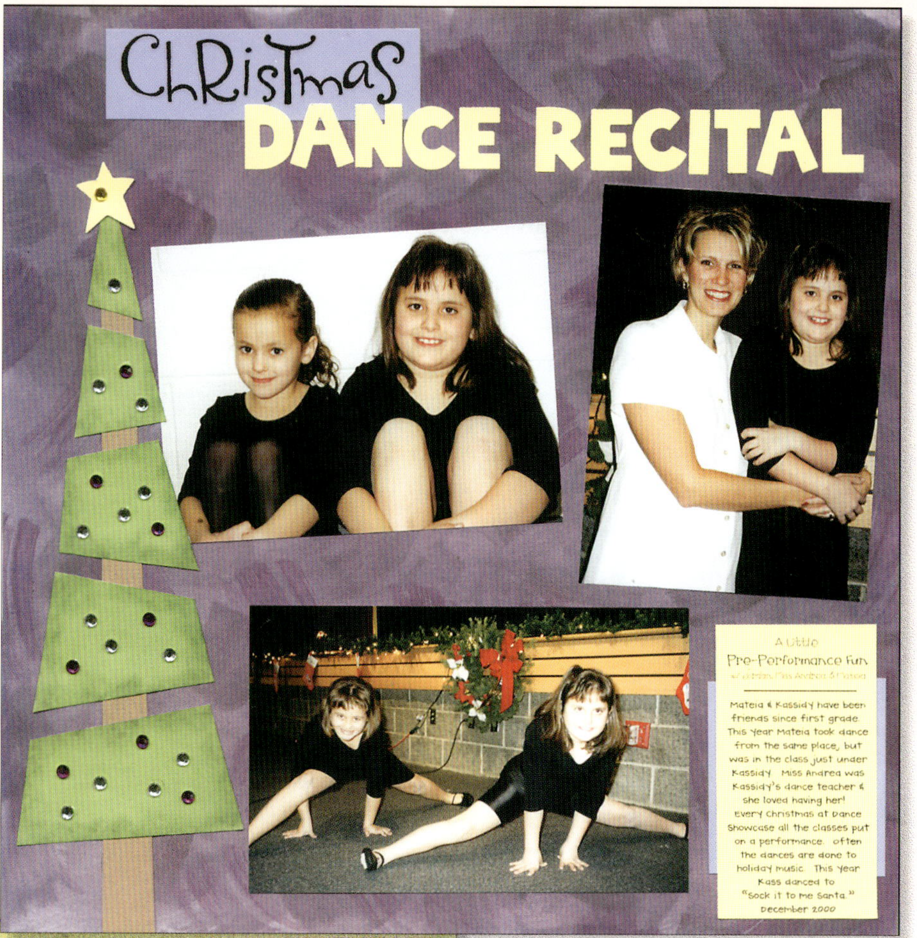

Christmas
DANCE RECITAL
A Little
Pre-Performance Fun
Mateia & Kassidy have been friends since first grade. This year Mateia took dance from the same place, but was in the class just under Kassidy. Miss Andrea was Kassidy's dance teacher & she loved having her! Every Christmas at Dance Showcase all the classes put on a performance. Often the dances are done to holiday music. This year Kass danced to "Sock it to me Santa."
December 2000

Christmas Dance Recital

Supplies

Patterned paper: Colorbök
Letter stickers: David Walker, Colorbök
Plastic craft gems: Westrim Crafts
Star punch: Emagination Crafts
Letter punches: EK Success
Computer fonts: CK Handprint, "The Best of Creative Lettering" CD Combo; CK Fun, "The Art of Creative Lettering" CD, *Creating Keepsakes*
Chalks: Craf-T Products

♥ **I Love It!:** *These plastic craft gems are perfect for re-creating the look and feel of Christmas or holiday lights.*

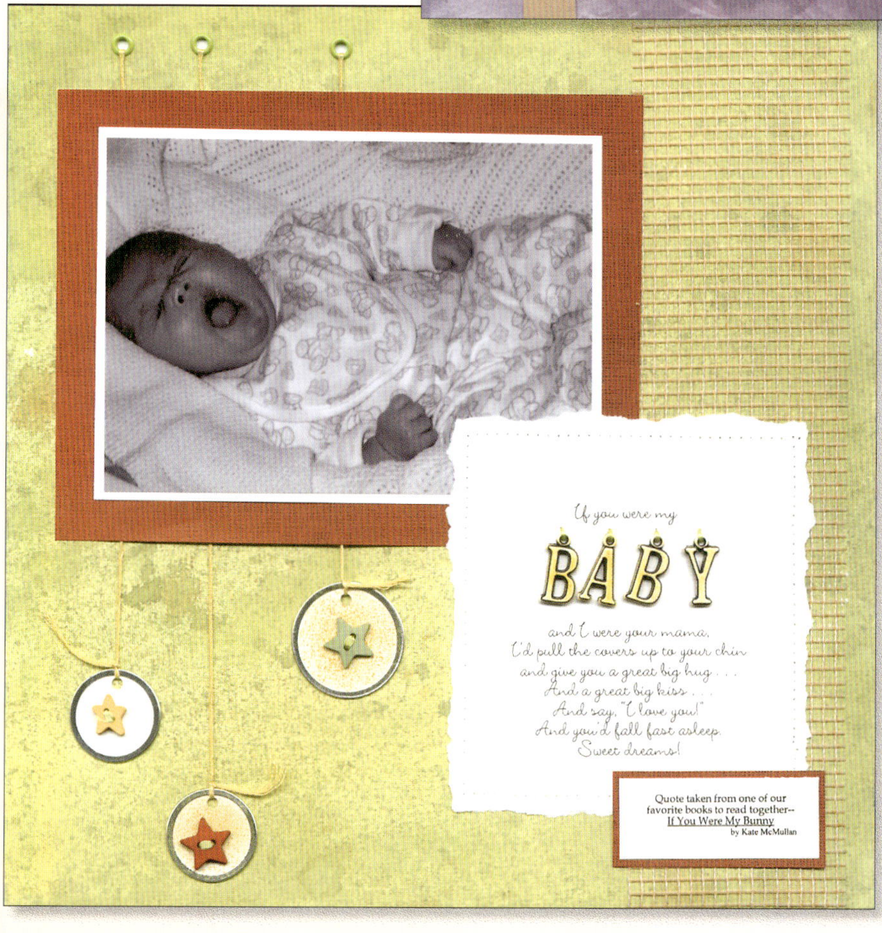

If you were my
BABY
and I were your mama,
I'd pull the covers up to your chin
and give you a great big hug . . .
And a great big kiss . . .
And say, "I love you!"
And you'd fall fast asleep.
Sweet dreams!
Quote taken from one of our favorite books to read together--
If You Were My Bunny
by Kate McMullan

If You Were My Baby

Supplies

Patterned paper: Provo Craft
Metal-rimmed tags and eyelets: Making Memories
Computer fonts: Garamond, Microsoft Word; Scrap Rhapsody, "Lettering Delights" CD, Inspire Graphics
Mesh: Magic Mesh
Buttons: Buttons Galore
Ink spritzer: Color Workshop

♥ **I Love It!:** *The mesh on the layout draws the eye to the texture of the loosely knit blanket in the black-and-white photograph.*

tip 9
highlight important aspects of your layout with pebble accents.

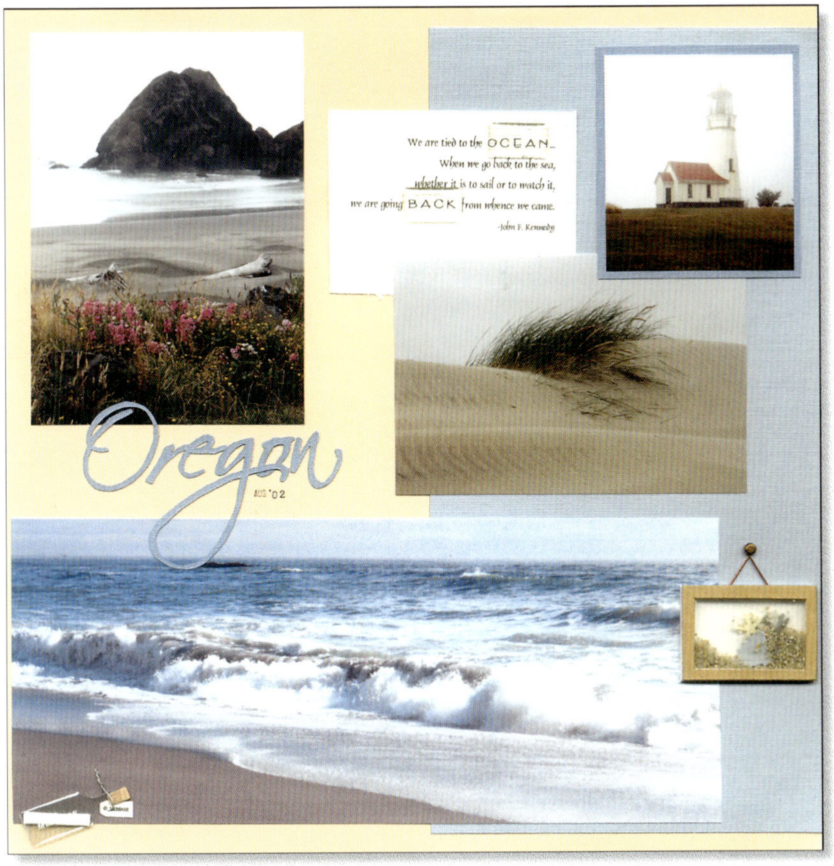
We are tied to the OCEAN.
When we go back to the sea,
whether it is to sail or to watch it,
we are going BACK from whence we came.
-John F. Kennedy
Oregon
AUG '02

Oregon

Supplies
Stickers: Jolee's Boutique, EK Success
Pebble accents: Making Memories
Stamping ink: Brilliance, Tsukineko
Computer fonts: Scriptina, downloaded from the Internet; Dauphin, Microsoft Word
Other: Date stamp

♥ **I Love It!:** *If you're ever in the market for a new camera, consider one that can take panoramic photographs. The beautiful photograph along the bottom of this layout eliminates the need for other complicated accents or patterns.*

♥ **I Love It!:** *Highlight key words in a favorite quote with attention-getting pebble accents.*

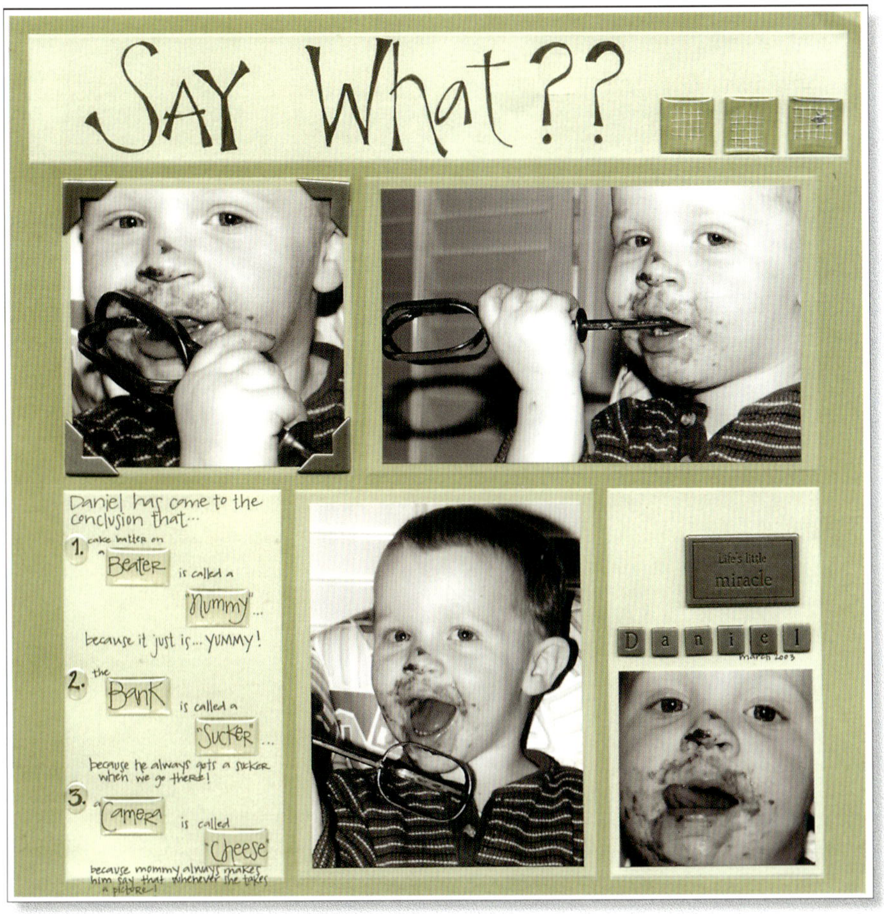
SAY What??
Daniel has come to the conclusion that...
1. a cake batter or "Beater" is called a "Yummy"...
because it just is... YUMMY!
2. the "Bank" is called a "Sucker"...
because he always gets a sucker when we go there!
3. a "Camera" is called "Cheese"
because mommy always makes him say that whenever she takes a picture!
Life's little miracle
Daniel
March 2003

Say What?

Supplies
Pre-formatted paper: All My Memories
Pebble and metal accents: Making Memories
Star punch: Fiskars
Mesh: Magic Mesh
Pen: Zig Writer, EK Success

♥ **I Love It!:** *Pebble accents aren't just for highlighting letters or words! Place textured paper, beautiful pressed flowers, tiny punches or other interesting items beneath the pebble for an eye-catching accent.*

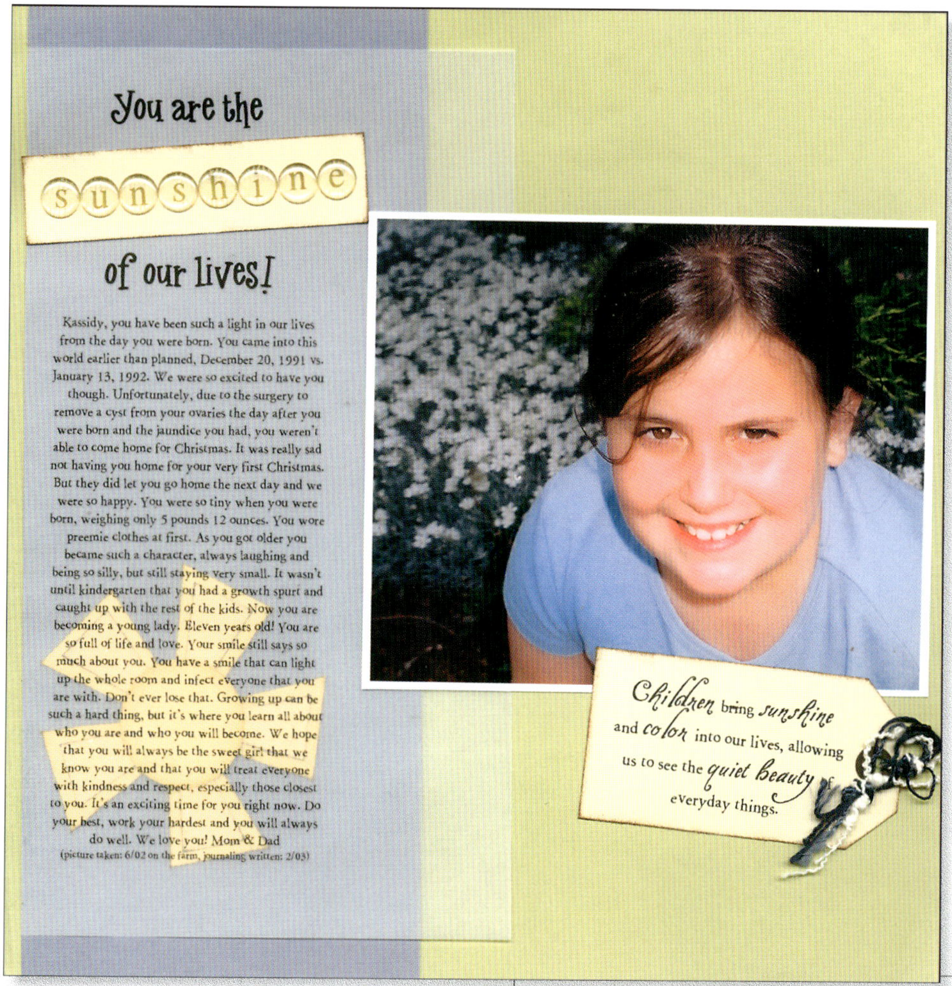
You are the
sunshine
of our lives!
Kassidy, you have been such a light in our lives from the day you were born. You came into this world earlier than planned, December 20, 1991 vs. January 13, 1992. We were so excited to have you though. Unfortunately, due to the surgery to remove a cyst from your ovaries the day after you were born and the jaundice you had, you weren't able to come home for Christmas. It was really sad not having you home for your very first Christmas. But they did let you go home the next day and we were so happy. You were so tiny when you were born, weighing only 5 pounds 12 ounces. You wore preemie clothes at first. As you got older you became such a character, always laughing and being so silly, but still staying very small. It wasn't until kindergarten that you had a growth spurt and caught up with the rest of the kids. Now you are becoming a young lady. Eleven years old! You are so full of life and love. Your smile still says so much about you. You have a smile that can light up the whole room and infect everyone that you are with. Don't ever lose that. Growing up can be such a hard thing, but it's where you learn all about who you are and who you will become. We hope that you will always be the sweet girl that we know you are and that you will treat everyone with kindness and respect, especially those closest to you. It's an exciting time for you right now. Do your best, work your hardest and you will always do well. We love you! Mom & Dad
(picture taken: 6/02 on the farm, journaling written: 2/03)
Children bring sunshine and color into our lives, allowing us to see the quiet beauty of everyday things.

You Are the Sunshine of Our Lives

Supplies

Letter pebble accents: Making Memories
Sun template: Coluzzle, Provo Craft
Computer fonts: P22 Garamouche, Impress Rubber Stamps; CK Elegant, "Fresh Fonts" CD, *Creating Keepsakes*; Whipper Basic, Whipper Snapper Designs
Fibers: On The Surface

I Love It!: *The sparkle and light reflecting from the pebble accents on this layout bring to life the word they spell: sunshine!*

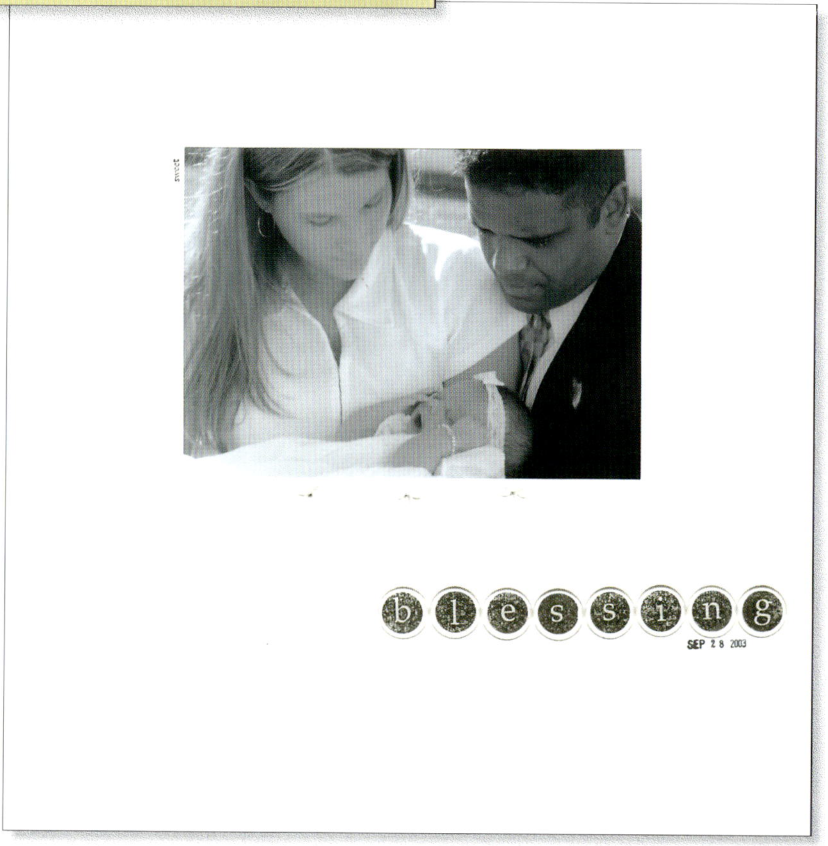
blessing
SEP 28 2003

Blessing

Supplies

Pre-formatted cardstock: Perspectives, Making Memories
Stickers: Jolee's Boutique, EK Success
Pebble accents: Making Memories
Letter stamps: Hero Arts
"Sweet" stamp: Stampin' Up!
Stamping ink: ColorBox, Clearsnap
Circle punch: Family Treasures

I Love It!: *This layout shows perfectly that "white space," or empty space, can be very good! Don't feel pressure to fill every blank space on a page with writing or accents. Instead, let sweet simplicity and beauty speak for itself.*

I Love It!: *Pebble accents come in several shapes and sizes, many of which coordinate with letter or small rubber stamps. Experiment with punches, stamps and other scrapbooking supplies to create new looks with pebble accents.*

tip 10

add a splash of color with embroidery floss.

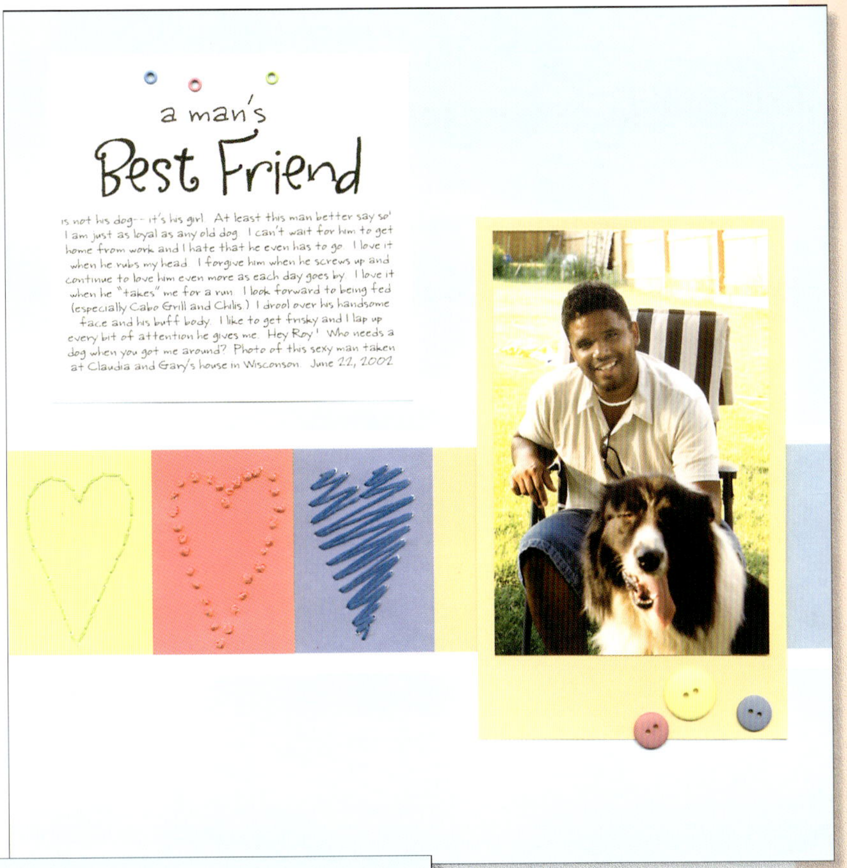

a man's
Best Friend
is not his dog-- it's his girl. At least this man better say so!
I am just as loyal as any old dog. I can't wait for him to get
home from work and I hate that he even has to go. I love it
when he rubs my head. I forgive him when he screws up and
continue to love him even more as each day goes by. I love it
when he "takes" me for a run. I look forward to being fed
(especially Cabo Grill and Chilis.) I drool over his handsome
face and his buff body. I like to get frisky and I lap up
every bit of attention he gives me. Hey Roy! Who needs a
dog when you got me around? Photo of this sexy man taken
at Claudia and Gary's house in Wisconson. June 22, 2002

A Man's Best Friend

Supplies

Patterned paper and buttons: SEI
Letter stickers: David Walker, Colorbök
Computer font: CK Sketch, "The Art of Creative Lettering" CD, *Creating Keepsakes*
Embroidery floss, buttons and eyelets: Making Memories

♥ **I Love It!:** *Embroidery is a craft that can come in handy for scrapbooking. This layout uses three different stitches: the backstitch, the spaced satin stitch and the French knot. Visit your local craft store to find resources on fun embroidery stitches you can incorporate onto your pages.*

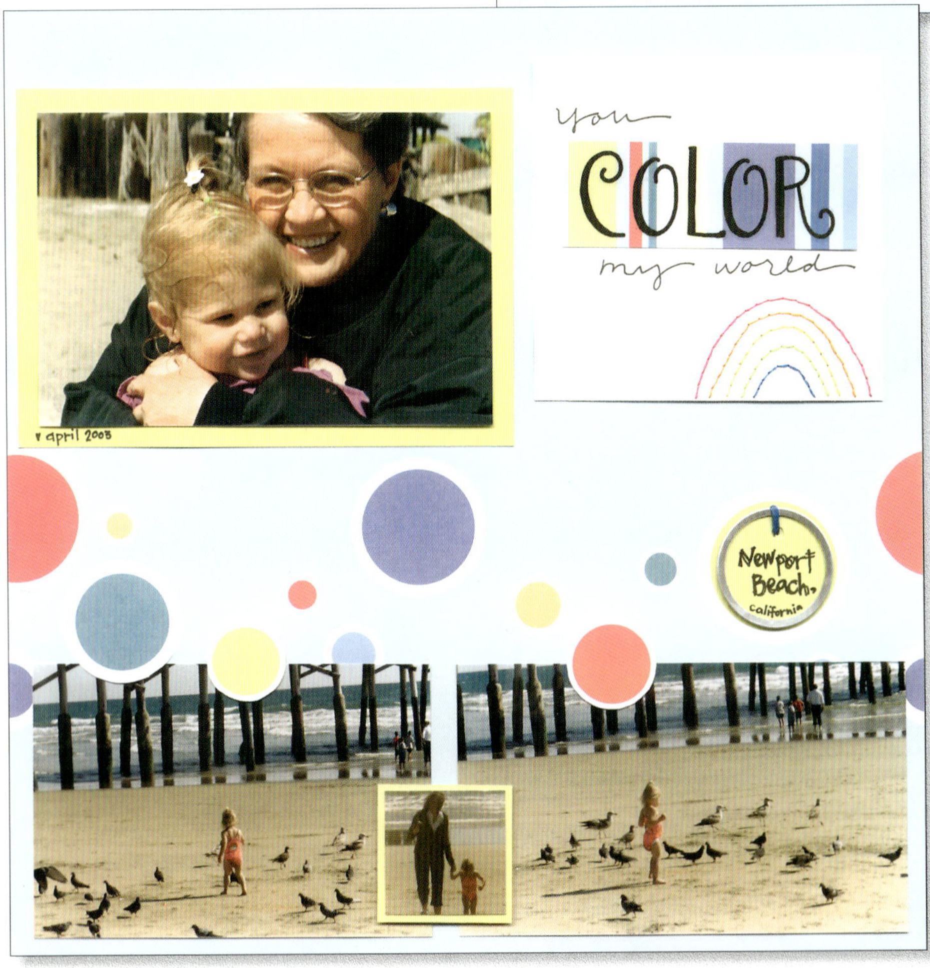

you
COLOR
my world
april 2003
Newport Beach, California

You Color My World

Supplies

Patterned paper: SEI
Letter stickers: Doodlebug Design
Metal-rimmed tag and embroidery floss: Making Memories

♥ **I Love It!:** *This simple stitched rainbow accent was created by penciling lines lightly on the layout, then using a backstitch along each line.*

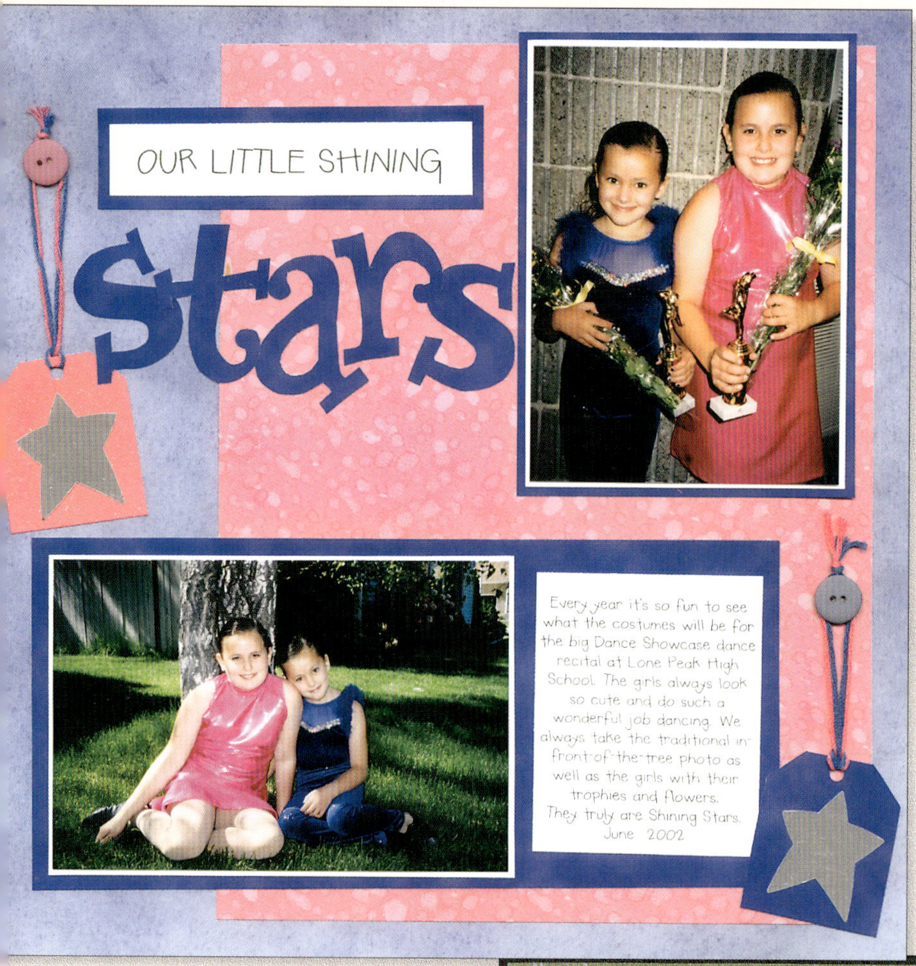
OUR LITTLE SHINING
Stars
Every year it's so fun to see what the costumes will be for the big Dance Showcase dance recital at Lone Peak High School. The girls always look so cute and do such a wonderful job dancing. We always take the traditional in-front-of-the-tree photo as well as the girls with their trophies and flowers.
They truly are Shining Stars.
June 2002

Our Little Shining Stars

Supplies
Patterned paper, buttons and embroidery floss: Making Memories
Star punch: Emagination Crafts
Computer font: CK Toggle, "The Best of Creative Lettering" CD Vol. 3, *Creating Keepsakes*
Lettering template: Party, ScrapPagerz

♥ **I Love It!:** *Use vivid embroidery floss to reinforce the color scheme of your layout. On this layout, matching shades of pink and blue embroidery floss were used to hang star tags from buttons.*

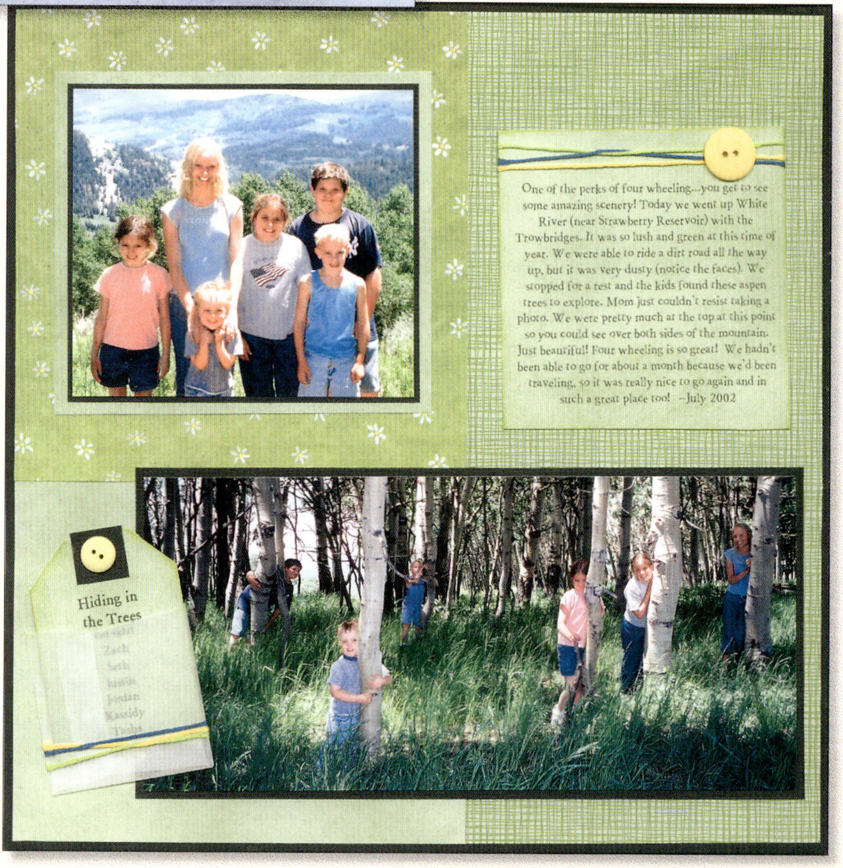
One of the perks of four wheeling...you get to see some amazing scenery! Today we went up White River (near Strawberry Reservoir) with the Trowbridges. It was so lush and green at this time of year. We were able to ride a dirt road all the way up, but it was very dusty (notice the faces). We stopped for a rest and the kids found these aspen trees to explore. Mom just couldn't resist taking a photo. We were pretty much at the top at this point so you could see over both sides of the mountain. Just beautiful! Four wheeling is so great! We hadn't been able to go for about a month because we'd been traveling, so it was really nice to go again and in such a great place too! --July 2002
Hiding in the Trees

Hiding in the Trees

Supplies
Patterned papers: Provo Craft (flower), Making Memories (plaid)
Buttons and embroidery floss: Making Memories
Stamping ink: Shadow Ink, Hero Arts
Computer font: P22 Garamouche, Impress Rubber Stamps
Envelope template: Coluzzle, Provo Craft

♥ **I Love It!:** *Buttons and thread are a natural pair. If you're considering using one or the other to accent a layout, try using them together for a polished look.*

tip 11

texturize your layouts with metal and mesh.

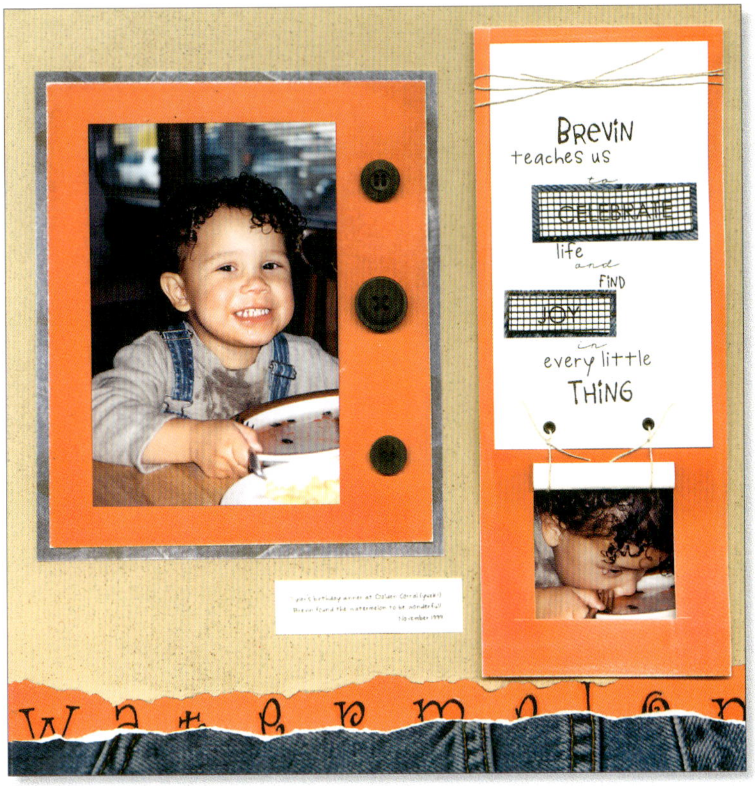
BREVIN
teaches us
to
CELEBRATE
life
and
FIND
JOY
in
every little
THING

Celebrate Life and Find Joy

Supplies
Patterned paper: Hot Off The Press
Photographic border: Shotz by Danelle Johnson, Creative Imaginations
Computer fonts: Scrap Brother, "Lettering Delights" CD, Inspire Graphics; CK Jot, "The Art of Creative Lettering" CD; CK Cursive, "The Best of Creative Lettering" CD Vol. 2, *Creating Keepsakes*
Letter stickers: Provo Craft
Eyelets: Making Memories
Other: Mesh, jute and buttons

♥ **I Love It!:** *Cut the sides and bottom (but not the top) of a square with a craft knife to create a frame. Roll up the flap to reveal a photograph underneath, and tie the roll with jute to keep it open.*

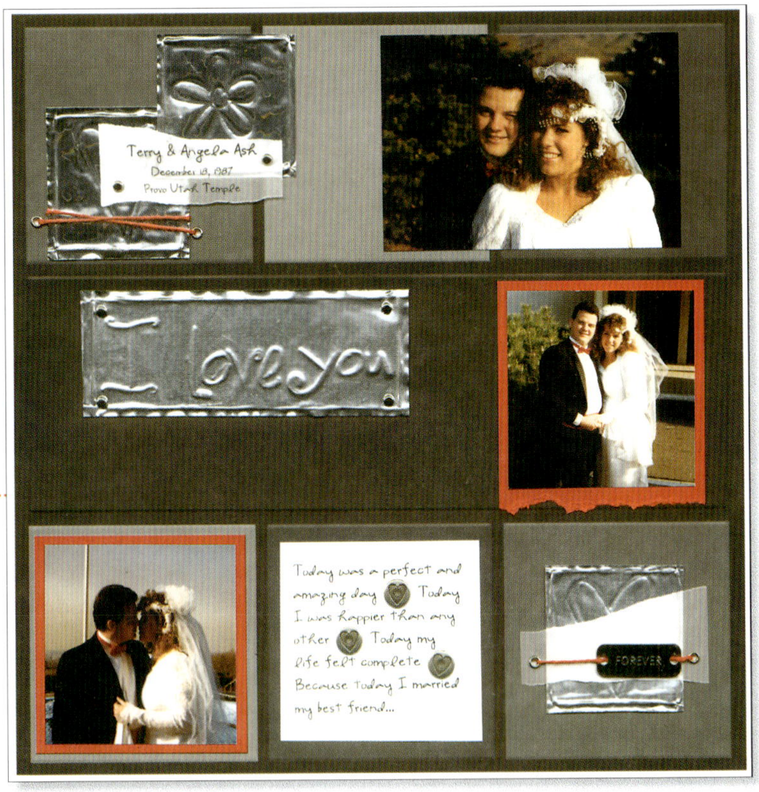
Terry & Angela Ash
December 18, 1987
Provo Utah Temple
I love you
Today was a perfect and amazing day Today I was happier than any other Today my life felt complete Because Today I married my best friend...
FOREVER

I Love You

Supplies
Pre-formatted paper: All My Memories
Vellum: Provo Craft
Metal paper: Magic Scraps
Metal accents: Making Memories
"Forever" charm: Colorbök
Computer font: CK Sloppy, Becky Higgins' "Creative Clips & Fonts" CD, *Creating Keepsakes*
Other: Red hemp string

♥ **I Love It!:** *The smooth, shiny metal, embossed with a stylus, provides a contrast to the silk dress in the photographs and symbolically conveys strength.*

Same Idea, Slightly Different: *This metal paper was etched with an etching tool instead of embossed. The edges of the metal paper were folded over to create a "frame" around the etched letter.*

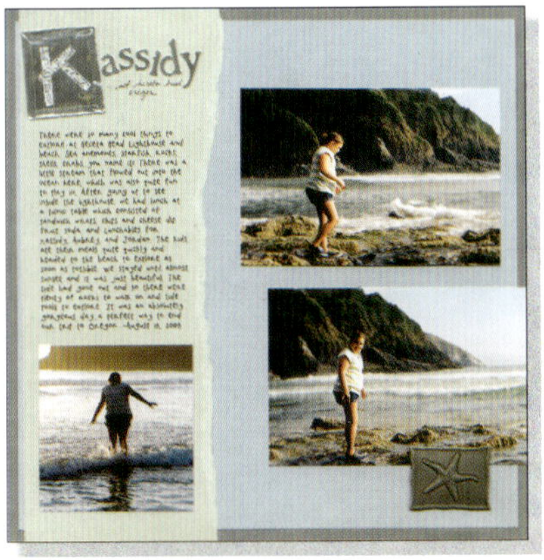
Kassidy

Kassidy

Supplies
Metal paper and engraver: Magic Scraps
Metal letter charms, metal starfish accent and eyelets: Making Memories
Computer font: 2Peas Chicken Shack, downloaded from *www.twopeasinabucket.com*
Pen: Pigma Micron, Sakura

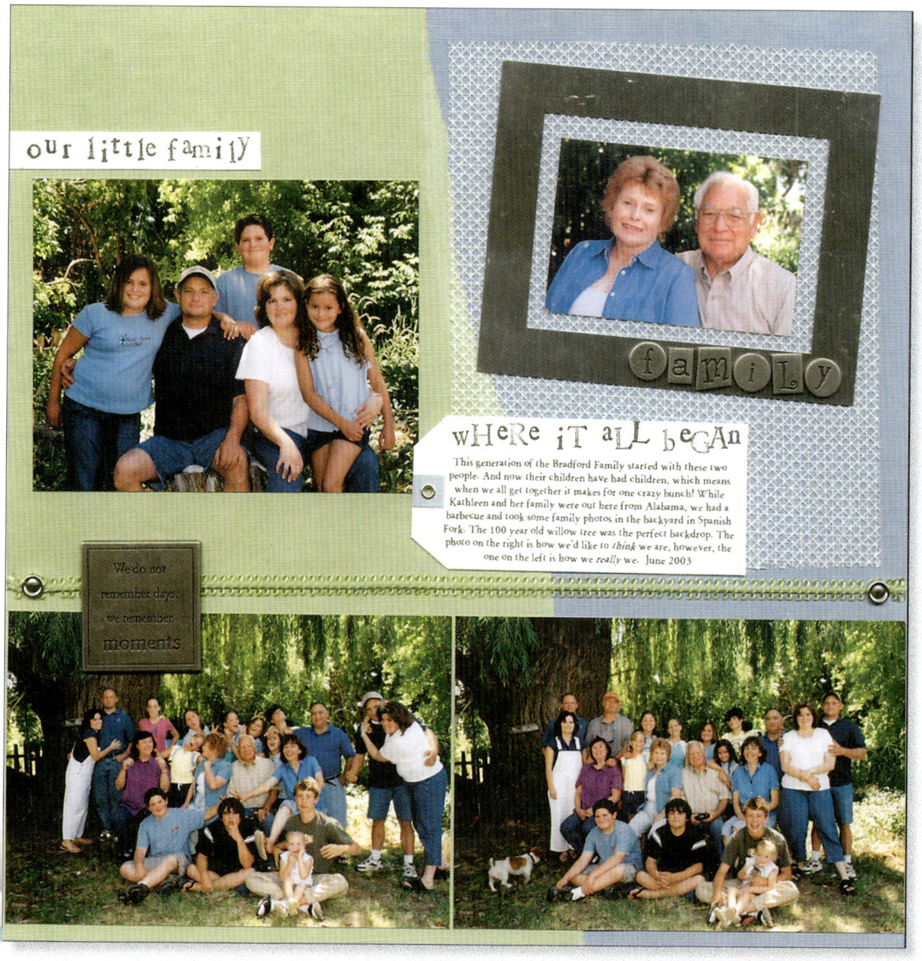
our little family
family
WHERE IT ALL BEGAN
This generation of the Bradford Family started with these two people. And now their children have had children, which means when we all get together it makes for one crazy bunch! While Kathleen and her family were out here from Alabama, we had a barbecue and took some family photos in the backyard in Spanish Fork. The 100 year old willow tree was the perfect backdrop. The photo on the right is how we'd like to *think* we are, however, the one on the left is how we *really* we. June 2003
We do not remember days, we remember moments

Our Little Family

Supplies
Metal accents: Making Memories
Letter stamps: PSX Design
Stamping ink: Stampin' Up!
Computer font: P22 Garamouche, Impress Rubber Stamps
Mesh: Magic Mesh
Other: Ribbon and studs

♥ **I Love It!:** *Crop a photograph to fit inside a metal frame, leaving a small gap between the photo and the frame. Fill the gap with uniquely textured items: mesh, window screening, corrugated paper or any other supply that matches or enhances the theme of your page.*

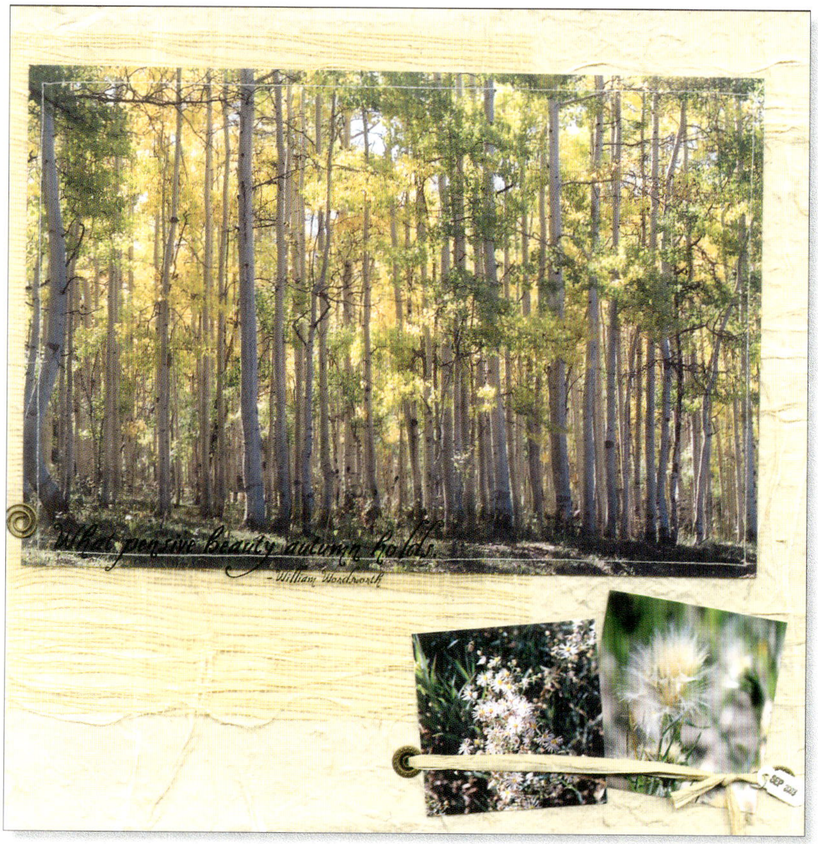
What pensive beauty autumn holds.
– William Wordsworth

Pensive Beauty

Supplies
Mesh: Magenta
Rivets: Chatterbox
Computer font: CK Elegant, "Fresh Fonts" CD, *Creating Keepsakes*
Other: Transparency paper, textured paper, spiral paper clip, raffia, mini-tag, date stamp and wire

♥ **I Love It!:** *Nature photographs contain so much beauty and rich texture. I love it when layouts with nature photographs mimic the same textures with handmade papers and mixed-media supplies.*

♥ **I Love It!:** *Print your favorite quote on transparency paper, then lay the paper over the bottom of the main photograph on your layout. The quote should be subtle—an afterthought for the beautiful photograph.*

tips

lisa's lessons on mixed media

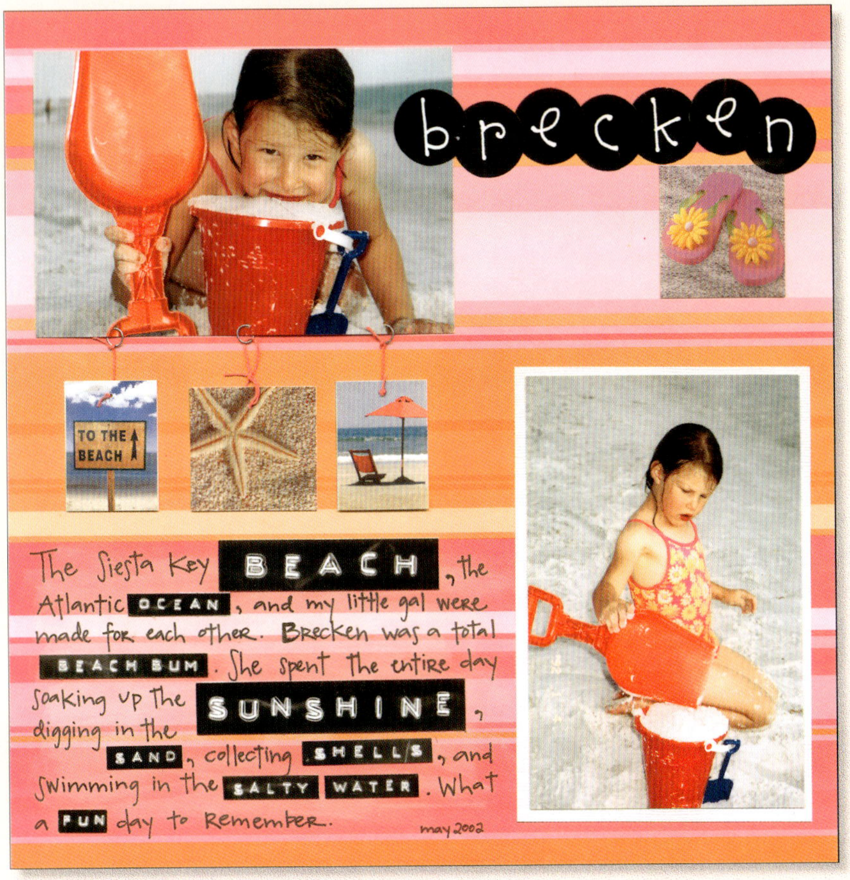
brecken
TO THE BEACH
The Siesta Key BEACH, the Atlantic OCEAN, and my little gal were made for each other. Brecken was a total BEACH BUM. She spent the entire day soaking up the SUNSHINE, digging in the SAND, collecting SHELLS, and swimming in the SALTY WATER. What a FUN day to remember.
may 2002

I'm amazed by the endless possibilities for layouts offered by mixed-media products! Here are two of my favorite mixed-media tips:

- If you're concerned about archival scrapbooking, educate yourself on what's safe and what's not for your layouts. I'm always surprised when I discover that a product not created for scrapbooking but used in the latest trends is actually okay to use! Still, my all-time favorite tip is to make copies of one-of-a-kind photographs to use on scrapbook layouts, then store the irreplaceable originals in acid-free envelopes or photo sleeves in a dark, safe place.
- Be a confident scrapbooker! I must admit, at the beginning of the trend of using mixed media on scrapbook pages, I was a little intimidated—even a little hesitant. But once I gave it a try, I realized how easy it is to find creativity when you're not limiting the range of products you can use on your pages. Of course, my voice of reason always reminds me that the focus of my layouts should always be the memories.

Three more favorite tips from this page:

- I wanted to paint a splash of white acrylic paint behind the journaling to help it stand out against the cheerful background, but I didn't have any paint. Instead, I grabbed a white stamp pad and lightly inked the area behind my journaling. I love the way it subtly made my journaling more prominent and increased the readability.
- Although they're small, metal jump rings add personality to your layouts. They're the perfect way to hang embellishments from your focal-point photo or title.
- Pre-printed photograph stickers are not only cute, they can also be incredibly helpful if you've missed "the perfect shot." They're also a great way to embellish pages that have heavy journaling but no photographs to accompany the memories.

Brecken

Supplies
Patterned paper and jump rings: Making Memories
Letter stickers: Doodlebug Design
Photograph and label-maker stickers: Pebbles Inc.
Stamping ink: ColorBox, Clearsnap
Twine: Waxy Flax, Scrapworks

lisa says:

"Mini-albums are a great ego booster for me. I love sitting down to scrapbook for a couple of hours and *finishing* a whole album! To make it even *easier,* I often use the same colors and products throughout the entire album—it looks great and cuts down the decisions I have to make. An added *bonus?* Mini-albums are smaller. That means they're more *portable,* so you can easily show them off to your friends and *family!"*

MINI-
ALBUMS

ch. 8

magnificent mini-albums

MINI *n. small in relation to others of the same kind*

ALBUM *n. a book with blank pages used for making a collection (as of stamps, autographs or photographs)*

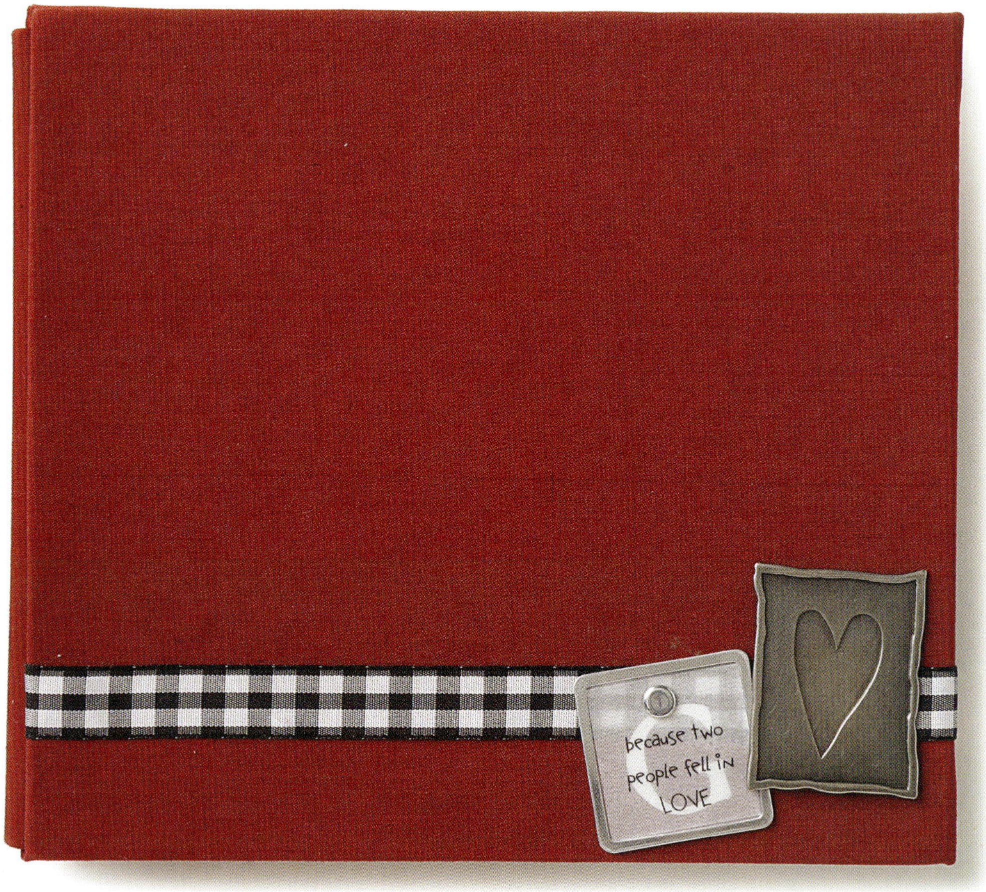

because two people fell in LOVE

Supplies
Metal-rimmed tag, metal accent and metal letter charm: Making Memories
Other: Gingham ribbon

Mini-albums are a fun, fast way to capture memories that are related to a brief event or a narrow theme. Embellish the cover of the album with materials appropriate to the album's theme.

album 1

first day of school

Remember the excitement, the nervousness, the anticipation you felt on your first day of each school year? This sentimental mini-album captures the first day of each year of school from a mom's perspective. Starting with kindergarten and following with each consecutive grade, the album, titled "Remember," details what was worn, what school it was, who else was there and feelings experienced that day by both mother and child.

All supplies from Making Memories except Quote: Wordsworth.

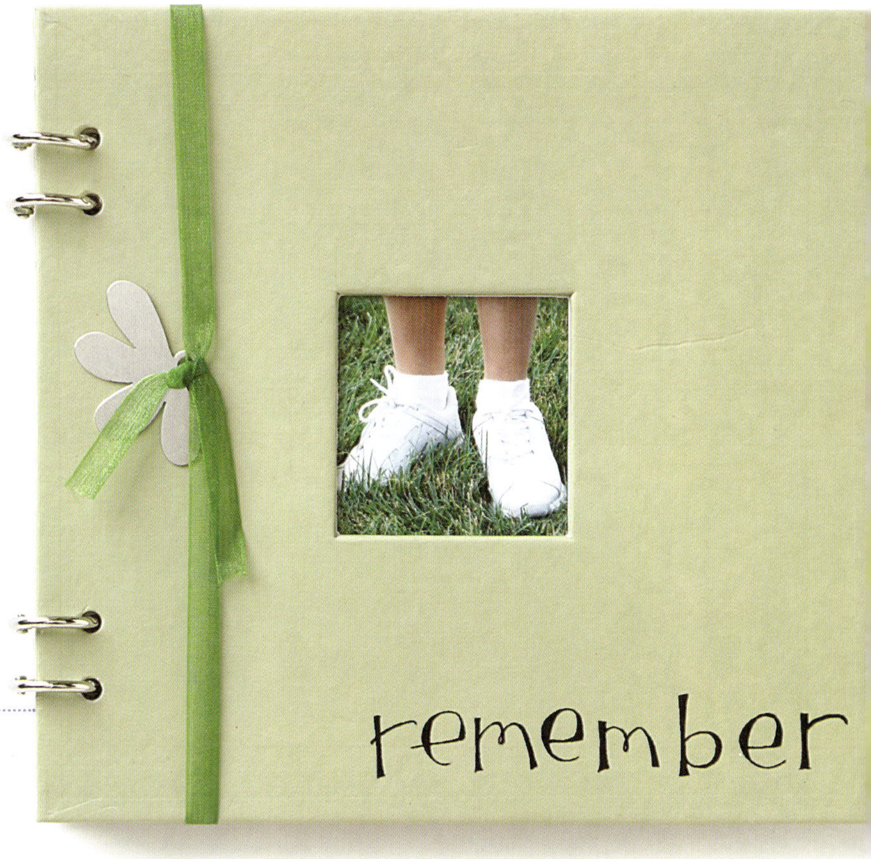
remember

New shoes are a part of every first day of school. Remembering little details like this will help keep memories vivid.

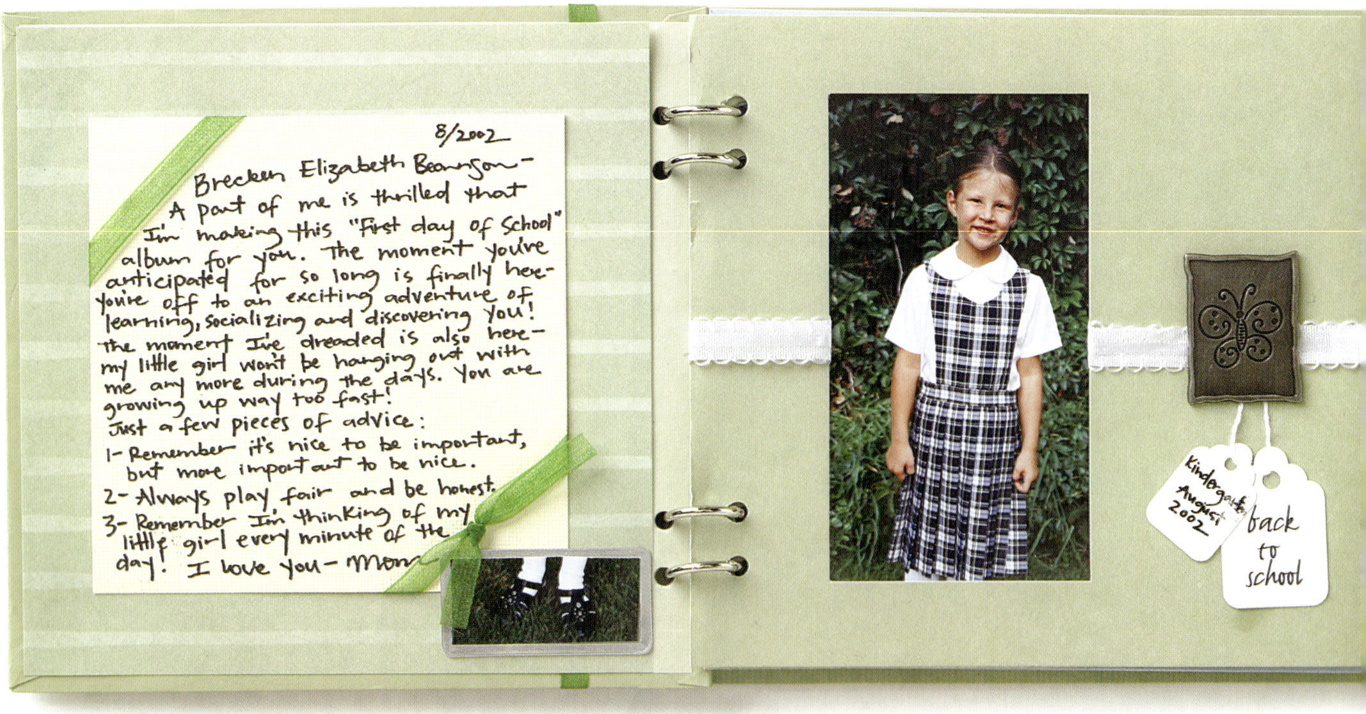
8/2002
Brecken Elizabeth Bearnson-
A part of me is thrilled that I'm making this "First day of School" album for you. The moment you've anticipated for so long is finally here- you're off to an exciting adventure of learning, socializing and discovering you! The moment I've dreaded is also here- my little girl won't be hanging out with me any more during the days. You are growing up way too fast!
Just a few pieces of advice:
1- Remember it's nice to be important, but more important to be nice.
2- Always play fair and be honest.
3- Remember I'm thinking of my little girl every minute of the day! I love you- Mom
Kindergarten August 2002
back to school

Include a heartfelt letter detailing your emotions as your children begin kindergarten. Don't forget to include any advice you want your kids to remember as they enter the big world!

What did your child wear on her first day of school? Why?

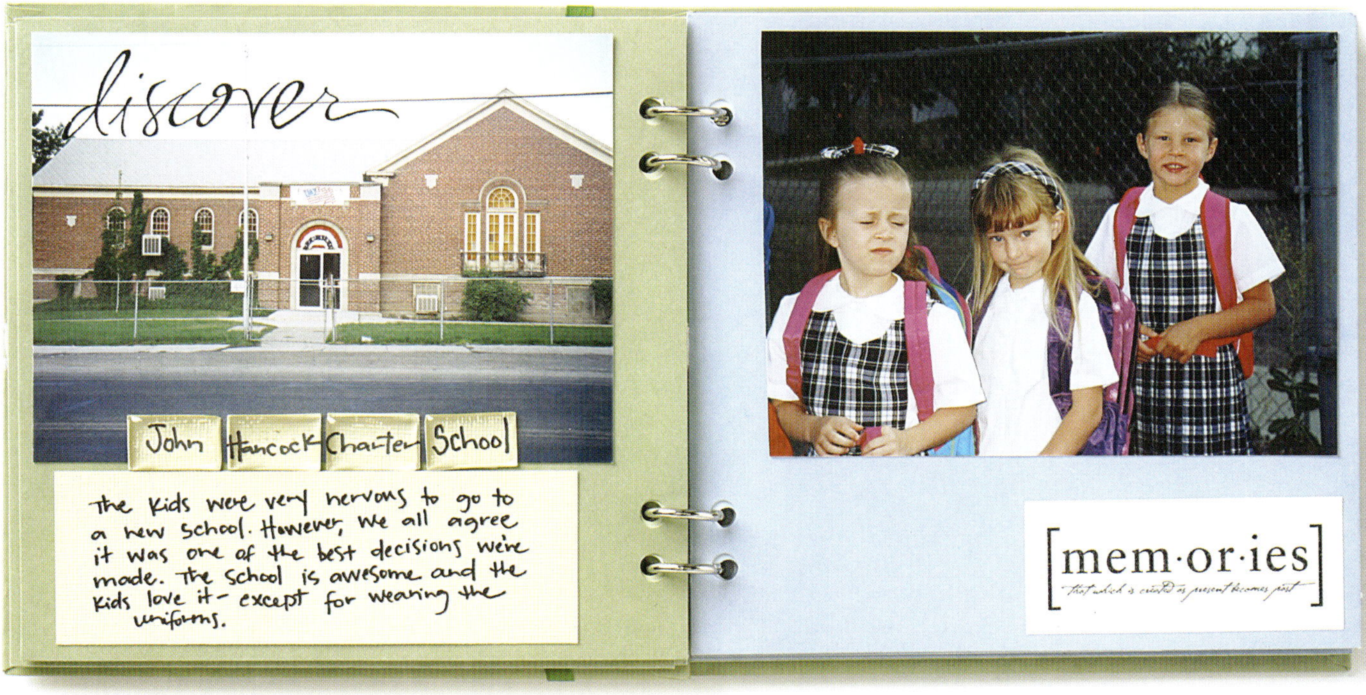
discover
John Hancock Charter School
the kids were very nervous to go to a new school. However, we all agree it was one of the best decisions we've made. The school is awesome and the kids love it - except for wearing the uniforms.
mem·or·ies

Take a photograph of your child's first school and each school your child attends. How did you pick that school? What are your favorite things about it? How did your child like it?

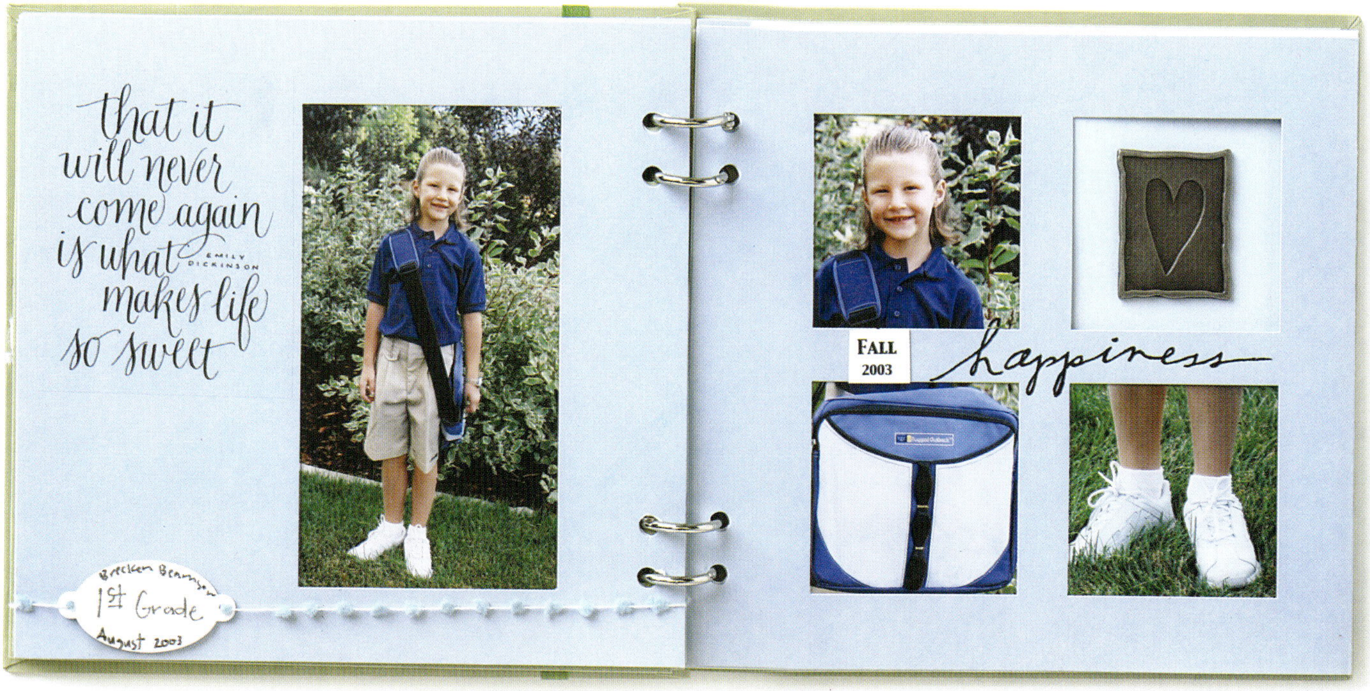
that it will never come again is what makes life so sweet
EMILY DICKINSON
1st Grade
August 2003
FALL 2003
happiness

Repeat the same information and details for each school year so you and your child can see how things change over time.

album 2
wedding memories

You probably have more than enough photographs from your own wedding, but have you ever wondered what your parents' wedding was like? This beautiful mini-album showcases heritage wedding photographs and memories from the big day. To maintain the heritage look and feel in the album, papers and products were aged with walnut ink, chalk and brass embossing powder.

All supplies from Making Memories except:
Computer fonts: CK Gutenberg and CK Constitution, "Fresh Fonts" CD, *Creating Keepsakes*
Date stamp: OfficeMax

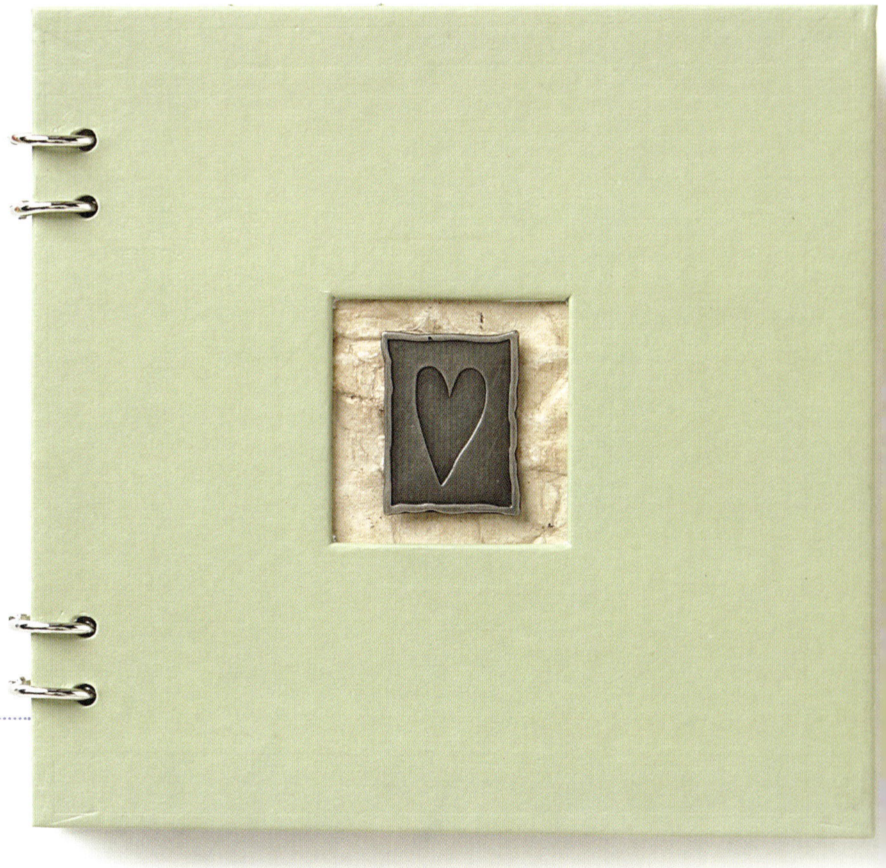

A simple metal heart accent backed with crumpled and chalked cardstock decorates the cover of this mini-album.

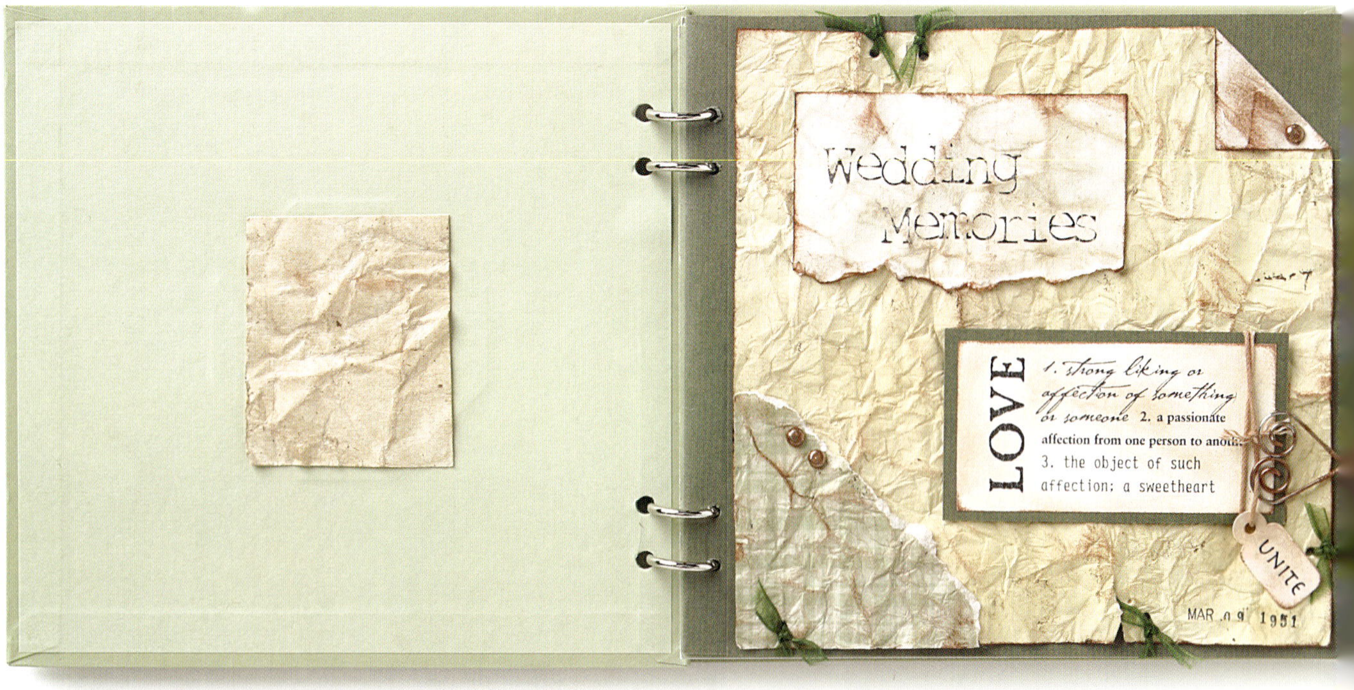
Wedding Memories
LOVE
1. strong liking or affection of something or someone 2. a passionate affection from one person to anoth
3. the object of such affection; a sweetheart
UNITE
MAR 09 1951

The title page introduces the album with a definition of love and the wedding date stamped in the lower corner.

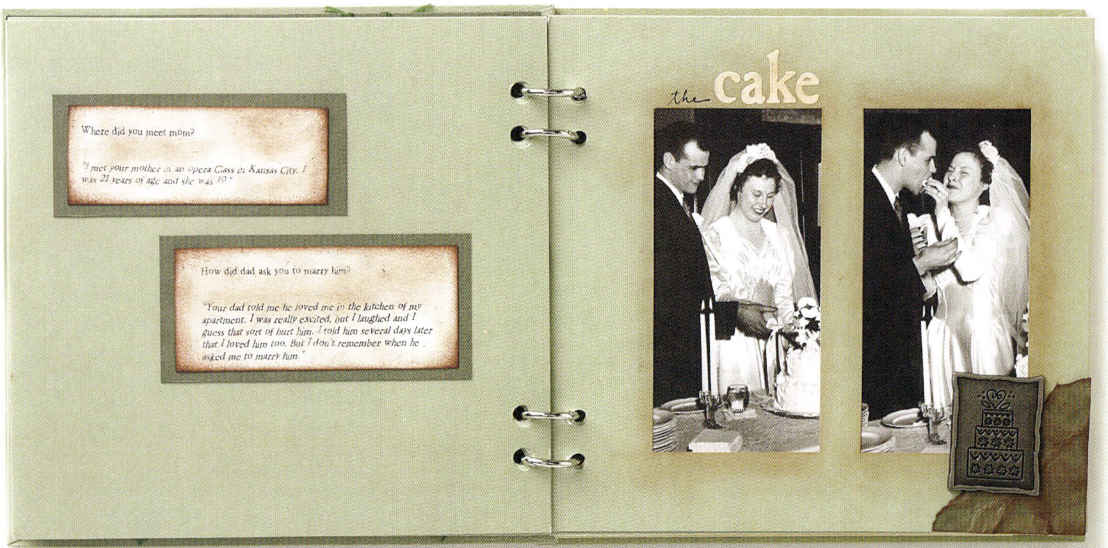
Where did you meet mom?
"I met your mother in an opera Class in Kansas City. I was 21 years of age and she was 19."
How did dad ask you to marry him?
"Your dad told me he loved me in the kitchen of my apartment. I was really excited, but I laughed and I guess that sort of hurt him. I told him several days later that I loved him too. But I don't remember when he asked me to marry him."
the cake

Include a page that explains why you created the album and how the story told inside begins.

Spotlight special photographs of the bride and groom, the location of the wedding and other details of the day.

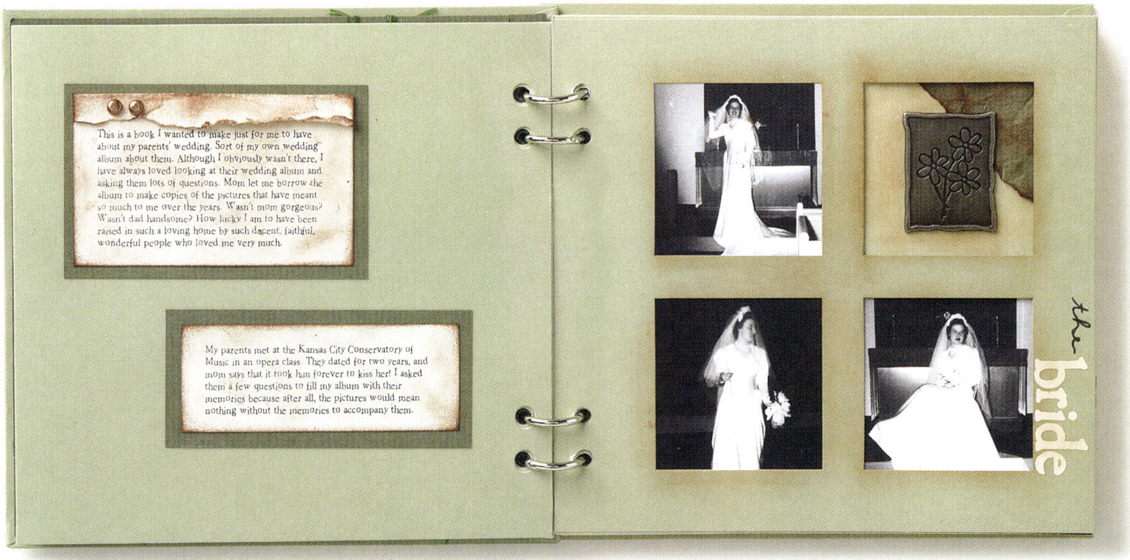
This is a book I wanted to make just for me to have about my parents' wedding. Sort of my own wedding album about them. Although I obviously wasn't there, I have always loved looking at their wedding album and asking them lots of questions. Mom let me borrow the album to make copies of the pictures that have meant so much to me over the years. Wasn't mom gorgeous? Wasn't dad handsome? How lucky I am to have been raised in such a loving home by such decent, faithful, wonderful people who loved me very much.
My parents met at the Kansas City Conservatory of Music in an opera class. They dated for two years, and mom says that it took him forever to kiss her! I asked them a few questions to fill my album with their memories because after all, the pictures would mean nothing without the memories to accompany them.
the bride

Ask each parent questions about his or her relationship and the wedding, then include the questions and answers in the album.

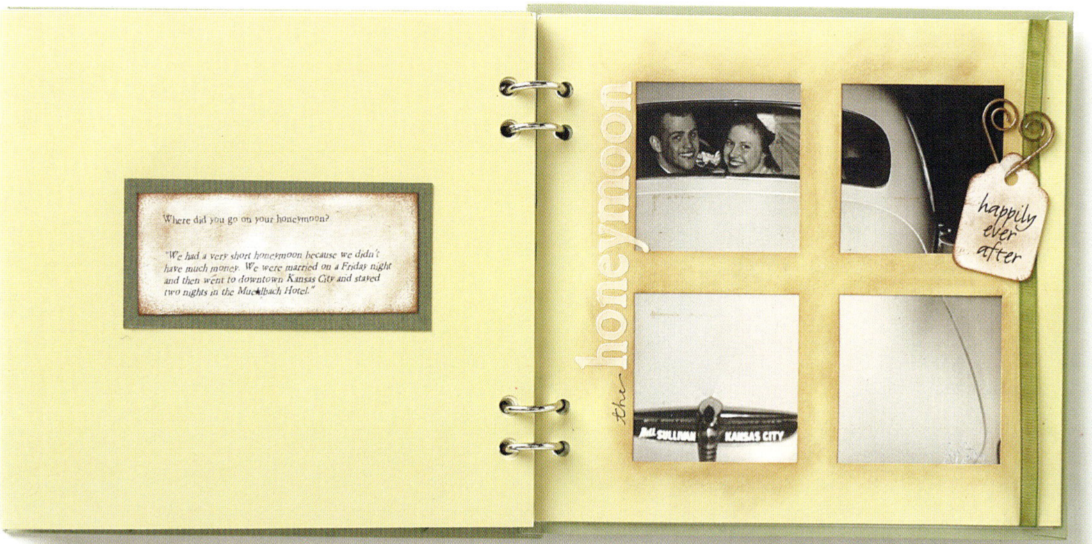
Where did you go on your honeymoon?
"We had a very short honeymoon because we didn't have much money. We were married on a Friday night and then went to downtown Kansas City and stayed two nights in the Muehlbach Hotel."
the honeymoon
happily ever after
KANSAS CITY

Don't forget information about the honeymoon, the first few years of marriage or funny mishaps and memories.

album 3

when you were five

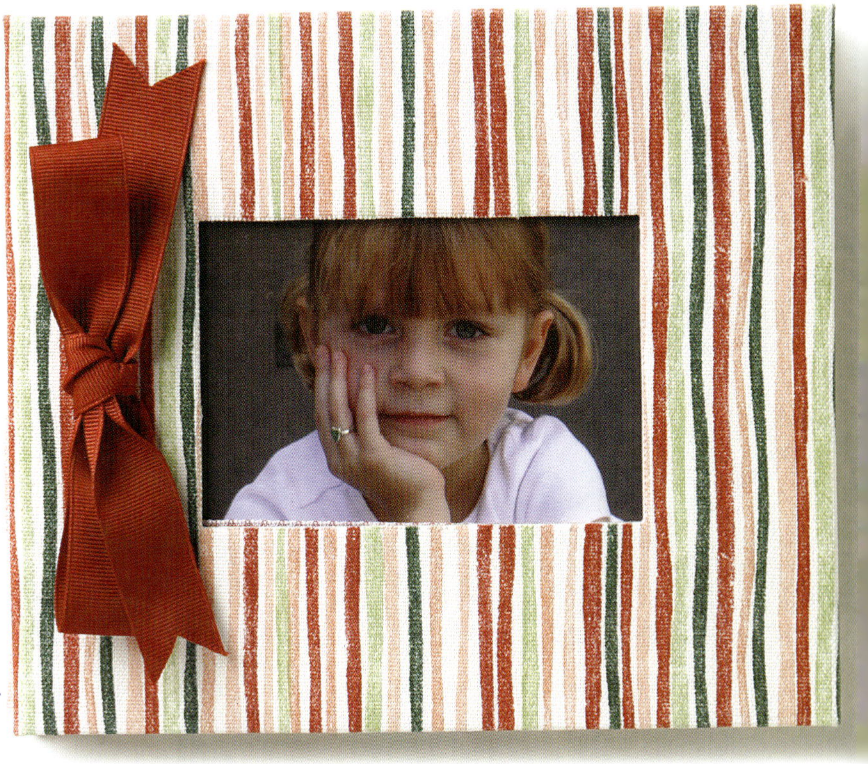

Freeze time by creating a mini-album all about your child at a certain age. From abilities and responsibilities to funny moments and friends, capture what makes your child unique. Include "scientific" information as well: what your child looks like, height, weight, number of brothers and sisters, and other facts your child will appreciate when he's grown.

All supplies from We R Memory Keepers except:
Ribbon: May Arts
Brads: Memory Lane Paper Company
Metal-rimmed tags: Avery
Eyelets: Creative Imaginations
Conchos: Scrapworks
Computer fonts: Tangerine, Macromedia; CK Fresh, "Fresh Fonts" CD, *Creating Keepsakes*

Choose a photograph for the cover that reveals your child's personality.

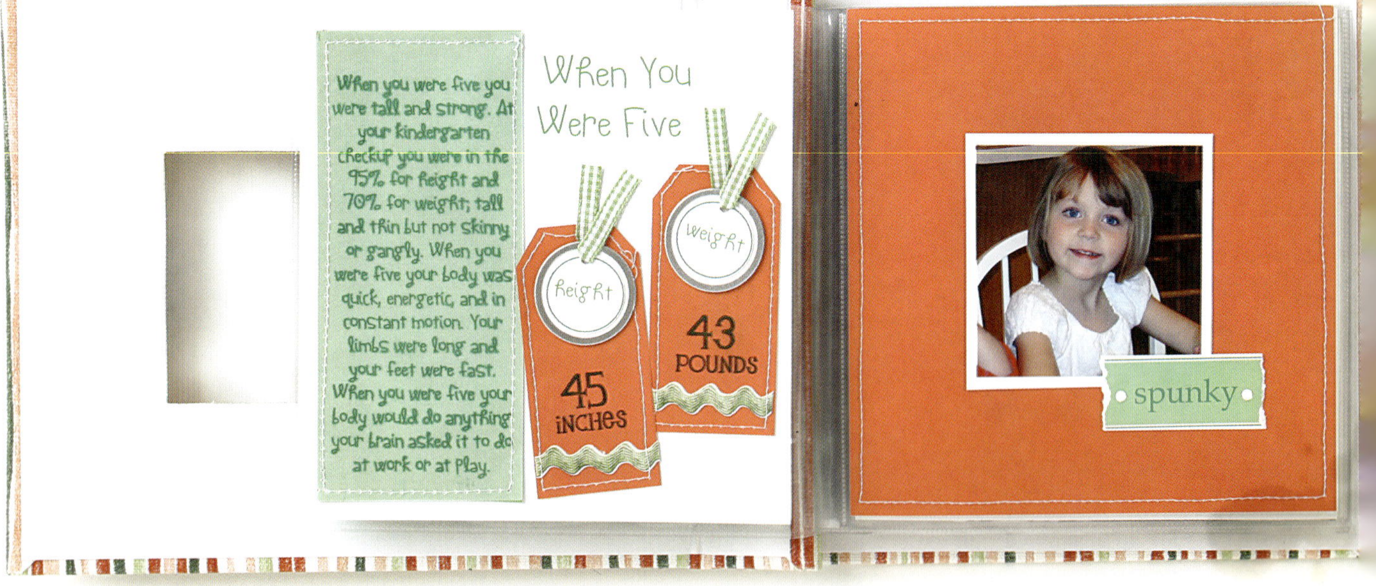

When you were five you were tall and strong. At your kindergarten checkup you were in the 95% for height and 70% for weight; tall and thin but not skinny or gangly. When you were five your body was quick, energetic, and in constant motion. Your limbs were long and your feet were fast. When you were five your body would do anything your brain asked it to do at work or at play.
When You Were Five
height
45 INCHES
weight
43 POUNDS
spunky

Include interesting information about your child's health and medical history.

Select your favorite photographs and accent them with words that represent your child's personality.

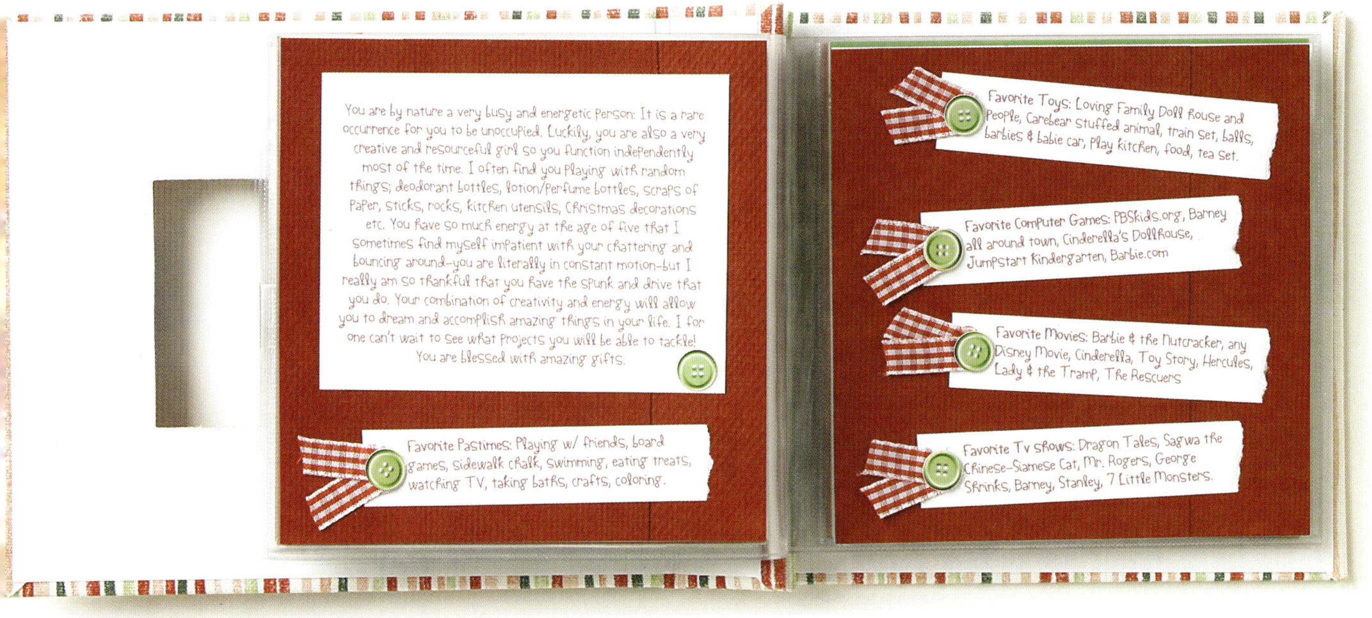

You are by nature a very busy and energetic person. It is a rare occurrence for you to be unoccupied. Luckily, you are also a very creative and resourceful girl so you function independently most of the time. I often find you playing with random things; deodorant bottles, lotion/perfume bottles, scraps of paper, sticks, rocks, kitchen utensils, Christmas decorations etc. You have so much energy at the age of five that I sometimes find myself impatient with your chattering and bouncing around—you are literally in constant motion—but I really am so thankful that you have the spunk and drive that you do. Your combination of creativity and energy will allow you to dream and accomplish amazing things in your life. I for one can't wait to see what projects you will be able to tackle! You are blessed with amazing gifts.
Favorite Pastimes: Playing w/ friends, board games, sidewalk chalk, swimming, eating treats, watching TV, taking baths, crafts, coloring.
Favorite Toys: Loving Family Doll house and people, Carebear stuffed animal, train set, balls, barbies & babie car, play kitchen, food, tea set.
Favorite Computer Games: PBSkids.org, Barney all around town, Cinderella's Dollhouse, Jumpstart Kindergarten, Barbie.com
Favorite Movies: Barbie & the Nutcracker, any Disney Movie, Cinderella, Toy Story, Hercules, Lady & the Tramp, The Rescuers
Favorite Tv shows: Dragon Tales, Sagwa the Chinese-Siamese Cat, Mr. Rogers, George Shrinks, Barney, Stanley, 7 Little Monsters.

Write a summary of your child's personality, talents and habits.

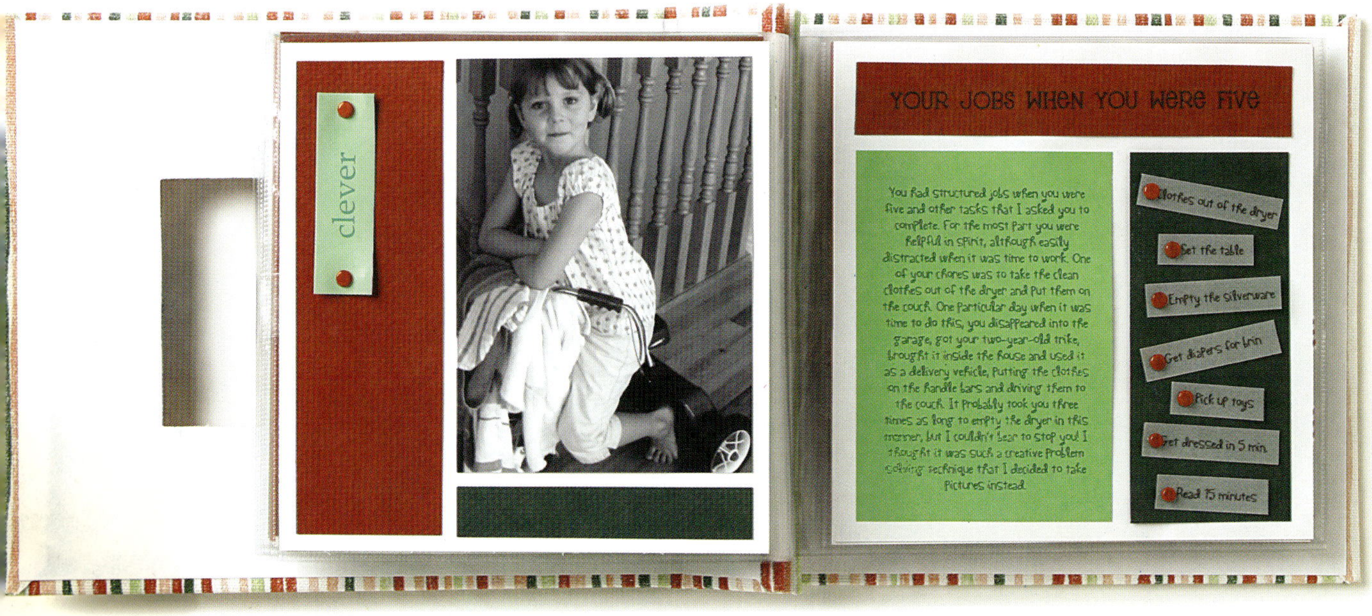

clever
YOUR JOBS WHEN YOU WERE FIVE
You had structured jobs when you were five and other tasks that I asked you to complete. For the most part you were helpful in spirit, although easily distracted when it was time to work. One of your chores was to take the clean clothes out of the dryer and put them on the couch. One particular day when it was time to do this, you disappeared into the garage, got your two-year-old trike, brought it inside the house and used it as a delivery vehicle, putting the clothes on the handle bars and driving them to the couch. It probably took you three times as long to empty the dryer in this manner, but I couldn't bear to stop you! I thought it was such a creative problem solving technique that I decided to take pictures instead.
Clothes out of the dryer
Set the table
Empty the silverware
Get diapers for Erin
Pick up toys
Get dressed in 5 min
Read 15 minutes

Share stories that illustrate your child's personality traits.

If your child is old enough to have chores or responsibilities, include a list of them and how well they are completed.

album 4

my three sons

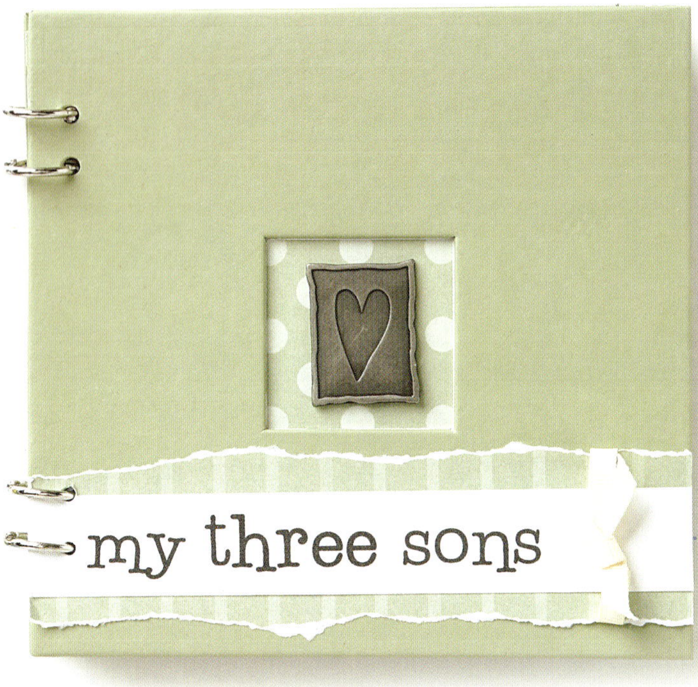
my three sons

Create a true parents' or grandparents' "brag book" by creating a mini-album about your children. Repeat the same format in a different color for each child to create a unified look and to save time. Include facts and fun tidbits—and add sentimentality by contrasting a baby photograph with a more recent photo of your child.

All supplies from Making Memories except: Computer font: CK Stenography, "Fresh Fonts" CD, *Creating Keepsakes*
Stamping ink: Rubber Stampede

An attractively layered cardstock strip tied with ribbon provides a title on the front of the album.

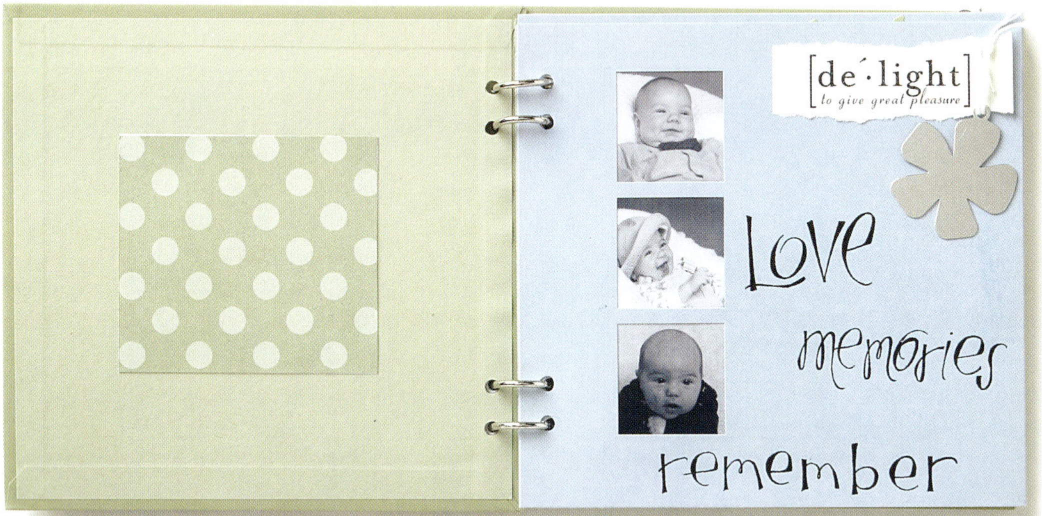
[de·light]
to give great pleasure
Love
memories
remember

The album opens with a page that includes a photograph of each child as a baby and sentimental words.

Each child's section begins with a black-and-white baby photograph.

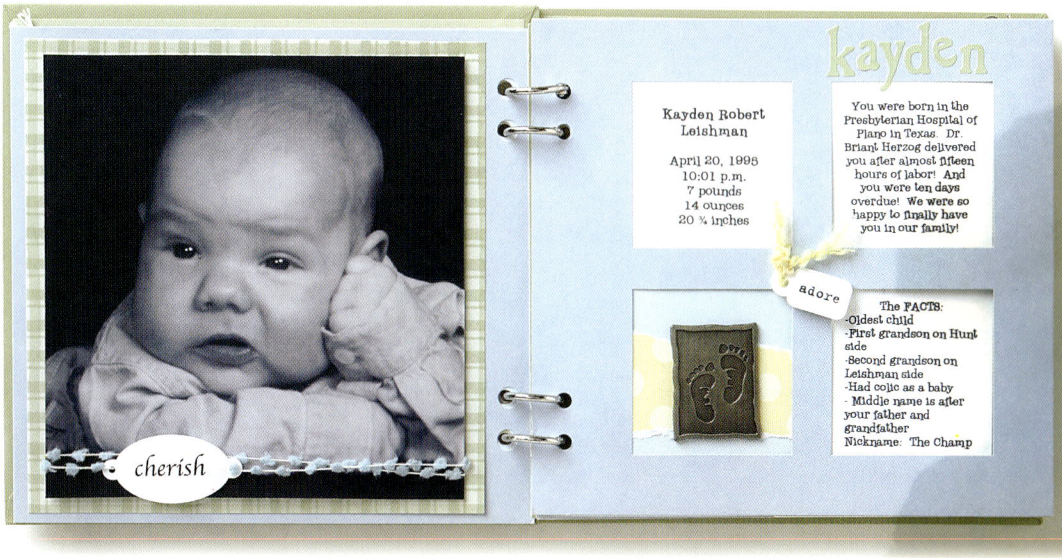
cherish
kayden
Kayden Robert Leishman
April 20, 1995
10:01 p.m.
7 pounds
14 ounces
20 ¾ inches
You were born in the Presbyterian Hospital of Plano in Texas. Dr. Briant Herzog delivered you after almost fifteen hours of labor! And you were ten days overdue! We were so happy to finally have you in our family!
adore
The FACTS:
-Oldest child
-First grandson on Hunt side
-Second grandson on Leishman side
-Had colic as a baby
- Middle name is after your father and grandfather
Nickname: The Champ

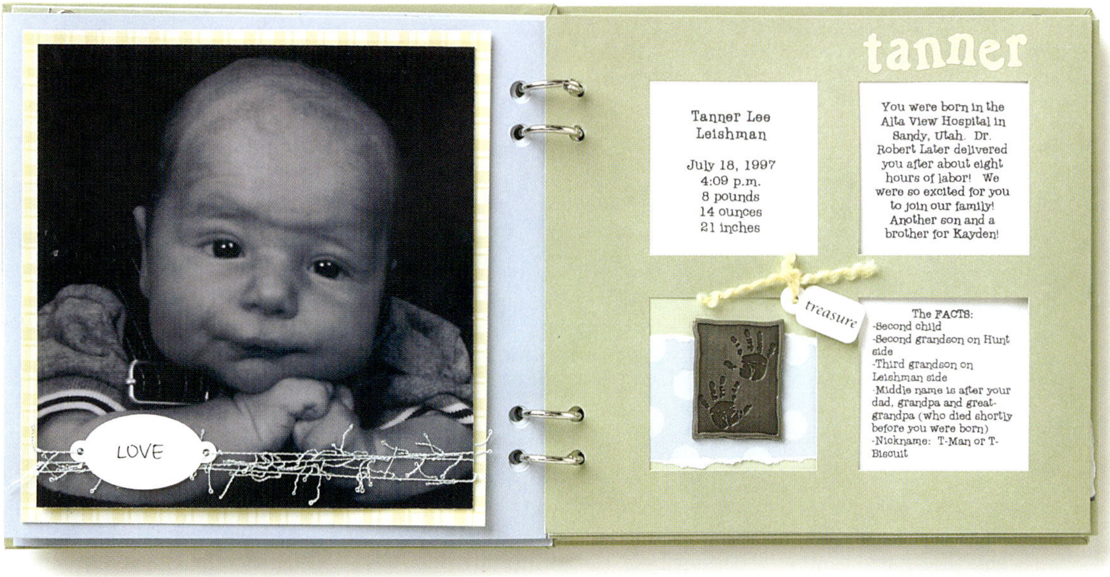

LOVE
tanner
Tanner Lee
Leishman
July 18, 1997
4:09 p.m.
8 pounds
14 ounces
21 inches
You were born in the Alta View Hospital in Sandy, Utah. Dr. Robert Later delivered you after about eight hours of labor! We were so excited for you to join our family! Another son and a brother for Kayden!
treasure
The FACTS:
-Second child
-Second grandson on Hunt side
-Third grandson on Leishman side
-Middle name is after your dad, grandpa and great-grandpa (who died shortly before you were born)
-Nickname: T-Man or T-Biscuit

A four-windowed page showcases information about the child's birth and facts about the child.

Express your feelings in a sweet letter to each child. They'll come to treasure your thoughts and impressions as they grow older.

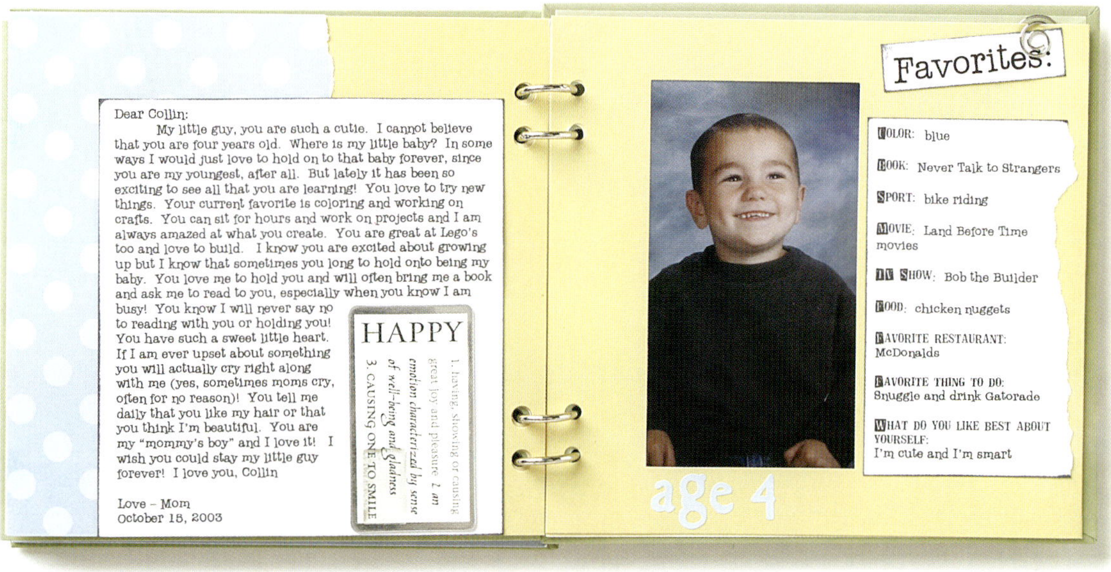

Dear Collin:
My little guy, you are such a cutie. I cannot believe that you are four years old. Where is my little baby? In some ways I would just love to hold on to that baby forever, since you are my youngest, after all. But lately it has been so exciting to see all that you are learning! You love to try new things. Your current favorite is coloring and working on crafts. You can sit for hours and work on projects and I am always amazed at what you create. You are great at Lego's too and love to build. I know you are excited about growing up but I know that sometimes you long to hold onto being my baby. You love me to hold you and will often bring me a book and ask me to read to you, especially when you know I am busy! You know I will never say no to reading with you or holding you! You have such a sweet little heart. If I am ever upset about something you will actually cry right along with me (yes, sometimes moms cry, often for no reason)! You tell me daily that you like my hair or that you think I'm beautiful. You are my "mommy's boy" and I love it! I wish you could stay my little guy forever! I love you, Collin
Love - Mom
October 15, 2003
HAPPY
1. having, showing or causing great joy and pleasure 2. an emotion characterized by sense of well-being and gladness 3. CAUSING ONE TO SMILE
Favorites:
COLOR: blue
BOOK: Never Talk to Strangers
SPORT: bike riding
MOVIE: Land Before Time movies
TV SHOW: Bob the Builder
FOOD: chicken nuggets
FAVORITE RESTAURANT: McDonalds
FAVORITE THING TO DO: Snuggle and drink Gatorade
WHAT DO YOU LIKE BEST ABOUT YOURSELF: I'm cute and I'm smart
age 4

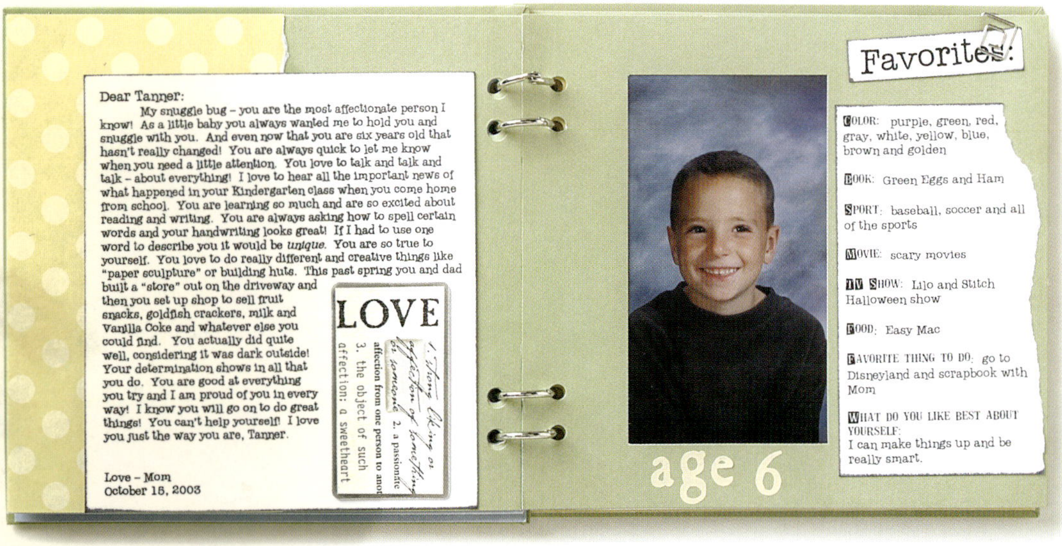

Dear Tanner:
My snuggle bug - you are the most affectionate person I know! As a little baby you always wanted me to hold you and snuggle with you. And even now that you are six years old that hasn't really changed! You are always quick to let me know when you need a little attention. You love to talk and talk and talk - about everything! I love to hear all the important news of what happened in your Kindergarten class when you come home from school. You are learning so much and are so excited about reading and writing. You are always asking how to spell certain words and your handwriting looks great! If I had to use one word to describe you it would be unique. You are so true to yourself. You love to do really different and creative things like "paper sculpture" or building huts. This past spring you and dad built a "store" out on the driveway and then you set up shop to sell fruit snacks, goldfish crackers, milk and Vanilla Coke and whatever else you could find. You actually did quite well, considering it was dark outside! Your determination shows in all that you do. You are good at everything you try and I am proud of you in every way! I know you will go on to do great things! You can't help yourself! I love you just the way you are, Tanner.
Love - Mom
October 15, 2003
LOVE
2. a passionate affection from one person to another 3. the object of such affection: a sweetheart
Favorites:
COLOR: purple, green, red, gray, white, yellow, blue, brown and golden
BOOK: Green Eggs and Ham
SPORT: baseball, soccer and all of the sports
MOVIE: scary movies
TV SHOW: Lilo and Stitch Halloween show
FOOD: Easy Mac
FAVORITE THING TO DO: go to Disneyland and scrapbook with Mom
WHAT DO YOU LIKE BEST ABOUT YOURSELF: I can make things up and be really smart.
age 6

Include a current photograph of the child, along with her age and a list of her favorite things at that age.

album 5

wedding day ABC's

Weddings and other life events are so detailed, they can be intimidating to try to capture in an album. Get your mind working and your creativity flowing by using the alphabet to capture the most meaningful memories from the day. Make one for your own wedding, then use the idea again and again to create gifts that will be treasured for a lifetime.

All supplies from K & Company except: Computer font: CK Elegant, "Fresh Fonts" CD, *Creating Keepsakes*

Keep a few non-specific but beautiful mini-albums on hand for your next mini-album projects.

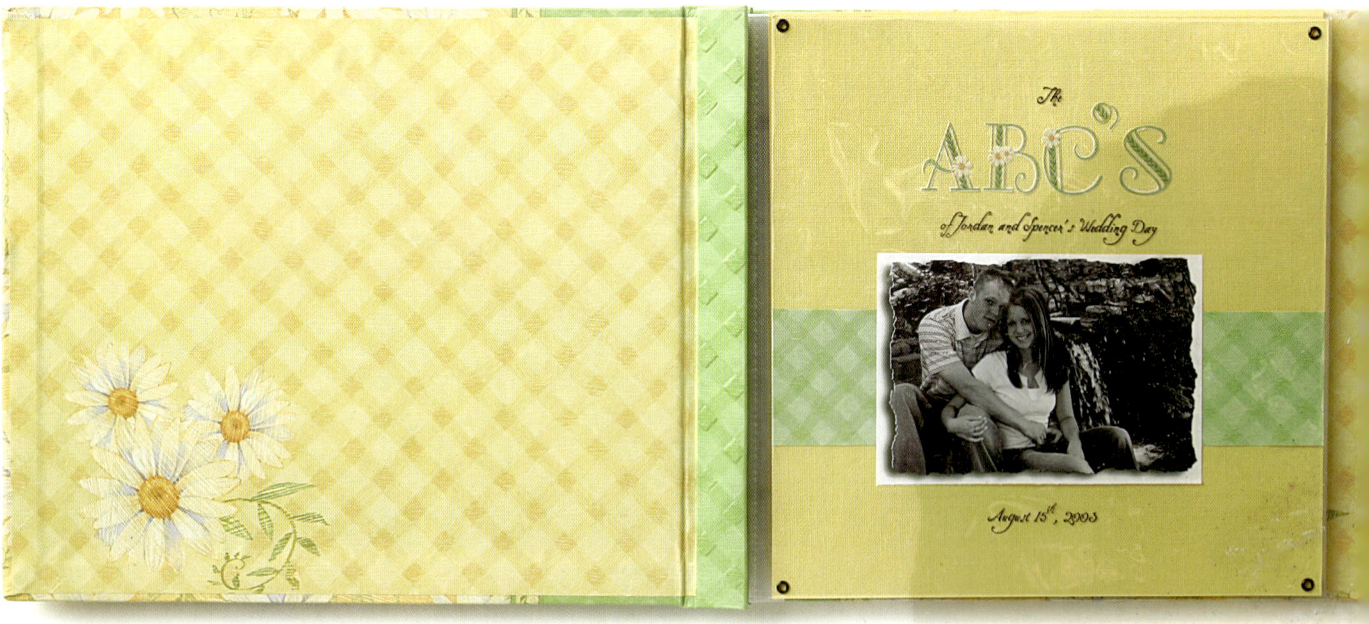
The
ABC'S
of Jordan and Spencer's Wedding Day

Include a photograph of the couple and the wedding date along with the title of the album on the title page.

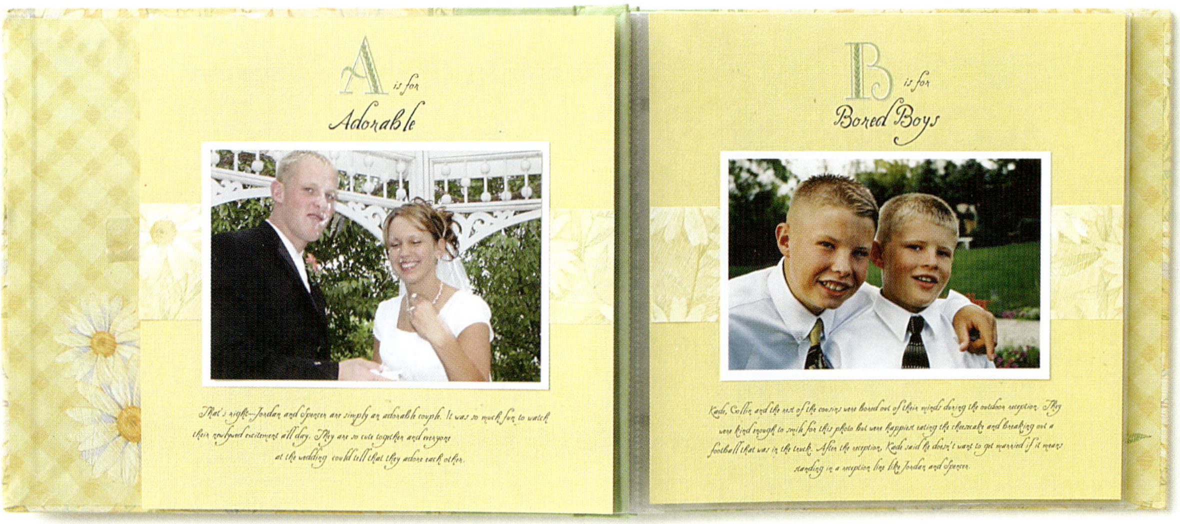
A is for
Adorable
That's right—Jordan and Spencer are simply an adorable couple. It was so much fun to watch their newlywed excitement all day. They are so cute together and everyone at the wedding could tell that they adore each other.
B is for
Bored Boys
Kade, Collin and the rest of the cousins were bored out of their minds during the outdoor reception. They were kind enough to smile for this photo but were happiest eating the cheesecake and breaking out a football that was in the truck. After the reception, Kade said he doesn't want to get married if it means standing in a reception line like Jordan and Spencer.

A simple strip of elegantly patterned paper and a letter sticker are the only embellishments the pages of this mini-album need.

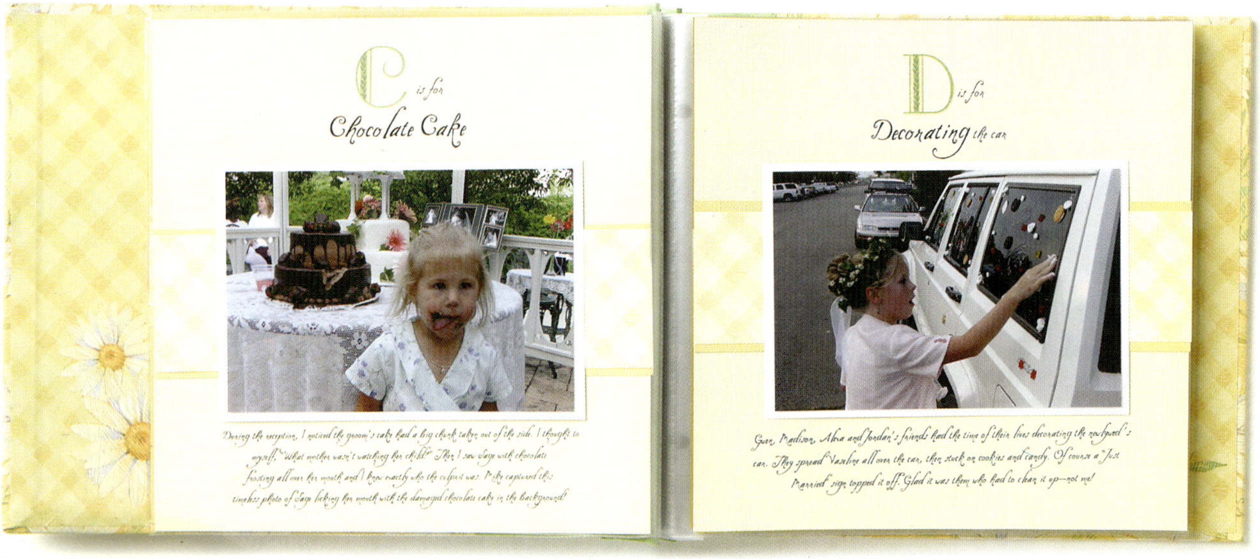
C is for
Chocolate Cake
During the reception, I noticed the groom's cake had a big chunk taken out of the side. I thought to myself, "What mother wasn't watching her child?" Then I saw Sage with chocolate frosting all over her mouth and I knew exactly who the culprit was. Mike captured this timeless photo of Sage licking her mouth with the damaged chocolate cake in the background!
D is for
Decorating the car
Gen, Madison, Alexa and Jordan's friends had the time of their lives decorating the newlywed's car. They spread Vaseline all over the car, then stuck on cookies and candy. Of course a "Just Married" sign topped it off. Glad it was them who had to clean it up—not me!

Be sure to include any sweet, charming or funny moments the bride and groom may have missed during the day.

Provide a behind-the-scenes look at how the day was executed so the bride and groom can look back and smile.

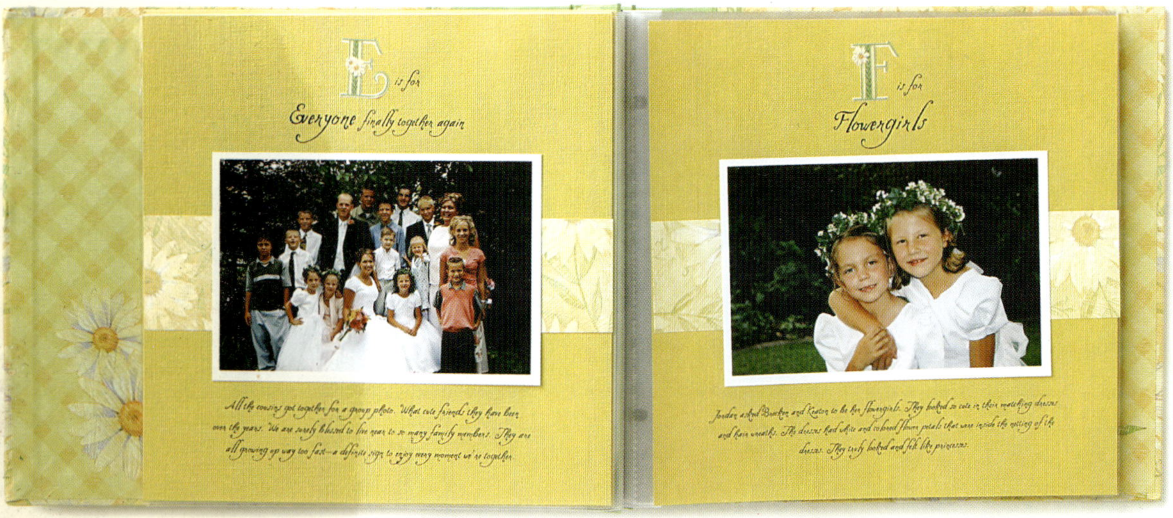
E is for
Everyone finally together again
All the cousins got together for a group photo. What cute friends they have been over the years. We are surely blessed to live near to so many family members. They are all growing up way too fast—a definite sign to enjoy every moment we're together.
F is for
Flowergirls
Jordan asked Brecken and Keaton to be her flowergirls. They looked so cute in their matching dresses and hair wreaths. The dresses had white and colored flower petals that were inside the netting of the dresses. They truly looked and felt like princesses.

Even if a professional photographer is present, keep your camera handy to capture sweet moments during the day, then include the photographs you took in the album. The bride and groom will appreciate the additional perspective.

www.creatingkeepsakes.com

album 6

my favorite photographs

When you're looking through your piles of photographs, pull out the ones that make you pause and think, "I love this picture!" Compile those favorite photographs into a mini-album along with favorite quotes, memories the photographs evoke, or a brief explanation of why those photographs hold a special place in your heart.

All supplies from Making Memories except:
Computer fonts: CK Stenography and CK Constitution, "Fresh Fonts" CD, *Creating Keepsakes*
Letter stamps: PSX Design
Stamping ink: ColorBox, Clearsnap
Other: Flower, bug, buttons and ribbon

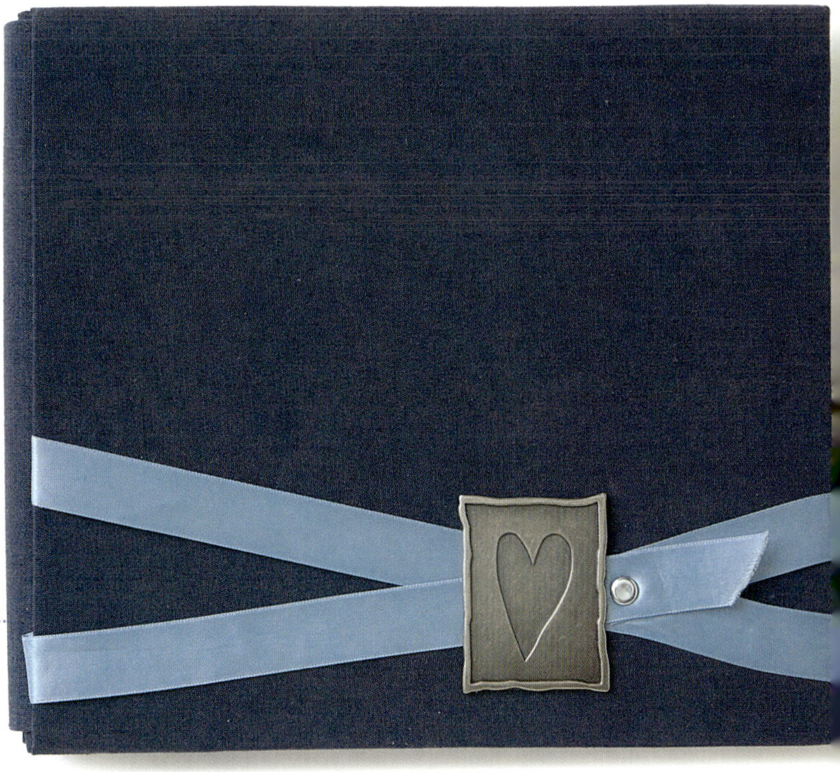

Smooth, simple ribbon and a metal accent decorate the cover of this album.

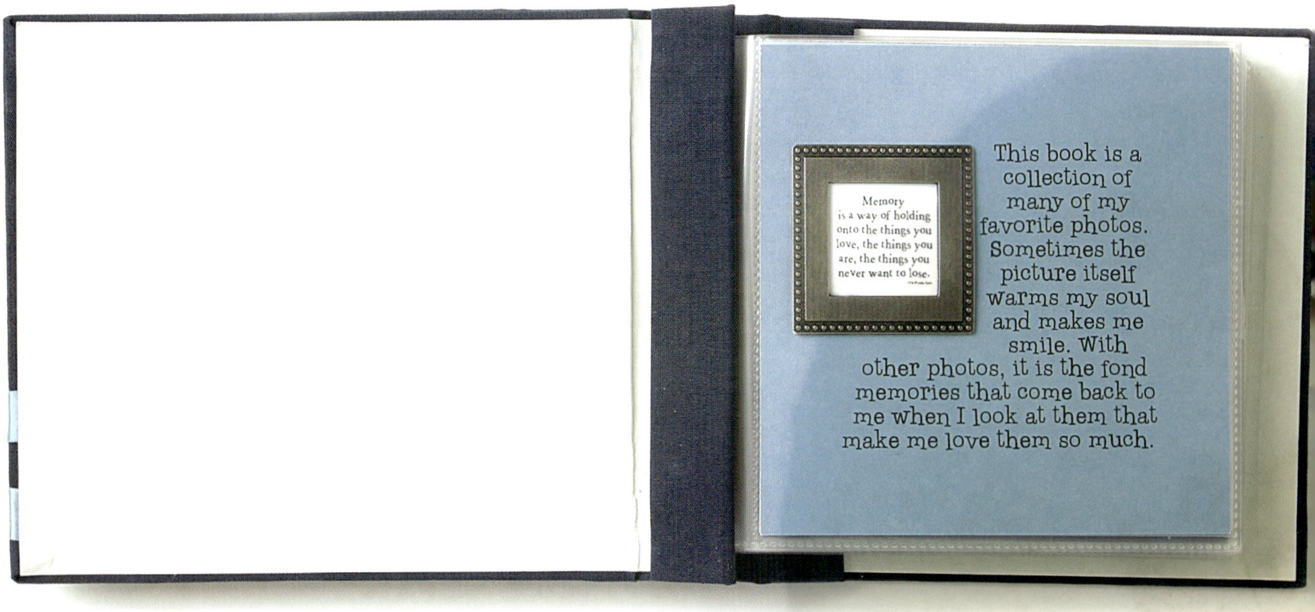
Memory is a way of holding onto the things you love, the things you are, the things you never want to lose.
This book is a collection of many of my favorite photos. Sometimes the picture itself warms my soul and makes me smile. With other photos, it is the fond memories that come back to me when I look at them that make me love them so much.

Create a title page that explains why you created the album and what the photographs inside mean to you.

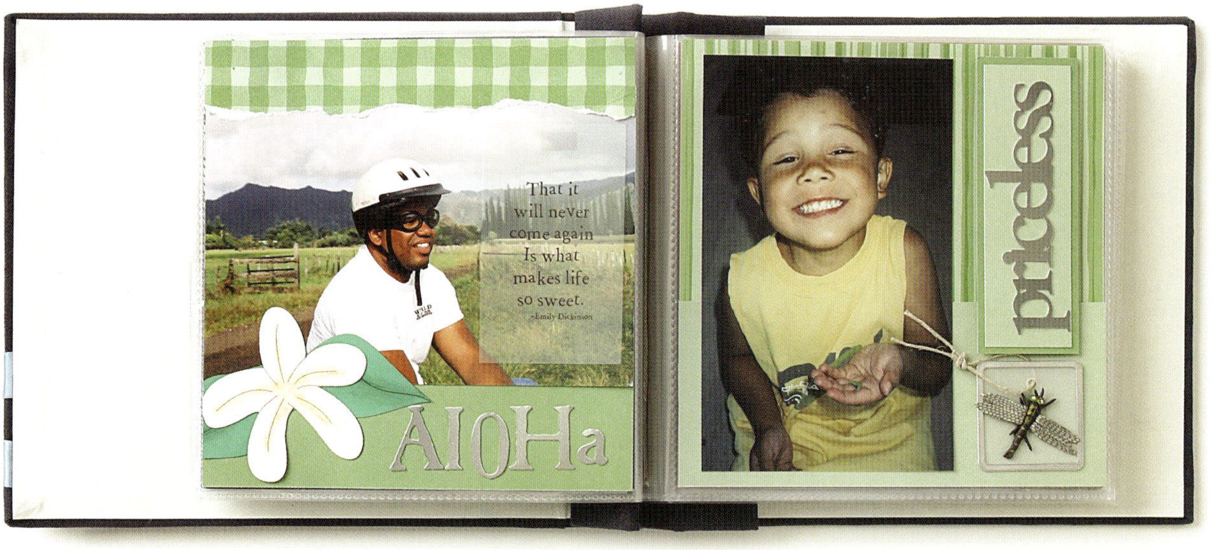
That it will never come again Is what makes life so sweet.
~Emily Dickinson
AlOHa
priceless

Draw elements from your photographs to include as accents on your page. Sum up how you feel about the photograph with one word using metal accents.

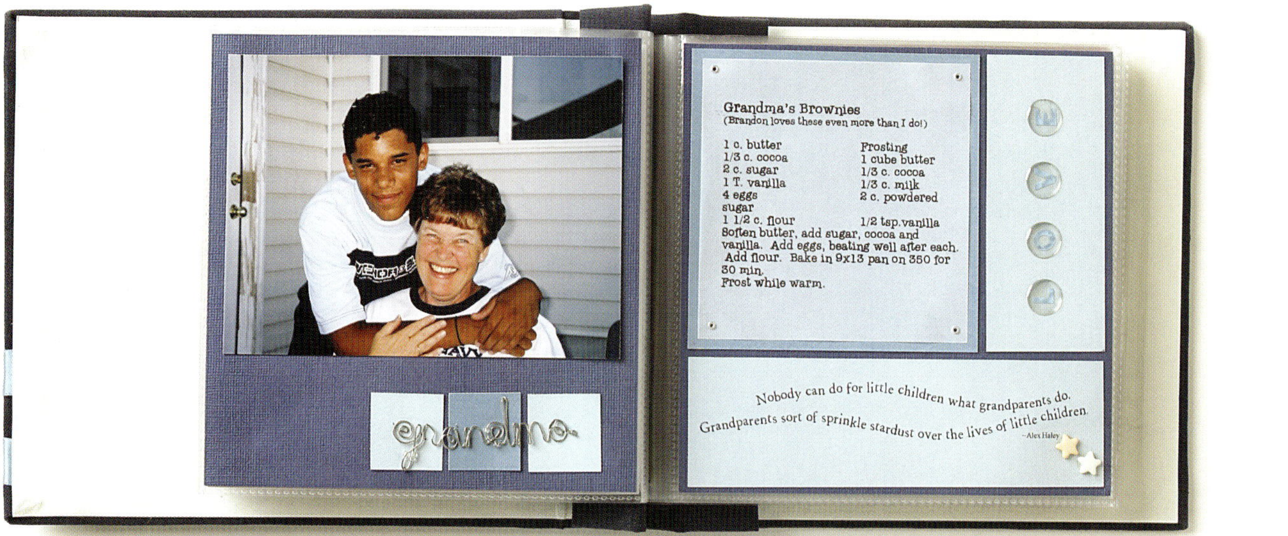
Grandma's Brownies
(Brandon loves these even more than I do!)
1 c. butter
1/3 c. cocoa
2 c. sugar
1 T. vanilla
4 eggs
sugar
1 1/2 c. flour
Frosting
1 cube butter
1/3 c. cocoa
1/3 c. milk
2 c. powdered
1/2 tsp.vanilla
Soften butter, add sugar, cocoa and vanilla. Add eggs, beating well after each. Add flour. Bake in 9x13 pan on 350 for 30 min.
Frost while warm.
grandma
Nobody can do for little children what grandparents do.
Grandparents sort of sprinkle stardust over the lives of little children.
~Alex Haley

Include photographs of loved ones sharing special moments.

Create a facing page for photographs that evoke special memories or information, such as recipes.

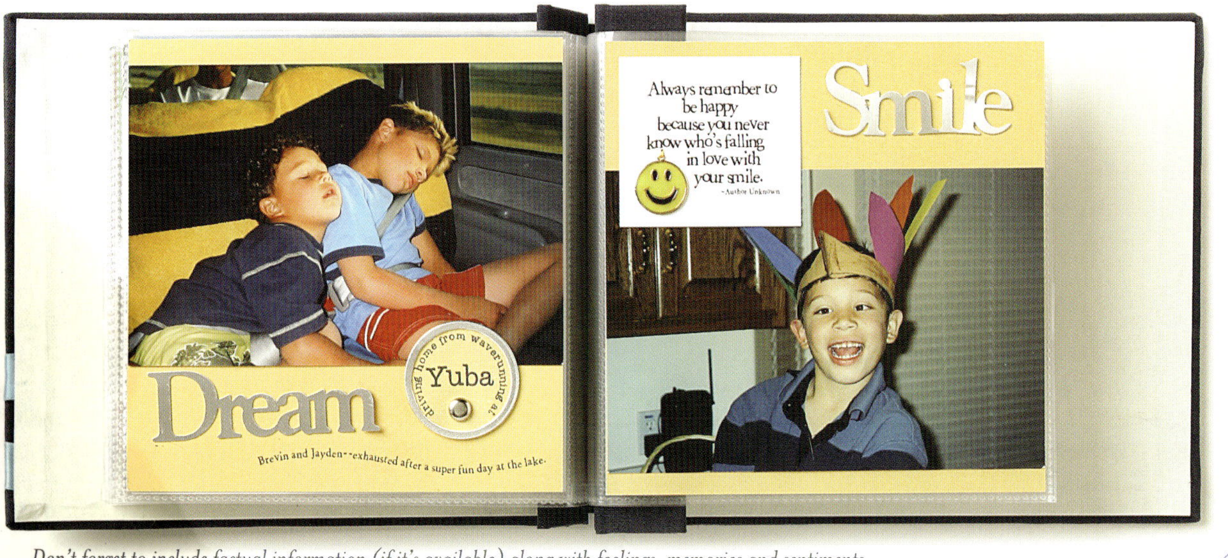
Always remember to be happy because you never know who's falling in love with your smile.
~Author Unknown
Smile
Dream
driving home from waverunning at
Yuba
Brevin and Jayden--exhausted after a super fun day at the lake.

Don't forget to include factual information (if it's available) along with feelings, memories and sentiments.

album 7
family vacation

Family vacations create too many memories to capture on a two-page layout but too few to fill a whole album—unless you use a mini-album, that is! Soon you'll have a library of keepsake mini-albums your family can glance through to remember the fun times you've had together while traveling. Include information about the kind of vacation it was: sightseeing, relaxing, visiting, etc. Then include details about activities, discoveries, endearing moments and other memorable experiences.

All supplies from Making Memories except: Computer fonts: Typewriter and CAC Leslie, downloaded from the Internet; 2Peas Gift, downloaded from *www.twopeasinabucket.com*
Letter stamps: PSX Design and Hero Arts
Stamping ink: StazOn, Tsukineko
Other: Transparency paper, shells, sand, string, metal mesh, acrylic paint, twine and bead

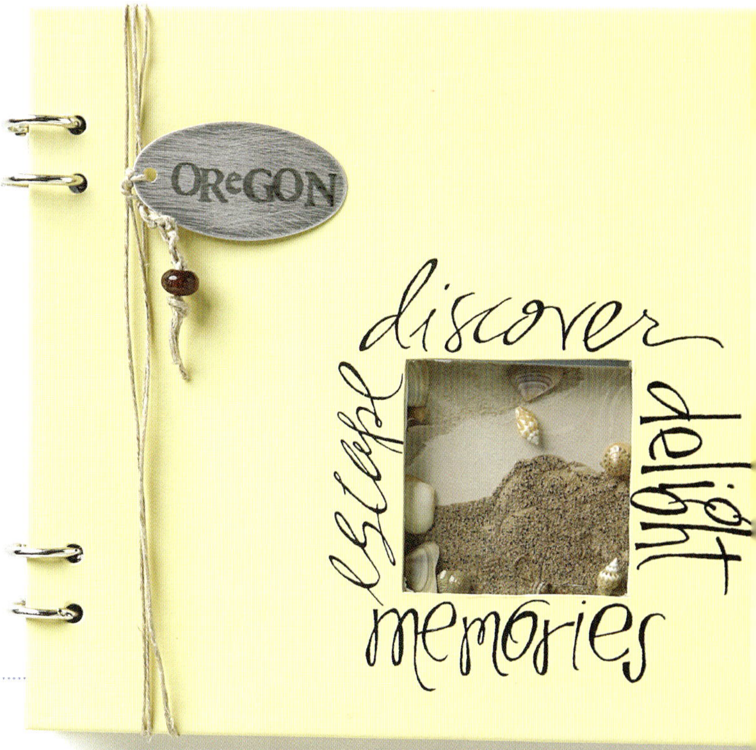

OReGON
discover
delight
memories
escape

A shadow box filled with shells and sand on the title page shows through the window on the album cover.

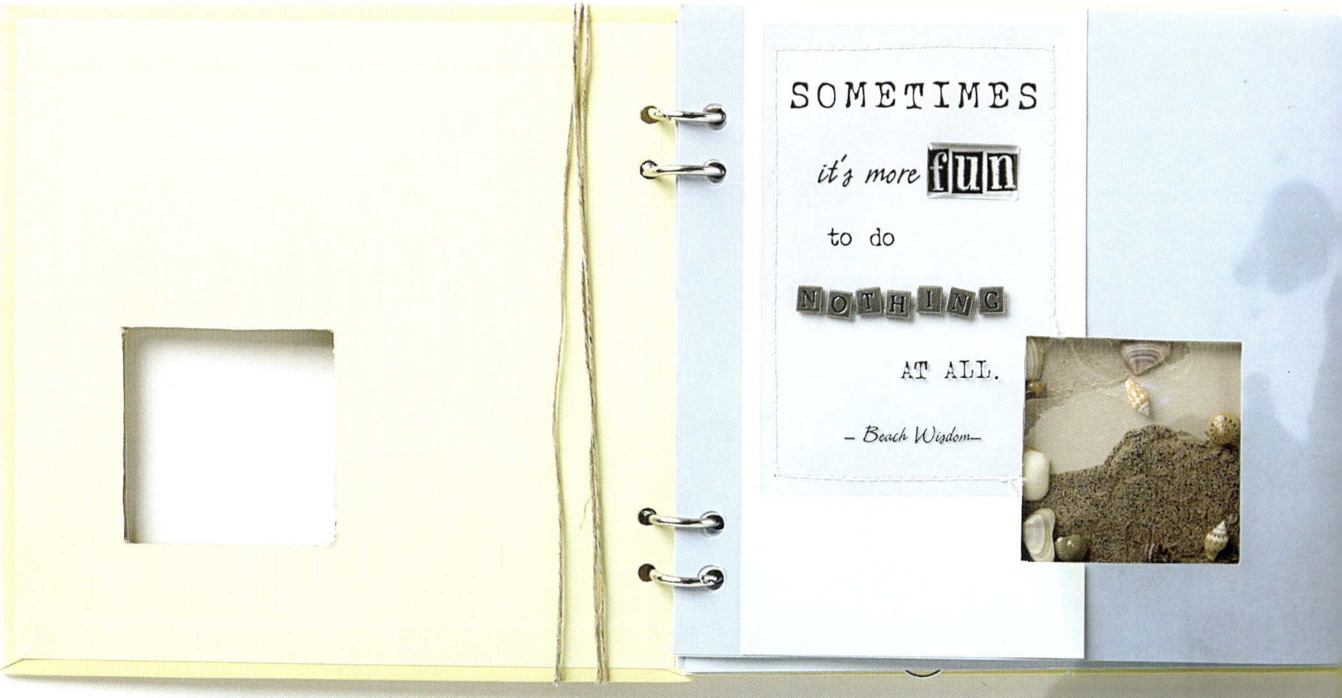

SOMETIMES
it's more FUN
to do
NOTHING
AT ALL.
– Beach Wisdom–

Begin your album with a quote or sentiment that sums up the vacation well.

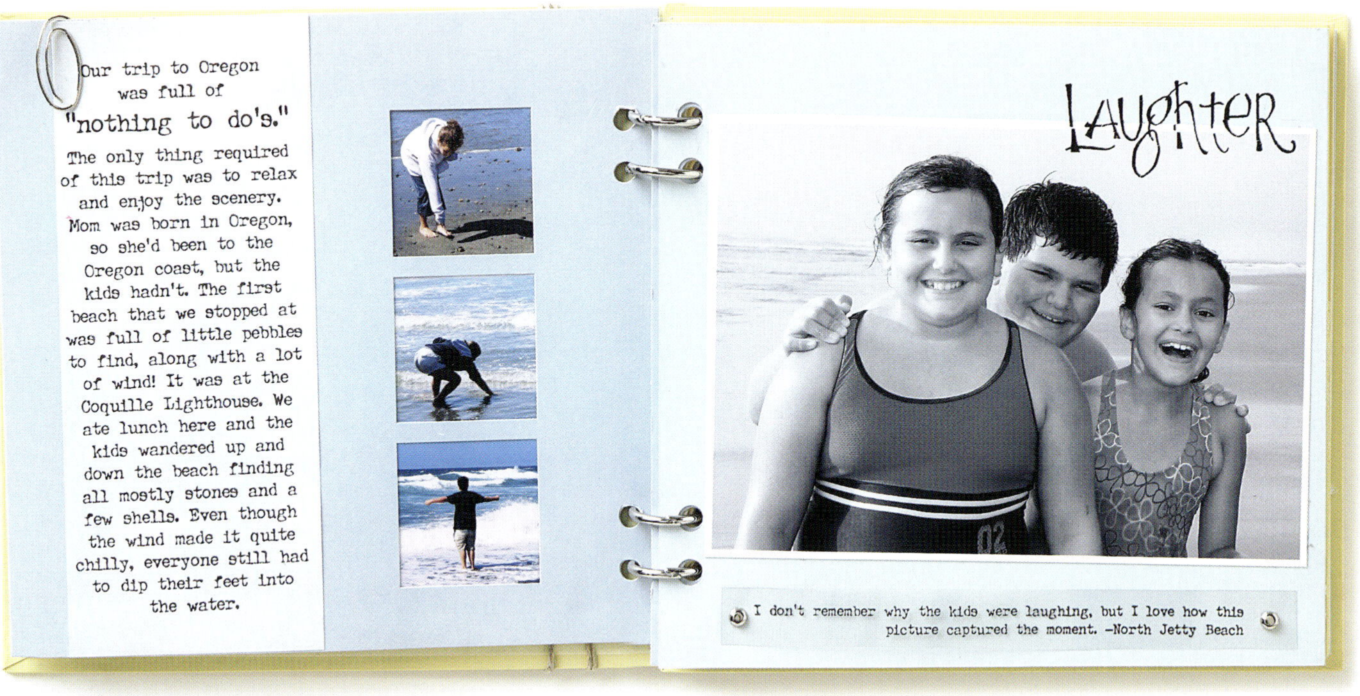
Our trip to Oregon was full of "nothing to do's." The only thing required of this trip was to relax and enjoy the scenery. Mom was born in Oregon, so she'd been to the Oregon coast, but the kids hadn't. The first beach that we stopped at was full of little pebbles to find, along with a lot of wind! It was at the Coquille Lighthouse. We ate lunch here and the kids wandered up and down the beach finding all mostly stones and a few shells. Even though the wind made it quite chilly, everyone still had to dip their feet into the water.
Laughter
I don't remember why the kids were laughing, but I love how this picture captured the moment. -North Jetty Beach

Write a brief summary of the vacation: who was there, where you went, how you chose the location, what the plans were and first impressions upon arriving.

Include your favorite photographs from your vacation and why you like them.

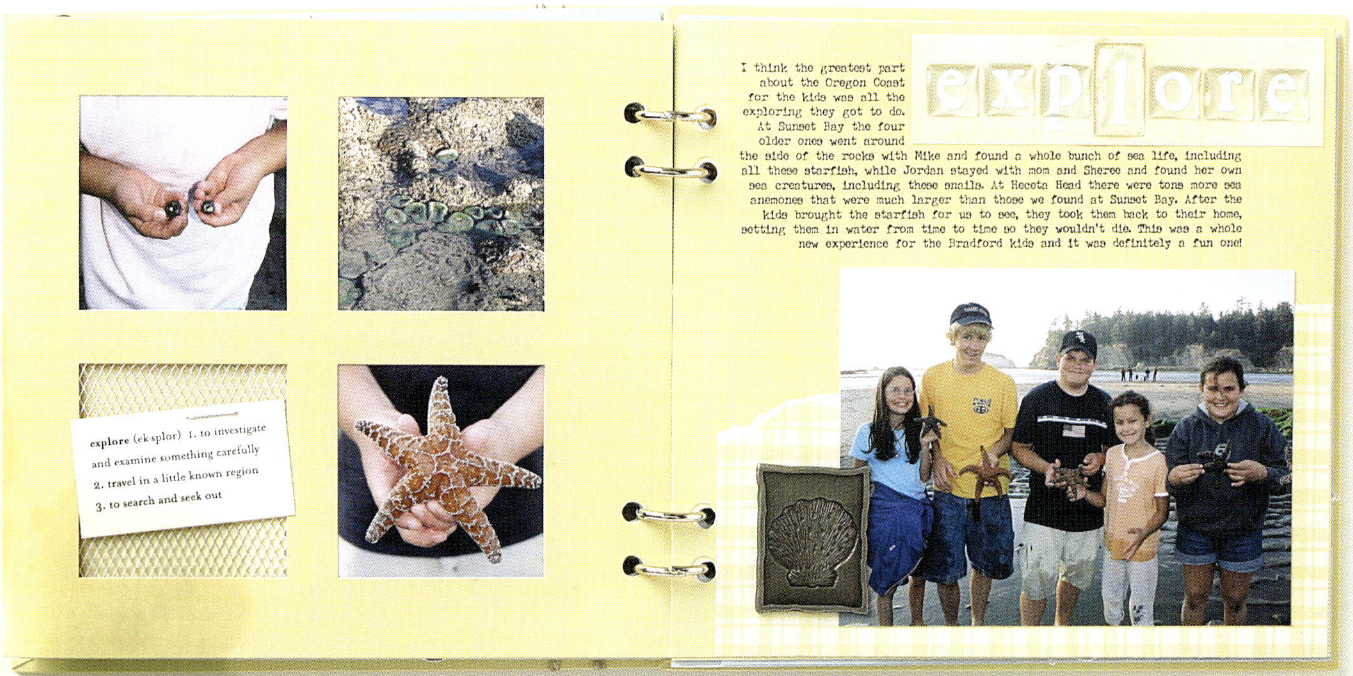
explore (ek·splor) 1. to investigate and examine something carefully 2. travel in a little known region 3. to search and seek out
explore
I think the greatest part about the Oregon Coast for the kids was all the exploring they got to do. At Sunset Bay the four older ones went around the side of the rocks with Mike and found a whole bunch of sea life, including all these starfish, while Jordan stayed with mom and Sheree and found her own sea creatures, including these snails. At Heceta Head there were tons more sea anemones that were much larger than those we found at Sunset Bay. After the kids brought the starfish for us to see, they took them back to their home, setting them in water from time to time so they wouldn't die. This was a whole new experience for the Bradford kids and it was definitely a fun one!

Use windows in the pages to highlight specific elements in your photographs you want to remember.

Include photos and memories of exploring new things, touring historic sights or visiting sentimental places.

lisa's lessons on mini-albums

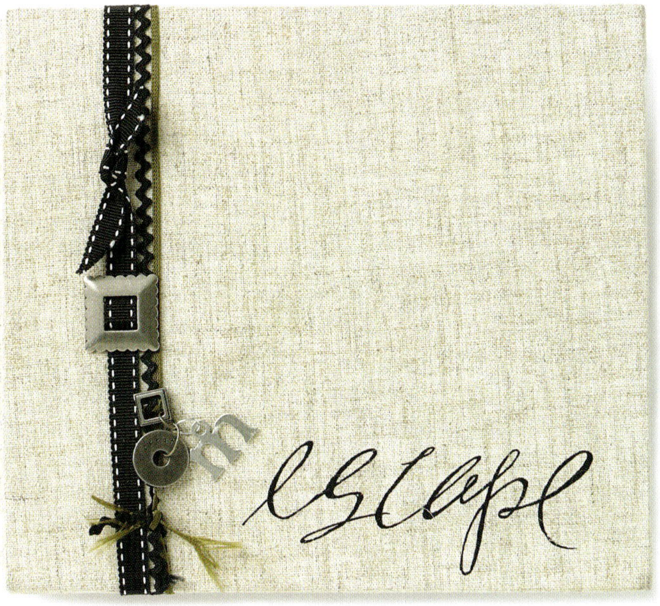

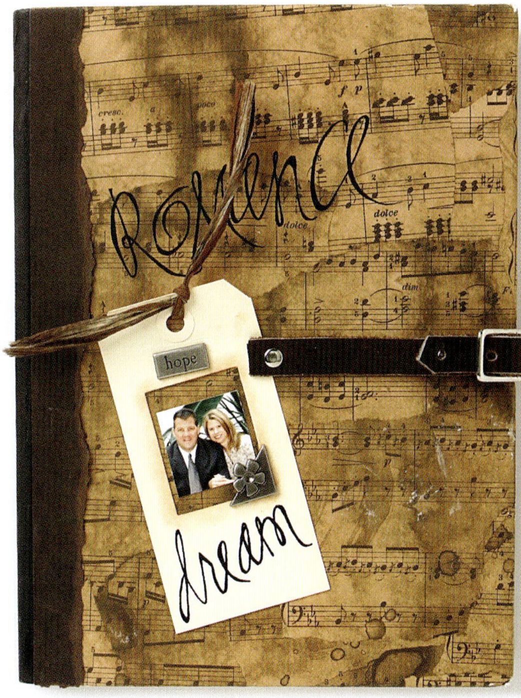

Escape

Supplies
All supplies: Making Memories

Romance

Supplies
Patterned paper: Source unknown
Metal accents and rub-on words: Making Memories
Other: Composition notebook, walnut ink, leather buckle and raffia

Creating mini-albums has really sparked my creativity and renewed my enthusiasm for scrapbooking. Here are my two favorite tips for using mini-albums to capture your favorite memories:

- Be selective about the photographs you include. As scrapbookers, we take a lot of photographs. The limited space of mini-albums helps you narrow down the huge pile of photos you need to scrapbook to a handful of your favorites that capture what you want to express. If you don't want to throw away the unused photographs, slip them into photo sleeves and put them away for future use.
- Set aside a block of time every once in a while as your regular scrapbooking time. A weekend is really all you need to conceptualize, start and finish a mini-album. Getting your memories organized, making them accessible to your loved ones and participating in a hobby you enjoy should be a priority to you, so schedule it in to make sure you'll remember it!

More great mini-album themes:

- Childhood Memories
- Lifelong Pursuits
- Things I Cherish
- Places from My Past
- Family Traditions
- Our Family
- Happy Times
- Hopes and Dreams
- The People I Love
- All about Me

lisa says:

"I continue to be amazed by the ideas scrapbookers around the world come up with for their pages. Great ideas can come from the simplest things—a color scheme you see during a drive in the country, the *positioning* of the text on the *label* of your shampoo bottle or a well-designed scrapbook *product* at the store. Above all, *trust* in your own *creativity* and let it shine on your pages!"

IDEA
GALLERY

gallery of great ideas

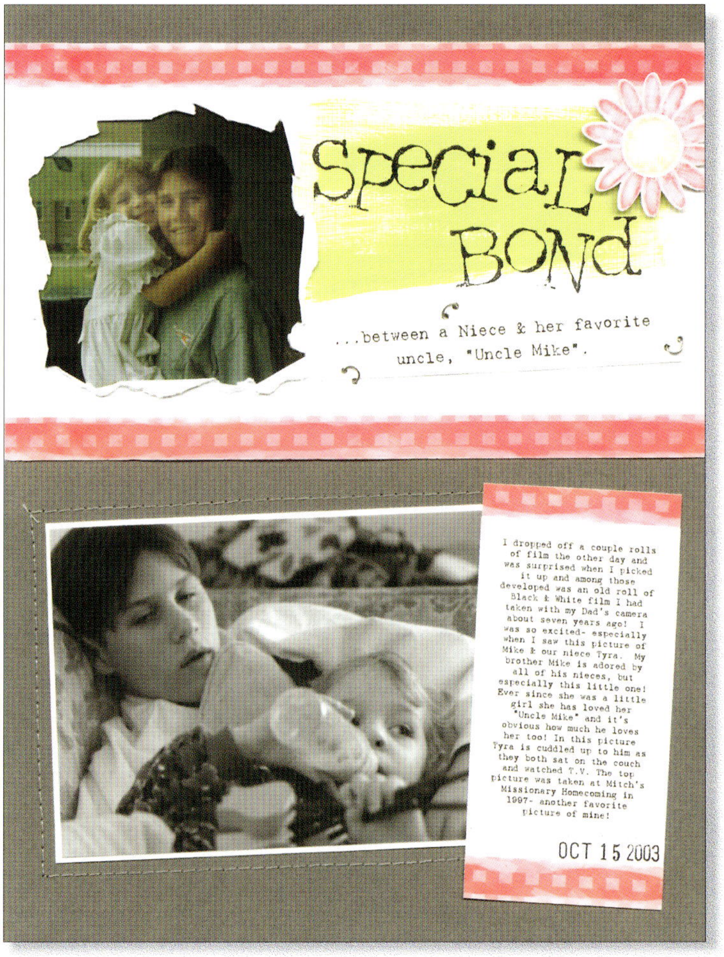
Special Bond
...between a Niece & her favorite uncle, "Uncle Mike".
I dropped off a couple rolls of film the other day and was surprised when I picked it up and among those developed was an old roll of Black & White film I had taken with my Dad's camera about seven years ago! I was so excited- especially when I saw this picture of Mike & our niece Tyra. My brother Mike is adored by all of his nieces, but especially this little one! Ever since she was a little girl she has loved her "Uncle Mike" and it's obvious how much he loves her too! In this picture Tyra is cuddled up to him as they both sat on the couch and watched T.V. The top picture was taken at Mitch's Missionary Homecoming in 1997- another favorite picture of mine!
OCT 15 2003

GREAT *adj. remarkable in magnitude, degree or effectiveness*

IDEA *n. a mental image or formulation of something*

Special Bond

Supplies
Stickers: Flavia, Colorbök
Letter stamps: Alphabet Set
Stamping ink: Ranger Industries
Computer font: Linenstroke, downloaded from the Internet
Jump rings: Making Memories
Acrylic paint: Delta
Other: 3-D foam adhesive

Great Idea!: *Add a vivid splash of color by brushing acrylic paint onto your layout, then stamping or printing a title on clear transparency paper.*

Great Idea!: *Most scrapbookers take photographs but don't scrapbook them for a while. Consider adding a "journaled on" date at the bottom of the journaling block if you write your journaling a while after the photographs were taken.*

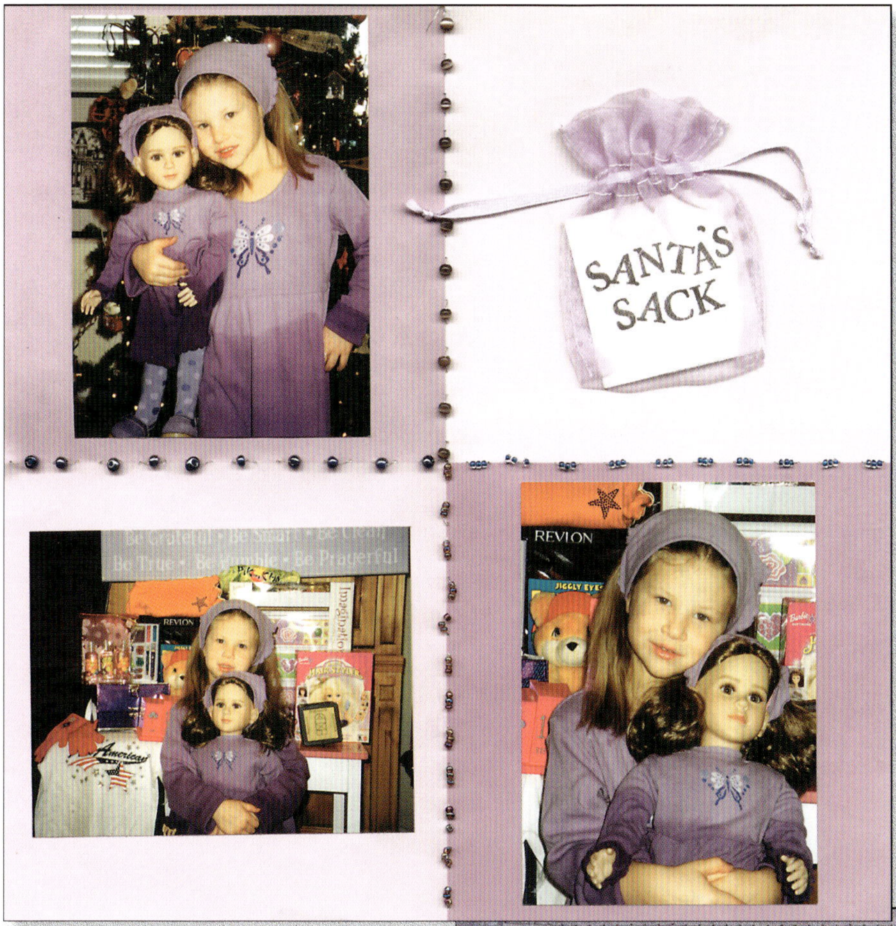
SANTA'S SACK
REVLON

Santa's Sack

Supplies
Patterned paper: Colorbök
Letter stamps: PSX Design
Stamping ink: Colorbox, Clearsnap
Other: Wire and drawstring bag
Beads: Westrim

Great Idea!: *Included in the drawstring bag is a list of everything Santa brought the subject of the layout for Christmas.*

Great Idea!: *During the winter holidays or at birthdays, arrange a quick "photo shoot" after the gifts are opened and snap shots of everyone with the gifts they received. These photographs will serve as a fun record as times change.*

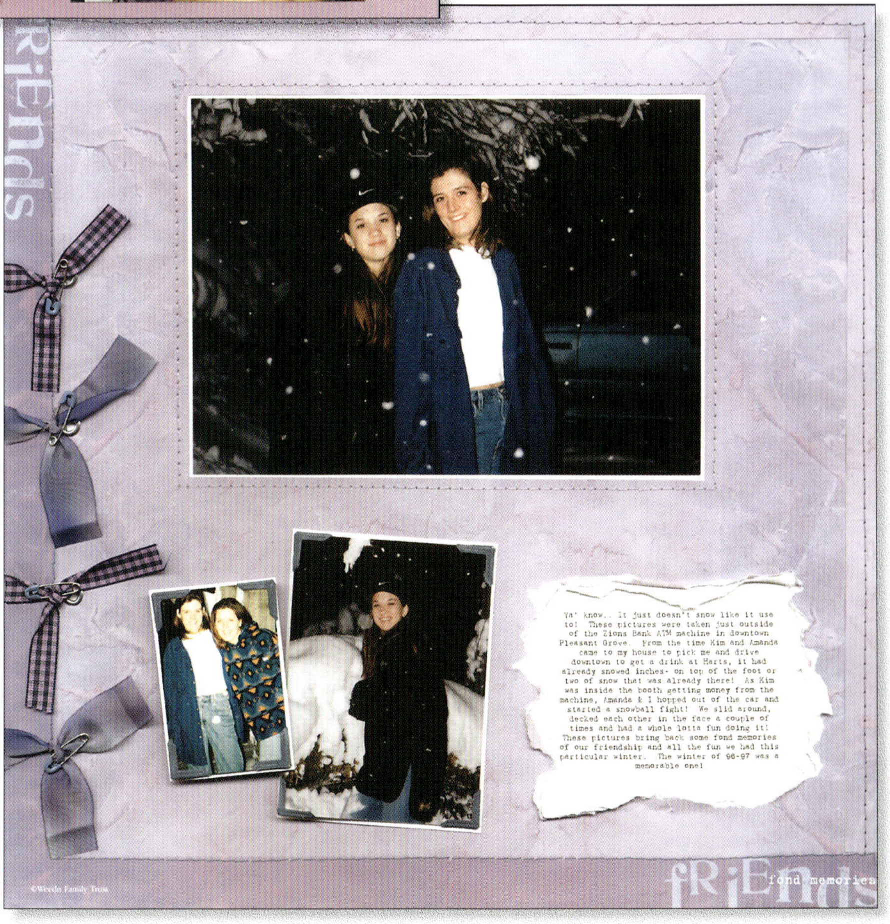
fRiEnds
Ya' know.. It just doesn't snow like it use to! These pictures were taken just outside of the Zions Bank ATM machine in downtown Pleasant Grove. From the time Kim and Amanda came to my house to pick me and drive downtown to get a drink at Harts, it had already snowed inches- on top of the foot or two of snow that was already there! As Kim was inside the booth getting money from the machine, Amanda & I hopped out of the car and started a snowball fight! We slid around, decked each other in the face a couple of times and had a whole lotta fun doing it! These pictures bring back some fond memories of our friendship and all the fun we had this particular winter. The winter of 96-97 was a memorable one!
fRiEnds
fond memories

Fond Memories

Supplies
Patterned paper: Flavia, Colorbök
Computer font: Typical Writer, downloaded from the Internet
Rub-on words, safety pins and eyelets: Making Memories
Photo corners: Kolo
Other: 3-D foam adhesive and ribbon

Great Idea!: *Cropping pictures closely around the subjects can sometimes leave you with a tiny photograph! Help the photograph hold its own by adhering it with 3-D foam adhesive. The added dimension will draw the viewer's eye to the photograph without allowing it to detract from the rest of the layout.*

Great Idea!: *Layer rub-on word accents over patterned papers with words already printed on them. Make sure the rub-on is smaller than the printed word so both are still readable.*

The Tale of Jordan and Peter Rabbit

Supplies
Patterned paper: Keeping Memories Alive
Stickers and letter stickers: Colorbök
Computer fonts: CK Wanted and CK Sassy, "Fresh Fonts" CD, *Creating Keepsakes*; Bernhard Modern BT, Microsoft Word
Stamping ink: VersaColor, Tsukineko
Fiber: Tidbits, Déjà Views
Brads: Making Memories

Great Idea!: *Add variety to your journaling by changing the voice to storybook format every once in a while. Children especially love to hear stories about themselves!*

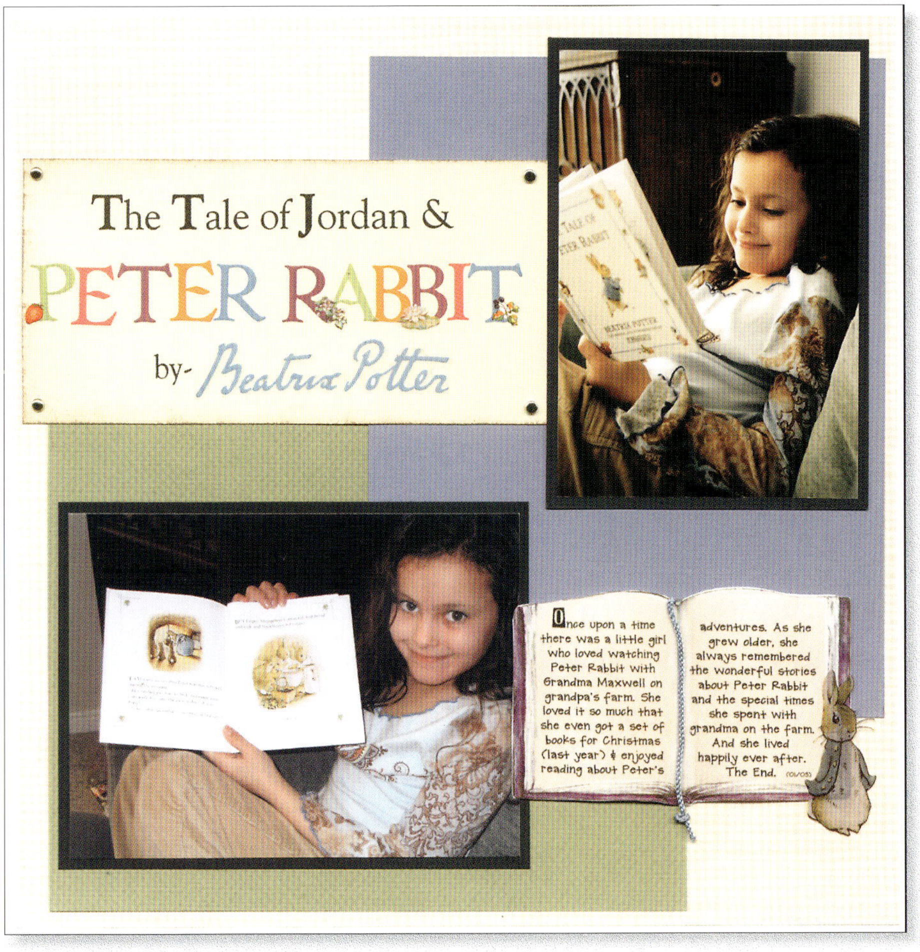

The Tale of Jordan &
PETER RABBIT
by- Beatrix Potter
Once upon a time there was a little girl who loved watching Peter Rabbit with Grandma Maxwell on grandpa's farm. She loved it so much that she even got a set of books for Christmas (last year) & enjoyed reading about Peter's
adventures. As she grew older, she always remembered the wonderful stories about Peter Rabbit and the special times she spent with grandma on the farm. And she lived happily ever after. The End.

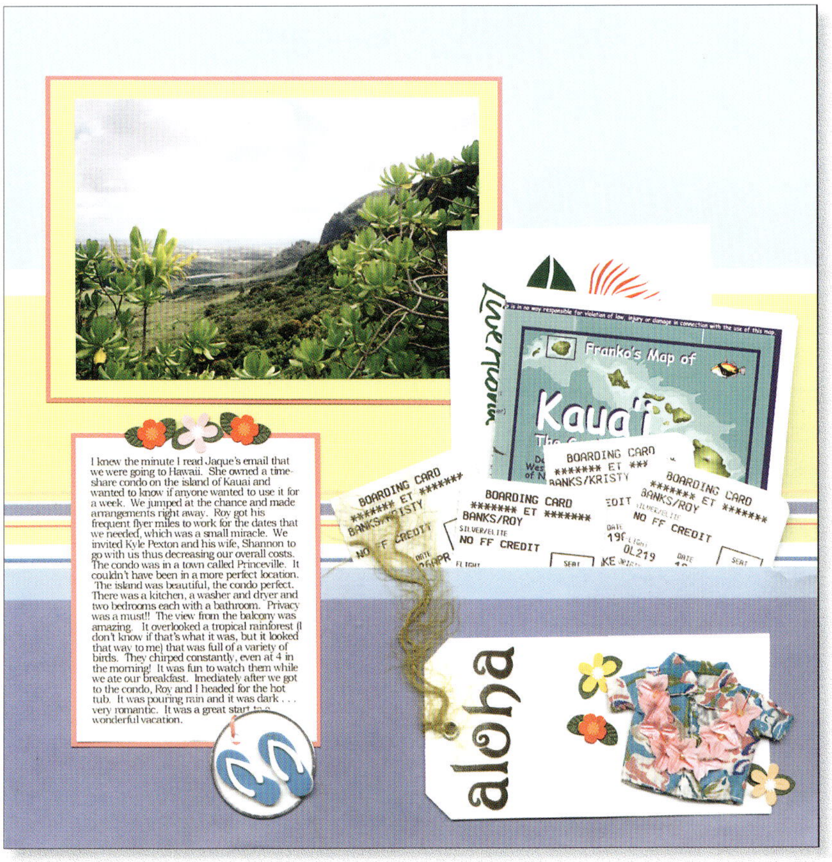

I knew the minute I read Jaque's email that we were going to Hawaii. She owned a time-share condo on the island of Kauai and wanted to know if anyone wanted to use it for a week. We jumped at the chance and made arrangements right away. Roy got his frequent flyer miles to work for the dates that we needed, which was a small miracle. We invited Kyle Pexton and his wife, Shannon to go with us thus decreasing our overall costs. The condo was in a town called Princeville. It couldn't have been in a more perfect location. The island was beautiful, the condo perfect. There was a kitchen, a washer and dryer and two bedrooms each with a bathroom. Privacy was a must!! The view from the balcony was amazing. It overlooked a tropical rainforest (I don't know if that's what it was, but it looked that way to me) that was full of a variety of birds. They chirped constantly, even at 4 in the morning! It was fun to watch them while we ate our breakfast. Imediately after we got to the condo, Roy and I headed for the hot tub. It was pouring rain and it was dark . . . very romantic. It was a great start
wonderful vacation.
Franko's Map of
Kaua'i
BOARDING CARD
BANKS/KRISTY
BOARDING CARD
BANKS/ROY
NO FF CREDIT
aloha

Aloha

Supplies
Patterned paper: SEI
Stickers: Jolee's Boutique, EK Success
Letter stickers: Provo Craft
Computer font: Garamond, Microsoft Word
Fibers: Adornaments, EK Success

Great Idea!: *Use strong scenic photographs and travel memorabilia to create an introduction page for your travel layouts. Many times this information is discarded and forgotten, but this layout shows what an asset these items can be to your albums.*

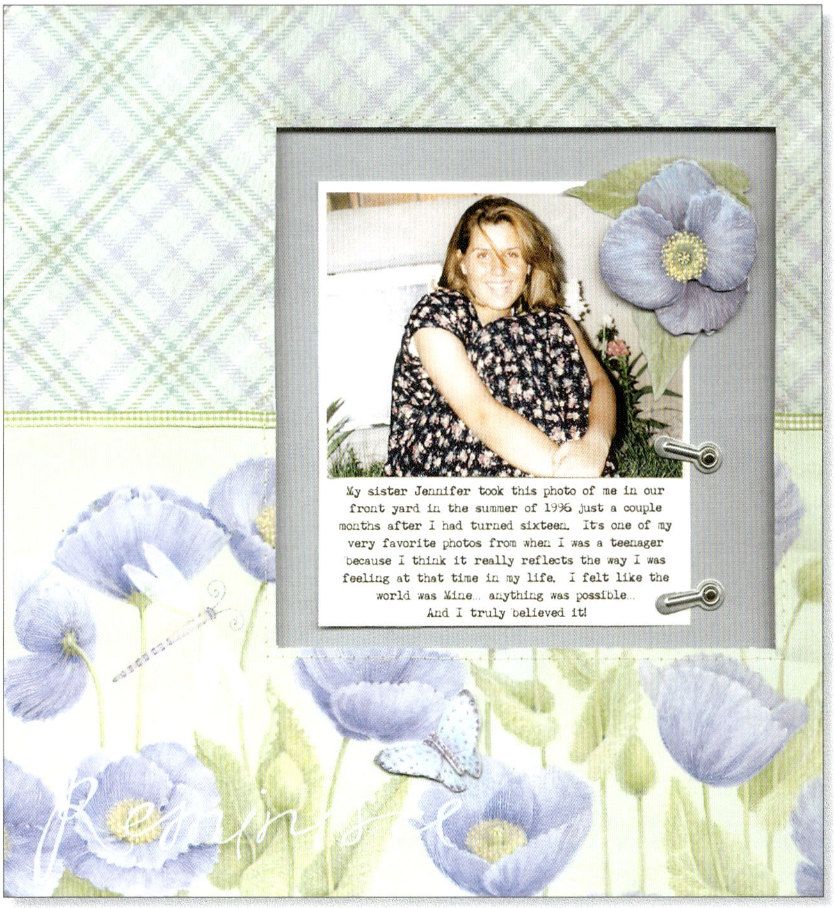
My sister Jennifer took this photo of me in our
front yard in the summer of 1996 just a couple
months after I had turned sixteen. It's one of my
very favorite photos from when I was a teenager
because I think it really reflects the way I was
feeling at that time in my life. I felt like the
world was Mine... anything was possible...
And I truly believed it!
Reminisce

Reminisce

Supplies

Patterned paper and stickers: K & Company
Computer font: Dyslexia, downloaded from the Internet
Photo hinges: 7 Gypsies
Rub-on word: Making Memories
Other: Foam core and gingham ribbon

Great Idea!: *Home decorating holds great inspiration for scrapbookers. The background papers on this layout were merged together by a strip of gingham ribbon—using the same concept as a chair rail or wallpaper border in home decorating. Practice translating ideas such as this one from non-scrapbooking sources until it begins to come naturally for you.*

Step-by-Step Instructions:

Create this beautiful shadowbox frame to highlight your favorite photographs in an artistic way.

Here's how:

1. If you plan to store the shadowbox-frame layout in a sheet protector, trim the paper you'll be using as a background for the layout by just over 1/4" on each side and 1/4" off the top. (For example, a 12" x 12" piece of paper would be trimmed to about 11 1/2" wide and 11 3/4" tall.)

2. Lay the trimmed background paper on a sheet of foam core and trace around the paper to create a pattern for the foam core. Use a craft knife and a sturdy ruler to cut along the lines (you may have to go over the line two or three times before the craft knife cuts all the way through the foam core).

3. Using your background paper, determine the location and size of the opening for the shadowbox frame. Cut that area out with a craft knife and ruler or a paper trimmer.

4. Lay the background paper on the foam core, lining up the edges, and trace the opening onto the foam core. Once again, cut the foam core along the lines with a craft knife and ruler.

5. Apply spray adhesive to the back of your background paper, line up the background paper on the foam core and adhere. Turn the foam core over, spray adhesive on the back of the foam core, and adhere a piece of paper to cover the opening in the foam core (providing a background for the shadowbox frame).

6. Decorate the shadowbox frame as desired!

This shadowbox technique is also a great way to include thicker items on your layouts, such as mini-albums.

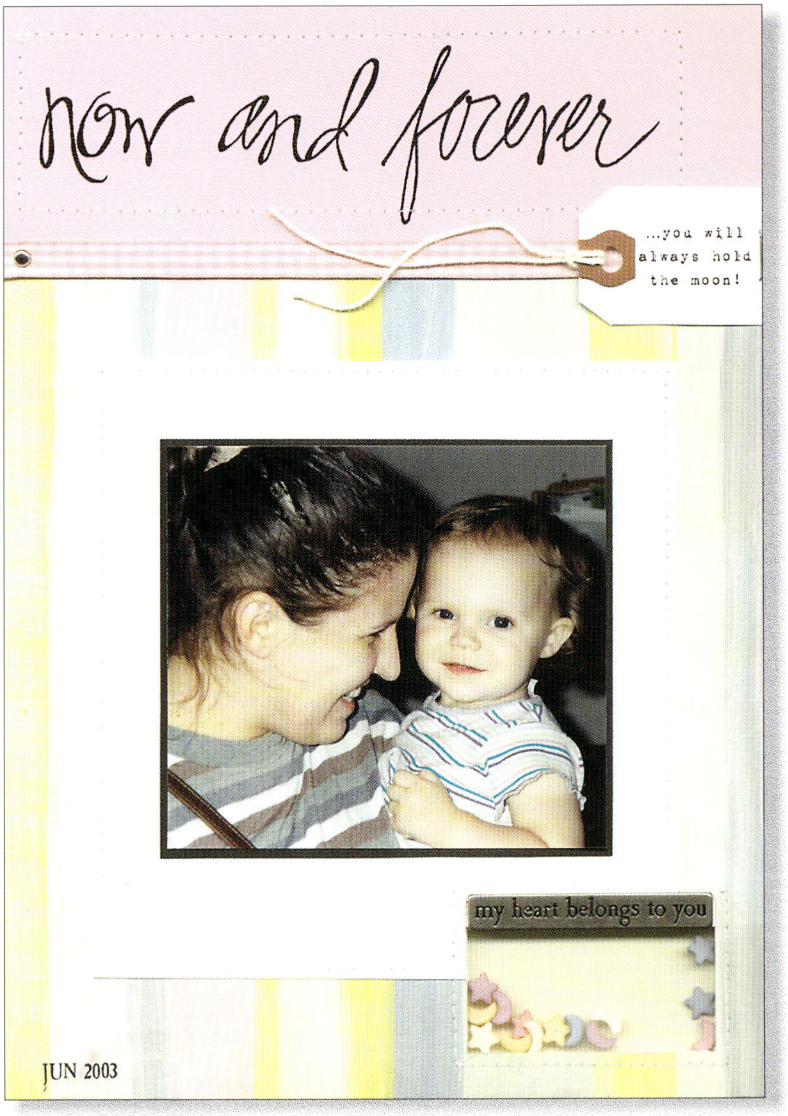
now and forever
...you will always hold the moon!
my heart belongs to you
JUN 2003

Now and Forever

Supplies
Patterned paper: K & Company
Rub-on word, metal accent, brad and date stamp: Making Memories
Computer font: Last Words, downloaded from the Internet
Buttons: Buttons Galore
Other: Transparency paper, gingham ribbon and string

Great Idea: *Use the dimension of foam core to create 3-D page accents, like this adorable shaker box. The foam core maintains the page's flat surface, ensuring that other layouts won't be affected by the art on the page.*

Great ideas for your shaker-box accents:

Transforming a shadow box into a shaker box is a great way to add dimension to your layout! Simply adhere a piece of transparency paper (to seal the items inside the box) to the foam core window before adhering paper to the front of the foam core layout. Here are some more fun ideas for creating fun and unique shaker boxes for your layouts:

- *A shaker box can be any size or shape: big or small, round or square. Try creating a shaker-box title by cutting letters or numbers into the foam core for the title, then filling them with various items.*
- *Use a photograph as the background for your shaker-box accent.*
- *Print a quote, journaling or a single word on the transparency paper that will cover your shaker box.*
- *Fill the box with creative items, such as: metal letter accents, beads, charms, buttons, silk flowers, sequins, confetti, game pieces, jewelry or sentimental memorabilia items. (See the example on the top of page 176 for a great shaker-box.)*

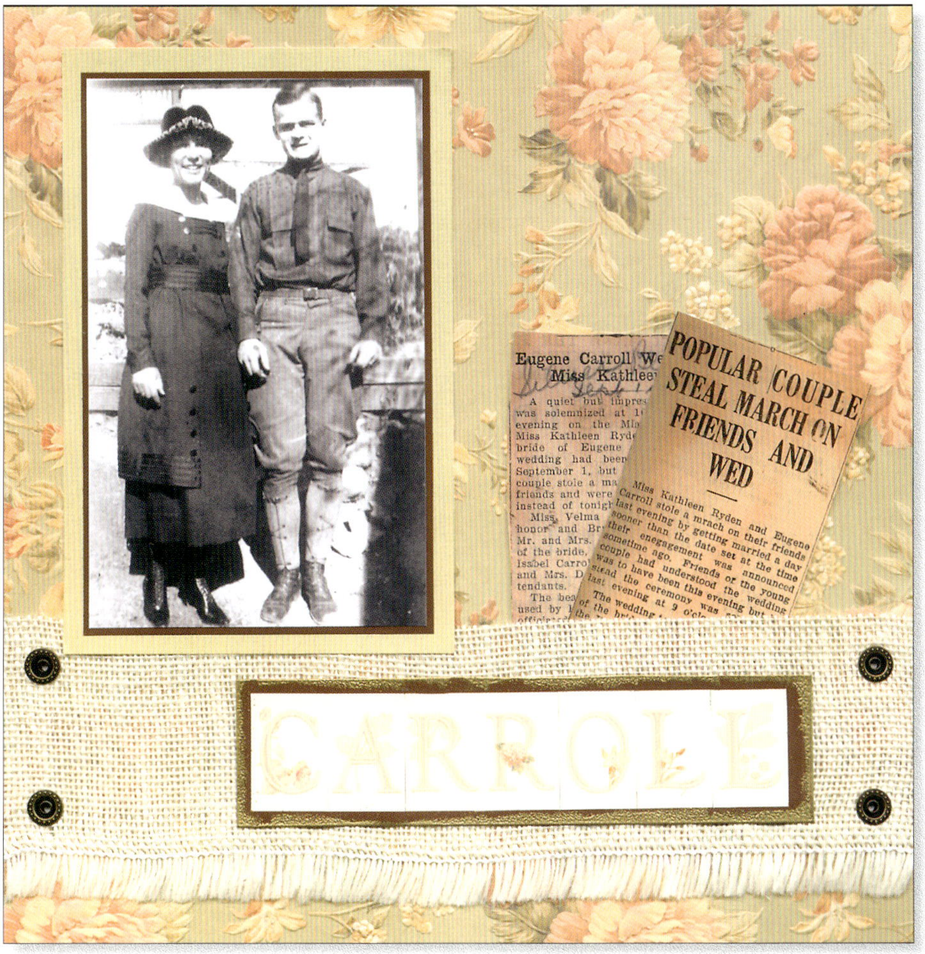
POPULAR COUPLE STEAL MARCH ON FRIENDS AND WED
Eugene Carroll We
Miss Kathleen
CARROLL

Carroll

Supplies
Patterned paper and letter stickers: K & Company
Rivets: Chatterbox
Embossing powder: Stamp-n-Stuff, Stampendous!
Other: Burlap

Great Idea!: *Use your computer scanner to make color copies of treasured memorabilia items, but instead of printing them on cardstock, print them on matte photo paper. The item will be sturdier and will look dressier on your layouts.*

Great Idea!: *Provide contrast for formal, feminine patterned papers by using a coarsely woven fabric to create a pocket on the layout.*

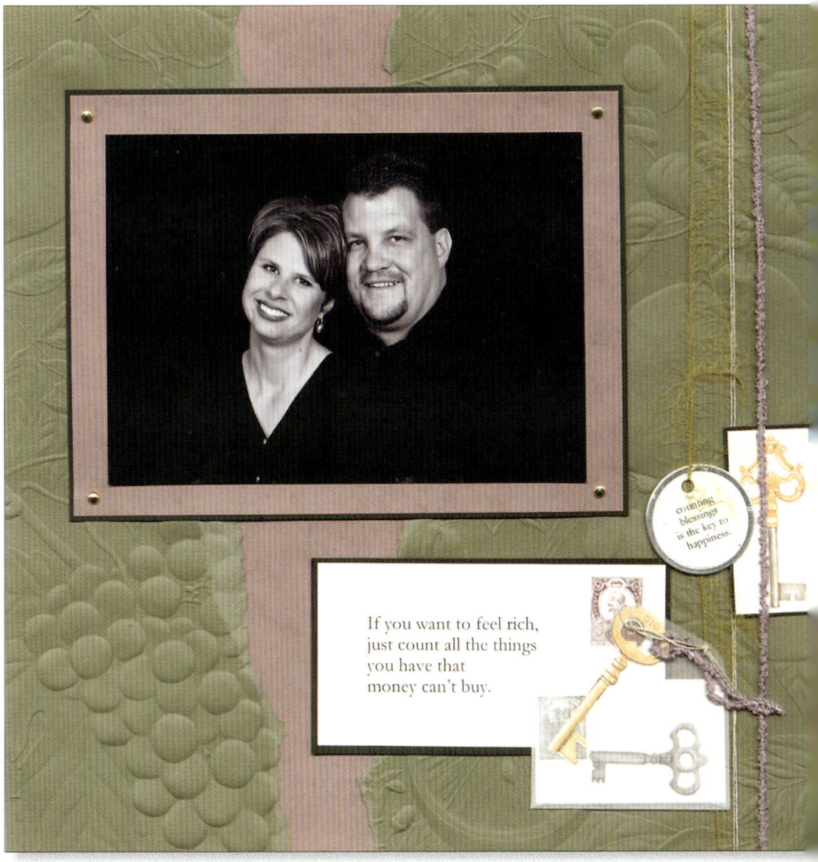
If you want to feel rich,
just count all the things
you have that
money can't buy.
counting blessings is the key to happiness.

Counting Blessings

Supplies
Embossed cardstock and stickers: K & Company
Metal-rimmed tag: Making Memories
Computer font: Garamond, Microsoft Word
Fibers: Adornaments, EK Success

Great Idea!: *Set up a black-and-white photo shoot with a black backdrop, and ask your subjects to wear black. This technique really draws attention to the subjects' faces.*

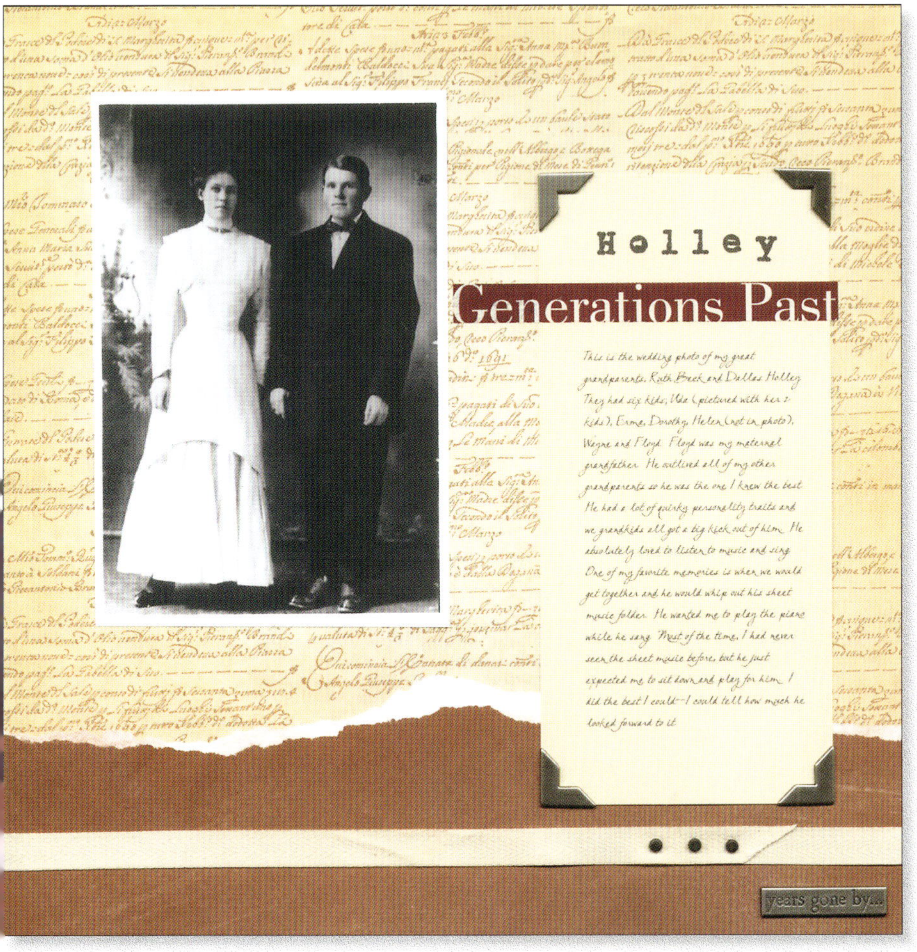
Holley
Generations Past
This is the wedding photo of my great grandparents, Ruth Beck and Dallas Holley. They had six kids; Ida (pictured with her 2 kids), Erma, Dorothy, Helen (not in photo), Wayne and Floyd. Floyd was my maternal grandfather. He outlived all of my other grandparents so he was the one I knew the best. He had a lot of quirky personality traits and we grandkids all got a big kick out of him. He absolutely loved to listen to music and sing. One of my favorite memories is when we would get together and he would whip out his sheet music folder. He wanted me to play the piano while he sang. Most of the time, I had never seen the sheet music before, but he just expected me to sit down and play for him. I did the best I could—I could tell how much he looked forward to it.
years gone by...

Holley Generations Past

Supplies
Patterned paper: Design Originals
Sticker: Phrase Café, EK Success
Metal accents: Making Memories
Computer font: CK Bella, "The Best of Creative Lettering" CD Vol. 5, *Creating Keepsakes*
Other: Ribbon

Great Idea!: *Don't let the size or shape of stickers or accents dictate the size of elements on your pages. Allowing elements to extend past the edges of journaling blocks or mats actually creates a wonderful flow on your layouts.*

Great Idea!: *When using patterned papers with handwriting on them, try to find computer fonts with similar characteristics for journaling and titles.*

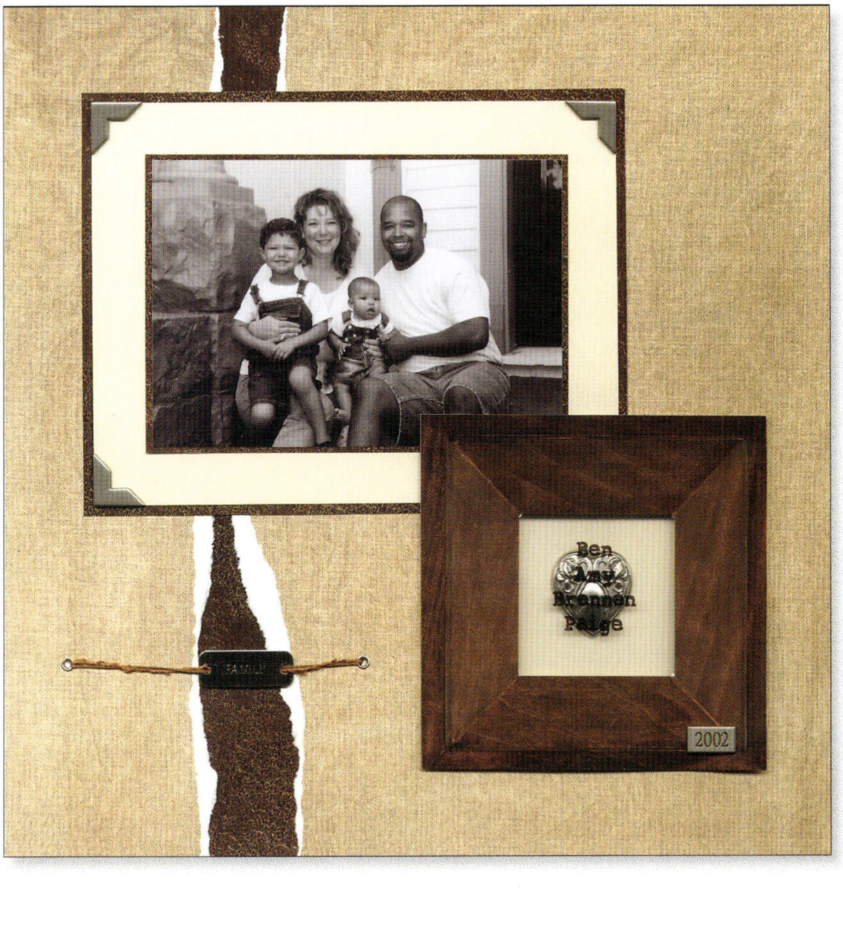
Ben
Amy
Brennen
Paige
FAMILY
2002

Family

Supplies
Patterned papers: SEI (light brown), Provo Craft (dark brown)
Preprinted frame: My Mind's Eye
Metal tag: Colorbök
"2002" metal accent and metal photo corners: Making Memories
Fibers: On The Surface
Computer font: CK Typewriter, "Fresh Fonts" CD, *Creating Keepsakes*
Other: 3-D foam adhesive, transparency paper, metal heart and eyelets

Great Idea!: *Printing journaling on transparency paper, adhering it to a pre-made frame, then adhering the frame over the metal heart accent using 3-D foam adhesive causes the journaling to appear in shadow on the background when viewed in direct light.*

Why We Love Our Man

Supplies

Patterned paper: Sue Dreamer, Colorbök
Heart punch: EK Success
Computer fonts: P22 Garamouche, Impress
Rubber Stamps: 2Peas Beautiful, downloaded from *www.twopeasinabucket.com*
Eyelets: Creative Imaginations
Fibers: Memory Lane Paper Company
Other: Swirl paper clip and page pebble

Great Idea!: *Highlight a word inside a word (like the word "fun" in "funny") by placing a pebble accent over the top of the word.*

Great Idea!: *Draw attention to a word in your title by changing the font color from the standard black to another color used on your layout. For a perfect match, scan the item you'd like to draw the color from, then (in Microsoft Word) select Format and Font. Click on the menu under Font Color, choose More Colors, and click New from File. Select the filename of your scan, and the color you scanned will be available to you as a new color choice.*

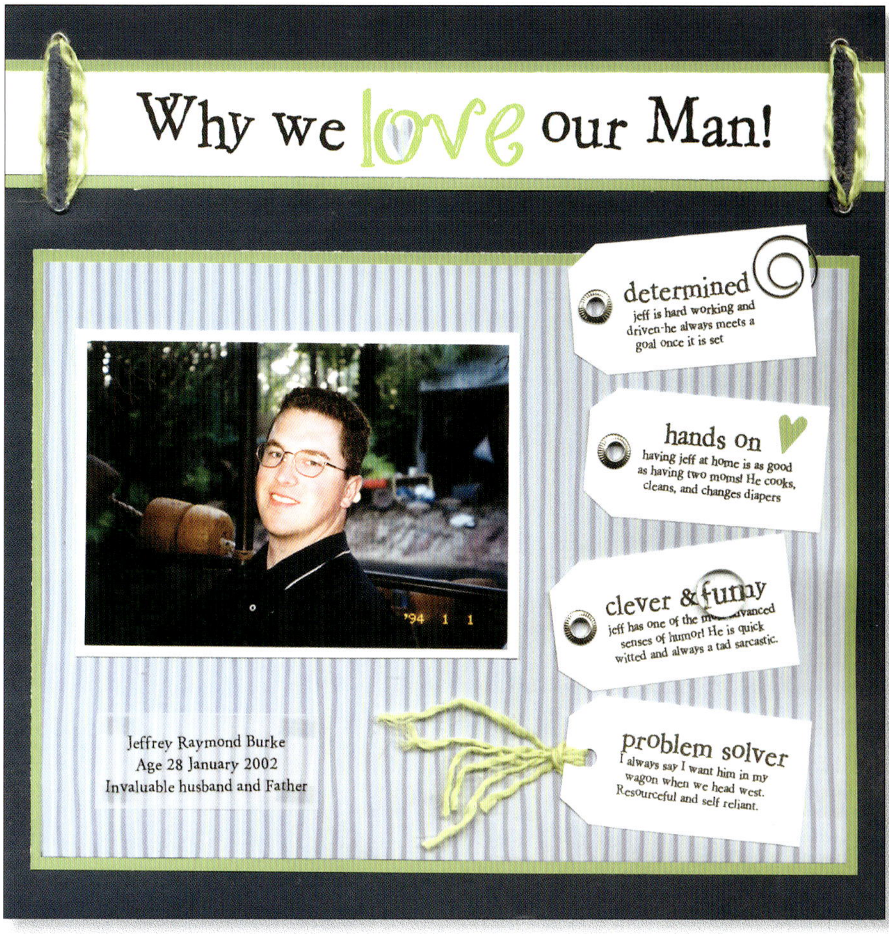

Why we love our Man!
determined
jeff is hard working and driven-he always meets a goal once it is set
hands on
having jeff at home is as good as having two moms! He cooks, cleans, and changes diapers
clever & funny
'94 1 1
Jeffrey Raymond Burke
Age 28 January 2002
Invaluable husband and Father
problem solver
I always say I want him in my wagon when we head west. Resourceful and self reliant.

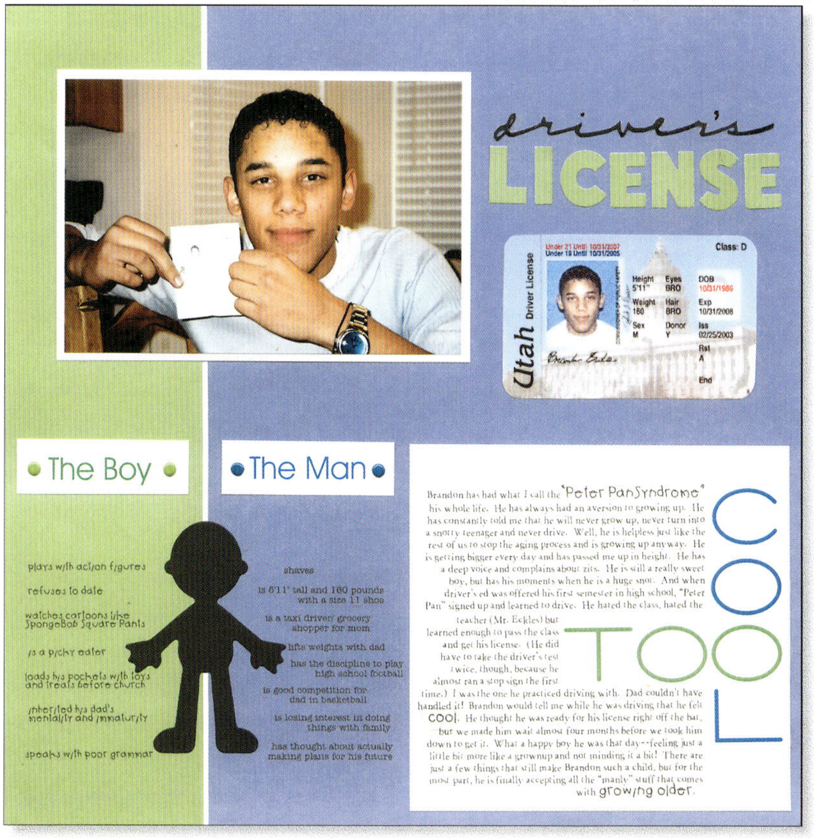

driver's LICENSE
Utah Driver License
Class: D
• The Boy •
• The Man •
plays with action figures
refuses to date
watches cartoons like SpongeBob Square Pants
is a picky eater
loads his pockets with toys and treats before church
inherited his dad's mentality and immaturity
speaks with poor grammar
shaves
is 6'11" tall and 160 pounds with a size 11 shoe
is a taxi driver/ grocery shopper for mom
lifts weights with dad
has the discipline to play high school football
is good competition for dad in basketball
is losing interest in doing things with family
has thought about actually making plans for his future
Brandon has had what I call the "Peter Pan Syndrome" his whole life. He has always had an aversion to growing up. He has constantly told me that he will never grow up, never turn into a snotty teenager and never drive. Well, he is helpless just like the rest of us to stop the aging process and is growing up anyway. He is getting bigger every day and has passed me up in height. He has a deep voice and complains about zits. He is still a really sweet boy, but has his moments when he is a huge snot. And when driver's ed was offered his first semester in high school, "Peter Pan" signed up and learned to drive. He hated the class, hated the teacher (Mr. Eckles) but learned enough to pass the class and get his license. (He did have to take the driver's test twice, though, because he almost ran a stop sign the first time.) I was the one he practiced driving with. Dad couldn't have handled it! Brandon would tell me while he was driving that he felt cool. He thought he was ready for his license right off the bat, but we made him wait almost four months before we took him down to get it. What a happy boy he was that day--feeling just a little bit more like a grownup and not minding it a bit! There are just a few things that still make Brandon such a child, but for the most part, he is finally accepting all the "manly" stuff that comes with growing older.
TOO COOL

Driver's License

Supplies

Sticker: Phrase Café, EK Success
Paper doll die cut: Sizzix
Letter punches: EK Success
Computer fonts: CK Cursive, "The Best of Creative Lettering" CD Vol. 2, *Creating Keepsakes*; DJ Crayon, package unknown, D.J. Inkers; P22 Garamouche, Impress Rubber Stamps; Arial and Times New Roman, Microsoft Word
Brads: Provo Craft
Pebble accents: Making Memories

Great Idea!: *Compare and contrast two different sides of a situation, experience or person in your journaling. Be sure to visually represent the difference between the two sides, too.*

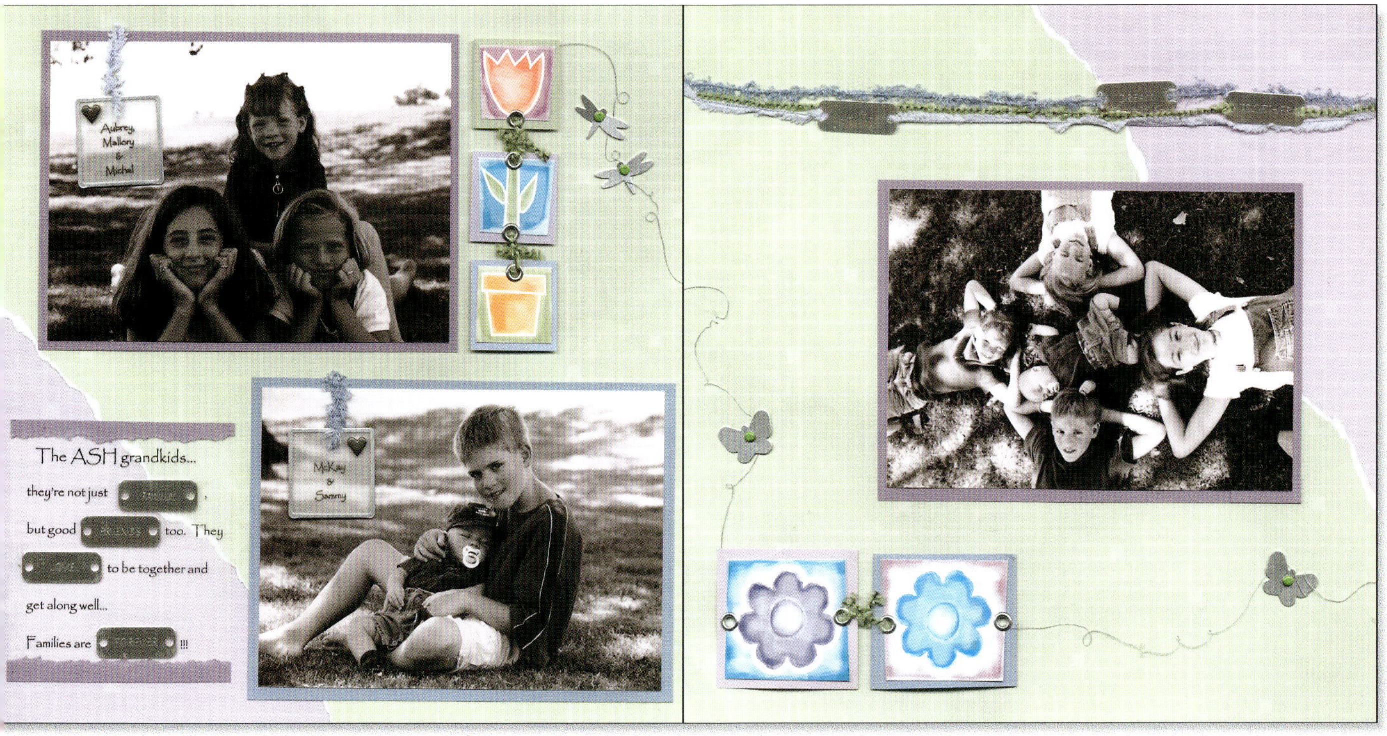
Aubrey, Mallory & Michel
The ASH grandkids...
they're not just
but good
too. They
to be together and
get along well...
Families are
!!!
McKay & Sammy

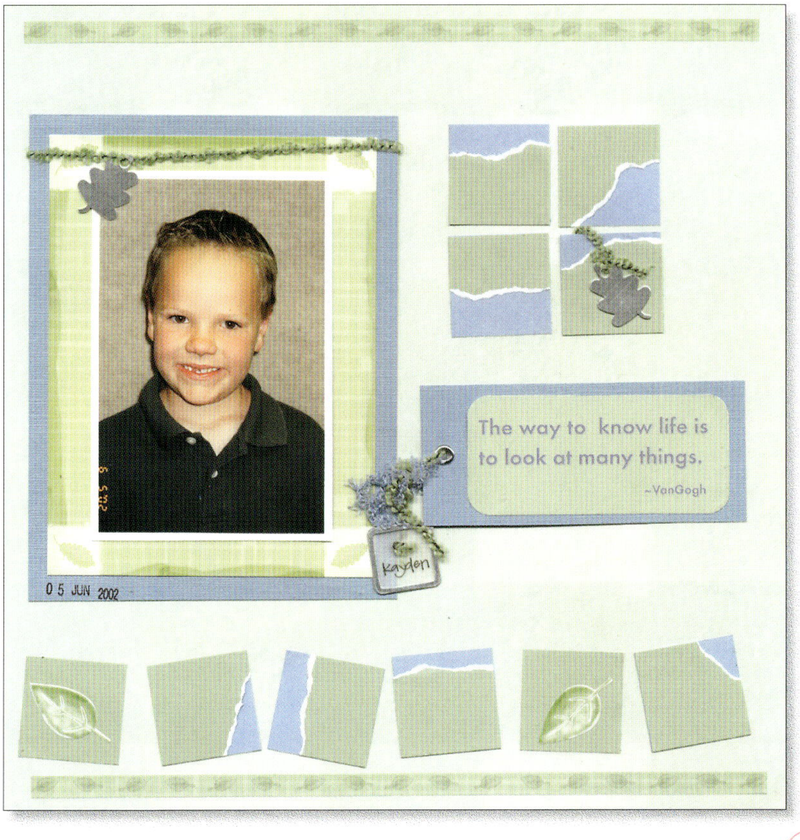
The way to know life is to look at many things.
~VanGogh
05 JUN 2002
Kayden

The Ash Grandkids

Supplies
Patterned papers, metal accents, preprinted accents and fibers: Colorbök
Craft wire: Westrim Crafts
Computer font: Papyrus, Microsoft Word

Great Idea!: *Have fun when photographing groups of children, especially when you're outdoors. In this eye-catching photograph, the kids lay on the grass with their hands behind their heads, each child's legs pointing a different direction. The photographer stood above the subjects on a picnic table to capture the shot.*

The Way to Know Life ...

Supplies
Preprinted frame, stickers, metal-rimmed tag, metal accents and fibers: Colorbök
Pen: Zig Writer, EK Success
Other: Date stamp

Great Idea!: *This serene but interesting border was created by cutting identically sized squares from blue cardstock and green-printed paper (with a white background). An edge was torn from each green square, then the green squares were adhered over the blue squares.*

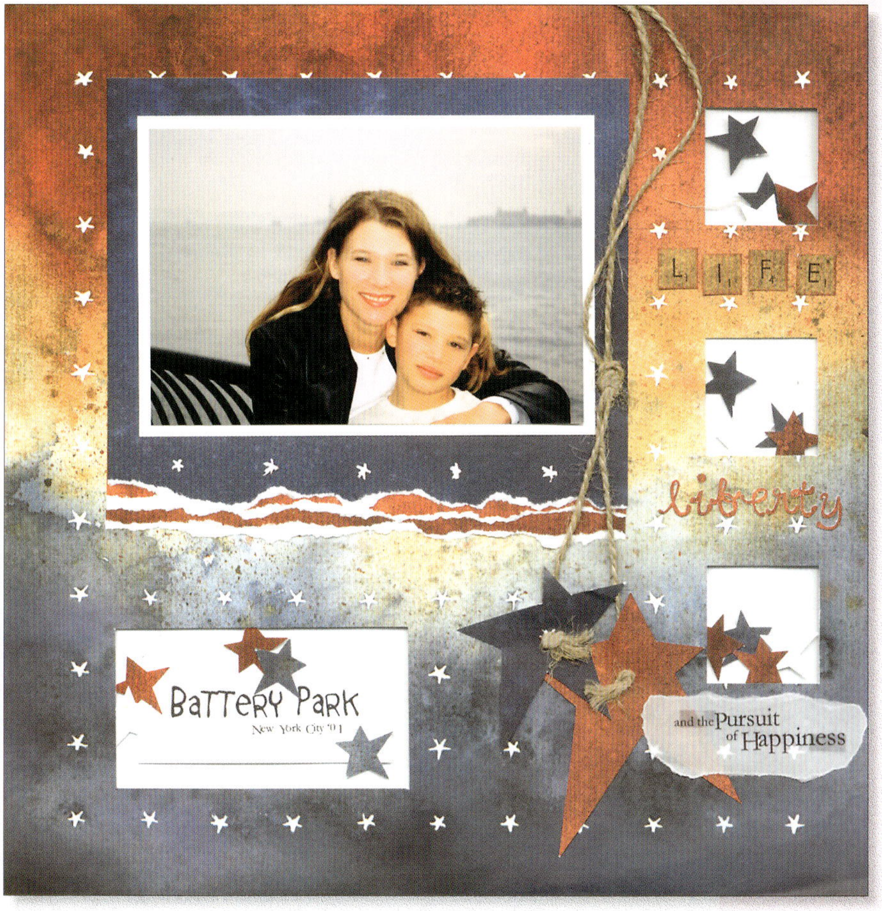

Battery Park

Supplies
Patterned paper: Provo Craft
Star template: Close To My Heart
Star punch: Posh Impressions
Computer fonts: Garamond, Microsoft Word; Roughedge, downloaded from the Internet; Doodle Cursive, package unknown, Cock-A-Doodle Design
Other: Jute and page protector

Great Idea!: *To create these see-through "windows," squares were removed from the background paper with a craft knife. Squares slightly larger than the squares cut from the background paper were cut from a sheet protector. Star punches were placed in between the layers of the sheet protector, the edges were adhered, and the sheet protectors were attached to the layout where the squares had been removed.*

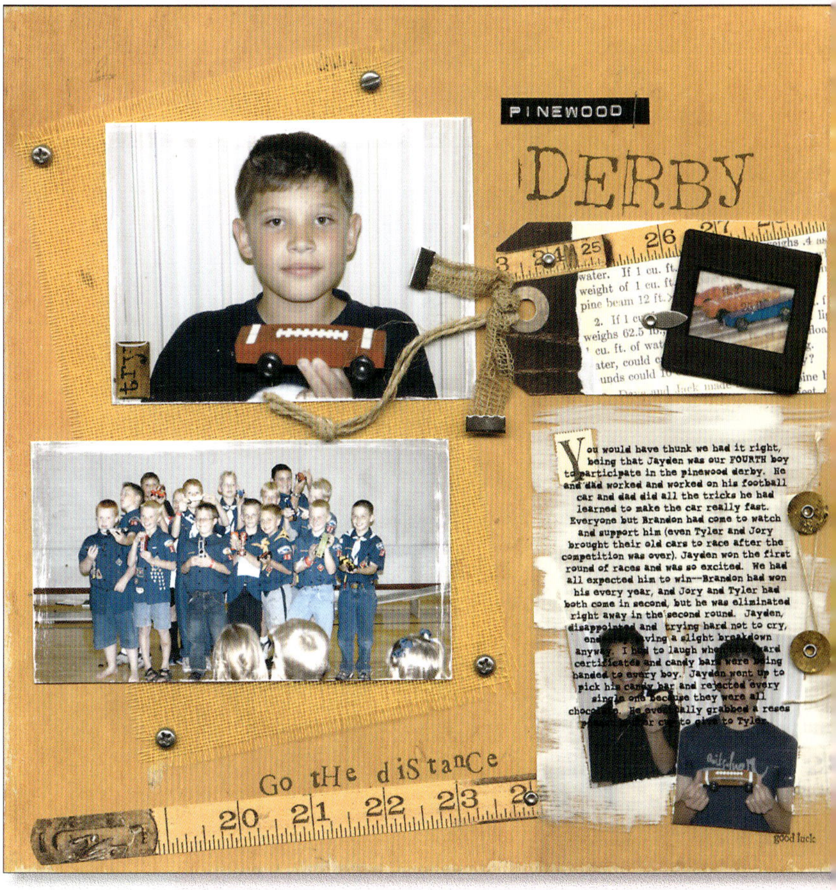

Pinewood Derby

Supplies
Patterned papers: Pebbles in my Pocket (background), Design Originals (on tag)
Stickers: Nostalgiques, EK Success
Preprinted tag: Pebbles in my Pocket
Metal accents: Making Memories
Mesh: Magenta
Letter stamps: Stampers Anonymous ("Derby"), PSX Design ("Go the Distance")
Rubber stamp: Stampin' Up! ("Good Luck")
Walnut ink: Postmodern Design
Computer font: CK Typewriter, "Fresh Fonts" CD, *Creating Keepsakes*
Other: Fibers, slide holder and acrylic paint

Great Idea!: *A photograph was printed onto vellum and placed in the slide holder, which was then placed on the tag and anchored with a metal photo anchor.*

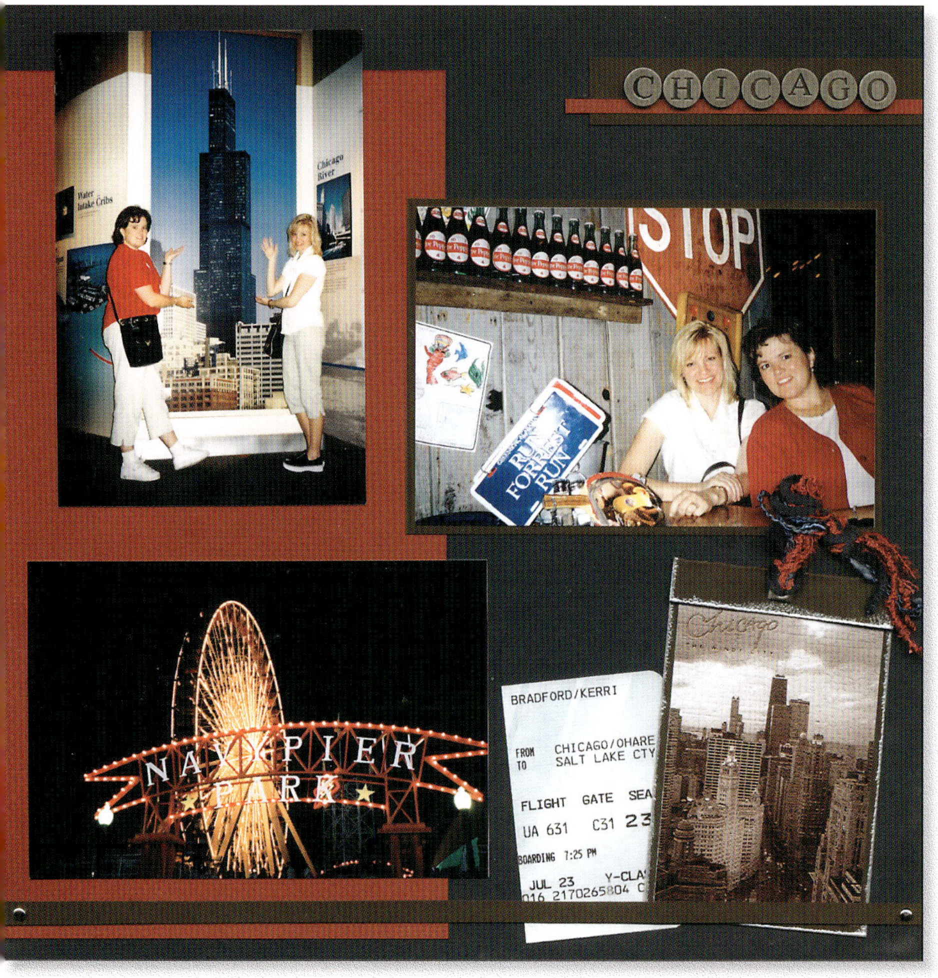

Chicago

Supplies
Metal accents: Making Memories
Embossing powder: Stamp-n-Stuff, Stampendous!
Fibers: Adornaments, EK Success

Great Idea!: *To create the tag at the bottom right of the layout, a postcard was scanned into a photo-editing program. The color of the postcard was changed to sepia, and the "crackle" feature in the photo-editing software was applied. The size of the postcard was reduced before it was printed and adhered to the tag. To match the metal accents used elsewhere on the page, the edges of the tag were heat-embossed with metallic embossing powder.*

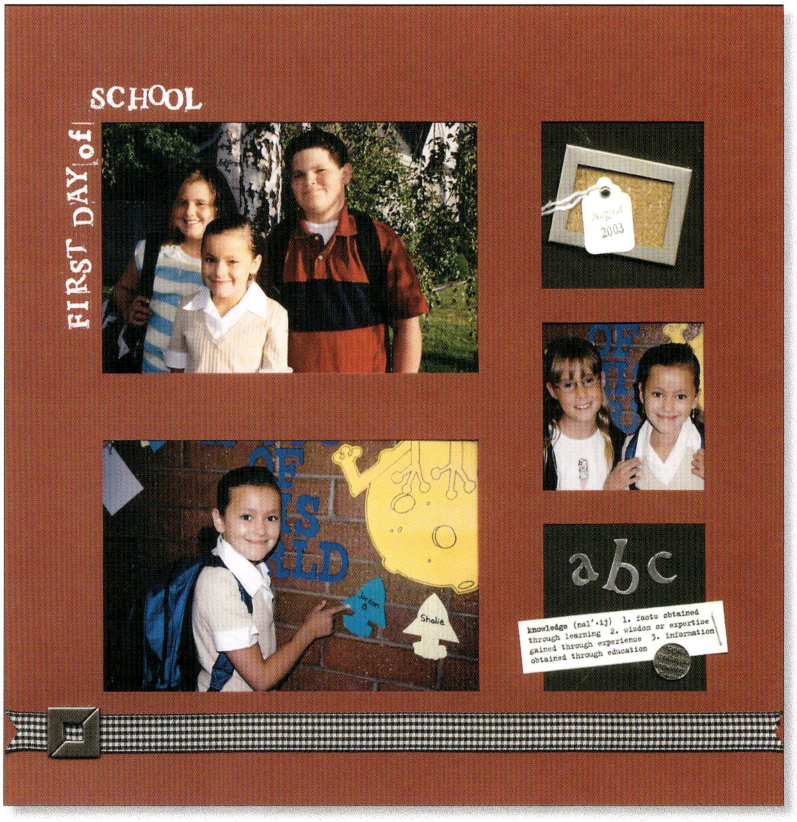

First Day of School

Supplies
Pre-formatted cardstock, definition accent, metal letter accents and charms, photo corners and date stamp: Making Memories
Metal frame: Scrapworks
Letter stamps: The Missing Link Stamp Co.
Embossing powder: Ranger Industries
"Knowledge" charm: Once Upon a Charm
Other: Ribbon, brad, staple, mini-tag and cork paper

Great Idea!: *Use cork paper and metal frames to create this fun bulletin board accent for school pages.*

Great Idea!: *Align two metal photo corners to create this adorable square accent.*

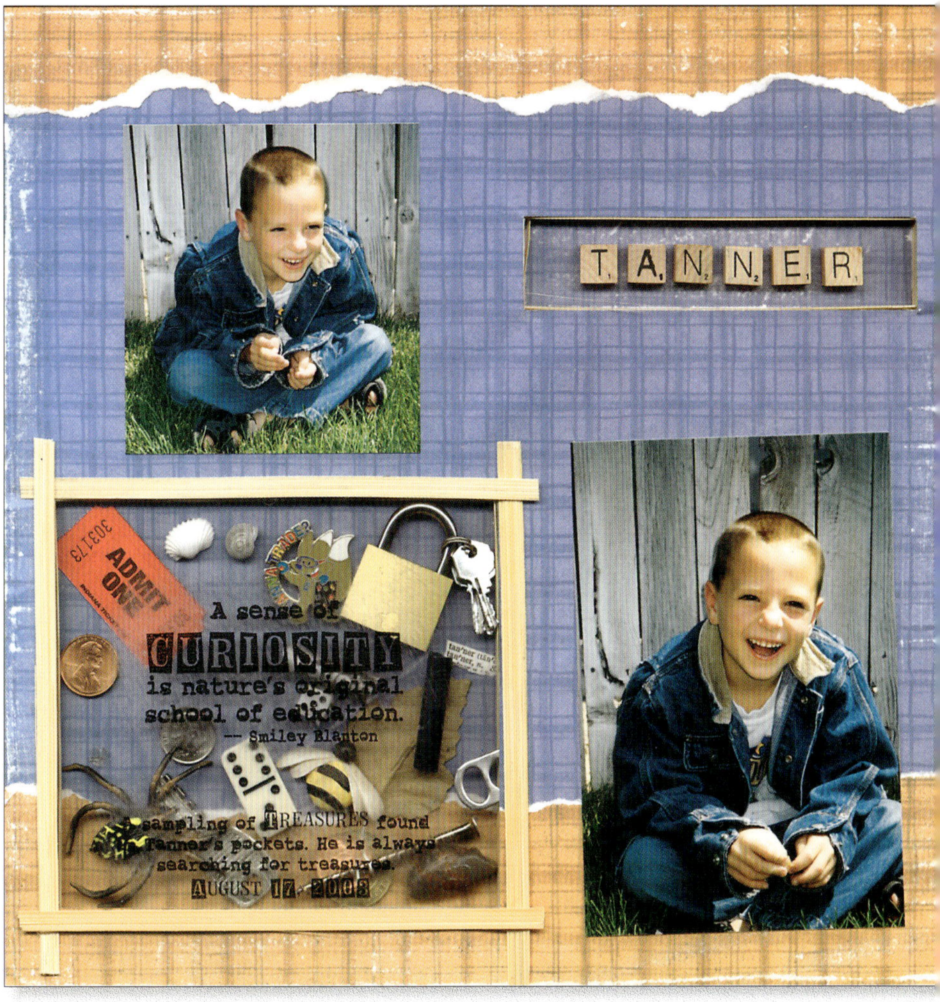

TANNER
ADMIT ONE
A sense of
CURIOSITY
is nature's original
school of education.
— Smiley Blanton
Tanner's pockets. He is always
searching for treasures.

Curiosity

Supplies
Patterned papers: Provo Craft
Scrabble letters: Impress Rubber Stamps
Computer fonts: CK Typewriter and CK Wanted, "Fresh Fonts" CD, *Creating Keepsakes*
Other: Transparency paper, bamboo pieces and foam core

Great Idea!: *A shadow box frame was created out of foam core to display the contents of a little boy's pockets.*

Great Idea!: *The journaling on the transparency paper wasn't visible enough, so the underside of the paper (underneath the journaling) was sanded with sandpaper to create a more opaque surface.*

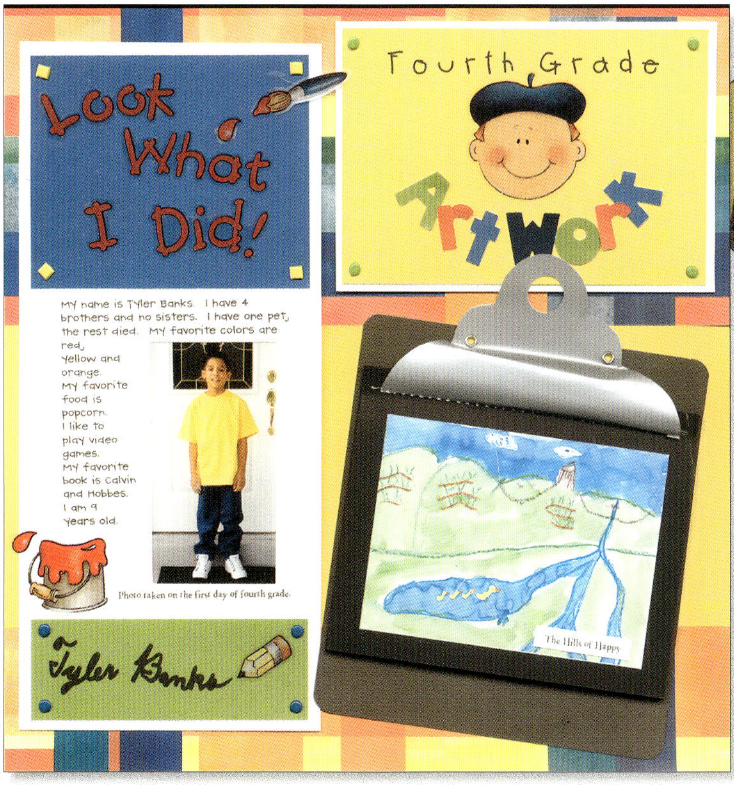

Look What I Did!
Fourth Grade
Artwork
My name is Tyler Banks. I have 4 brothers and no sisters. I have one pet, the rest died. My favorite colors are red, yellow and orange. My favorite food is popcorn. I like to play video games. My favorite book is Calvin and Hobbes. I am 9 years old.
Photo taken on the first day of fourth grade.
Tyler Banks
The Hills of Happy

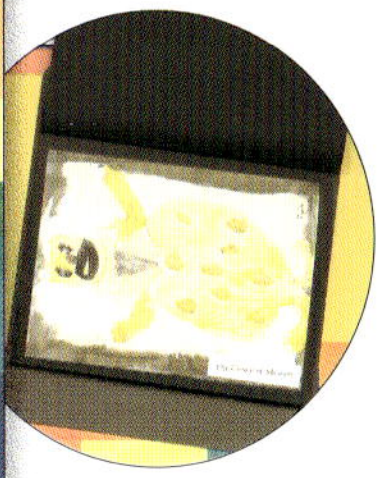

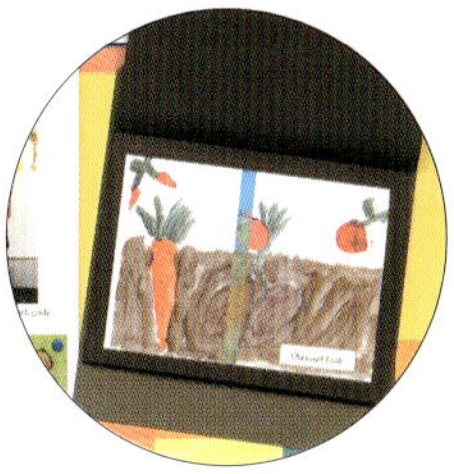

Fourth Grade Artwork

Supplies
Patterned paper: Sandylion
Stickers and brads: Provo Craft
Letter punches: EK Success
Computer fonts: DJ Crayon, package unknown, D.J. Inkers; CK Handprint, "The Best of Creative Lettering" CD Combo, *Creating Keepsakes*; P22 Garamouche, Impress Rubber Stamps

Great Idea!: *The cute clipboard accent on this layout displays color copies of artwork with each piece's title. Once all of the artwork was recorded on the layout, the originals could be given away as gifts, framed and placed on the wall, or discarded as needed.*

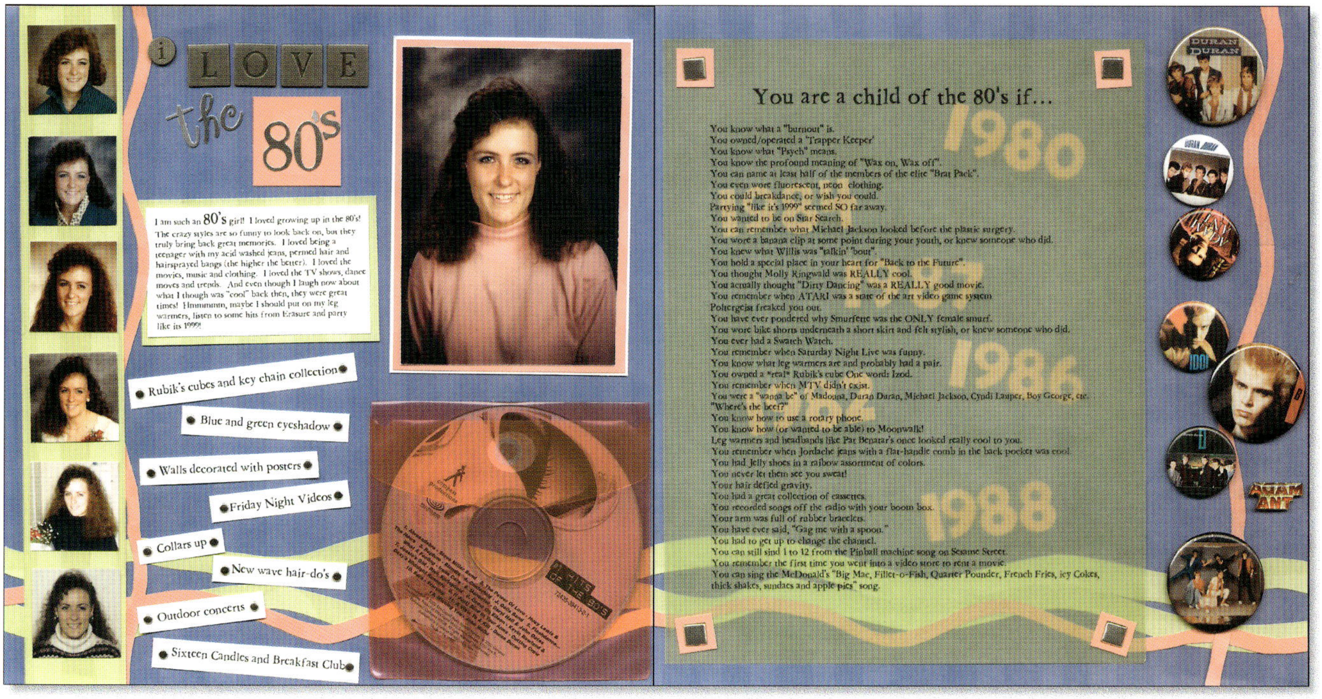
i LOVE the 80's
I am such an 80's girl! I loved growing up in the 80's! The crazy styles are so funny to look back on, but they truly bring back great memories. I loved being a teenager with my acid washed jeans, permed hair and hairsprayed bangs (the higher the better). I loved the movies, music and clothing. I loved the TV shows, dance moves and trends. And even though I laugh now about what I though was "cool" back then, they were great times! Hmmmmm, maybe I should put on my leg warmers, listen to some hits from Erasure and party like its 1999!
Rubik's cubes and key chain collection
Blue and green eyeshadow
Walls decorated with posters
Friday Night Videos
Collars up
New wave hair-do's
Outdoor concerts
Sixteen Candles and Breakfast Club
You are a child of the 80's if...
You know what a "burnout" is.
You owned/operated a 'Trapper Keeper'
You know what "Psych" means.
You know the profound meaning of "Wax on, Wax off".
You can name at least half of the members of the elite "Brat Pack".
You even wore fluorescent, neon clothing.
You could breakdance, or wish you could.
Partying "like it's 1999" seemed SO far away.
You wanted to be on Star Search.
You can remember what Michael Jackson looked before the plastic surgery.
You wore a banana clip at some point during your youth, or knew someone who did.
You knew what Willis was "talkin' 'bout".
You hold a special place in your heart for "Back to the Future".
You thought Molly Ringwald was REALLY cool.
You actually thought "Dirty Dancing" was a REALLY good movie.
You remember when ATARI was a state of the art video game system
Poltergeist freaked you out.
You have ever pondered why Smurfette was the ONLY female smurf.
You wore bike shorts underneath a short skirt and felt stylish, or knew someone who did.
You ever had a Swatch Watch.
You remember when Saturday Night Live was funny.
You know what leg warmers are and probably had a pair.
You owned a *real* Rubik's cube One word: Izod.
You remember when MTV didn't exist.
You were a "wanna be" of Madona, Duran Duran, Michael Jackson, Cyndi Lauper, Boy George, etc.
"Where's the beef?"
You know how to use a rotary phone.
You know how (or wanted to be able) to Moonwalk!
Leg warmers and headbands like Pat Benatar's once looked really cool to you.
You remember when Jordache jeans with a flat-handle comb in the back pocket was cool.
You had Jelly shoes in a rainbow assortment of colors.
You never let them see you sweat!
Your hair defied gravity.
You had a great collection of cassettes.
You recorded songs off the radio with your boom box.
Your arm was full of rubber bracelets.
You have ever said, "Gag me with a spoon."
You had to get up to change the channel.
You can still sind 1 to 12 from the Pinball machine song on Sesame Street.
You remember the first time you went into a video store to rent a movie.
You can sing the McDonald's "Big Mac, Fillet-o-Fish, Quarter Pounder, French Fries, icy Cokes, thick shakes, sundaes and apple pies" song.
1980
1986
1988
DURAN DURAN
IDOL
ADAM ANT

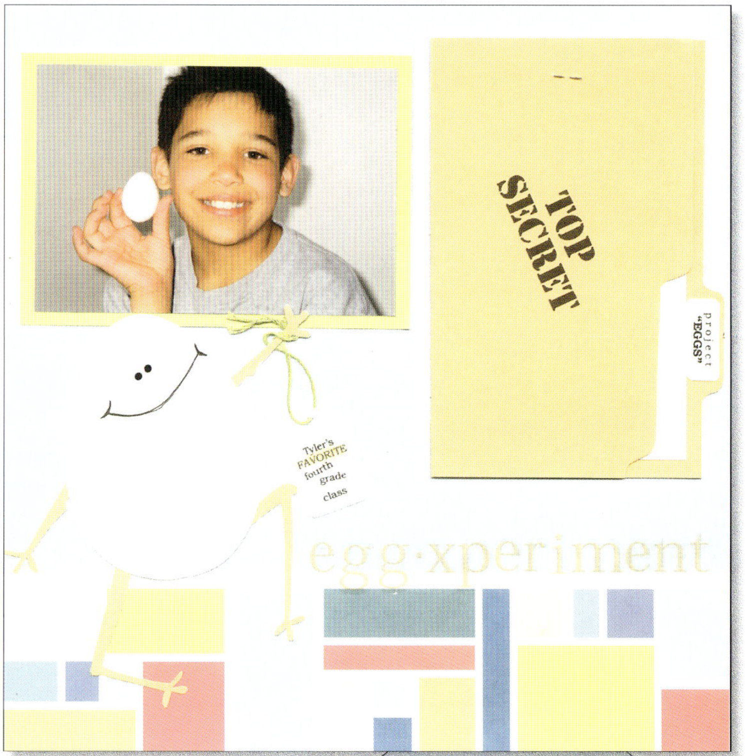
TOP SECRET
project "EGGS"
Tyler's FAVORITE fourth grade class
egg·xperiment

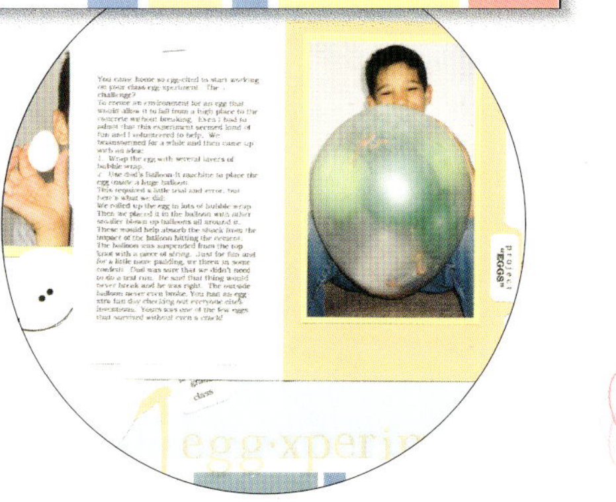
project "EGGS"
egg·xperi

I Love the '80s

Supplies
Patterned paper: Lasting Impressions for Paper
Vellum: Provo Craft
Memorabilia pocket: Xyron
Metal letters and mini-brads: Making Memories
Square brads: All My Memories
Number punches: EK Success
Square punch: Emagination Crafts
Computer font: CK Fraternity, Becky Higgins' "Creative Clips & Fonts" CD, *Creating Keepsakes*

Great Idea!: *Create a layout to commemorate each decade you've lived through. These layouts are a great place to put all that memorabilia you knew you'd never use again but just couldn't get rid of!*

Great Idea!: *Slide a CD of favorite songs from the era into a large memorabilia pocket on a layout.*

Project Eggs

Supplies
Patterned paper and letter stickers: SEI
Computer font: Garamond, Microsoft Word
"Top Secret" graphic: WordPerfect
Embroidery floss: Making Memories
Pen: Zig Writer, EK Success

Great Idea!: *Create a file folder on your layout that opens to reveal "classified" information.*

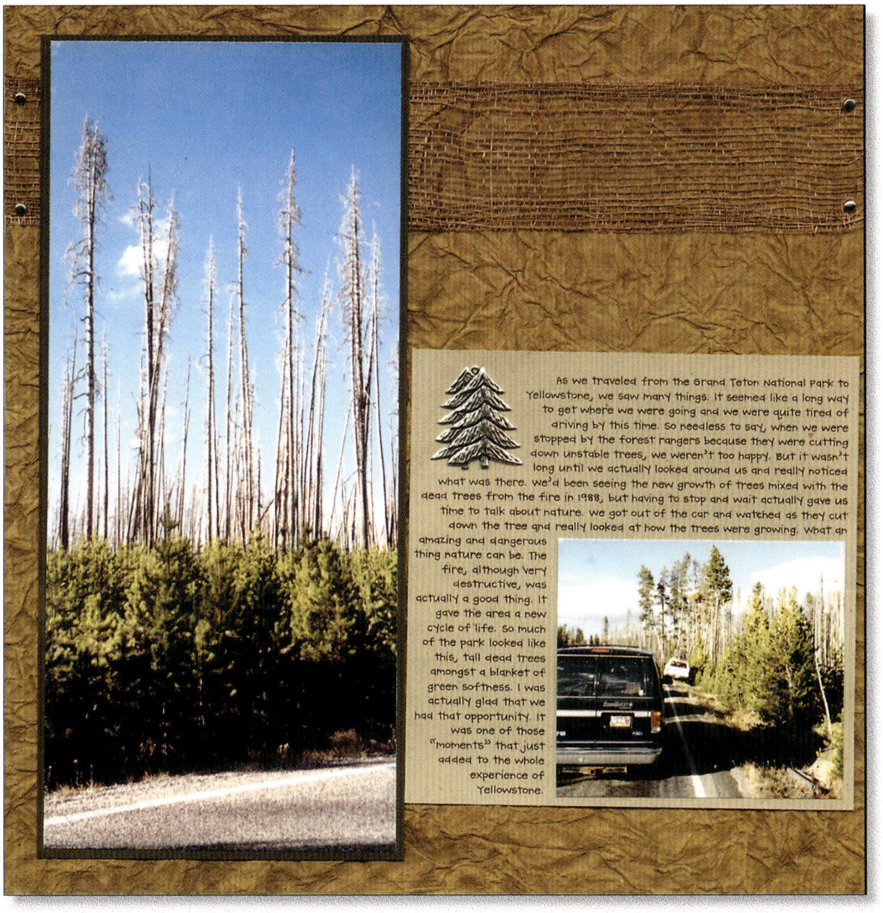
As we traveled from the Grand Teton National Park to Yellowstone, we saw many things. It seemed like a long way to get where we were going and we were quite tired of driving by this time. So needless to say, when we were stopped by the forest rangers because they were cutting down unstable trees, we weren't too happy. But it wasn't long until we actually looked around us and really noticed what was there. We'd been seeing the new growth of trees mixed with the dead trees from the fire in 1988, but having to stop and wait actually gave us time to talk about nature. We got out of the car and watched as they cut down the tree and really looked at how the trees were growing. What an amazing and dangerous thing nature can be. The fire, although very destructive, was actually a good thing. It gave the area a new cycle of life. So much of the park looked like this, tall dead trees amongst a blanket of green softness. I was actually glad that we had that opportunity. It was one of those "moments" that just added to the whole experience of Yellowstone.

Trees

Supplies
Crumpled paper: Provo Craft
Tree charms: Buttons Galore
Computer font: CK Handprint, "The Best of Creative Lettering" CD Combo, *Creating Keepsakes*
Brads: Making Memories
Other: Mesh, Ribbon

Great Idea!: *Imitate the look of a panoramic photograph using your scanner, printer and paper trimmer. Enlarge a photograph to about 1" less than the height or width of your background paper (depending on how the photograph is oriented and how it will be positioned on the page). Print the photograph, then trim it to create a long and narrow strip, and mat with a coordinating color!*

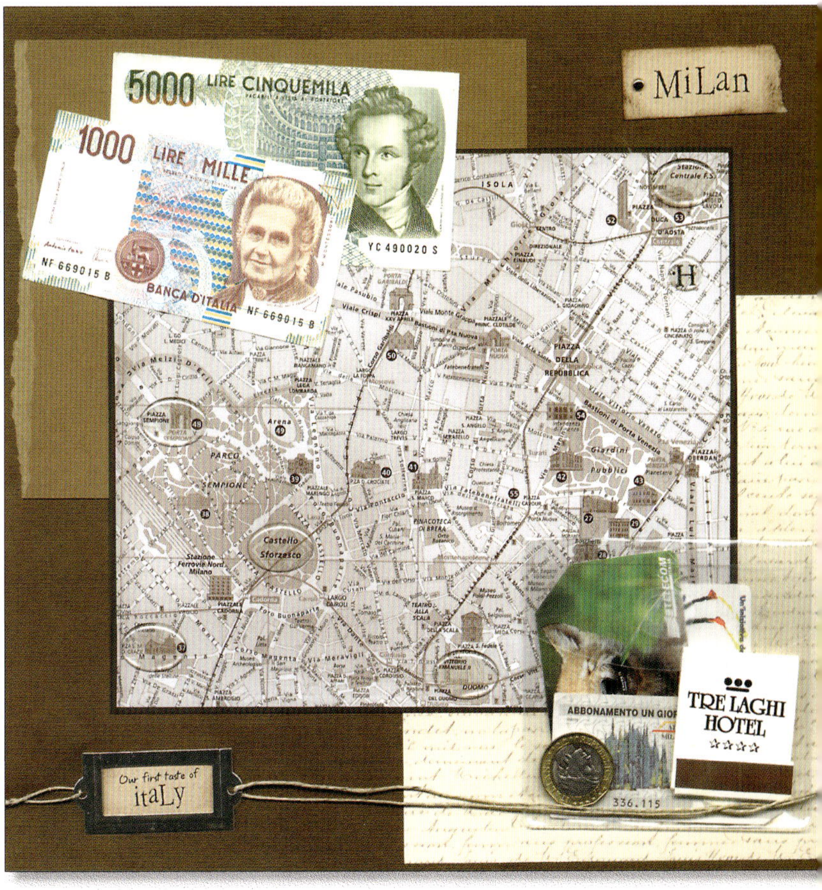
MiLan
Our first taste of
itaLy
TRE LAGHI
HOTEL

Milan

Supplies
Patterned paper: 7 Gypsies
Pebble accents: Making Memories
Memorabilia envelope: Xyron
Bookplate: Magic Scraps
Letter stamps: PSX Design
Stamping ink: Brilliance, Tsukineko
Computer fonts: CK Extra, "Fresh Fonts" CD; CK Artisan, Becky Higgins' "Creative Clips & Fonts" CD, *Creating Keepsakes*
Other: Brad and jute

Great Idea!: *Pebble accents highlight each location on the map the tourists traveled to.*

Great Idea!: *Attractively arrange various memorabilia items from your vacation in a memorabilia envelope for display on your layout.*

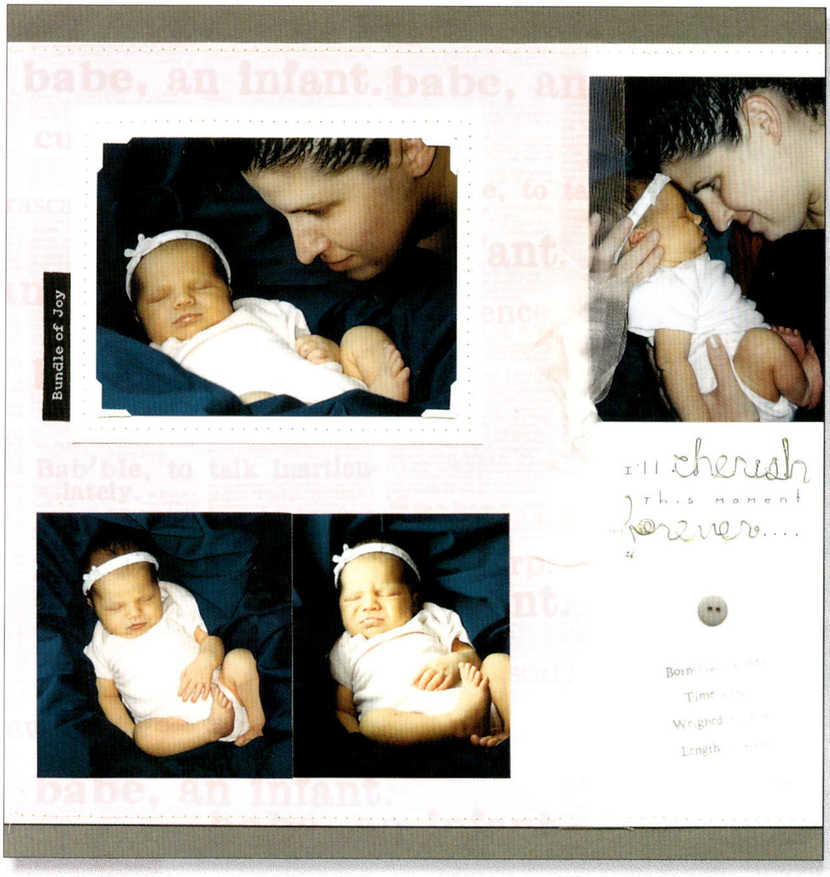

Cherish This Moment

Supplies
Patterned paper: 7 Gypsies
Wire word accents and button: Making Memories
Printed label: me & my BIG ideas
Photo corners: Kolo
Computer fonts: 2Peas Think Small, downloaded from *www.twopeasinabucket.com*; CK Jot, "The Art of Creative Lettering" CD; CK Constitution, "Fresh Fonts" CD, *Creating Keepsakes*
Other: Ribbon and vellum envelope

Great Idea!: *Include birth statistics and information in a delicate vellum envelope.*

Great Idea!: *Select a sheer ribbon to use as a border between two different papers—the contrast will still be visible through the ribbon, creating interest and variation.*

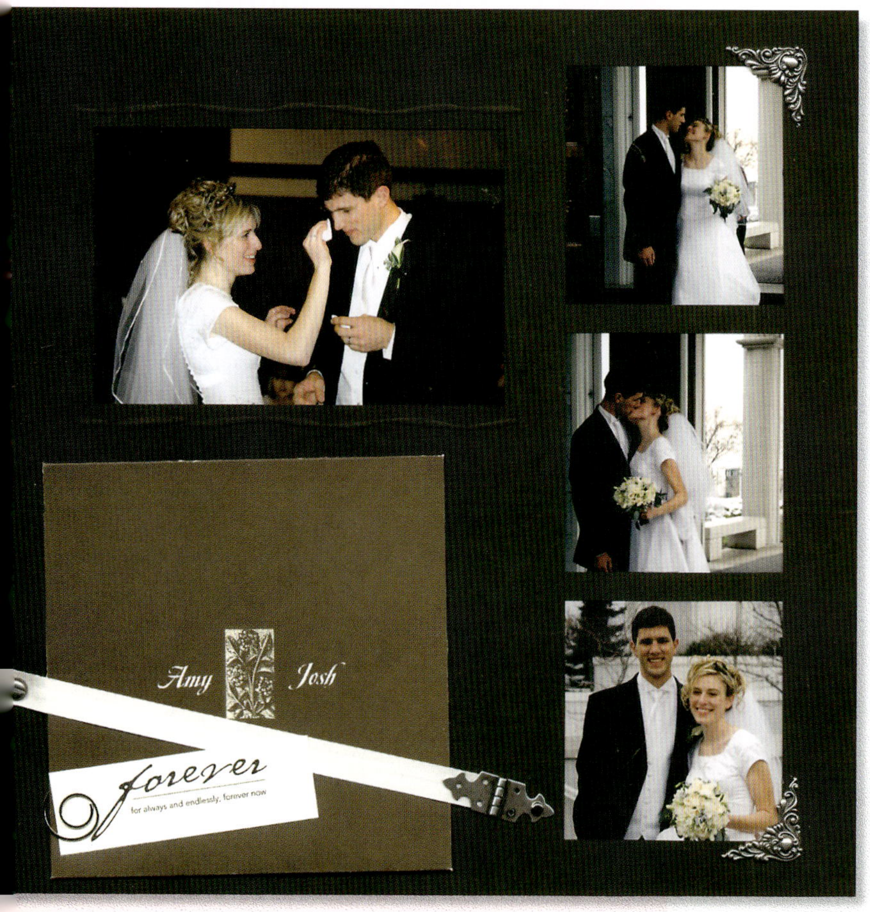

Forever

Supplies
Pre-formatted cardstock, definition accent and screw eyelet: Making Memories
Embossing template: Lasting Impressions for Paper
Metal corners and hinge: Once Upon a Charm
Other: Ribbon and spiral paper clip
Embossing template: lasting Impressions

Great Idea!: *A delicate border was embossed around the opening for the main photograph on the layout.*

Great Idea!: *Tuck a beautiful wedding invitation behind a length of elegant ribbon attached to the layout with an ornate metal hinge.*

"Where is home? Home is where the heart can laugh without shyness. Home is where the heart's tears can dry at their own pace."

— VERNON G. BAKER

"A friend is someone who knows the song in your heart and can sing it back to you when you have forgotten the words."

— UNKNOWN

"Life itself is the proper binge."

— JULIA CHILDS

"No day is so bad it can't be fixed with a nap."

— CARRIE SNOW

"Love the moment, and the energy of that moment will spread beyond all boundaries."

— CORITA KENT

"Earth's crammed with heaven and every common bush afire with God."

— ELIZABETH BARRETT BROWNING

"Children are the living messages we send to a time we will not see."

— JOHN H. WHITEHEAD

"There is more to life than increasing its speed."

— GANDHI

"God has given us our memories that we might have roses in December."

— J.M. BARRIE

"A mother's arms are made of tenderness and children sleep soundly in them."

— VICTOR HUGO

"Whatever you can do or dream you can, begin it. Boldness has power, genius, and magic in it. Begin it now."

— GOETHE

"Once in a lifetime one should be allowed to have as much sweetness as one can possibly want and hold."

— JUDITH OBREY

"Where there is great love, there are always miracles."

— WILLA CATHER

"Faith is the bird that feels the light and sings when the dawn is still dark."

— RABINDNANATH TAGORE

"Seek not outside yourself— heaven is within."

— MARY LOU COOK

"Imagination is more important than knowledge."

— ALBERT EINSTEIN

"Life's truest happiness is in the friendships we make along the way."

— ANONYMOUS

"Life isn't a matter of milestones, but of moments."

— ROSE KENNEDY

"Family faces are magic mirrors. Looking at people who belong to us, we see the past, present and future."

— GAIL LUMET BUCKLEY

"Babies are such a nice way to start people."

— DON HEROLD

"Alone we can do so little, together we can do so much."

— HELEN KELLER

"A baby is God's opinion the world should go on."

— CARL SANDBURG

"A mother's love for her child is like nothing else in the world. It knows no law, no pity, it dares all things and crushes down remorselessly all that stands in its path."

— AGATHA CHRISTIE

"THE ONLY WAY TO HAVE A FRIEND IS TO BE ONE."

— RALPH WALDO EMERSON

"We've had bad luck with our kids–they've all grown up."

— CHRISTOPHER MORLEY

"There are only two ways to live your life. One is as though nothing is a miracle. The other is as if everything is."

— ALBERT EINSTEIN

"Seek the wisdom of the ages, but look at the world through the eyes of a child."

— RON WILD

"If there is anything better than to be loved it is loving."

— ANONYMOUS

"Your only obligation in any lifetime is to be true to yourself."

— RICHARD BACH

"Think big thoughts but relish small pleasures."

— H. JACKSON BROWN, JR.

"I AM BEGINNING TO LEARN THAT IT IS THE SWEET, SIMPLE THINGS OF LIFE WHICH ARE THE REAL ONES AFTER ALL."

— LAURA INGALLS WILDER

"The only thing worth stealing is a kiss from a sleeping child."

— JOE HOULDSWORTH

"Life is a paradise for those who love many things with a passion."

— LEO BUSCAGLIA

"A true friend is one soul in two bodies."

— ARISTOTLE

"A heart in love with beauty never grows old."

— TURKISH PROVERB

"Enjoy the little things in life, for one day you may look back and realize they were the big things."

— ANONYMOUS

"A dream is a wish your heart makes—when you're fast asleep."

— CINDERELLA

"And forget not that the earth delights to feel your bare feet and the winds long to play with your hair."

— KAHLIL GIBRAN

"Children are the keys of paradise."

— RICHARD STODDARD

"Be glad of life, because it gives you the chance to love and to work and to play and to look up at the stars."

— HENRY VAN DYKE

"When you love someone all your saved-up wishes start coming out."

— ELIZABETH BOWEN

"The art of being happy lies in the power of extracting happiness from common things."

— HENRY WARD BEECHER

"Some people, no matter how old they get, never lose their beauty—they merely move it from their faces into their hearts."

— ANONYMOUS

"One of the secrets of a happy life is continuous small treats."

— IRIS MURDOCH

"Love every day. Each one is so short and they are so few."

— NORMAN VINCENT PEALE

"If you obey all the rules, you miss all the fun."

— KATHARINE HEPBURN

"There is no such thing in anyone's life as an unimportant day."

— ALEXANDER WOOLLCOTT

"Just living is not enough. One must have sunshine, freedom and a little flower."

— HANS CHRISTIAN ANDERSON

"The road to a friend's house is never long."

—DANISH PROVERB

"Children are living jewels dropped unsustained from heaven."

—ROBERT POLLOK

"Never, Never, Never give up."

— WINSTON CHURCHILL

"A FRIEND IS SOMEONE WITH WHOM YOU DARE TO BE YOURSELF."

— FRANK CRANE

"Home is a place where the small are great and the great are small."

— ANONYMOUS

"Where there is love, there are always miracles."

— WILLA CATHERDDDD

"We should show life neither as it is or as it it ought to be, but only as we see it in our dreams."

— COUNT LEO TOLSTOY

"Children are living jewels dropped unsustained from heaven."

—ROBERT POLLOK

"Now join your hands, and with your hands your hearts."

—WILLIAM SHAKESPEARE

"What is a friend? A single soul dwelling in two bodies."

— ARISTOTLE

"Whatever our souls are made of, his and mine are the same."

— EMILY BRONTE

"There comes a time in every rightly constructed boy's life when he has a raging desire to go somewhere and dig for hidden treasure."

— MARK TWAIN